30ˢ

All-American Ads

1. **Zeke:** "Yes, I got my first part today, Cousin Ezra. Just wait till the folks back home see me in Superba Pictures' new jungle thriller!"

Ezra: "Well...I'm a little afraid they won't recognize you, Cousin Zeke!"

Acknowledgements

This volume of historical material would never have been completed without the help of numerous individuals. Among them are Cindy Vance of Modern Art & Design, who continues to labor on these massive volumes with her enthusiasm intact while infusing them with her design and image-editing expertise; Nina Wiener who managed to keep this project and countless others at Taschen on track, in order and beautifully edited; Steven Heller for his impeccable and swift writing; and Sonja Altmeppen, Tina Ciborowius, Andy Disl, Horst Neuzner, and the rest of the Taschen staff in Cologne for their help and guidance in consistently producing a quality product.

As always, special thanks are due to all of those who provided the magazines and material that eventually wound up in this book, including Dan DePalma, Ralph Bowman, Gary Fredericks, Jeff and Pat Carr, Jerry Aboud, Cindy and Steve Vance, Richie Strell, and all the other dealers of paper ephemera. I couldn't have done it without you.

And doing it one more time, the folks at Artworks—Blue, Liz, Adrian, and Eric—who pulled it off again.

And lastly, a hearty "Schnitzelbank" cheer to Benedikt and Angelika Taschen for their continuing friendship and support.

Jim Heimann

Cover: Sperry Flour, 1939
endpapers: Outdoor Advertising Industry, 1934
pages 2–3: Ten High Whiskey, 1939
pages 4–5: Buick, 1935
pages 6–7: General Electric, 1931
pages 8–9: Paramount, 1932
pages 10–11: Arrow Shirts, 1935
pages 12–13: Heinz, 1932
pages 14–15: Thompson Products, 1935
pages 16–17: Westinghouse, 1936
pages 18–19: Italian Line, 1934

Imprint

© 2003 TASCHEN GmbH
Hohenzollernring 53, D–50672 Köln
www.taschen.com

Art Direction & Design: Jim Heimann, L.A.
Digital Composition & Design:
Cindy Vance, Modern Art & Design, L.A.
Cover Design: Sense/Net, Andy Disl, Cologne
Production: Tina Ciborowius, Cologne
Editorial coordination: Sonja Altmeppen, Cologne
German translation: Harald Hellmann, Cologne
French translation: Philippe Safavi, Paris
Spanish translation: Gemma Deza Guil for LocTeam, S.L., Barcelona
Japanese translation: Maiko Masujima, Kanagawa

Printed in Spain
ISBN: 3-8228-1620-5
ISBN: 4-88783-203-6
(edition with Japanese cover)

All-American Ads

Edited by Jim Heimann
with an introduction by Steven Heller

TASCHEN

KOLN LONDON LOS ANGELES MADRID PARIS TOKYO

Steven Heller:

Alcohol &
Tobacco
44

Automobiles
118

Consumer
Products
282

Entertainment
356

Fashion &
Beauty
416

Food &
Beverage
502

RICAN

Industry
590

Travel
720

Interiors
656

Advertisements of the Thirties:
From Modernism to Shirt-Sleevism

by Steven Heller

American advertising of the thirties was born in 1925 in Paris along the banks of the Seine. The *Exposition Internationale des Arts Décoratifs et Industriels Modernes*, a playground of modernity, was laid out in boulevards lined with pavilions decorated with geometric ornamentation and neo-classical friezes. The world's leading clothing, furniture, and houseware manufacturers, along with many grand emporia, exhibited their latest products and designs. But one player was noticeably absent.

The United States, the world's greatest industrial nation, declined an invitation to participate. The leaders of American industry believed, as historian Terry Smith explained, "that they could not match the French designers either in making a stripped Arts and Crafts 'modernism' or by boldly countering with a national style."

And they were right. American products were either nondescript or laden with beaux-arts ornament to camouflage a mass-produced look. Although mass production was the foundation on which the modern American economy was built, many cultural critics argued that items coming off the assembly line lacked good taste. While the Bauhaus

and other European modern avant-gardes had embraced the machine, American industrialists, who could easily afford to improve their products aesthetically, were apathetic. What they did not resist, however, were marketing strategies that would stimulate higher profits. So industry frantically tried to find a new means of increasing sales through the art, science, and hucksterism of advertising.

The man who helped revolutionize American advertising from the mid-twenties through the thirties was Earnest Elmo Calkins, an advertising pioneer, design reformer, and founder of the New York-based Calkins and Holden Advertising Co. Inspired by the *Exposition Internationale des Arts Décoratifs et Industriels Modernes*, he described the array of cubistic and futuristic graphics, packages, and displays in the department-store pavilions thus in a treatise on the subject: "It is extremely 'new art' and some of it too bizarre, but it achieves a certain exciting harmony, and in detail is entertaining to a degree." Upon returning to the United States he proffered a vision of how American advertising could benefit from European modernism and modern art.

In Paris Calkins witnessed an approach to illustration—at that time the primary means of creating and disseminating images—that was not sentimentally representational but used symbols and metaphors to create a "magical" atmosphere for consumables. Boxes and bottles were not mere utilitarian vessels, but rather signifiers of the essence of a product. Calkins wrote: "Modernism offered the opportunity of expressing the inexpressible, of suggesting not so much a motor car as speed, not so much a gown as style, not so much a compact as beauty." And if this had a similar ring to one of F. T. Marinetti's futurist manifestoes, it was because Calkins borrowed his language from the European avant-garde, while at the same time he eschewed its radicalism.

No other advertising man was more responsible for the American consumerist revolution than Calkins, who looked more like a Mid-western preacher than a New York huckster. Yet he was instrumental in such progressive modern marketing concepts as "consumption engineering," "forced obsolescence," and "styling the goods". And these buzzwords were the core of an adver-

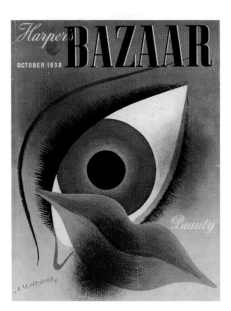

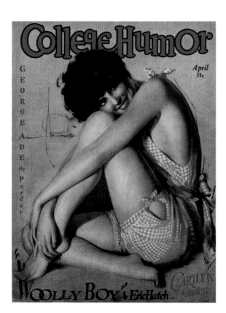

tising strategy that insinuated modern art and graphic design into a heretofore copy-ruled, devoutly conservative profession whose primary service was purchasing ad space from magazines and newspapers.

It was no longer possible "to make an advertisement striking, conspicuous and attractive by still pictures and realistic groups," asserted Calkins, who sought to take advantage of new color printing technologies, photographic effects, and aesthetic trends to make "art" that was memorable and monumental. By integrating modern art into stodgy mainstream commercial culture, Calkins revived interest in old products and also forced consumers to anticipate a bright future filled with consumables. Nonetheless, his so-called radical ideas met with opposition from those who wanted to sell in a less artsy manner. His ideas were indeed making headway, but the vast majority of advertisements were copy-laden tracts designed to avoid misperception and ambiguity of any kind.

Conservative ad men argued that fancy advertising images were elitist distractions, unresponsive to the tastes of ordinary consumers, and therefore doomed to fail.

Calkins, they said, had a conflated sense of his own class values as opposed to a reflection of the whole society. To the contrary, Calkins felt that "artistic advertising" could be a democratizing force in terms of the middle classes. Indeed, he targeted solely an economic class that he called "people of taste," rather than inducing unattainable longings in the so-called have-nots.

Calkins believed that cluttered design (Wheaties, p. 526), comic strips (Camel, p. 53) puerile drawings, and copy (Saráka, p. 299) were demeaning and confusing. Instead he proffered techniques that created mystiques through stylized, symbolic, and abstract forms. This meant that advertising could be less dependent on copy because the image was the primary mode of communication. More important, this model also elevated the art director above the copywriter in the hierarchy of advertising. Calkins felt that the so-called "art expert" was just as important as a literate copy chief. Throughout the twenties and thirties agency art directors acquired new-found prominence—indeed, art directors used illustration to create modern auras. Given Calkins' method, commonplace objects—toasters, refriger-

ators, pencils, shortening and coffee tins—were presented against dynamic patterns and at skewed angles; and contemporary industrial wares were often shown in surrealistic and futuristic settings.

Modern art was a value additive and valuable camouflage. "When the uglier utilities of business cannot be beautified," wrote Calkins, "art is used to make them disappear." Suggesting a special relationship between the advertisement and goods by graphic style was something Calkins called "atmosphere," a fetishistic trait that ultimately rubbed off on the product itself.

Nonetheless, Calkins was a pragmatist. The cleverness of advertising could not exceed the public's capacity to understand what was being advertised—and be hooked in the process. He sought to raise the overall standard, yet this was accomplished in the "most advanced yet acceptable" manner and "style" was the means, not the end. Advertisements for Camay (p. 288), Kinsbury Pale (p. 75), and Thompson Products (pp. 14–15), to name but a few, were a true synthesis of the modern style and traditional commercial art. This was not simply a pyrrhic victory; Calkins was honestly content to create mod-

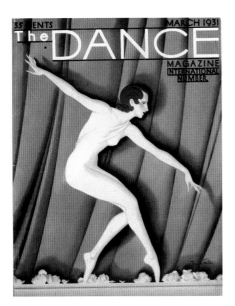

ernistic allusions because, he explained, "Improving the physiognomy of advertising had a twofold result. It directly influenced the taste of the public and indirectly conditioned the production of goods."

In some quarters the new commercial advertising style increased sales, which triggered greater production, which then stimulated the economy. Manufacturers and retailers were happy, and designers and artists were major contributors to this bounty. A commercial artist of the day once wrote, "I've seen this styling idea coming closer and closer to the thing that really counts... a container that millions of hands stretch out to buy because it says something to them that they can't resist!"

But there was a downside to the success of Calkins' approach. In the early thirties American industry was actually producing *too many* goods to sustain high levels of repeat consumption. Moreover, the mammoth stock market crash of 1929 had, to say the least, put a huge crimp into mass buying power. By 1933 Calkins' style engineering reached its point of diminished return. Overzealous advertising and product manufacturing during the earlier bull market did

not directly cause this catastrophic economic downslide—triggering America's Great Depression—but it was symptomatic of what N. W. Ayer's Harry Batten describes as economic overconfidence, "a sort of gambling fever [that] spread into every level of society." By the mid-1930s, still stinging from the Depression, advertisers and advertising had adopted what was called shirt-sleeve advertising, which fills much of this volume.

As the rising tide of the Depression washed away all the impressive economic gains of the postwar boom years, Calkins' agency and the scores of other big New York "shops" had to give clients what they wanted: sales. Certain "modernisms" were retained in post-Depression advertising, but the vast majority of advertisements returned to hard-sell techniques, including celebrity testimonials (for cigarettes), multi-image pictorials (for cars), sentimental landscapes (for travel), and well-stocked, glistening refrigerators (for food and drink). The most progressive art in the world was not going to sell detergent, toothpaste, deodorant, vegetable oil, or light bulbs. Subtlety was out, irony was barely a consideration, and comedy—unless in the form of easy-to-

comprehend comics—was useless if the goods stayed on the shelves.

Calkins charged copywriter-artist/art director teams with the job of making creatively balanced advertisements and campaigns, but in the wake of the Depression shrill displays of screaming headlines and purple testimonials replaced any artistic nuances. Before the age of television, print advertising in newspapers, magazines, and on billboards (and radio, of course) was the most effective way of directly tempting the consumer. But advertising could not afford the luxury of the subtle tease. Ads had to make bold claims followed by stark promises, ending with memorable taglines. For example, an ad for Jantzen swimwear (p. 482), illustrated by the master of soft-core allure, George Petty, promised women they'd have gorgeous men while promising men the prize of similarly endowed women if only they bought the product. The suggestive headline "Perfectly suited by Jantzen" further demonstrates that someone with a flair for clever phraseology was involved in the campaign.

The Jantzen ad was actually more artful than most in its genre. Conversely, the

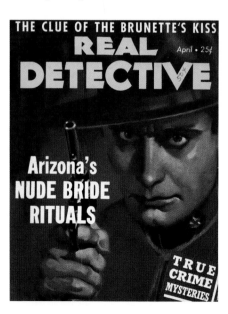

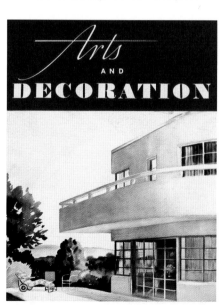

artless Chipso ad (p. 284) for a curiously named laundry detergent was a more common sort. Here a color photograph showing a children's tea party with a freshly coifed homemaker and three happy lassies in clean party clothes sits above the lengthy title: "Our clothes look new for more than one season's wear... thanks to Chipso," says the mother of happy little girls. It is a typically unimaginative testimonial type of ad. The grammatically challenged tagline "Chipso makes clothes wear—longer" (under a photo of mom in her apron at the slop sink with a box of the magical flakes) further reinforces the idea that happiness is cleanliness and cleanliness comes in a box.

Chipso may have been at the lower rung of the creative ladder but it was nonetheless influenced by better-known, more solidly financed national campaigns, like the one for Coca-Cola that left nothing to the imagination. "Home... to the pause that refreshes" (p. 586) is laden with layers of text and visual effluvia. A headline featuring Coca-Cola's venerable tagline sits atop a stylized painting of two happy, sugar-crazed pre-teen siblings (although the face of the girl perhaps intentionally looks much older and wiser than her body would suggest). Mom has just returned home from a shopping spree with arms full of packages (wishful thinking during the Depression) to receive the joyful greeting of her youngest child (presumably already sated by Coca-Cola and cookies). As if the painting doesn't offer enough narrative, two ancillary photographs show a "real life" mom buying and serving the dark, sweet elixir. And if all this is not enough reinforcement, think again. The text block, "When you shop you get something you don't bargain for. You get tired... and thirsty," knocks the reader over the head and brands the famous logo "Drink Coca-Cola" onto the cerebral cortex.

Advertisements like this filled the pages of *Life*, *Look*, *The Saturday Evening Post*, *Collier's*, and countless other weekly and monthly magazines. Despite the falling fortunes brought on by the Depression, commercial magazines rode crests of success—like movies they were diversions from the humdrum of the everyday. The ads not only sold the goods, they provided a sense of normalcy that helped consumers find their respective centers amid social turmoil.

Advertising of the thirties ultimately served two important functions: to stimulate want, thus generating sales; and to exhort American capitalism, thereby instilling a sense of optimism during dark times. To look at the advertisements in this volume one would never guess that Americans were suffering from severe hardships. The more artful specimens of the early thirties gave way to hard-selling (a symbolic indicator of hard times) but advertising for most commodities and a few luxuries was just as ubiquitous, and indeed exuberant, as before the crash. By the end of the decade, as war clouds formed over Europe, advertising helped artificially stimulate American consumerism. The shirt-sleeves had been rolled up, the economy was beginning to chug along, and then came World War II. Every aspect of American life would be forever altered and advertising would change its demeanor once again.

Steven Heller is the co-Chair of the MFA/Design program at the School of Visual Arts, New York and author of over eighty books on design and popular culture.

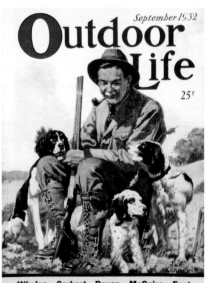

Anzeigen in den dreißiger Jahren:
Von der Modernen Kunst zur Hemdsärmeligkeit

von Steven Heller

Die amerikanische Werbung der dreißiger Jahre erblickte 1925 an den Ufern der Seine das Licht der Welt. Auf der *Exposition Internationale des Arts Décoratifs et Industriels Modernes*, einem Schaufenster der Moderne, wurden großzügige Boulevards von Pavillons gesäumt, die mit geometrischen Ornamenten und neoklassizistischen Friesen geschmückt waren. Die weltweit führenden Produzenten von Bekleidung, Möbeln und Haushaltswaren stellten hier gemeinsam mit vielen großen Warenhäusern ihre neuesten Produkte und Designs vor. Ein wichtiger Mitbewerber am Markt glänzte jedoch durch Abwesenheit.

Die Vereinigten Staaten, die bedeutendste Industrienation der Welt, hatten die Einladung zur Teilnahme ausgeschlagen. Die Marktführer der amerikanischen Wirtschaft fürchteten, so der Kunsthistoriker Terry Smith, „sie hätten den französischen Designern nichts entgegenzusetzen, weder sachliche Arts-and-Crafts-Modernität noch einen eigenständigen Stil".

Und damit hatten sie Recht. Amerikanische Produkte waren entweder gesichtslos oder sie waren mit Schnörkeln überfrachtet, was ihre Produktion am Fließband verschleiern sollte. Obgleich die Massenferti-

gung das Fundament der modernen amerikanischen Wirtschaft war, bemängelten viele Kritiker die Fließbandprodukte als geschmacklos. In Europa hatten das Bauhaus und andere avantgardistische Strömungen die maschinelle Fertigung als Herausforderung begriffen. Die amerikanische Industrie, die ihre Produkte ohne großen Aufwand ästhetisch hätte aufwerten können, verhielt sich hingegen passiv. Für neue Marketingstrategien, die Umsatzsteigerungen versprachen, war sie jedoch empfänglich.

Maßgeblich an der Revolutionierung der Werbung in den USA beteiligt war von Mitte der zwanziger bis Ende der dreißiger Jahre Earnest Elmo Calkins, ein Pionier auf dem Gebiet der Werbung, ein Designreformer und Gründer der in New York ansässigen Agentur Calkins and Holden Advertising Co. Beflügelt von der *Exposition Internationale des Arts Décoratifs et Industriels Moderne*, beschrieb Calkins die vielen kubistisch und futuristisch inspirierten Werbegrafiken, Verpackungen und Displays in den Pavillons der Warenhäuser: „Es ist zwar alles ausgesprochen ‚modern', einiges auch zu bizarr, erzielt jedoch immer eine gewisse spannende Harmonie und ist bisweilen sogar unter-

haltsam." Calkins nahm eine Vision davon, wie die amerikanische Werbung von der europäischen Moderne profitieren könnte, mit zurück in die Staaten.

In Paris hatte Calkins eine Herangehensweise an die Illustration – damals das wichtigste Mittel der Bildproduktion und -verbreitung – kennengelernt, die sich nicht sklavisch ans reine Abbilden hielt, sondern Symbole und Metaphern benutzte, um Gebrauchsgütern eine „magische" Atmosphäre zu verleihen. Kartons und Flaschen waren mehr als nur zweckmäßige Behältnisse, sie verwiesen auf den Charakter eines Produkts. Calkins schrieb: „Die Moderne bietet die Gelegenheit, das Unausdrückbare auszudrücken, nicht auf ein Auto, sondern auf Geschwindigkeit zu verweisen, nicht auf ein Kleid, sondern auf Stil, nicht auf eine Puderdose, sondern auf Schönheit." Wenn das an eines der futuristischen Manifeste von F. T. Marinetti erinnert, liegt das daran, dass Calkins seine Terminologie der europäischen Avantgarde entlehnte, deren Radikalität er allerdings vermied.

Kein anderer Werbefachmann hat die Werbung in den USA derart revolutioniert wie Calkins, der eher einem Prediger aus

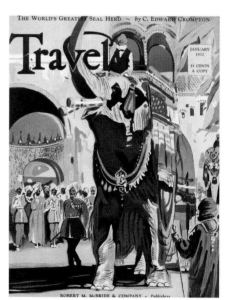

dem Mittelwesten als einem ausgefuchsten Reklameprofi aus New York ähnelte. Dennoch war er maßgeblich an der Entwicklung moderner Werbekonzepte und -termini wie „consumption engineering", „forced obsolescence" und „styling the goods" beteiligt. Diese Schlagworte standen im Mittelpunkt einer Werbestrategie, die moderne Kunst und modernes Grafikdesign geschickt in eine Profession einbrachte, die bis dahin textorientiert und durch und durch konservativ gewesen war, und deren Dienstleistung hauptsächlich darin bestand, Anzeigenplatz in Illustrierten und Zeitungen zu buchen.

Calkins setzte auf moderne Farbdruckverfahren, fotografische Effekte und ästhetische Trends, um eine einprägsame und herausragende „Kunst" zu erschaffen. Indem er modernes Artwork in die fade Standardwerbung integrierte, frischte Calkins das Interesse an bereits eingeführten Produkten auf und brachte darüber hinaus den Verbraucher dazu, freudig einer Zukunft voll schöner Konsumgüter entgegenzusehen. Seine „radikalen Ideen" stießen jedoch auf Ablehnung bei denen, die eine weniger kunstorientierte Werbung bevorzugten. Seine Ideen waren in der Tat bahnbrechend, doch die große

Mehrheit der Anzeigen zeigte weiterhin Bleiwüsten, die tunlichst jedes erdenkliche Missverständnis, jede Zweideutigkeit ausschließen sollten.

Konservative Werbeleute vertraten die Ansicht, eine so fantasievolle Werbung sei elitär und ginge am Geschmack der breiten Masse vorbei. Sie fanden, Calkins könne sich nicht von den Wertvorstellungen seiner eigenen Klasse frei machen und die Gesellschaft im Ganzen sehen. Calkins hingegen glaubte, dass „künstlerische Werbung" eine demokratisierende Kraft für den Mittelstand sein könnte. Seine eigentliche Zielgruppe waren „Menschen von Geschmack", wie er sagte; ihm lag nichts daran, in den so genannten Habenichtsen unerfüllbare Wünsche zu wecken.

Für Calkins waren eine zu unruhige Gestaltung (Wheaties, S. 526), Bildergeschichten (Camel, S. 53) und läppische Zeichnungen und Texte (Saráka, S. 299) eine Zumutung, die den Verbraucher nur verwirrten. Er propagierte Techniken, die durch stilisierte, symbolische und abstrakte Formen eine geheimnisvolle Aura erzeugten. Da die Bildaussage nun im Vordergrund stand, verlor der Text für die Werbung zwangsläufig an Bedeutung. Während der zwanziger und

dreißiger Jahre kamen die Artdirectors daher zu bislang nicht gekanntem Ansehen – ja, sie verliehen den Dingen durch die optische Gestaltung tatsächlich ein modernes Gesicht. Nach Calkins Rezeptur wurden alltägliche Gebrauchsgegenstände vor einem dynamisch gemusterten Hintergrund und aus ungewohnten Perspektiven präsentiert; zeitgenössische Industrieprodukte wurden oft in einem surrealistischen und futuristischen Kontext gezeigt.

Das moderne Artwork war ein Surplus, das sich auszahlte, und es diente der Camouflage. „Wenn man die hässlicheren Gebrauchsgegenstände nicht verschönern kann", so Calkins, „hat das Artwork die Aufgabe, sie unsichtbar zu machen." Eine durch grafische Mittel angedeutete besondere Beziehung zwischen Produkt und Anzeige war das, was Calkins „Atmosphäre" nannte, ein Fetischcharakter, der letzten Endes auf das Produkt selbst abfärbte.

Doch Calkins blieb ein Pragmatiker. Die Werbung durfte den Verbraucher nicht überfordern, sondern musste ihn fesseln. Er wollte das allgemeine Niveau heben, doch obwohl das mit den „fortschrittlichsten Methoden" geschehen sollte, war der Stil

nur Mittel, nicht Endzweck. Anzeigen für Camay (S. 288), Kingsbury Pale (S. 75) und Thompson Products (S. 14–15), um nur einige zu nennen, stellen eine echte Synthese von modernem Stil und traditioneller Werbegrafik dar. Dies war kein Pyrrhussieg; Calkins war vielmehr überzeugt: „Wenn man das Erscheinungsbild der Werbung optimiert, erreicht man zweierlei. Es beeinflusst unmittelbar den Geschmack der Öffentlichkeit und wirkt sich indirekt positiv auf die Warenproduktion aus."

Calkins erfolgreiche Methode hatte jedoch auch einen Nachteil. In den frühen dreißiger Jahren produzierte die amerikanische Industrie einfach mehr als der Markt aufnehmen konnte. Darüber hinaus wirkte sich der katastrophale Börsenkrach von 1929 nicht eben positiv auf die Kaufkraft aus. 1933 kam Calkins Pionierarbeit in Sachen Stil an den Punkt, an dem sie sich einfach nicht mehr rentierte. Übereifriges Werben und Überproduktion während des Wirtschaftsbooms früherer Tage waren nicht unmittelbar für den Niedergang der amerikanischen Wirtschaft und die große Depression verantwortlich, aber sie waren symptomatisch für das, was Harry Batten von der renommierten Werbeagentur N. W. Ayer als einen übertriebenen wirtschaftlichen Optimismus beschreibt, eine „Art von Spielsucht", die alle gesellschaftlichen Bereiche erfasst hatte. Mitte der dreißiger Jahre hatten sich die immer noch von der Wirtschafskrise gebeutelten Anzeigenkunden und Werbefachleute auf den so genannten hemdsärmeligen Werbestil besonnen, für den sich im vorliegenden Band die meisten Beispiele finden.

Als die bedrohliche Flut der Depression alle Profite der Boomjahre vor dem Krieg fortgespült hatte, musste Calkins Agentur wie alle anderen großen New Yorker „Shops" ihren Klienten nur noch eins verschaffen: reißenden Absatz. Eine gewisse Modernität wurde nach der Wirtschaftskrise beibehalten, aber der überwiegende Teil der Werbung offenbarte eine Rückkehr zur Holzhammermethode. Man warb mit Prominenten (für Zigaretten), mit zahllosen Einzelbildchen (für Automobile), mit romantischen Landschaften (für die Reisebranche) und mit gut gefüllten, glänzenden Kühlschränken (für Lebensmittel). Subtilität war out, Ironie nicht minder und witzige Einfälle – außer in Form leicht verständlicher Comics – sinnlos, wenn die Waren in den Regalen liegen blieben.

Calkins betraute Teams von Werbetextern und Illustratoren oder Artdirectors damit, kreativ ausbalancierte Anzeigen und Kampagnen zu entwerfen, aber im Gefolge der Wirtschaftskrise verdrängten marktschreierische Slogans und Lobeshymnen „zufriedener Kunden" jedwede künsterischen Zwischentöne. Die Werbung konnte sich den Luxus der subtilen Verführung nicht mehr leisten. Anzeigen mussten markige Behauptungen aufstellen, vollmundige Versprechen folgen lassen und mit einem einprägsamen Slogan enden.

Eine Anzeige für Jantzens Bademoden (S. 482), illustriert von George Petty, dem Großmeister der erotischen Illustration, versprach den Frauen ganze Männer und den Männern kurvige Frauen, wenn sie das Produkt kauften. Die doppelsinnige Headline „Perfectly suited by Jantzen" zeigt, dass ein Texter mit Sprachgefühl an der Kampagne beteiligt war. Damit war die Anzeige von Jantzen anspruchsvoller als die meisten anderen in diesem Genre.

Die anspruchslose Anzeige für Chipso (S. 284), ein Waschmittel mit skurrilem Namen, entsprach da schon eher der Regel. Ein Farbfoto zeigt Kinder, die Kaffeeklatsch

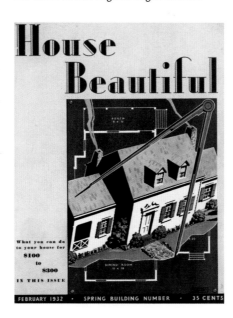

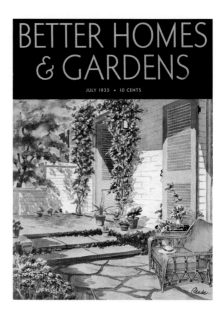

spielen, eine frisch frisierte Hausfrau und drei strahlende Mädchen in blitzsauberen Partykleidchen, während die zu lang geratene Unterzeile verrät: „Our clothes look new for more than one season's wear... thanks to Chipso." Das ist die klassische, einfallslose Anzeige mit der Aussage einer zufriedenen Konsumentin. Der grammatikalisch zweifelhafte Slogan „Chipso makes clothes wear – longer" (unter dem Foto von Mutter, die in ihrer Schürze am Waschbecken steht, in der Hand einen Karton des Zaubermittels) unterstreicht noch die Botschaft, dass nur Sauberkeit wahres Glück bedeutet und diese Sauberkeit in dem Karton steckt.

Chipso mag kein kreatives Highlight gewesen sein, aber die Anzeige lässt durchaus den Einfluss bekannterer und besser finanzierter Werbekampagnen erkennen, etwa der für Coca-Cola, die es auch tunlichst vermied, Fragen offen zu lassen. „Home... to the pause that refreshes" (S. 586) erschlägt einen mit Text und Bildern. Der klassische Coca-Cola-Slogan prangt als Headline über einer stilisierten Illustration, die zwei kleine, glückliche, zuckersüchtige Geschwister zeigt. Mom kehrt gerade schwer bepackt vom Einkauf zurück (reines Wunschdenken in Zeiten

der Rezession) und wird von ihrem jüngsten Kind begeistert begrüßt. Als wäre dies noch nicht Narration genug, zeigen zwei begleitende Fotografien eine „echte" Mom dabei, wie sie das dunkle, süße Elixier einkauft und kredenzt. Und wer es noch immer nicht kapieren will, bekommt als Nachschlag den Textblock „When you shop you get something you don't bargain for. You get tired... and thirsty" an den Kopf geschmissen, der ihm das berühmte Logo „Drink Coca-Cola" in die Großhirnrinde brennt.

Anzeigen dieser Machart füllten die Seiten von *Life, Look, The Saturday Evening Post, Collier's* und zahlloser anderer wöchentlich oder monatlich erscheinender Illustrierten. Trotz der wirtschaftlichen Misere ging es den Illustrierten gut – wie das Kino lenkten sie die Menschen von ihrem tristen Alltag ab. Die Anzeigen halfen nicht nur, Produkte zu verkaufen, sie schufen auch eine Atmosphäre der Normalität, die den Menschen half, im allgemeinen gesellschaftlichen Chaos nicht die Orientierung zu verlieren.

Die Werbung der dreißiger Jahre erfüllte zwei wichtige Aufgaben: zum einen förderte sie natürlich die Kauflust und folglich den Absatz, zum anderen beschwor

sie die Selbstheilungskraft des amerikanischen Kapitalismus und weckte so in düsteren Zeiten einen gewissen Optimismus. Wenn man die Anzeigen in dem vorliegenden Band betrachtet, würde man niemals vermuten, dass Amerika damals in einer ernsthaften Krise steckte. Die stilvolleren Anzeigen der frühen dreißiger Jahre wichen aggressiveren Werbekonzepten (immer ein Indikator für düstere Zeiten), aber die Werbung für die meisten Gebrauchsgegenstände und einige wenige Luxusartikel blieb so allgegenwärtig und überschwänglich wie vor dem Börsenkrach. Und gegen Ende des Jahrzehnts, als bereits düstere Kriegswolken über Europa aufzogen, gelang es der Werbung, die Nachfrage in Amerika künstlich zu steigern. Man krempelte die Ärmel hoch, die Wirtschaft fand wieder Tritt – und dann kam der Zweite Weltkrieg. Alle Aspekte amerikanischen Lebens sollten sich für immer ändern, und auch die Werbung sollte wieder ein neues Gesicht bekommen.

Steven Heller ist Co-Chair des MFA/Design-Programms an der School of Visual Arts, New York, und Autor von mehr als achtzig Büchern zu Design und Populärkultur.

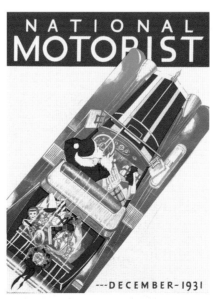

Les publicités des années 30 :
Du modernisme à la méthode coup-de-poing

de Steven Heller

La publicité américaine des années trente est née en 1925 à Paris. L'*Exposition internationale des arts décoratifs et industriels modernes*, creuset de la modernité, s'étirait de part et d'autre de la Seine dans des pavillons ornés de motifs géométriques et de frises néoclassiques. Venus du monde entier, les principaux créateurs de prêt-à-porter, de mobilier et d'articles ménagers, ainsi que de nombreux grands magasins, y exposaient leurs derniers produits et leurs dernières inventions. Toutefois, l'un des acteurs brillait par son absence.

Les Etats-Unis, la plus grande nation industrielle, avaient décliné l'invitation. Comme l'explique l'historien Terry Smith, les barons de l'industrie américaine « se sentaient incapables de rivaliser avec les créateurs français en produisant un ‹ modernisme › dépouillé à la Arts and Crafts ou en osant créer un style propre ».

A juste titre. Quand ils n'étaient pas insipides, les produits américains étaient surchargés d'ornements censés dissimuler le fait qu'ils étaient fabriqués en série. Bien que l'économie américaine moderne reposait entièrement sur la production de masse, nombreux étaient les critiques décriant le mauvais goût des articles sortant des chaînes de montage. En Europe, le Bauhaus et d'autres mouvements d'avant-garde avaient intégré la machine, mais les industriels américains restaient apathiques alors qu'ils avaient largement les moyens d'améliorer l'esthétique de leurs produits. En revanche, ils n'étaient pas indifférents aux stratégies commerciales susceptibles d'accroître leurs profits.

L'homme qui contribua le plus à révolutionner la publicité américaine à partir du milieu des années 20 et jusque dans les années 30 fut Earnest Elmo Calkins, publicitaire de la première heure, réformateur du design et fondateur de l'agence new-yorkaise Calkins and Holden Advertising Co. Enthousiasmé par l'exposition parisienne de 1925, il rédigea un traité décrivant les graphismes, les emballages et les étalages cubistes et futuristes présentés dans les pavillons des grands magasins : « C'est un art extrêmement ‹ nouveau ›, parfois bizarre mais atteignant un degré d'harmonie fascinant, qui, dans le détail, est plutôt divertissant. » De retour aux Etats-Unis, il tenta de démontrer comment la publicité américaine pouvait tirer profit du modernisme et de l'art moderne européens.

A Paris, Calkins avait été frappé par une nouvelle forme d'illustration – alors principal vecteur de création et de diffusion d'images – qui n'était plus figurative, mais qui recourait à des symboles et à des métaphores pour entourer les biens de consommation d'une aura « magique ». Les boîtes et les flacons n'étaient plus de simples contenants utilitaires, mais les signifiants de l'essence d'un produit. Calkins note dans ses écrits : « Le modernisme permet d'exprimer l'inexprimable, d'évoquer non pas une automobile mais la vitesse, non pas une robe du soir mais l'élégance, non pas un poudrier mais la beauté. » Si cela n'est pas sans rappeler le futurisme de Marinetti, c'est parce que Calkins empruntait au langage de l'avant-garde européenne sans pour autant approuver son radicalisme.

Aucun publicitaire ne contribua autant que lui à la révolution consumériste des Etats-Unis. Calkins ressemblait davantage à un prédicateur de l'Amérique profonde qu'à un publicitaire new-yorkais. Il joua pourtant un rôle crucial dans l'avènement de concepts de marketing progressistes comme « l'ingénierie de la consommation », « l'obsolescen-

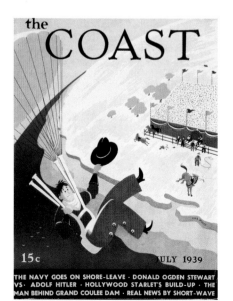
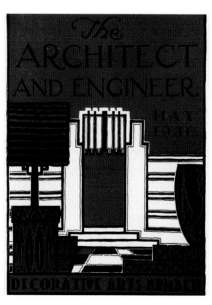

ce forcée » et « l'habillage de produits ». Ces mots clés formaient le noyau dur d'une stratégie publicitaire qui fit entrer l'art moderne et la création graphique dans un univers farouchement conservateur et dominé jusqu'alors par le texte, dont l'activité première était d'acheter de l'espace publicitaire dans les journaux et les magazines.

Calkins chercha à mettre à profit les nouvelles technologies d'impression en couleur, les effets photographiques et les dernières tendances esthétiques pour créer un « art » mémorable et monumental. En intégrant l'art moderne dans l'indigeste culture commerciale grand public, Calkins ranima l'intérêt pour les produits anciens et obligea les consommateurs à imaginer un avenir radieux rempli de biens de consommation. Cependant, ses idées « radicales » se heurtèrent à l'opposition de ceux qui voulaient vendre « sans faire de chichis ». Si sa vision gagnait du terrain, la grande majorité des publicités n'étaient encore que des tracts surchargés de textes conçus pour lever toute ambiguïté quant à la nature du produit proposé.

Les publicitaires conservateurs estimaient que les images publicitaires sophis-tiquées étaient élitistes et qu'elles ne correspondaient pas aux goûts du consommateur moyen. Pour eux, Calkins avait un sens exagéré de ses propres valeurs sociales qui ne reflétaient pas la société dans son ensemble. De son côté, Calkins pensait que la « publicité artistique » pouvait être un facteur de démocratisation pour les classes moyennes. Plutôt que de susciter des désirs nécessairement frustrés chez les plus démunis, il s'adressait exclusivement à une classe socioéconomique qu'il appelait « les gens de goût ».

Calkins considérait comme bêtifiants et déroutants les affiches surchargées (Wheaties, p. 526), les bandes dessinées (Camel, p. 53), les dessins et les slogans puérils (Saráka, p. 299). A leur place, il préconisait des techniques capables de créer une mystique par le biais de formes abstraites, stylisées et symboliques. La publicité pouvait donc s'affranchir du texte, l'image devenant le principal vecteur de communication. Tout au long des années 20 et 30, les directeurs artistiques des agences de publicité – recourant à l'illustration pour créer des auras modernes – acquirent un rôle de premier plan. Suivant la méthode de Calkins, ils commencèrent à présenter des objets courants de guingois et sur des fonds aux motifs dynamiques. De même, les articles industriels étaient souvent mis en scène dans des décors surréalistes et futuristes.

L'art moderne constituait une valeur ajoutée et un précieux camouflage. « Lorsque les nécessités du commerce ne peuvent être embellies, écrit Calkins, l'art sert à les faire disparaître. » Il appelait « atmosphère » le style graphique suggérant un lien privilégié entre la publicité et le produit, un trait fétichiste qui finit par déteindre sur l'article lui-même.

Toutefois, Calkins était un pragmatique. Une publicité qui péchait par excès d'ingéniosité risquait de perdre son public qui, ne comprenant plus ce qu'on cherchait à lui vendre, ne se laissait plus séduire. Il cherchait à relever le niveau général de la manière « la plus moderne possible, et néanmoins acceptable » ; le « style » était un moyen, et non une fin. Les publicités pour Camay (p. 288), Kinsbury Pale (p. 75) et Thompson Products (p. 14–15), pour n'en citer que quelques-unes, constituent une véritable synthèse du style moderne et de la création

publicitaire traditionnelle. Il ne s'agit pas là que d'une victoire à la Pyrrhus. Calkins expliquera plus tard que « l'amélioration de l'aspect de la publicité a eu deux effets : elle a directement influencé le goût du public et indirectement conditionné la production des biens de consommation ».

Cependant, le succès de la démarche de Calkins eut également son revers. Au début des années 30, l'industrie américaine produisait *trop* pour entretenir un niveau de consommation élevé et continu. En outre, le krach de 1929 avait sérieusement entravé le pouvoir d'achat des Américains... quand il ne l'avait pas totalement anéanti. En 1933, la réforme de Calkins atteignit ses limites et la tendance commença à s'inverser. Certes, le soin excessif apporté aux campagnes publicitaires et à la fabrication des produits pendant la période d'euphorie d'avant 1929 n'était pas directement responsable de la débâcle économique, mais il était symptomatique de ce que Harry Batten, de chez N. W. Ayer, a décrit comme un excès de confiance économique, « une sorte de fièvre du jeu [qui] s'était propagée dans toutes les couches de la société ». Au milieu des années 30, dans un monde

encore en pleine dépression, les publicitaires se rabattirent sur ce qu'on a appelé « la publicité coup-de-poing », que cet ouvrage vise à illustrer.

Face au raz-de-marée de la crise de 1929, qui balaya toutes les grandes avancées économiques de l'immédiat après-guerre, l'agence de Calkins et les nombreuses autres « boutiques » new-yorkaises durent donner à leurs clients ce qu'ils réclamaient : des ventes. Au lendemain de la Grande Dépression, certaines publicités conservèrent quelques aspects modernistes, mais la plupart des annonceurs renouèrent avec leurs techniques de vente agressives, faisant de nouveau appel aux témoignages de célébrités (pour les cigarettes), aux planches d'illustrations (pour les automobiles), aux paysages romantiques (pour les voyages) et aux réfrigérateurs rutilants et bien remplis (pour les produits alimentaires). Si les produits restaient dans les rayons, la subtilité devenait hors sujet, l'ironie inconcevable, et l'humour (hormis dans des bandes dessinées faciles à comprendre) inutile.

Calkins confia à des équipes de rédacteurs-artistes-directeurs artistiques le soin de créer des annonces et des campagnes

publicitaires créatives et équilibrées, mais, dans un contexte de dépression économique, les slogans tonitruants et les témoignages ampoulés remplacèrent toutes les nuances artistiques. Toutefois, la publicité ne pouvait plus s'offrir le luxe de séduire avec finesse. Les annonces lançaient des affirmations grandiloquentes, suivies de promesses saisissantes, et s'achevaient sur un mot de la fin mémorable. Ainsi, une publicité pour les costumes de bains Jantzen (p. 482) illustrée par George Petty, maître de l'érotisme chic, assure aux femmes qu'elles séduiront des hommes superbes tout en promettant aux hommes de tomber des créatures de rêve. Et l'accroche affirme : « Jantzen vous va comme un gant. »

A dire vrai, cette publicité pour Jantzen était plus sophistiquée que la plupart des autres du même genre. Plus représentative de l'époque, la publicité pour une lessive au nom sans ambiguïté, Chipso (de « cheap », bon marché, p. 284), ne fait pas dans la dentelle. Une photographie en couleur montre un goûter : trois fillettes radieuses et endimanchées sont accompagnées de leur maman qui semble sortir de chez le coiffeur et qui déclare : « Nos vêtements

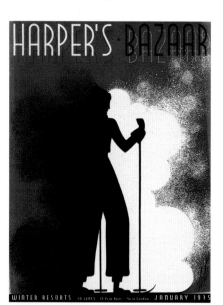

semblent neufs alors qu'ils ont plus d'une saison… grâce à Chipso. » Le manque de créativité de cette publicité-témoignage est typique. La légende finale « Chipso fait durer les vêtements plus longtemps » (sous une photo de Maman en tablier devant l'évier avec un paquet de cristaux magiques), vient renforcer l'idée que la propreté fait le bonheur et qu'elle s'achète en boîte.

Chipso se trouvait peut-être en bas de l'échelle de la créativité, mais elle n'en était pas moins influencée par des campagnes plus connues et mieux financées, comme celles de Coca-Cola, qui ne laissaient rien à l'imagination. « A la maison… pour la pause fraîcheur » (p. 586) est surchargée de textes et de visuels. La vénérable accroche de la marque couronne une illustration stylisée montrant deux enfants radieux se gavant de sucreries (le visage de la fille semble, peut-être intentionnellement, plus mûr que son corps ne le laisse penser). Maman, qui rentre des courses les bras chargés de paquets (un pur fantasme en cette période de grave récession), est accueillie par sa petite dernière (apparemment déjà repue de Coca-Cola et de gâteaux). Comme si l'image n'était pas déjà suffisamment expli-

cite, deux photographies montrent une « vraie » maman en train d'acheter et de servir le fameux élixir sucré. Au cas où l'on n'aurait toujours pas compris, la légende assène : « Faire les courses n'est pas toujours une partie de plaisir. Cela fatigue… et donne soif. » Le célèbre logo « Buvez Coca-Cola » est ensuite marqué au fer rouge sur le cortex cérébral du lecteur.

Des publicités de ce genre remplissaient les pages de *Life, Look, The Saturday Evening Post, Collier's* et d'innombrables autres hebdomadaires et mensuels. Malgré des recettes fortement réduites par la Grande Dépression, les magazines florissaient. A l'instar du cinéma, ils offraient une distraction toujours bienvenue dans la grisaille ambiante. Les publicités faisaient non seulement vendre, mais elles entretenaient l'illusion que rien n'avait changé, donnant aux consommateurs une impression de normalité dans une époque de grands bouleversements sociaux.

La publicité des années 30 joua deux rôles principaux : elle stimula la demande, et donc les ventes, et elle encouragea le capitalisme américain, servant de vecteur d'optimisme pendant cette période sombre. A voir

les publicités publiées dans cet ouvrage, qui aurait pensé que les Américains subissaient à l'époque de dures épreuves ? Les exemples plus artistiques du début de la décennie cédèrent le pas à des réclames plus agressives (indicateur symbolique d'une grave récession), mais la publicité pour la plupart des biens de consommation et certains produits de luxe resta aussi omniprésente, voire envahissante, qu'avant le krach boursier. A la fin des années 30, alors que le spectre de la guerre planait au-dessus de l'Europe, la publicité contribua à stimuler artificiellement la consommation américaine. Chacun avait retroussé ses manches et l'économie commençait à reprendre du poil de la bête… quand survint la Seconde Guerre mondiale. La vie américaine sous tous ses aspects allait s'en trouver à jamais altérée et, une fois de plus, la publicité allait devoir s'adapter.

Steven Heller est codirecteur du département MFA/Design à la School of Visual Arts de New York et l'auteur de plus de quatre-vingts ouvrages sur le design et la culture populaire.

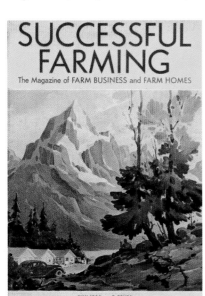

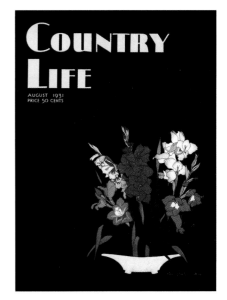

La publicidad en los años treinta:
de las vanguardias a las «mangas arremangadas»

por Steven Heller

La publicidad norteamericana de los años treinta nació en París, en 1925, a orillas del Sena, en la «Exposition Internationale des Arts Décoratifs et Industriels Modernes», centro de recreo de la modernidad, durante la cual varias avenidas quedaron franqueadas por pabellones ornamentados con motivos geométricos y frisos neoclásicos. Los fabricantes de prendas de vestir, mobiliario y menaje del hogar más prestigiosos del mundo, junto a otros muchos grandes emporios comerciales, exhibieron sus últimos artículos y diseños. Pero hubo un jugador cuya ausencia se hizo notar...

Estados Unidos, la nación industrial más importante del mundo, declinó la invitación a participar en la exposición. Los dirigentes del sector industrial norteamericano consideraban, en palabras del historiador Terry Smith, «que no podían equipararse a los diseñadores franceses, ni creando un "modernismo" Arts & Crafts desnudo ni desplegando un estilo nacional propio».

Y tenían razón. Los artículos norteamericanos que no eran totalmente anodinos presentaban una decoración excesiva bajo la que intentaban camuflar su aspecto de producto salido de una cadena de montaje.

Pese a que la producción en serie era la base sobre la que se fundamentaba la economía norteamericana moderna, muchos críticos culturales argüían que los objetos que salían de las cadenas de montaje carecían de buen gusto. Mientras que la Bauhaus y otras vanguardias europeas habían sabido sacar partido de la mecánica, los industriales norteamericanos, quienes fácilmente podían permitirse incrementar el nivel estético de sus productos, se mostraban apáticos. Pero a lo que no opusieron resistencia fue a las estrategias de márketing para aumentar sus beneficios. La industria estadounidense encendió los motores para hallar nuevos medios con los que aumentar las ventas a través del arte, la ciencia y la palabrería de la publicidad.

El hombre que contribuyó a revolucionar la publicidad en Estados Unidos a partir de mediados de los años veinte y durante la década de 1930 fue Earnest Elmo Calkins, un pionero de la publicidad, reformador del diseño y fundador de la agencia Calkins and Holden Advertising Co., afincada en Nueva York. Inspirado por la «Exposition Internationale des Arts Décoratifs et Industriels Modernes», describió, en un tratado

sobre la materia, el despliegue de escaparates, embalajes y gráficos cubistas y futuristas expuestos en los pabellones de los grandes almacenes con las siguientes palabras: «Se trata de un "arte radicalmente nuevo" y quizá algo raro, pero logra una bella armonía y, en detalle, es sumamente divertido». A su regreso a Estados Unidos, presentó su visión de cómo la publicidad norteamericana podía sacar partido del arte moderno y modernista de Europa.

En París, Calkins descubrió un nuevo enfoque de la ilustración, por entonces el principal medio para crear y difundir imágenes, un enfoque que en lugar de representar y apelar a los sentimientos, empleaba símbolos y metáforas para crear un ambiente «mágico» en el que envolver los bienes de consumo. Las cajas y las botellas no eran meros recipientes utilitarios, sino significantes de la esencia del producto. Calkins escribió: «El Movimiento Moderno ofreció la oportunidad de expresar lo inexpresable, de sugerir no tanto un vehículo a motor sino más bien la velocidad, no un vestido de noche sino estilo, no un estuche de maquillaje sino la belleza». Y si aquellas palabras recordaban a uno de los manifiestos futuristas de F. T. Marinetti,

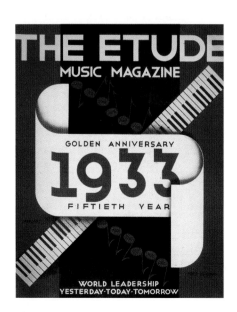

era precisamente porque Calkins adoptó el lenguaje de las vanguardias europeas, si bien eludió su radicalismo.

Ningún otro publicista fue tan relevante para la revolución del mercado de consumo norteamericano como Calkins, quien parecía más un predicador de la región central de Estados Unidos que un agente de publicidad de Nueva York. Y sin embargo, fue una figura capital para el progreso de algunos conceptos modernos de márketing, como «ingeniería del consumo», «obsolescencia forzada» y «objetos con estilo», palabras de moda todas ellas que devinieron el corazón de una estrategia publicitaria que introdujo el arte moderno y el diseño gráfico en una profesión hasta entonces devotamente conservadora y basada en textos descriptivos insertados en espacios publicitarios de revistas y periódicos.

Ya no era posible «dotar de sorpresa o atractivo a un anuncio mediante imágenes fijas y fotografías corales realistas», sentenció Calkins, cuyo deseo era aprovechar las nuevas tecnologías de impresión en color, los efectos fotográficos y las tendencias estéticas para crear un «arte» memorable y monumental. Integrando el arte moderno en la aburrida cultura comercial, Calkins reavivó el interés por productos de antaño e indujo a los consumidores a vislumbrar un futuro esperanzador, repleto de bienes de consumo. Mas sus ideas, tachadas de radicales, toparon con la resistencia de quienes preferían utilizar técnicas comerciales menos artísticas. Y mientras sus ideas se abrían camino, la inmensa mayoría de los anuncios seguían siendo octavillas repletas de texto cuyo fin era evitar todo malentendido o ambigüedad.

Los publicistas conservadores esgrimían que aquellas imágenes llenas de florituras no eran más que distracciones elitistas, ajenas al gusto de los ciudadanos de a pie, los principales consumidores, y que, por lo tanto, estaban abocadas al fracaso. En su opinión, Calkins había extrapolado al conjunto de la sociedad los valores de la clase a la que pertenecía. Pero lo que ocurría era lo contrario. Calkins consideraba que la «publicidad artística» podía convertirse en una fuerza democratizadora y generadora de una clase media uniforme. Más aún, su objetivo era dirigirse a la clase que él denominaba «gente con buen gusto», en lugar de crear nuevos deseos inasequibles entre los menos pudientes.

Calkins consideraba que los diseños recargados (Wheaties, pág. 526), los dibujos pueriles de las tiras cómicas (Camel, pág. 53) y los anuncios de texto (Saráka, pág. 299) eran degradantes y confusos. En su lugar, propuso utilizar técnicas que crearan un ambiente místico a través de formas estilizadas, simbólicas y abstractas. De este modo, la publicidad rompía sus vínculos de dependencia con el texto y la imagen devenía el medio primordial de comunicación. Y lo que es más importante, este modelo elevaba, además, al director de arte por encima del *copy* en la jerarquía del mundo de la publicidad. Para Calkins, el llamado «experto en arte» era tan importante como el *copy* más erudito. Durante los años veinte y treinta, los directores de arte adquirieron una prominencia hasta entonces inusitada en las agencias publicitarias. En sus trabajos, recurrieron a la ilustración para crear auras modernas. Aplicando el método de Calkins, los objetos cotidianos –tostadoras, frigoríficos, lapiceros, envases de lácteos, cafeteras, etc.– se presentaban en diseños dinámicos y en ángulos sesgados, mientras que las herramientas industriales de la época se integraron en una estética surrealista y futurista.

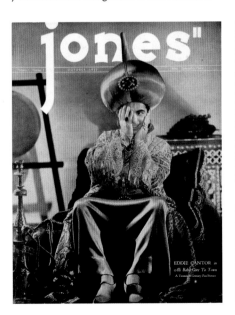

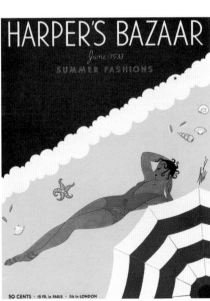

Sin embargo, Calkins era ante todo un hombre pragmático y sabía que la agudeza de la publicidad no podía superar la capacidad del público de entender lo que se anunciaba y, en el proceso, atraer su atención. La intención de Calkins era elevar el estándar general, pero había que hacerlo de la manera «más avanzada y, al mismo tiempo, aceptable posible», utilizando el «estilo» como un medio, y no como un fin. Los anuncios para Camay (pág. 288), Kinsbury Pale (pág. 75) y Thompson Products (pág. 14–15), por mencionar tan sólo algunos, eran una verdadera síntesis de estilo moderno y arte comercial tradicional.

El nuevo estilo de publicidad comercial aumentó las ventas, lo que disparó la producción y, así, se estimuló la economía. Fueron épocas felices para los fabricantes y los vendedores, y los diseñadores y artistas contribuyeron enormemente a aquella dicha. Un artista comercial de la época escribió: «He notado cómo esta idea adquiría cada vez mayor nitidez... hasta convertirse en algo verdaderamente importante: un envase que sostienen millones de manos porque les comunica algo a lo que no pueden resistirse».

No obstante, la propuesta de Calkins tenía un inconveniente. A principios de los años treinta, la industria norteamericana estaba produciendo *demasiados* artículos para mantener los elevados niveles de consumo reiterado. El espectacular colapso de la Bolsa en el año 1929 había disminuido, por decirlo suavemente, el poder adquisitivo del pueblo. En 1933, la ingeniería estilística de Calkins alcanzó un punto de inflexión. El entusiasmo desmedido de la publicidad y la producción de artículos durante el período alcista precedente no constituyó una causa directa del descalabro económico con el que se inició la Gran Depresión de Estados Unidos, pero sí fue sintomático de lo que Harry Batten de N. W. Ayer describió como un exceso de confianza económica. A mediados de los años treinta, heridos aún por la Gran Depresión, los publicistas adoptaron lo que se dio en llamar una publicidad «de mangas arremangadas», cuyos ejemplos componen gran parte de este volumen.

A medida que la marea de la Gran Depresión iba engullendo las impresionantes ganancias de los años de auge económico de la posguerra, la agencia de Calkins y las cuentas de otras grandes «tiendas» neoyorquinas tuvieron que dar a sus clientes lo que les demandaban: ventas. Y aunque algunos anuncios de los años posteriores a la Gran Depresión contenían aún ciertos toques modernos, la inmensa mayoría de ellos volvieron a recurrir a las técnicas de publicidad agresiva: caras célebres (para anunciar cigarrillos), ilustraciones de múltiples imágenes (para presentar automóviles), paisajes emotivos (para promocionar viajes) y frigoríficos refulgentes llenos a rebosar (para presentar alimentos y bebidas). El arte más avanzado del mundo no iba a vender detergente, pasta de dientes, desodorante, aceite vegetal ni bombillas. Se eliminaron las sutilezas, se desterró la ironía, y la comedia resultaba inútil si los artículos seguían en las estanterías.

Calkins encargó a varios equipos compuestos por un director de arte y un *artista-copy* concebir anuncios y campañas publicitarias equilibradas y creativas, mas, tras la Gran Depresión, los titulares llamativos y los testimonios grandilocuentes acabaron con todo matiz artístico. Antes de la era de la televisión, la publicidad impresa en periódicos, revistas y vallas, (y las cuñas radiofónicas) había constituido el medio más eficaz para tentar al consumidor. Sin embargo, ahora la publicidad debía contener afirmaciones contundentes, seguidas de promesas fiables, y

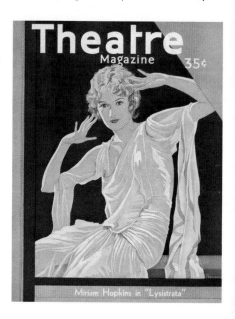

concluir con una frase memorable. Así, por ejemplo, un anuncio para trajes de baño Jantzen (pág. 482) prometía a las mujeres hombres fascinantes y a los hombres, mujeres esculturales con sólo comprar el producto.

Con todo, el anuncio de Jantzen exhibía una dosis artística más elevada que la mayoría de los de su género. En contraposición, el austero anuncio de Chipso (pág. 284) para un detergente de ropa era más común. En una fotografía en color aparecían un ama de casa recién salida de la peluquería y sus tres hijas vestidas con trajes impolutos sobre un titular que rezaba: «La ropa del año pasado sigue pareciendo nueva... gracias a Chipso». Un anuncio testimonial típico, sin el más mínimo atisbo de imaginación. El eslogan «Chipso hace que su ropa dure más» reforzaba la idea de que la felicidad es limpieza y la limpieza se condensa en una caja.

Y aunque es posible que Chipso se encontrara en el peldaño más bajo de la escalera creativa, no es menos cierto que acusaba la influencia de campañas nacionales más conocidas y de mayor presupuesto, como la de Coca-Cola, que no dejaba nada a la imaginación. El anuncio con el lema «Disfruta en casa... de la pausa que refresca» (pág. 586)

está repleto de capas de texto y efectos visuales. Un titular en el que aparecía el venerable lema de Coca-Cola recorría el margen superior de una estilizada ilustración de dos felices hermanas preadolescentes. Tras un día de compras desenfrenadas, su madre regresa a casa cargada de bolsas, donde la recibe cariñosamente su hija más pequeña. Por si la ilustración no fuera en sí lo bastante elocuente, dos fotografías auxiliares muestran una madre «real» comprando y sirviendo ese elixir oscuro y dulce... Pero no queda ahí la cosa. El texto «Cuando se va de compras, hay algo con lo que siempre se vuelve: cansancio... y sed» golpea al lector con el famoso logotipo «Beba Coca-Cola».

Anuncios como éstos poblaron las páginas de *Life*, *Look*, *The Saturday Evening Post*, *Collier's* y otras tantas revistas. Pese a la recesión económica que conllevó la Gran Depresión, las revistas comerciales alcanzaron la cumbre de su éxito: al igual que las películas, se convirtieron en diversiones que distraían de la rutina diaria. La publicidad no sólo vendía artículos, sino que transmitía una sensación de normalidad que ayudaba a los consumidores a encontrar un punto de anclaje en medio del desconcierto social.

En última instancia, la publicidad de los años treinta cumplió dos fines importantes: estimular el deseo y, con ello, las ventas, y exhortar al capitalismo norteamericano, infundiendo cierto optimismo en aquellos negros años. Al contemplar los anuncios de este libro resulta imposible imaginar el sufrimiento de los norteamericanos en aquella época de penurias. Si bien los ejemplos más artísticos de principios de los años treinta dieron paso a una publicidad más agresiva, los anuncios continuaron estando tan presentes y siendo tan exuberantes como en la época previa al crack del 29. A finales de la década, cuando las nubes de la guerra encapotaban el cielo en Europa, la publicidad contribuyó a estimular el consumo en Estados Unidos. Con las mangas arremangadas y la economía dando indicios de reactivación, estalló la Segunda Guerra Mundial. La vida en Norteamérica cambiaría de manera irreversible y la publicidad volvería a caminar por nuevos senderos.

Steven Heller es codirector del programa de diseño MFA/Design en la School of Visual Arts de Nueva York y autor de más de 80 libros sobre diseño y cultura popular.

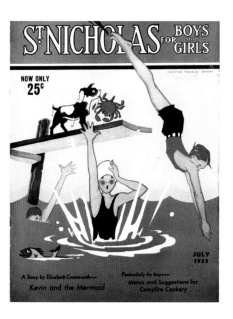

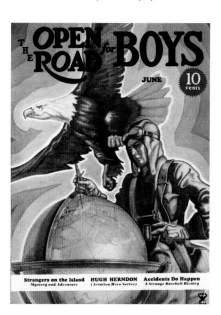

アメリカン・アドバタイジング30s

モダニズムから実践主義へ

スティーヴン・ヘラー

30年代のアメリカ広告は、1925年にパリのセーヌ川両岸で誕生した。〈現代装飾・工業美術国際展（通称アール・デコ展）〉は、近代性が発揮された舞台となって、大通りに連なる展示館で繰り広げられた。それぞれの展示館は幾何学的な装飾や、新古典様式のレリーフの装飾帯で飾り付けされていた。世界一流の服飾、家具、家庭用品メーカーが、多数のおもだった小売店とともに最新の製品とデザインを出展していた。だが、あきらかに役者がひとり欠けていた。

合衆国は世界最大の産業国ながら、展覧会参加の招きを断った。アメリカ産業界のリーダーたちは、「アメリカはアーツ・アンド・クラフツ運動を“モダニズム”に変容させようにも、アメリカ的独自様式で果敢に対抗しようにも、フランスのデザイナーには太刀打ちできない」という歴史学者テリー・スミスの説を信じていた。

事実、それは正しかった。アメリカ製品はなんの変哲もないか、大量生産品だと分からないように過剰に装飾してあるかのどちらかだった。大量生産は近代アメリカ経済の基盤だが、文化評論家の多くが主張するように、工場のラインから生産される品物は趣味が悪かった。バウハウスやヨーロッパの近

代前衛主義は、機械を称賛していた。一方、アメリカ産業界は製品を芸術的に進化させられるほど豊かだったというのに、まったく芸術には無関心だった。が、抗えなかったのはさらなる利益を上げるためのマーケティング戦略だった。そこで産業界は広告における芸術、科学、コピーライティングを通して、売上増加のための新たな方法を必死で模索した。

アメリカの広告を1920年代半ばから30年代にかけて革新的に変化させたひとりの人物がいた。その人物とはアーネスト・エルモ・カルキンである。彼は広告業界の先駆者であり、デザインの革命家であるとともにニューヨーク拠点のカルキン・アンド・ホールデン・アドバタイジング社の創立者だった。彼は〈現代装飾・工業美術国際展〉に着想を得て、ずらりと並んだキュビズム的で未来主義的なグラフィックアートやパッケージ、百貨店の展示について論文の中でこのように描写した。「これはまさに“ニューアート”だ。いささか奇妙だが、確実にある刺激的な調和に到達していて、細部においてはかなり興味深い」。彼は合衆国へ帰国すると、どうすればヨーロッパ的モダニズムとモダンアートをアメリカの広告に役立てられるか、ある未来像を提示した。

カルキンはパリでイラストの取り組みを目の当

たりにした。当時はそれがイメージを創造し普及させる一番の手段であった。イラストとは情趣あふれる絵画的なものではなく、シンボルやメタファーを駆使して「不思議な」雰囲気を消耗品に与えるものであった。箱やボトルは単なる実用的な器ではなく、製品の本質的要素を物語るものであった。カルキンはこう説明している。「モダニズムは、表現し得ないものを表現する機会を与えた。つまり自動車ではなくそのスピードを、ガウンではなく優雅さを、化粧用コンパクトでなくその美しさを示唆することだ」。これが未来派の詩人Ｆ・Ｔ・マリネッティの未来主義宣言を思い起こさせるとしたら、それはカルキンがこのヨーロッパ前衛主義者の言葉や過激さを覆い隠して拝借したからである。

広告業界でアメリカ的な消費者革命を招いたのはほかでもなくカルキンだった。彼はニューヨークの広告ライターというよりむしろ中西部の伝道者のようだった。彼は、「消費工学」、「陳腐化」、「商品のスタイリング」といったような進歩的な近代的マーケティング・コンセプトの一役を担った。そしてこれらのもったいぶった用語は広告戦略の核となり、主に雑誌や新聞の広告スペース確保に従事していた従来型の広告コピー至上主義の保守的な職業に、モ

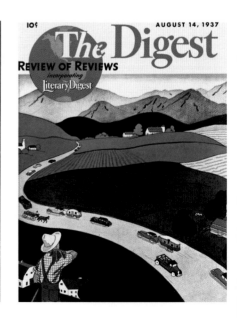

ダンアートとグラフィックデザインを知らず知らず浸透させた。

　もはや「静止写真や現実的なものの寄せ集めで、広告を衝撃的で魅力的にすること」は不可能だとカルキンは力説した。彼は新しいカラープリント技術、フォトグラフィック効果、美的トレンドを利用して不朽の「アート」を生み出そうとした。モダンアートを没個性的広告文化の本流に引き込むことで、カルキンは昔からある商品を再び興味深いものに仕立て上げた。同時に、消費者に消費できる商品で、なおかつ輝かしい未来を期待せずにはいられないように仕向けた。それでもなお、彼の過激ともいえるアイデアはもっと実用的なやり方で売ろうとする人々の反対にあった。実際、彼のアイデアは進捗していたものの、大多数の広告は、勘違いやあいまいな表現を徹底的に排除するような広告文にあふれていた。

　保守的な広告業界人は、洒落た広告イメージはエリート主義者の気晴らしで、一般消費者の意に沿うものではない、だから失敗するに決まっている、と主張した。彼らに言わせれば、カルキンは社会全体の反映と、対立する自分のクラス階級の価値観をない交ぜに考えていた。それとは逆に、カルキンは

「アーティスティックな広告」が中産階級層には一般受けすると考えた。実際に、彼は「趣味の良い人々」と呼ばれた経済上のクラス階級をターゲットにしたに過ぎず、いわゆる持たざる人々に手の届かないような憧れを引き起こすつもりはなかった。

　カルキンは乱雑なデザイン（Wheaties,p.526）、漫画（Camel, p.53）、子供の落書きのような絵と広告コピー（Sharaka, p.299）は低俗で分かりにくいと考えた。その代わりに、彼は様式化されたシンボリックで抽象的な形式を使った秘法的技術を編み出した。それは広告が広告コピーにそれほど頼らなくてもやっていけることを意味した。というのもイメージとは意思伝達の基本形だからだ。もっと重要なことは、このような事例は広告業界のヒエラルキーにおいてアートディレクターを格上げし、コピーライターよりも上に位置づけた。いわゆる「アートエキスパート」は、広告コピーを取り仕切る者と同等に重要であるとカルキンは悟った。1920年代から30年代を通して、アートディレクターは新発見のすばらしいものを手に入れた。事実、アートディレクターはイラストレーションを利用してモダンな雰囲気を漂わせた。カルキンの手法によって、トースター、冷蔵庫、鉛筆、ショートニング、コーヒーの缶

といったありふれた日用品は力学的パターンに逆らって、斜めのアングルで提示された。そしてその時代の工業製品はシュールレアリズム的・未来主義的な道具立ての中に展示されることが多かった。

　モダンアートは付加価値的なもので、カムフラージュには欠かせなかった。カルキンはこう述べている。「醜悪な有用性を美化することは不可能だ」「アートはそういったものを消し去るために使用される」。グラフィックアートによる広告で、商品との関係を独特にほのめかすことは、カルキンが「ムード」と名づけたもので、最終的には製品そのものに投影されるフェティッシュな特性になった。

　しかし、カルキンは実利派であった。巧妙に仕組まれた広告は何が宣伝されているのか大衆が理解できる範囲内であったし、そしてわかってもらえれば製品は売れた。彼は全体的な基準を引き上げようと努めたが、それも「最も進歩的でありながら許容範囲内の」やり方で遂行された。そして「スタイル」はその手段であって、目的ではなかった。キャメイ（p.288）、キンズベリー・ペール（p.75）、トンプソン・プロダクツ（p.14-15）などのいくつかの例は、まさに近代的なスタイルと従来型のコマーシャルアートの統合といえる。これについて、成功ではあるが

失うものも多いとは単純に言えない。カルキンはモ
ダニズム的ニュアンスを創造できたことに心から
満足していた。というのも、彼は次のように述べて
いたからである。「広告観相学を発展させることは2
重の結果をもたらす…直接的には大衆の趣向に影
響を与え、間接的には製品の生産を左右する」

　季節を重ねるうちに新しい広告宣伝スタイルは
売り上げを伸ばし、そしてそれが生産増加の誘引と
なり、ひいては経済を活性化した。メーカーや小売
業者は満足していた。そしてこの恵まれた結果に大
いに貢献したのはデザイナーとアーティストだった。
当事の広告アーティストはこのように説明している。
「私は、この演出するという考え方が徐々に重要な
ものになっていくのを目の当たりにした…売り場で
何百万もの手が商品に伸びる。それは、何が何でも
欲しくなるような演出だからだ！」

　しかしカルキンのアプローチの成功にも陰り
が見えた。1930年代初頭、アメリカ産業界は、消費
の反復を高水準で維持するために、実にあまりにも
多くの商品を生産しようとしていた。そのうえ1929
年の巨大株式市場の破綻は、控えめに言えば、大衆
の購買力の大きな足かせとなっていた。1933年ま
でに、カルキンの広告工学的手法は縮小転換期を

迎えた。これまでの買い手市場の中で過熱していっ
た広告と製品生産は、アメリカ大恐慌の引き金とな
るこの経済不況の直接の原因ではなかったが、それ
はN・W・エイヤーのハリー・バトンが経済過信とし
て「社会のあらゆる層に浸透した一種の投機熱」と
表現した事態の兆候だった。1930年代半ばまで広
告業界人と広告は大恐慌の痛手を引きずってはい
たものの、本書の大半を占める現実主義広告と呼
ばれていた広告を取り入れていった。

　大恐慌の上げ潮が、戦前の好景気時代のすば
らしい経済利益を根こそぎ洗い流してしまった。そ
のため、カルキンの広告代理店と多数のニューヨー
クの大きな「ショップ」は顧客が欲しいと思うものを
与えること、つまり販売活動をする必要があった。確
固たる「モダニズム」精神は大恐慌後の広告に引き
継がれたが、大多数の広告業界人はハードセルに回
帰し、有名人の推奨（タバコ広告）、マルチイメージの
絵（車）、情緒ある風景（旅行）、そしてものがいっぱ
い詰まってきらきら輝く冷蔵庫（食料・飲料）といっ
た手法が取り入れられていた。世界最先端のアート
では洗剤、歯磨き粉、デオドラント用品、植物油や電
球は売れなかった。含蓄ある表現は影を潜め、アイ
ロニーはかろうじて見受けられたものの、分かりや

すい漫画は別として、陳列棚に置いてあるだけのコ
メディー商品は役立たずであった。

　カルキンはコピーライターとアートディレクター
のチームに、クリエイティブな調和が取れた販売促
進広告の制作を課した。しかし、大恐慌が起こったこ
とで、けたたましい見出しと絢爛たる推奨文がアー
ティスティックなニュアンスに取って代わった。テレ
ビ登場以前は新聞の折り込み広告や雑誌、屋外看
板、（そしてもちろんラジオ）が単刀直入に消費者の
気をそそる最も効果的な方法であった。しかし、広
告はもはや、もったいぶってじらすような贅沢はして
いられなかった。広告は記憶に残る決まり文句で終
わるように、徹底した約束事に従って主張を明確に
しなければならなかった。例えば、ジャンセンの水
着広告（p.482）は、ソフトさが魅力の巨匠ジョージ・
ペティのイラストである。商品を購入しさえすれば、
女性に素敵な男性を確約し、一方で同じように女性
を手に入れられると男性に約束する。「実にお似合
い──ジャンセン」という思わせぶりな見出しはさら
に、巧みな表現能力を持つ人物がこの販売促進に
かかわっていることを示している。

　ジャンセンの広告はこの手の広告の中では技巧
的な部類に入る。反対に、変わった名前の洗濯洗剤、

チブソーの素朴な広告(p.284)はかなり一般的である。ここに子供たちのティーパーティーのカラー写真がある。こざっぱりと髪をスカーフでまとめた母親と、清潔でおしゃれな服を着た3人の幸せそうな娘たちが冗長なタイトルの上で座っている。幸福な少女たちの母親は言う。「私たちの服は何シーズン着ても下ろしたてのよう…チブソーのおかげで」。これは想像力不要の典型的な推薦型の広告である。この文法的に難しいキャッチコピー「チブソーで服が着られる——もっと長く」(魔法の粉の箱を手に洗い場のシンクにいるエプロンをした母親の写真下)はさらに、幸福とは清潔さであり、その清潔さはこの箱の中にあるという考えをも強調している。

チブソーは創造性では及びもつかなかったといえるが、それでも有名で予算豊富な全米中の販売促進キャンペーンの影響を受けていた。想像力をさしはさむ余地のないコカ・コーラの広告はその一例だ。「くつろぎ…リフレッシュするひととき」(p.586)は、たたみかける文章と強い影響力を放つ視覚的効果が盛り込まれていた。コカ・コーラの頭が下がるキャッチコピーの入った見出しが、楽しげな甘いもの好きの10代になる前の2人の子供たち(少女の顔はおそらく意図的に身体よりも年長で賢そうに

描かれている)というお決まりの絵の一番上に載っている。母親はショッピングを楽しんで帰宅したばかりで、たくさんの包みを抱えて(大恐慌時代の願望的思考だ)、末っ子のうれしそうな出迎えを受けている(もうコカ・コーラとクッキーで大満足したのだろう)。まるでこの絵だけでは説明不足といわんばかりに、「実物の」母親が黒くて甘い魔法の液体を買って出している2枚の写真がついている。これでも足りないというなら、もう一度見てみよう。「買い物に行くと思いがけないことがある。疲れる…のどが渇く」というひとかたまりの文章が読み手の頭を直撃し、大脳皮質に有名なトレードマーク「コカ・コーラを飲もう」を刻みつける。

こういった広告が『ライフ』『ルック』『サタデー・イブニング・ポスト』『コリアーズ』そのほか数え切れないほどの週刊誌や月刊誌のページを埋めた。大恐慌が富の衰退をもたらしたにもかかわらず、商業雑誌は成功を極めていた。映画がそうであるように、雑誌も単調な日常生活における気晴らしだった。広告は商品を売るだけでなく、社会的混乱のただなかにあって、消費者が各自のよりどころを見出せるような正常感覚を供給したのだ。

30年代の広告は最終的にふたつの重要な機能

を果たした。欲望を刺激し、ひいては販売を促進すること、そして、アメリカ資本主義を熱心に説き、それにより暗い時代に楽観主義を知らず知らず浸透させることだった。この本の広告を見ると、アメリカが艱難辛苦にあっていたとは想像もつかないことだろう。30年代初期のもっとアーティスティックだったお手本は、ハードな時代を象徴的に示しているハードセルに取って代わった。贅沢品の広告は少数で、多くが日用品のためであったが、経済破綻前と同じようにどこにでも存在し、豊かな繁栄を遂げたことは事実である。30年代後半は、戦争がヨーロッパに暗い影を落としていた頃だが、広告は人為的な助けとなってアメリカの消費主義を活気づけた。すでに物事は着々と進んでいて、経済は音を立てて動き始めようとした。そこへ第2次世界大戦が始まった。アメリカの生活があらゆる点で永遠に変わってしまうかのようであった。そして広告は再びその様相を変えていくことになる。

スティーヴン・ヘラーはニューヨーク・ビジュアルアーツ・スクールのMFAデザイン学科の共同主任。デザインと大衆文化に関する80冊を超える本の著者でもある。

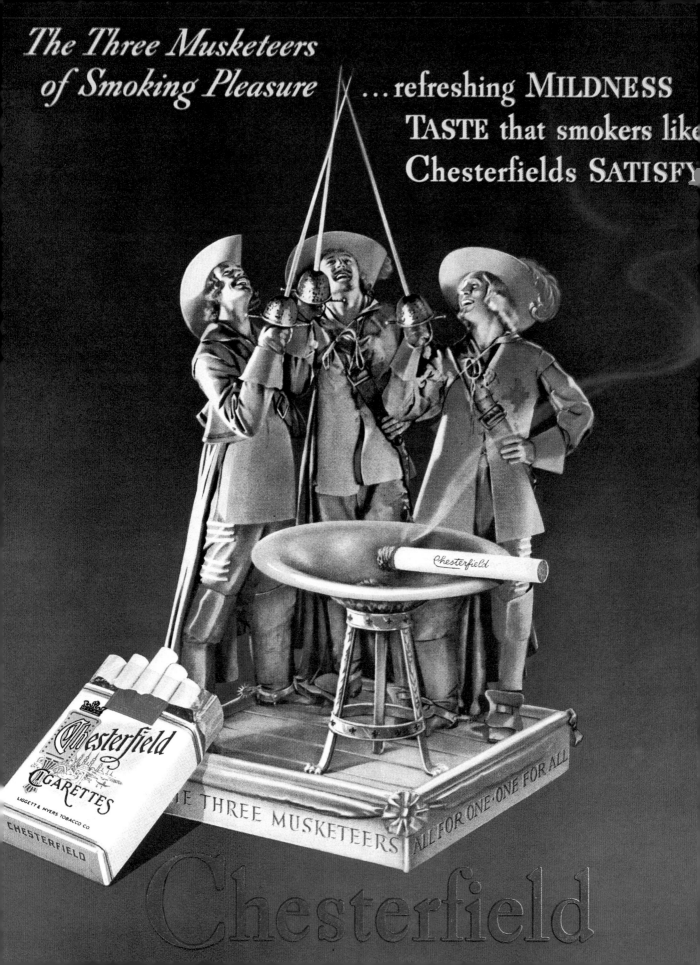

Chesterfield, 1937

Chesterfield, 1937

Philip Morris, 1934 ◄◄ *Chesterfield, 1937* ◄ *Chesterfield, 1937*

Chesterfield, 1937

Chesterfield, 1939

Chesterfield, 1938

Chesterfield, 1938

Chesterfield, 1931

▶ *Chesterfield, 1937*

friendly green parrot has become my boon
companion and gives me so much pleasure
I call him Colonel SATISFY... the best
name I know for pleasure.

Chesterfields will give you more pleasure

They Satisfy

"I like a FRESH cigarette –*don't you?*"

THE true source of delicate mildness and agreeable flavor in a cigarette is choice, full-mellow, sun-ripened tobaccos.

Tobaccos of such fine mild quality are *naturally* soothing to the throat, and delightful to the taste – it takes no harsh or violent processing to make them so.

Camels are blended of tobaccos like that – fine Turkish and mild sun-ripened Domestic tobaccos – and they are never parched or toasted.

Camels go into the package clean, dust-free, *fresh* with natural moisture – the Camel Humidor Pack brings them to you that way, in prime condition, *fresh* to smoke.

There is so much difference between *fresh* Camels and the hot smoke of parched dry-as-dust tobaccos that millions of men and women are switching to Camels with grateful relief.

If you want to see how much that difference means in unalloyed smoke-enjoyment, try Camels for just one day – then leave them – if you can!

R. J. REYNOLDS TOBACCO COMPANY, *Winston-Salem, N. C.*

"Are you Listenin'?"

R. J. REYNOLDS TOBACCO COMPANY'S COAST-TO-COAST RADIO PROGRAMS

CAMEL QUARTER HOUR, Morton Downey, Tony Wons, and Camel Orchestra, direction Jacques Renard, every night except Sunday, Columbia Broadcasting System

PRINCE ALBERT QUARTER HOUR, Alice Joy, "Old Hunch," and Prince Albert Orchestra, direction Paul Van Loan, every night except Sunday, N. B. C. Red Network

See radio page of local newspaper for time

Smoke a FRESH cigarette

CAMELS

Made FRESH — Kept FRESH

● *Don't remove the moisture-proof wrapping from your package of Camels after you open it. The Camel Humidor Pack is protection against perfume and powder odors, dust and germs. In offices and homes, even in the dry atmosphere of artificial heat, the Camel Humidor Pack can be depended upon to deliver fresh Camels every time*

Camels, 1932

"You like them FRESH? So do I!"

YOU don't have to tell the woman who has switched to Camels the benefits of *a fresh* cigarette.

She knows all about it — that's the reason she stays switched.

She has learned that the fine, fragrant, sun-ripened choice tobaccos in Camels have a perfectly preserved delicate mildness all their own.

She knows by a grateful throat's testimony what a relief this smooth, cool, slow-burning *fresh* cigarette means to sensitive membrane.

Camels are fresh in the Camel Humidor Pack because they are *made* fresh, fresh with natural moisture and natural flavors—they are never parched or toasted.

If you don't know what the Reynolds method of scientifically applying heat so as to avoid parching or toasting means to the smoker — switch to Camels for just one day, then leave them — if you can.

R. J. REYNOLDS TOBACCO COMPANY, *Winston-Salem, N. C.*

"Are you Listenin'?"

R. J. REYNOLDS TOBACCO COMPANY'S COAST-TO-COAST RADIO PROGRAMS

CAMEL QUARTER HOUR, Morton Downey, Tony Wons, and Camel Orchestra, direction Jacques Renard, every night except Sunday, Columbia Broadcasting System

PRINCE ALBERT QUARTER HOUR, Alice Joy, "Old Hunch," and Prince Albert Orchestra, every night except Sunday, N. B. C. Red Network

See radio page of local newspaper for time

CAMELS

Made FRESH — Kept FRESH

● *Don't remove the moisture-proof wrapping from your package of Camels after you open it. The Camel Humidor Pack is protection against perfume and powder odors, dust and germs. In offices and homes, even in the dry atmosphere of artificial heat, the Camel Humidor Pack can be depended upon to deliver fresh Camels every time*

© 1932, R. J. Reynolds Tobacco Company

Smoke a FRESH cigarette

Camels, 1932

▶ *Camels, 1935*

HERE'S WHY CAMEL'S MILDNESS APPEALS TO OUT-OF-DOORS PEOPLE

"They Never Get on Your Nerves"

Henry Clay Foster, explorer, tiger hunter, and steady Camel smoker. He has struggled for many a weary mile through bush and jungle...faced many a tense moment when nerves were tested to the limit. Speaking of nerves and smoking, Foster says: "My idea of a mild cigarette is Camel. I've been in some tough spots, but Camels have never thrown my nerves off key, although I'm a steady Camel smoker and have been for years. Camels give me the mildness I want—better taste—the fragrance and aroma of choice tobaccos."

"Get a Lift with a Camel"

Erwin Jones, Boulder Dam engineer, says: "If I'm tired, a Camel refreshes me in a few minutes. What a swell taste Camels have! You can tell they are made from choice tobaccos."

"Camels don't get your Wind"

Miss Judy Ford, of New York and Florida, says: "Wishing to keep in the best of condition, I prefer Camels! They are so mild that they never disturb my wind or fray my nerves."

COSTLIER TOBACCOS!

CAMEL
TURKISH & DOMESTIC BLEND CIGARETTES
CHOICE QUALITY

● Camels are made from finer, MORE EXPENSIVE TOBACCOS—Turkish and Domestic—than any other popular brand.

(*Signed*) R. J. REYNOLDS TOBACCO COMPANY
Winston-Salem, North Carolina

"They Never Tire Your Taste"

Lieutenant Commander Frank Hawks, U.S.N.R., holder of 214 speed records, says: "Camels taste better—mild, cool, and mellow. They are never harsh or irritating to my throat."

© 1935, R. J. Reynolds Tob. Co.

"MARVELOUS MUSIC—
AND MY FAVORITE CIGARETTE, CAMELS"

CAMEL
TURKISH & DO
BLE
CIGA

Camels are made from finer, MORE EXPENSIVE tobaccos than any other popular brand

Women are very critical of flavors—it is part of their training.

Even when tea is iced most women, by its flavor, can price it withi a few cents. So when it is a question of cigarettes women are doubl critical. That is why more and more women are changing to the fine more expensive tobaccos in Camels.

Leaf tobacco for cigarettes can be bought from 5¢ a pound t $1.00, but Camel pays the millions more that insure your enjoymen

The fine, rich flavor of Camels will delight your taste—light on and enjoy its fragrant, mellow mildness.

*Jade jewels by Marcus, Fifth Avenue • Orchids by Irene Hayes, Park Avenue
Flavor and mildness by Camel.*

Camels, 1939

Camels, 1939

Camels, 1933 ◄ Camels, 1937

Camels, 1937

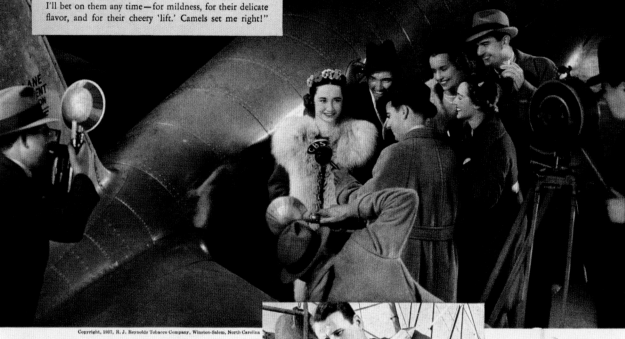

For Digestion's Sake... Smoke Camels

"I'll back that to the limit," says Miss Dorothy Kilgallen, spunky globe-circling girl reporter

AROUND THE WORLD IN 24 DAYS. "It was a breathless dash," said Miss Dorothy Kilgallen, famous girl reporter, back at work (*above*) after finishing her assignment to circle the world by air in record-breaking time. (*Right*) Her exciting arrival at the Newark Airport. "I snatched meals anywhere," she says, "ate all kinds of food. But Camels helped me keep my digestion tuned up. 'For digestion's sake—smoke Camels' meant a world of comfort to me. I'll bet on them any time—for mildness, for their delicate flavor, and for their cheery 'lift.' Camels set me right!"

Copyright, 1937, R. J. Reynolds Tobacco Company, Winston-Salem, North Carolina

Camels help you go through a day with a sense of well-being

IN every job—reporter or housewife, explorer or laborer—tension and upsets are to be expected. Healthy nerves and good digestion enable you to glide over trying incidents and get the full enjoyment out of working, eating, and playing. No wonder that so many who make their mark in the world today are steady Camel smokers!

At mealtimes—enjoy Camels for the aid they give digestion. By speeding up the flow of digestive fluids and increasing alkalinity, Camels contribute to your sense of well-being. Between meals—get a "lift" with a Camel. Camels don't get on the nerves, or irritate the throat. Join the vast army of smokers who say: "Camels set you right!"

ABOUT TO SHOOT AN OIL-WELL WITH T. N. T. "My business makes me mighty careful about my nerves and digestion," says B. C. Simpson. "Camels have what I like. They don't get on my nerves. And they put a heap more joy into eating."

CAMEL
TURKISH & DOMESTIC BLEND CIGARETTES

COSTLIER TOBACCOS Camels are made from finer, MORE EXPENSIVE TOBACCOS — Turkish and Domestic — than any other popular brand

IT'S A *THRILLING LIFE!*

Folks who risk their lives as a matter of course are careful in their choice of a cigarette. They say:

"CAMELS NEVER GET ON YOUR NERVES"

MAN THROWS LION! Mel Koontz, noted lion and tiger tamer, schools "big cats" for Hollywood films. Sketch (*left*) shows Mel meeting the lunge of a savage 450-pound beast. That's where nerve-power tells—as Mel *knows!* He says this: "Camels don't jangle my nerves—my mind is at rest as to that! Camels are *milder*. They have the real natural mildness that's *grown* right in the tobacco. We animal tamers stick pretty well to Camels!"

(*Right*) CRASHING A PLANE [th]rough a house is the spectacular [sp]ecialty of Stunt Pilot Frank Frakes. [An]d, at this writing, he's done it [—] *times*—on movie locations, at [ex]hibitions. Time after time, with [his] life actually in his hands, it's [ea]sy to understand why Pilot Frakes [sa]ys: "I take every precaution to [ke]ep my nerves steady as a rock. [N]aturally, I'm particular about the [ci]garette I smoke. And you can bet [my] choice is Camel. I can smoke [as] many as I want and feel fresh [—] never a bit jittery or upset."

(*Above*) THREE TIMES Lou Meyer won the Indianapolis auto-racing classic—only driver in history to achieve this amazing triple-test of nerve control. He says: "My nerves must be every bit as sound as the motor in my racer. That's why I go for Camels. They never get on my nerves a bit. Camels take first place with me for *mildness!*"

(*Left*) THRILLING STUNTS for the movies! Ione Reed *needs healthy nerves!* Naturally, Miss Reed chooses her cigarette with care. "My nerves," she says, "must be right—and no mistake! So I stick to Camels. Even smoking Camels steadily doesn't bother my nerves. In fact, Camels give me a grand sense of comfort. And they taste so good! Stunt men and women I know favor Camels."

Camels are [a] matchless blend of finer, [M]ORE EXPENSIVE TOBACCOS —Turkish and Domestic

Copyright, 1938
R. J. Reynolds Tob. Co.
Winston-Salem, N. C.

PEOPLE **DO** APPRECIATE THE COSTLIER TOBACCOS IN CAMELS

THEY ARE THE LARGEST-SELLING CIGARETTE IN AMERICA

Meet these men who **live** [w]ith tobacco from planting [t]o marketing — and note [t]he cigarette **they** smoke

"Most tobacco planters I know prefer Camels," says grower Tony Strickland, "because Camel buys the fine grades of tobacco —my own and those of other growers. And Camel bids high to get these finer lots. It's Camels for me!"

Planter David E. Wells knows every phase of tobacco culture . . . the "inside" story of tobacco quality. "At sale after sale," he says, "Camel buys up my finest grades at top prices. It's only natural for most planters like me to smoke Camels."

"I ought to know finer tobaccos make finer cigarettes," says grower John T. Caraway. "I've been smoking Camels for 23 years. Camel buyers pay more to get my finest tobacco—many's the year. Camels are the big favorite with planters down here."

Camels, 1939

Camels, 1939

Camels, 1938

Alcoa Aluminum, 1939

Camels, 1937

Camels, 1938

Camels, 1937

Lucky Strike, 1938

Lucky Strike, 1935

Lucky Strike, 1936

Lucky Strike, 1937

▶ *Lucky Strike, 1932*

Her Throat Insured For $50,000.

DOLORES DEL RIO* tells why it's good business for her to smoke Luckies...

"That $50,000 insurance is a studio precaution against my holding up a picture," says Miss Del Rio. "So I take no chances on an irritated throat. No matter how much I use my voice in acting, I always find Luckies gentle."

They will be gentle on *your* throat, too. Here's why... Luckies' exclusive "Toasting" process expels certain harsh irritants found in all tobacco. This makes Luckies' fine tobaccos even finer... a *light* smoke.

Sworn records show that among independent tobacco experts—men who know tobacco and its qualities—Luckies have twice as many exclusive smokers as all other cigarettes combined.

WITH MEN WHO KNOW TOBACCO BEST IT'S LUCKIES—2 TO 1

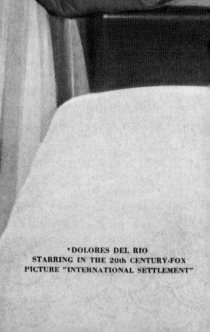

*DOLORES DEL RIO STARRING IN THE 20th CENTURY-FOX PICTURE "INTERNATIONAL SETTLEMENT"

Lucky Strike, 1938

Lucky Strike, 1938

Lucky Strike, 1938 ◄ Lucky Strike, 1937

Lucky Strike, 1938

Lucky Strike, 1935

▶ *Lucky Strike, 1935*

Just can't be Weather-Beaten!

Just like
Betty Petty . . .
Old Golds love the
April Showers
For the bloom they
Give to May flowers.
But like smart Betty,
Old Golds are
Doubly Protected
Against the
Spring dampness
That steals the
Freshness of a
Girl's curls or a
Cigarette.
Working together
Like slicker and
Umbrella . . . those 2
Cellophane jackets
On every pack
Just can't be
Weather-beaten,
They keep O. G's'
Extra choice, extra
Long-aged tobaccos
As fresh and fragrant
As the Tulips of
Spring . . . ready to
Delight your
2 lips in any
Climate
Anywhere!

Every pack wrapped in 2 jackets of Cellophane; the OUTER jacket opens from the BOTTOM.

ATTENTION! YOU PETTY FANS!
Send 10c and 2 Old Gold wrappers for a beautiful 4-color reproduction of this picture of "Betty Petty," without advertising, suitable for framing. Address: OLD GOLD, 119 West 40th St., New York City.

For Finer *FRESHER* Flavor . . . Smoke Double-Mellow Old Golds

TUNE IN on Old Gold's "Melody and Madness" with ROBERT BENCHLEY and ARTIE SHAW'S Orchestra, every Sunday night, Columbia Network, Coast-to-Coast

Old Gold, 1939

DOUBLE ENJOYMENT *Guaranteed!*

Old Gold CIGARETTES
THE TREASURE OF THEM ALL

ZIPS OPEN IN A JIFFY!
Outer Cellophane Jacket opens from the Bottom.
Inner Cellophane Jacket opens from the Top.

MAYBE you have a "crush" on another cigarette. But wait 'til you taste those prize-crop-tobacco Old Golds! Brought to you *factory-fresh,* in the new "Double-Cellophaned" package. If you don't say *"Delish!"* you get double your money back . . . as per offer in your daily newspaper.

2 PRIZE CROP TOBACCOS make them DOUBLE-MELLOW
JACKETS, *DOUBLE "CELLOPHANE,"* keep them FACTORY-FRESH

Old Gold, 1935 ◄   *Old Gold, 1936*

Camels, Prince Albert, 1937

Camels, Prince Albert, 1936

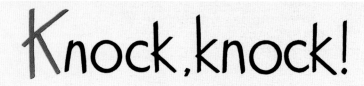

Knock, knock!

Who's there?
Wetherby!
Wetherby who?

Wetherby hanged, Lady! "Weather" gets the ha-ha from Double-Mellow Old Gold's *double*-Cellophane package. Rain or shine! Hot or cold! Any climate! Anywhere! Any time!...you'll find Double-Mellow Old Golds are always factory-fresh. Thanks to those 2 jackets of the finest moisture-proof Cellophane on every package. And don't forget O. Gs. are blended from the choicest of the *prize crop* tobaccos!

ZIPS OPEN DOUBLE-QUICK!

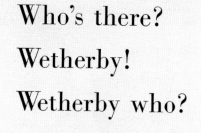

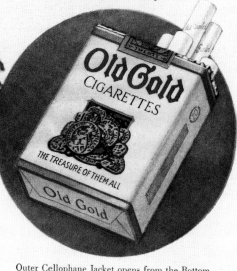

Outer Cellophane Jacket opens from the Bottom.
Inner Cellophane Jacket opens from the Top.

Copyright, 1936, by P. Lorillard Co., Inc.

PRIZE CROP TOBACCOS MAKE THEM **DOUBLE-MELLOW**
2 JACKETS OF "CELLOPHANE" KEEP THEM **FACTORY-FRESH**

Old Gold, 1936

► *Lucky Strike, 1937*

Tobaccoland's Finest Gift

Joan Crawford

takes time out from her part in M-G-M's "Mannequin" to play the part of Mrs. Santa Claus.. Joan Crawford has smoked Luckies for eight years, has been kind enough to tell us: "They always stay on good terms with my throat."

In this season of joyful giving, when you offer friends the ever-welcome gift of cigarettes, remember two facts . . .

First, that among independent tobacco men, Lucky Strike has twice as many exclusive smokers as all other brands combined.

Second, that Lucky Strike not only offers the finest tobacco but also the throat protection of the exclusive process "It's Toasted".

With men who know tobacco best..

It's Luckies—2 to 1

ALUMINUM FOIL SAYS THEY'RE FRESH!

Foil that is non-toxic, safe to use on foods, should be the best kind for cigarettes, too. That's one reason why the makers of Kools and Raleighs wrap them in *Aluminum* Foil.

Another is to *extra*-protect their freshness. Aluminum Foil excels as a guardian of goodness because it wards off light and air. Helps, also, to keep tobacco's moisture content just right for real enjoyment.

The full name of this *extra*-protection is Alcoa Aluminum Foil, made by Aluminum Company of America, 2153 Gulf Building, Pittsburgh, Pa.

ALCOA Aluminum

FRIENDLY TO FOOD *Foil*

Alcoa Aluminum, 1939

▶ *Philip Morris, 1938*

TO MEN...who have *not* smoked cigars

YES, smoking habits of men are changing . . . Look about and you will see men in business—on the street—at your club in town and country are smoking a long, graceful cigar.

That long, genteel cigar, working the change, is the Robt. Burns Panatela—*The New Idea in Smoking.*

It is the manly, modernistic expression of smoking. It belongs with latest fashions—sophisticated ideas of living—in smart settings. . . . For the Robt. Burns Panatela puts style into smoking.

You—who have not tried Robt. Burns Panatelas—mix them with your customary smoking, and experience their pleasing flavor, and manly smartness.

Robt. Burns
THE *New Idea* IN SMOKING

Panatela 10¢

Panatela, 1930

BE "Mouth-Happy"

Surprising . . . how that "wrong side of the bed" feeling can be charmed away with Spud! Full-bodied flavor as you smoke . . . and cool, clean taste that lasts the live-long day.

SMOKE SPUDS

MENTHOL-COOLED CIGARETTES

Kool, 1934 ◄ Spuds, 1932

CALL FOR PHILIP MORRIS

For Good Reasons—

Every day millions actually confirm what a distinguished group of doctors discovered:

WHEN SMOKERS CHANGED TO PHILIP MORRIS, EVERY CASE OF NOSE OR THROAT IRRITATION DUE TO SMOKING, CLEARED COMPLETELY OR DEFINITELY IMPROVED.

This means *complete* smoking pleasure . . . unmarred by throat irritation.

AMERICA'S FINEST CIGARETTE

CREATORS OF FAMOUS CIGARETTES FOR 90 YEARS, ALWAYS UNDER THE PHILIP MORRIS NAME

Philip Morris, 1939

Kool, 1934

Kool, 1935

United Beer Brewers, 1939

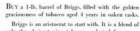

Briggs Tobacco, 1937

▶ *Kool, 1935*

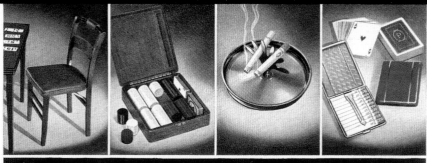

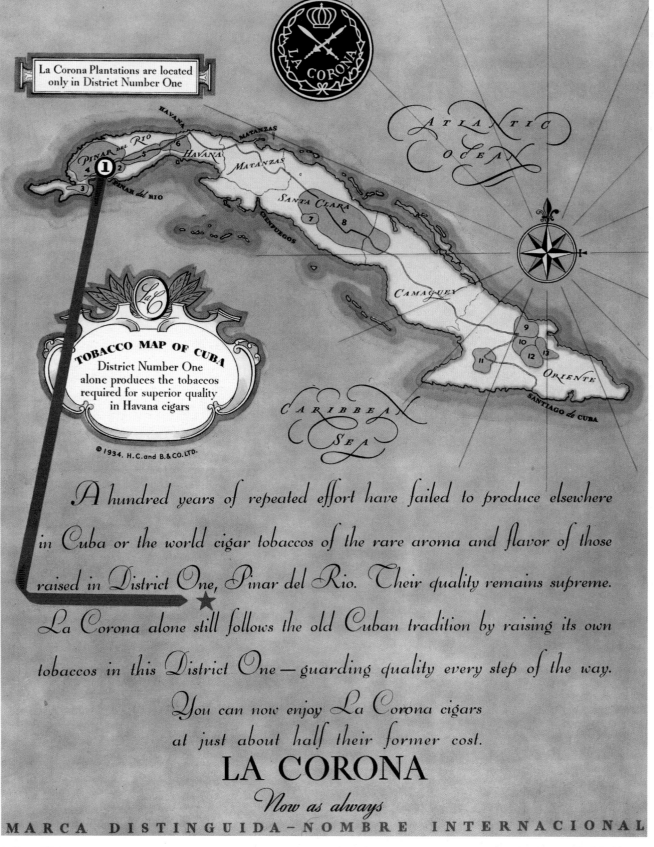

The Beer That Made Milwaukee Famous

Today...It's Schlitz in "Steinies"

TASTE SCHLITZ TODAY ... in the new, compact, easy-to-handle "Steinie" Brown Bottle. It is reminiful of olden days ... of beer sipped from the cool depths of stone steins.

Old-time brewmasters never enjoyed the facilities of modern science to assure uniform deliciousness to their brew but Schlitz has expended millions of dollars in research and development to make each glass uniformly delicious, appetizing and healthful.

With the first sip you instantly recognize the difference between Schlitz and other beers. That delightful, satisfying difference is old-time flavor

which Schlitz brews with scientific uniformity into every sparkling drop.

It's the full-bodied flavor of rich barley-malt wedded to the piquant tang of the finest hops the world affords...brewed to the peak of ripe, mellow perfection under Schlitz Precise Enzyme Control. You may choose from the modern "Steinie" Brown Bottle ...tall Brown Bottle...or Cap-Sealed Can...whichever suits your needs. Each brings you Schlitz at its best with the health benefits of Sunshine Vitamin D.

Schlitz "Steinie" Brown Bottles are compact—light in weight—easy to carry—take less space in your refrigerator. Contents same as regular bottle.

JOS. SCHLITZ BREWING CO. Milwaukee, Wis.

Schlitz, 1937

TO GOOD HEALTH & GOOD CHEER

LET Pabst Blue Ribbon Beer grace the festive board, it's hearty and healthy, sociable and sensible, the best of the better beers... And after you order it once, it will become your standing order—for holidays and other days as well.

PABST BLUE RIBBON

Pabst Blue Ribbon, 1933

When Smart America Steps out—

PABST GETS THE CALL

For Keener Refreshment...

Leave it to gay young America to pick the one Beer for the peak of Pleasure . . . Pabst Blue Ribbon. It's the Lighter, Brighter, Brisk-bodied beer—streamlined For Keener Refreshment in Every delicious, thirst-quenching Drop . . . Because there's Nothing heavy or syrupy to Slow up its delightfully Refreshing action, as it Smoothes away dull care. And there's a fortune of flavor

In every glass . . . a lasting Sparkle and tang like that of Rare old champagne. The Result of thorough Aging, plus the master's Golden touch—a Pabst Secret for 95 years. That's why, the world over, Smart company perks-up With Pabst. So when you Step out, demand the brand That says BLUE RIBBON . . . The Class of all Beers—in A Class by Itself.

Pass the word...you want
Pabst BLUE RIBBON

Pabst Blue Ribbon, 1939

▶ *Budweiser, 1933*

Because it fits so gracefully and so gaily into the scheme of good living, BUDWEISER is recognized as the King of Bottled Beer. Millions who welcomed beer back, are finding there is only one BUDWEISER — brewed and fully aged in the world's largest brewery.

Budweiser
KING OF BOTTLED BEER

ANHEUSER-BUSCH ~ ST.LOUIS

Their grain won first prize...for you!

WHAT BECOMES of this country's finest rye, corn and barley—the kind of grain that wins prizes at Fairs?

We don't know what happens to *all* of it. But we do know that a goodly share of it comes to our distillery . . . to be made into Four Roses. In fact, that's the only kind of grain we buy.

True, it costs more. But without it, Four Roses just wouldn't be Four Roses. Without it, Four Roses wouldn't have the flavor that has made it so famous.

But even the finest grain, before it can be used for Four Roses, must season—

until the moisture is gone, until the grain is dry, flinty, sound. For only then can the rich, clean kernels impart their full goodness to the several whiskies that eventually will be combined to give you Four Roses.

Eventually? Yes—for these straight whiskies must slumber and slowly mellow in their oaken casks for at least 4 years before they may share the illustrious name Four Roses! Then these superb whiskies are *combined* into *one* whiskey that is finer than any of them could be alone.

Four Roses is ALL whiskey—America's finest whiskey...made for you from America's finest grain. Try it today! *Frankfort Distilleries, Inc., Louisville and Baltimore.*

FOUR ROSES

EVERY DROP IS WHISKEY AT LEAST 4 YEARS OLD

A BLEND OF STRAIGHT WHISKIES—90 PROOF—THE STRAIGHT WHISKIES IN FOUR ROSES ARE FOUR YEARS OR MORE OLD

Four Roses, 1939

▶ *Four Roses, 1938*

**WHAT MORE
COULD A MAN ASK?**

*...than to come home to his
books...his dog...and
Four Roses*

Four Roses is a blend of straight whiskies,
90 proof, made by Frankfort Distilleries,
Incorporated, Louisville & Baltimore.

Four Roses, 1937

Four Roses, 1939

Four Roses, 1938

Four Roses, 1937

At Boston's Swank Copley-Plaza
PABST gets the Call!

For *Keener* Refreshment . . . It's Lighter . . .
Brighter . . . Brisk-Bodied, Not Logy!

● You certainly step out in smart company when you order Pabst Blue Ribbon. From coast to coast—in America's finest restaurants, hotels, clubs and lounges—*Pabst Gets the Call!* . . . Because Blue Ribbon is the more delicious beer that's lighter . . . brighter . . . brisk-bodied, not logy. Nothing heavy to slow up its delightfully refreshing tingle.

That's why Pabst is more *keenly* refreshing and thirst-quenching. It permits you to enjoy glass after glass, for it has a sprightlier golden goodness you *never* tire of. . . . This master-blended formula is a 93-year Pabst secret. So don't expect to find it in any other beer. When you want keener refreshment—remember . . . give *Pabst* the call. Demand BLUE RIBBON, the beer that's tuned to America's *smarter* taste!

America's Homes, too, Give Pabst the Call! From coast to coast, Pabst is first in America's homes! This overwhelming preference for family and guests is the truest measure of years being. And 93 years of Pabst quality has won this leadership. Order Pabst Blue Ribbon today. Your choice of bottles or handy, spout-saving cans.

At The Mark Hopkins on Nob Hill—hub of pleasure in San Francisco's finest social life . . . Towering above the Golden Gate and World's Fair grounds. Here the gay younger set gathers for keener refreshment. And the choice—of course—is Pabst Blue Ribbon.

KEENER REFRESHMENT

Copyright 1939, Pabst Sales Company, Chicago

Pass the word...you want
Pabst BLUE RIBBON

Pabst Blue Ribbon, 1939

"Canada's Finest"

General James Wolfe ONE OF "CANADA'S FINEST"
Mortally wounded on the Plains of Abraham, General Wolfe's last words, when told that the French had been decisively beaten, were: "Now, I can go in peace!" His famous victory in 1759, won for Great Britain all of French Canada. A military genius, a deep thinker, a great humanitarian, General Wolfe ranks high among "Canada's Finest."

The Most Delicate of all Whiskies

ALONE AMONGST DISTILLERS, the House of Seagram, we believe, has the background of blending experience and the craftmanship necessary to make a Canadian Whisky as light, as low proof (86.8) and as delicate as Seagram's "V.O." Taste "V.O." Compare it with any other Canadian Whisky. Only then will you be able to realise and appreciate its true fineness. Seagram's "V.O." is the supreme achievement of Seagram's master craftsmen. It is truly a masterpiece of the blenders' art —"Canada's Finest" Canadian Whisky.

Seagram's V.O. CANADIAN

Deliciously Delicate — Yet Deeply Satisfying

Seagram's "V.O." Canadian rare old blended whisky, 6 years old—Distilled, aged and blended under the supervision of the Canadian Government.

A MASTERPIECE OF THE BLENDERS ART
6 years old—86.8 proof

Seagram-Distillers Corporation, Offices: N. Y.

Seagram's V.O., 1939

A Truly Great Whiskey

Four Roses, 1938

Our search led us to an old distillery
on the banks of the River Dee...

A NOBLE SCOTCH
"Gentle as a Lamb"

WE TRACED this highly praised whisky to its source, the old and honored firm of Train & McIntyre Ltd., whose Strathdee Distillery on the River Dee supplies Highland malts that go into this rare blend. We arranged with Train & McIntyre to bring Old Angus to America—unchanged, the same superb whisky the Scots and English favor . . . Try Old Angus—the whisky whose smooth liqueur quality and mild taste can best be described by calling it "A Noble Scotch—Gentle as a Lamb."

OLD ANGUS
Liqueur
BLENDED SCOTCH WHISKY

YOUR GUIDE TO GOOD LIQUORS

Old Angus, 1938

END YOUR THANKSGIVING DAY DINNER
IN AN OLD-FASHIONED BLAZE OF GLORY!

FOUR ROSES
WHISKEY
MADE BY FRANKFORT
LOUISVILLE • BALTIMORE

Frankfort makes a whiskey for every taste and purse: **PAUL JONES**, Antique, Old Oscar Pepper, Shipping Port.

IT'S your first Repeal Thanksgiving—so celebrate it right!

Over a fat plum pudding, pour Four Roses Whiskey until the pudding is fairly soaked with the fragrant liquor. Then set it aflame, and bear the masterpiece to the table in a blue blaze of glory. What an ending for your dinner! No whiskey was ever used to better purpose.

And no *finer* whiskey could be used for this purpose. For the Four Roses of today has all the rich aroma and dulcet flavor that made it famous in the old days.

Four Roses is a product of Frankfort, a company that has been making fine whiskey for four generations. And it is made in their traditionally painstaking way—from mellow, hand-made, aged-in-the-wood whiskies. *No tricks!*

Right now, lay in a supply of Four Roses for Thanksgiving. Mix your pre-dinner cocktails with it—use it for your after-dinner highballs. Ask for Four Roses, too, in hotels and restaurants. You can be certain of its purity. For it comes sealed in the patented Frankfort Pack *that must be destroyed* before the bottle within it can be removed.

"Irvin S. Cobb's Own Recipe Book," written as only Mr. Cobb could write it, is now ready. Send 10¢ in stamps for your copy. Address Frankfort Distilleries, Incorporated, Dept. 443, Louisville.

This advertisement is not intended to offer alcoholic beverages for sale in any state wherein the sale or use thereof is unlawful

Four Roses, 1934

Four Roses, 1937

Why Kentucky Derby winners live forever

A HORSE immortal? Yes—if he has borne the victorious wreath of roses at historic Churchill Downs—the honor turfdom reserves for *the champion of champions!*

Immortal—because *his* forthright virtues, blended with those of *other* brilliant champions, will be passed on—to give us Derby winners of tomorrow.

Many virtues blended together—that is the secret of greatness in a thoroughbred. And it's also the secret of the greatness of Four Roses. This is what we mean ... Four Roses is *all whiskey*—whiskey, every drop. But here's the point—

Four Roses is more than just a *single* fine straight whiskey.

It is *several* straight whiskies, each of which is outstanding for some *particular* quality. Blended together, with almost loving care, these whiskies merge *all* their individual virtues in *one* glorious whiskey—Four Roses—a whiskey we believe is America's *finest*, regardless of age or price!

Frankfort Distilleries, Incorporated, Louisville and Baltimore, also make Paul Jones (92 proof), Old Oscar Pepper brand, and Mattingly & Moore (both 90 proof)—all blends of straight whiskies.

FOUR ROSES

We believe Four Roses is America's Finest Whiskey, regardless of age or price

A blend of straight whiskies
—90 proof

Seagram's, 1939

Seagram's, 1939

Seagram's, 1937

"AMERICA'S FINEST"

a Salute to
MICHIGAN
"The Auto State"
ONE OF "AMERICA'S FINEST"

State Capital is Lansing — State
Population is 4,808,000 — Largest
City, Detroit — Its Pop. 1,569,000.

Do You Know . . . that 3,710,000
automobiles were manufactured
in Michigan last year? . . . *that*
94% of all the motor cars in
America are "made in Michigan"?
. . . *that* Detroit is the fourth largest city in the U.S.A.? . . . *that*
there are more than 6,000 lakes
in Michigan?

★

Watch for other advertisements in this series saluting the 48 states — "America's Finest"

Why the Rare Taste of "*America's Finest*" Never Varies, Never Changes

No matter when you buy a bottle of
Seagram's 7 or 5 Crown . . . this afternoon,
next month or in the years to come . . . the
taste and the quality will be identical.

With a skill in the art of blending that
comes only through long years of practice and experience, Seagram's master
blenders are able to perpetuate the fa-

mous Crown taste with infinite exactness.

The next time you mix a hearty highball
with the richer 7 Crown or a silky-smooth
Manhattan with the milder 5 Crown —
notice that delicious taste. It's "America's
Finest" — and it never changes.

At the bar or the package store, say Seagram's . . . and be sure.

CROWNS TASTE BETTER — BECAUSE THEY'RE MASTER BLENDED

Seagram's Crown Whiskies
"America's Finest"

"AMERICA'S FINEST"
Seagram's Crown Whiskies

90 PROOF

Seagram's, 1938

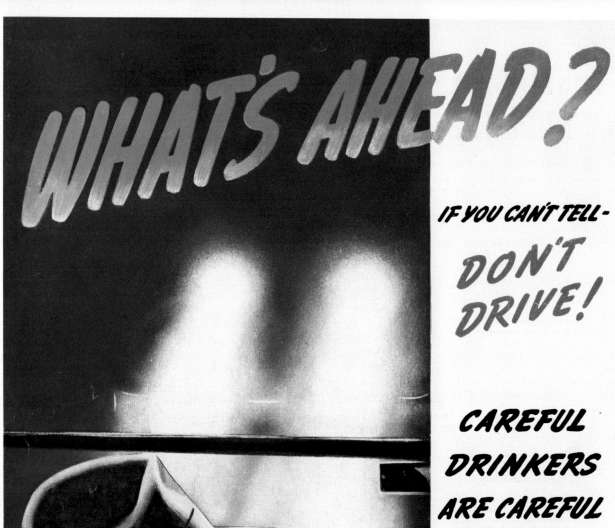

WHAT'S AHEAD?

IF YOU CAN'T TELL—

DON'T DRIVE!

CAREFUL DRINKERS ARE CAREFUL DRIVERS!

90 PROOF

LAIRD & CO.

SCOBEYVILLE, NEW JERSEY

This advertisement is published by Laird & Company, America's oldest family of Brandy Distillers, in the interest of safe driving.

Laird's, 1939

▶ *Four Roses, 1937*

A HIGHBALL AT NIGHTFALL

Ah, to relax at nightfall over a whiskey-and-soda!

A drink with sparkle and zest and tang—a drink to be sipped slowly . . . so that the enjoyment of it may be prolonged!

But be mighty careful, in making *your* highball, to use a whiskey worthy of this congenial drink— a whiskey that *holds* its flavor, as you sip it, to the very end.

In short—make your highball with Four Roses! For Four Roses gives *life* to a whiskey-and-soda. Four Roses *holds* its delicate aroma and forthright flavor down to the last drop!

That's easy to understand. For while Four Roses is *all whiskey*, it's not just *one* fine straight whiskey —it's a glorious combination of *several* selected American straight whiskies. Several whiskies, so blended together, that they unite their noblest qualities in *one* illustrious whiskey—a whiskey greater than any one of them alone could ever be!

FOUR ROSES

A blend of straight whiskies—90 proof

We Believe Four Roses is America's finest whiskey, regardless of age or price

Frankfort Distilleries, Inc., Louisville & Baltimore, also make Paul Jones, Old Oscar Pepper brand, Mattingly & Moore —all blends of straight whiskies, 90 proof.

Canadian Club, 1939

Penn Whiskey, 1935

Seagram's, 1938

► Canadian Club, 1937

A Tale of Two Countries

TABEPNA MΠAPMΠA ΓIANNH

ΕΛΕΓΧΟΣ ΔΙΑΒΑΤΗΡΙΟ
ЦАРИНСКА УПРАВА
CUSTOMS INSPECTIO

SKOPLJE 161 KMS.
SALONIKA 82 KMS.
ATHENS 594 KMS.

"Crossing borders was our specialty on our motor trip through the Balkans," writes H. T. Hudson of Texas. "When we arrived at the fourth one in two days, with our front wheels in Greece and our rear wheels in Yugoslavia, we were hot and thirsty. I wanted a whisky and soda— but my Greek dictionary offered the discouraging comment that the 'Greeks had no word for it'! Then I noticed that on the local inn there was a sign and it read 'Canadian Club'! It wasn't long before we were enjoying the mellow flavor of your very fine whisky. So it seems that, like us, the Greeks do have a word for it—or, rather two words . . . 'Canadian Club'! Lucky Greeks!"

"Canadian Club" is the only whisky of its kind. But Hiram Walker also makes ryes, bourbons, gins—whatever you like, at whatever you like to pay. At dealers, clubs, bars, hotels. Hiram Walker & Sons, Peoria, Ill. Walkerville, Ont. Glasgow, Scotland

AMBASSADOR OF GOOD WILL TO 87 COUNTRIES

Hiram Walker's "CANADIAN CLUB"

"Seems like they're all calling for a DRY whiskey!"

Paul Jones, 1937

AN ESTABLISHED IDENTITY

Kentucky Tavern, 1935

Take it over on the alkaline side

It's good sense to take drink-things with White Rock. The drink-wise way. White Rock's over on the alkaline side. Helps neutralize the acidity of whatever you mix it with . . . Furthermore, White Rock brings out a good taste. Doesn't bury it.

. . . better for you

Cointreau, 1934 ◄ White Rock, 1933

WHERE THERE'S LIFE . . .

Budweiser, 1933

What whiskey was born 10 years before the first Kentucky Derby?

IN 1875, when Aristides galloped to immortality by winning the first Kentucky Derby, a certain other Kentucky thoroughbred had already been famous for ten years.

This thoroughbred was Paul Jones—a blend of straight whiskies—born in 1865, and named for the gentleman who first made it—Colonel Paul Jones.

Today, this grand whiskey is made by the direct descendants of the old Colonel. And every drop is made the way he made it—by the slow, costly old-fashioned method.

Get a bottle of Paul Jones and discover what inherited skill and choice ingredients mean in flavor and smoothness. Ask that your drinks be made with Paul Jones. A product of Frankfort Distilleries of Kentucky and Maryland.

There is a Frankfort whiskey for every pocketbook: FOUR ROSES, OLD OSCAR PEPPER—a blend of straight whiskies. SHIPPING PORT—straight whiskey. ANTIQUE, MATTINGLY & MOORE—whiskey, a blend.

Send 10¢ for "Irvin S. Cobb's Own Recipe Book".

Lovers of fine gin will appreciate the rare flavor of Paul Jones ★★★★ Gin

Paul Jones
A BLEND OF ALL STRAIGHT WHISKIES

Under his fingers...the reason you'll like Paul Jones!

YES, those three letters...D-R-Y...spell one big reason why so many men of discerning taste find Paul Jones Whiskey very much to their liking!

For Paul Jones, you see, is a truly DRY whiskey — hearty and robust (as a man's whiskey *should* be!)...yet without a trace of sweetness in its make-up.

And this crisp, clean-flavored quality of

DRYNESS is just one of *many* reasons why Paul Jones has been famous as "A Gentleman's Whiskey" since 1865. Try Paul Jones— discover *all* the reasons! Frankfort Distilleries, Incorporated, Louisville & Baltimore.

★ ★ ★ ★

A blend of straight whiskies.
100% straight whiskies — 90 proof

When it Pours—
CHEERFULNESS *Reigns* INSIDE

THERE'S a lot of sunshine in a bottle of vermouth—it seems as if you could taste it. Do you think that's imagination?—well, try a glass. Try it straight (chilled) so you can get the full spicy, bitter-sweet flavor—and you'll think of vineyards and herb farms under the warm Italian sun. Try it straight and you'll *find out what makes a cocktail taste good.* You'll realize why vermouth is enjoyed in every country on the globe—the great appetizer before meals, and one of the most universal of drinks.

Straight or in a cocktail it will make your lunch or dinner look more inviting. With soda, it's the conservative drink for a long evening—vermouth is versatile! But make sure you taste it straight—for vermouth, one of Europe's oldest drinks, is the newest drink of America! We mean Martini & Rossi, of course—it's the standard.

SOLE AGENTS FOR U. S. A., W. A. TAYLOR & CO., NEW YORK

Alcohol by vol.
Italy, 15.95%
Dry, 18%

3 MOODS IN 1 BOTTLE
(Either Bottle)

1. Be gay—have a Manhattan or Martini.
2. Be moderate—have vermouth straight. Served chilled in cocktail glass.
3. Be conservative—have vermouth and soda. Mixed like a highball, using vermouth instead of whiskey.

MARTINI & ROSSI
VERMOUTH

Paul Jones, 1938 ◄ *Martini & Rossi, 1939*

Bonded Belmont, 1938

Bonded Belmont, 1938

▶ Bonded Belmont, 1938

Ten High, 1939

Ten High, 1939 ◄ Glenmore, 1939

Ten High, 1939

Ten High, 1939

The egret in his tropic lair
Proudly preens his plumage rare;
If you'd take pride in what you serve
Get CALVERT'S "SPECIAL" or "RESERVE"!

America is learning how to drink!

You have, no doubt, observed it, too . . . a definite trend in American drinking habits. A trend toward moderation. A sensible trend toward lighter, blended whiskies . . . *better whiskies.*

Americans are learning how to drink . . . how to enjoy in wise moderation the pleasant flavor and bouquet of truly fine blended whiskies. And so, more and more, the call is for Calvert.

American good taste and judgment have created a nation-wide demand for these light, smooth, fine-flavored whiskies . . . Calvert's "Reserve" and "Special." They are whiskies you, too, will drink appreciatively . . . in pleasant moderation.

BLENDED FOR BETTER TASTE

Call for Calvert *The Whiskey of Good Taste*

Copr. 1938 Calvert Distillers Corp., Distilleries: Baltimore, Md., and Louisville, Ky., Executive Offices: Chrysler Bldg., N. Y. C. Calvert's "Reserve" Blended Whiskey—90 Proof—65% Grain Neutral Spirits . . . Calvert's "Special" Blended Whiskey—90 Proof—72½% Grain Neutral Spirits.

Calvert, 1938

WHY IS A WRENCH CALLED A "MONKEY" WRENCH?

Glenmore, 1939

Canadian Club, 1939

The Spirit of Old Kentucky

Kentucky Tavern, 1935 ▶ *Canadian Club, 1939*

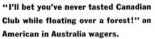
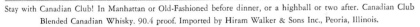

Shanghai

WHEREVER you go, you will find the preference is for Three-Star Hennessy. And wherever you are . . . Shanghai, Paris, London, New York . . . you will find that same unvarying quality in Hennessy that has won it world leadership. Warm the glass in the hands, then sip it s-l-o-w-l-y . . . to fully enjoy its delightful bouquet and flavour.

SOLE AGENTS FOR THE UNITED STATES: Schieffelin & Co., NEW YORK CITY, IMPORTERS SINCE 1794

THREE STAR **HENNESSY** COGNAC BRANDY

Hennessy, 1934

Cairo

COLORFUL Cairo appreciates the matchless quality of Three-Star Hennessy, the finest naturally matured brandy in the world. Sipped slowly, after warming the glass in the hands, its wonderful bouquet and "clean" taste make it supreme among liqueurs . . . consequently, perfect for brandy-and-soda, cocktails and other mixed drinks made better with good brandy.

SOLE AGENTS FOR THE UNITED STATES: Schieffelin & Co., NEW YORK CITY. IMPORTERS SINCE 1794

THREE STAR HENNESSY
COGNAC BRANDY

Hennessy, 1934

Rhum Negrita, 1939

Old Grand-Dad, Old Taylor, Mount Vernon, Old Overholt, 1939

Old Grand-Dad, Old Taylor, Mount Vernon, Old Overholt, 1938

Hennessy, 1933

Hennessy, 1935

Schenley's, 1939 ◄ Old Crow, 1938

Martini & Rossi, 1939

Holiday Greetings with Great Western

Make good cheer during the holiday season this year with a dashing, sparkling, convivial champagne—a wine "that maketh glad the heart of man." ★ Such a champagne is Great Western Champagne. ★ Six times honored since 1867 in foreign competition and winner of the Diploma of Honor, highest award ever given to any champagne in a European Exposition…it is made after the time-honored French method of slow fermentation in the bottle. ★ Serve Great Western all through the holiday season and be assured that your guests are enjoying one of the world's fine champagnes.

Won Europe's   *Highest Honors*

Great Western AMERICAN CHAMPAGNE
PLEASANT VALLEY WINE COMPANY, RHEIMS, NEW YORK
GREAT WESTERN FOR GREAT MOMENTS

Great Western Champagne, 1935 ◄ *Great Western Champagne, 1937*

Drinks never taste thin with Gordon's Gin

Gordon's Gin has Liqueur Quality and High Proof, 94.4. That means richer flavor—velvety smoothness—drinks that never taste thin. Obey your sense of discrimination—always ask for Gordon's—you'll be amazed at the finer, richer, smoother taste of your gin drinks.

Gordon's Gin

100% NEUTRAL SPIRITS DISTILLED FROM GRAIN • 94.4 PROOF

COPYRIGHT 1937, GORDON'S DRY GIN COMPANY, LIMITED... LINDEN, N. J.

Gordon's Gin, 1937

For a perfect MANHATTAN *Cocktail*

USE OLD OVERHOLT WHISKEY

In a zestful Manhattan, vermouth finds its perfect affinity in Old Overholt, a bottled in bond straight rye whiskey...rich and robust... as different as day and night. It belongs to that distinguished company of fine whiskies, brandies, wines and liqueurs, produced in America or brought from abroad by National Distillers, that have won an enviable world-wide repute.

Like the hallmark on sterling, the National Distillers emblem is a symbol of unquestioned quality. National Distillers Products Corporation, Executive Offices, 120 Broadway, New York.

YOUR GUIDE TO NATIONAL DISTILLERS GOOD LIQUORS

Old Overholt, 1937

GABRIEL HEATTER...FAMOUS RADIO COMMENTATOR, PRESENTS A

19th Hole Broadcast

"THE VOTE'S IN! By an overwhelming majority, Tom Collins has been elected America's No. 1 Summer drink. And Hiram Walker gins are the choice of the people when they make this tall, cool thirst-quencher! Actual records show that America buys more Hiram Walker gins than any other kind."

How to make a Tom Collins for Two

AMERICA BUYS MORE HIRAM WALKER GINS THAN ANY OTHER KIND

Hiram Walker, 1938

Carried for nearly a century
to every corner of the earth

GILBEY'S *the* GIN *that made the* Collins *famous*

Lurching camels in the Sahara and tossing junks on China seas...kinky-headed carriers in mid-Africa and dogsleds in the icy North...they're strange reasons, aren't they, for your saying "make it with Gilbey's" wherever you order a Tom Collins? And yet...there's no more amazing proof of Gilbey's quality than the way it has spread to the very ends of the earth!

But even more amazing is the way Gilbey's has changed the world's conception of gin drinks. Not only the Collins but many another international drink owes its fame to the silken perfection Gilbey's gives. And you need only one little sip of a Gilbey's Tom Collins to know what a delicious difference it makes. Ask for Gilbey's wherever you go.

THE "INTERNATIONAL GIN" PRODUCED BY GILBEY IN THE U.S.A.—AS WELL AS IN...ENGLAND...AUSTRALIA...CANADA

Copyright 1939 — National Distillers Products Corp., New York City   YOUR GUIDE TO GOOD LIQUORS   Gilbey's Gin — 90 Proof — made from 100% grain neutral spirits

Gilbey's Gin, 1939   ▶ *Gordon's Gin, 1938*

Gordon's has the Advantage

OF LIQUEUR QUALITY & HIGH PROOF, *94.4*

It's an advantage worth having! For Liqueur Quality means richer flavor, velvety smoothness. And High Proof. 94.4, means sustained flavor—drinks that never taste thin.

DRINKS NEVER TASTE THIN WITH **Gordon's Gin**

THE HEART OF A ♥ GOOD COCKTAIL

Discriminating people automatically accept some few names as standards of excellence. In gin, DIXIE BELLE enjoys the enviable favor of those whose taste is unquestioned. Flawless smoothness. Restrained but definite bouquet. Flavor that blends gracefully without overplaying its part. Such superior qualities are the result of surpassing

equipment and scientifically controlled distilla in America's Largest Distillery. DIXIE BEL merit, not its moderate price, won overwhel preference this first year of Repeal. Distilled bottled by Continental Distilling Corporat Philadelphia. Another Continental quality liqu Rittenhouse Square 100 proof Straight Rye Whi

Cocktail hour at the Waldorf

In The Oasis Room

DIXIE BELLE distilled dry GI

THE GOOD

Companion

Among those whose standards demand more
than superficial merit, the distinguished quality of
DIXIE BELLE Dry Gin is a revelation. Such refinement of bouquet, such gracious smoothness, such
readiness to merge discreetly with your chosen cocktails and highballs, are instant tokens of a gin of
the highest character . . . "Distilled by Continental."

Also distillers of Sweep Stakes, Snug Harbor and Envoy
Club Blended Whiskies and Cavalier Distilled Dry Gin

CONTINENTAL DISTILLING CORPORATION, Philadelphia

This advertisement is not intended to offer alcoholic beverages for sale or delivery in any state
wherein the sale or use thereof is unlawful.

DIXIE BELLE
DISTILLED DRY
Gin

And the winner is...

The Celebrity Sell

In copy impossible to print by today's standards, advertisers trumpeted the perceived benefits of smoking to consumers of the 1930s. In this ad targeted at female smokers, Miss Lombard's voice teacher advises her to smoke as much as she wants without fear of damaging her throat. This claim is reinforced by "experts" who state that Luckies® "toasted" technology removes certain throat irritants found in tobacco. Surrounded by all this glamour and vague hints of a healthy pastime, who would not be seduced into smoking?

Paffen mit Prominenten

Heute undenkbar, aber dieser Werbetext preist die Vorzüge des Rauchens! Miss Lombards Lehrer für Sprech- und Atemtechnik, so möchte diese Anzeige einer weiblichen Klientel weismachen, habe garantiert, dass sie ohne Sorge um ihre Stimme so viel rauchen könne, wie sie wolle. Unterstrichen wird die Behauptung durch „Expertenstimmen", die der speziellen Verarbeitungstechnik der Luckies® bescheinigen, sie entziehe dem Tabak die Kehle reizende Schadstoffe. Bei so viel Glamour und vagen Hinweisen auf einen gesundheitlich unbedenklichen Zeitvertreib, wer würde sich da keine anzünden wollen?

La célébrité fait vendre

Avec des textes qui nous paraissent aujourd'hui impensables, les annonceurs vantaient aux consommateurs des années 30 ce qu'on croyait être les bienfaits du tabac. Dans cette publicité s'adressant aux fumeuses, le professeur de chant de Miss Lombard affirme qu'elle peut fumer autant qu'elle veut sans craindre pour sa gorge. Cette déclaration est appuyée par des « experts » selon lesquels la technologie de « torréfaction » de Luckies élimine certains irritants de la gorge présents dans le tabac. Devant tant de glamour, comment ne pas céder à une tentation si saine ?

Caras conocidas

En un texto que resultaría imposible publicar hoy en día, los anunciantes vendían al público de los años treinta los beneficios demostrados de fumar. En este anuncio dirigido a las mujeres fumadoras, el profesor de voz de la Sra. Lombard le recomendaba fumar tanto como gustara sin temor a dañar sus cuerdas vocales. Dicha afirmación aparecía sustentada por la opinión de «expertos», quienes aseguraban que la tecnología de «tueste» aplicada en la elaboración de los cigarrillos Luckies® eliminaba los irritantes de garganta detectados en las demás marcas de tabaco. ¿Quién podía resistirse a fumar en una época en la que el tabaco no sólo estaba rodeado de *glamour,* sino que además se vendía como un pasatiempo saludable?

有名人の売り込み

広告制作者は現代的な基準からすると考えられないような広告文で、喫煙がもたらす恩恵を1930年代の消費者たちに吹聴した。女性の喫煙者に的を絞ったこの広告では、女優ロンバードのボイス・トレーナーが、のどをつぶす恐れはないので好きなだけタバコを吸いなさいと彼女に進言している。この主張を、「専門家」が援護する。彼らはラッキーズ®(ラッキー・ストライク)の「健康を祝した」技術が、タバコというものにつきものの、ある種ののどの刺激を取り除くと述べている。これは健康的な娯楽ですよという、すべてが魅惑的であいまいな暗示にかかってはタバコを吸わずにはいられないだろう!

Her Singing Coach Advised A Light Smoke

CAROLE LOMBARD* **PREFERS LUCKIES BECAUSE THEY'RE EASIER ON HER THROAT**

"WHEN I had to sing in a recent picture," says Carole Lombard, "I considered giving up smoking. But my voice teacher said I needn't if I'd select a light smoke—Luckies.

"I soon found that even when singing and acting 12 hours a day, I can smoke as many Luckies as I like . . . without the slightest throat irritation."

The reason Luckies are easy on Miss Lombard's throat is because the process "It's Toasted" takes out certain throat irritants found in all tobacco—even the finest.

And Luckies do use the finest tobacco. Sworn records show that among independent tobacco experts—auctioneers, buyers, warehousemen, etc.—Lucky Strike has twice as many exclusive smokers as have all other cigarettes combined.

In the honest judgment of those who spend their lives buying, selling and handling tobacco...with men who know tobacco best . . . it's Luckies—2 to 1.

*Star of the new Paramount production "True Confession"

A Light Smoke

EASY ON YOUR THROAT—"IT'S TOASTED"

LUCKY STRIKE *"IT'S TOASTED"*

CIGARETTES

LUCKY STRIKE

WITH TOBACCO EXPERTS...
WITH MEN WHO KNOW TOBACCO BEST
It's Luckies 2 to 1

Lucky Strike, 1937

117

Illustrated above: The 2-Door Sedan ~ Body by Fisher

NEW SERIES PONTIAC BIG SIX

Beautiful New Bodies by FISHER *for the* Greatest CHEVROLET *in Chevrolet History*

WOMEN everywhere helped design the new Chevrolet Six—with its beautiful new bodies by Fisher. Their letters have come from every part of America—now with a suggestion, now with a request, now praising this or that feature. And every one of these letters was carefully considered by Chevrolet and Fisher. The steering wheel should be set lower ... the brakes should be easier to apply ... the gasoline gauge should be on the dash ... seats should be made deeper. Others asked that certain features be retained—the adjustable driver's seat ... the smooth clutch action ... the easy steering ... the harmonious design of the fittings ... the comfortable and stylish interiors. Every worthwhile suggestion was adopted. For women are using Chevrolet cars more widely every day—and their tastes, their desires, their suggestions are entitled to the utmost consideration. Chevrolet and Fisher believe you'll like the new Chevrolet Six. Its design, in every particular, is meant to be better suited to a woman's taste and needs.

CHEVROLET MOTOR COMPANY, DETROIT, MICHIGAN
Division of General Motors Corporation

Chevrolet, 1930

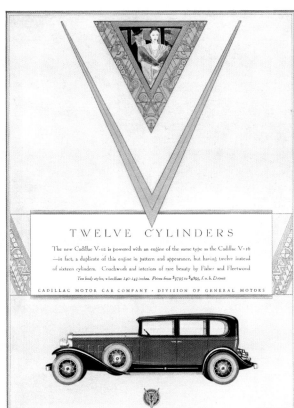

TWELVE CYLINDERS

The new Cadillac V-12 is powered with an engine of the same type as the Cadillac V-16 —in fact, a duplicate of this engine in pattern and appearance, but having twelve instead of sixteen cylinders. Coachwork and interiors of rare beauty by Fisher and Fleetwood

Ten body styles; wheelbase 140–143 inches. Prices from $3795 to $4495, f.o.b. Detroit

CADILLAC MOTOR CAR COMPANY · DIVISION OF GENERAL MOTORS

Oldsmobile, 1933 ◄◄ *Pontiac, 1930* ◄ *Cadillac, 1930*

This Young Couple is about to make an important decision...... *and* it probably will be wrong

THIS young man and his wife are about to make one of their most exciting dreams come true—they are about to buy an automobile.

They want a Reo, and want it badly. But every time they look longingly at it, Old Man Budget wags a warning finger. And Old Man Budget probably will wheedle them into buying a cheap car, on the pretext that it is the only car they can afford.

If they do buy a cheap car, here's what probably will happen. For a few months, it will be quite thrilling. True, there will be petty annoyances and petty expenses. True, every time they mention the name of the car their own, it will be accompanied by something that sounds suspiciously like an apology.

But at the end of a year, or maybe two, that thrill is completely missing—their car is definitely on the downward trail. So they trade it in—and take a staggering loss in depreciation. Their cheap car has cost them dearly.

BUT—suppose this young couple makes the right decision—suppose they do buy a Reo Flying Cloud. Let's see what will happen then!

At the end of a year—yes, and at the end of three, four, or five years, their Reo Flying Cloud will still be running sweeter than the cheaper car would have at any time. The Reo is good—really

good—for 100,000 miles. Why?

Why does the Reo outlive all cars of American make and origin, regardless of price? Let's find out—let's see what's under the paint.

Reo pays 10% to 25% more for parts, so that these parts will stand a strain 50% to 100% greater than you ever will ask a car to take. Reo axles and springs are so sturdy that Reo gives them a test that is the equivalent of shooting the car off a four-foot ledge at 60 miles an hour.

Performance? Reo climbs from a standing start to 60 miles an hour in 26 seconds. You may never want to go that fast. But think of the ease and safety of driving a car with such acceleration

The Reo Flying Cloud Model 20 Standard Sedan $1495 f.o.b. Lansing, Michigan. Spare tire extra.

and flexibility. That's one reason why Reo is known as the easiest car in the world to drive.

And Reo's marvelous brakes will bring the car from 60 down to a dead stop in 4 seconds, with never a skid or swerve even on a shiny-wet road. Reo brakes cannot become unequalized. Water cannot affect them. And they've been known to function on their original bands for 50,000 miles!

And looks? Reo lines give to the Reo Flying Cloud the kind of classic beauty usually found only in the higher priced cars—beauty that does not fade—beauty that does not demand the frequent, radical body changes that cause heavy depreciation.

Come, Budget, give these young people a break. Their Reo will be a *really* economical investment—not for just a year, but for 100,000 miles.

BUDGET—LET THEM HAVE THEIR REO

REO FLYING CLOUD

GOOD for 100,000 miles

REO MOTOR CAR COMPANY, LANSING, MICHIGAN

Reo Motor Car Co., 1930

© 1930 The Texas Company

RESEARCH ... THE GUIDE TO PROGR[ESS]
Anticipating every development; insuring ever higher standard[s of] quality ... Texaco Laboratories are the source of Texaco progr[ess]

The "Pride of the Navy" served by Texaco...

Sailing high above the clouds or battling raging headwinds, the Los Angeles has demonstrated again and again its ability to meet every test.

For more than four years the motors of this leviathan of the air have been lubricated efficiently with Texaco Airplane Oil. Here again, as with Hawks on his record breaking flights from Coast to Coast — as with the Sun-God on its epoch making non-stop refueling flight, specialized Texaco

Aviation Products have demonstrat[ed] their dependability.

On land, at sea and in the air — in ea[ch] of our 48 States, in 46 foreign countri[es] the name Texaco has become a symbol [of] quality for petroleum products.

Motorists everywhere can assure the[m-] selves of this same uniform quality an[d] dependable performance by stoppin[g] under the Texaco Red Star with the Gree[n] T when they need gasoline and motor o[il.]

TEXACO

The mark of quality for petroleum products

THE TEXAS COMPANY

Refiners of a complete line of Texaco Petroleum Products, including Gasoline, Motor Oil, Industrial Lubricants, Railroad and Marine Lubricants, Farm Lubricants, Road Asphalts and Asphalt Roofing.

SIXTEEN CYLINDERS

The Cadillac sixteen-cylinder engine goes far beyond the contemporary conception of brilliant performance. It multiplies power and subdivides it into a continuous flow . . . constantly at full-volume efficiency . . . flexible . . . instantly responsive. This, plus complete individuality in styling, is—in brief—the story of the "V-16"

CADILLAC MOTOR CAR COMPANY   DIVISION OF GENERAL MOTORS

Texaco, 1930 ◄ *Cadillac, 1930*

DISTINCTION...

Everywhere in America where great achievement is appreciated, people are unhesitatingly acclaiming Franklin. The introduction by Franklin of the first airplane-type engine in a motor car—an engine which in tests has flown an airplane—is heralded as a great forward step in the automobile's march of progress. A vision of the future—the turning point of a new era.

Even more important and dramatic is this engine's tremendous power-ability. Delivering the greatest power for cylinder capacity of all automotive power plants, it brings air-cooling engineering into undisputed leadership. It throws down the bars and sweeps aside all previous conceptions of motor-car performance. Sixty, seventy, eighty miles an hour are quickly, quietly and comfortably reached without the slightest engine

exertion. Now riding is gliding. You get a new thrill every time the Franklin does things you thought impossible before. Last year Franklin gained the distinction of holding all major road records. This year many of these same records have been sensationally re-broken by the new Franklin.

Distinguished for its airplane performance, the new Franklin also enjoys nation-wide distinction for its authoritative appearance. Darting-arrow horizontal louvres, each lower and behind the other as if shot consecutively from a bow. Modishly fashioned embossed paneling—the streamlining of aircraft reflected in the low hung doors concealing the running boards—the gracefully arched hood front, ribbon-wide, with slender skyscraper effect of its highlighted vertical shutters—the whole ensemble is modern, smart, fleet-looking.

When you see the car—when you drive it—when you are thrilled by the performance of its airplane-type engine, you will enthusiastically award Franklin highest motor car honors for 1930. Franklin Automobile Company, Syracuse, New York.

AIR·COOLED

FRANKLIN

Franklin, 1930

Lovejoy
HYDRAULIC
SHOCK ABSORBERS

IN VIEW of the present-day stress upon comfort, it is especially significant that the finest cars in every price class are equipped with Lovejoy Hydraulic Shock Absorbers. For the builders of such cars select their shock absorber equipment solely for its capacity to heighten motoring enjoyment. On this uncompromising basis, the foremost manufacturers in each group—in fact, the majority of *all* car manufacturers—have chosen Lovejoys as standard equipment. DELCO PRODUCTS CORPORATION, DAYTON, OHIO

Lovejoy Shock Absorbers, 1930

THE

AIR-FLIGHT

PRINCIPLE

Makes Riding as Smooth as Flying

Seven Points of Superiority in the FISK *AIR-FLIGHT* Principle

1. Larger air chamber—your car rides less on the rubber, more on the air.
2. All-Cord material reduces internal friction and adds strength without rigidity or weight.
3. Multiple cable bead gives more strength at the rim while increasing side-wall flexibility.
4. Increased length of flex area at the side-wall provides greater use of the air cushion.
5. Rim-width, streamline tread eliminates useless overhanging tread rubber and allows greater air cushioning.
6. Greater road contact results in better and longer-lasting non-skid qualities.
7. The newly perfected *AIR-FLIGHT* balance between air and materials achieves the *maximum air-cushioning and mileage.*

Within the last few years the world has learned a new kind of travel comfort—*in swift, luxurious airplanes.*

Motorists who experienced the smooth sensation of flying wanted this air-flight comfort brought to them for their cars. They pictured more luxurious riding, made possible by a tire that carried its load *more on the air.*

Working along these lines, Fisk engineers found the way to build a true *air-flight* tire. They developed new principles of tire design, making full use of the cushiony content of air. They perfected a better balance of materials, without bulky masses of misplaced rubber that lessen riding comfort. The result is a tire that floats your car smoothly along on air, with the effortless ease that is typical of flying.

Visit your Fisk Dealer today and see these remarkable new tires. They are more flexible yet more durable—combining *air-flight* comfort with exceptional mileage. Try these Fisk *Air-Flight* Principle Tires and experience a different driving sensation...surer traction and greater comfort than you have ever known before.

Time to Re-tire GET A FISK!

FISK
mileage

Texaco, 1930 ◄ *Fisk, 1930*

Luxury-loving ladies of Merrie England in Robin Hood's
day journeyed forth in gayly draped and softly pillowed litters,
borne by two stout horses and accompanied by men-at-arms

Packard engineering leadership — again impres-
sively proved by the epochal development of
the Diesel aircraft engine — has long rested on
the distinguished and luxurious Packard Eight.

The same talent and resourcefulness which produced the Packard-Diesel — acknowledged the
greatest advance in aircraft power in the history
of aviation—developed the famous eight-in-line
powerplant which has contributed so largely to
Packard's supreme reputation in the fine car field.

Only an organization thus skilled in the theory
and practice of fine engine building could have
conquered the baffling problems of Diesel aircraft engine design. And, conversely, the only
organization which could design and build a successful aircraft Diesel—in competition with the
engineering talent of the world—must be pre-
eminently fitted to determine the ideal type of
power for *luxurious* motor car transportation.

It is not accidental that the Packard Straight
Eight is the largest selling car in the world in
the field above $2,000.

Luxurious Transportation

PACKARD
ASK THE MAN WHO OWNS ONE

Packard, 1930

COROC
GAVE MOTOR CAR MANUFACTURERS
A DISTINCTIVE FINISH FOR
DISTINGUISHED MODERN CARS

COROC
IS THE TRADE-NAME OF A
VARIETY OF FINISHES FOR
SPECIFIC USES, PLEDGED
ALWAYS TO DO EXACTING JOBS
PERFECTLY...AND ECONOMICALLY

COOK'S products have solved some of the
most difficult finishing problems in aviation and
in the automobile industry, as well as in many
other industries which are exacting in their demands for finishes that stand up longest
under the most trying conditions. ¶ Such a
product is COOK'S COROC maroon finish,
which for the first time provides a sturdy, durable, solid-covering **maroon finish** needing no
special ground coats, as formerly required, and
fewer finishing coats than previously necessary.
Thus a manufacturer can now offer a model in
maroon finish at no higher price than for ordinary
colors. ¶ The COOK'S COROC label appears
on a variety of special finishes, each pledging to
solve a particular industrial finishing problem well.

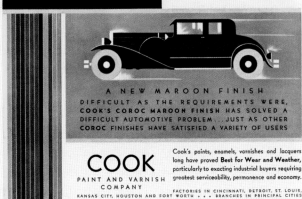

A NEW MAROON FINISH
DIFFICULT AS THE REQUIREMENTS WERE,
COOK'S COROC MAROON FINISH HAS SOLVED A
DIFFICULT AUTOMOTIVE PROBLEM...JUST AS OTHER
COROC FINISHES HAVE SATISFIED A VARIETY OF USERS

COOK
PAINT AND VARNISH
COMPANY

Cook's paints, enamels, varnishes and lacquers
long have proved **Best for Wear and Weather**,
particularly to exacting industrial buyers requiring
greatest serviceability, permanence and economy.

FACTORIES IN CINCINNATI, DETROIT, ST. LOUIS,
KANSAS CITY, HOUSTON AND FORT WORTH • • • BRANCHES IN PRINCIPAL CITIES

Cook Paint & Varnish Co., 1930

The New Ford Convertible Cabriolet

PROUDLY you will drive the new Ford Cabriolet because of its distinctive grace of line and alert, capable performance. It has
the further advantage of being a most practical car. • • • • • • • •

On clear, brisk days, the blue sky overhead, you can enjoy the airy freedom of a roadster. When dark clouds come, it takes
but a few moments to raise the top and command the snug comfort of a coupe. It is thus a splendid car for all the year, for
every changing mood of mind or weather. • • • • • • • •

Ease of control, comfort, the safety of fully enclosed four-wheel brakes and a Triplex shatter-proof glass windshield,
reliability, economy and long life are among the other outstanding features of the new Ford Cabriolet. • • • •

Ford, 1930

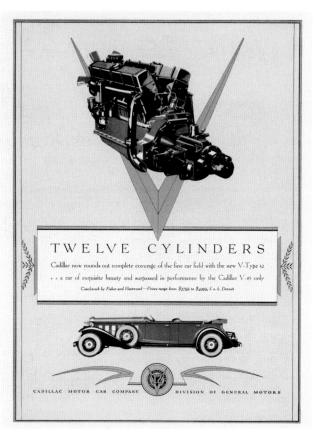

TWELVE CYLINDERS

Cadillac now rounds out complete coverage of the fine car field with the new V-Type 12
• • a car of exquisite beauty and surpassed in performance by the Cadillac V-16 only

Coachwork by Fisher and Fleetwood • Prices range from $3795 to $4595, f. o. b. Detroit

CADILLAC MOTOR CAR COMPANY   DIVISION OF GENERAL MOTORS

Cadillac, 1930

A joyous car for golden summer days

MANY are the delights of the Ford Roadster these golden summer days. Short the miles and pleasant because of its alert and sprightly performance, its safety and its easy-riding comfort.

And what a joy it is to travel along the way with the top down, the blue sky overhead and the fresh, cool air brushing a rosy glow upon your cheeks! Rare indeed the woman who has not hoped that some day such a car might be her very own.

That dream, long cherished, may now come true. For the new Ford Roadster, with all its beauty of line and unusual mechanical excellence, is most conveniently priced. Many months of glorious motoring await your beckoning.

THE NEW FORD ROADSTER

S P E E D

FIRESTONE Gum=Dipped Tires have always been associated with speed. They have been on all the winning cars in that classic of automobile racing, the 500=Mile Indianapolis Race, for ten consecutive years. They hold all world records on road and track for speed, safety, endurance and mileage. The new Supreme Balloon with its heavier Gum=Dipped cord construction, more rubber and broader nonskid tread, is the safest tire ever built for comfortable travel at any speed. Its superb workmanship and striking appearance will enhance the finest motor cars.

Firestone
Supreme Balloon

DISTINCTION

AS DISTINCTIVE as the Bird of Paradise, the New Firestone Supreme Balloon adds a definite beauty to the finest of motor cars. Constructed entirely of superlative materials, built slowly and painstakingly, it represents the final word in dependability, riding comfort and mileage. The tread is wider, thicker, tougher. The Gum-Dipped cord construction has never been equalled for strength and stamina. The polished, ebony-black appearance, enhanced by two rich gold stripes around the side-walls, makes the Supreme Balloon look as good as it really is. A tire to match the finest, fleetest motor cars.

Firestone
Supreme Balloon

Copyright, 1930, The Firestone Tire & Rubber Co.

Firestone, 1930

SURE-FOOTED

THE FIRESTONE SUPREME BALLOON is sure-footed—the strongest, safest tire ever built. Its rugged tread grips the road and provides safety against skidding—its Gum-Dipped cords provide strength and unfailing dependability at high speeds. ¶Here is tire equipment of ultra performance—freedom from troubles and insurance of long mileage. Supreme Balloons are appearing in ever increasing numbers on America's finest, fastest cars. The Firestone Dealer will gladly equip your car today.

Firestone
Supreme Balloon

Copyright, 1930, The Firestone Tire & Rubber Co.

Firestone, 1930

FOR A DISCRIMINATING CLIENTELE
Through all the ages fine things have been produced because there were those who could appreciate their ownership. The celebrated Goya tapestries executed in Spain in the late 18th century, were woven under royal patronage. Today Packard builds fine cars for those who appreciate and are satisfied only with the truly beautiful and luxurious in transportation.

Most popular of all Packard cars is the distinguished and luxurious Standard Eight Five-Passenger Sedan. The Sedan pictured below is of the new 826 series —characteristically Packard in lines and general appearance but embodying added power and beauty, new improvements and refinements in many of its details. It costs no more to own this beautiful and distinctive new Packard than to drive any car of similar size and power, whatever its price. Operating expenses are little if any less for a car of similar size but lesser excellence and lower price.

And depreciation, the major cost of motoring, totals no more for the Packard —if the owner keeps it a little longer than he has been accustomed to drive

PACKARD
ASK THE MAN WHO OWNS ONE

other cars. There is nothing unusual in this, for most Packard owners *do* keep their Packards far longer, both in months and miles, than the cars they previously owned. Not for economy's sake —but because they want to keep them! Why not buy a Packard Standard Eight Sedan and provide your family with the beauty, comfort and distinction of luxurious transportation? Any Packard man will chart Packard ownership costs for you side by side with those of your present Packard-size car. You will find, undoubtedly, that you are *paying* for a Packard. Why not *have* one?

Firestone, 1930 ◄   Packard, 1930

Fifteen years ago, Myron Perley painted the Pierce-Arrow portrait shown in miniature above. Time's changes are increasingly revealed in the artist's 1930 portrayal of the same scene, alongside.

PIERCE ARROW

THERE are deep and personal gratifications in Pierce-Arrow ownership which have no counterpart in the possession of any other motor car, however fine.

A Pierce-Arrow, for example, commands a gracious right-of-way wherever it moves. It meets always a certain prideful recognition which America reserves for things that are particularly fine—and that are its own.

There is reassurance, too, in the knowledge that one's automobile has *individual character* —a quality so inherent with Pierce-Arrow that it is apparent in every phase of the car's distinguished performance, in every line of its slender beauty and grace.

The fame of Pierce-Arrow goes back to the beginning of quality automobiles. The name has always borne the distinction of belonging to *America's finest motor car.*

THREE NEW GROUPS *of* STRAIGHT EIGHTS
132 to 144-inch Wheelbases
$2695 to $6250 at Buffalo
(Custom-built Models up to $10,000)

Pierce Arrow, 1930

CAPTAIN HAWKS buys an air-cooled FRANKLIN

Have you ever flown an airplane? Flashed through space at 125 miles an hour—yet felt the pace to be much slower? Glided from cloud to cloud with perfect ease and comfort? It's all fascinating and thrilling.

Captain Hawks—speed monarch of the sky—knows every thrill of the air. Knows the great superiority of the air-cooled engine, which has made possible famous flights and dramatic aircraft progress. In his first Franklin ride, Captain Hawks sensed that Franklin, too, through the superiority of the air-cooled engine, has achieved brilliant performance and comfort. For the first time, he found the *airplane feel* in a motor car. He enjoyed the ease with which Franklin could be *directed*. The riding like gliding,

with 80 miles an hour like 50, thrilled him.

Franklin—America's truly airplane-type car—presents a bright picture for the future of the automobile. Because of the great progress of air-cooling, many automobile authorities are saying, "Eventually all cars will be air-cooled."

Try a Franklin ride. Put the car to every test. You'll find new comfort and a new feeling of safety. The exclusive Franklin features, made possible by air-cooling, are translated into the finest motoring the world has ever known.

In outward beauty, Dietrich has styled the new De Luxe Franklin to be as modern and progressive as

Captain Hawks, his airplane and his new Franklin Convertible Speedster

Franklin engineering. Through its lower price level Franklin is now available to a greatly widened group of fine car buyers. Call your local dealer for a trial ride. Franklin Automobile Company, Syracuse, N. Y.

THE   AIR-COOLED   AIRPLANE-TYPE   CAR

Franklin, 1930

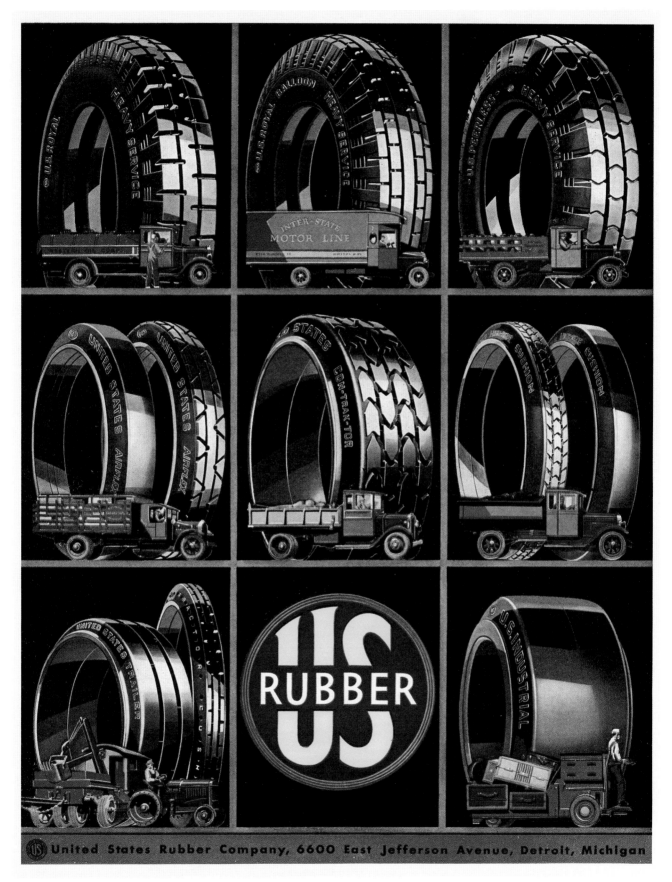

United States Rubber Company, 6600 East Jefferson Avenue, Detroit, Michigan

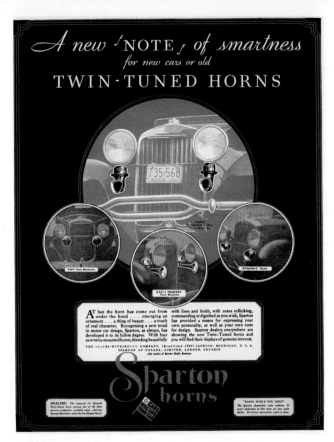

Sparton Horns, 1931

La Salle, 1931

IN ALL THE FOUR FACTORS OF ECONOMY
THE NEW OLDSMOBILE STANDS HIGH

First cost . . . operating expense . . . long life . . . and service costs . . . these are the four fundamental factors which determine how economically you can acquire and own a motor car. And in all four of these fundamental factors of economy the new Oldsmobile stands high.

First, it is economical to buy—for its new lower price now makes it possible for you to enjoy Oldsmobile's fine-car advantages for as little as $845, f. o. b. Lansing. And many of these advantages, including the famous Syncro-Mesh non-clashing transmission, are now made available for the first time in any car at such low price.

Second, the new Oldsmobile is economical to drive, because its cost of operation, month after month, is uniformly low. Demands on fuel, oil and tires . . . and, hence, on the pocketbook . . . are unusually light.

Third, it is economical to own because its proved design and sturdy

construction contribute to remarkable durability . . . as proved in the hands of nearly a quarter of a million owners during the past three years.

Finally, the new Oldsmobile is economical to operate due to a fair and equitable owner service policy. This policy is explicit in its terms . . . and as broad in its application as any in the industry.

These four factors are responsible, in no small way, for the widespread popularity which Oldsmobile has enjoyed in the past. And they are sound reasons why the new Oldsmobile represents a logical and economical investment—a good buy from every standpoint.

OLDSMOBILE

PRODUCT OF GENERAL MOTORS

Oldsmobile, 1931

In creating a fully convertible Landau Phaeton for the Chevrolet Six, Fisher adds another brilliant triumph to its long record of achievement in coachcraft.

Heretofore, this distinctive body type has been offered solely in the costly custom field. Today, in a spirited interpretation, solidly constructed and handsomely finished, it is available at Chevrolet's low price.

The Landau Phaeton is racy in its design, with bold moulding treatments, wide doors, and rakish roof line. The ingenious top mechanism is solid and

rattleproof, but lowers easily and compactly. Upholstery in leather, deep, restful cushions, side arm rests, and recessed ash trays are among its fine-car features. Thus Fisher's skill in design and craftsmanship plus the resources of Chevrolet and General Motors brings a model long popular for custom use within the reach of every car buyer.

Fisher is proud to have had a part in this achievement and to join with Chevrolet in offering for the first time at modest cost a car of such pronounced charm, all-season utility, and high value.

FISHER BODY CORPORATION · DETROIT, MICHIGAN
Division of General Motors

Chevrolet, 1931

▶ *Chrysler, 1931*

CHRYSLER IMPERIAL

WITH PATENTED
FLOATING POWER

AUTOMATIC CLUTCH • SILENT GEAR SELECTOR • FREE

WHEELING • INTERNAL HYDRAULIC BRAKES

ALL-STEEL BODY • OILITE SQUEAK-PROOF SPRINGS

DOUBLE-DROP GIRDER-TRUSS FRAME

New Chrysler Imperial Custom Eight Phaeton

New Chrysler Imperial Custom Eight Sedan

CHRYSLER'S FINEST MOTOR CARS

TAKE THE WHEEL . . . enjoy the most unforgettable ride you've ever had

The new Chrysler Imperial Eights are everything the word "Imperial" signifies . . . as the dictionary says, "fit for an emperor; magnificent; imposing; superior in size or quality."

Styled, appointed and engineered for those who want the finest—and only the finest motor cars—these new Imperials have a "luxury" of performance heretofore unknown in *any* motor car at *any* price.

In these cars you get the last word in up-to-date engineering. We promise you a new sensation. We promise you the easiest, silkiest, quietest ride to be had on wheels.

Floating Power engine suspension works a seeming miracle in performance. Creates an altogether new *feeling* in motoring. Wipes out power tremor completely at all car speeds. Eliminates all sense or suggestion of engine effort.

Even if you have a chauffeur, you'll want to do most of the driving. For these cars have an Automatic Clutch that is *absolutely* automatic. They have the latest and finest in Free Wheeling. They have a new Silent Gear Selector—enabling an instant, silent change to a higher or a lower gear at any car speed with no more effort than moving a lead pencil.

They have Oilite Squeak-Proof Springs—patented springs that *never* need lubrication, and *never* squeak. And Chrysler's world-famous Hydraulic Brakes for quick, positive, *cushioned* stopping—with new Centrifuse brake drums of steel with a lining of cast iron fused permanently to the steel. Resulting in cooler brakes. Safer brakes. Longer-lasting brakes.

The new Chrysler Imperial Eight with 125-horsepower engine may be had in two chassis sizes—a 135-inch wheelbase, carrying Chrysler's All-Steel Bodies, and a 146-inch wheelbase, carrying custom bodies by Chrysler and Le Baron.

•

A new Chrysler Imperial Custom Eight, six body models, $2895 to $3595; a new Chrysler Imperial Eight, three body models, $1925 to $2195; a new Chrysler Eight, five body models, $1435 to $1695; a new Chrysler Six, five body models, $885 to $935 (Automatic Clutch and Oilite Squeak-Proof Springs on all Sixes at slight extra cost). F. O. B. Factory. Duplate Safety Plate Glass standard on Custom Eights. Obtainable on Six and Eight Sedans, $17.50; on Imperial Sedans, $20; all 2-passenger Coupes, $9.50.

You'll be happier with a Chrysler

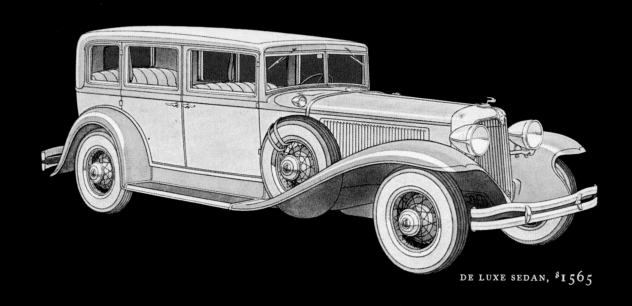

Chrysler Eight De Luxe

PATTERNED AFTER THE CHRYSLER IMPERIAL EIGHT

DE LUXE SEDAN, $1565

De Luxe Style—De Luxe Comfort—De Luxe Performance

CHRYSLER, so often the pioneer to better things, has now pioneered with an entirely new and better kind of luxury and performance in a car of moderate price—the new Chrysler Eight De Luxe, available in five magnificent body models.

It is a *de luxe* car through and through, from start to finish, inside and outside.

The de luxe power of a bigger engine. The de luxe comfort of bigger bodies and longer springs. The de luxe smartness of a divided windshield with *inside* adjustable sun visors. De luxe upholstery of Bedford cord. De luxe interior panels and mouldings of dark walnut finish. De luxe fitments . . . Everything about the car suggests a car of much higher price.

Its big, quiet engine is completely insulated from the frame by live rubber; has a large, perfectly balanced crankshaft, fully counterweighted—and develops with velvety ease a good 95 horsepower.

Eighty miles an hour—if you like speed—but whether you travel that fast or not, the power that makes such speed possible enables

you to glide along at moderate speeds without consciousness of engine effort.

This de luxe performance owes much to Chrysler's exclusive Multi-Range four-speed transmission with Dual High gears. *Both are internal-mesh gears which make it possible to shift instantly at any time from one to the other, at any car speed, without clashing.* Two high gears *double* the range of high gear performance. There is one high gear for flashing pick-up and bursts of speed in traffic, and another higher gear for the open road.

Drive this Chrysler. Learn from it th[e] fascinating difference between Chrysler pe[r]formance and other performance. Enjoy th[e] difference in the way it clings to the road a[t] all speeds; the way it takes the turns; th[e] way it soars up the hills; the ease of its piv[-]otal steering; the positive control and safety o[f] its internal self-equalizing hydraulic brake[s].

Chrysler's fine quality, Chrysler's geni[us] for engineering progress, Chrysler's carefu[l] craftsmanship, all have made this Chrysle[r] Eight De Luxe a motor car you'll drive wit[h] unending pride and supreme satisfaction.

This is a case of fine automobile value mad[e] almost unbelievably finer. See for yourself[.]

CHRYSLER SIX	. . . . .	$885 to $93[5]
CHRYSLER "70"	. . . .	$1245 to $129[5]
CHRYSLER EIGHT	. . . .	$1495 to $166[5]
CHRYSLER EIGHT DE LUXE		$1525 to $158[5]

(Five wire wheels standard; six wire wheels $35 extra)

CHRYSLER IMPERIAL EIGHT	$2745 to $314[5]

(CUSTOM MODELS $3150 TO $3575)

All prices f.o.b. factory; special equipment extra.

THE EIGHT AS BUICK BUILDS IT

An enlarged reproduction of this painting by George Biggs, in full color, suitable for framing, will be mailed upon request. Dept. P. Buick Motor Co., Flint, Michigan

Some day your boy will own a Buick

You who have a boy, with mischief in his eye and wings upon his feet, are one of the rich men of this world, regardless of your rating in Dun or Bradstreet.

He may pester you with questions, may make more noise than a dozen boys ought to, may even mar the upholstery of your brand new automobile. But he is *your* boy—and all your heart is his.

Many men who drive Buicks today were boys when Buick began building automobiles twenty-seven years ago. Some lifted the hoods of their fathers' Buicks and studied that pioneer Valve-in-Head engine as boys now study Buick's Valve-in-Head Straight Eight.

They went on to fine careers . . . and Buick went along with them . . . developing, improving, refining, year after year.

The tie of friendship between these owners and Buick is very close. Some have owned as many as five, ten, even twenty Buick cars. More than eighty-eight per cent—almost nine out of ten—purchase Buicks again and again.

Buick hopes for this same friendship with your boy when he reaches man's estate, and is more than willing to pay the price in constant progress.

Buick will go forward with that boy, *grow* with him, seek to interpret his desires in transportation, as it interprets the desires of present-day motorists.

Just as surely as Buick fulfills this responsibility, and proves worthy of his favor, some day your boy will own a Buick.

The new Buick Straight Eights, in four series and four price ranges, are offered in 20 luxurious models. from $1025 to $2035, f.o.b. Flint, Mich.

A GENERAL MOTORS VALUE
BODY BY FISHER

WHEN BETTER AUTOMOBILES ARE BUILT . . . BUICK WILL BUILD THEM

Buick, 1931

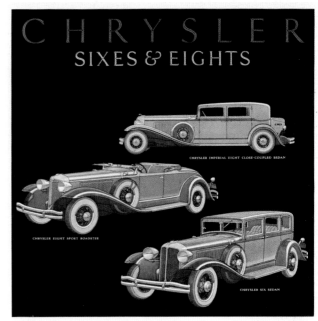

CHRYSLER
SIXES & EIGHTS

CHRYSLER IMPERIAL EIGHT CLOSE-COUPLED SEDAN

CHRYSLER EIGHT SPORT ROADSTER

CHRYSLER SIX SEDAN

Own a Chrysler—Enjoy the Difference

OWN a Chrysler and you have a car you'll *really* enjoy—because there is a very real difference between a Chrysler and all other cars.

Sit at the wheel of a Chrysler—*any* Chrysler—and you will discover things about Chrysler performance that will stir your pulse and make your eyes sparkle. A distinctly different sensation of almost boundless power. A difference in breath-taking pick-up. A different kind of smoothness. And thrilling speed with a complete feeling of security and ease of control.

Chrysler is giving this vividly different performance in a wide range of Chryslers priced within the reach of practically every purse and income. All smart cars that inspire pride—and challenging all comparison in value.

An entirely new Chrysler Six styled like the smart Chrysler Eights—a fine, big Six with a 116-inch wheelbase; a double-drop frame; a 70-horsepower engine and safety bodies of strong steel.

And the Chrysler "70"—with its 93-horsepower engine and its Multi-Range 4-speed transmission, which together have made it world-famous for performance.

And the Chrysler Eight—with its distinguished appearance, low center of gravity, safety steel bodies, Dual High gears and quick, quiet gear shift.

And the Chrysler Imperial Eight—the embodiment of all motoring luxury—a magnificent car with a 145-inch wheelbase and a 125-horsepower engine—a car for the connoisseurs of motor cars.

Drive a Chrysler—*any* Chrysler—and learn what a difference there is in favor of Chrysler.

CHRYSLER SIX . . . . . $885 to $895
CHRYSLER "70" . . . . . $1245 to $1295
CHRYSLER EIGHT . . . . $1495 to $1665
CHRYSLER IMPERIAL EIGHT $2745 to $3145
(CUSTOM MODELS $3575 to $3575)
All prices f.o.b. factory; special equipment extra.

Chrysler, 1931

Through such gigantic chasms of rock as this, the fleet of the Yellowstone Park Transportation Company carries thousands and ten thousands each year in safety and comfort

There is no greater kaleidoscope in nature than the Grand Canyon of the Yellowstone—rainbows, ambers, ochres, cobalts—splashed with pure wine and shot with lemon, vermillion hue, snow white and silver gray

You feel particularly intimate with nature, for the wild life of Yellowstone meets you trustingly at every turn

Then there is the ghostly glory of the geysers—hundreds of them. To hear them roar with eager vehemence into the sky—to watch them gush aloft with feathery fierceness, is an experience never forgotten

Friendly bear and bison, deer and beaver roam unafraid beside the roads you travel in Yellowstone, adding the final touch of completeness to this land of marvels

YELLOWSTONE PROVES
that it pays to decide: the
"I WILL BUY ONLY A LEADING MAKE OF TIRE"

Soon after the jingling horse team and stage coach gave way to motor transport in Yellowstone Park, all other tires yielded place to Goodyears on the great Yellowstone fleet. ¶ Unchallenged, Goodyears have held that place for fourteen years. ¶ During almost exactly the same period of time, Goodyears have led all other tires in sales to the public. Since 1915, it has been consistently true that

"more people ride on Goodyear Tires than on any other kind." ¶ There is, in these two facts, more than coincidence. ¶ For the responsibility of transportation through the world's most magnificent wilderness and wonderland, Yellowstone chooses only *the* leading make of tire . . . Isn't there, in this method of choosing tires, a mighty sound thought for you?

THE GREATEST NAME IN RUBBER

GOOD YEAR

Copyright 1931, by The Goodyear Tire & Rubber Co. Inc

Chrysler, 1931 ◄ *Goodyear, 1931*

The silent, smooth performance of La Salle V-8 is admirably reflected in the long, flowing lines of the 2-Passenger Coupe, with body by Fisher, illustrated below. La Salle V-8 prices range from $2195, f. o. b. Detroit. G. M. A. C. terms available on all body styles.

So completely is the ideal of fine workmanship ingrained at the Cadillac plant that, no matter whether it be for Cadillac or for La Salle, every detail of design and manufacture is approached with the same meticulous care. There is only *one* standard of excellence, regardless of the task to be done. As a result, the La Salle V-8 provides a degree of quality and a type of performance far beyond those suggested by its moderate price — for it is built with the same exactitude as Cadillac itself.

LA SALLE V-8

Cadillac, 1931

To ride in the Cadillac V-12 is to know at once why it is ranked so highly among the fine cars of the world—for the appeal of its 12-cylinder performance is well-nigh irresistible. Even those who are accustomed to the foremost automobiles, are finding in the V-12 a new conception of motoring luxury. In fact, a V-12 demonstration, almost without exception, makes conventional cars seem commonplace.

CADILLAC V 8 12 16

Cadillac, 1931

Arch of Titus
Rome

TIME yields generous tribute to the work that is sound and fine. This can be true of an automobile tire, as of a triumphal arch. It is true of the Goodyear Double Eagle—first of the *super*-tires—today far more highly esteemed than at any previous time. Tire of tires in the beginning, the Double Eagle has been imitated, copied, patterned after, of course; but in its matchless excellence it continues to stand steadily first in reputation, as it does in sales.

The
DOUBLE EAGLE
by
GOODYEAR

Goodyear, 1931

for speed on the court
A DRY BALL
for speed on the road
A DRY GAS

DRY
lively

WET
sluggish

Just as the spectacular playing of a tennis star may be marred by a wet, sluggish ball, so the sparkling performance of even the finest car may be impaired by wet gas.

Texaco-Ethyl is the "dry" Ethyl gasoline. It is dry as it leaves the manifold—dry as it enters the cylinders—completely responsive to every spark flash.

There are no fuel-starved cylinders to impair the performance of your engine, for Texaco-Ethyl serves each with a uniform mixture of dry, live gas and smooth, anti-knock compound. Your daily shopping tours are made easier. No coughing, sputtering starts, no stalling in traffic.

Make your neighborhood Texaco man headquarters for servicing your car. If you need tires checked, radiator filled, or windshield cleaned, drop in. He will be glad to attend to these details without any obligation whatsoever.

THE TEXAS COMPANY · *Texaco Petroleum Products*

TEXACO-ETHYL
THE "DRY" ETHYL GASOLINE

Texaco, 1931

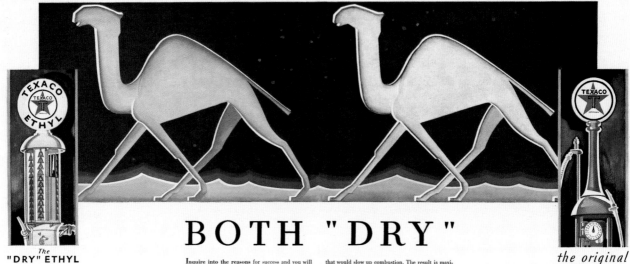

The
"DRY" ETHYL
Gasoline

BOTH "DRY"

Inquire into the reasons for success and you will usually find something simple and fundamental. Ask the reason for the marked superiority of the *new* and *better* Texaco Gasoline and Texaco-Ethyl and the answer is simply, "They're both 'dry'."

"Dryness" in gasoline is that quality which permits quick and complete vaporization. It means the even distribution to all cylinders of a completely "dry" vapor containing no wet drops of gasoline

that would slow up combustion. The result is maximum power delivered to the cylinders—instant response to the spark flash—quicker starting and pick-up—and more miles for your gasoline dollar.

That's what **Texaco** means to every motorist who uses it—and there are thousands of them—in every one of our 48 States. Some use the *new* and *better* Texaco Gasoline and some use Texaco-Ethyl. One should be yours. Both are "dry."

THE TEXAS COMPANY   *Texaco Petroleum Products*

the original
"DRY" GAS

The NEW and BETTER
TEXACO-ETHYL *and* TEXACO GASOLINE

Texaco, 1931

▶ *International Motor Truck, 1931*   ▶ ▶ *Chevrolet, 1931*

THE INTERNATIONAL MOTOR TRUCK—1931

Product of a Full Century of Manufacturing Experience

Today the service of International Harvester in the field of Transportation goes far beyond Agriculture. Three-fourths of its great annual output in trucks is absorbed by Commerce and Industry—a striking demonstration of universal acceptance, proof of the merit in manufacture that grows out of generations of accumulated experience.

1831

1931

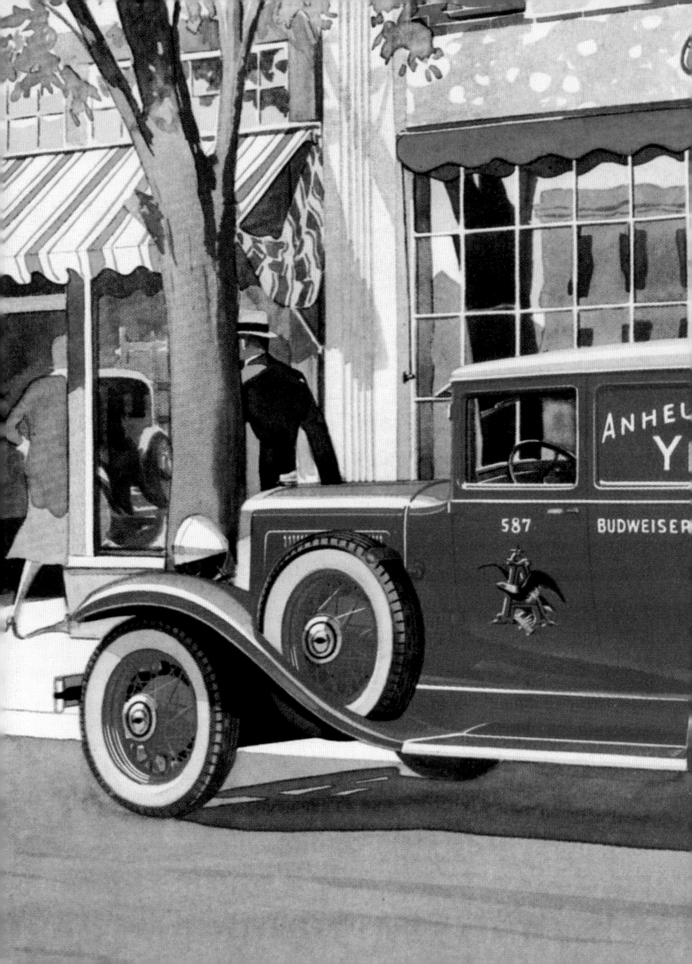

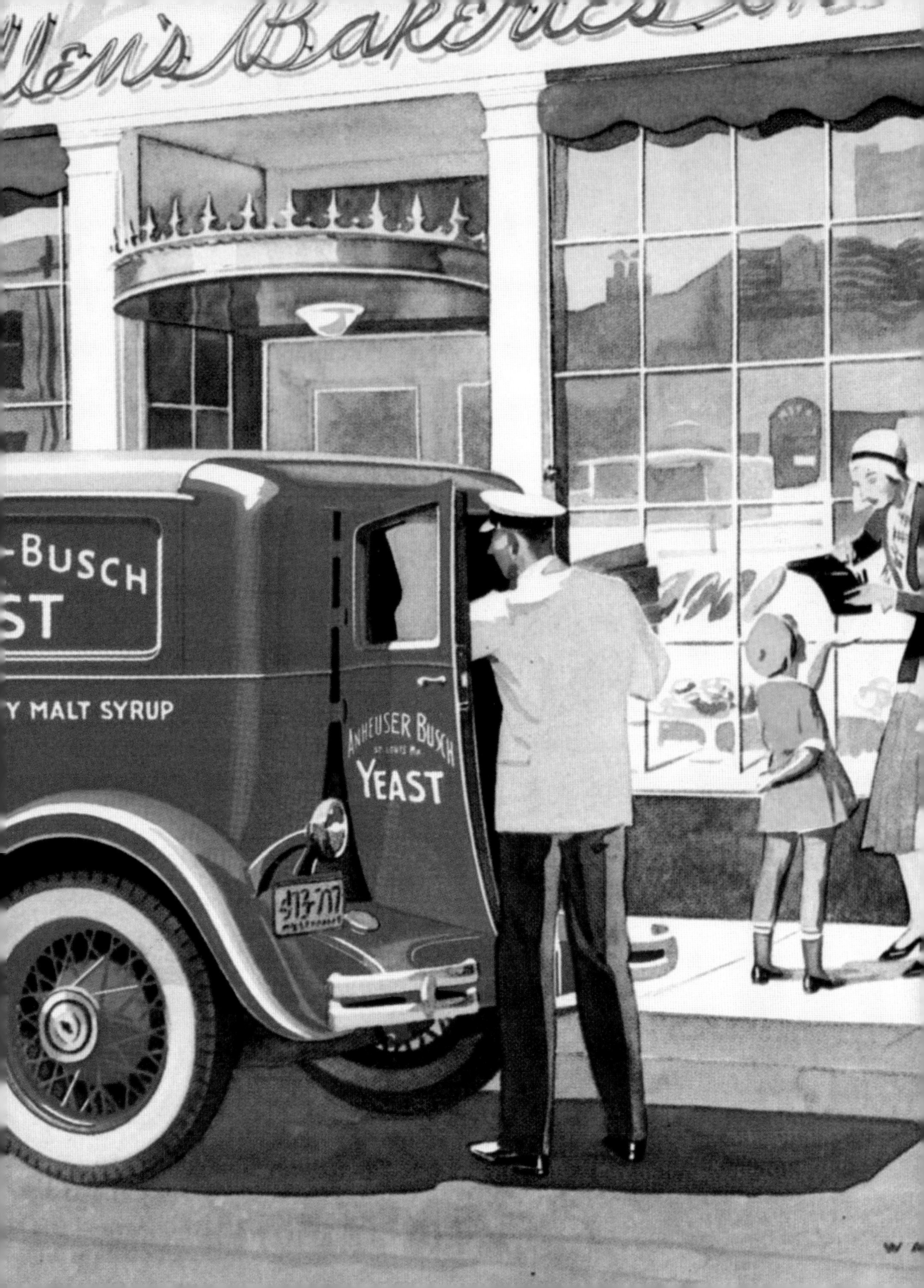
-BUSCH
ST
Y MALT SYRUP
ANHEUSER BUSCH
ST. LOUIS MO.
YEAST

MARMON
SIXTEEN

The Marmon Sixteen is the modern automobile. Its beauty of line and appointment is the beauty of the simplicity and efficiency of today. Its 200-horsepower engine is an achievement of great importance. Both in action and appearance the Marmon Sixteen redefines the motor car in terms of the present. Wheelbase, 145 inches. Prices under $5000. Marmon Motor Car Company, Indianapolis, Ind.

Marmon Motor Car Co., 1931

▶ *Chrysler, 1931*

THIS IS THE LIFE!

MAYBE it's because convertible cars have a particular swank; maybe it's because they have two-in-one utility—in either case, or both, it is obvious that convertible sedans and coupes are strongly in vogue.

The increasing popularity of these smart and useful body types finds Chrysler in the forefront, with convertibles meeting every desire. Chrysler has created outstanding convertible sedans and coupes in four different chassis sizes—ranging all the way from $935 to $3595.

The convertible sedan pictured above is that of the Chrysler Imperial Eight, listing at $2195. Wheelbase, 135 inches; engine, 125 horsepower . . . a magnetic and magnificent motor car. Just to look at it makes you want to drive it.

Together with all the style and luxury of Chrysler's new convertibles, and of all other Chrysler models, there is an entirely new sensation in Chrysler performance. New results due to Floating Power engine mountings. Smoothest, quietest power you have ever experienced. Not the slightest engine tremor at any car speed. Not the slightest suggestion of engine effort.

The most refreshing of all cars to drive. Shock-proof steering. Effortless gear shifting. Squeak-proof springs. Strongest, safest bodies. Surest, safest brakes. Chrysler's unrivaled Hydraulic Brakes are always self-equalizing, and have Centrifuse drums that give *five times* the wear of ordinary brakes.

There's everything about a Chrysler to make you like it—and keep on liking it. There's just no equaling Chrysler engineering or Chrysler results.

A new Chrysler Imperial Custom Eight, six body models, $2895 to $3595 • a new Chrysler Imperial Eight, three body models, $1925 to $2195 • a new Chrysler Eight, five body models, $1435 to $1695 • a new Chrysler Six, five body models, $885 to $935 F. O. B. Factory • (On Sixes, the Automatic Clutch is optional at $8 extra and Oilite Squeak-Proof Springs are optional at $10 extra) • Duplate Safety Plate Glass standard on Custom Eights. Obtainable on Six and Eight Sedans, $17.50; on Imperial Sedans, $20 • all 2-passenger Coupes, $9.50. All closed models wired for PHILCO-TRANSITONE RADIO.

FLOATING POWER · AUTOMATIC CLUTCH · SILENT GEAR SELECTOR · FREE WHEELING · INTERNAL
HYDRAULIC BRAKES · OILITE SQUEAK-PROOF SPRINGS · DOUBLE-DROP GIRDER-TRUSS FRAME

CHRYSLER
IMPERIAL

WITH PATENTED
FLOATING POWER

Tune in on CHRYSLER MOTORS RADIO PROGRAM "Ziegfeld Radio Show" personally conducted by Flo Ziegfeld — Columbia Coast-to-Coast Network; every Sunday evening

Reo-Royale, 1931

MANY A FINE CAR OWNER
IS SELECTING OAKLAND
FOR PERSONAL USE . . .

There are several reasons for the present trend toward Oakland V-8 as a personal car. For your personal car has a place all its own. It need not be as long or weighty perhaps as the largest cars you own, but it must meet your personal ideas of taste and style, and it must have the ability on the road to do the things that you ask.

We find that owners accustomed to fine automobiles see much in Oakland V-8 to meet their approval. They know its V-8 motor is in the certain trend of today's engine design for fine cars, boats or aircraft. They see the Syncro-mesh transmission as an evidence of thoughtfulness for their convenience.

In the Fisher-built bodies they find an understanding of their tastes and standards —a feeling of thorough care and of work well done.

It is an added virtue that a car like this may be had at a moderate price. Its expense for running and maintenance, too, comes within a sensible budget.

We want to turn one of these fine cars over to you for a two or three days' trial. Drive it anywhere you wish, and give it a real test.

THE SPORT COUPE

MAKING NEW FRIENDS AND KEEPING THE OLD

The Convertible Coupe

OAKLAND
PRODUCT OF GENERAL MOTORS · BODY BY FISHER

Oakland, 1931

AS POWERFUL AS ETHYL GASOLINE

THE leaping, racing flight of the sailfish is a breath-taking display of power under perfect control.

To put the power of gasoline under control, leading oil refiners add Ethyl fluid. This prevents the uneven explosions that cause power-waste, harmful "knock" and overheating. It *controls combustion*, delivering power to the pistons with a smoothly increasing pressure.

Controlled combustion makes such an improvement in car performance that Ethyl Gasoline is now the biggest selling motor fuel in the country. Practically all leading refiners add Ethyl fluid to good gasoline to form Ethyl Gasoline, and nearly every filling station now has one or more Ethyl pumps. Look for the Ethyl emblem. Ethyl Gasoline Corporation, New York City.

FOR SUMMER DRIVING — Ethyl Gasoline keeps the motor cooler because combustion is controlled. In summer, as in other seasons, Ethyl fluid is mixed with base gasoline that is best suited to the season.

THE ACTIVE INGREDIENT USED IN ETHYL FLUID IS LEAD

Ethyl, 1931

examine value

The General Motors Corporation maintains a creative staff known as the Art and Color Section to aid and counsel the division engineers in the style development of General Motors cars. The special province of this staff embraces style, color and appointments, and under its skillful handling, lines and proportions yield to fashion influences well in advance of the prevailing mode. Through the activities of the Art and Color Section, General Motors is kept abreast of style changes, and in co-operation with division engineers conscientious effort is made to secure the most pleasing effects. Thus the divisions of the General Motors Corporation are supported in their creative work by unusual art and style facilities which contribute deeply to the outstanding values in General Motors cars.

General Motors, 1931

GENERAL MOTORS CARS
HAVE OUTSTANDING VALUE

CHEVROLET · PONTIAC · OLDSMOBILE · OAKLAND · BUICK · LA SALLE · CADILLAC · BODIES BY FISHER

147

A NEW FRIEZE UPHOLSTERY

by Chase

ZENOBIA- A NEW FABRIC AND DESIGN AS USED IN A SPECIAL NASH EIGHT SEDAN

THE revolt against lustreless, monotones in motor car upholstery is here evidenced in this interesting car interior.

Here, indeed, is a striking example of a modern application of an old-world art . . . hand block-printing on a beautiful Mohair Frieze. The elegance of the design . . . a rich floral motif . . . the superb pastel colorings employed and the enduring nature of the fabric, are indicative of a new upholstery trend.

The noticeable swing-back to fine, mohair fabrics for motor cars is evidence of growing dissatisfaction with delicate upholstery materials which are only adaptations for automobile use and are not pre-eminently "travel fabrics" . . . a distinction enjoyed for many years by Chase Angora mohair fabrics.

There is one of a variety of unusual Chase Velmo fabrics which will enhance the beauty of your car. Full co-operation offered to your dealer in its selection or samples for the asking.

Product of . . . . . SANFORD MILLS: *Selling Agents:* L. C. Chase & Co., Boston, New York . . Detroit . . San Francisco . . Chicago

The unique Frieze Upholstery, used so effectively in the interior of this de Luxe motor car owned by Mr. J. C. Tills of the Pittsburgh Plate Glass Company is complemented by a solid color sidewall and deck-lining Chase Frieze and also Imperial Mohair floor rug . . . both of the same ground tone as the seat covering.

CHASE
Velmo
UPHOLSTERY FABRICS

The New Chevrolet Sedan Delivery, $575

Over 400 prominent fleet operators use Chevrolet Six equipment

ALLIED MILLS INCORPORATED
AMRADA PETROLEUM CORPORATION
AMERICAN GAS & ELECTRIC COMPANY
AMERICAN WATER WORKS & ELECTRIC COMPANY, INC.
ANHEUSER-BUSCH INCORPORATED
ARMOUR AND COMPANY
ARMSTRONG CORK COMPANY
ASSOCIATED TELEPHONE UTILITIES CO.
THE BORDEN COMPANY
BYLLESBY ENGINEERING & MANAGEMENT CORPORATION
THE CELOTEX COMPANY
THE CITIES SERVICE ORGANIZATION
COLGATE-PALMOLIVE-PEET COMPANY
THE COMMONWEALTH & SOUTHERN CORPORATION
CRANE COMPANY
DE LAVAL SEPARATOR COMPANY
GENERAL OUTDOOR ADVERTISING COMPANY, INCORPORATED

Wherever men or materials must be transported at minimum cost per mile, you will find Chevrolet six-cylinder cars and trucks in service. A roster of the fleet operators who use Chevrolets includes over 400 leading firms, representing practically every phase of American commerce and industry. A few are listed herewith. These names will serve to indicate the size and caliber of the organizations using Chevrolet equipment.

GENERAL ELECTRIC COMPANY
THE GOODYEAR TIRE & RUBBER COMPANY, INC.
KELLY-SPRINGFIELD TIRE COMPANY
P. LORILLARD COMPANY, INCORPORATED
MIDDLE WEST UTILITIES SYSTEM
MISSOURI STATE HIGHWAY DEPARTMENT
PILLSBURY FLOUR MILLS COMPANY
PORTLAND CEMENT ASSOCIATION

THE PURE OIL COMPANY
SHELL PETROLEUM CORPORATION
SINCLAIR REFINING COMPANY
SKELLY OIL COMPANY
STANDARD BRANDS INCORPORATED
STANDARD OIL COMPANY OF CALIFORNIA
STANDARD OIL COMPANY OF INDIANA
STANDARD OIL CO. OF NEBRASKA
STANDARD OIL CO. OF NEW YORK
STONE & WEBSTER ENGINEERING CORPORATION
SUN OIL COMPANY
SWIFT & COMPANY
UNITED BISCUIT CO. OF AMERICA
UNITED LIGHT & POWER COMPANY
UNITED STATES RUBBER COMPANY
UNITED STATES TOBACCO COMPANY
WESTERN ELECTRIC COMPANY, INC.
WESTINGHOUSE ELECTRIC & MFG. COMPANY
WILSON & CO., INC.
THE YOUNGSTOWN SHEET & TUBE COMPANY

Chevrolet passenger car prices range from $475 to $650. Chevrolet truck chassis are priced from $355 to $590. All prices f. o. b. Flint, Michigan. Special equipment extra. Product of General Motors. Low delivered prices and easy terms. Chevrolet Motor Company, Detroit, Michigan.

NEW CHEVROLET SIX
The Great American Value

Chevrolet, 1931

MILES FROM HOME...
miles from help

She was perfectly capable of changing a flat. But today she was dressed for a luncheon—and the tire was muddy—the jack smeared with grease. Then (it seemed like a miracle to her)—a Texaco tank truck drove up—and changed the tire for her.

This is a typical example of the willing cooperation which inspires every Texaco employee, on the road or at a Texaco Service Station. Even if you drive in only for air, or a windshield to be cleaned—Texaco welcomes you. Feel free to stop, not only for "dry" Texaco-Ethyl Gasoline and Texaco Motor Oil, but also for any service you desire. THE TEXAS COMPANY · Texaco Petroleum Products.

© 1931, The Texas Company

TEXACO
GASOLINE...MOTOR OIL

Texaco, 1931

Ask the man who owns one

To you who appreciate luxurious transportation Packard extends a cordial invitation to examine its remarkable New Series cars. You should do more than merely admire their beauty in the showroom. Inspect them critically. Drive them yourself. Ride in them as a passenger. For the new Packards are *entirely* new—new in everything save straight-eight motor principle and the characteristic "Packard" appearance. ¶ Never before has Packard offered new models with so many new features and important improvements. Body lines are refined and modernized. Interiors are newly insulated against sound and temperature—more luxuriously upholstered. Wheelbases are longer—tread wider. Power is greater, smoother. Transmission is Packard-built, four-speed, synchro-mesh. And outstanding among all improvements are the dash-controlled, adjustable hydraulic shock absorbers affording *Ride Control*—an exclusive feature. ¶ The new Packards are more beautiful, more distinguished than ever—and you will find them the easiest driving, most comfortable riding cars you have ever known.

PACKARD

Velmo Upholstery Fabrics, 1931 ◄ *Packard, 1931*

THE EIGHT AS BUICK BUILDS IT

Come, travel the long fine road of Buick ownership

A long, smooth, carefree road, winding through the years, is the road of Buick ownership. It starts the day you take delivery of your Buick. It leads to scores of thousands of miles of glorious motoring enjoyment.

You do not have to be wealthy to travel this road. And yet many people of wealth are choosing it because it's so fine. You may make the journey in any one of Buick's four Straight Eights listing from $1025 to $2035.

Only those who follow the road know its joys. The thrill of masterly performance, of riding luxury, of day-in-and-day-out dependability comes with actual possession of a new Buick with its Valve-in-Head Straight Eight Engine, Silent-Shift Syncro-Mesh Transmission and Insulated Body by Fisher. But you can judge how wonderful the road must be by the great number of motorists who travel it.

Over 700,000 more men and women are driving Buicks today than any other car of Buick's price or higher.

More than 50 out of every 100 buyers of the fourteen eights in Buick's price class have chosen the Eight as Buick Builds It during the several months since its introduction.

More than eighty-eight per cent of these owners—almost nine out of every ten—have bought Buicks again and again over a long period, clinging happily to the Buick road.

It has to be a great road to attract and hold so many discriminating motorists, year after year—now, doesn't it?

We who build this car, your Buick dealer, and the great body of men and women who give Buick such decisive preference, all invite you: Come, travel the long fine road of Buick ownership.

The new Buick Straight Eights, in four series and four price ranges, are offered in 22 luxurious models, from $1025 to $2035, f. o. b. Flint, Michigan.

A GENERAL MOTORS VALUE

WHEN BETTER AUTOMOBILES ARE BUILT, BUICK WILL BUILD THEM

Buick, 1931

ESSEX $595 *f.o.b. Detroit*
The Value Sensation in a Year of Sensational Values

The New Essex Super-Six Challenger Coupe

Restful Comfort in the New Essex

Rare Riding Comfort
in the finest performing six Hudson ever built

Essex now competes with the *lowest* in price—and yet it challenges the *finest* in quality! It is a full-sized car, big and roomy—and it introduces Super-Six smoothness to the lowest price field.

With its 60-horsepower motor and 70 miles an hour speed, it challenges the performance of *any* six at *any* price! It is quicker in get-away, more powerful on hills, faster on the road and it matches the economy of cars most noted for their low operating cost.

It possesses aristocratic beauty that fills every owner with pride and pleasure. From its chromium-plated radiator grid to its large rectangular rear window it is smartly styled. Interior appointments, too, are tastefully done.

Essex has always been world-famous for performance. This new car now surpasses that of

any previous model. It is ruggedly built to assure enduring reliability and give lasting satisfaction.

These advantages mark Essex as the outstanding motor car value. But in addition you get *Rare Riding and Driving Comfort* such as you never before experienced in a car of its low price. Seats are wide and deep. Head-room and leg-room are greater. Bodies are insulated against weather and noise. Doors are wider. There is lots of room for comfort while riding.

Go to your nearest dealer and see this Essex. Drive it and make your own tests. *Compare it point for point, dollar for dollar, with any other cars on the market.* Then you will agree it is the Value Sensation in a year of sensational values.

$595 ESSEX
COACH OR BUSINESS COUPE

Other body models as attractively priced. Special Equipment Extra. All prices f. o. b. Detroit

Essex, 1931

EVIDENCE: how the Right Trucks
Do produce EXTRA PROFITS

MORGAN LINEN SERVICE

103 GENERAL MOTORS TRUCKS

Earn More for Morgan Service, Inc.—Nation-Wide Laundry Chain

THE right trucks, and the right truck *methods*, are producing extra profits—often amounting to hundreds of dollars yearly per truck—for firms in nearly every line.

This 103-truck fleet of Morgan Laundry and Linen Service of New York, Boston, Chicago, Los Angeles and 12 other principal cities, is a good example.

It may also suggest unlooked-for profits in your own truck operation—obtainable through the unusual service General Motors Truck Company provides.

A. K. Morgan, President, tells about the performance of their General Motors Trucks and why they have standardized on them for 1931:

"We bought our first General Motors Truck in 1927 because that name—General Motors—to us meant the most modern, proved design and construction.

"We have gradually added 102 more, in four years' time, and have standardized on them this year because:

"*These trucks have consistently proved their ability to 'pick up' and deliver more laundry and linen than other units of comparable size. They are doing this per day, per week and per year.*

"General Motors Truck representatives studied our delivery operations closely. This insured the correct equipment for our varied types of work. And it brought us highly profitable suggestions on loading, routing, dispatching, and driver supervision.

"Last year our General Motors Trucks rolled up more than a million miles; 'picked up' and delivered more than 298 million pieces of laundry.

"With the exception of one or two cities, we maintain no mechanics in our garages—only car washers. All maintenance is handled by General Motors Truck branches. This has meant substantial savings for us."

Look to your truck operation for increased profits. You can have printed results of a nation-wide survey of

truck methods, costs, economies, profits. Or, experienced men will study your trucks at work, giving all possible suggestions for making them more profitable—without cost or obligation.

Our nation-wide truck research has aided us in the other big part of our job. That is, providing a line so complete that there is a modern 6-cylinder General Motors Truck having ample speed, power and ruggedness for any delivery or hauling job.

Put it up to us to help you make more money with your trucks. Telephone your branch or dealer. Or drop a post-card to the factory.

GENERAL MOTORS TRUCK COMPANY, Pontiac, Mich. (Subsidiary of Yellow Truck & Coach Mfg. Co.) GENERAL MOTORS TRUCKS, YELLOW CABS and COACHES. Factory branches, distributors, dealers, in over 2200 principal cities and towns. Time payments through our Y.M.A.C.

What This Performance Means to Driver-Salesmen

"When my General Motors Truck was assigned to me, it gave me extra time to go after new business—because it covers my route faster and performs reliably all day long. It's had a healthy effect upon my sales production and commissions."

—E. DORGAN
One of the Leading Driver-Salesmen of Morgan's Chicago Branch

GENERAL MOTORS TRUCKS

General Motors, 1931

riding comfort

...YOU GET REAL MOTORING COMFORT WITH LOW PRICE

... Costing only a little more than the lowest-priced cars, Pontiac gives you riding comfort.

Pontiac's seat cushions have more than just softness and form-fitting depth. . . . They rest on springs of the "tied down" type which furniture makers put into fine chairs.

The hydraulic shock absorbers, instead of working independently, are designed to soften and equalize spring action.

Built into Pontiac at 43 important points are thick rubber pads—they take up vibration that escapes springs and shock absorbers.

The Fisher body is tightly insulated against heat, cold and dampness. . . . The driver's seat adjusts to the position most comfortable for you. . . . There is indirect ventilation . . . a non-glare windshield . . . a "smoked" rear-vision mirror.

And out on the road you learn that Pontiac has weight and balance for secure steadiness—steers at a light touch—brakes easily and positively.

BEAUTY, TOO

Built low to the ground and ample in length, Pontiac has the sweeping lines you want today. The deep "V" radiator with its chrome screen makes the front view distinctive. Heavy single-bar bumpers add a lot—so do tailored splash aprons and neat built-in fender lamps. Fine whipcord or mohair upholstery gives the interior genuine quality. Fittings and finish are impressive.

Drive this smart car with its powerful, dependable engine—learn its low fuel consumption—feel the unusual comfort. Pontiac is indeed an outstanding value. And the value is still greater when you consider that Pontiac's price, delivered to you, includes complete factory equipment—front and rear bumpers, hydraulic shock absorbers, five wire wheels, and extra tire, tube and tire lock. Remember, too, that if you purchase on time, you have the advantage of G. M. A. C. convenient terms.

OAKLAND 8—PONTIAC 6
TWO FINE CARS

PONTIAC
AN OUTSTANDING GENERAL MOTORS VALUE

Pontiac, 1931

▶ *Chevrolet, 1931*

STYLE LEADERSHIP

that does not rest on price

THE SMOOTHNESS OF AN EIGHT · THE ECONOMY OF A FOUR

NEW PLYMOUTH
FLOATING POWER
and FREE WHEELING

Coupe (with rumble seat), $610
(special equipment extra)

$535
and up, f.o.b. Factory

"SPEAKING OF OPERATIONS"

LOOK these facts squarely in the face:—

Fours have one-half as many pistons, connecting rods, valves, cams, wrist-pins, valve springs, connecting rod bearings, piston rings, valve stem guides, spark plugs and cylinders as eights.

Maybe you don't even know what all those things are, but any mechanic will tell you they are all *working* parts.

They cost money; most of them need lubrication; all of them have to stand constant wear.

When it comes to simple operation, the Four is the most economical, sturdiest and, dollar for dollar, the highest quality car you can get in the lowest-price field. Certainly the same cost will buy better labor and materials when the manufacturer has to buy only half as much.

The only trouble with the old-style Fours is vibration.

Until Chrysler Motors engineering genius perfected Plymouth's new and exclusive "Floating Power," there was that "interrupted torque" of the four to send tremors up through the frame and body to driver and passengers.

Now the New Plymouth gives the Smoothness of an Eight with the Economy of a Four.

Floating Power does away with the vibration that is found in old-time Fours. It gives the New Plymouth a power-flow as smooth as satin, as soft as velvet. So completely does Floating Power eliminate vibration in the New Plymouth that even experts could not tell how many cylinders were under the hood; most of them guessed eight.

Plymouth's Floating Power also gives 56 brake-test horsepower, with actual stop watch speeds of 65 to 70 miles an hour and pick-up from a standing start to 40 miles in 9.7 seconds.

Free Wheeling in Plymouth brings to the field of lowest price this thrilling feature of high-priced cars. You can shift between all forward speeds without declutching—easily, quickly, smoothly.

Plymouth also gives a new easy-shift transmission. You can shift quickly from second to high and back again at speeds of 35 and 45 miles an hour without clashing or grinding of gears even with Free Wheeling locked out.

Plymouth is the only car of lowest price which has self-equalizing, internal hydraulic 4-wheel brakes—simplest and unexcelled for safety and smoothness.

Chrysler Motors engineers have given the Plymouth a double-drop frame for lower center of gravity, greater safety and roadability, and finer style.

And when you see the New Plymouth, yet another thrill awaits you. From radiator to tail light you will find eye-compelling beauty of line and color—comparable in artistic perfection with far costlier cars.

Plymouth challenges the world of lowest-price cars—in appearance, in full size, in performance, in smoothness, in economy, in value.

Here at last is a real quality car for millions—a supreme engineering achievement with the Smoothness of an Eight and the Economy of a Four.

We invite you to prove the superiority of the New Plymouth. It welcomes your most critical examination. Ride in it. Drive it. Compare it with any car at or near its price. Plymouth accepts the challenge.

New Plymouth Body Styles—Roadster $535, Sport Roadster $595, Sport Phaeton $595, Coupe $565, Coupe (with rumble seat) $610, Convertible Coupe $645, Sedan (2-door) $575, Sedan (4-door 3-window) $635, f. o. b. factory. Wire wheels standard at no extra cost. Convenient time-payments may be arranged.

NEW PLYMOUTH IS SOLD BY ALL CHRYSLER, DODGE AND DE SOTO DEALERS

Plymouth, 1931

Two New
REO FLYING CLOUDS
Eight $1395
Six $1295

Standard Model Prices
f. o. b. Lansing

The 7-Passenger Custom Model Sedan

You have a right, today, to expect the most distinguished motor cars in history, at prices that would have been impossible, even a year ago. These new Reos meet both tests. They are the best Flying Clouds ever built. They are sold at the lowest prices.

REO MOTOR CAR COMPANY, LANSING · TORONTO.

Reo Motor Car Co., 1931

The Great American Value for 1932

SMARTER FISHER BODIES · SILENT SYNCRO-MESH SHIFT
SIMPLIFIED FREE WHEELING · IMPROVED SIX-CYLINDER
ENGINE · 60 HORSEPOWER (20% INCREASE) · 65 TO 70 MILES
AN HOUR · FASTER, QUIETER GETAWAY · SMOOTHER OPERATION
GREATER COMFORT AND VISION · UNEQUALLED ECONOMY

Special Sedan
Standard Five-Window Coupe
De Luxe Sport Coupe
De Luxe Convertible Cabriolet
De Luxe Five-Passenger Coupe
De Luxe Convertible Landau Phaeton
De Luxe Coach
Convertible Landau Phaeton
De Luxe Five-Window Coupe
De Luxe Coupe

Cadillac, 1931 ◄ *Chevrolet, 1931*

A genuinely good motor car

...hen it comes to selecting the family car, women ...e naturally partial to Chevrolet from the ...ry start. Who doesn't love to drive a smart, ...orful automobile, with plenty of spirit and ...sh! But what finally *decides* a woman on ...evrolet, probably more than anything else, is a ...ality that appeals to her *practical* nature. It's the ...echanical *goodness* of the car—its exceptional ...lity to keep on running, and stay out of trouble.

...is goodness is thoroughly ingrained in every ...rt of the Chevrolet that has to do with owner-...isfaction. The starter, for instance, is soundly ...nstructed, of excellent materials, then carefully ...ted to make sure it will always work properly. ...e Fisher bodies are built in the same rigid, solid ...y that custom cars are built, to prevent the ...currence of annoying squeaks and rattles. The ...ering gear is designed to turn easily at all ...es. The big, powerful, 4-wheel brakes are made ...ather-proof and trouble-proof. The engine, ...ng a smooth-running Six, can be throttled ...wn to very low speeds, in high gear, without ...dency to stall. And this engine requires the ...y minimum of stops at the gasoline station. ...day, in thousands of households, this depend-...lity of the Chevrolet Six is making the daily ...tine both easy and pleasant for women—and ...aving them money, as well. Isn't it a fine thing ...the American family that there *is* such a car. ...d that the price is well within the means of all.

NEW CHEVROLET SIX
The Great American Value

Chevrolet, 1931   ► *Lincoln, 1931*

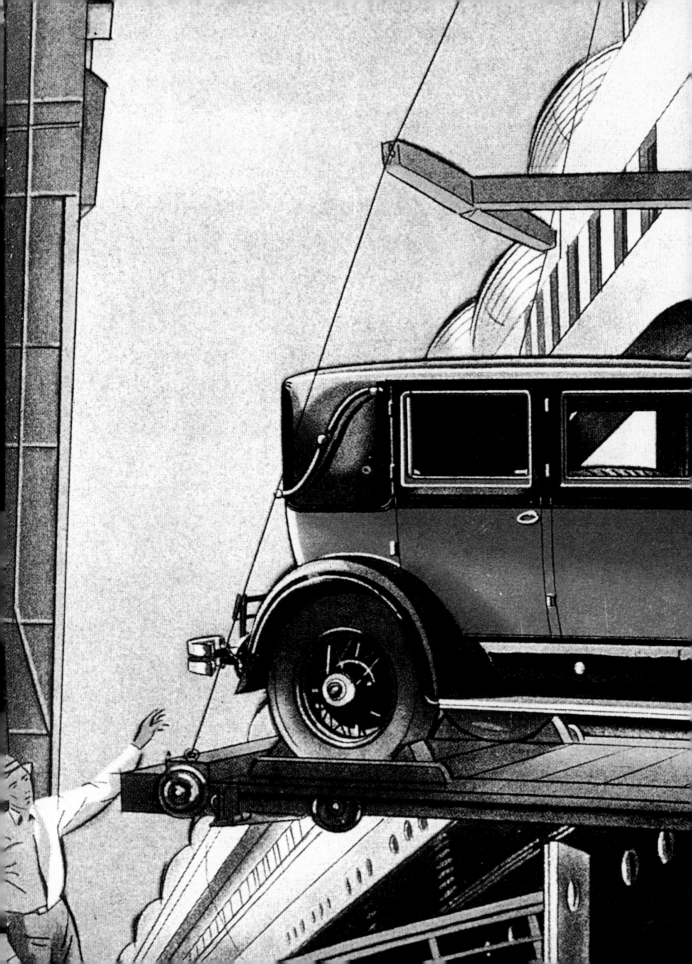

A genuinely good motor car

When it comes to selecting the family car, women are naturally partial to Chevrolet from the very start. Who doesn't love to drive a smart, colorful automobile, with plenty of spirit and dash! But what finally *decides* a woman on Chevrolet, probably more than anything else, is a quality that appeals to her *practical* nature. It's the mechanical *goodness* of the car—its exceptional ability to keep on running, and stay out of trouble. This goodness is thoroughly ingrained in every part of the Chevrolet that has to do with owner-satisfaction. The starter, for instance, is soundly constructed, of excellent materials, then carefully tested to make sure it will always work properly. The Fisher bodies are built in the same rigid, solid way that custom cars are built, to prevent the occurrence of annoying squeaks and rattles. The steering gear is designed to turn easily at all times. The big, powerful, 4-wheel brakes are made weather-proof and trouble-proof. The engine, being a smooth-running Six, can be throttled down to very low speeds, in high gear, without tendency to stall. And this engine requires the very minimum of stops at the gasoline station. Today, in thousands of households, this dependability of the Chevrolet Six is making the daily routine both easy and pleasant for women—and is saving them money, as well. Isn't it a fine thing for the American family that there *is* such a car. And that the price is well within the means of all.

The New Chevrolet Specia

NEW CHEVROLET SIX
The Great American Value

"CRACK-PROOF" TEXACO

in your crankcase *now*
means a quieter engine this summer

DRAIN FILL *then* LISTEN

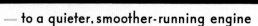

——to a quieter, smoother-running engine

Summer means hard, hot driving! Save your engine. Avoid that unexpected repair bill that so often results from the use of an oil not made for summer driving. Drain today. Fill with the proper grade of crack-proof Texaco. Then listen to a quieter, smoother engine.

Texaco Motor Oil is made crack-proof by special refining processes. Because it's crack-proof, Texaco will not break down or lose its lubricating qualities during the hardest driving. It maintains its oiliness long after

ordinary motor oils have become thin and lifeless. It is free from hard-carbon-forming impurities—free from *all* impurities. Crack-proof Texaco gives positive, full protection to your engine any time, anywhere.

Drive into a Texaco Station today. Fill with crack-proof Texaco—then listen. You'll immediately sense the security of smooth performance that saves your car—and saves you money.

THE TEXAS COMPANY · *Texaco Petroleum Products*

Texaco, 1931

RIVERSIDE BATTERIES
TRADE MARK
COST LESS ·· FOR ALL CARS

SUPER POWER

2-Year Guarantee

Chevrolet, 1931 ◄ *Riverside Batteries, 1931*

PONTIAC IS THE NEW CAR IN THE LOW PRICE FIELD

IT'S A BIG *straight* 8 — $585

AND UP—F. O. B. PONTIAC, MICHIGAN

Whether your purse be big or little, you owe it to yourself to ride in this new big Pontiac Straight 8.

It is in the high price field in everything but price.

The smooth-flowing power of its big 77-horse-power Straight 8 engine gives you performance such as you'd never dream of finding in a low cost car—78 real miles per hour. Its 115-inch wheelbase, coupled with the beautiful new Fisher Bodies, gives you roomy comfort and easy riding such as never offered before in the low price field.

Closed models have the new Fisher No-Draft Ventilation, individually controlled—the greatest advance in comfort and pleasure since closed cars were developed. It stops drafts, prevents window fog and allows for draftless ventilation in front and rear seats.

Pontiac is winning its new owners from every class—on its sheer value, outstanding performance, low cost and long-lived operating economy.

Whatever you've paid for cars before—this year drive a Pontiac before you buy—the big Straight 8 in the low price field. It's the car you'll like to drive, be proud to own, and it is easy to buy and run.

ENGINE CUSHIONED IN RUBBER
FISHER NO-DRAFT INDIVIDUALLY CONTROLLED VENTILATION

The two-door Sedan, $635, f. o. b. Pontiac, Mich. Special equipment extra. Easy G.M.A.C. terms.

LOOK - DRIVE - COMPARE

CHECK THESE FEATURES	PONTIAC STRAIGHT 8	OTHER CARS		
		CAR No. 1	CAR No. 2	CAR No. 3
STRAIGHT EIGHT ENGINE	YES			
FISHER NO-DRAFT VENTILATION (Individually Controlled)	YES			
WHEELBASE	115			
WEIGHT	3175			
FULL PRESSURE LUBRICATION (Rifle-drilled connecting rods)	YES			
SPEED	78			
HORSEPOWER	77			
DELIVERED PRICE (Your favorite model)				

PONTIAC STRAIGHT 8

Pontiac, 1931

A NEW SIX

that brings the important developments of the year to the low-price field . . . .

A NEW V-EIGHT

that offers the distinction of V-Eight performance, at a list price under eight hundred and fifty dollars . . . .

Both offer the following new developments of major importance:

SYNCRO-MESH
·
QUIET SECOND
·
FREE WHEELING
·
RIDE CONTROL
·
LONGER WHEELBASE
·
INCREASED POWER AND HIGH SPEED
·
GREATER ECONOMY
·
NEW, ROOMIER FISHER BODIES
·
RUBBER CUSHIONING
·
ENCLOSED SPRINGS

RIDING COMFORT. Pontiac is the kind of car you are glad to drive or ride in all day long. With its Ride Control, you can adjust shock absorber action according to varying road conditions and the number of people the car is carrying. Then, at 47 chassis points, there is rubber cushioning, completely insulating the motor, frame, springs, axles, body—absorbing minor shocks, preventing metal-to-metal contacts, and deadening noise.

The springs are a superior enclosed type, self-lubricating and easy-flexing at all times. Ample wheelbase and evenly distributed weight assure the fine balance you require, both for comfort and for security in high speed driving. The seat-cushions are deep and form-fitting. The Fisher bodies are tightly insulated against outside heat, cold and noise.

With this genuine fine-car riding comfort Pontiac also gives you brilliant speed, great reserve power, and new pleasure in every type of driving. You enjoy remarkable economy, too, both in low first-cost and in running expense.

See these two splendid cars—inspect them—drive them. You will agree that the 1932 Pontiac, either the Six or Eight is indeed AN OUTSTANDING GENERAL MOTORS VALUE

riding comfort

CHIEF OF VALUES

NEW PONTIAC
SIXES *and* V-EIGHTS

Pontiac, 1931

▶ *Mobiloil, 1932*

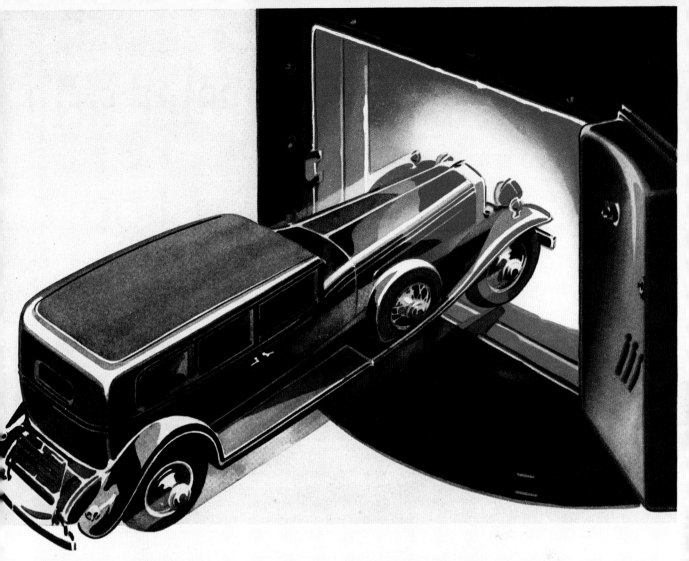

ULL PROTECTION at 400°F !
saves your Engine !

quick starting alone is not enough. Many so-called
ter oils" may give you easy starting. But they can't
up. They are not *double-range* winter oils.

biloil Arctic is the unique *double-range* winter oil.
not only get a quick start below zero but a few
tes later, when engine temperatures may run up to
F. you get *full, rich protection*.

biloil Arctic does not thin out dangerously when you
its protection most. It stands up! It maintains its
ubricating quality.

e world leaders in scientific lubrication have chosen

crudes and refining processes that give Mobiloil Arctic its
unique ability to stand up. You will find no other winter
oil like it, because no other winter oil is made in just the
same way!

Your Mobiloil dealer is ready to drain your crankcase
and refill with Mobiloil Arctic. See him today. While
you are there, insure easy gear-shifting by having him put
Mobiloil "CW" in your gears.

We invite you to listen to the Mobiloil Concert, broadcast coast to coast
each Wednesday evening from WEAF and 53 associated N. B. C. stations
at 9:30, Eastern Standard Time.

Mobiloil Arctic

MEETING · THE · NEW · TIME

WITH GREATER HUPMOBILE SIXES AND EIGHTS
26 MODELS ....$795 AND UP
AT THE FACTORY

Two views of the Cabriolet-Roadster. Note how top completely disappears, leaving just a smooth expanse of gleaming metal.

AN UNMISTAKABLE AIR OF QUALITY

When it comes to turning out smart personal transportation—count on Chevrolet always to keep a step ahead of the rest of the industry. Last year's car won a most distinguished following—with its air of quality and character. This year's product carries out the same atmosphere to such a point that many people are actually comparing the new Chevrolet Six with leading custom-built creations. The lines are clean, smooth, and well-poised, with just the right amount of sparkle to give them freshness and individuality. The treatment of chromium-plate and bright color has been handled with skill and effectiveness. The bodies are by Fisher—which, to the man familiar with custom cars, is just about as much as you could say for *any* coachwork. Moreover, you have your choice of 20 different models, each with that matchless driving combination of Free Wheeling and silent, easy Syncro-Mesh shifting.

Priced as low as $475, f. o. b. Flint, Michigan. Special equipment extra. Low delivered prices and easy G. M. A. C. terms. Chevrolet Motor Co., Detroit, Michigan. Division of General Motors

NEW
CHEVROLET
SIX

THE GREAT AMERICAN VALUE FOR 1932

Chevrolet, 1932

ORDINARY GASOLINE burns unevenly, *incompletely*. Follow the pictures above from left to right. First the spark. In the next four pictures, the flame spreads across the cylinder.	Notice the progressive formation of "carbon yellow." In the sixth picture—BANG! All remaining gasoline exploded. That is knock. The last picture shows only afterglow, waste.	ETHYL GASOLINE burns evenly, *completely*. Follow the smooth spread of power right from the spark in the first picture—clear through to the end of combustion. There is no knock—	no unevenness—no "carbon yellow." This means that *more* of Ethyl's power is delivered to the piston and *less* heat is left to pass out through exhaust valves or into the cooling water

Climb down inside your Engine
SEE *the difference Ethyl makes*

FOR the most important act in its life, gasoline has always hidden behind steel walls. But Detroit engineers put a quartz window in the top of an engine and took high-speed photographs of what actually happens.

You can now SEE the difference Ethyl Gasoline makes. Look at the pictures above. At the left, the uneven combustion of regular gasoline. At the right, the smooth combustion of Ethyl Gasoline. Compare these two strips of pictures. The next to the last picture of each strip is enlarged for your convenience below. Compare! Here are gasoline facts, straight from the *inside* of an engine.

Next time you drive into a filling station—stop at the Ethyl pump. *Experience* the greater power, the freedom from harmful knock and overheating, the faster pick-up, and the smoother, sweeter-running motor that Ethyl gives. On this page you *see* the difference. Buy Ethyl Gasoline and you will FEEL the difference! Ethyl Gasoline Corporation, New York.

LEFT—Ordinary gasoline at the instant of knock. Partly burned gases exploded—wasted power in harmful heat. Particles of free carbon show as the "carbon yellow"—caused by *incomplete* combustion.

RIGHT—Ethyl Gasoline delivers greater power smoothly—with less waste heat and less strain on the engine. Notice the *complete* combustion. No knocking. No "carbon yellow."

Buy ETHYL GASOLINE

Ethyl, 1932

EXTRA? EXTRA?
No... *it's all in the Standard Edition*

WILL everybody who likes the nice little conveniences that make driving easy and comfortable please stand up and say—HUDSON!

Things like the new ride controls, that spread lullaby smoothness on every road; the thermostatic carburetor heat device, that spurs the great engine to 101 horse and away on the coldest morning—

Important things, like automatic starting and anti-stalling, that see you swiftly out of traffic and safely across the railway tracks—

Cute little tricks like the two-finger ivory pendulum that opens or shuts the full-opening windshield; or the shift lever button through which you can go selective free wheeling at just the hop o' your thumb...or the wrist-level door pulls... or the arc-slide fasteners that draw a yawning

pocket taut and trim after the heaviest stuffing. Pay extra for these and them and those? Oh, no; they're all our treat on the standard Hudson Pacemaker models for 1932!

We'd as soon think of charging you extra for the flashing jewel-like colors, the airplane "speeds and streams" styling, the pastel-tinted interiors, the arm rests and foot rests, the new quick-vision instrument panel, the full-range selective transmission, the 30 times stronger frame, and the solid-unit steel body itself.

No, the instantly appealing features of the 1932 Hudson are not "extras." We know you want them and so we offer them as the finishing touch of extra value, of premium quality, at no increased price, in the Pacemaker car for 1932.

HUDSON MOTOR CAR COMPANY, DETROIT, MICHIGAN
HUDSON-ESSEX OF CANADA LIMITED, TILBURY, ONTARIO

SOME OF THE 71 STANDARD FEATURES THAT MAKE HUDSON *PACEMAKER* FOR 1932

RIDE CONTROLS—A simple dash adjustment that permits you to regulate shock absorber action instantly and evenly to both road condition and number of passengers. Makes all roads boulevard-smooth for the Pacemaker Hudson!	FULLY ADJUSTABLE SEATS—Are you long-legged? Short-legged? Hudson seats, both front and rear, can be instantly adjusted in height and depth to the position you find most natural, providing true easy-chair comfort and relaxation.	"TELL-TALE" OIL AND GENERATOR SAFETY SIGNALS—Two electric ruby-jeweled lights, mounted on dash. Should oil supply or generator charge fall below safe levels, a red light flashes an instant warning you cannot fail to heed.	AUTOMATIC SELF-STARTER—Starts the engine when you turn the switch key, and re-starts it—instantly—should you stall in traffic or on grades. Enables the novice to drive with veteran confidence under all conditions.	SUPER ACCELERATOR—Shoots a maximum fuel charge into manifold when throttle is suddenly depressed, insuring instant power response to meet road emergencies. Accelerates? Get-away? It's like stepping on a wildcat's tail!	SIMPLIFIED SELECTIVE FREE WHEELING—No new operations to master. The control is mounted where it belongs—in the shift-lever knob. A finger's pressure, and you free wheel through all forward speeds, in the New Pacemaker Hudson.

HUDSON

——THREE SPLENDID NEW SERIES OF GREATER EIGHTS——

MAJOR SERIES	STERLING SERIES	STANDARD SERIES
These richly appointed large, imposing cars are replete with every convenience and the many extras that add so much to comfort and pride of ownership.	Especially designed to meet the requirements of those who desire an extra roomy and luxurious car with approximation in keeping.	Complete in every essential detail with many features not to be had in other cars priced hundreds of dollars higher, the series will appeal to a vast army of buyers.
LISTING FROM $1445 TO $1595 F. O. B. DETROIT	LISTING FROM $1275 TO $1295 F. O. B. DETROIT	LISTING FROM $995 TO $1095 F. O. B. DETROIT

PACEMAKER—Hudson Eight Standard Sedan for five passengers $1095 F. O. B. Detroit

Hupmobile, 1932 ◄ *Hudson, 1932*

THE SPIRIT OF BUICK OWNERS . . .

"We're certainly proud of our Buick!"

The family that owns a Buick Straight Eight takes natural pride in possession of a motor car on which the whole world has placed its seal of approval.

Theirs is the *complete* satisfaction of people who know they have a truly fine car. They find it a pleasure to invite friends to accompany them in their Buick. The Body by Fisher is beautiful, spacious, comfortable, appointed with the same perfect taste which characterizes the homes of discerning families.

And riding in a Buick is a joy to everyone. The car moves so smoothly and steadily, the Buick Valve-in-Head Straight Eight Engine reels off the miles with such swift, silent power, that passengers are delighted with every minute of the trip. There is cause for pride, too, in Buick's quick responsiveness to the will of the driver—because Wizard Control, combining Automatic Clutch, Controlled Free Wheeling and Silent-Second Syncro-Mesh, makes operation effortless.

Most pleasing of all is that long-lived reliability which is the very heart of Buick—the capacity to give *more and better miles*—to keep on serving finely and faithfully, as so many Buicks have done, for 150,000 miles and more.

You will understand, when you own a Buick, why so many motorists favor this car so enthusiastically.

The thought which is in their minds will find echo in the minds of yourself and family—"We're certainly proud of our Buick."

STRAIGHT **BUICK** EIGHTS

PRODUCT OF GENERAL MOTORS WITH BODY BY FISHER

The fine car in the $1000 to $2000 field.
Available on the liberal G. M. A. C. payment plan.

WHEN BETTER AUTOMOBILES ARE BUILT, BUICK WILL BUILD THEM

Buick, 1932

The Ambassador Hotel, Los Angeles, where smart Californians gather nightly in the famous Cocoanut Grove. The new Oldsmobile Straight Eight and Six in the foreground.

Where life is most brilliant
YOU'LL FIND THE STYLE LEADERS

Wherever those who know and do the *smart* thing gather, you will find, this year, two new motor cars. They are the new Oldsmobiles—the new Six and the new Eight. Strikingly original, thoroughly modern throughout, these cars display an individuality of line and of manner that has made them the recognized Style Leaders for 1933. . . . Moreover, this leadership goes deeper than appearance. Advanced engineering has contributed to these new cars a smoothness of power, a sparkle in action, and a downright dependability that distinguish Oldsmobile *more than*

ever as "the car that owners recommend." . . . Why deny yourself the joy of owning and driving one of the handsome Style Leaders? Oldsmobile prices are *the lowest in a decade*—Oldsmobile style is the smartest in the field—Oldsmobile performance is more brilliant than ever—and Oldsmobile durability never was more certain! . . . See your dealer today. He will gladly place a car at your disposal for a trial drive. **OLDSMOBILE**

GREATER VALUE THROUGHOUT—Both the new Oldsmobile Six and Straight Eight are bigger, roomier, more powerful cars. The Six four-door Sedan weighs 3325 lbs.; the Eight four-door Sedan, 3482 lbs.—curb weight. The engines develop 80 h. p. and 90 h. p. respectively, and the Six will do 75 to 80 miles an hour—while the Eight is capable of 80 to 85, actual stop-watch speeds. Scientific new 3-point engine mountings of live rubber absorb all vibration from the power plants. Oldsmobile's improved automatic choke and carburetion advancements facilitate starting, quicken acceleration, and effect economies in operation. Syncro-Mesh and Silent Second gear make shifting easy and pleasant. Steering and braking are now practically effortless. A tremendously strong new double-drop X-type frame allows a lower center of gravity and gives remarkable driving stability. Completely new Fisher bodies . . . built throughout to a standard of excellence not previously expected in motor cars priced so low . . . afford every modern comfort and convenience . . . most important of which is the sensational new improvement, Fisher No Draft Ventilation, Individually Controlled.

TWO GENERAL MOTORS VALUES • **THE SIX $745 AND UP** • **THE EIGHT $845 AND UP** • **G. M. A. C. TERMS**
PRICES F. O. B. LANSING

Oldsmobile, 1932

▶ General Motors, 1932

In the background—Hall of Science, Century of Progress International Exposition, Chicago, 1933

Eminent In Quality—Thrifty In Price

Nash is committed unalterably to the quality ideal. And for 1933, the five new series of Nash cars unmistakably represent the very best that Nash ever has built—in design, engineering, appearance and performance.

No one, this year, or any other year, ever will be able to say of Nash, "they don't build them as well as formerly."

The solid, substantial worth of a Nash car, the unusual brilliance of its performance, will be remembered long after price is forgotten.

And the price of a 1933 Nash car will not soon be forgotten. Nash prices for 1933 are the

lowest ever placed on cars of comparable qua

The Nash Standard Eight Sedan, one of the fi performing Eights in America today, is $ lower than in 1932. The 116-inch wheelbase horsepower, Nash Big Six Sedan is now $695, $ *under 1932.* The big Special Eight and the Tw Ignition, Underslung=Worm=Drive Advan and Ambassador Eights likewise offer the N owner maximum quality at minimum price.

Nash for 1933 — cars you would rather drive prices you would rather pay!

*Do you know
for what a moderate sum
you can own a New
La Salle?*

Because of their deep regard for LaSalle's high place among the fine cars of the world, many people do not realize that LaSalle is not a costly car to own. The initial expenditure is very little more than the price of many automobiles of less distinguished character. As a result of the thorough quality Cadillac creates with its fine design and precise craftsmanship, the expense for LaSalle's operation and maintenance is surprisingly small. And, finally, LaSalle's faultless style and faithful performance inspire an unusual span of ownership. One is happy to keep a LaSalle over a much greater length of time and drive it a great deal farther than a lesser automobile. In fact, the actual figures often prove that many who are now driving lower-priced cars might very *profitably* be enjoying the prestige and satisfaction of owning a LaSalle. Why not get the facts from your Cadillac-LaSalle dealer today? LaSalle prices from $2395, Cadillac from $2795, f. o. b. Detroit.

LA SALLE
V

The New La Salle V-8 Front-End Ensemble

*A man is known
by his automobile*

Of all those material possessions which bespeak a man's place among his fellow men—none is more instantly recognized than his automobile. Wherever he goes and whatever he does, his car has come to be accepted as a symbol of his tastes, his standing and his business success. Because of this, there has grown up about Cadillac and LaSalle a degree of respect which is unusual in America's business life. Men who have given the problem serious thought will have no other automobile; for here is the "Standard of the World"—the car which has stood, for thirty years, as the emblem of all that is fine. They know, when they drive a Cadillac or LaSalle, that they have the masterpiece itself—and that it is given the recognition which a masterpiece always inspires. LaSalle prices range from $2395, Cadillac from $2795, f. o. b. Detroit.

CADILLAC
V 8 12 16

The Cadillac V-8 Two-Passenger Coupé

La Salle, 1932

Cadillac, 1932

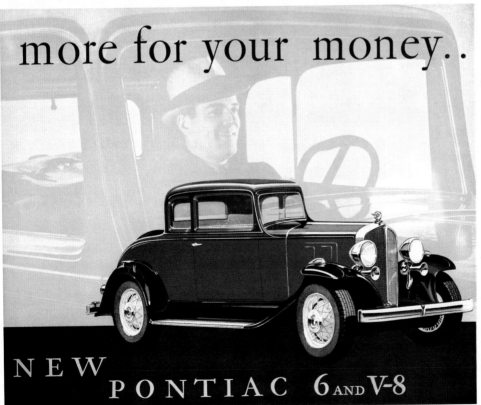

more for your money..

N E W
PONTIAC 6 AND V-8

more size
more performance
more economy
more real value

If you have driven a lot of cars—and if you've made up your mind this year to buy the most you can for your money—then consider these definite reasons why Pontiac should be your choice:

PONTIAC OFFERS MORE SIZE AND COMFORT. Pontiac's cost is small—but Pontiac's dimensions are *not* "small-car" dimensions. The wheelbase of the Six is 114 inches—making it *the largest car on the market at its price!*

This large size means much in smooth riding. It means too, that the Fisher bodies of both the Six and the V-Eight are extra long and roomy. Seats are wider and deeper, luxuriously cushioned for genuine comfort.

PONTIAC OFFERS MORE PERFORMANCE . . . Pontiac's large, easy-working motors are more powerful than ever before. You will thrill to Pontiac's getaway—its top speed—its ability on hills. The Six gives well over 70 *real* miles an hour, and does it smoothly. The V-Eight—much faster—is one of the most thrilling performers on the road today.

Then, for comfort, there's Ride Control—adjusting shock absorber action to any road. Also, improved Syncro-Mesh, with quiet second, and Free Wheeling. With these highly desirable features, Pontiac provides 47-point rubber cushioning in chassis and body, absorbing vibration, and smoothing your ride.

PONTIAC OFFERS MORE ECONOMY. With all its flashing performance, Pontiac retains its low running costs. The new cars have improved carburetion, with automatic heat control and fuel economizer. There is full-pressure lubrication—as in all the finest cars. Every one of these features aids in long life as well as in low running expense.

PONTIAC OFFERS MORE REAL VALUE. Look into Pontiac thoroughly. You will find, in point after point, a margin of excellence so wide that you cannot ignore it—find, in fact, that Pontiac offers the desirable features of larger cars at a much lower cost.

* * *

It is economy to buy a Pontiac. For then you have a new, modern car—free from repair or maintenance costs—and a car which you can enjoy and be proud of. The purchase price is low, and running expense no greater than that of cars built for economy alone.

CHIEF OF VALUES

Tune in on PAUL WHITEMAN and his "Pontiac Chieftains" every Friday evening—NBC coast-to-coast Blue Network at 10 o'clock E.S.T.

Nash, 1933 ◄ *Pontiac, 1932*

A FINER AND FAR MORE DISTINGUISHED LaSALLE
. . . at an even more moderate price

It was an occasion for great rejoicing among men and women who admire fine possessions when the new La Salle V-Eight appeared upon the American scene a few weeks ago. For here was something they had been seeking. Here was a motor car of proud lineage, enriched throughout in its quality—yet offered at prices in perfect keeping with the current economic scheme. . . . No need to question the correctness of the youthful grace which is the dominating note in its appearance—for the style of the new La Salle was created by the most accomplished designers at the command of the Fisher studios. No need to wonder about its mechanical fitness or the nature of its performance—for La Salle is the product of the same skilled craftsmen who build those magnificent motor cars, the Cadillac V-Eight, V-Twelve, and V-Sixteen. . . . The new La Salle is powered by the 115-horsepower Cadillac V-type eight-cylinder engine. Throughout chassis and body are many refinements and developments of major importance, including the new Fisher No-Draft Ventilation system, individually controlled. Yet the standard five-passenger sedan is now reduced to $2245, f.o.b. Detroit—a price most attractively reasonable for a car of Cadillac design, Cadillac construction, and genuine Cadillac quality.

La Salle v-8
A GENERAL MOTORS VALUE

La Salle, 1933

▶ *Packard, 1932* ▶ ▶ *Firestone, 1934*

EAR OF BLOWOUTS

tone High Speed Tires

years every winner in the Indianapolis 500-Mile Race has equipped his car with Firestone Tires.

Firestone Tires were on the Ford V-8 Truck that recently established a new Coast-to-Coast record, traveling 2,945 miles in 67 hours 45 minutes 30 seconds running time.

Only Firestone Tires are built with Gum-Dipped *high stretch* cords. *Only* Firestone Tires have the cotton fibers, cords, plies and body safety-locked with rubber.

See the Firestone Service Dealer or Service Store in your community. Investigate the high quality of Firestone Tires, Tubes, Batteries, Spark Plugs, Brake Lining, Anti-Freeze and the many other Firestone motoring necessities designed for your comfort and safety.

●

Listen to the
Voice of Firestone
Every Monday Night
Over N.B.C.—WEAF
Nation-wide Network

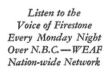

Firestone
PATENTED
Gum-Dipping
PROCESS

DRYING TOWER

CALENDERING
EXTRA RUBBER IS APPLIED
ON EACH SIDE OF GUM-
DIPPED CORDS PREVENTING
FRICTION AND PROVIDING
EXTRA CUSHION BETWEEN
CORD PLIES.

GUM-DIPPING

The Firestone patented Gum-Dipping process by which eight extra pounds of rubber are added to every 100 pounds of cord was demonstrated to more than ten million people who went through the Firestone Factory and Exhibition Building at "A Century of Progress" last summer.

Firestone has again accepted the invitation of "A Century of Progress" to represent the Rubber Industry at the World's Fair in 1934—and we extend to you a cordial invitation to see at that time the Gum-Dipping process and how Firestone Tires are made.

© 1934, F. T. & R. Co.

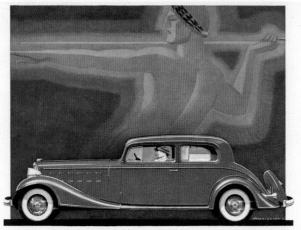

BUICK GIVES MORE AND BETTER MILES
—its record provides the proof

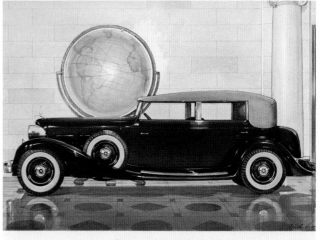

STANDARD OF THE WORLD

After all, when it comes to choosing a motor car, you want *proof* of value, instead of claims. And there is ample proof that *Buick gives more and better miles* in the acts of the car itself. You have only to drive a Buick Eight a short distance to know that it gives *better miles*. Its long wheelbase means a far smoother ride; its size and weight assure real comfort and security at all speeds; the performance of its Valve-in-Head Straight Eight Engine is the kind of performance you've always wanted in a car. And Buick gives *more* miles, too. Witness the number of Buicks that have travelled 200,000 miles and more—and that are still serving with true Buick reliability after five, ten, even fifteen years of use. You can't go wrong buying a Buick—you never could. It's a wise, economical investment.

The recently new Buick models are offered at moderate prices in liberal and convenient G. M. A. C. terms. All are Buick-straight and through. They have new Bodies by Fisher, Valve-in-Head Straight Eight Engines, and new Fisher No-Draft Ventilation, Individually Controlled. All are fine, economical motor car investments.

THE CROIX DE GUERRE — **"CAR THAT TIME FORGOT"** — **THE DESERT MAIL** — **CIRCLING THE GLOBE** — **MEDAL OF AWARD**

WHEN BETTER AUTOMOBILES ARE BUILT, BUICK WILL BUILD THEM . . . A GENERAL MOTORS VALUE

Buick, 1932

Of few products can it be said with truth that they actually set the standard for others of their kind. And among these few, most surely, is a Cadillac automobile.

For almost twenty-five years, Cadillac cars have occupied this unusual position in the automotive industry—in fact, since 1908, when Cadillac was awarded the famous Dewar Trophy for perfect interchangeability of parts.

Year after year, the public has grown more aware of Cadillac's position, until today you hear it affirmed on every hand.

"She's a little *Cadillac*, isn't she?" boasts the owner who has just taken possession of one of the smaller motor cars.

"She has a little the 'feel' of a *Cadillac*," says the new possessor of a medium-priced car.

"This performs more like a *Cadillac* than any other car I ever drove," explains another owner.

And, again, you hear the good-natured apology, "Of course, it's not a *Cadillac!*"

A moment's reflection will serve to recall that you have heard these very remarks, time and time again. Practically never is any other car used as the standard of comparison—almost always a Cadillac.

This, of course, did not "just happen." Reputations such as this do not "grow up," like Topsy. They have their basis, always, in an actual superiority of fact. And back of this superiority is usually found an *ideal*, religiously adhered to, year after year.

In the case of Cadillac, the will to leadership has become a greater spur to achievement than any creed or law could possibly be. It simply never occurs to anyone at Cadillac that Cadillac is privileged to do anything else than excel in all things.

It is out of this spirit that has come Cadillac's long list of basic contributions to the motor car industry. The self-starter, precision manufacture, the closed body, the Synchro-Mesh transmission, the 16-cylinder engine, the 90-degree V-type engine—all of them came, and could have come only, from the Cadillac will to achievement.

We feel certain that most buyers in the fine-car field appreciate the position that Cadillac occupies. Cadillac sales, at least, certainly indicate as much. But for those who may not have had occasion to give the matter particular thought, we wish merely to suggest that the "Standard of the World" is always a safe measure to follow in choosing any commodity.

Cadillac, 1933

A Single Standard of Excellence

YEARS ago the Lincoln tradition was established—to make as fine an automobile as it is possible to produce. That ideal has never for a moment been lost sight of. It is stronger today than ever before.

The new Lincoln V-8 cylinder car measures up to the same high standards that have always governed the Lincoln. Like the V-12, it is built of the best materials available by the most skilled labor. Advanced engineering, precision manufacture, careful testing of operations, characterize both cars equally.

The V-8 cylinder Lincoln is fleet-looking and richly furnished. Smooth abundant power, secure ease of driving, unusual riding comfort—with new free-wheeling, synchronized gear shifting, remarkably soft but sure braking—such are only a few features of this new Lincoln.

Like all Lincolns of the past, the V-8 cylinder Lincoln is a modern motor car of balanced excellence that has been designed and built for your complete satisfaction.

THE LINCOLN

THE NEW LINCOLN EIGHT IS PRICED FROM $2900 AT DETROIT

Lincoln, 1932

ED WYNN says ~

SO-O-O-O

... he filled up with Texaco Fire-Chief and drove happily ever after"

Every day more motorists are ending *their* winter starting troubles with *quick-starting* Texaco Fire-Chief Gasoline.

Texaco *Fire-Chief* is actually a fire-engine gasoline. It was originally developed to meet U. S. Government specifications for—"a grade of motor fuel suitable under adverse conditions of starting and acceleration." That's *your* guarantee of sure-fire action from your car in any kind of weather!

Try a tankful today. *Quick-starting* Texaco *Fire-Chief* is available at Texaco Stations in every one of our 48 States—at *no extra price*.

THE TEXAS COMPANY · Texaco Petroleum Products

ED WYNN
(THE FIRE-CHIEF)
Tuesday Nights, Coast-to-Coast, N.B.C.

TEXACO FIRE-CHIEF GASOLINE
Developed for fire engines - - - Yours at no extra price

Texaco, 1933   ▶ *International Trucks, 1934*

First Shown at the World's Fair in June
Now Ready for the Road:

A new and greater line of

INTERNATIONAL
TRUCKS

Latest and finest of trucks...A new high in style and distinction...New values in utility and performance...*A complete new line of Internationals!* The powerful 4- to 5-ton unit below is one of a beautifully streamlined series of trucks that are *all-truck*, embodying new engineering features and new mechanical excellence throughout. Take Harvester's word for it—the quality apparent on the surface is more than matched by the quality underneath. It is the *EXTRA quality* that International Truck owners have banked on *for more than thirty years.* See these new Internationals. All models, from ½-ton up, now on display at International branches and dealers. For details, write International Harvester Company of America, Inc., 606 S. Michigan Ave., Chicago, Ill.

INTERNATIONAL HARVESTER's new half-ton, 6-cylinder truck is far more than a routine new model. An International chassis priced at $360 is real news for every truck user. Backed by the International reputation for quality and service — here is an outstanding value in performance and economy. Call at any International branch or dealer's showroom and see how exceptional quality has been clothed in style and beauty. In the light-truck field we offer you the new International Model D-1 as a value beyond comparison. You are cordially invited to inspect this new truck.

INTERNATIONAL HARVESTER COMPANY
606 S. Michigan Ave. OF AMERICA (INCORPORATED) Chicago, Illinois

INTERNATIONAL TRUCKS

International Trucks, 1933

YOU SAVE WITH A NEW CHEVROLET

and you'll always be proud to own it

All those in favor of spending less money on their cars—less for gas and oil, less for upkeep, less for repairs—say "Chevrolet!" And all in favor of owning one of the smartest, most refreshing style creations on the road —just repeat "Chevrolet!" For *that's* the name of the one low-priced car that covers both extremes of the motor car scale. On the practical side, it saves you more money than any other automobile you can buy. On the pleasure side, it offers all the newest, keenest thrills of driving. And these include nearly everything you've hoped for in your next automobile: The kind of dashing beauty that brings delight to every eye. The same kind of coachwork as on many expensive cars: *wood-and-steel bodies by Fisher*. The newest boon to travel comfort and safety: *Fisher No Draft Ventilation!* The latest, most successful means of wiping out annoying vibration: *Chevrolet's cushion-balanced engine mounting*. That wonderful new idea in simplified car-starting: *The Starterator*. And many other surprises, thrills, *all* of them—mind you—in a *Chevrolet*—a tried and tested six of known dependability and unbeatable economy! Doesn't a combination like that make you want to visit a Chevrolet dealer—say "good-bye" to your old, worn automobile—then say "hello" to a sparkling new Chevrolet *of your own?*

CHEVROLET MOTOR COMPANY, DETROIT, MICHIGAN

$445 TO $565

All prices f. o. b. Flint, Mich. Special equipment extra. Low delivered prices and easy G. M. A. C. terms. A General Motors Value.

Chevrolet, 1933

Spring Motoring Thrills

The open road is calling! Desert flowers... green hills and rain-washed trees... crisp Spring sunshine ...clean, fresh, blossom-scented air, and the lure of distant beauty spots. Let nothing mar your fullest enjoyment of this western Spring outdoors.

Driving pleasure depends upon motor performance...instant starting, economical mileage, power and smoothness at all speeds. In emergency vehicles, *human life* depends upon these same factors.

Texaco *FIRE-CHIEF* Gasoline exceeds highest United States Government specifications for "emergency" fuel. It gives you "emergency performance" —*plus* added Tetraethyl Lead for extra smoothness — and the cost is the same as that of ordinary gasolines.

For a sample of "emergency performance," and a happier outing, stop at the nearest Texaco *FIRE-CHIEF* pump before starting on your next motor trip.
THE TEXAS COMPANY . . . A California Corporation

LAUGH WITH ED WYNN, 9:30 PACIFIC TIME, TUESDAY NIGHTS, N.B.C

TEXACO *FIRE-CHIEF*

WITH TETRAETHYL LEAD ★ NO EXTRA COST

Buick, 1933 ◄ Texaco, 1934

BRUNN BROUGHAM

The LINCOLN

BUILDERS of the Lincoln never compromise with quality. At all times, irrespective of price trends, cost of materials and manufacture, the Lincoln is built to the highest standards of mechanical excellence. . . . The Lincoln factory is a model of efficiency. Skilled craftsmen work unhurriedly. Rigid tests control each step of manufacture within precision limits almost unbelievably minute. . . . The Lincoln of today provides the unsurpassed power and smoothness of the 150-horsepower, V-12 cylinder Lincoln engine. It offers new features of safety, new ease of handling, greater economy of operation, and important refinements of body design and finish that bring to owners a new appreciation of motoring comforts. . . . The Lincoln is today available in two wheelbase lengths, in standard and custom body types, at prices that range from $3200 at Detroit.

Lincoln, 1934

Firestone, 1934

Texaco, 1934

► *Chevrolet, 1932*

CHEVROLET

America's leading dailies rely on Chevrolet

From men to machinery, everything about a metropolitan newspaper moves consistently at a swifter pace than in any other business. And, as a matter of course, most dailies that are regularly first with the news entrust deliveries to Chevrolet trucks. For Chevrolets are built to fit naturally into this picture of incessant, punishing speed. The special truck-type engine is the most powerful in the low-price field. Because it is a six, the power-flow is smooth and effortless, even at racing speeds. And generously oversize vital parts, combined with six-cylinder freedom from wearing vibration, reduce repairs to a minimum, and insure continuous service regardless of hauling conditions. The flying starts, skidding stops and spectacular dashes that make up the day of a newspaper truck may have no counterpart in your business. But you will find it well worth while to standardize on a truck that can meet these strenuous conditions. For this stamina, plus minimum fuel and oil consumption and low first cost, make Chevrolet trucks the most economical you can buy!

CHEVROLET MOTOR COMPANY, DETROIT, MICHIGAN. *Division of General Motors*

Passenger cars priced as low as	**$445**	½-ton models with bodies priced as low as **$460**
Truck chassis priced as low as	**$345**	1½-ton models with bodies priced as low as **$670**

Prices f.o.b. Flint, Mich. Special equipment extra. Low delivered prices and easy G.M.A.C. terms.

CHEVROLET
IX CYLINDER PASSENGER CARS AND TRUCKS

There is no

MISTAKING

a

PIERCE ARROW

. . . PARTICULARLY, THE NEW TWELVES AND EIGHTS OF 1934 . . .

THE FINEST, THE EASIEST-RIDING CARS EVER BUILT BY PIERCE-ARROW

"HERE COME THE HOYTS"

THERE is something about a Pierce-Arrow that brings a friendly wave of the hand from traffic-officers... Even truckmen pull over a little more quickly, and doormen salute a little more smartly.

This instinctive deference is not due to the distinctive appearance of the car... nor its extraordinary comfort... nor the unparalleled control of its full-power brakes... nor even the quiet smoothness of its engine, so superb that it recently broke 14 world records for speed and endurance.

No one feature is responsible. The only explanation is that Pierce-Arrows are Pierce-Arrows. And the new models of 1934 will tend to deserve and to extend this deference.

PIERCE-ARROW

Pierce Arrow, 1934

LIKE fine wine... a fine car should be tried. The only way to form an opinion of the new Pierce-Arrow is by actual trial, yourself at the wheel. Then you will know the fleetness, the easy riding, the smooth handling, the responsiveness... amazing even to those long accustomed to Pierce-Arrow.

Pierce Arrow, 1934

The first step toward having a Packard

THE FIRST STEP toward having a Packard car is one you can take privately and with no investment other than a little of your time.

● Your Packard dealer will be pleased to give you a booklet which will allow you to decide whether you want to drive or ride in one of the newest Packards and have your old car appraised.

● The booklet, presenting the most confident offer in the motor car industry, introduces a new method of fine car buying. We say buying because we believe

fine cars should be bought rather than sold. You will be delighted to find the Packard salesman working with you toward this end.

● In the booklet you will find a list of those in your own community who have bought Packard cars; a suggested list of questions for you to ask them; and blank pages on which to record the answers you get.

● We suggest that you select a jury of your friends and neighbors, twelve good men and true, who

own Packard cars, and then let your purchase of a Packard stand or fall on what they tell you.

● Only a great car could make such an offer. Only a great car makes it. Why not 'phone or call for your copy of the booklet? The sooner you get it, the sooner, we believe, you will have a Packard and then—"Ask The Man Who Owns One" will apply to you.

PACKARD

ASK THE MAN WHO OWNS ONE

Pierce Arrow, 1934 ◀ *Packard, 1934*

1½ ton, six-cylinder ... $545 STANDARD CHASSIS ... 60 miles an hour

THIS sensational truck is offered by one of the oldest manufacturers in the industry to buyers who know the difference between a real truck and a delivery car.

It embodies that excellence of design and honesty of construction which have earned Diamond T a position of leadership in the heavy-duty truck field. It is truly a truck, built for long life in truck service, with no passenger car association in any part.

Diamond T has built only heavy-duty trucks for more than twenty years. During all this time it has operated continuously under one management, whose standards of engineering and manufacture have made Diamond T trucks the choice of many of America's leading fleet operators.

Several years ago, Diamond T engineers began development of a new 1½-ton model, fast, powerful, and distinguished in appearance.

Thousands of these trucks are already in service. Millions of trouble-free miles testify to their conspicuous superiority.

Now, Diamond T meets the light-duty vehicle in its own field of pure price, bringing to this low-price field the real truck builder's standards of quality, stamina and fine truck appearance—a sensational value at $545!

See this great truck and try it out against any other vehicle of similar rating. Call your Diamond T dealer. He will be glad to send one to your place of business.

DIAMOND T MOTOR CAR COMPANY
CHICAGO, ILLINOIS

Manufacturers of motor trucks exclusively since 1911

Compare before you buy ... These "high-light" specifications give only the barest outline of the speed, strength, and power built into this truck. They do, however, provide positive proof that it is the largest, strongest, and most substantially built truck at its price—the greatest truck value in the world.

Gross capacity 8500 lbs., including weight of chassis, cab, body and load. Stripped chassis weight 3100 lbs.

Six-cylinder truck engine, 3¼" x 4½"; piston displacement 228 cubic inches, 7 main bearings, pressure lubrication, 80 horsepower developed on brake test, rated 60 horsepower in truck service.

7-inch truck frame, 4-speed truck transmission.

Heavy-duty rear axle, one-piece cast steel housing; full-floating axle with dual tires at extra cost.

Four wheel hydraulic brakes, non-warping cast brake drums.

Long, wide springs of alloy steel with helper springs rear and silent spring shackles; no lubrication required.

Standard wheelbase 135", longer wheelbases at extra cost. Price $545, standard chassis at the factory, tax extra.

DIAMOND·T

Other models, 1 to 10 tons capacity, including six-wheelers.

Dealers throughout the United States and 48 foreign countries.

Diamond-T, 1933

Body by Fisher

Possession ··· **Makes the Heart Beat Faster** ◆ ◆ ◆

BUICK this year is widening the tremendous favor it holds with people who live in the modern manner. Its beauty, its luxury, its air of quiet sophistication, are in their language and their mode, as its sturdy dependability and mighty performance are in the universal language of motoring.

In today's Buicks, engineering creates a different and finer kind of motoring—the Buick kind. It adapts Knee-Action wheels to Buick's own requirements for the gliding ride.

But it doesn't stop there. It goes all the way to the gliding ride as only Buick gives it. It builds in a new balance of weight and springing, and a new ride stabilizer; it equips with new air-cushion tires.

Then it provides center-point steering for your greater surety of control; vacuum power brakes for your greater safety; automatic starting and other operations for your greater convenience and ease, and your car's increased efficiency.

In less than an hour you can learn why Buick is cresting the flood of popularity—and discover that just the thought of possessing it for your own makes your heart beat faster.

· BUICK ·

WHEN · BETTER · AUTOMOBILES · ARE · BUILT — BUICK · WILL · BUILD · THEM

Buick, 1934

HOW DAD WON

He was respected for his analytical ability. He had inspected the 1934 Auburn's rigid frame. He was impressed with the fact that the chassis contains no untried experiments. He had had years of experience with Lycoming engines; in passenger cars, airplanes, boats, and trucks. His business acumen convinced him Auburn offers the greatest value. But it would appear that the feminine influence predominated in his home. So, Daughter got behind the wheel. The ample room, luxurious interior, and ventilation control won Mother and Sister over instantly.

When they came home from a demonstration, amazed at Auburn's easy riding, the way the car clung to the road, the absence of side-sway, and the advantages of the Extra High gear of Dual-Ratio—well, the Auburn had sold itself.

AVBVRN

6 CYLINDER MODELS (119" WHEELBASE) $695 TO $745; 8 CYLINDER MODELS (126" WHEELBASE) $945 TO $1125; SALON 12 MODELS $1395 TO $1545
All prices at the factory, subject to change without notice. • Equipment other than standard, extra
AUBURN AUTOMOBILE COMPANY, AUBURN, INDIANA, Division of Cord Corporation

Auburn, 1934

BIGGER · SMOOTHER · FINER

...and Only $715*

The new Pontiac is an *Eight*—it's a *beauty*—and it does *travel!* . . . Its superb Straight Eight engine—the *smoothest* in the industry—develops 84 horsepower, delivers 85 miles an hour, and many owners report more than 16 miles to the gallon of gas! . . . Enclosed Knee-Action Wheel springing and luxurious Fisher bodies—with Fisher ventilation, of course—give you the *easiest* and most comfortable ride you've ever had in any car at anywhere near Pontiac's price. . . . Yet the Pontiac lists at hundreds of dollars below the average Straight Eight and only a few dollars above the list price of the average Six! Why not get a Straight Eight for your money?

PONTIAC MOTOR COMPANY, PONTIAC, MICHIGAN

Illustrated, the 4-door Sedan. List price at Pontiac, Michigan, $805. List prices of other models at Pontiac, Michigan, $715 and up. With bumpers, spare tire, metal tire cover, tire lock and spring covers, the list price is $32.00 additional. . . . The new Pontiac is a General Motors Value.

PONTIAC

The Economy Straight Eight

Pontiac, 1934

► La Salle, 1934

and Dad gave us a new La Salle

Leisure ahead!

One of the wisest fathers it is our privilege to know, recently wrote this in a letter to the Pontiac Motor Company..."I wish to buy for my daughter a new Pontiac Cabriolet. She will be graduated with her class in June, and in her leisure hours from this time on, I want her to say where she will go—and when. I dislike the idea of her having to depend upon others for all her transportation."... We have nothing to add, of course, to what he wrote —for it constitutes a complete sales argument, entirely within itself. We might add, though, that we once got a letter almost precisely like this from the father of a growing-up boy!

PONTIAC MOTOR COMPANY, PONTIAC, MICHIGAN

PONTIAC

Pontiac, 1934

A FAMOUS SLOGAN GOES TO WORK

FOR MORE than 30 years, Packard advertising has carried the slogan—Ask the man who owns one.

● Now this slogan has gone to work. It is helping motorists select their next fine car.

● This is how it can help you. We have prepared an unusual little book which your Packard dealer will gladly send you. This book contains the names of people in your community—many of them friends and neighbors of yours—who have purchased Packards. The book contains, too, a list of questions covering every phase of motor car performance and upkeep.

● From this book, choose any number of those "who own one." Ask them the questions given, and any others you may think of. Then follow their verdict.

● If it's unfavorable, dismiss Packard from your mind. But if it's what we're sure it will be, phone your Packard dealer and have him bring one of the new Packards to your door. Drive it—see how thrillingly it lives up to what its owners say about it. Notice, too, that in appearance, as in performance, this car is unmistakably a Packard ... one American fine car that has maintained its individuality and distinction.

PACKARD
ASK THE MAN WHO OWNS ONE

Packard, 1934

TO A CERTAIN HARD HITTING NUMBER THREE
Now starring on Long Island

You, who take so keen a delight in an agile, fast-stepping horse, will be glad to know that you can now get the same responsive performance in a motor car. The Chevrolet answers you like something alive—sweeping up to 80 miles an hour in a flash—stopping in an instant—taking every road without a jolt in the body or steering wheel—doing all these things for miles on end with practically no attention. There is no use to expect quite the same performance from any other automobile. Only Chevrolet combines fully-enclosed Knee-Action, the Blue-Flame engine, cable-controlled brakes, shock-proof steering, and Body by Fisher. And it takes exactly this ideal combination to make the ideal personal car. For proof, we point to the overwhelming preference your own friends are showing for the 1934 Chevrolet.

CHEVROLET MOTOR COMPANY, DETROIT, MICHIGAN
Compare Chevrolet's low delivered prices and easy G.M.A.C. terms

CHEVROLET MASTER SIX
SPORT COUPE

CHEVROLET
FOR 1934

A GENERAL CHEVROLET MOTORS VALUE

General Tires, 1934 ◄ *Chevrolet, 1934*

To a famous
COLLECTOR OF TROPHIES
at
Narragansett Bay

You are one of those rare skippers who play no favorites. You have seen the virtues of every kind of sailing craft and won signal victories with them all. It is as much for that as for your fame as a master of sail, that we address this to you. Because we believe your constant search for new thrills will be gratified once more when you first take the wheel of a Chevrolet. Your scorn for engines will be dispelled by the soundless responsiveness of the Blue-Flame motor. Your delight in a ship that is able in any breeze, will be renewed with the Knee-Action ride. In fact, we can promise you much the same pleasure you get from sailing a snug craft in which you are both master and crew. We say this so confidently because so many people have told us that the Chevrolet is the best form of personal transportation on land.

CHEVROLET MOTOR COMPANY, DETROIT, MICHIGAN
Compare Chevrolet's low delivered prices and easy G.M.A.C. terms

CHEVROLET MASTER SIX
SPORT COUPE

CHEVROLET *for* 1934

A GENERAL CHEVROLET MOTORS VALUE

Chevrolet, 1934

TOUR WITH TEXACO!

*L*AVISH NATURE packed this western land with beauty spots . . . forested mountains . . . rushing streams and dusky canyons . . . flowering plains, picturesque seashore and desert oases. Men laced this playground empire with roads like great, smooth ribbons. There's romance, and youth and joy around the bend of the open road.

Hundreds of users declare TEXACO *FIRE-CHIEF* Gasoline performance makes motoring definitely more enjoyable. Quick starts, abundant power, and economical mileage are built into *FIRE-CHIEF* at the refinery, by following—and *exceeding*—highest U.S. Government specifications for "emergency" motor fuel. Addition of *tetraethyl lead* rounds out this famous gasoline used by more tourists than any other kind.

FIRE-CHIEF is available wherever you go, in all our 48 states—and in 106 foreign countries. Drive into your nearest TEXACO station today, and learn why the wisest motorists *tour with Texaco!*

THE TEXAS COMPANY
A CALIFORNIA CORPORATION

HEAR ED WYNN · EVERY TUESDAY NIGHT
5:30 PACIFIC TIME · NBC · COAST-TO-COAST

TEXACO *FIRE-CHIEF*

UST IT . . FOR IT'S *Cadillac* BUILT

You will feel much more at *ease* in the beautiful streamlined La Salle than you have *ever* felt in other automobiles. . . . You will experience greater *mental* comfort and greater *physical* comfort as well. . . . You will have the same feeling of assurance whether you happen to be parking at a fashionable club—or traveling over a rough road—or climbing a steep mountain trail far from human habitation. . . . In all of these situations, *peace of mind* is the constant companion of the man or woman who drives a new streamlined La Salle.

. . . You can trust it implicitly —for it is Cadillac-built. *La Salle*

$1595 AND $1695
AT DETROIT
PRICES SUBJECT TO CHANGE WITHOUT NOTICE

LE BARON CONVERTIBLE ROADS

THE LINCOLN

The Lincoln appeals first to the sophisticated motorist. Those who know the most about motor cars, who need not compromise with price, are its loyal adherents. They have owned four, six, or ten Lincolns. . . . Even more than its predecessors, the new Lincoln merits the allegiance of owners, old and new. This year, the powerful V-12 cylinder engine is placed forward several inches in the frame. As a result the luxurious body becomes roomier, and rear-seat passengers ride poised ahead of the axle, rather than directly over it. Thus the new Lincoln is a more comfortable car than ever before. . . . And it is an easier car to handle. It surges lightly, swiftly ahead with a touch of the accelerator. Shifting is smoother. Springs are more flexible. . . . Modern beauty has been achieved without the sacrifice of the dignity traditional with Lincoln. Eighteen body types designed to meet every motoring requirement, formal or informal, are available

THE NEW FORD V·8 FOR 1935

Modern Comfort and Modern Beauty

ONE OF THE most important features of the New Ford V-8 for 1935 is its remarkable riding comfort—especially in the back seat. This is achieved by fundamental changes in weight distribution, new seat position, and longer springs of unusual flexibility. You ride forward, toward the center of the car—center-poised between the springs. This gives rear-seat passengers the comfort of a "front-seat ride" and makes every road a smoother road. . . . There's increased leg room, body room and luggage room and the front seats are 4 to 5½ inches wider. . . . New and modern also are the distinctive lines and colors of the New Ford V-8 and the luxurious upholstery and appointments of the De Luxe body types. . . . The all-steel bodies are equipped with Safety Glass throughout at no additional cost. . . . Ease of steering, new easy-pressure clutch, improved quick-stopping brakes, and the dependable, economical performance of the V-8 engine are additional reasons why it is such a satisfactory choice for the woman motorist. . . . The New Ford V-8 for 1935 is modern in every detail.

Ford, 1934

THE FORD V·8

THE FORD IS PART OF THE PICTURE

The alert, capable Ford V-8 is part of the picture of every activity. . . . For the gay, glad spirit of Youth is in it—an eagerness to be doing things and going places in a thoroughly modern manner. . . . You catch a suggestion of this as you watch the Fords go by—trim, lithe and colorful. You are very sure of it as you drive the car and note how swiftly, silently and comfortably you travel along. . . . Smooth power flows through quiet gears—the quick response of the car commands your confidence—you realize that it makes quite a difference when there's a V-8 cylinder engine under the hood. . . . Truly, a new thrill in motoring awaits you in the Ford V-8.

Ford, 1934

Don't GAMBLE
with their Safety!

WHAT man would knowingly jeopardize the safety of his family? Yet many men thoughtlessly permit their wives and children to ride behind car windows of ordinary, easy-to-break glass . . . despite the fact that Duplate Safety Glass is so much safer, and the extra cost of it, thanks to car manufacturers, almost negligible. For the sake of your family's greater security, insist on Duplate Safety Glass in every window of the next car you buy. Pittsburgh Plate Glass Company, 2267 Grant Bldg., Pittsburgh, Pennsylvania.

To replace glass in your present car with Duplate, look for the name of your nearest Duplate dealer in the "Where to Buy It" section of your local Telephone Directory under "Glass . . . Safety"

YOUR FAMILY RIDES IN GREATER SECURITY BEHIND WINDOWS OF DUPLATE SAFETY GLASS

Duplate Safety

Lincoln, 1935 ◀   *Duplate Safety, 1934*

THE WILLOUGHBY LIMOUSINE

The LINCOLN

THE LINCOLN, a versatile car, continually astonishes loyal owners who put it to supreme tests of one kind, and then, on another occasion, find that it can meet wholly new and different tests. Thus, a rancher in Wyoming, accustomed to mountain and desert driving, learns from his wife of the car's agility in city traffic. A business man, to whom the Lincoln is a triumph of engineering, suddenly realizes, as he emerges from the opera, how beautiful a car he drives. The Lincoln is all things to all people. . . . This is a luxurious car, a safe car, with a V-12 cylinder, 150-horsepower engine powerful enough to take steep hills in high and at an almost incredible pace. Lincoln engineers affirm it the finest they have yet designed, and experience on the road confirms that judgment. And it is a car which imparts to the owner, no less than to the maker, pride in its beauty and pleasure in its high achievements. Available in twenty-three standard and custom-built body types.

Lincoln, 1934

IT BRINGS VACATION JOYS TO TOWN!

SUMMER SPENT, you turn again toward the city. Places you visited and the pleasures of being away are still in your mind. If you own a Lincoln-Zephyr you can bring vacation joys back with you! This car will satisfy on city streets near home as it did on the open road!

The V-type 12-cylinder engine that responded with confident power up a mountain now idles quietly in traffic. You move smoothly when lanes are crowded. Emergency speed is there if you need it. And for all the stops and starts at lights, the

Lincoln-Zephyr will go along with thrift and ease!

This is a big car. Three of you can ride comfortably from home to office or theater on the front seat. Yet the Lincoln-Zephyr handles lightly. Parking places are not so small as they seem! And the wide windshield gives you a clear view of what goes on.

The unique body-and-frame, exclusive to Lincoln-Zephyr, is built for comfort. In all closed types, steel panels are welded to a framework of steel trusses. The whole is

suspended over soft transverse springs inches apart. The Lincoln-Zephyr's cen of gravity is low; the car holds to ground. Passenger and car weight is b anced toward the center.

This car is justly called "style leade Its graceful streamlines have influenc the designs of an industry. But look *bene* the style! Here, for travel in country town, is a combination of features at dium price not to be matched at any pri Lincoln Motor Company, Division of F Motor Company.

BENEATH ITS OUTWARD BEAUTY

Lincoln-Zephyr V-12

A combination of features that makes the Lincoln-Zephyr the only car of its kind. 1. *Unit-body-and-frame—steel panels welded to steel trusses.* 2. *V-type 12-cylinder engine—smooth, quiet and economical power.* 3. *High power-to-weight ratio—low center of*

THE STYLE LEADER

The 1935 Packard Super Eight Club Sedan for Five Passengers

Yours Sincerely —

BUICK

WHEN · BETTER · AUTOMOBILES · ARE · BUILT · BUICK · WILL · BUILD · THEM

Body by Fisher

At the bottom of a thousand letters a day, the writers sign off, *"Yours sincerely."* · · · Your Buick is yours sincerely for a thousand days and nights—and as many more as you like. · · · This quality of faithfulness is inseparable from Buick. It is the constant and dominant thought in the minds of Buick's engineering designers and builders. *It is the great heart of a great car.* · · · It is clothed in smart beauty, in the most modern of windstream styling. Luxury and generous size surround and enhance it. Out of it spring an agility of performance and a comfort of riding so unique and superior as to make you believe you have never before known really fine motoring. · · · Choose any Buick for your own, from the new Series 40 at its list price of $795, on up to the top price of $2175 for the Series 90. Any and all of them will serve you with the same unwavering fidelity. For each one is a *Buick;* and there is only one kind of dependability in Buick—the highest.

Series 40—$795 to $925. Series 50—$1110 to $1230. Series 60—$1575 to $1675. Series 90—$1875 to $2175. List prices at Flint, Mich. All prices subject to change without notice. Illustrated above is model 48, $865 at Flint. Special equipment extra.

The new 1935 PACKARD has four surprises for you

FOUR SURPRISES? Yes, four *big* surprises!

Surprise No. 1 is the sheer beauty of this new Packard. Here is modern streamlining at its finest. Yet the famous identifying Packard lines are still there. They have even been accentuated.

Surprise No. 2 will come when you open the door of this new car. Was any other car ever so easy to enter? And the roominess of the interior! Packard designers have given you the widest, most comfortable seats you ever sat in.

Surprise No. 3 you'll get when you drive this car. For Packard engineers, by increasing the tread and redistributing weight, have made the new Packard easier to handle even than last year's car. They have made it the easiest riding car you ever rode in. And by redesigning windshield and windows, they have given you greater vision than ever before.

Surprise No. 4 is one that will make you gasp. Last year's Packard motor and chassis were hailed as the finest in the world. Yet, by utilizing new materials and redesigning parts, Packard engineers have actually made this 1935 car still more wonderful. They have created a motor so perfect that, were the equator a road, you could drive the car half-way around the world *in a week* without affecting the motor in any way.

But learn about the new Packard first-hand! Visit your Packard dealer's—see this new car and drive it. We sincerely believe that, after that, you will never again be contented with any other car.

ON THE AIR: *Packard presents Lawrence Tibbett, John B. Kennedy and a distinguished orchestra every Tuesday evening, 8:30 to 9:15 E.S.T., W.J.Z. Network, N.B.C.*

PACKARD

ASK THE MAN WHO OWNS ONE

Buick, 1934

Packard, 1935

Lincoln, 1935 ◄ Chevrolet, 1935

Mr. A. Atwater Kent *of Philadelphia*
is one of more than 1000 distinguished owners through whose gateways
Packards have passed for 21 years or more

The Packard Twelve Coupe Roadster for Two or Four Passengers

IN EVERY well-established family, certain traditions have grown up . . . Daughters follow mothers to the same finishing schools. Sons follow fathers into the same exclusive clubs.

In many of America's most distinguished families, the Packard motor car has become one of the most firmly grounded traditions. More than 1000 of these families have owned Packards continuously for 21 years or more.

Such a record—the greatest testimonial, we believe, ever accorded a fine motor car—could not have been created by salesmanship alone. It could only have been built up by the car itself—by the service Packard

gives, by the luxury Packard affords, by the prestige Packard carries.

From every indication, thousands of fine car owners who have driven their old cars years longer than usual are choosing 1935 as the time to replace their old cars with new ones. And from every indication, a majority of these owners are deciding to make their new car the finest of the year's new big fine cars—the 1935 Packard.

PACKARD EIGHT · SUPER EIGHT · TWELVE

· Ask the man who owns one ·

Packard, 1935

Pontiac, 1935

It
would take
17 years
to replace him

The greatest value that can be built into a tire is HUMAN MILEAGE—extra quality that makes the tire itself last longer and extra safety that makes you last longer, too. That's what we mean by HUMAN MILEAGE. Only in the General Tire are all of these protective features present.

BLOWOUT-PROOF PROTECTION
SKID-SAFE TRACTION
LOW PRESSURE COMFORT
SHOCKLESS RIDING
TENSION-FREE DRIVING

THE NEW
GENERAL
*Dual-*BALLOON
"THE BLOWOUT-PROOF TIRE"

General Tires, 1935

*Here's the top R.P.S.
for 1935*

R.P.S. means Ride, Performance, Style . . . and Nash is the 1935 car that people the country over point to as leading in all three! At last it can be said that perfect streamlining can also be perfectly beautiful —that's the new Nash Aeroform design. At last a motor car "ride" has been developed that's so smooth, so level, it's like having "a new road under the wheels"—that's synchronized springing, a patented new principle in springing, plus a 50-50 balance in car weight and mid-section seating.

And if you would enjoy something really new, really different in performance —drive this Nash. Test its Twin Ignition Flying Power, the sort of power airplanes have. Feel the straight-pull, quick-stop safety control of its super-hydraulic brakes. Get the thrill that comes when the automatic cruising gear cuts in above 40—giving *faster* car speed at *slower* engine speed. See how amazingly far you travel on a gallon of gasoline! Acquaintance with a Nash means an instant friendship for the car. See and drive the car with the year's finest R. P. S.

NASH ADVANCED SIX—6-PASSENGER VICTORIA $825
120-inch Wheelbase—90 Horsepower

NASH ADVANCED EIGHT—6-PASSENGER VICTORIA $1045
125-inch Wheelbase—102 Horsepower

NASH AMBASSADOR EIGHT—6-PASS. VICTORIA $1170
125-inch Wheelbase—102 Horsepower

1935 LAFAYETTE—built by Nash—eight different models in the lowest price field—$580 to $710— lowest priced sedan with trunk in the world, with only one exception!

(All Prices F. O. B. Factory—Subject to change without notice) Special Equipment Extra

$825

1935 *Nash*

AEROFORM DESIGN · FLYING POWER (DEVELOPED FROM TWIN IGNITION) · SUPER-HYDRAULIC BRAKES · AUTOMATIC CRUISING GEAR · ALL-STEEL, ONE-PIECE BODIES · SYNCHRONIZED SPRINGING · MID-SECTION SEATING · BALANCED RIDE · BALL-BEARING STEERING

Nash, 1935

► La Salle, 1935

Today a brilliant
NEW La SALLE
with flashing new performance
ENTERS A LOWER-PRICE FIELD

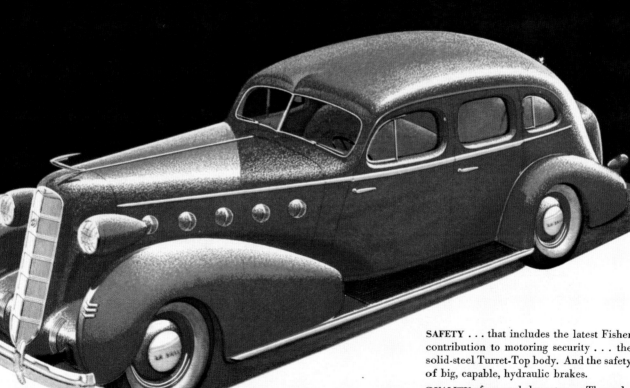

$1225

CADILLAC is proud today to announce its latest achievement . . . a brilliant, flashing new La Salle, with . . .

PERFORMANCE of an inspiring new type . . . responsively eager in traffic, swift and unlabored on the hills, faster and smoother on the open road. Yet performance that carries with it new economies of operation.

STYLING . . . that is smarter than that of the style-setting La Salle of last year.

SAFETY . . . that includes the latest Fisher contribution to motoring security . . . the solid-steel Turret-Top body. And the safety of big, capable, hydraulic brakes.

QUALITY of unusual character. . . . Throughout its sturdy chassis and throughout its luxurious interior, trimly tailored in quality fabrics, the new La Salle is a tribute to fine car ideals. This is but natural . . . for it is designed and built by Cadillac.

The new La Salle is now on display at the salesrooms of your Cadillac-La Salle dealer. You are cordially invited to see it and to drive it . . . to judge its exceptional value and its brilliant performance for yourself.

CADILLAC MOTOR CAR COMPANY

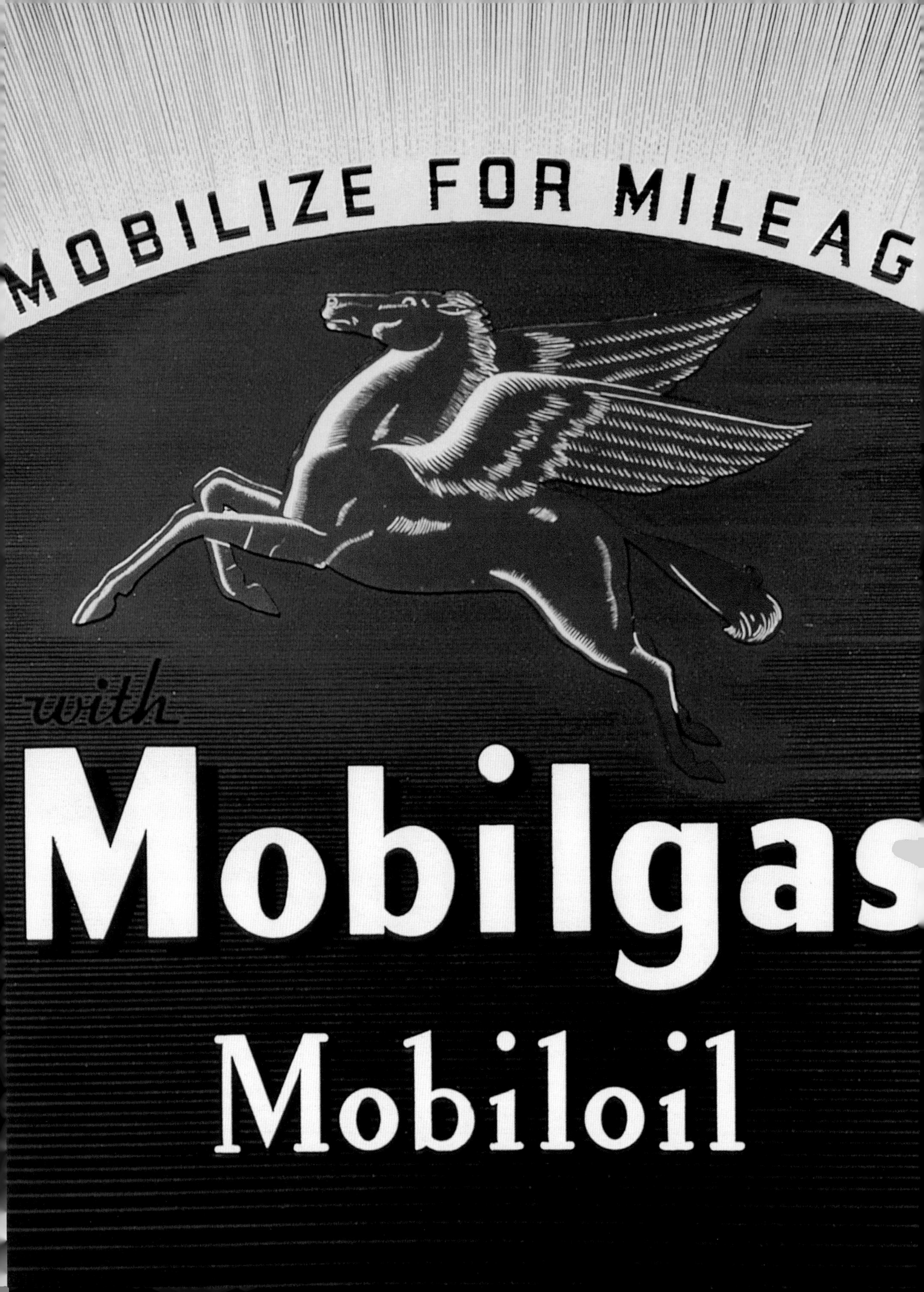
MOBILIZE FOR MILEAG
with
Mobilgas
Mobiloil

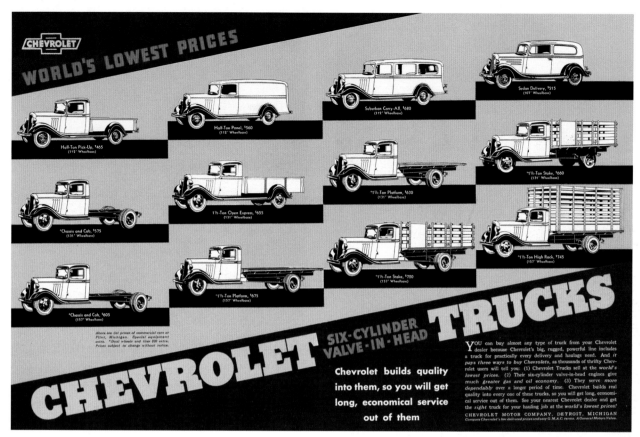

Chevrolet, 1935

Happy Days Ahead

The Ford V-8 is an invitation to enjoy many thousands of miles of motoring. For the mother in the home. The young woman in business. The June Bride. And the girl graduate who has been longing for a car of her own. . . . For the purchase of a Ford V-8 is in itself something of a graduation — a step upward to a higher plane of motor car performance and all-around satisfaction. . . . Formerly you had to pay more than $2000 for a car with a V-8 engine. The Ford has brought it within your reach at a low price. And provided beauty, comfort, safety and richness of upholstery and appointment to match that fine car performance. . . . The Ford V-8 is thoroughly modern throughout. It stands at the head of its class in everything that means top honors for a motor car.

Mobiloil, 1935 ◄ *Ford, 1935*

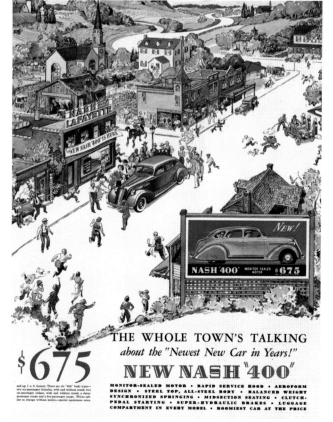

THE WHOLE TOWN'S TALKING
about the "Newest New Car in Years!"
NEW NASH "400"

$675

and up, f. o. b. factory. There are six "400" body types — two six-passenger victorias, with and without trunk; two six-passenger sedans, with and without trunk; a three-passenger coupe and a five-passenger coupe. Prices subject to change without notice—special equipment extra.

MONITOR-SEALED MOTOR • RAPID SERVICE HOOD • AEROFORM DESIGN • STEEL TOP, ALL-STEEL BODY • BALANCED WEIGHT SYNCHRONIZED SPRINGING • MIDSECTION SEATING • CLUTCH-PEDAL STARTING • SUPER-HYDRAULIC BRAKES • LUGGAGE COMPARTMENT IN EVERY MODEL • ROOMIEST CAR AT THE PRICE

Nash, 1935

THE MOST BEAUTIFUL THING ON WHEELS

HAS A WONDERFUL STORY TO TELL!

There isn't much difference between the cost of a Pontiac and the cost of the lowest priced car you can buy. Just a matter of a few cents a day. But what a world of difference there is in what you get for what you pay!

When you step into the most beautiful thing on wheels you step right into the fine-car class, for every Pontiac feature is the finest money can buy. Pontiac's solid steel "Turret-Top" Bodies by Fisher are the safest bodies built today. Pontiac's big hydraulic brakes—triple-sealed to bar out dirt and moisture—have yet to be surpassed. Big-car weight and size, and scientific springing give you steadiness and security you simply cannot get

in smaller, lighter cars. Silver-alloy bearings and a completely sealed chassis keep the Pontiac young for years on end. And when it comes to performance, Pontiac asks no odds of any car at any price!

We do not ask you to take these remarkable statements on faith. On the contrary we urge you to let the Pontiac tell its own wonderful story of quality and value. Spend just 10 minutes behind the Silver Streak. That's all it takes to prove beyond a doubt that if you plan to buy a low-priced car you can't do better than a Pontiac in 1935.

PONTIAC MOTOR COMPANY, PONTIAC, MICHIGAN

PONTIAC

List prices at Pontiac, Michigan, begin at $615 for the Six and $730 for the Eight (subject to change without notice). Standard group of accessories extra. Available on easy G. M. A. C. Time Payments. $615

Pontiac, 1935

Smart to be seen in
Smarter to buy

NEW 1936 STUDEBAKERS · · · PRICED AS MUCH AS $300 LOWER

You are looking at a picture of the thrilling new automobile that is the toast of motoring America ... the big, thrifty, incomparably beautiful, new 1936 Studebaker Champion ... offering 97 advancements that you have not seen combined in any other car!

New prices—as much as $300 less—give these Champions a buy appeal so decisive that, once you see them, ride in them and drive them, you'll wonder how anybody could possibly make any choice but Studebaker.

Beneath this new Champion's glowing harmony of suave, smooth, competent-looking exterior line, flows the lovely melody of America's smartest fittings and appointments ... gracing interiors so roomy, you feel almost lost in their spaciousness when you

drive alone ... and so restful, on any road or at any speed, you unqualifiedly award the comfort of the 1936 Studebaker ride your first prize.

New Studebaker engines, brilliantly responsive and tremendously powerful, wring every ounce of energy out of every drop of fuel so efficiently, your oil as well as your gasoline costs stay under your budget, week after week and month after month. And with feather-touch hydraulic brakes, finger-tip straight-line steering and the world's strongest, quietest all-steel bodies, reinforced by steel, you are safer than you've ever been in a motor car before. Choose the Champion you prefer ... a matchless new 90-horsepower Dictator Six ... a superb new 115-horsepower President Eight.

Studebaker, 1935

U.S. Royal Tires, 1935

▶ *Chevrolet, 1935*   ▶▶ *Chevrolet, 1935*

From 1911 to 1935
PIONEER OF QUALITY
in the low price field

The Master De Luxe Town Sedan

CHEVROLET

TURRET-TOP BODY BY FISHER (WITH FISHER NO DRAFT VENTILA-
TION) . . . IMPROVED KNEE-ACTION RIDE . . . BLUE-FLAME VALVE-
IN-HEAD ENGINE WITH PRESSURE STREAM OILING . . . WEATHER-
PROOF CABLE-CONTROLLED BRAKES . . . SHOCK-PROOF STEERING.

For nearly a quarter of a century—from the building of the first
Chevrolet to the building of the 1935 Master De Luxe models—
Chevrolet has led the way in bringing modern, up-to-date transportation to the low-price field. Turn your mind back over the years
and you will find that Chevrolet has pioneered improvement after
improvement in low-priced cars. Smartly-styled closed bodies . . .
the Syncro-Mesh Transmission . . . the Knee-Action Ride . . . solid
steel Turret-Top construction, and many other improvements of the
first importance, all have originated with Chevrolet. Many motor
car builders have pioneered one new feature or a series of new
features, but it is perfectly true to say that Chevrolet has pioneered
quality for the entire low-price field. And, of course, you get the
highest development of Chevrolet beauty, comfort, performance
and economy in the Master De Luxe Chevrolet for 1935. Examine
this distinguished motor car . . . ride in it . . . and choose *Chevrolet* for quality at low cost!

CHEVROLET MOTOR COMPANY, DETROIT, MICHIGAN
Compare Chevrolet's low delivered prices and easy G. M. A. C. terms. A General Motors Value

CHEVROLET *for* 1935

...d motor car - like the ...iend ... is the motor car that wears well !"

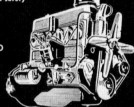

Master De Luxe Coupe

La Salle Two-Door Touring Sedan—$1185

THE NEW
LA SALLE

Illustrated above is the beautiful new La Salle, captivating member of the Royal Family of Motordom. La Salle is really one of the marvels of this great manufacturing age. It is endowed with Cadillac engineering and Cadillac manufacturing throughout, and offers the priceless advantage of Cadillac prestige—yet it is priced so low that it is a prudent choice for even the modest budget. We believe sincerely that there is no other car like La Salle— none other that offers so much of luxury and elegance and distinction, at a price so remarkably low. Your Cadillac-La Salle dealer would welcome an opportunity to demonstrate its exceptional performance—today.

La Salle, 1935

▶ *Firestone, 1935*

Your guide to safety

In this day of fast-moving motor cars, safety from blowouts and skidding is of vital importance. To assure motoring safety for you and your family, Firestone builds tires that are made blowout-proof by the patented process of Gum-Dipping. The scientifically designed tread will stop a car 15% to 25% quicker than other well known makes.

Take no chances, equip your car now with Firestone High Speed Tires — *the Masterpiece of Tire Construction.*

Listen to the Voice of Firestone featuring Richard Crooks, Nelson Eddy, Margaret Speaks. Monday evenings over Nationwide N.B.C.—WEAF Network

Firestone

Body by Fisher, 1936

Nash, 1935 ◄ *Goodyear, 1934*

Body by Fisher, 1935

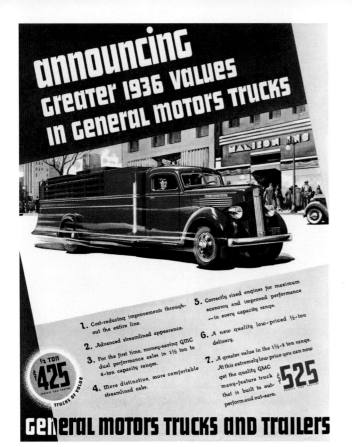

General Motors, 1936

Studebaker, 1936

Ethyl, 1936

Plymouth, 1936

▶ *Duesenberg, 1934*

He drives a Duesenberg

THE NEW FORD V·8 FOR 1936

The New Ford V-8 for 1936 is beautifully timed for these modern days. It is personable without being pretentious—as up-to-date in performance as in appearance. . . . The V-8 engine maintains its leadership in power, acceleration, smoothness and all-round efficiency—gives you many advantages formerly available only in high-priced cars. This V-8 engine is an important reason why the Ford is such a satisfying car to drive. . . . You will find, too, that there is something equally outstanding about the safety, comfort and roominess of the 1936 Ford V-8. . . . You drive with unusual security because of ease of handling, the welded steel body, big powerful brakes that stop the car with ease and certainty, and Safety Glass (all around in all Ford body types at no additional cost). . . . The compact design of the V-8 engine means extra inches of body room and makes the Ford a really big car inside. Center-Poised seat position contributes to easy riding comfort on every type of road—in the back seat as well as in the front. . . . You will like everything about the New Ford V-8 for 1936. For it has everything you would like to have in a modern motor car.

Oldsmobile, 1936

Ford, 1936 ◄   Pontiac, 1936

Smart to be seen in
Smarter to buy

AND THIS BEAUTIFUL 1936 STUDEBAKER COSTS ALMOST AS LITTLE

It's America's best looking coupe

There isn't another 1936 automobile that even half approaches the luxury beauty of this big thrifty new 3-passenger Dictator. And you will have to take our word for that. If you've seen all the other new cars you know! In that sweeping rear deck there's the largest carrying compartment you've ever seen in a coupe . . . more room for baggage than most people ever require . . . so much room in fact that many motorists are choosing this Dictator coupe for its carrying capacity wholly aside from its luxury and beauty.

AS LOWEST PRICE CARS

$665
and up
at the factory

NOW priced as low as $665 at the factory, this big, thrifty, thoroughly new Studebaker sells itself on sight. Exquisitely appointed, styled by the gifted Helen Dryden, it won two first places in the Gilmore Yosemite 352-mile Run—the national gas economy classic . . . an average of 24.27 miles per gallon for the Dictator Six—20.34 miles per gallon for the President Eight!

Sedan rear seats are chair-height with 58⅜ inches of elbow room . . . and 3 extra inches of toe room on the flat, comfortable rear floor. The beautifully contoured steel body is the world's strongest — with the world's largest one-piece solid steel top. Feather-touch hydraulic brakes! Straight-line steering! Swift acceleration!

But for real proof, you must drive this matchless new Studebaker. Dictator prices begin at $665 — President prices at $965. And the new Studebaker C. I. T. 6% plan offers a new low in time payments. The Studebaker Corporation, South Bend, Indiana.

World's only car with
AUTOMATIC HILL HOLDER
The most gratifying experience you ever had in driving . . . prevents your rolling back when you come to a stop on any upgrade . . . the most important safety advancement of 1936.

Spectacular economy with
GAS-SAVING OVERDRIVE
With this invention, a development of Studebaker free wheeling, your engine uses gas only 2 miles while your car is traveling 3 miles.

★ ★ ★
SAFER ALL-STEEL BODIES . . . ROOMIER
INTERIORS . . . FLAT, COMFORTABLE FLOORS

NEW 1936
Studebaker
SMART TO BE SEEN IN . . . SMARTER TO BUY

Studebaker, 1936

The imposing entrance of the Brazilian Embassy, one of the twenty-six Embassies and Legations in Washington in which Packards are owned

Washington prefers Packards

Washington, the political and social capital of the country, is more than a city of lovely homes. It is a city of fine motor cars as well.

And of all these fine cars, 55.3 per cent are the larger Packards!

This is not surprising. Packard, long the most popular of American fine cars, still further increased the margin of its preference during the past twelve months, when nearly half of all the fine cars purchased in this country were Packards.

Many of these owners are among the more than a thousand distinguished families who have driven Packards continuously for twenty-one years or more. Such a record of owner loyalty is unmatched in the motor car industry.

The British Embassy residence of His Excellency, the Honorable Sir Ronald Lindsay, P.C., G.C.M.G., K.C.B., C.V.O. A Packard graces this beautiful setting.

The residence of Mr. and Mrs. C. Mathews Dick of Washington and Newport. Mr. Dick has owned Packards for twelve years.

The lovely home of Mrs. James Freeman Curtis of Washington and Roslyn. It is widely known as the 1925 F. Street Club. Mrs. Curtis' present car is one of a long succession of Packard ownership.

PACKARD

EIGHT
SUPER-EIGHT
TWELVE

Ask the man who owns one

Packard, 1936

CADILLAC
Fleetwood
TOWN CABRIOLET

THE SPEAR-HEAD OF MOTORING PROGRESS

Surely it is not assuming too much to suggest that all cars are better cars today as a result of the high standards established by Cadillac thirty years ago and progressively maintained ever since. ∙ ∙ Motorists generally have always recognized, and even required, that Cadillac should give unmistakable evidence of its right to a distinct leadership in engineering, in handling, in riding, and in luxury. ∙ ∙ Yet much as all cars have improved as a result of example and public requirement, Cadillac in the Royal Family of Motordom has held fast and even emphasized these distinguished differences. ∙ ∙ It is a pleasant thing that Cadillac attains the peak of its thirty years of achievement at the same time that it records the lowest prices in more than two decades. ∙ ∙ If you are disposed to question the almost universal admission that Cadillac's cars surpass others in riding and driving, in comfort and in beauty—that Cadillac is still the spearhead of motoring progress—the briefest demonstration will reassure you. ∙ ∙ Cadillac has never done as well by its public in performance, in appearance, in value, as in the current cars.

Prices list at Detroit, subject to change without notice. Special equipment extra. Offered on G.M.A.C.'s new 6% Time Payment Plan.

LaSALLE $1175
CADILLAC $1645
CADILLAC
FLEETWOOD $2445

The Royal Family of Motordom

Cadillac, 1936

The years will prove how right you were *to choose a* PONTIAC

BUILT TO BE AMERICA'S
MOST DEPENDABLE
LOW-PRICED CAR

SATISFY YOURSELF WITH SOMETHING BETTER

Illustrated—the De Luxe Eight Four-Door Touring Sedan—$840

WE ARE naturally gratified to hear the 1936 Silver Streak Pontiac referred to as America's most distinctive car. We are proud of its recent victory in the Gilmore-Yosemite Valley Economy Run, where it defeated all entrants in its class with an average of 23.9 miles per gallon over 252 miles of hill and dale roads. But our greatest satisfaction comes from a fact which you, as a Pontiac owner, will be years in discovering: The Pontiac is built to *stand out* through sheer ability to *stand up.* Not only is every Pontiac feature the finest money can buy; engineering and materials meet the same exacting standard. As a result, we can point to a record that is probably unique in the industry. Over 83 per cent of all the more than a million Pontiacs ever built are still in daily use—and an astonishing number have now gone well over 200,000 miles. We confess to a special motive in thus assuring you of almost endless miles of care-free, trouble-free driving. Our eyes are on the future. We want your Pontiac to serve you so well that when you again buy a car there will be no question of choice—you will naturally and inevitably buy another Pontiac.

ALL PONTIAC CARS CAN BE BOUGHT ON G.M.A.C.'S NEW 6% PLAN, WHICH GREATLY REDUCES THE COST OF BUYING ON TIME

$615

1936
1937
1938
1939
1940

Pontiac, 1936

Shell, 1936

Packard, 1936

Chevrolet, 1936

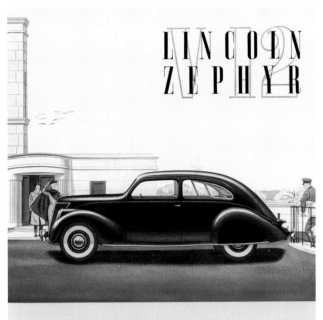

LINCOLN ZEPHYR V12

TWELVE CYLINDERS POWER THIS NEW CAR OF MANY-SIDED APPEAL

The first person who bought a LINCOLN-ZEPHYR was the president of a railroad. A fair cross-section of owners reveals, also, eminent physicians . . . executives who travel much . . . society matrons with children of school age. Their reasons for buying this car are varied and practical. Underlying them all, typical of them all, is this: "It is a new *kind* of car. It offers a new kind of value!"

It is an unusual idea to place a 12-cylinder engine in a car of medium price. The engine itself is new. Designed by Lincoln, built by Lincoln, it is the culmination of years of research and experiment. It develops 110 horsepower. Because of its exclusive design; because of its great power and flexibility; because it pulls a car low in weight for its size, *owners are getting 14 to 18 miles a gallon!*

It is a new idea to streamline a car as fully as this car is streamlined. But the graceful, flowing contours simply grow out of the body structure beneath. Steel trusses form a rigid bridge over which steel panels are welded—top, sides, bottom. Six passengers, or one, are gently cradled in the framework, and poised forward of the rear axle. You ride near the center even when in the back seat.

It is a new idea, finally, to provide so much power, size, comfort in a car selling for $1275.

But a conviction of the builder is that engineering experience, precision methods, and vast resources, applied intelligently, can do what otherwise could not be done. This car combines Ford ability to give great value at low cost with the Lincoln tradition to build without regard to cost. It does for the medium-price field what these other cars do for their own fields.

Learn, today, what outstanding value Lincoln has built into a car new in idea, new in performance!

PRICED FROM $1275 F.O.B. DETROIT
Available in Two Sedan Body Types

Lincoln, 1936

The Modern Car With The V·8 Engine

You will have a feeling that you are driving a truly fine car when you drive the 1936 Ford. And you are! For today's Ford is a fine car in everything but the price. It is modern in line and style and appointment. . . . Comfortable and roomy. . . . An unusually safe car to drive because of ease of handling, welded steel body, Safety Glass throughout (at no extra cost), and sure, dependable, quick-stopping brakes. . . . And it has a modern V·8 engine. . . . You will find that this makes quite a difference in driving enjoyment—it is smoother, quieter and more responsive, with a comforting reserve of power. There is something thrilling, too, about the way a V·8 helps you to step out ahead at traffic lights. . . . It is never any effort to drive a Ford—that is why it is so kind to your nerves and disposition. Two new features for 1936 are easier steering and easier gear shifting.

FORD V·8 FOR 1936

$25 A MONTH, WITH USUAL DOWN-PAYMENT, BUYS ANY NEW FORD V·8 CAR ON UCC ½ PER CENT PER MONTH FINANCE PLANS

Ford, 1936

THE *Difference* IS MORE MARKED THAN EVER

Those who are not able to avail themselves of the rare privileges which Cadillac and La Salle owners enjoy, can still be better served than ever before by a number of excellent cars of lower price. . . . The whole industry has moved forward—mostly in the direction of massed demand and sprightly appearance and performance; but, of course, Cadillac has been, as always, in the forefront of that forward movement. . . . But the difference and the distinction in Cadillac and La Salle have

become more marked than ever, for Cadillac has deliberately planned its 1936 creations to widen the gap between the Royal Family of Motordom and all other cars in the world. . . . Those who revel in the special ease and elegance and the pronounced distinction which Cadillac and La Salle provide for their owners, simply cannot satisfy themselves with anything else. . . . The briefest of experiences, either at the wheel or as a chauffeured passenger, will prove this to your entire satisfaction.

Model illustrated 5720. Monthly payments to suit your purse. Prices list at Detroit, Michigan, subject to change without notice. Special equipment extra.

La Salle CONVERTIBLE COUPE

La Salle $1175   *Cadillac* $1645
CADILLAC *Fleetwood* $2445

THE ROYAL FAMILY OF MOTORDOM

Cadillac, 1936

THRILLING BIG-CAR LUXURY
with small-car economy!

"STEP ON IT" to better times—to exciting new thrills in motoring! Take the wheel of a 1936 Reo Flying Cloud. Give it "the gun". Then discover how amazingly little more it costs to enjoy genuine big-car luxury, riding ease and performance in *America's Finest Six!*

Look for *every* fine-car feature—every worth while advancement in this new Reo. You'll get real cash savings and a world of satisfaction out of Reo's new Economy Overdrive. This great improvement drastically reduces gas and oil bills; eliminates motor strain at high speeds. And

Reo gives you the strength and safety of all-steel bodies, the sure, positive action of sealed hydraulic brakes—*plus* a vast reserve of power in the smooth, responsive Reo-built engine.

Strikingly streamlined, *America's Finest Six* is a car with individuality—one you'll be proud to own and drive. The deluxe interior is deeply cushioned and spacious enough for six adults to ride at ease. Draftless ventilation keeps air properly circulated—makes driving more comfortable and enjoyable.

Call your nearest Reo dealer today. Ask him to send over a big, luxurious new Flying Cloud for a trial without obligation. You'll agree it's America's greatest value—in first price, operating cost and typical Reo dependability. The new Reo C. I. T. 6% Plan now makes it possible for you to buy *America's Finest Six* on most favorable terms.

New Economical Overdrive

$795 and part c.o.b. Lansing, subject to change without notice. Special equipment and tax extra.
*Money-saving overdrive available at slight additional cost.

America's Finest Six

REO FOR ECONOMY AND LONG LIFE

Reo Motor Car Co., 1936

A full color reproduction of this picture, suitable for framing, will be sent you free upon request. Write Dodge Division of Chrysler Corporation, Detroit, Mich.

"My Goodness!... what a Grand Car!"

says SHIRLEY TEMPLE

Star of "Captain January"

"IN selecting a car to take Shirley to and from the studio," says Mrs. George Temple, mother of the talented child cinema star, "we were primarily interested in safety. The new 1936 Dodge, with its rugged steel body and amazing brake action, proved a happy solution to this problem."

You, too, are entitled to the greatest protection your money can buy . . . and Dodge gives you that protection with its safety-steel body . . . and *genuine* hydraulic brakes that have more than eight years of experience in hydraulic brake building behind them.

The new 1936 Dodge, however, gives you more than these very necessary safety features. Praised by famous fashion authorities for its breath-taking beauty, Dodge is already smashing economy records . . . owners report 18 to 24 miles to the gallon of gasoline . . . savings up to 20% on oil.

Dodge also gives you the Airglide-Ride . . . redistribution of weight *evenly* to all four wheels . . . Chair-Height seats . . . patented Floating Power engine mountings . . . and all this for less money—now only $640* and up!

See this big, new Dodge today. *And don't fail to make the free economy test!*

———— D O D G E ————

Division of Chrysler Corporation

BIG, NEW, MONEY-SAVING DODGE priced from $640 to $995. *List prices at factory, Detroit, subject to change without notice. Special equipment extra.

Shirley Temple, starring in "Captain January," a Twentieth Century—Fox Picture (Darryl F. Zanuck in charge of production) soon to be shown at your favorite theatre.

Big Money-Saving **DODGE** AT NEW LOW PRICE - NOW ONLY **$640*** Through the Official Chrysler Motors Commercial Credit Company New 6% Time Payment Plan you will find it easy and less costly to arrange time payments to fit your budget.

"WHY SHOULD I BUY AN EXPENSIVE CAR-

When the New Dodge offers such Unusual Beauty and Economy?"

says GINGER ROGERS

LIKE many another who could afford a more expensive car, the combination of beauty and economy won Miss Rogers to the big, new, Money-Saving Dodge. Acclaimed by fashion authorities the "Beauty Winner" of 1936, Dodge is smashing economy records . . . owners report 18 to 24 miles to the gallon of gas and oil savings up to 20%.

But with a Dodge you get more than style and economy. Dodge gives you the protection of safety-steel bodies, pioneered by Dodge, and *genuine* hydraulic brakes, plus a wealth of expensive-car features such as the Airglide-Ride . . . redistribution of weight equally to all four wheels . . . Chair-Height seats . . . patented Floating Power engine mountings . . . and many other advancements.

See the new Dodge today. Drive it. See the free economy test . . . And bear in mind that it is not unusual that dependable Dodge cars give their owners up to 200,000 and even more miles of service. And don't forget, Dodge—at new, low prices—now costs only a few dollars more than the lowest-priced cars.

————DODGE————

Division of Chrysler Corporation

Ginger Rogers

who skyrocketed to new popularity in such films as "Gay Divorcee" and "Top Hat" is appearing with Fred Astaire in "Follow the Fleet," the new RKO film musical, now being shown at your neighborhood theatre.

g, Money-Saving **DODGE** *new low price--only* $640*

Priced from $640 to $995. *List prices at factory, Detroit, subject to change without notice. Special equipment extra.

Through the Official Chrysler Motors Commercial Credit Company New 6% Time Payment Plan you will find it easy and economical to arrange time payments to fit your budget.

General Motors, 1936

Studebaker, 1936

International Trucks, 1936

Studebaker, 1936　　　▶ *International Trucks, 1936*

"Time Marches On"
with
INTERNATIONAL
TRUCKS

The next time you see The March of Time in your favorite theater, imagine another installment in the making. As you travel across the sound screen watching today's events, The March-of-Time's cameras are catching new people and places for the news of tomorrow.

Here is a March-of-Time International Half-Ton Truck cleverly equipped to advance the efficiency of its sound-and-camera crews. As the editors keenly follow the trend of the world's news this truck with its cameras and microphones is constantly in range of the dramatic events the editors are recording for the screen.

The March of Time uses Half-Ton Internationals for their heavy-duty quality and stamina, and also for *nation-wide service*. International Harvester maintains the largest Company-owned truck service organization in the world. Wherever duty calls these trucks, they will always be near an International branch or dealer.

INTERNATIONAL HARVESTER COMPANY
606 S. Michigan Ave.   (INCORPORATED)   Chicago, Illinois

The Half-Ton International chassis, on
113-in. wheelbase, is priced at
$400 f. o. b.
factory
There is a full range of other International
sizes up to powerful 6-wheelers. See the
nearby branch or dealer.

INTERNATIONAL

"We arrived in New York at Midnight...and the Lincoln-Zephyr knows all about traffic"

THIS new kind of car conquers all roads, all circumstances of travel. In city or country, on roads good and bad, the LINCOLN-ZEPHYR rolls up new records of performance.

Ask, as you consider this car, what it offers that other cars in its price field do not. The LINCOLN-ZEPHYR has a 12-cylinder engine—the V-type. Twelve cylinders mean greater smoothness . . . greater flexibility. And twelve cylinders, here, *mean 14 to 18 miles per gallon!*

The LINCOLN-ZEPHYR has a unique body structure. *This is the only car of its kind.* Body and frame are one, welded together. You ride surrounded by steel. And you ride amidships. This car flows along like a sloop in a favoring breeze.

The LINCOLN-ZEPHYR has extra roominess. It is a big car. The wheelbase is 122 inches. The engine is compact, and interiors thus longer. There are no conventional running boards; seats, like divans, are wider. Three may sit comfortably

on the front seat or the back. THE LINCO ZEPHYR, finally, has the Lincoln background is built in the Lincoln plant. Lincoln preci methods are LINCOLN-ZEPHYR precision meth Mechanical standards for the one are mechan standards for the other.

Prices now are lower. Convenient terms can arranged through Authorized Universal Cr Company Finance Plans. *Lincoln Motor Compo builders of the Lincoln and Lincoln-Zeph*

LINCOLN-ZEPHYR V·12

THIS IS THE CAR THAT IS PRIC
BELOW ITS SPECIFICATIO

A CRUDE CHALLENGE

to every motor oil in the world

Veedol MOTOR OIL

100% PENNSYLVANIA AT ITS FINEST

"Veedol provides lubrication protection to the modern motor, unmatched by any motor oil in the world." That is the challenge... and here is the proof.

Today, motor parts are smaller, clearances are finer. That means the lubricating oil film must be *thinner!* Motors operate for longer periods at greater speeds. That means the oil film must be *smoother!* Motors generate higher internal heat and friction. That means the oil film must be *tougher!*

And the thinnest, smoothest, and toughest of all oil films is the Veedol "Film of Protection." Veedol is made exclusively from Bradford Pennsylvania crude oil... the finest, the costliest crude in all the world (as shown by daily market quotations). Veedol is made by the world's largest refiner of Pennsylvania lubricants (as shown by government statistics).

It is that combination of the world's finest raw material and the matchless experience of its refiner that makes Veedol possible... that makes it the world's finest motor oil.

No wonder Veedol brings your modern motor a positive protection against costly wear and tear! No wonder Veedol, with its modest price, dares to challenge any oil at any price.

Tide Water Oil Company, 17 Battery Place, New York City

THE FILM OF PROTECTION

INDESTRUCTIBLE

VEEDOL MOTOR OIL

MADE 100% FROM PENNSYLVANIA'S COSTLIEST CRUDE

Veedol Motor Oil, 1936

THE NEW FOUR-PASSENGER CLUB CABRIOLET

"Watch The Fords Go By"

Most often "it's a Ford" that steps out ahead at the traffic light. And does it so easily! No fuss or effort. Seems to just glide away in a smooth-flowing surge of power. . . . There's no surprise at this alert acceleration—you've come to expect it of a V-8. For many months, motorists have seen the Ford set the pace in traffic, on hills and on the open road. Frequently, you have heard it said—"The V-8 engine is the finest engine Ford has ever built." . . . Today's Ford gives you modern V-8 performance, with outstanding reliability and low cost. Its economy has been proved on the road by nearly three million Ford V-8 owners. . . . Each year the Ford brings you more in value—each year it costs less to run.

THE FORD V·8

$25 A MONTH, WITH USUAL DOWN-PAYMENT, BUYS ANY NEW FORD V-8 CAR ON NEW UCC ½% PER MONTH FINANCE PLANS

Ford, 1936

Yesterday's tiresome journey

IS JUST A REFRESHING JAUNT!

CHRYSLER AIRFLOW EIGHT SEDAN

To PEOPLE who haven't experienced it before, the effortless ease of riding in an Airflow Chrysler is nothing short of astonishing.

As you ride, you are conscious, of course, that the trip is smooth. But after 500 miles, you'll be downright amazed at the lack of fatigue you feel.

The reason is purely scientific . . . the effect of a rhythm which scientists know is most pleasing to human nerves. All the little jiggles and jounces are gone. The car takes the big bumps in long, easy glides . . . so slowly and softly that your nerves are scarcely conscious of the motion at all.

To this magnificent ride is added the magic of Chrysler's Automatic Overdrive† which cuts engine speed one-third at road speeds over 40. It's a sensation as smooth and silent as sailing . . . and you actually get as much as 5 more miles from every gallon of gas.

Your nearby Chrysler dealer cordially invites you to get acquainted at first hand with the greatest luxury in travel today . . . the spacious roominess, the scientific economy, the unmatched safety, the glorious ease and comfort of the world's most modern motor car. Accept his invitation to ride in an Airflow Chrysler.

☆ CHRYSLER SIX . . . 93 horsepower, 118-inch wheelbase, $760 and up.
☆ DE LUXE EIGHT . . . 110 and 115 horsepower, 121 and 123-inch wheelbase, $825 and up.
☆ AIRFLOW EIGHT . . . 115 horsepower, 123-inch wheelbase. All models, $1345.
☆ AIRFLOW IMPERIAL . . . 130 horsepower, 128-inch wheelbase. All models $1475.
☆ AIRFLOW CUSTOM IMPERIAL . . . 130 horsepower, 137-inch wheelbase, $3075 and up.
†Standard on Airflow Imperial. Available on all 1936 Chryslers at slight additional cost.

All prices list at factory, Detroit; special equipment extra.

Ask for the Official Chrysler Motors-Commercial Credit Company Time Payment plan. Available through all Chrysler dealers.

Chrysler's on the Air! . . . Big Star Program . . . Every Thursday, 8 P.M. Eastern Daylight Saving Time . . . Columbia Network. You're invited to listen.

AIRFLOW CHRYSLER

Lincoln, 1937 ◄ Chrysler, 1936

Lady, Relax!

A ride in a Ford these days is a journey in contentment. Everything is just right—everything is just as you would like to have it. Many times you will find yourself leaning back and saying— "It's a grand car to drive." For there's something calm and restful about traveling in a Ford V-8. . . . Ease of handling takes the trouble out of traffic. Smooth-surging V-8 power makes mole-hills out of mountains. Center-Poise Riding turns rough roads into boulevards. Big, powerful brakes bring the car to a swift, swerveless stop. You drive relaxed in the roomy, comfortable Ford V-8— sure of its safety—confident of its performance and dependability over many thousands of miles. . . . This kind of driving adds a great deal to motoring enjoyment—explains the popularity of the Ford V-8—tells why it is the first choice of so many women nowadays. V-8 is the mark of the modern car.

THE FORD V·8

$25 A MONTH, WITH USUAL DOWN-PAYMENT, BUYS ANY NEW FORD V-8 CAR ON NEW UCC ½% PER MONTH FINANCE PLANS

Ford, 1936

V·8 Is The Mark Of The Modern Car

The Ford is an exceptionally good choice for the woman motorist because it is so dependable and easy to handle. That has always been so. These days there is still another reason for its ever-widening popularity—it is a thoroughly modern car. The Ford is as up-to-date in performance, comfort and safety as in appearance and appointment. Here are some modern features of the Ford . . . V-8 ENGINE (fine-car acceleration, power and smoothness—increased motoring enjoyment). . . . CENTER-POISE RIDING (greater comfort, front and rear—you ride near the center of the car instead of over the axles). . . . SAFETY GLASS all around at no extra cost (an important reason why the Ford is such a safe car to drive). . . . NEW STEEL WHEELS (distinctive design—large hub caps—big tires). . . . COMPLETE LINE OF BODIES (seventeen types, including new Convertible Sedan with trunk, illustrated above).

FORD V·8 FOR 1936

$25 A MONTH, WITH USUAL DOWN-PAYMENT, BUYS ANY NEW FORD V-8 CAR ON NEW UCC ½% PER MONTH FINANCE PLANS

Ford, 1936

"Good looking" DOESN'T HALF DESCRIBE THIS STUDEBAKER $665*

...and it's priced close to the lowest!

ABOVE you see a candid camera shot—of a Studebaker snapped off-guard and without benefit of make up! A truthful color photograph that tells more than pages of words could, about the distinction of Studebaker design!

Page through this magazine or any other magazine and you won't find a car with the charm in every line that gifted Helen Dryden has styled into this Studebaker. And the interiors are equally thrilling. Smart new-type upholstery and fittings! Seats that are roomy lounges! Flat, restful floors!

The air-curved Studebaker top is the largest one-piece sheet of steel ever used in an automobile. Feathertouch hydraulic brakes! Lightning fast acceleration! And Studebaker operating economy isn't theoretical . . . it's official . . . 24.27 miles per gallon under A.A.A. supervision in the national classic of this year!

See for yourself that Studebaker's eye appeal is matched by its drive appeal! *Dictator prices begin at $665—President prices at $965, list at factory, South Bend, Indiana. And Studebaker's C.I.T. 6% plan offers new low time payments.

YOU GET FREE GAS ONE MILE OUT OF THREE

That's exactly what happens when Studebaker's Car-Saving Automatic Overdrive is in use. Studebaker is one of the few cars offering this advancement in all models. Quickly pays back its slight extra cost.

REAR SEATS HAVE 58% INCHES OF ELBOW ROOM

That's more roominess from side to side than any other car. And there's one-third 3 extra inches of hat room. You ride restfully inside a sheath of quiet steel tremendously reinforced by steel girders.

Studebaker

SMART TO BE SEEN IN...SMARTER TO BUY

Studebaker, 1936

Mighty Sweet

A mighty sweet new Studebaker President at a mighty sweet low price!

You don't have to own a polo pony stable to appreciate the eye-appeal and charm of this exciting new 1937 Studebaker President. • But if you are blessed with that kind of good fortune, you're probably a smart enough money manager to realize that it isn't good business to pay more than this President's price* for any car. • With its 125 inches of wheelbase and its 115-horsepower eight cylinder engine, it matches any car built in impressiveness, comfort and performance. And it isn't any stepchild of a fine family either. It's Studebaker's incomparable best. • It takes an 84-page book to picture and describe the features that this thrilling President offers which you cannot get in any other car.

Studebaker, 1936

These Famous Stars can Afford the most Expensive Cars—YET THEY DRIVE THE DODGE "BEAUTY WINNER"

A RARE COMBINATION of smart styling, performance and record-breaking economy . . . that's what "sold" these world-famous stars on Dodge! . . . And that very same combination has sold Dodge to thousands . . . to men and women who can afford even the most expensive cars . . . and who discovered in the big, new Dodge "Beauty Winner" so many extra-value features that they decided that paying more for a car was literally a waste of money.

In what other car priced within $500 of Dodge can you find such an amazing combination of beauty, safety, luxury and record-smashing economy? . . . genuine hydraulic brakes . . . the famous Airglide-Ride . . . safety-steel body . . . Chair-Height seats . . . equalized weight distribution and many other advancements!

See this new Dodge! Make the free economy test! See with your own eyes how Dodge saves gasoline . . . and don't forget Dodge now costs only a few dollars more than the lowest-priced cars!

DODGE
Division of Chrysler Corporation

BIG MONEY-SAVING *Dodge* AT NEW LOW PRICE...ONLY $640

Dodge, 1936

▶ *Firestone, 1936*

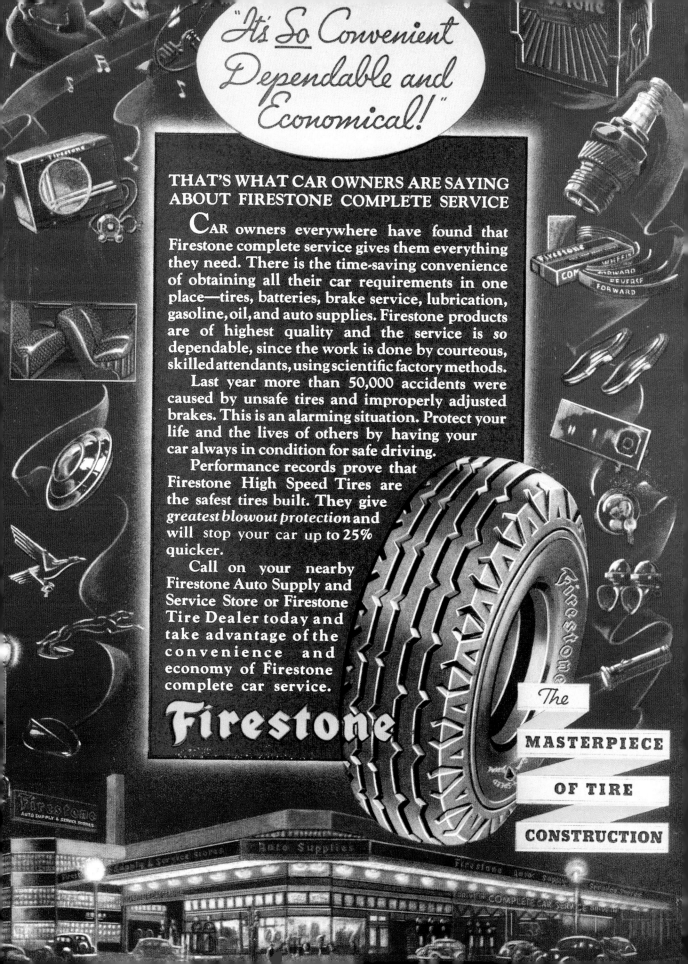

"It's _So_ Convenient
Dependable and
Economical!"

THAT'S WHAT CAR OWNERS ARE SAYING ABOUT FIRESTONE COMPLETE SERVICE

CAR owners everywhere have found that Firestone complete service gives them everything they need. There is the time-saving convenience of obtaining all their car requirements in one place—tires, batteries, brake service, lubrication, gasoline, oil, and auto supplies. Firestone products are of highest quality and the service is _so_ dependable, since the work is done by courteous, skilled attendants, using scientific factory methods.

Last year more than 50,000 accidents were caused by unsafe tires and improperly adjusted brakes. This is an alarming situation. Protect your life and the lives of others by having your car always in condition for safe driving.

Performance records prove that Firestone High Speed Tires are the safest tires built. They give _greatest blowout protection_ and will stop your car up to 25% quicker.

Call on your nearby Firestone Auto Supply and Service Store or Firestone Tire Dealer today and take advantage of the convenience and economy of Firestone complete car service.

Firestone

The
MASTERPIECE
OF TIRE
CONSTRUCTION

Buick, 1937

Graham, 1937

Packard, 1937 ◄ *Chevrolet, 1937*

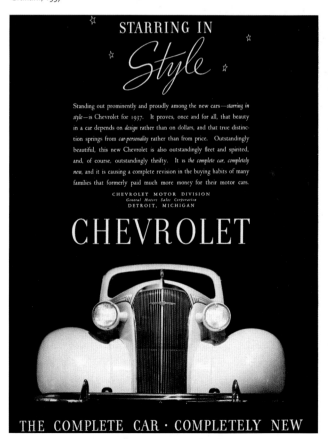

Chevrolet, 1937 ► *De Soto, 1937*

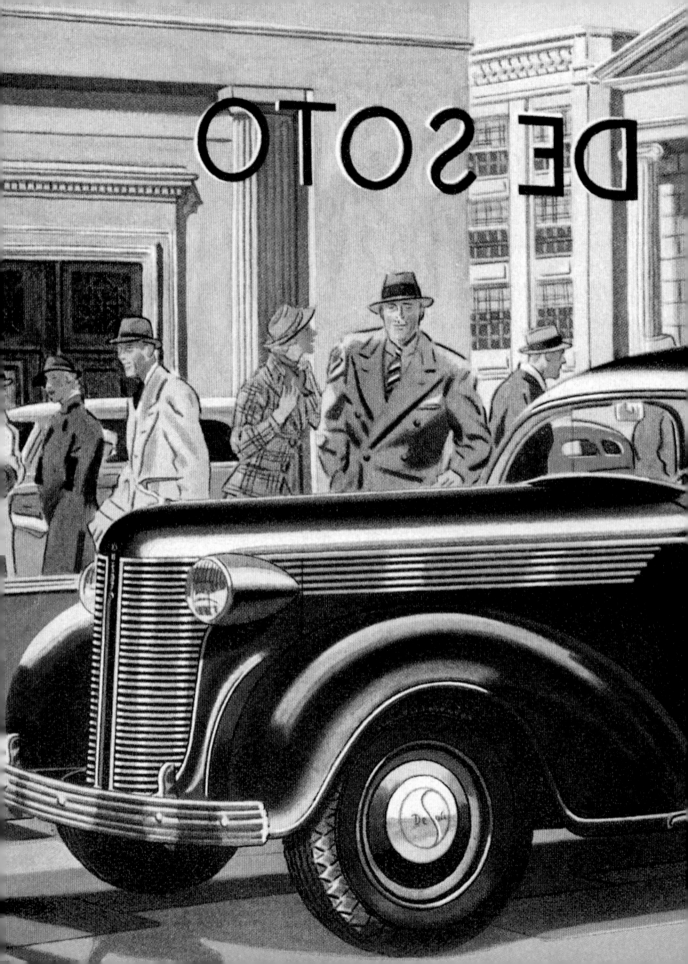

Ethyl, 1936

Lincoln, 1937

Any way you measure it…TERRAPLANE *proves itself*
No.1 CAR of the Low Price Field

OF ALL the leading low priced cars, Terraplane is tops in wheelbase … you can measure *that.* Tops in power … the specifications show you *that.* Tops in roominess … and a yardstick tells you *that.* Tops in performance and endurance…official records give you the measure of *that.* You needn't depend on claims or guesswork.

Here are some of Terraplane's more than forty No. 1 advantages … you'll find the rest at your nearest Hudson and Terraplane dealer's:

No. 1 in Size, with wheelbase increased to 117 inches … longest *by nearly 5 inches* of the low priced leaders.

No. 1 in Roominess and Luxury. 55 full inches of front seat comfort for three … at least 3½ inches more than any of the others. And interior richness always thought "too fine" for a low priced car.

No. 1 in Power, increased to 96 and 101

pedal. The car almost drives itself! Front floor all clear of gear or brake levers. (Conventional gear lever available without extra cost.) Amazing accuracy and responsiveness in steering with new roller tooth gears … not found in any of the other low priced leaders.

No. 1 in Endurance and Economy. Eight official A.A.A. Contest Board endurance records smashed by a 1937 Terraplane! 1,000 miles at 86.54 miles an hour in the most punishing "torture test" a stock car ever endured. And top economy *proved* in official tests, made at everyday driving speeds.

No. 1 in Safety. Body *all* of steel, with roof of solid steel … pioneered by Terraplane. Duo-Automatic Hydraulic

smooth horsepower … tops among low priced leaders by *at least 11 horsepower.* With *proved* performance, certified by Contest Board, American Automobile Association.

Brakes … *two* separate braking systems from the *same* pedal. Safety proved in official tests, stopping in *half* the legally required distance.

Come to any Hudson and Terraplane dealer's. Make these *two* comparisons:

First—match Terraplane against other low priced cars. Let your own measurements be the proof that not another one can stand with this No. 1 CAR, any way you want to measure it.

Second—match Terraplane against cars priced *above* the low price field. See for yourself how far up the price scale you must go to equal the important advantages you get in Terraplane.

Why do without *anything* you want

in an automobile … even though you're buying in the low price field? And why pay a premium high up the price scale for the things you get at Terraplane's low price? *Drive* the No. 1 CAR of the Low Price Field … find how much more your money buys in Terraplane.

HUDSON MOTOR CAR COMPANY, Detroit, Michigan
Hudson Motors of Canada, Ltd., Tilbury, Ontario

Ask about the new low cost Hudson–C. I. T. Time Payment Plan—terms to suit your income.

$595

and up, f. o. b. Detroit, Texas, delivery, handling and standard group of accessories extra.

Drive CARS BUILT BY HUDSON

Hudson, 1937

▶ Buick, 1937

I T ISN'T the setting that makes the jewel, nor is it alone Buick's modern line

and finish that make it seen so increasingly often in distinguished company.

The plain fact is that Buick's stimulating pace and brilliant behavior have

brought international recognition of its flawless mechanical excellence. When

such excellence is further adorned in style that sparkles with lustrous freshness, what

other choice is left for the sensible traveler who wants the most in his motor car?

"It's Buick again!"

Limited
ONE OF FOUR GREAT
BUICKS

THE MODEL SHOWN IS A LIMITED SERIES 90 SIX-PASSENGER
FOUR-DOOR SEDAN WITH 130 HORSEPOWER, VALVE-IN-HEAD
STRAIGHT-EIGHT ENGINE AND 138 INCH WHEELBASE.

Who cares where the highway leads when you have a Buick Roadmaster to take its measure in moments of pure and perfect pleasure? Who frets about the flight of Time, when in this magnificent traveler you're ready to assert your dominion over Time's flight! By any test of action, ease or enjoyment, by force alike of beauty and of staunch mechanical goodness, Roadmaster rates high among the greatest of the world's fine cars. And it is a car of today — its spirit is in tune with the eager outlook of today's modern-minded folk. That is why they have taken it to their hearts in such noticeably growing numbers.

"It's Buick again!"

Buick 8

Roadmaster one of four great BUICKS

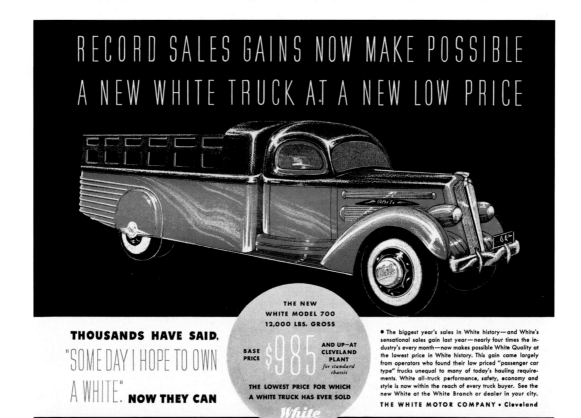

RECORD SALES GAINS NOW MAKE POSSIBLE A NEW WHITE TRUCK AT A NEW LOW PRICE

THOUSANDS HAVE SAID, "SOME DAY I HOPE TO OWN A WHITE." **NOW THEY CAN**

THE NEW
WHITE MODEL 700
12,000 LBS. GROSS

BASE
PRICE **$985** AND UP—AT
CLEVELAND
PLANT
*for standard
chassis*

THE LOWEST PRICE FOR WHICH
A WHITE TRUCK HAS EVER SOLD

White

● The biggest year's sales in White history—and White's sensational sales gain last year—nearly four times the industry's every month—now makes possible White Quality at the lowest price in White history. This gain came largely from operators who found their low priced "passenger car type" trucks unequal to many of today's hauling requirements. White all-truck performance, safety, economy and style is now within the reach of every truck buyer. See the new White at the White Branch or dealer in your city.

THE WHITE MOTOR COMPANY • Cleveland

White Trucks, 1937

Smart America HAS MADE THIS
1937 STUDEBAKER ITS SPOTLIGHT FAVORITE

$665*

GAS AND OIL ECONOMY OF LOWEST PRICED CARS

It's the world's only car with the double safety of the built-in automatic hill holder and feather-touch hydraulic brakes! Its new steering gear halves the turning effort of parking! Its great engines with their lightning fast acceleration, give driving a new thrill!

And speaking of engines . . . you travel mile after mile and day after day for less money in a Studebaker than many do in small, lower priced cars!

That's because Studebaker, alone among all cars, makes available the dual economy of the Fram oil cleaner and the gas-saving automatic overdrive.

Gleaming in a paint finish twelve coats deep, the air-curved steel-reinforced-by-steel Studebaker body has the world's largest one-piece steel top . . . and lavishly roomy interiors inimitably styled in the best of good taste by gifted Helen Dryden!

Called smarter in every flowing contour than any other 1937 car by critical motorists, the new Studebaker sells for as little as $665* and up at factory, South Bend—and the Studebaker C. I. T. budget plan assures low cost time payments.

DOORS LIGHTLY CLOSED ARE TIGHTLY SHUT . . . IN 1937 STUDEBAKERS ONLY! *You never need slam the door of a 1937 Studebaker! They have revolutionary and exclusive new rattle-proof rotary door latches which engage securely at a light pressure and each movement of the car shakes the doors more tightly shut—a protection provided only by Studebaker!*

WORLD'S ONLY CARS WITH
DUAL ECONOMY OF FRAM OIL CLEANER AND
GAS-SAVING AUTOMATIC OVERDRIVE

EXTRA ROOMY INTERIORS
WITH CHAIR HEIGHT SEATS AND SMART
HELEN DRYDEN STYLING

ENORMOUSLY SPACIOUS LUGGAGE
COMPARTMENTS

WORLD'S ONLY CARS
WITH BUILT-IN AUTOMATIC HILL HOLDER
PLUS HYDRAULIC BRAKES

*Exciting 1937
Studebakers*

*Has Nash Started a new
Vogue in Motoring?*

AT PALM BEACH! *And at smart places everywhere, you'll see the people that other people copy stepping out in Nash cars this year!*

The swing to Nash grows stronger . . . thousands realize it's no longer smart to be *too* thrifty . . . when you can get such big cars for so *little* more than small cars cost!

● A few years ago it was the "style" to scrimp and save on the family automobile. But not this year. Thousands are getting out of the "small car" class. They are changing to Nash . . . stepping out in style again!

And never before have such big cars cost so little. The Nash La-Fayette-"400" is a great big 117-inch wheelbase car . . . much bigger than any of "all three" small cars. But compare prices on the 4-door sedan models. *You'll be astonished!* This big Nash costs just a few dollars more.

And all Nash cars give you over-sized hydraulic brakes, strong steel bodies, wide seats, extra headroom and legroom—*plus* those vital engineering features that make Nash cars run smoother and "sweeter" for years.

Go to your Nash dealer. See how much more Nash gives you for your money. Then you'll know *why* thousands are changing to Nash.

From Actual Photograph of Nash Ambassador Six 4-Door Sedan with trunk

NASH

DELIVERED PRICES! *Go Nash delivered price. Compare with sale-price, low but Nash saves you money. Delivered price about a new light on the remarkable value Nash is offering this year. Easy budget plans. Terms low as $18 monthly. Automatic Cruising Gear available on all models at slight extra cost.*

ASK ABOUT THE CONVENIENT TERMS AND LOW RATES AVAILABLE THROUGH THE NASH-C. I. T. BUDGET PLAN

NASH LAFAYETTE-"400" *117-inch wheelbase* **NASH AMBASSADOR SIX** *121-inch wheelbase* **NASH AMBASSADOR EIGHT** *125-inch wheelbase*

ON THE AIR! Floyd Gibbons as Master of Ceremonies with Vincent Lopez and Orchestra. Famous guest stars! C. B. S. stations coast to coast every Saturday, 9 P. M. EST. Tune in!

1937 X-RAY SYSTEM NOW READY! The first complete summary available to the public of all the facts about all the new cars. Reveals some astonishing differences in cars of the same price. See it at any Nash showroom. Buy with your eyes open this year!

Buick, 1937 ◄   Studebaker, 1937   Nash, 1937

Nash, 1937

Chevrolet, 1937

De Soto, 1937

International Trucks, 1937

A NEW SERVANT OF TRANSPORTATION FOR RAIL AND HIGHWAY

THE AUTO-RAILER "HANDYMAN" TO THE RAILROADS..
Serves a Hundred Uses with Flexibility, Safety and Unprecedented Economy

Operating on steel rails, the rubber tires of the Auto-Railer have six times the relative traction of steel wheels! This fact alone makes the Auto-Railer a highly efficient railroad unit. Its low first cost, plus remarkable operating economy when compared to conventional rail equipment, enables the railroads to compete effectively with buses and trucks for traffic on short hauls.

Equally at home on rails or highways, the Auto-Railer can move from one to the other in just a few seconds by a simple adjustment of the retractable pilot wheels, which are lowered for rail travel and raised for highway travel. Manufactured as a locomotive, as a freight-carrying unit, as a passenger coach or as a vehicle for maintenance and light service work, the Auto-Railer saves time and money in many different ways. It accomplishes store-door pickup and delivery without expensive re-handling of loads. Likewise, continuous point-to-point transporta-tion of passengers, using both city streets and rails, is now available for interurban service.

Railroads are now using Auto-Railer locomotives for switch-engine and short-line use—in average day-to-day train service the locomotive will handle 8 to 14 freight cars. Automotive economy and flexibility are now brought to the railroads by the same company which for more than twenty years has supplied a large percentage of their loading and shipping requirements.

PRODUCTS MANUFACTURED: Auto-Loaders . . . Auto-Railers . . . Auto-Shifters . . . Auto-Stops . . . Automobile Loading Materials . . . Battery Separators . . . Thermerons . . . Wood Block Flooring . . . Evanair Heaters . . . Ventilating-Heating Systems . . . Venetian Blind Materials • PLANTS: Bandon, Oregon . . . Detroit, Michigan . . . Marshfield, Oregon . . . Brighton, Michigan . . . Jackson, Mississippi . . . Vancouver, British Columbia . . . Coquille, Oregon

EVANS PRODUCTS COMPANY. Detroit, Michigan
Products engineered for Safer, more Economical and Efficient Transportation

Evans Products Co., 1935

BOTH HAVE

Rhythm

AND PERFECT PERFORMANCE

The world applauds the perfect performance. Perfect performances don't "just happen." For twenty-five years, the Electric Auto-Lite Company has been the foremost builder of Starting, Lighting and Ignition systems for the leading motor cars of America. . . . With this record of knowledge and experience, Auto-Lite engineers now introduce the perfected spark plug —the final link in perfect ignition performance—the Auto-Lite Spark Plug, Ignition Engineered by Ignition Engineers. Now you can get the most out of motoring—Greater Economy, Increased Acceleration and —Perfect Performance. Replace with Auto-Lite Spark Plugs today. Merchandising Division, The Auto-Lite Company, Toledo, Ohio.

AUTO-LITE SPARK PLUGS

Ignition Engineered by Ignition Engineer

International Six-Wheeler with dump body of Boulder-Dam type. Armor-plate shield protects cab and driver.

The ALL-STEEL CAB— one of the many advanced features in the new International line. Illustration at the right shows the interior of the roomy, well-appointed de luxe cab. Driver comfort, clear vision, and safety are assured in every International model, Half-Ton up.

THE *New* INTERNATIONAL

Heavy-duty champion of the truck world at the top of his form—another of the new Internationals, a powerful six-wheeler shown with armored dump body.

International Harvester presents to users of trucks the latest and finest products of its automotive plants—trucks at the peak of today's efficiency with a styling of exterior that is yours to judge. *All the new Internationals are as NEW in engine and chassis, in structural refinement, in every vital detail, as they are NEW in streamlined distinction for the highway. All are ALL-TRUCK, and all are as modern as today's fine cars.*

The International line offers a trim, streamlined unit for the Half-Ton field and a wide range of sizes for every type of load and hauling requirement. Here at the far end of the *complete line* is a truck for big tonnage, brute performance, and economy on an impressive scale—a finer product for the heavy-duty field to which International sells *twice as many trucks as any other manufacturer.*

See the new Internationals. Whatever your own exact hauling needs, there is the right model and size awaiting your pleasure in the new array of trucks now on display at all International branch and dealer showrooms.

INTERNATIONAL HARVESTER COMPANY
606 S. Michigan Ave. (INCORPORATED) Chicago, Illinois

Read what this driver writes:

International Harvester Company,
Chicago, Ill.

As one of the drivers in the Payne fleet at Grand Coulee Dam, I was very much interested in your recent ad on the subject.

I am majoring in mechanical engineering at the University of Washington. I earn my expenses driving and repairing heavy trucks during vacations and other times. I have worked for practically all of the major trucking contractors in this part of the country, driving all the more popular brands of heavy dump trucks.

I am a most enthusiastic booster for the International six-wheelers. I drove the one belonging to Goodfellow Bros., Wenatchee, Wash., during its term of operation at Coulee Dam. Operating side by side with other dual-drives, the International was invariably picked for the toughest assignments. It became known without question as the toughest, most dependable, yet cheapest truck to operate per yard-mile of any truck on the project.

Yours respectfully,

Seattle, Wash.   Harold T. Smith
February 13, 1937   4014 Brooklyn St.

INTERNATIONAL TRUCK

HERE WE ARE.... *ENVYING*

Did we envy the Dexters in their new Packard? The honest answer is...*yes!* Emphatically, *yes!* We had always wanted a Packard. We felt we'd almost give our good right arms to be sitting there like the Dexters, heads in the clouds, with people saying "Hmm, they sure must be making good."...Then

we got to thinking—I made as much as Ed Dexter. If he could afford a Packard, why couldn't I? Well, why *couldn't* I?...So we marched down to the Packard showroom to look at the new Packard 120 and the new Packard Six, and to ask a lot of questions...

HERE WE ARE.... *BEING ENVIED*

And as a result, we're no longer on the outside, envying. We're on the *inside* being envied. On the inside of our new Packard. We found out that our old car took full care of down payment, and that this new Packard was ours for only *$35 a month!* We've found out it costs no more to service than the small car we

used to own. You can't imagine the kick we're getting out of owning and driving a Packard. We're as thrilled as a couple of kids. And we're telling our friends to get wise...to learn how easy it is now to *be* the man who owns one!

★ ASK THE MAN WHO OWNS ONE ★

General Motors Trucks, 1937

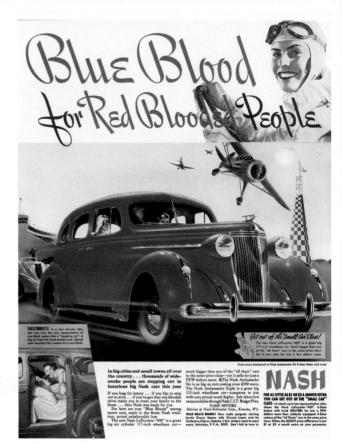

Nash, 1937

Pontiac, 1937

▶ De Soto, 1936

FLORIDA HIGHLIGHTS

SKETCHED IN AND AROUND MIAMI BY FLOYD DAVIS

THE NATION'S SOCIAL CAPITAL moves South. And social leaders coming for rest find themselves caught in a furious round of revelry...the gayest season Florida has seen since the Twenties.

LONG ISLAND MALLET STARS arrive *via Airflow* to try the turf of Florida's leading polo center ...the scenic Phipps Fields at Gulf Stream. The Sunday games are always gala events.

YACHTSMAN CARTER divides his life between boat and DeSoto Airflow III. "Every one," he says, "should have the safety of Airflow's genuine hydraulic brakes, steel unit frame-and-body."

THE MOTORING THRILL THAT'S STILL UNMATCHED

TWO YEARS AGO, DeSoto introduced the famous Airflow car...predicted that *all* cars would follow its lead.

Today, its scientific weight distribution...equalized springing...seating for six ... are still the most talked-about features in cars. And many are the efforts to copy them.

But any DeSoto owner will quickly tell you...America's lowest-priced Airflow car is *still* years ahead.

Spend a few minutes with DeSoto's Airflow III. Feel the utter relaxation of travel that's silent, swift and sure ...on any road, at any speed. Test the economy of its Gas-Saver Transmission. See the charming intimacy of its custom-styled interiors...the new beauty of its extended front and modern trunk.

Sedan or coupe, $1095, list at factory, Detroit. Special equipment extra. Ask about the new 6% Time Payment Plan.

DE SOTO
Product of the Chrysler Corporation

Airflow III

Companion Car to Airstream DeSoto

MIAMI'S SPORTING calendar is studded with sailing events, which reach their climax in the annual St. Petersburg Race, held late in March.

DANCING AT THE DEAUVILLE...and demonstrating the mode in wide-cut evening frocks. Slippers are in vivid reds, greens and blues.

Nash is Winning the Women's Vote!

GOOD TASTE! The beautiful simplicity of Nash design is winning with people of discriminating taste

Car illustrated is Nash Ambassador Six 4-Door Sedan.

WHEN YOU'RE GOING PLACES you'll appreciate the 13 cu. ft. of space in this extra large trunk. Enough room for all the luggage you'll ever need to take along. Trunks are standard equipment on all Nash sedans ... no extra charge!

WOMEN were the first to notice it. Men were quick to agree. Nash is smartly styled without being "tricky" or "freakish". Everywhere it's winning people of *good taste!*

And plus all its style and smartness, the new Nash LaFayette-"400" is now more than sixteen feet long from bumper to bumper. It gives you extra headroom, elbow room, legroom.

The Nash Ambassador Six is now an extra long 121-inch wheelbase car,

the Eight has a 125-inch wheelbase. Both cars give you the surging power of the famous Nash Twin Ignition engine. And all Nash cars give you oversized hydraulic brakes, steel bodies, plus a list of costly engineering features. See the new X-Ray system now at all Nash Showrooms.

NASH SPEED SHOW Floyd Gibbons as M. C. with Vincent Lopez and his Orchestra. Famous guest stars of stage, screen, radio. C.B.S. stations coast to coast Saturday, 9 P.M. EST. Tune in!

NASH $595 AND UP*

All prices f. o. b. factory. Special equipment extra. Automatic Cruising Gear available on all models at slight extra cost. NEW NASH-C. I. T. BUDGET PLAN. Low, convenient terms.
IMPORTANT! ALL PRICES SUBJECT TO CHANGE WITHOUT NOTICE!

NASH LaFAYETTE-"400" $595 and up*
117-inch wheelbase

NASH AMBASSADOR SIX $755 and up*
121-inch wheelbase

NASH AMBASSADOR EIGHT $855 and up*
125-inch wheelbase

Nash, 1937

▶ *Oldsmobile, 1937*

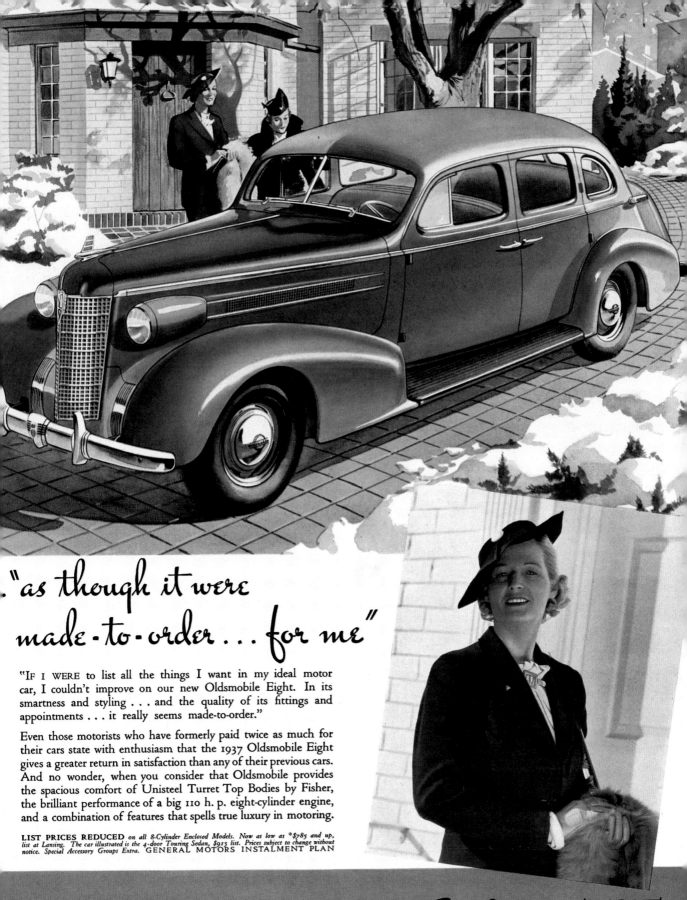

Wayne Computing Pumps, 1937

De Soto, 1937

International Trucks, 1937

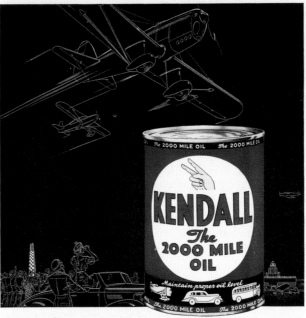

Kendall Refining Co., 1937

LINCOLN-ZEPHYR V·12

TRAVEL THE MODERN WAY!

RUNNING in luxury through blue waters, a modern ruler of the seas joins two continents in four days. . . . Cleaving white highways, a modern ship of the land, the LINCOLN-ZEPHYR, brings far places together with an ease not known before!

This car has four wheels, but there the similarity between the LINCOLN-ZEPHYR and others ends. The LINCOLN-ZEPHYR is different in design, different in the way it behaves on the roads, different in its effect upon owners. People talk about this advanced type of transportation as they talk about a fine horse, a trip abroad, a new home. Something stimulating has come into their lives!

First in their conversation is the LINCOLN-ZEPHYR engine. It has twelve cylinders in V-style, develops 110 horsepower. It gives 14 to 18 miles to the gallon, an extraordinary record. But this is an extraordinary car! From the unique all-steel body and frame combined in a single piece, to the inclusion of so many fine-car features, the car stands out in *value* as it stands out along a country-club driveway.

Have you thought, up to now, that all cars are basically alike? *Travel the modern way!* Lincoln Motor Company, builders of Lincoln and Lincoln-Zephyr V-12 motor cars.

Lincoln, 1937

▶ *De Soto, 1936*

A NOSE FOR NEWS!

THAT'S WHY LOWELL THOM PICKS DESOTO AS CAR OF YI

EVENT 32
1st PLACE 4

America's Ace Radio Commentator has a Big Story about his new De Soto Car

"It's AMERICA'S SMARTEST low-priced car!" That's the motor news of the year—flashed to you by De Soto-owner Lowell Thomas.

Here's what he says: "The great new De Soto is news because it *interests* people. It attracted thousands at the auto shows and it's being talked about all over America! I'm certainly sold on mine!"

No wonder! This great car is more luxurious than ever...both inside and out. Faster pick-up...easier han-dling...bigger, *genuine* hydraulic brakes...more comfort-able Safety Interior...the year's smartest styling—every

great new De Soto feature is a page one headline

And here's the best news yet: De Soto is price a few dollars above the lowest! This *big* car a costs no more to run than most *small* cars!

It's easy to own! See your De Soto dealer. D DIVISION OF CHRYSLER CORPORATION, Detroit,

"LOWELL, YOUR NEW DE SOTO CERTAINLY LOOKS GREAT!"

"IT IS—YET IT'S PRICED JUST ABOVE THE LOWEST!"

IT'S AMERICA'S SMARTEST LOW-PRICED CAR

QUICK FACTS: 1. "Lightning-fast" pick-up... Improved 93-h.p. "Economy Engine." 2. Patented Floating Power engine mountings. 3. Longer wheelbase...119 inches. 4. Bigger hydraulic brakes. 5. Easier shifting. 6. Safety-steel body rubber-mounted on a bigger, stronger frame. 7. Luxurious Safety Interior. 8. "Cush-ioned" ride with airplane-type shock-absorbers. 9. Easier steering...no "road-shock." Ask for Official Commercial Credit Company Finance Plan.

TUNE IN MAJOR BOWES' AMATEUR HOUR—COLUMBIA NETWORK—THURSDAYS, 9 TO 10 P. M., E. S. T.

SEE YOUR DE SOTO DEALER

FOR A
GREAT CAR, FINE SERVIC
AND A SQU Rd DEAL

A DISTINGUISHED OLD NAME
ON A BRILLIANT NEW CAR :

NEW HUPMOBILES FOR 1938! A Six and a Custom Six—each on a 122" wheelbase, each powered by another famous Hupp engine, of 101 hp. A bigger, more luxurious Custom Eight—on a full 125" wheelbase, with a rugged, responsive, 120-horsepower, eight-in-line engine. Smooth, flashing performance and owner-satisfying economy reach new highs in these brilliant new Hupps. Safe, all-steel bodies, double-action hydraulic brakes, extra-roomy interiors, and super-width doors feature every model.

STEP UP WITH HUPP
The 1938 Hupmobiles are *now* on display in Hupp dealers' showrooms everywhere! And these new cars, like all their famous forebears, will be enthusiastically welcomed by *their own* public—those for whom Hupmobiles are especially designed and built.

For no Hupmobile was ever planned like a variety show—to please everybody —to meet every purse. Hupmobiles have always had a distinctive clientele. Hupp builds for those who want a bigger car, one more luxurious in its roominess and appointments, modern without being extreme in its body lines, built to last for years and yet modestly priced in the middle brackets.

The 1938 Hupmobiles are for those people. If you are one of them—if you are tired of the cars that the millions drive—if you can't recognize your own in a parking lot without reading the license number—see and drive the *distinctive* 1938 Hupmobile. Or if you are tired of paying fancy prices for the power and weight and room and precision-built excellence you demand, and yet want a *fine* car with a famous name, see and drive the big 1938 Hupmobile.

These brilliant new cars are better looking, better performing and more comfortable, safe and enduring than any previous Hupmobile. Anyone who *ever* owned a Hupp will tell you that is saying a great deal!

HUPP MOTOR CAR CORPORATION, DETROIT, MICHIGAN

"HUPP HAS ALWAYS BUILT A GOOD CAR"

THE 1938 HUPMOBILE
SIXES and EIGHTS

Hupmobile, 1937

The Girl Delivers the Message...
INTERNATIONALS
DELIVER THE GOODS

Everywhere you go, smiling girls remind you of "the pause that refreshes" with ice-cold bottles of Coca-Cola. And have you noticed, too, how people turn to look at the Internationals that are used to deliver Coca-Cola? This eye-arresting quality is a real prestige builder in the bottled beverage business.

On top of that, Internationals deliver Coca-Cola on a rock-bottom economy basis. More and more businesses with years of hauling experience are turning to International Trucks.

Sound ALL-TRUCK construction in every model of the complete International line insures low operating costs in every hauling field. And from lowered costs come increased profits—*plus the prestige* of International Trucks. Traveling advertisements for your business!

If the hauling of any type of load is a load on your mind, it will pay you to get an International demonstration. The International dealer or branch in your city will work it out for you without obligation.

INTERNATIONAL HARVESTER COMPANY
180 North Michigan Avenue · Chicago, Illinois

International Cab-Over-Engine Model D-300—the ideal truck for this work in crowded traffic. Short turning radius, maximum loading space, perfected load distribution, and a completely comfortable cab make this truck a stand-out in the low-price 1½-ton field.

INTERNATIONAL TRUCKS

International Trucks, 1938

STUDEBAKER'S CROWNING ACHIEVEMENT
NEW 1938 STUDEBAKERS
Lowest priced Commander...lowest priced President... in Studebaker history and a new Six...the greatest dollar values Studebaker has ever offered

YOU PAY SO LITTLE FOR SO MUCH MORE

STUDEBAKER, world's oldest vehicle manufacturer, dramatizes its eighty-sixth consecutive year with three great new 1938 automobiles . . . three glamorous new luxury cars that emphasize low price!

Studebaker has spent millions to give you three 1938 Studebakers that are completely new in every vigorous, flowing line . . . original creations of the world's foremost designers and finest craftsmen . . . strikingly different in appearance and appeal . . . and brilliantly representative of the operating economy for which Studebaker is famed.

In these new low-priced luxury cars, Studebaker, for the first time in the history of automobiles, introduces solid, symmetrical, balanced design that is as functional and devoid of meaningless ornamentation as the rhythmical clean-cut architecture of the modern skyscraper.

New Miracle Ride plus many brilliant innovations!
You have more wonderful new things to see and to try in these great new Studebakers of 1938 than you have ever found in any new automobiles.

All models combine Independent Planar Wheel Suspension with finest Hydraulic Shock Absorbers to give you the unforgettably comfortable Studebaker Miracle Ride. All models have Exceptionally Wide New Interiors, New Oversize Luggage Compartments, New Non-Slam Safety Door Latches, New Flat Transmission Gears, New Acceleration and Hill-climbing Performance and the Improved 1938 Fram Oil and Motor Cleaner. The Automatic Hill Holder is standard on the Commander and President. The New Studebaker Miracle Shift and Gas-Saving Automatic Overdrive are available on the Commander and President at slight extra cost.

Cars that bring luxury down to earth in price!
Only by seeing and driving these three great new luxury cars of 1938 can you do justice to them or to yourself.

In the face of rising prices, Studebaker has invested millions of dollars in dies, tools and new equipment and succeeded in making these great new 1938 cars the greatest dollar values that have ever glorified the Studebaker name.

There's so much to discover, so much to admire, you'll want to spend a lot of time getting acquainted with everything they offer for so little. Purchasable on Studebaker's C.I.T. budget plan. Studebaker Corporation, South Bend, Indiana.

NEW MIRACLE RIDE · NEW FLAT TRANSMISSION GEARS · NON-SLAM SAFETY DOOR LATCHES · EXTRA ROOMY LUXURY INTERIORS · OVERSIZE LUGGAGE COMPARTMENTS · SAFETY GLASS ALL AROUND · FRAM OIL AND MOTOR CLEANER · NEW SUPER-STRONG FRAMES · BRILLIANT NEW ACCELERATION AND HILL-CLIMBING PERFORMANCE · AUTOMATIC HILL HOLDER STANDARD ON COMMANDER AND PRESIDENT · NEW MIRACLE SHIFT AND GAS-SAVING AUTOMATIC OVERDRIVE AVAILABLE ON COMMANDER AND PRESIDENT AT SLIGHT EXTRA COST

De Soto, 1937 ◄ *Studebaker, 1937*

243

GMC

1½-2 TON
CAB-OVER-ENGINE

½-TON

¾-TON

1½-2 TON

3-TON

From the SMALLEST to the LARGEST

5-TON

8-TON

and all with the same Good Name

General Motors trucks and trailers overspread the entire field of commercial haulage. If you have no everyday trucking problem but only occasional loads to haul, use the new GMC "Trailabout" which attaches to your car! For *half-ton* trucks with most spacious bodies—see GMC! For all *medium-duty* haulage, check both the *standard* GMC models and the new *cab-over-engine* types with their almost unbelievable advantages! For cumbersome, weighty loads, enlist the strong-backed "heavy" GMC's! And the *matched* GMC tractor-trailer combinations meet all other needs! Also important—*GMC prices now crowd the lowest!*

Time payments through our own Y. M. A. C. Plan at lowest available rates

GENERAL MOTORS TRUCKS & TRAILERS

GENERAL MOTORS TRUCK & COACH, DIVISION OF YELLOW TRUCK & COACH MANUFACTURING CO., PONTIAC, MICH.

12-TON

General Motors, 1937

▶ *Autocar Trucks, 1937*

A low-priced, light-duty truck is one thing . . . but a medium-priced, light-duty Autocar is a thing apart.

"FOLLOW THE LEADERS FOR THEY KNOW THE WAY"

UTOCAR TRUCKS, Ardmore, Pa. *Branches in Leading Cities*

The new 1938 Packard Eight

The Touring Sedan, one of the nine beautiful Packard Eight models for 1938

TEAR OUT THESE CLAIMS .. AND MAKE US PROVE THEM!

This year, be a cynic.

Say that no car could be as good as we claim the new Packard Six and the new Packard Eight to be. Tear out the following claims, bring them to a Packard showroom. Say: *"I dare you to make good on these statements"*...

For the new Packard Six and Eight, we claim...

1 That these new Packards give you the *gentlest* ride you ever had in a motor car; that they make bad roads seem smooth, and smooth roads seem even smoother than they are. *Make us prove it.*

2 That Packard has designed an exclusive new rear suspension which, through a combination of ingenious engineering principles, now gives the *rear wheels* the superb riding effect of independent wheel suspension. *Make us prove it.*

3 That increasing the wheelbase of the Six from 115 to 122 inches, and the Eight from

120 to 127 inches; that adding more beautiful interiors... have made these cars the most luxurious ever offered at their respective prices. *Make us prove it.*

4 That Packard, working with a great University, has developed the first really quiet all-steel body with an all-steel top. *Make us prove it.*

5 That these cars have a new feeling of security on curves and wet pavements, that side-away on turns is minimized, that the danger of skidding is reduced. *Make us prove it.*

6 With normal mileage you need to lubricate these cars only twice a year, and then at only 15 points. *Make us prove it.*

7 That these new Packards are the only cars in their price classes to offer *both* long mechanical life and long style life. *Make us prove it.*

8 That if you ride in a Packard, you'll want one more than you have ever wanted any car. *Make us prove it.*

9 That you—right now—can afford one. *Make us prove it.*

These are our statements—and we mean every word of them. Your nearest Packard dealer is waiting for you to come in and challenge them.

1938 PACKARD SIX & EIGHT*

Formerly called the Packard 120

Each Tuesday night at 9:30 E.S.T. over the NBC Coast-to-Coast Red Network, Lanny Ross and Charles Butterworth have as their guest one of the topmost stars of radio, stage or screen. Don't miss Packard's big star-studded full hour show.

ASK THE MAN WHO OWNS ONE

Packard, 1937

FOR AMERICA'S FIRST FAMILIES

FOR THOSE whose prestige in the community calls for a car in keeping with their position . . .

For those whose importance and responsibilities demand the utmost in safety, comfort and quiet . . .

In short, for all those to whom a motor car is more than mere transportation . . .

Packard presents the 1938 edition of the motor cars that have been the choice of America's first families for more than a quarter of a century.

You will find them roomier, more luxurious than ever—the safest, quietest, most comfortable cars in the world . . .

SOCIALLY—AMERICA'S *FIRST* MOTOR CAR

Packard, 1937

MEET HUDSON FOR 1938

HUDSON *Terraplane* · HUDSON *Six* · HUDSON *Eight*

117-INCH WHEELBASE . . . 96 AND 101 HORSEPOWER   122-INCH WHEELBASE . . . 101 AND 107 HORSEPOWER WITH SIX STAR MOTOR   122 AND 129-INCH WHEELBASE . . . 122 HORSEPOWER

3 Brilliant New Cars

That cost you less for what you get than any other cars in the world!

BIGGER ★ ROOMIER ★ WITH NEW LUXURY ★ NEW DRIVING EASE

Today, Hudson proudly announces three really unusual new automobiles . . . all under the Hudson banner.

With prices starting close to the very lowest, these new Hudsons have been designed from the ground up with the one idea of giving you more for your money than you can get anywhere else. Each of them, we believe, tosses overboard every previous idea as to what its price should buy.

Each brings you brilliant new style and luxury,

and more size and room than ever . . . backed by performance, economy and long life hard to match no matter how much more you might pay.

And, in a year when automatic gear shifting is the brand new feature of other cars, Hudson's Selective Automatic Shift Transmission . . . made greater still for 1938 . . . stands alone as the only automatic shift that has proved itself in three years of use, by over 150,000 owners and more than a billion miles of driving.

When you meet the three new Hudsons for 1938, at any of thousands of Hudson showrooms, it is our confident belief that you will meet cars unequalled anywhere for downright *value*. Then *drive* Hudson for the biggest, happiest surprise of your motoring life. And . . . best of all . . . see how little it costs to own a Hudson. America's No. 1 Cars!

Complete line of new 1938 Hudson Terraplane Business Cars also on display

IT'S "BARGAIN YEAR" IN HUDSON SHOWROOMS

NEW LUXURY INTERIORS *and* A STYLE IDEA NEVER SEEN BEFORE!
1938's GREATEST DRIVING FEATURE . . NEW SELECTIVE AUTOMATIC SHIFT TRANSMISSION

(Optional at low extra cost . . . conventional gear shift available at no cost if desired)

(LEFT) A hint of the ultra modern style . . . with contrasting chromium trim . . . in Hudson Six and Eight models . . . while the Hudson Eight Custom series and the big Country Club Sedan present an even more luxurious style design. Again, in Hudson Terraplane . . . new and different luxury interiors! The art of leading designers has been at work on every detail of every model . . . seat widths, leg and head room, fabrics, finish, fittings . . . combining beauty with thoughtful attention to your comfort and convenience.

(RIGHT) Shift by merely flicking a finger up at the wheel and lifting your toe from the accelerator. You never need to use the clutch pedal. Yet shift to any gear you want, at any car or engine speed. Enjoy a clear floor in front . . . no gear or brake levers to stumble over.

Hudson, 1937

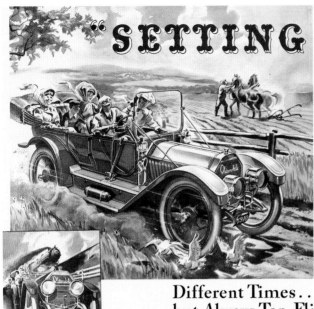

"SETTING THE PACE!"

Different Times.. ..Different Models
but Always Top-Fli ght Performance!

IN 1901, when a young mechanic drove a curved-dash Oldsmobile runabout from Detroit to New York in the extraordinary time of seven and one-half days, Oldsmobile was setting the pace. In 1905, when two curved-dash Oldsmobiles flashed 4,400 miles across the continent in exactly 44 days, Oldsmobile re-

corded another pace-setting performance. And in 1910, when the powerful, rugged Oldsmobile Limited gave mastery of the road to thousands of owners throughout America, Oldsmobile's reputation as a pace-setting car was carried to still greater heights. Today, Oldsmobile's 1938 Six and Eight are winning fresh laurels for

advanced engineering . . . for dashing, resourceful, economical action. And with the development and introduction of Oldsmobile's new Automatic Safety Transmission, which opens an entire new realm of flashing, flowing performance, Oldsmobile steps out ahead again . . . as the car that is setting the pace!

FREE SHEET MUSIC!
"In My Merry Oldsmobile," the popular waltz song of 1905 and today a favorite in radio and pictures, has recently been reprinted both in waltz and fox-trot tempo. For a free souvenir copy of the sheet music, write to Oldsmobile, Department M, Lansing, Michigan.

Sensation of Its Day! The "Oldsmobile Limited" of 1910 set the style and luxury and performance trends of its times. Celebrated for its power, its brute strength and its silken smoothness, the lines and action of this sturdy Oldsmobile touring model have been preserved to posterity in that most famous of all automobile paintings, "Setting the Pace," by William Harnden Foster.

Sensation of Today! The 1938 Oldsmobile—the Eight above and the Six below—again step out ahead in Style-Leader styling and in all the modern features for comfort, convenience and safety. The painting, just above, is a modern companion piece to Foster's "Setting the Pace" and, like its famous predecessor, suggests the top-flight performance for which Oldsmobile cars have long been noted.

OLDSMOBILE

1897 *America's Oldest Motor Car Manufact urer Celebrates Its 40th Anniversary.* **1937**

Oldsmobile, 1937

Simple as ABC
to pick a *Good* Used Car

A Go to your OLDSMOBILE dealer

B Look for the orange *Safety-Tested* used car tag

C Note the Special Bargain Prices

OLDSMOBILE DEALERS
now offer "*Safety-Tested*" Used Cars
in many makes · many models · all on easy terms

NOW you can buy a used car with utmost confidence! The special, orange-colored Safety-Tested Tag, used by Oldsmobile dealers throughout America as the mark of a good used car, is your assurance of sound and reliable value. Go to your nearest Oldsmobile dealer at once and examine his splendid stock of Safety-Tested Used Cars. You will find he is offering

choice selections of the popular 1935 and 1936 Oldsmobiles, as well as late-model cars of other makes. Many of these cars embody such modern features as Knee-Action Wheels, Hydraulic Brakes and Turret Top Bodies. Many have been driven but a few thousand miles. All are specially priced for quick sale and immediate delivery. Act now, and get the pick of them all!

Safety-Tested MEANS
that the car which carries the Safety-Tested Tag has been carefully inspected, and reconditioned where necessary, with regard to the features that make for safe driving—tires, brakes, steering, engine and electrical system—as indicated by your Oldsmobile dealer's check marks appearing on the Safety-Tested Tag.

LOOK IN THE CLASSIFIED SECTION OF YOUR TELEPHONE DIRECTORY FOR THE NAME OF YOUR NEAREST OLDSMOBILE DEALER!

Oldsmobile, 1937

CADILLAC leads the *world*
in the field above $1500!

Model illustrated—Cadillac Series 60 5-Passenger Touring Sedan, $1660

Cadillac sells more cars priced above $1500 than any other motor car manufacturer in the world.

In fact, Cadillac sells almost as many cars in this price field as all the other American manufacturers combined. This has been true for a long time—and it is increasingly true today.

Surely, here is the final proof of how America ranks its motor cars. Seven builders offer cars in this field—and the buyer can take his choice.

Cadillac is made the big favorite for an obvious reason—an unchallenged reputation for prestige, quality and performance.

Always, Cadillac has held to its standards. Not once has its name been given to a car in the lower price range.

Yet, due to advanced manufacturing practices, Cadillac has been able to lower its prices drastically. The Cadillac Series "60" today costs approximately half what a Cadillac cost four years ago.

Why not ask your dealer to demonstrate this remarkable car? Learn for yourself why Cadillac leads the world in the quality field!

$1555 AND UP

Delivered price at Detroit, Michigan, subject to change without notice. Prices include all standard accessories. Transportation, State and Local Sales Taxes, Optional Accessories and Equipment—Extra.

Cadillac, 1937

Two New Beauties!

BETTER *Engineered* ... BETTER *Made!*

Chrysler for 1938

CHRYSLER Royal
MORE FOR THE MONEY
IN THE LOW-PRICED FIELD!

CHRYSLER Imperial
PHENOMENAL PERFORMANCE
AT A REMARKABLE PRICE!

BIGGER . . . and a beauty. That's the new Chrysler Royal for 1938. Three inches more wheelbase than the 1937 Royal which invaded the low-priced field with such spectacular success.

Look at that proud, commanding radiator . . . the jewel-like modeling of the radiator grille . . . the graceful union of hood and fenders and streamlined headlamps.

Inside, beauty greets you again. The instrument panel sets the keynote . . . rich, smart, luxurious . . . blending in color harmony with the striking new steering wheel and its ring-type horn control . . . complementing the superb upholstery in new short-nap mohair or broadcloth.

A new, larger 95 horsepower Gold Seal engine . . . amazingly thrifty . . . silky smooth with Floating Power.

Glorious roominess! 119 inches of wheelbase. 96¼ inches from windshield to rear window! A 49 inch rear seat! The most spacious luggage capacity you ever saw!

High-priced riding comfort! Safety *All-Steel* Bodies . . . time-tested hydraulic brakes . . . finger-touch steering . . . toe-touch stopping . . . synchronized gear-shifting. A big, beautiful, luxurious car that tops everything in the low-priced field.

The Luxurious Imperial

The beautiful, high-powered Chrysler Imperial for 1938! More fine car for the money than America has ever seen!

Long famous as Chrysler's top-rank-ing car, the magnificent Imperial is now in the medium-priced field.

The proud, commanding beauty that comes from added length and size! Wheelbase increased to 125 inches . . . for low-swung smartness and grace . . . for the roominess of true fine-car luxury.

Deep, wide, chair-high seats! Beautiful appointments! Matchless riding ease . . . the buoyant, gliding smoothness of longer wheelbase . . . balanced weight distribution . . . independently sprung front wheels . . . slow-recoil springs and Aero Hydraulic Shock Absorbers.

Under that long, impressive hood, the electrifying response of 110 horse-power . . . cradled by Floating Power.

The safety and reliability of Chrysler great engineering features . . . all at their finest expression. Safety *All-Steel* Bodies . . . hydraulic brakes . . . steering and gear-shifting perfection that makes this big, powerful car as effortless as the breeze.

See this great, new Imperial . . . you'll thrill to its beauty . . . marvel at its price.

* * *

Easy to buy on convenient terms with the official Commercial Credit Company plan.

☆ **NEW 1938 ROYAL** . . . 95 horsepower, 119-inch wheelbase. Ten body types.

☆ **NEW 1938 IMPERIAL** . . . 110 horsepower, 125-inch wheelbase. Six body types.

☆ **NEW 1938 CUSTOM IMPERIAL** . . . 130 horsepower, 144-inch wheelbase. Three body types.

Tune in on Major Bowes, Columbia Network, every Thursday, 9 to 10:00 P. M., E. S.

★ CHRYSLER SWEEPS ON IN THE LOW-PRICED FIELD!

"WIFE TELLS HUSBAND AND *How!*"

The Lady ... wears a smart black moire afternoon dress. Dress and jewels from Bergdorf Goodman. The Car ... is a smart Chrysler Royal Sedan.

"JACK, you're in a rut! You're a man and you ought to know all about motor cars! But you don't, or you'd never be content with that antique chariot we ride around in. When we drive alongside one of those new Chryslers I turn simply green with envy!

"Can't you see the style and beauty of those tapered Airflow streamlines, with no headlamps sticking out in front and no bulging trunk breaking the rear-end sweep? You've never seen the inside...so you don't know about the gorgeous ivory plastic instrument panel and fittings... the beautiful upholstery and the great wide seats!

"You wouldn't know that the body is four inches wider at the windshield, with broad, uncluttered floors and plenty of room for those long legs of yours! And the biggest clear-vision windows!

"How much longer are you going to ask a 108-pound woman to drive a car she can't park? I want an easy-steering, easy-braking, easy-riding car like Chrysler! And I want a steering wheel gear-shift, too!

"Get up-to-date! Find out about superfinished parts and how they double engine life! Just drive a car once that really loves to GO!

"And look at the gas our old car burns! When I shop, I *shop* ... and I know that this Chrysler is modestly priced and very economical to operate. So, get out of the rut...let's buy a Chrysler!

1939 CHRYSLER ROYAL ... 100 horsepower, 119-inch wheelbase. **1939 CHRYSLER IMPERIAL** ...135 horsepower, 125-inch wheelbase. Also Chrysler's famous Custom Imperial in five and seven passenger sedans and limousines...with Chrysler's amazing new transmission advancement, the Fluid Drive. ★ Tune in on Major Bowes, Columbia Network, Every Thursday, 9 to 10 P.M., E. S. T.

BE WISE *Buy Chrysler!*

Chrysler, 1939

WAKE UP AND DRIVE THE SMARTEST CAR OF 1938!

Alice Faye skims over the hills back of Hollywood in her big new De Soto

A BEAUTIFUL GIRL and a beautiful car—both going places! Wherever you look you'll find it's true—smart people are picking this wonderful new De Soto!

The answer? Simple as ABC. Today, De Soto gives you *fine-car* features at *small-car* cost. Superb appearance...the luxury of a "cushioned" ride...thrilling performance...and plenty of room for six people!

You get "lightning-fast" pick-up with the improved 93-h.p. "Economy Engine." Easier shifting and easier steering—no "road-shock." Bigger hydraulic brakes stop you quickly, surely. You ride in a Safety-steel body rub-

ber-mounted on a stronger, heavier frame. This new De Soto gives you *plus*-value, right straight through!

Yet this *big* car is priced just above the lowest...and costs no more to run than most *small* cars! Don't wait any longer—see your De Soto dealer now! De Soto Division of CHRYSLER CORPORATION, Detroit, Michigan.

SEE YOUR DE SOTO DEALER
FOR A GREAT CAR, FINE SERVICE AND A SQUARE DEAL

It's America's Smartest Low-Priced Car

QUICK FACTS: 1. "Lightning-fast" pick-up. 2. Improved 93-h.p. "Economy Engine." 3. Patented Floating Power engine mountings. 4. Longer wheelbase...119 inches. 5. Bigger hydraulic brakes. 6. Easier shifting. 7. Luxurious Safety Interior. 8. "Cushioned" ride with airplane-type shock absorbers. 9. Easier steering...no "road-shock." Ask for the Commercial Credit Company Finance Plan.

TUNE IN MAJOR BOWES' AMATEUR HOUR—COLUMBIA NETWORK—THURSDAYS, 8 TO 9 P.M., E.S.T.

De Soto, 1937

Just arrived...and what a welcome it's getting

NEW STUDEBAKER
State President

OF COURSE, it's designed as if you had money to burn...but you don't need that kind of money to buy it...the refreshingly new Studebaker State President that came with this Spring and that's been going like the wind in sales! ★ The only fine car premium that's missing from this latest masterpiece of Studebaker structure and Helen Dryden styling is the customary fine car premium of high price! ★ It has fine car glow lamps on its fenders...fine car chromium strips on its running boards and sills...fine car custom pillow-type upholstery of the finest fine car fabrics...door latches that click lightly and tightly and silently...a gas-saving automatic overdrive that rests your engine and the outgo from your income besides! ★ Yet the price of this State President is just a shade above that of the low priced standard Studebaker President. And it's sold of course on the convenient Studebaker C.I.T. budget plan.

RIDE IN STATE IN A STATE PRESIDENT

Studebaker, 1937

WHEREVER SMART PEOPLE GATHER...

As the crowds leave America's smartest sporting events, more people drive off in large Packards than in any other fine car. It is a dramatic confirmation of a significant statistic—that nearly half of all the large fine cars being sold in America today are Packards.

PACKARD...SOCIALLY, AMERICA'S FIRST MOTOR CAR
• THE TWELVE • THE SUPER • EIGHT

Packard, 1937

A necessity in airplanes ...a big help in cars

Follow the lead of major air lines and fill your car's tank at pumps marked "Ethyl." Here you get—

1 More anti-knock fluid (containing lead tetraethyl) at pumps marked "Ethyl" than you get in the best regular-grade gasoline.

2 All-round quality (including quick starting) that is *double-tested*—by the oil company and by the Ethyl Gasoline Corporation.

3 100% performance from your high compression engine.

4 Saving on oil as well as gas by preventing knock and overheating.

More than 100,000 gasoline dealers say, "Our best grade is marked Ethyl."

NEXT TIME GET ETHYL...A BETTER RUN FOR YOUR MONEY

Ethyl, 1937   ▶ *Packard, 1937*

PRESENTING THE SENSATIONAL NEW

CADILLAC *Sixty* SPECIAL

THE NEWEST CAR IN THE WORLD

THERE HAS NEVER BEEN a car like the *new* Cadillac Sixty Special . . . a car with such definite modernity of line, yet so obviously right in taste . . . a precedent-breaking car prophetic of motor cars not yet on other drawing boards, yet a car wholly devoid of freakish trappings.

THERE HAS NEVER BEEN anything like the vivid, spirited performance of this car . . . with its inexhaustible vitality, its eager-flowing power, its quiet,

obedient responsiveness! There has never been anything like its inviting, all-embracing comfort . . . davenport seats, with extra width and extra depth. There has never been anything like the vision with which you drive the Cadillac Sixty Special . . . there is more outward vision than in any closed car ever built heretofore.

THERE ARE BOLD STROKES OF INSPIRED DESIGN in the Sixty Special. There are no runningboards

—you step right in, through doors of ge[...] width. From every angle—the Cadillac Sixty S[...] is, beyond dispute, *the newest car in the wor[...]*

IF YOU ARE TIRED OF THE COMMONPLACE —[...] want the only really different car of the year—[...] by all means accept our invitation to driv[...] matchless Cadillac Sixty Special. Its perfor[...] . . . in your own hands . . . will make the[...] extravagant description seem faint praise in[...]

There is also a new Cadillac Sixty in more conventional mold, and selling at a price we believe represents the greatest value in the motor car market. It differs from the Special in app[...] and appointment—it is one with the Special in quality and in performance. And as to performance . . . the Cadillac Sixty is unquestionably America's finest-performing eight cylinder car!

International Trucks, 1938

Ford, 1938

Cadillac, 1938 ◄ Daytonian Tires, 1938

MILLIONAIRES WILL BUY IT !

But you can easily afford it...
Actually, it costs you but little more
than the low-priced cars!

GRAHAM   NOW ON DISPLAY AT ALL GRAHAM SHOWROOMS

Graham, 1938   *► Plymouth, 1938*

Great Value at an A...

INVEST IN "THE CAR THAT STANDS UP BEST"

nazing Low Price !

you the *extra value* of "live" rubber mountings that block out road noise vibration..."radio studio"sound-proof-airplane-type shock-absorbers...and ted Floating Power engine mountings.

ere's *extra value* in Plymouth's safety, Plymouth's *double-action* hydraulic s stop you smoothly, safely. Around over you, under you, is the security of -steel body...welded into one rigid unit. e 1938 Plymouth steers faster, handles

easier...the windshield has 12% more vision. And the whole interior is Safety-Styled.

In every way, this is the greatest Plymouth ever built. You cannot know this car until you've ridden in it—driven it. See it today—and find out about Plymouth's great value. See any Dodge, De Soto or Chrysler dealer. PLYMOUTH DIVISION OF CHRYSLER CORPORATION, Detroit, Michigan.

TUNE IN MAJOR BOWES' AMATEUR HOUR...COLUMBIA NETWORK, THURSDAYS, 9 TO 10 P. M., E.S.T.

OS GREAT CARS

And you'll even like the price tag !

YOU'LL like the 1938 Standard Ford V-8. It's a better car in many ways than the 1937 Ford V-8 which was bought by more people than any other make.

You'll like its clean, new curves . . . its neatly tailored interiors . . . the easy way it starts and steers and stops. You'll like the privilege of picking the V-8 engine size you need . . . 85 horsepower for unusually high performance . . . 60 horsepower for unusually low operating cost. (Hundreds of "thrifty 60" owners report averages of 22 to 27 miles a gallon—or even more.)

Best of all, your liking for the Standard Ford will include the price tag! It is priced low—even for 1938—and its prices cover equipment for which you have too often had to pay extra. . . . You'll save money the day you buy your Standard Ford V-8 and every mile you drive it. You can bank on that.

F O R D   V · 8   F O R   1 9 3 8

The De Luxe Ford V-8 is built on the same chassis as the Standard, with the sa basic Ford features. It has richer appointments and a little more room in the seds. Above is the Club Coupe, which seats five inside and leaves a very large luggage sp

Ford, 1938

MASTER DE LUXE SPORT SEDAN
also available in Master model

MASTER DE LUXE TOWN SEDAN
also available in Master model

MASTER DE LUXE COACH
also available in Master model

MASTER DE LUXE SEDAN
also available in Master model

"You'll be AHEAD with a CHEVROLET !"

Take your choice of any one of these beautiful new Chevrolet models and you will own the choice motor car of the low-price field.

For only Chevrolet brings you all of Chevrolet's modern features at such low delivered prices and with such outstanding all-round economy.

1938 CHEVROLET

FOR 27 YEARS
CHEVROLET
THE SYMBOL OF SAVINGS

"THE CAR THAT IS COMPLETE"

Chevrolet, 1938

Every Motoring Family will applaud

"I'm glad we came in the Cadillac"

There is far more than mere coincidence in the fact that those who have "arrived" socially, so often arrive at social gatherings in . . . a Cadillac-Fleetwood!

To people of innate good taste, there is simply no substitute for Cadillac-Fleetwood. For these people know that no other car can bestow quite the same degree of enduring distinction as does a car built by

Cadillac, and appointed and embellished by Fleetwood.

The new Cadillac-Fleetwoods are a fitting climax to Cadillac's 36 years of building *only* fine cars. Their gracious beauty, spacious luxury, uncramped comfort, and their quiet, brilliant performance . . . make them, by far, the most magnificent V-8's in Cadillac history.

Why not drive one of these superb creations . . . soon?

Twelve individual body styles to express any preference are available on the new Cadillac-Fleetwood chassis.

Cadillac · Fleetwood
A GENERAL MOTORS VALUE

Cadillac, 1938

2 good reasons for stepping up to the V·8 class

THE two new 1938 Ford cars are different in appearance, appointments and price. But they have the same chassis, the same mechanical excellence, and the same basic Ford features.

Their modern V-8 power-plants provide smooth 8-cylinder satisfaction which only much more expensive cars can equal. 85 horsepower in the De Luxe Ford. A choice of 85 horsepower or 60 horsepower in the Standard Ford.

The De Luxe has more room in the Sedans and finer fittings. The Standard costs a little less to buy and, with the thrifty "60" engine, offers the lowest operating cost in Ford history.

Both of the new Ford cars are priced low. And both include, without extra charge, the equipment you need for driving comfort. Pick the one that meets your personal preferences, and step up to the V-8 class! . . . There's a Ford dealer near you.

Above, the Standard Ford V-8 Tudor . . . Below, the De Luxe Ford V-8 Fordor

THE TWO NEW FORD V·8 CARS FOR 1938

Ford, 1938

THERE'S *ADDED JOY* IN *ADDED CYLINDERS*

People who have never driven a twelve-cylinder car may think of it, primarily, as capable of high speed. The Lincoln-Zephyr is that, most certainly, but the joy of driving it comes in many ways. It has power in reserve. In traffic, or on the open road, it goes evenly and gently.

Every move of this powerful car inspires confidence and encourages better driving. New owners discover that familiar trips are made more quickly—but that they drive less fast than before. Having picked up an even pace, they maintain it—without pressure, without fatigue.

And many people who have never driven a twelve-cylinder car think of it as inherently expensive to operate. Lincoln-Zephyr performance is both efficient and economical. Owners report from 14 to 18 miles to the

gallon, under a wide variety of traffic, road and driving conditions; and up-keep cost is low because of sound design and precision manufacture.

Some people jump to the conclusion that the Lincoln-Zephyr must be an expensive car to buy. It is medium in price. Wholly new in beauty, in balance, in riding ease, and safety, this modern "twelve" is the only car of its kind at any price.

Choose from six handsome body types, including the two new convertibles, Sedan and Coupe. Lincoln Motor Company, builders of Lincoln and Lincoln-Zephyr V-12s.

Prices begin at $1395, delivered at Detroit factory. State and federal taxes extra. Sedan illustrated is $1395, delivered at Detroit factory; price includes white side-wall tires.

LINCOLN - ZEPHYR V·12

Texaco, 1938 ◄ Lincoln, 1938

Action!

To be a dozen places in a day . . . as you often are; to keep going with good grace and an eye on the clock . . . you need wings on your ankles or a Mercury 8 at your door!

The Mercury 8 is the fine new Ford-built motor car priced between the Ford V-8 and the Lincoln-Zephyr.

There's a serene elegance about this car that is thoroughly satisfying. It *looks* unhurried yet moves forward with fleet V-8 power.

It's long and low . . . as streamlined as a ribbon in the wind. And it's luxuriously large inside . . . completely cushioned for lounging . . . remarkably silenced for rest.

And *driving* this "Eight" is sheer delight! A Californian writes that "my wife is particularly pleased with the steering . . . makes the car so easy to park. On our first trip, we did better than 20 miles to the gallon of gasoline . . . in traffic, have not fallen below

17 miles to the gallon." The Mercury has money-sense along with style! As a lady of action, you'll phone for a demonstration.

MERCURY FEATURES SUMMED-UP

Streamlined length more than 16 feet over all on 116-inch wheelbase . . . Very wide, deep seats . . . Scientific soundproofing . . . Balanced weight and center-poise design for smooth riding . . . A 95-horsepower V-type 8-cylinder engine . . . Hydraulic brakes . . . Large and accessible luggage locker.

FORD MOTOR COMPANY—FORD, MERCURY, LINCOLN-ZEPHYR AND LINCOLN MOTOR CARS

MERCURY EIGHT

Mercury, 1939

THEODORA GOES WILD ABOUT HER NEW DESOTO

IRENE DUNNE, NOW STARRING IN THE RKO PICTURE "THE JOY OF LIVING" WITH HER NEW DESOTO.

Irene Dunne Demands Value and Economy— She Gets Both in this GREAT DE SOTO!

LOOK AT these two big reasons why smart car buyers are choosing De Soto: (1) VALUE—you get more for your automobile dollar. (2) OPERATING ECONOMY —De Soto fits in with today's budgets!

Think of it! You get faster pick-up with De Soto's 93-h.p. "Economy Engine." Greater safety, too, with its deeper, stronger frame and bigger, GENUINE hydraulic brakes. Greater comfort...with independent front wheel springing and airplane-type shock-absorbers that smooth even the roughest roads. Chrysler Corporation engineering gives you complete sound-proofing...Floating Power engine

mountings...effortless handling—DOZENS of FINE-CAR features that all add up to EXTRA VALUE!

De Soto is smart to LOOK AT and smart to OWN. This BIG car is now priced just above the lowest... costs no more to run than most SMALL cars! Investigate De Soto's EXTRA VALUE today! De Soto Division of Chrysler Corporation, Detroit, Michigan.

"YOUR NEW DE SOTO CERTAINLY IS A BIG CAR, MISS DUNNE!"

"BIG IN EVERYTHING BUT PRICE!"

IT'S AMERICA'S SMARTEST LOW-PRICED CAR
QUICK FACTS: 1. "Lightning-fast" pick-up...Improved 93-h.p. "Economy Engine." 2. Powered Floating Power engine mountings. 3. Longer wheelbase ...119 inches. 4. Bigger hydraulic brakes. 5. Easier shifting. 6. Safety-steel body rubber-mounted on a bigger, stronger frame. 7. Luxurious Safety Interior. 8. "Cushioned" ride with airplane-type shock-absorbers. 9. Easier steering....no "road-shock." See De Soto today —discover how easy it is to own this smart car.

TUNE IN MAJOR BOWES AMATEUR HOUR—COLUMBIA NETWORK—THURSDAYS, 9 TO 10 P.M., E.S.T.

SEE YOUR DE SOTO DEALER
FOR A
GREAT CAR, FINE SERVICE AND A SQUARE DEAL

De Soto, 1938

This year, greet Summer in a Lincoln-Zephyr

Now, under skies of water-color blue, outbound roads call the traveler. Change of season brings the desire for change of scene . . . for mountain, painted desert, and skyline, long dreamed of but unvisited.

This year, owners of a new car, the Lincoln-Zephyr, will reach places which before were only names on a map. They will cover longer distances than they would have attempted last year. Traveling by 12 cylinders, they will go in new comfort, new ease, new confidence!

A "twelve," to many people, still denotes a car for the wealthy alone. In times past, that has been true. Today it is no longer true. This "twelve" is medium in price. It is still true, however, that a "twelve" is a smoother, gentler,

and a more luxurious ride—and more fun!

This "twelve" is not only ahead in number of cylinders. It is advanced in all ways. It is a new idea for a 12-cylinder engine to give 14 to 18 miles to the gallon. Yet this engine does, cheerfully. It is a new idea to provide so much size, safety and luxury at medium price. Yet this car provides them.

Modern in appearance and performance, the Lincoln-Zephyr is today's new transportation. It will give more pleasure than you thought a car could ever give. It will open roads you thought you might never see. It offers the kind of travel you thought might not come for years! Lincoln Motor Company, builders of Lincoln and Lincoln-Zephyr V-12s.

Lincoln-Zephyr V-12

Lincoln, 1938

It's got what they call— "Box Office"

From Actual Photograph of Nash Ambassador Eight 4-Door Sedan

In the show business, a star that clicks with the crowd and packs the house has "box office". This year, Nash set a new style and clicked with America! Every day, hundreds more are discovering that Nash offers much bigger, more luxurious cars for the money.

● It's a new kind of car for the money. Bigger. Smarter. More luxurious than popular priced cars have ever been before. Look at that car in the picture! Wouldn't you be proud to own it? No wonder thousands are changing to Nash this year.

The new Nash LaFayette "400" is now a great big 117-inch wheelbase car with the famous 90 horsepower "400" engine. It's a much bigger car, a more powerful car than any of "all three" small cars. But compare the delivered prices on 4-door sedan models. Actually, this great big Nash costs just a few dollars more than any of "all three" small cars.

Nash Ambassadors. The Nash Ambassador Six is a luxurious 121-inch wheelbase car with a thrilling 95 horsepower "Twin Ignition" engine. Actually, it's as big as other cars costing as much as $400 more.

The Nash Ambassador Eight is the last word in luxurious motoring. A thrilling 105 horsepower "Twin Ignition" engine, 125 inches of wheelbase. Make your own comparisons—you'll find that the Nash Ambassador Eight is as big as other cars costing from $100 to $300 more.

Nash gives you more for your money. Nash gives you bigger cars, more luxurious cars for the money. And all Nash cars are equipped with oversized hydraulic brakes, the strongest type of steel body construction in the industry—plus all the vital engineering features you'd expect to find only in the highest priced cars. See these big, beautiful new Nash cars before you make any decisions.

NASH SPEED SHOW Floyd Gibbons as M. C. with Vincent Lopez and his Orchestra. Famous guest stars of stage, screen, radio. C. B. S. stations coast to coast Saturday, 9 P.M. EST. Tune in!

NASH
LaFAYETTE "400" 117-inch wheelbase
AMBASSADOR SIX 121-inch wheelbase
AMBASSADOR EIGHT 125-inch wheelbase

Automatic Cruising Gear available on all models at slight extra cost. New Nash C.I.T. Budget Plan. Low, convenient terms.

1937 X-RAY SYSTEM NOW READY!
The first complete summary available to the public of all the facts about all the new cars. Reveals some astonishing differences in cars of the same price. See it at any Nash showroom. Buy with your eyes open this year!

Nash, 1939

▶ A C Spark Plug, 1938

"SPARK PLUGS NEED CLEANING, TOO!"

Had your plugs cleaned lately?

Plug cleaning *by the AC Method* completely and thoroughly removes the gas-wasting, power-stealing soot, carbon, and oxide coating. The cost is only 5c a plug.

Quality Spark Plugs
or peak performance

years of building quality
lugs—for the car maker and
car owner—are behind these
products. For full spark plug
ction, install a set of new
ark plugs every 10,000 miles.

"There's enough oxide coating on your plugs to steal 10% of your gas."

Many a doctor has arrived "in time" thanks to clean, reliable plugs.

REGISTERED
AC
SPARK PLUG
CLEANING STATION

THIS SIGN identifies Registered AC Spark Plug Cleaning Stations. Look for it.

SPARK PLUG DIVISION • *General Motors Corporation* • FLINT, MICHIGAN

✳ Let these traffic signs prove — your next car should be a 1939 Packard

* Each sign dramatizes how completely the behavior of a motor car is changed—thanks to Packard's exclusive T & T ENGINE and FIFTH SHOCK ABSORBER

DOES IT sound far-fetched—that your local traffic signs will make you prefer a Packard above all other cars?

All right, hurry to your Packard dealer's, borrow either a new 1939 Packard Six or Packard One Twenty—and prepare to learn new lessons in safety and comfort.

Lesson 1—at the first light

Roads being what they are, you probably won't go far before you stop at a traffic light. It turns green—and here you get your first thrill.

For you flash away from that light with a new and exciting surge of power! Your Packard leaps ahead—for it's powered with an improved and spirited motor known as the TRAFFIC & TRAVEL ENGINE. Why TRAFFIC & TRAVEL? Because it's the most efficient motor-car engine at *both* traffic and touring speeds—that Packard has designed in 40 years of engine building!

Lesson 2—a new experience!

There's your next sign—*Railroad Crossing*. Should you grab the seat and wait for the bumps? Not in this car! For this Packard is the first car ever to tame shocks which have been reaching you since the original automobile was built . . . the first car ever to check *cross-shocks*.

Think a minute and you'll realize what this means. For almost all road shocks hit *partly* up-and-down and *partly* cross-wise. If the cross-wise shocks get through, you sway. But now Packard, with an exclusive FIFTH shock absorber, has smothered these hitherto-unabsorbed shocks!

At a dozen other traffic signs, this fifth shock absorber goes into action. It makes your Packard round S-curves without side-stepping, steer with greater accuracy

—and greatly reduces a car's tendency to *side-skid*!

Shift gears—for two surprises

"Stop," the sign says. You do so, swiftly and surely. Then you shift gears—and are delighted by two things.

First, you no longer reach down and feel for a gear lever. For you're using the handiest gear shift lever that ever blessed a car—the Packard HANDSHIFT. It's an improved lever under your steering wheel, leaving your front floor clear, and it's *standard equipment* on both the Packard Six and One Twenty. **Second,** you've never experienced such velvety shifting! That's because your gears are in constant mesh—thanks to the Packard UNIMESH

Transmission, a transmission design taken from the Packard 12!

But—words are a poor substitute for the real thing. Go now to your Packard dealer's. Look your fill at the smartest, most beautiful lines in motoring—the lines that say "Packard" the world over. Get the facts on how easy a Packard is to own. Then borrow either a Packard Six or Packard One Twenty—and let the Traffic Sign Test make you a proud and happy owner!

New! Another Packard plus!

It's Packard's ingenious Econo-Drive—optional at additional cost. This new and perfected fourth-speed gear lets your engine turn 27.8% more slowly at speeds over 30 miles an hour. Think what this saves you in gas and oil, and in decreased

engine wear. Yet Econo-Drive is more than worth its extra cost—in smoother, quieter, more pleasurable motoring.

THE NEW 1939 PACKARD SIX and 120*

(Also known as Packard Eight)

How Much . . . ? You can expect a most agreeable surprise when your Packard dealer shows you how *little* it costs to buy one of these new Packards—delivered right to your door. He will tell you the exact local price on whatever model you prefer—the small down payment, which very likely will not require any cash outlay—and the astonishingly low monthly payment figures that prove how easily you can own and drive a 1939 Packard.

ASK THE MAN WHO OWNS ONE

Packard, 1938

More people the world around ride on GOODYEAR TIRES than on any other kind

Goodyear, 1938

► *Nash, 1938*

EXCITING NEW NASH "HURRICANE POWER"! Even in lowest priced models you flash from 15 to 50 M.P.H. in 13 seconds *in high!* And with this performance, economy is even better than last year.

CONDITIONED AIR for Winter Driving—now made *automatic!* "Tune in" the comfort you want . . . the "Weather Eye" keeps it constant.

SOMETHING'S GOING TO HAPPEN TO YOU

On the Road Today . . . a New 1939 Nash . . . with the Ride and Drive of Your Lifetime !

Y OU'LL see it pass you on the road . . . sometime this week. A sudden rush of wind . . . a silver streak, snaking ahead of traffic, silent as a shadow.

Then you'll know that the first new 1939 Nash is in town.

If you thrill to a thoroughbred, you, too, will soon drive a Nash.

In sober truth, *you have never had your hands on such a car in all your life.* It has glamour, character. It is lithe, low and *fire* on four wheels.

Simply touch that throttle . . . and in three fast shifts you can break the hearts of the best of them.

Then a *fourth speed forward* is like "wings" on your car!

Want to try the "Weather Eye"?

Just set that dial in front, and you ride all winter in fresh, balmy June air—*automatically* kept at your comfort level!

Ten old driving peeves have been abolished. You start, stop, shift, and steer with new ease, *speed!*

Spacious interiors . . . seats that quickly make up into a big double bed . . . exquisite appointments. Literally, it's a home on wheels.

It is, we believe, the world's most modern car. Certainly, it is the most exciting. And prices are something to cheer about!

See your Nash Dealer, *drive it!* NASH MOTORS DIVISION, Nash-Kelvinator Corp., Detroit, Mich.

NOW ON DISPLAY . . . FOUR SERIES OF GREAT CARS . . . 21 MODELS
Nine of Them Priced Right Next to the Lowest . . . See them today

500 MILES a day is an easy, delightful trip. Then you can sleep in your Nash—in a double bed.

It's that New NASH

CAROLE LOMBARD TELLS WHY SH[E] PICKED DE SOT[O]

1 SCENE: MALIBU BEACH. Time: the present. The lovely lady i[s] none other than the glamorous Carole Lombard who has ju[st] arrived in her new Streamline Styled De Soto. Miss Lombard [is] now starring in David O. Selznick's "Made for Each Other[."]

MY STORY

Carole Lombard

"I wanted a Smart Car that was easy to drive and economical to own —I chose De Soto."

2 "STYLE COMES FIRST with me. I like De Soto's Streamline design, the fascinating headlamps...thank heavens, there's no old-fashioned trunk bustle.

3 "THEN I DISCOVERED De Soto's new Handy-Shift—simplest gear shift I've ever used. It's mounted right on the steering post. More room in front."

4 "FRONT AND BACK, the seats a[re] wide as sofas. Room for six peo[ple.] That Streamlined Lugga[ge] Locker has plenty of room, to[o.]"

5 "I LIKE DE SOTO'S Five Speeds Forward. It's thrilling...well worth the modest extra cost. And that new 'passing gear' just zooms you ahead.

6 "I LIKE DE SOTO'S economy, Safety-Steel body and hydraulic brakes; my friends say I used good judgment getting such a dependable car.

7 "I WATCH my check stubs. De Soto's low price is good news." *De Soto Division of Chrysler Corporation, Detroit, Mich.*

SEE YOUR
DE SOTO DEALER

FOR A GREAT CAR...FIN[E] SERVICE & A SQUARE DEA[L]

Built for those who would be missed in the community

To provide the utmost in safety General has developed the Dual 10 tire. The unusual tread design of flexible ribbons of rubber makes it possible to stop a car quicker at 60 in the rain than ordinary tires stop at 50 in dry weather. One experience in preventing an accident that might have been fatal to you or others will make you quickly forget the somewhat higher cost of this remarkable tire. Property damage as well as human damage are further removed from reality when you ride on these tires. From the standpoint of year around safety everyone should have the protection the General Dual 10 provides.

The General Tire & Rubber Co., Akron, Ohio

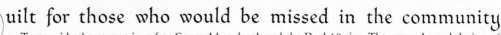

De Soto, 1938 ◄ *General Tire Co., 1937* ► *De Soto, 1939*

HERE is the way to end those upkeep worries that take the fun out of motoring. With Shellubrication you know that your car has been serviced according to manufacturer's specifications. That every point has received the proper lubricant from Shell's line of sixteen special oils and greases.

Shell's exclusive "blue print" style receipt tells you whether the battery has been checked . . . lights checked . . . squeaks silenced . . . and other extra services performed.

Talk to your neighborhood Shellubrication dealer about this modern upkeep service today.

ALL THESE EXTRAS
WITHOUT EXTRA CHARGE

Your tires and running boards rubber-dressed . . . upholstery vacuumed or brushed out . . . windows polished . . . chromium shined . . . body wiped off . . . lights checked . . . battery checked . . . lenses cleaned . . . and many other extras — all without extra charge

SHELLUBRICATION
The Modern Upkeep Service

Indian Motocycle, 1938 ◄ *Shell, 1938*

"NOW I'LL SHOW YOU HOW TO FLY ON LAND!"

A GENERAL MOTORS VALUE

MOST PEOPLE WHO purchase the Cadillac Sixty Special are attracted, first of all, by its striking appearance. Without doubt, it is the most distinctive car in America.

But when they take the wheel, they find yet *another* reason for choosing the Sixty Special . . . and a big one, too. We refer to its unduplicated performance. It is not merely that the Sixty Special is dynamic in acceleration and unbelievably smooth in operation—the *whole conception* of its performance is different. The way it rides . . . the way it hugs the road

. . . the way it handles in traffic . . . *everything* is delightfully different.

Only a ride can fully reveal what this difference means in terms of additional satisfaction. It actually makes all other performance seem commonplace by comparison.

May we prove this—by an extended road demonstration? Your Cadillac dealer has the car. Just tell him the time—and place. He will do the rest.

THE NEW

CADILLAC
Sixty
SPECIAL

Also, see the new Cadillac Sixty-One—the lowest-priced Cadillac for 1939—available in four body types. Its remarkable performance and luxurious riding comfort make it a worthy companion car to the famous Sixty Special. Your Cadillac dealer will be happy to demonstrate both cars at your convenience.

Cadillac, 1938

▶ *Shell, 1938*

"I WON'T NEED YOU TODAY— *I'M* DRIVING!"

THE CADILLAC SIXTY SPECIAL is the most fascinating car to drive in all the world.

This is the verdict of owners without number—many of whom have driven every car of reputation the market affords.

Indeed, hundreds who had vowed they would never again drive a motor car have gone back to the wheel with a whoop—in charge of their Cadillac Sixty Specials.

It is hard to explain what happens in a Sixty Special that *doesn't* happen in other cars—for the difference encompasses *everything*.

First of all, there's the marvelous smoothness of the engine. The throttle feels like velvet under your foot, and the steering wheel is as kind to your hand as a chamois glove.

Then there's the way the car rides the road. You don't bobble, you don't side-sway, you don't roll. You just settle down like Man o' War on the home stretch and stick tight to the pavement. It's a tremendous sensation.

And how you snuggle down into those seats! Your favorite chair at the club was never more inviting. It's the most *relaxing* ride you can imagine.

And the *time* you make is terrific—yet you do it without once showing a heavy foot. The car is simply so quick and nimble and well-balanced that you post a high average without excessive speed.

Yes—this car is an experience. And it's an experience no man who loves a motor car should ever think of missing.

How about it for you? Your Cadillac dealer has the Sixty Special. All you need do is provide the time—and name the place.

THE NEW

CADILLAC
Sixty
SPECIAL

Also, see the Cadillac Sixty-One—the lowest-priced Cadillac for 1939. Its remarkable performance and luxurious riding comfort make it a worthy companion car to the famous Sixty Special. Your Cadillac dealer will be happy to demonstrate both cars at your convenience.

International Trucks, 1939

International Trucks, 1939

Cadillac, 1939 ◄ Lincoln, 1939

Chevrolet, 1935

Why Spencer Tracy Owns a DeSoto!

De Soto, 1939

▶ *International Trucks, 1939*

CLEVELAND POLICE ★★
MOTORIZED

MOBILE PATROL OF INTERNATIONALS COVERS CITY DAY AND NIGHT

City Divided Into Twelve Zones

Each International Truck in Cleveland's Emergency Mobile Patrol is assigned to cover one zone, twenty-four hours a day. No matter in what part of a zone a Patrol...

Crime Records Lowest In 10 Years. Traffic Fatalities Down 47%

GREATER SAFETY AND PROTECTION

Through the motorization and reorganization of the Cleveland Police Force by the Director of Public Safety, in the past six months, a great improvement is accomplished...unit, combining...equipped to...ambulance...accident...scene...and...the...fort...d in...ose...trol...ous...t-aid...ce of...eedy...police...by th...ency...velar...hen a...ation...ted...r serv...or n

Cleveland's Emergency Mobile Patrol, a fleet of speedy, specially equipped International Trucks, is already famous for increased police protection, faster service, quicker...

The brilliant performance of this most...Internationals is equalle...of the carefully trained o...Mobile Patrol duty. Wor...an eig...men are ready for any emergency da...Each automotive u...combining sp...comfort, has been specially equipped...purpose...b

ABOVE: One of Cleveland's famous twelve Emergency Mobile Patrols . . . a speedy International Model D-2 panel body truck, designed for both ambulance and patrol service. All twelve have radio receiving sets, heaters, sirens, spotlights, and police identifying lights.

LEFT: Interior of specially built, two-seated Emergency Mobile Patrol Truck showing steel floor, special rear step, barred rear doors, heavy screen partition behind driving compartment.

CLEVELAND is prouder than ever of its Police Force which is now entirely motorized with the exception of the traffic detail.

The city's Emergency Mobile Patrol is making history by helping daily in the reduction of crime and traffic fatalities. The entire nation is focusing its attention on this masterly stroke of police-pioneering.

Twelve motor units, fully equipped for double-duty service as ambulances and patrols, are manned by officers all of whom have hospital and first-aid training. Many of them are college graduates. The proved results in greater safety and service of this innovation in patrol work are spectacular.

All twelve of these new Cleveland Police Patrols are International Model D-2 panel body trucks. And the performance of these Internationals is thoroughly in keeping with the reputation Internationals have established for

economy, durability and dependability in every line of work.

That kind of performance and that reputation explain why International Harvester sells more heavy-duty trucks, 2-ton and up, than any other three truck manufacturers combined.

What does *your* business require in truck service or hauling? Whether you're a grocer or a farmer, a baker or a builder, there's an International designed for your special needs. The International Dealer or Branch nearest you is ready at any time to demonstrate International top performance, rock-bottom economy, and brilliant appearance.

INTERNATIONAL HARVESTER COMPANY
(INCORPORATED)
180 North Michigan Avenue   Chicago, Illinois

ABOVE: Each unit is a complete ambulance with finest riding comfort. Equipment includes first-aid kit, inhalator, stretcher, and all other accessories required for emergency rescue work.

INTERNATIONAL TRUCKS

Young Henry Ford went to the Fair

It was summer, 1893. The Chicago World's Fair was crowded, clamorous, exciting. But a thirty-year-old mechanic named Ford forgot everything else as he studied a small gasoline engine mounted on a fire hosecart. He had been working a long time to develop just such a power-plant. Here was proof that his plans were sound! He hurried home to his little shop in Detroit, and by 1896 produced a horseless carriage that would really run.

OUT of that early Fair came a Ford *conviction*, as well as a Ford car. The conviction that expositions are *education*. The conviction that if you show men's most advanced ideas to the minds of other men, progress is inevitable and everybody benefits.

That's why the Ford Motor Company has been a big exhibitor at every important fair since its founding. And that's why Ford is one of the largest industrial exhibitors at the New York World's Fair this year.

Mr. Ford believes that all these exhibits will help eager young people to gain inspiration and knowledge for inventions that will be as important to the world of

tomorrow as mass motor car production has been to the world of today.

You are cordially invited to visit the Ford Building, shown below.

Here a ride on the Road of Tomorrow will give you a grand view of the entire Fair. Here you can watch the complete cycle of Ford production on a tremendous turntable, with striking lighting and moving figures. Here, too, you'll see the world's first animated mural, and many actual production and testing operations which highlight the quality of all Ford-built cars.

The Ford Building, above, also appears in section D6 of the World's Fair Map which occupies the next two pages. This view shows part of the Road of Tomorrow and the elm-shaded patio, where visitors may rest and relax.

Prestone, 1939

To see why *Packard for 1940 represents an all-time high in value, please turn the page...*

Ford, 1939 ◄ Packard, 1939

Firestone, 1939

New International
DELIVERY TRUCKS

with All-Steel
... Streamlined **METRO** *Bodies*

TWO NEW CHASSIS

These new International Trucks with Metro Bodies are new in every respect— completely International designed and built. They are not so-called body-builders' conversions.

D-2-M
½-ton Chassis in 2 wheelbase lengths: 102-inch, for the 7½-foot body; and 113-inch, for the 9½-foot body.

D-15-M
¾- to 1-ton Chassis in 2 wheelbase lengths: 102-inch, for the 7½-foot body; and 113-inch, for the 9½-foot body.

Double the cubic capacity of the standard panel body on the same wheelbase length is now offered you in these new International Trucks with the new Metro Bodies.

And only in these two International Trucks can you get these new Metro Bodies.

There are no fenders, no running boards, no hood. There is a smooth floor, a greater area for loads, better distribution of weight. Modern insulation throughout; refrigerator insulation also available.

These new trucks handle easier, park easier and in less space. They are easier on the driver, because they are easier to drive, easier to get in and out of, easier to load and unload. There are wider doors, there is more headroom, the driver is farther front, the gear-shift control is on the steering column, and there is greater visibility.

Never before, to our knowledge, have streamlined beauty, increased utility, and absolute economy been combined to greater advantage for multi-stop service.

If this does not happen to be the type of truck you need in your business; if you need just a small half-ton pick-up or a great powerful 6-wheel dump, or any size or type in between, you will find it in the complete International line.

There's an International Dealer or Branch in your immediate vicinity—ready and eager to demonstrate the right International chassis and the correct International body for increasing your trucking efficiency and profit.

INTERNATIONAL HARVESTER COMPANY
(INCORPORATED)
180 North Michigan Avenue   Chicago, Illinois

Copyright 1939, by International Harvester Company, Incorporated

INTERNATIONAL TRUCKS

New! BIG *Beautiful*
CAB-OVER-ENGINE TRUCKS

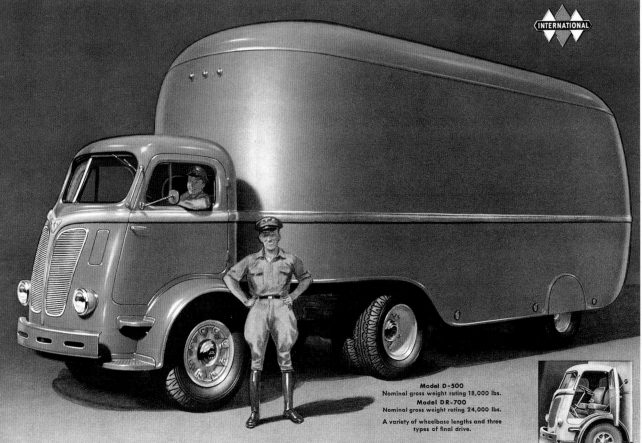

INTERNATIONAL

Model D-500
Nominal gross weight rating 18,000 lbs.
Model DR-700
Nominal gross weight rating 24,000 lbs.

A variety of wheelbase lengths and three
types of final drive.

Enter the handsome, spacious cab of
this International — take the individual spring-filled bus-type seat — all
set for a ride-drive that will be a revelation to the experienced truck driver.

New vision, maneuverability, and
safety ride with the operator of these
new cab-over-engine Internationals.
Perfectly placed controls and wide
view of the road give a new and genuine sense of comfort and efficiency.

Here's a *first view* of the new International *heavy-duty* cab-over-engine trucks!

International Harvester brings you a product of *new and superior design — a new high in cab-over-engine efficiency — a traffic-type truck that will soon be the talk of the industry.*

STYLING and LINES — let this picture and your first sight of the trucks themselves be Exhibit A.

BASIC DESIGN — the International Models D-500 and DR-700, like the popular D-300, are true engine-under-seat units, engineered from stem to stern for full cab-over-engine efficiency. Ideal ⅓-⅔ load distribution, for tractor or straight truck operation.

DRIVER COMFORT, EASY RIDING, VISION, SAFETY — a genuine surprise is in store for every man who takes the wheel and tests the superb spring-suspension in these new trucks.

ACCESSIBILITY — all minor repairs easily handled through floor and from underneath. Major overhaul made surprisingly easy.

MECHANICAL EXCELLENCE — by *International Harvester.*

Inspect and drive a D-500 or DR-700 yourself — or assign your most experienced driver to a test-tryout. Put the truck through its paces and compare it with all competition. Then render a verdict as frankly as you like. What we mean is — *we've really got something here in these new cab-over-engine Internationals!*

See the nearest International Dealer or Branch.

INTERNATIONAL HARVESTER COMPANY (INCORPORATED)
180 North Michigan Avenue   Chicago, Illinois

INTERNATIONAL TRUCKS

International Trucks, 1939 ◄   *International Trucks, 1939*

And the winner is...

A Dollar Saved Is a Dollar Earned

Known primarily for their motorcycles, Indian Motorcyle Co. offered a three-wheeled vehicle that both dispatched mechanics on calls and served as an advertising device and status symbol. Selling the image of a modern, efficient business was deemed as important as the dependability of a vehicle in the lean 1930s. Novelty factor withstanding, the claims of this ad serve as a reminder to the gas-guzzling twenty-first century that you don't need a Hummer® to get the job done.

Ein gesparter Dollar ist ein verdienter Dollar

In erster Linie für ihre Motorräder bekannt, bot die Indian Motorcycle Co. auch dieses dreirädrige Gefährt an. Es sollte Mechaniker zu ihren Notfällen kutschieren und gleichzeitig als Werbemittel und Statussymbol dienen. In den finanziell klammen Dreißigern war ein modernes, effizientes Image mindestens so verkaufsfördernd wie die Zuverlässigkeit eines Fahrzeugs. Vom Skurrilitätsfaktor einmal abgesehen: Die Anzeige ist für die verschwendungssüchtigen Amerikaner auch insofern nicht uninteressant, als sie daran erinnert, dass benzinschluckende Monster eine lange Tradition haben.

Un dollar épargné est un dollar gagné

Surtout connu pour ses motos, Indian Motorcycle Co. proposa dans les années 30 un véhicule à trois roues servant à la fois de moyen de transport aux mécaniciens dépanneurs, de support publicitaire et de signe extérieur de réussite. En ces années de vaches maigres, afficher une image d'entreprise moderne et efficace était aussi important que de pouvoir dépendre d'un véhicule fiable. Au-delà de l'aspect gadget, cette publicité rappelle au 21e siècle grand amateur de pétrole qu'on peut être efficace sans consommer beaucoup d'essence.

Un dólar ahorrado es un dólar ganado

Conocida principalmente por sus motocicletas, Indian Motorcyle Co. presentaba un vehículo de tres ruedas que no sólo incluía los últimos adelantos mecánicos, sino que, además, servía como instrumento publicitario y como símbolo de estatus. En los años treinta, años de vacas flacas, la imagen de un negocio moderno y rentable era tan eficaz como la seriedad de un vehículo. Y dejando a un lado el factor novedoso, lo extraordinario de este anuncio es que defendía que no era necesario tener un cochazo para poder desplazarse, una idea que se podría reutilizar perfectamente en el mundo del siglo XXI, plagado de vehículos con un consumo de gasolina desorbitado.

わずかな利益も逃さない

インディアン・モーターサイクル社は主にオートバイ生産でその名が知られていたが、3輪自動車を発表した。これは、顧客の要望に応じて整備工を派遣するためのもので、広告宣伝やステータス・シンボルにもなる商品であった。近代的・効率的な企業イメージを売りこむことは、不況の30年代においては自動車の信頼性と同様に重要であると考えられていた。目新しさが功を奏して、この広告の主張は仕事を片付けるのにハマー®（4輪駆動車）はいらない、と高燃費の21世紀を再認識させる役目を果たしている。

GREATEST MONEY MAKER EVER OFFERED SERVICE STATIONS

1 *man does the work of* **2**

YOUR NAME HERE

Indian DISPATCH-TOW

PROGRESSIVE SERVICE STATIONS use this modern equipment to *speed service, save time, cut costs*. Indian Dispatch-Tow makes pick up and delivery just a one-man job—releasing a man for more profitable work. Outside servicing costs are cut two-thirds through lower overhead, saved time, saved man-power. Dependable Dispatch-Tow costs only about 1c a mile to operate, turns idle hours into profitable working time.

BIG ADVERTISING VALUE—MONEY MAKER
Service stations are judged by the equipment they keep. Your name on an Indian Dispatch-Tow flashing about town is not only great advertising — it also stamps your station as efficient and modern. You can give better service at smaller cost—win new customers, make more money—with snappy Indian Dispatch-Tow service. *Write for proof based on experience*, and complete information. Address Dept. SS-7.

INDIAN MOTOCYCLE CO., *Springfield, Mass.*

Indian Motocycle Co., 1937

UNRETOUCHED PHOTOGRAPH IN NATURAL COLORS TAKEN IN THE HOME OF MRS. GEORGE J. O'BRIEN, PROVIDENCE, R. I.

"Our clothes look new for more than one season's wear . . . thanks to Chipso"

says young mother of three happy little girls

Mrs. George J. O'Brien looks too carefree to know about the actual work of housekeeping. "But I do," she assured us. "I do my own housework and all the children's washing, besides washing my own housedresses and underwear and good linens.

"I use CHIPSO for everything. It makes washing easy because it soaks the children's dirtiest clothes clean. I don't have to wear them out with rubbing. And Chipso leaves colors bright and fresh. Our clothes look new for more than one season's wear.

"I used to think I could not use my general

laundry soap for things like the children's knitted sweaters, but I found that Chipso leaves woolens beautifully soft.

"Chipso is fine for dishes and cleaning, too. It doesn't coarsen my hands or make them sore. A soap that is so safe for the skin is bound to be all right for nice fabrics, I think, even if it is such a practical soap for getting dirt out in a hurry."

Chipso is not adulterated with harsh, "dirt-cutting" ingredients. It cleans with richer, thicker SUDS. Dirt cannot withstand its penetrating SOAPINESS, but colors, and even delicate silks and woolens are safe in it. Get Chipso from your grocer before another washday goes by. The low cost of this big package of concentrated rich SAFE soap makes Chipso the best soap value on the market today.

Chipso *makes clothes wear* — longer

Chipso, 1933

"Our clothes get their wear on our backs . . . *not in the wash*," smiles mother of six

In Baltimore's mild climate, wash-clothes get year-round wear. Unretouched color photograph taken last summer at the home of Mrs. R. Giblin.

MRS. GIBLIN had to look at the size tag in Jack's blouse to tell how old it was. "Hum—it's more than a year since I bought him that size," she meditated, "yet it looks as unfaded and as good as his new ones.

"Our clothes are washed with CHIPSO," she continued. "They don't get any rough treatment on washday. Chipso makes such grand suds (I always say my tub looks like an ice cream soda!) that the dirt *soaks* right out. No hard rubbing. Saves a lot of wear! The white clothes come perfectly white; we never boil them. And yet Chipso doesn't fade the colored clothes."

Chipso is quick, yet SAFE, because it is SOAPIER! It is not adulterated with the harsh, "dirt-

cutting" substances which cause inferior soaps gradually to weaken your clothes and dull their color. Chipso loosens dirt harmlessly with its RICHER SUDS. "It is safe even for silks . . . makes my blankets fluffy . . . and it's so economical! I certainly feel I get my money's worth out of Chipso," says Mrs. Giblin.

You, too, will find your big box of SAFE Chipso a wonderful soap value. Get it from your grocer.

Chipso *makes clothes wear* — longer

Chipso, 1934

RUBBING is RUIN

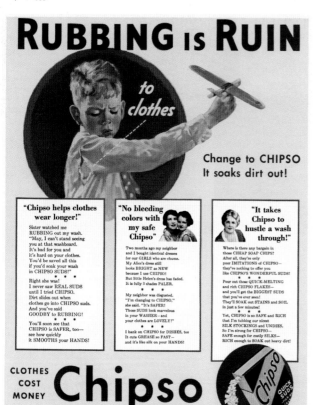

to clothes

Change to CHIPSO
It soaks dirt out!

"Chipso helps clothes wear longer!"

Sister watched me RUBBING out my wash. "May, I can't stand seeing you at that washboard. It's bad for you and it's hard on your clothes. You'd be saved all this if you'd soak your wash in CHIPSO SUDS!"

Right she was! I never saw REAL SUDS until I tried CHIPSO. Dirt slides out when clothes go into CHIPSO suds. And you've said GOODBY to RUBBING!

You'll soon see that CHIPSO is SAFER, too—see how quickly it SMOOTHS your hands!

"No bleeding colors with my safe Chipso"

Two months ago my neighbor and I bought identical dresses for our GIRLS who are chums. My Alice's dress still looks BRIGHT as NEW because I use CHIPSO! But little Helen's dress has faded. It is fully 3 shades PALER.

My neighbor was disgusted. "I'm changing to CHIPSO," she said. "It's SAFER!" Those SUDS look marvelous in your WASHER—and our clothes are LOVELY!"

I bank on CHIPSO for DISHES, too. It cuts GREASE as FAST—and it's like silk on your HANDS!

"It takes Chipso to hustle a wash through!"

Where is there any bargain in those CHEAP SOAP CHIPS? After all, they're only poor IMITATIONS of CHIPSO—they're nothing to offer you like CHIPSO'S WONDERFUL SUDS!

Pour out those QUICK-MELTING and rich CHIPSO FLAKES—and you'll get the BIGGEST SUDS that you've ever seen! They'll SOAK out STAINS and SOIL in just a few minutes!

Yet, CHIPSO is so SAFE and RICH that I'm tubbing our nicest SILK STOCKINGS and UNDIES. So I'm strong for CHIPSO—SAFE enough for costly SILKS—RICH enough to SOAK out heavy dirt!

CLOTHES COST MONEY

Chipso
MAKES CLOTHES WEAR LONGER

Chipso, 1938 ◄ *Chipso, 1932*

$1¹⁵ Silk Stockings for only 50¢!

MADE BY THE GOTHAM SILK HOSIERY CO.

Special Offer Send 50¢ and 3 Ivory Flakes box-tops and get these beautiful "Adjustables" patented and made by The Gotham Silk Hosiery Co., never sold for less than $1.15

(MAIL WITH COUPON BELOW)

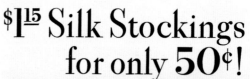

IMPORTANT—This coupon brings you $1.15 stockings for only 50¢ and 3 Ivory Flakes box-tops. Paste your 50¢ between two of the Ivory Flakes box-tops to prevent loss in mail.

Procter & Gamble, Dept. VC-98, Box 877, Cincinnati, O.

"What is the best Stocking Insurance?"
Make this test on fine sheer hosiery

Hurry! For this one time only, we're offering you this special chance to test Ivory Flakes on a pair of clear chiffon stockings of beautiful quality, so that you will see how perfectly all "washables" are protected by pure Ivory Flakes suds. These stockings are first quality—the famous "Adjustables" patented and made by The Gotham Silk Hosiery Co., the largest manufacturer of branded and advertised hosiery.

"Adjustables" never sell for less than $1.15 in department stores and hosiery shops. Yet for 50¢

and 3 Ivory Flakes box-tops, they're *yours*! You save 65¢—on these lovely sheer all-silk stockings!

Wear them. Wash them with Ivory Flakes

"Stocking satisfaction" (beauty and longer wear) comes from fine stockings cared for by a fine soap. Wash your "Adjustables" after each wearing with Ivory Flakes. Lukewarm Ivory suds will keep them clear, springy, "new-dyed" in color, because Ivory Flakes are pure—safe for even a baby's skin.

Hurry! Get your Ivory Flakes from your dealer today. See how much *more* soap you get in the big Ivory Flakes box, than of any other fine-fabrics soap! Clip coupon—get a pair of "Adjustables" at this thrillingly low price!

The Gotham Silk Hosiery Co. says: "We recommend IVORY FLAKES"...99⁴⁴/₁₀₀% Pure

Ivory Flakes, 1935 ► *Ivory Flakes, 1937*

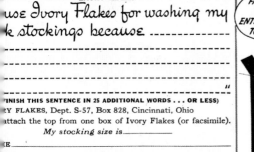

AS YOU DESIRE ME

Olive oil has a flattering way of putting youth into your skin

"THERE are no ugly women!" said a great Frenchman, "only those who stop trying to make themselves beautiful." Don't ever stop trying. Dare to be lovely. Work to keep skin smooth, soft, fine. Age needn't show. Youth *can* be yours.

Use olive oil

Olive oil has the most flattering way of bringing youth into your skin, of keeping it there. It softens and soothes the skin, melting away the sight of those fine, age-betraying lines. Beauty experts are in perfect accord about olive oil . . . and also about the way you should use it. Over 20,000 of them advise Palmolive

Soap—the one soap, you know, that tells what it's made of; the one leading soap made with a lot of olive oil.

Try this youth—test

Just do this, won't you? For thirty days, morning and evening, work a lather of Palmolive and warm water into your skin. Rinse with warm water, then with cold. Follow this treatment for the bath, too.

Now, let the years march on. Keep pace with youth, confidently . . . secure in the knowledge of a youthful skin—a skin that's firm, smooth, appealing . . . a skin that makes you infinitely desirable.

This much Olive Oil goes into every cake of Palmolive Soap

Keep that Schoolgirl Complexion

Palmolive, 1933

Palmolive, 1937

Curity, 1939

Ivory, 1937

Boraxo, 1936

Bon Ami, 1935

Old Dutch Girl, 1931

Sunbrite Cleanser, 1933

Camay, 1934

► *Bon Ami, 1937*

Rub-a-dub-dub...
Three men...and one tub
Bon Ami is the answer

Bon Ami makes short work of cleaning up after "the men" of the family. First it cleans quickly—*and polishes at the same time.* Then it washes away easily . . . leaving your bathtub smooth and unscratched! You'll find Bon Ami not only protects the surface of your tub, but also helps you avoid drain trouble. For unlike coarse cleansers, Bon Ami leaves no gritty sediment behind to clog up pipes or drains. That's another reason why you'll like this "polishing cleanser." Try Bon Ami!

Bon Ami for Bathtubs
..."hasn't scratched yet!"

Copr. 1936, The Bon Ami

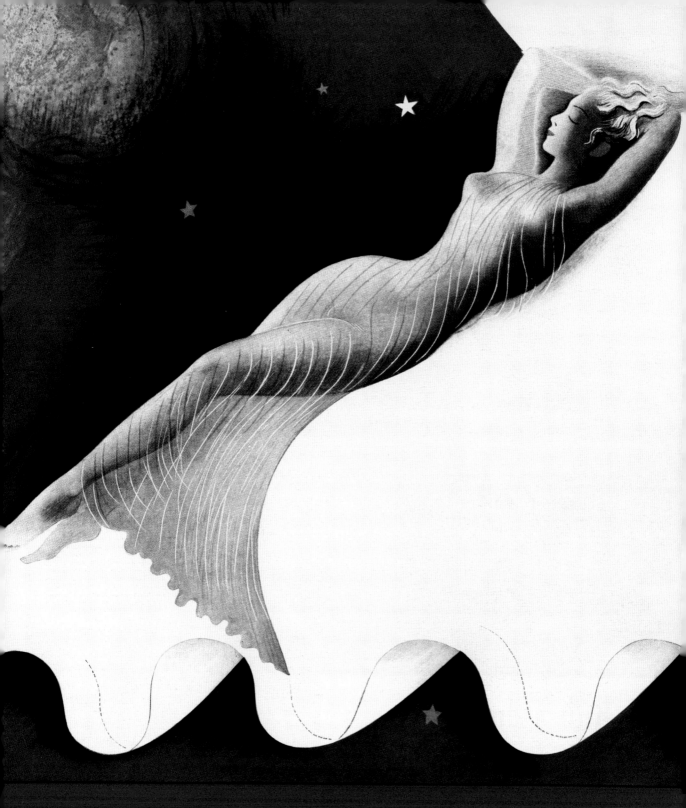

S.O.S., 1938

Bab-O, 1931

Cannon, 1937 ◄ Ivory Flakes, 1938

Sunbrite Cleanser, 1931

... THEN AT LAST SHE GOT A JOB!

Rinso, 1933

CLARA TAKES "THE BLUE" OUT OF MONDAY

SUPER SUDS

THE BIG BOX OF SOAP FOR 10¢

Can *any* toothbrush actually provide a pleasant surprise?

With one of these replace the brush you used this morning —then compare results

If your toothbrush gives you whiter, cleaner teeth it does you a lot of good for a very small sum of money.

And the right brush, properly used, will do exactly *that* for you. It will *not* make you a million dollars, or turn you into a movie star overnight. *But it will give you whiter teeth—*

Just get the right brush—one *small* enough and of proper shape to do the best possible job of cleaning teeth.

Then—*don't keep it in service after honest wear has impaired the cleansing and polishing qualities.* Most people do. That is why we offer this reminder to everyone who uses a toothbrush.

This brush—Dr. West's—is famous for the polishing action made possible by its correct design. Now it has been made doubly effective by the use of still finer materials.

These snowy, springy bristles are the costliest the world's markets supply. Only Dr. West's new brushes have them. They are specially trimmed and spaced to enter and sweep clean all crevices— as well as to polish the surfaces.

America's most sensational dentifrice success Dr. West's tooth pas —an advance as great the famous toothbrus

Your druggist has new Dr. W toothbrushes for every member c family. Adult's size, 50c; youth' child's, 25c; "professional brush, Each brush thoroughly sterilize sealed. And each is fully guara Get some today. *Results may rea prise and delight you.*

The Easy, Correct W *to brush teeth*

Brush always away from gums t the cutting edges of the teeth; *with* the crevices, never across. what dentists advise. And they mend Dr. West's because it is o shape and size to make correct br easy. Do this twice daily, and soon have whiter teeth.

Why It Cleans *every tooth ana* This diagram shows how Dr. Wes rect design enables you to swee crevice clean—and to cleanse the ous inside curve of teeth, or t back, as thoroughly as those in fro

CLEANS TEETH BETTER WECO Product **Dr. West's TOOTH BRUSH** WECO Product STERILIZED MADE IN USA REG U.S. PAT. OFF. PENETRATES AND CLEANS EVERY CREVICE: POLISHES EV

© 1930, W.

NEW TOOTH BRUSH DISCOVERY

Tek
Now lasts 6 times longer

GENUINE NATURAL BRISTLES...RESIST WEAR AND WATER!

Now you can throw away your soggy tooth brush!

Here's an amazing, new kind of Tek that gives you the stimulating spring of *genuine natural bristles*—and keeps that spring and cleaning power more than *6 times longer than before!* That's 6 times longer protection for your teeth and gums.

Not a waterproof coating that will wear off or wash out. But a permanently improved, genuine bristle, transformed by an exclusive Tek process so that it will stand up under the

wear-and-water of your daily brushing at least *6 times longer!*

And you'll find Tek so easy to use. Its small, scientific shape cleans even the hard-to-reach curve behind your front teeth. Cleans your teeth and massages your gums.

Gay colored handles for each of the family. In new, silver-and-blue carton, on sale today. Tek 50¢. Tek Jr. 25¢. Tek Professional (2 tooth) 50¢. *Double Tek,* two brushes packed together, one for morning, one for night, specially priced.

Johnson & Johnson
NEW BRUNSWICK, N. J.   CHICAGO, ILL.

Tek Toothbrush, 1939

YES! IT HAS NO BRISTLES*!

Cannot shed—

Cannot grow soggy—

Cannot fail to clean!

SEALED IN GLASS—SURGICALLY STERILE

50¢ *In the Regular size and the smaller, 2-row Professional size. Three textures: hard, medium, soft*

Dr. West's Miracle-Tuft

Made possible by this triumph of modern chemistry—the discovery of sensational Du Pont EXTON! Used exclusively in DR. WEST'S Miracle-Tuft...

Try to pull it out! No bristle shedding! Exton is non-porous and water-repellent! This new bristle-like filament doesn't split or pull out and fail to clean your teeth.

99% Waterproof Water is the natural enemy of your toothbrush. But Exton is non-porous and water-repellent! This new bristle-like filament doesn't get soggy in use and fail to clean your teeth.

Lasts Longer Scientific tests show that a Miracle-Tuft will outlast animal bristle brushes many times over. In use, 6000 works on a laboratory testing machine destroyed the animal bristle brush (shown) but scarcely harmed the Miracle-Tuft (below).

Throw away your present toothbrush! It's made with *animal bristles* unless it's a *Miracle-Tuft.* Science has at last brought you a surer way to lovelier, more attractive teeth—this toothbrush *without bristles* and without bristle troubles.

It is made with Exton, a unique bristle-like filament now produced by Du Pont exclusively for Dr. West's. Exton has none of animal bristle's undesirable qualities. It cannot break off, split or pull out. It does not go limp or soggy during brushing. It cleans teeth with a thorough-

ness never before possible except by a dentist. And it's ideal for massaging the gums.

One brushing with a *Miracle-Tuft* will convince you that this remarkable toothbrush will do amazing things for your teeth. Try it. At 50¢ it's a bargain in good looks, attractive smiles, lovelier teeth!

WORLD'S FINEST NATURAL-BRISTLE TOOTHBRUSH—DR. WEST'S WATER-PROOFED

Packed in new style Blue and Yellow Carton . . . Sterilized. The same famous brush that has outsold all others for years at 50¢. Made of finest natural-bristle, water-proofed against sogginess. ...35¢

Also try DR. WEST'S Tooth Paste—an amazingly effective aid to brilliant white teeth!

Mustachios on all toothbrushes have been made with animal bristles. Now, after years of research, DU PONT EXTON BRISTLE—a product of Du Pont Chemistry—has been developed and is used in DR. WEST'S Miracle-Tuft Toothbrush exclusively.

Copr. 1939 by Weco Products Company

Dr. West's Toothbrush, 1939

how to keep ROMANCE aflame

Mary Jean (below) knows that Lux helps any girl's game. Ted and Tim are beaten before they start by a swanky pink shantung. Lux keeps Mary Jean's cottons and summer silks fresh and gay, her sweaters soft as down.

At parties, Sally (below) is always the center of things. Her lovely yellow organdie, fresh from its Lux bath, panics the boys. "The sweetest femme on the floor," they agree. Never would Sally trust dainty washables to ordinary harsh soaps or cake-soap rubbing. "Mercy no! Lux is a girl's best friend!"

"That dress is a knockout!" compliments Ralph (below), married five years. Stepping out with his wife always gives him a kick. "You darling," purrs Fran, delightedly. "I do adore this blue printed silk even if it is made over. It's silly to let things get faded and dowdy when you can keep colors looking gorgeously new with Lux."

Of course, you want romance—dates by the dozen—an adoring husband through the years. Lux helps to make all this come true! Lux is made to keep you attractively dressed at little cost—to keep colors like new. Avoid ordinary soaps with harmful alkali and cake-soap rubbing. They're apt to fade colors, shrink woolens, mar the adorable freshness of cottons and linens, wear out things far too soon. But Lux, you remember, is safe for everything safe in water alone!

Connie (above) is pleased with her green peasant linen—color-fresh, like new, thanks to last night's Luxing. "Looks like a million," thinks Jerry, the new man at the office. Connie knows how to keep her pet frocks gloriously colorful—always ready for a big moment. That out-of-the-bandbox look brings down the strongest men! Moral: Stick to Lux!

LUX

Woman's Home Companion   July 1935

Dr. West's Toothbrush, 1930 ◄   *Lux, 1935*

Can your mouth pass the *ACID TEST?*

ACID MOUTH   NORMAL MOUTH

* **THE ACID TEST...place a litmus paper in your mouth.** If it turns *purplish red* . . . your mouth is acid. If it remains *blue* . . . your mouth is alkaline, free from acids that may imperil teeth and gums. *After a mouth-rinse with GLYCO-Thymoline the litmus paper remains blue,* evidence that the mouth acids have been neutralized.

For your convenience in making this test, the coupon below will bring you a generous sample of GLYCO-Thymoline and litmus paper. Fill out and mail coupon now.

Demand more of your mouthwash than merely a pleasant taste or tingle. Don't let a strong, irritating solution mislead you into believing that effective action has taken place. Acidity is one of the gravest dangers your mouth must combat. GLYCO-Thymoline gently flushes the mouth clean and ends the fermentation that helps create acid.

Morning and night, you will like the pleasant, refreshing effect of a mouth-rinse with GLYCO-Thymoline. It restores clean taste instantly...it bathes and tones the mem-

brane lining of your mouth...you feel the glow of complete cleanliness. And you know that acidity has been counteracted.

Used and prescribed by physicians and dentists for over 30 years. GLYCO-Thymoline should be handy in every bathroom cabinet, for the use of every member of the family. Just ask your nearest druggist for "GLYCO"...or, send coupon below for a trial...and make the acid test. Kress and Owen Company, New York.

GLYCO-THYMOLINE
(Trade Mark)

This Coupon Brings a Sample Bottle

KRESS & OWEN CO., 361 Pearl Street, New York City

Gentlemen: Kindly send me a generous sample of GLYCO-Thymoline and litmus paper to make the *acid test.* Enclosed find 4¢ to cover postage.

NAME _____

ADDRESS _____

CITY _____ STATE _____

L.H.C.6-46

USED AND PRESCRIBED BY PHYSICIANS AND DENTISTS FOR OVER THIRTY YEARS

Glyco, 1931

Colgate, 1932

Colgate, 1937

Durham Safety Razor, 1937

Colgate, 1933

▶ *U.S. Savings Bonds, 1935*

A Gift

increasing in cash value every year for ten years

UNITED STATES SAVINGS BONDS

DIRECT OBLIGATIONS OF THE UNITED STATES GOVERNMENT

$18.75 . . . . *increases in 10 years to* $25
$37.50 . . . *increases in 10 years to* $50
$75.00 . . . *increases in 10 years to* . . . $100
$375.00 . . *increases in 10 years to* . . . $500
$750.00 . . *increases in 10 years to* . . $1000
Redeemable in cash at any time after 60 days from date issued

United States Savings Bonds are a form of remembrance which will please any one of any age. They will be issued in the name of the person for whom you purchase them, and so registered on the records of the Treasury Department.

In your shopping trips this season, include your Post Office— there, upon cash payment, you may secure the actual bonds. Personal check accepted subject to collection.

AS EASY TO BUY AS A MONEY ORDER ★ AT YOUR POST OFFICE ★

He took his girl swimming and gave her Athlete's Foot

HE WAS A
CARRIER ★

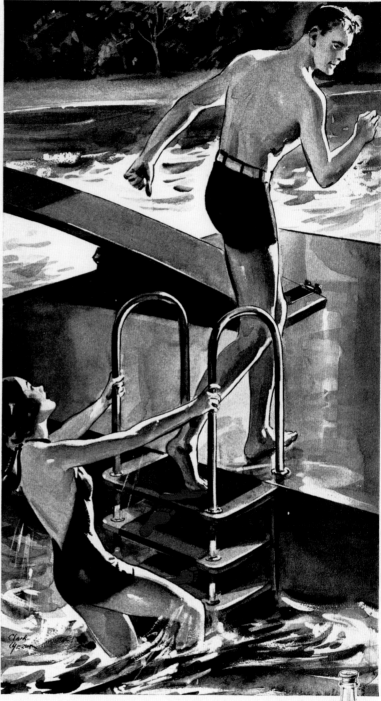

NO ONE is safe in the company of a victim of Athlete's Foot, when their bare feet tread the same surfaces.

For a single carrier of Athlete's Foot—a woman, child or man—may infect scores of other people who are so luckless as to follow in the bath house at the beach, in the shower or locker-room at the club, on the edge of a swimming pool, or even in the family bathroom.

Red skin is the mark of the Carrier

If you suspect you have a case of Athlete's Foot, you may be in danger as grave to yourself as to others who may contract it from you; use Absorbine Jr. promptly.

Don't take chances. Examine the skin between your toes. If it looks red, itches, stings or burns, you'll welcome the cooling, soothing relief brought by applications of Absorbine Jr. You may save yourself a lot of painful trouble.

For Athlete's Foot is caused by an insidious fungus that digs and bores deeper into the skin, when neglected—resulting in unwholesome whiteness and moistness, peeling skin, cracks and painful rawness.

Absorbine Jr. destroys the fungus

Even in advanced stages, Absorbine Jr. relieves the condition and helps to soothe and heal the damaged tissues. If, however, you feel your case is really serious, by all means consult your doctor in addition to the use of Absorbine Jr., morning and night.

When you buy, insist upon genuine Absorbine Jr. and accept no imitations offered as being "just as good." This famous remedy has been tested and proved for its ability to kill the fungus when reached, a fungus so stubborn that infected socks must be boiled 20 minutes to destroy it.

Absorbine Jr. is economical to use because it takes so little to bring relief. Also wonderful for the bites of insects, such as mosquitoes and jiggers. At all druggists, $1.25 a bottle. For free sample, write W. F. Young, Inc., 362 Lyman Street, Springfield, Massachusetts.

★ "Carrier" is the medical term for a person who carries infection. People infected with Athlete's Foot are "carriers." And at least one-half of all adults suffer from it (Athlete's Foot) at some time, according to the U. S. Public Health Service. They spread the disease wherever they tread barefoot.

ABSORBINE JR.

Relieves sore muscles, muscular aches, bruises, sprains and Sunburn

Absorbine Jr., 1937

AN ADVERTISEMENT **Your Dentist** Wants You TO READ AND STUDY

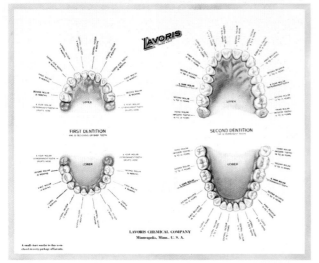

Lavoris, 1930

HERE is an unusual illustration for a full-page advertisement in such a big and important publication. It isn't pretty, perhaps, but it can be mighty valuable to you and your family.

It is intended to make you mindful of the value of dental service and oral hygiene.

See the "baby teeth." Many times the "six year molar" is mistaken for a "baby tooth" and allowed to decay. Early loss of a "six year molar" may affect contour of the jaw and face throughout life.

Decay, or other dental disorders, may affect your health. Frequently, ailments of stomach, heart, nerves, eyes, are directly traceable to dental conditions.

Your dentist wants to help you. His trained eye, supplemented by the "x-ray," detects sources of possible trouble.

Do not allow anybody to tell you that "once a year" or "twice a year" is often enough to visit the dentist. Only your dentist can tell you how often you should see him. He, better than anybody else, knows the char-

acteristics and tendencies of your mouth.

Brush your teeth, of course. And after brushing, sluice from the spaces and tissue every trace of food and dentifrice debris. Do this with plain water—cold, or warm, as you prefer—to which a bit of Lavoris may be added. (One part Lavoris to four parts of water.)

Your dentist may prescribe a stronger Lavoris solution if you have some disorder of oral tissue.

Know your dentist. Know your teeth. Know the delightful, freshing effect that follows the use of Lavoris, the scientific oral detergent that has gained world-wide popularity through what it *is* and what it does rather than by advertising.

Again, we urge you to study this page, to be sure that it is studied and understood by your entire family. If you want additional copies, write us. Again we say: "Do As Your Dentist Tells You."

LAVORIS CHEMICAL COMPANY
MINNEAPOLIS · TORONTO

This page is a part of the Lavoris Reciprocation Program tendered the American Dentist in recognition of more than 25 years' acceptance and good will

Itching, Cracking Feet
Ringworm and Athlete's Foot Curbed by Special Treatment

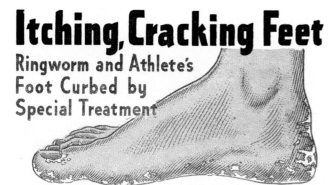

Do your feet itch so badly that they nearly drive you crazy? Does the skin on your feet crack and peel? Are there blisters between your toes and on the soles of your feet? Do your feet get so sore at times that they actually bleed? If you suffer from these foot troubles you should realize that the real cause often is a germ-like fungus and that you can not get rid of your trouble until you kill the fungus or germ.

Doctor's Treatment Fights the Cause

Ordinary ointments and liquids can not do much good to overcome foot troubles such as these because they do not fight or kill the underlying cause of the trouble. Fortunately it is now possible to combat these foot troubles and even the most stubborn ringworm infection with the doctor's formula called Nixoderm, based on the prescription of a famous English skin specialist. Nixoderm is swift and positive and has these 3 definite actions: 1. It quickly starts

killing the germs, parasites, or fungus responsible for many foot infections and ringworm. 2. It stops the terrible itching and soothes and cools the skin usually in 7 to 10 minutes. 3. It helps Nature promote healing and a naturally soft, clear, smooth skin.

Guaranteed Results

Get Nixoderm from your druggist today. Apply it tonight and see for yourself the tremendous improvement in the morning. In just a few days' time Nixoderm must have proved to your entire satisfaction that it is removing the germs, parasites, and fungus cause of foot trouble and be completely satisfactory in every way, or you merely return the empty package and the full purchase price will be refunded. Don't put up another day with the agony and the danger of itching, cracking, bleeding feet infected by this highly contagious fungus. No matter what you have tried or used or how long you have suffered, Nixoderm must do the work to your entire satisfaction or cost nothing. Get Nixoderm from your druggist today. The guarantee protects you.

Nixoderm, 1937

Says gay ULI-ALI of TIMBUCTOO
Phone Bali 222
(Meaning *"No-No-Me no need Saráka"*)

BUT . . . Millions of civilized people do need SARÁKA and hundreds of thousands use this NEW DISCOVERY upon Doctors' advice for thorough and safe relief from habitual

CONSTIPATION

Uli Ali's active outdoor life and the abundance of natural fresh foods she eats precludes her suffering from constipation. But for you highly civilized people, whose sedentary lives and refined foods make you the victim of habitual constipation, there is good news for you in this new discovery.

Developed from the sap of a tropical tree—tested and perfected for many years by a famous laboratory —Saráka* was first introduced

through the American medical profession.

Samples of Saráka were sent to doctors all over the United States. Tests were made by tens of thousands of physicians. They, having satisfied themselves as to its merits, began recommending Saráka to their patients.

Today, hundreds of thousands of people all over the country use it, at doctors' advice, for relief from habitual constipation.

Costs 10¢ to Try

Saráka is now on sale in most drug stores in large and medium size and in the 10¢ trial-size. If your doctor has not given you a trial package, get one from your druggist or mail the coupon below. See what a safe and pleasant way Saráka is to gain relief from habitual constipation.

*Trade Mark Reg. U.S. Pat. Off.

Copyright 1934
Schering Corporation

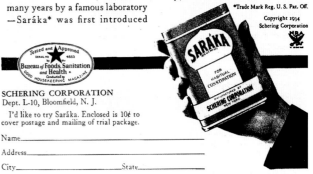

SCHERING CORPORATION
Dept. L-10, Bloomfield, N. J.

I'd like to try Saráka. Enclosed is 10¢ to cover postage and mailing of trial package.

Name_____

Address_____

City_____State_____

Saráka, 1934

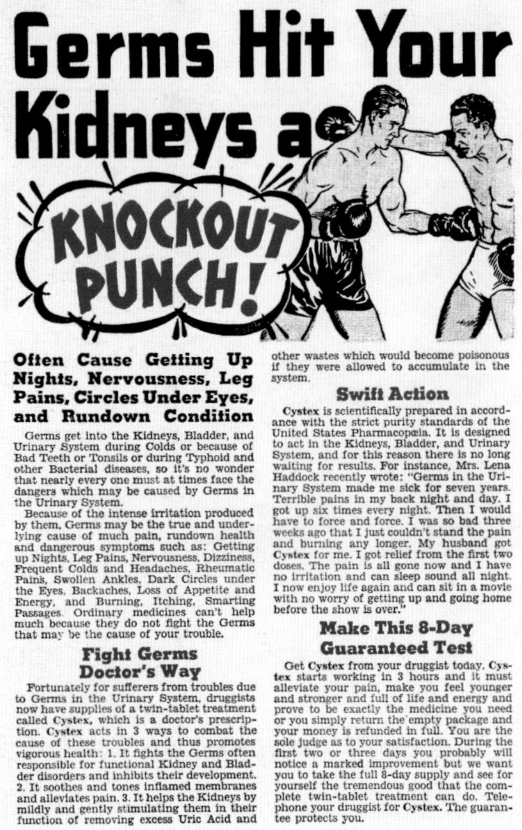
Germs Hit Your Kidneys a
KNOCKOUT PUNCH!
Often Cause Getting Up Nights, Nervousness, Leg Pains, Circles Under Eyes, and Rundown Condition
Germs get into the Kidneys, Bladder, and Urinary System during Colds or because of Bad Teeth or Tonsils or during Typhoid and other Bacterial diseases, so it's no wonder that nearly every one must at times face the dangers which may be caused by Germs in the Urinary System.
Because of the intense irritation produced by them, Germs may be the true and underlying cause of much pain, rundown health and dangerous symptoms such as: Getting up Nights, Leg Pains, Nervousness, Dizziness, Frequent Colds and Headaches, Rheumatic Pains, Swollen Ankles, Dark Circles under the Eyes, Backaches, Loss of Appetite and Energy, and Burning, Itching, Smarting Passages. Ordinary medicines can't help much because they do not fight the Germs that may be the cause of your trouble.
Fight Germs Doctor's Way
Fortunately for sufferers from troubles due to Germs in the Urinary System, druggists now have supplies of a twin-tablet treatment called Cystex, which is a doctor's prescription. Cystex acts in 3 ways to combat the cause of these troubles and thus promotes vigorous health: 1. It fights the Germs often responsible for functional Kidney and Bladder disorders and inhibits their development. 2. It soothes and tones inflamed membranes and alleviates pain. 3. It helps the Kidneys by mildly and gently stimulating them in their function of removing excess Uric Acid and other wastes which would become poisonous if they were allowed to accumulate in the system.
Swift Action
Cystex is scientifically prepared in accordance with the strict purity standards of the United States Pharmacopœia. It is designed to act in the Kidneys, Bladder, and Urinary System, and for this reason there is no long waiting for results. For instance, Mrs. Lena Haddock recently wrote: "Germs in the Urinary System made me sick for seven years. Terrible pains in my back night and day. I got up six times every night. Then I would have to force and force. I was so bad three weeks ago that I just couldn't stand the pain and burning any longer. My husband got Cystex for me. I got relief from the first two doses. The pain is all gone now and I have no irritation and can sleep sound all night. I now enjoy life again and can sit in a movie with no worry of getting up and going home before the show is over."
Make This 8-Day Guaranteed Test
Get Cystex from your druggist today. Cystex starts working in 3 hours and it must alleviate your pain, make you feel younger and stronger and full of life and energy and prove to be exactly the medicine you need or you simply return the empty package and your money is refunded in full. You are the sole judge as to your satisfaction. During the first two or three days you probably will notice a marked improvement but we want you to take the full 8-day supply and see for yourself the tremendous good that the complete twin-tablet treatment can do. Telephone your druggist for Cystex. The guarantee protects you.

Cystex, 1937

Don't Let
Dry, "Dead Skin"
Make You A Wall Flower
WRINKLES
LINES
BLACKHEADS
SHINY NOSE
DRYNESS ROUGHNESS
CREPEY THROAT
Here's The AMAZING Beauty Cream That's Thrilling ALL America
• Skin beauty is the soul of romance—the power to attract. The key to a woman's charms—happiness—success . . . At last a way has been found to aid nature restore softer, smoother, younger-looking skin.
Give Your Skin These Thrilling New Beauty Benefits To Help Nature Restore Smooth Younger Looking Skin.
Make This Guaranteed
3 Day Test
That Is Showing Thousands of Women How To Combat Dry, Rough Skin, Shiny Nose, Blackheads, Lines, Wrinkles
• The most advanced beauty development known to the cosmetic art to aid nature uncover new, live, fresh, clearer skin. Beauty editors are writing about it! Thousands praise it! The very first application of this new beautifier, TAYTON'S CREAM, releases precious triple-whipped ingredients to specially combat Dryness, Roughness, Shiny Nose, Pimples, Blackheads, Enlarged Pores and fight tragic wrinkles—Tired Lines. Like nature's own oils of youth helps keep the skin soft and supple. TAYTON'S CREAM quickly melts and dissolves the dry, scaly, dead skin cells. Cleans. Lubricates. Smooths. By stimulating the underskin, arousing the oil glands, freeing clogged pores, the cause of blackheads, dryness and premature wrinkling is combated in nature's own way. That's why TAYTON'S CREAM is succeeding in the most stubborn cases. Get a jar today.
Make Your Sleepy Skin Wake Up and Live
• Every day newspapers report how Hollywood beauty experts are making women appear more beautiful. How they care for the skin. Make it look younger, more appealing. Give it stimulation. Cleanse. Lubricate. Fight dryness, roughness, tired lines and wrinkles. Make it wake up and live. Now, right in your own home, and for only a few cents, you can give your skin these thrilling new beauty benefits.
Make Your Guaranteed Test
• Make this positive proof test. Let your own mirror tell you the results. Ask for TAYTON'S CREAM at your drug, Department, or 10c store. Cleanse with it and also use it as a night cream for 3 days. It must make your skin softer, smoother, clearer and younger-looking, or money back on return of empty jar. If your dealer cannot supply you, don't accept a substitute. TAYTON'S CREAM, being the very latest beauty development, some stores may not as yet have it, but if you will speak to the manager and insist he order for you, he can quickly get it from his headquarters, or wholesaler. The guarantee protects you.
TAYTON
"An Old English Name"
New Glamour Make-up
TAYTON'S FACE POWDER
TAYTON'S LIPSTICK
TAYTON'S ROUGE

Tayton, 1937

Many Meals Fall Short On Vitamins
People Don't Know Whether They Are Getting Enough Vitamins—Until Ill Health Shows It. But Add ONE FOOD to Your Diet EVERY DAY and You Can Be Sure of a Regular EXTRA Supply of These Four Vitamins
G
Too Little Vitamin G Means Poor Growth
Diet Abundant in Vitamin G
THIN, nervous children are often found to be undersupplied with Vitamin G—the GROWTH VITAMIN. A generous supply of this vitamin is needed by all growing children to aid in the proper development of a strong, healthy body. Fleischmann's Yeast is rich in Vitamin G. Children from 5 to 12 years can be given 1 to 2 cakes daily.
D
MISSHAPEN, poorly formed teeth (like those in plaster cast at left) can come from a lack of Vitamin D—the BONE VITAMIN. Growing children, especially, need plenty of Vitamin D to help in the formation of strong, attractive teeth. Fleischmann's fresh Yeast provides a rich supply of this BONE VITAMIN. Children from 5 to 12 years can be given 1 to 2 cakes each day.
Not Enough Vitamin B
B
Ample Vitamin B
A
INCREASED SUSCEPTIBILITY TO COLDS can occur when you are getting too little Vitamin A. Lack of this vitamin weakens the membranes lining nose and throat. Eat Fleischmann's Yeast daily to add to your regular supply of Vitamin A.
DISTENDED bowels (see picture at left above), impaired digestion, sagging stomach may all result from too little Vitamin B.
Ample Vitamin B—the NERVE VITAMIN—is needed to help keep your nerves, intestinal tract, stomach and bowels normal and healthy. Eat Fleischmann's fresh Yeast to add to your daily supply. It is one of the richest known natural food sources of Vitamin B.
ROBUST HEALTH, a sturdy, well-built body like that of Red Rolfe, brilliant Yankee third baseman, show he receives his full daily quota of the 4 essential vitamins, A, B, D and G.
EVERYDAY MEALS are often uncertain in providing enough of all the vitamins the body needs to keep it really healthy!
As a result, there are many people today who suffer from some degree of vitamin deficiency.
By the addition of just one food—FLEISCHMANN'S fresh YEAST—to your diet, you can increase your daily intake of these 4 essential vitamins—A, B, D and G.
Fleischmann's fresh Yeast is the only natural food that gives you such a rich supply of these 4 combined health-building vitamins.
Eat 3 cakes regularly, every day—one cake about ½ hour before each meal. Eat it plain—or dissolved in a little water. Begin right now to secure an EXTRA supply of these important vitamins in addition to what your meals provide. It's a good plan to order two or three days' supply at a time from your grocer. Fleischmann's Yeast keeps perfectly in the icebox.
Copyright, 1937, Standard Brands Incorporated

Fleischmann's Yeast, 1937

A UNIQUE RECIPE SERVICE
For AMERICAN HOME READERS
When, a little more than a year ago, the Editor of The American Home proposed printing the recipes so that they could be easily filed, she also devised the Menu Maker—an all-steel cabinet in four colors as illustrated which we offer our readers, complete with a card index and a supply of Cellophane envelopes.
The Menu Maker is large enough to hold all your recipes. The Cellophane envelopes permit you to file your recipes with the picture side out and the recipe itself visible on the reverse side, and fit the American Home recipes without extra cutting, allowing of leeway in case you want to replace the recipe. The envelopes are, of course, washable. The index consists of the classification of all foods as well as for each day of the week, and the use of the American Home Menu Maker permits you to plan your meals for a week in advance with all recipes filed for quick reference.
In short, the Menu Maker is a sensible, workable recipe file that only a practical housewife could have designed from actual experience, and in offering it to our readers we believe it to be the first practical recipe idea ever offered by a magazine.
40,000 SATISFIED USERS
40,000 American Home readers have adopted the American Home Menu Maker and are using it to file the recipes which appear monthly in The American Home. We offer you the Menu Maker in your choice of colors, the complete index, and 50 Cellophane envelopes for only $1.00. If you live west of the Mississippi, please add 25c to cover additional postage.
78 Recipes and Envelopes
For new readers and those who have not been filing the American Home recipes, the Editor recently went through all recipes published in The American Home and selected those she thought worthy of a permanent place in our Menu Maker. In addition she has supplied us with personal favorites from many years' culling and sampling.
We now offer the Editor's Favorite Recipes—78 of them—and Cellophane envelopes to hold them, postpaid for only 50¢. If you have the Menu Maker and want these Favorite Recipes, send only 50¢ in stamps, and if you are ordering the Menu Maker, add 50¢ and get the complete service.
Postpaid only $1.00 Complete
add 25c west of Mississippi
PLEASE USE THIS COUPON
THE AMERICAN HOME, 251 Fourth Ave., New York City
I am enclosing $1.00 for the complete Menu Maker in Blue, Black, Yellow, Green (check color), this to include 50 Cellophane envelopes, indices, etc.
Name
Street
City State
Add 25¢ if west of the Mississippi, in Canada or U. S. Possessions. AH 2-36

American Home, 1936

▸ *Sheaffer's, 1939*

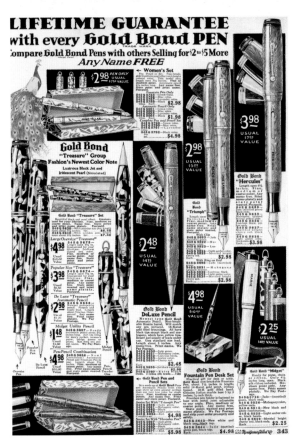

Gold Bond Pen, 1931

Carter's Ink, 1937

Waterman's, 1937 ◄ *Sheaffer's, 1938*

Sheaffer's, 1930

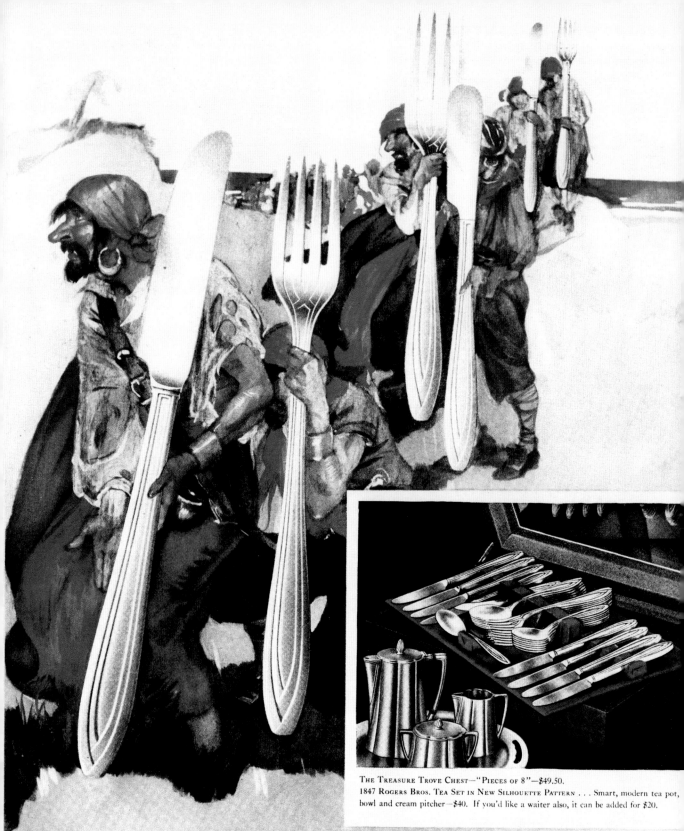

THE TREASURE TROVE CHEST—"PIECES OF 8"—$49.50.
1847 ROGERS BROS. TEA SET IN NEW SILHOUETTE PATTERN . . . Smart, modern tea pot,
bowl and cream pitcher—$40. If you'd like a waiter also, it can be added for $20.

·1847 ROGERS BROS

SILVERPLATE

INTERNATIONAL SILVER CO.

Write International Silver Co., Factory E, Meriden, Conn., for booklet X-28. "What the well-dressed table will wear in silverware."

Looking ahead to a November Wedding

Leonora Ormsby of Saks-Fifth Avenue plans an informal wedding of ultra-smartness. She puts the bride into gleaming Bemberg* satin lamé, with V-tail jacket and train (and makes it very practical, too, for without the jacket, the dress is a daring, backless evening frock). Then slips the bridesmaid into a pink dinner suit with an Irene Hayes floral muff and scores another "different" wedding.

Ask your 1847 Rogers Bros. dealer about the exciting new trends in wedding invitations and announcements. About the newest ideas as to the bride's gifts to her bridesmaids. And be sure to tell him your choice of the lovely 1847 Rogers Bros. patterns, so he can pass the hint—well in time—to your friends. Then every lovely piece will match. Better see him at once.

1847 ROGERS BROS.
Meriden, Conn.
"AMERICA'S FINEST SILVERPLATE"

Irene Hayes, New York's smart-world florist, chooses a Louis Sherry wedding-ring cake to hold her centerpiece of Mahaja roses and snapdragons, and with this, uses green-banded Wedgwood plates, clearest Baccarat Crystal glasses, and the bride's mother's lovely 1847 Rogers Bros. silverplate. "Like many fine traditions," says Irene Hayes, "the taste for 1847 Rogers Bros. runs in families. The bride who is accustomed to the best on her mother's table naturally wants 1847 Rogers Bros. silverplate for her own."

1847 Rogers Bros. poses the hardest question a fall bride has to answer—which pattern? For 1847 patterns are all so lovely! "First Love" brings to the world of silverplate, for the first time, the high-raised motif, the deep-etched detail of sterling. "Lovelace" borrows orange blossoms to wreathe its pierced motif. And "Legacy" has a fine, early New England quality. In any of the eight 1847 Rogers Bros. patterns, a service for six costs but $29.50. Easy terms of payment make it possible to have all the pieces one needs.

*TUNE IN—Sunday, October 3—hear 9:11:15 ILLIAM POWELL opens the "SILVER THEATER" featuring leading Hollywood stars every Sunday. C.B.S. coast-to-coast, 6 P.M., E.S.T.—5 P.M., C.S.T.—4 P.M., M.S.T.—3 P.M., P.S.T.

1847 Rogers Bros., 1938

Rosalind Russell gives spring's best tip to the Bride-To-Be

ROSALIND RUSSELL, M-G-M's brightest star in smart-world dramas, has this to say to brides-to-be:

"A wedding means so many things to decide!

"First, choosing him (though he thinks he chose you!) . . .

"Then selecting your wedding dress (I'd have the dress pictured here for myself) . . .

"And then, choosing your silver pattern—the one that will grace your table all your days.

"The one I specially want you to see is the pattern I named—

"'First Love.'

"It's 1847 Rogers Bros. newest—and it's beautiful!

"And when I think of how you can get 50 pieces and a gorgeous Bridal Chest besides for the price of 40 pieces, if you'll just hurry to your silver dealer's . . . You will hurry, won't you?"

Dresses by Irene—hat by Lilly Daché

Such patterns—until now—have been possible only in sterling! 1847 Rogers Bros. broke all precedents when "Lovelace" appeared with its orange blossoms and piercing, for such a pierced pattern had, until then, meant sterling. Again, in "First Love," tradition was upset, for it had been thought that only sterling could have so high-raised a motif—such depth of detail. Choose from these and six other 1847 Rogers Bros. patterns when you get your Bridal Chest.

It's true! For a limited time only you can buy this beautiful 50-piece service for eight, in the Bridal Chest pictured above, for the price of 40 pieces. It's as though the ten pieces you see in the top and the handsome chest itself were a gift to you. Every piece is 1847 Rogers Bros. silverplate, with the year-mark 1847 on the back. In pieces it. The price—but $49.75. Other sets as low as $36.50. Easy terms will be arranged by your dealer.

What does the year-mark 1847 mean, on the back of silverplate? It means the finest silverplate that one can buy—1847 Rogers Bros. Gaytime silverplate. Many old families in America treasure heirlooms in this fine plate—pieces that once adorned pre-Civil War tables in homes of the wealthy, or that went West in covered wagons, bobbing away with a few treasured possessions. Today—as these 1847 Rogers Bros. patterns, a service for six costs

1847 Rogers Bros.
INTERNATIONAL SILVER COMPANY
Meriden, Conn.
1847 Rogers Bros. silverplate is the choice of brides who know.

1847 Rogers Bros., 1930 ◄ *1847 Rogers Bros., 1938*

5 years of the WORLD'S WORST LAUNDRY

and still these sheets wore on!

Out of a Panama jungle comes this remarkable story of sheets that refused to wear out!

"IT WAS in 1910," writes Dr. Henry V. Johnston, now of Washington, D. C., "that my wife purchased these Pequots. I was stationed in the Santo Tomas Hospital of Panama City. Alfreda Gomez, our native Panama washerwoman, laundered our sheets and pillow cases for five years in a muddy jungle stream, using home-made soap, and a stone as a washboard.

"We returned to Virginia in 1914—but it wasn't till 1929 that my wife cut up these Pequot sheets—after 19 years of the hardest kind of usage!"

THE JOHNSTONS, of course, got extra long service from their sheets. But *anybody* can get long wear from Pequots! Thousands of housewives have told us so.

Every woman who wants her money's worth will be glad to know that Pequot's extra wear has been confirmed by an impartial laboratory. The United States Testing Co. recently tested 9 leading brands of sheets. Here are its findings: Pequot was *strongest*, both before and after 100 washings. Pequot was most *uniform* in strength and weight. Pequot *shrank less* than average, and had *least* "sizing". No wonder Pequot has such a wonderful reputation for wear!

Of course, you'll discover and enjoy other qualities in Pequot sheets—qualities no laboratory can measure. You'll love their true whiteness, their straight, well-sewn hems, their soft, caressing "old linen" feel.

You will appreciate that new Pequot convenience—the Quick-Pick tab. Even when the sheets are folded and stacked, this little permanent signal sticks out and shows you which sheet fits each width bed. No sheets but Pequots offer this convenience.

Many stores are featuring Pequots right now. It's a thrifty time to buy. PEQUOT MILLS, SALEM, MASS.

PEQUOT SHEETS AND PILLOW CASES

REG. U.S. PAT. OFF.

NRA Code No. 1

4 Reasons Why Your New Sheets Should Be PEQUOTS

1 The experience of 4 generations of American housewives proves that Pequots consistently *wear longer*.

2 Impartial laboratory tests prove Pequot *strongest* and most *uniform*.

3 Pequots are caressingly soft, clear white, carefully made, and easy to wash.

4 Pequots have the handy Quick-Pick Tab, which shows the width, even when the sheets are folded on the shelf.

PEQUOTS ARE AMERICA'S MOST POPULAR SHEETS . . . BECAUSE THEY WEAR LONGER!

Pequot, 1934

▶ *Community Plate, 1935*

The Exquisite Tribute

Christmas morning, let her eyes feast on loveliness. Give Community Plate ...of all Silverware the loveliest ... and you have given beauty for all the years to come. You may choose from six distinguished designs, awaiting you wherever fine Silver is sold. Gift pieces are priced at $1.50 and up.

OMMUNITY PLATE
Leadership in Design Authority

Franciscan Ware, 1937

Vernon Pottery, 1938

Telechron, 1937

Big Ben, 1931

▶ Oriental Novelties, 1931

ORIENTAL and AMERICAN NOVELTIES

Descriptions on Opposite Page

CHOICE $1.00 EACH

A $1.35
H $1.25
FF $1.75 A PAIR
GG 49¢
Z 65¢ SET
PP 42¢
R 75¢
J $4.50
HH 65¢ SET
Y $3.45
K $1.00
S $1.00
AA $1.00
JJ 55¢
SS $2.75
L $1.95
D $1.25
T $1.00
BB $1.00
KK 23¢
TT $1.00
M $1.00
E 55¢
U $1.00
CC $1.00
LL $2.25 SET
N 83¢ SET
F 98¢
O $1.00
V $1.50 SET
DD $1.39
MM $2.48 SET
VV 65¢
WW 98¢
W $1.00 SET
XX 50¢
YY 48¢
ZZ 69¢
P 65¢
EE $1.00 SET
NN $1.25
AAA 59¢
X $1.25
FFF 98¢
DDD $3.33 SET of 6
OOO $1.79
HHH 98¢
EEE 98¢
MMM $2.89
SSS $5.00
NNN 43¢
PPP
JJJ

Cannon, 1939

Cannon, 1931

McCalls, 1937 ◄ *Nashua Blankets, 1930*

Chatham Blankets, 1938

IF YOU HAD BEEN AWAY
THREE YEARS~

A ND returned to New York just before
dinner one evening—what would you
do? Where would you dine; what play or
movie would you see; where would you
dance and have an early breakfast? Or,
if you stayed in (which you probably
wouldn't), what book (if any) would you
read?

THE NEW YORKER, considering you reasonably intelligent, would tell you. Reading it is
the only way you could find out, unless you knew
and talked with all THE NEW YORKER
writers and all the people they write about. And
they are a great many.

So if you turned to THE NEW YORKER
you would find a conscientious guide of all
current amusement offerings worthwhile—*theatres, motion pictures, musical events, art exhibitions, sports,* and *miscellaneous entertainment*
—providing a ready answer to the prevalent
query, "What shall we do this evening?" You
would be apprised of what is going on in the
public and semi-public smart gathering places—
clubs, hotels, cafés, supper clubs, cabarets, and
other resorts. You would be told where to lunch
and dine and dance.

THE NEW YORKER is published avowedly
for a metropolitan audience. Its character is perfectly expressed by its art which has set a new
standard in American publishing.

In addition, it prints *prose* and *verse, humor,
satirical paragraphs,* and *stories* about the people
and events that make New York the most fascinating island in the world. These you will find
in no other publication.

THE
NEW YORKER,
25 WEST 45TH STREET,
NEW YORK

Superb Bindings

THE TRAVELS OF MARCO POLO

GEOFFREY CHAUCER — CANTERBURY TALES IN MODERN ENGLISH — Illustrated by ROCKWELL KENT

SELECTED PROSE & POETRY OF RUDYARD KIPLING — Edited by MANUEL KOMROFF

THE COMPLETE WORKS OF O. HENRY

Which of these
DE LUXE BEST SELLERS

(Many Originally Published at $5, $6.50, $10.50 and Even Up to $25)

do you want for only 59¢ to $1.98 Each?

LOOK at the amazing list of book BARGAINS on this page and the next! Books you have always wanted. Books that belong in every modern American's library. At only one-half, one-fifth, even ONE-FIFTEENTH their original prices!

And these are not books that didn't sell, or publisher's "left-overs"—but gorgeous new editions of books which have sold hundreds of thousands of copies at the former prices!

See which ones you want. Then send coupon on next page—without money—NOW!

Turn Over for More of These Amazing Book Bargains..

Deluxe Best Sellers, 1937

For Friends who have EVERYTHING

A YEAR OF
Fortune
IS THE PERFECT
Christmas Gift

—a magazine whose unsurpassed beauty and stimulating content will stir among your friends, both men and women, the same enthusiasm that you and countless others have so often voiced.

Xmas Gift Rates

1 Subscription $10
Additional . . . . each $7

FORTUNE is the only magazine I have ever felt worthy to send to friends as a gift. — CHARLES F. NOYES, *President*, Charles F. Noyes Co., Inc.

The New Yorker Magazine, 1936 ◄ *Fortune Magazine, 1934*

Will their Dream come True, or will Sex Ignorance Mar Their Happiness

Thousands of marriages end in misery and divorce because so many married people are ignorant of the Art of Love. Is *your* marriage on the brink of ruin? Do *you* search for the joy of a perfect union? Now YOU can change despair into heavenly happiness—if you know the secrets of the intimate physical contacts of marriage.

Dr. Marie Stopes, in the preface to her world-famous book, says, "In my own marriage I paid such a terrible price for sex ignorance that I felt that knowledge gained at such a price should be placed at the service of humanity." This volume, "Married Love," courageously fulfills this noble purpose.

MARRIED LOVE

A Solution of Intimate Sex Difficulties
by Dr. Marie Stopes

With remarkable frankness, and in simple, understandable language, Dr. Stopes explains the intimate and important details of wedded life. Point by point, and just as plainly as she would tell you in private confidence, Dr. Stopes takes up each of the many troublesome factors in marriage. She makes clear just what is to be done to insure contentment and happiness. She writes directly, forcefully, concretely, explaining step by step every procedure in proper sex relations.

Partial Contents

- The practice of restraint to please the wife.
- Surest way to prepare wife for union.
- The marital rights of the husband.
- What the wife must do to bring her husband's physical desires in harmony with her own.
- Regulation of physical marital relations.
- Sleeplessness from unsatisfied desires.
- Nervousness due to unsatisfied desires.
- Charts showing periodicity of natural desire in women.
- The essential factors for the act of union.
- Greatest physical delights in marital life.
- How some women drive their husbands to prostitutes.
- Natural desire for physical union.
- Joys of the honeymoon.
- Ignorance of the bride and unwise actions of the groom.
- The man who has relations with prostitutes before marriage.
- Causes for unhappiness in marriage.
- Frequency of marital relations.
- Stimulation of physical desires.
- The problem of the strong-sexed husband and the weak-sexed wife.
- Positions.
- Physical relations during pregnancy.
- Problems of childless unions.

"Married Love" contains 192 pages printed on fine antique paper, handsomely bound in cloth. Actual size is 5¼ x 7⅝ inches.

You must read this valuable book to understand why over 1,000,000 copies have been sold in Europe and America! ORDER YOUR COPY TODAY!

American Biological Society
319 East 34th Street   Dept. M169   New York, N. Y.

1,000,000 COPIES SOLD

Men and women by the thousands eagerly paid the original published price of $5 a copy. The enormous sale made possible a $3 edition—and thousands more availed themselves of this bargain. All told, more than a million copies of "Married Love" have been sold in Europe and America. And now—for a limited time (this announcement may not appear again) —this same book is yours for only 98c! A new world of happiness may be in store for you! A new dawn of joy and health and energy and—the success that comes with them.

Order at Once

Send in your order at once to be sure to secure a copy of this famous book dealing with the intimate contacts of love in marriage. Take advantage of this special offer made to the readers of *Pictorial Review* to secure a copy of "Married Love" at this amazingly low price of only 98c.

MARRIED LOVE Dr. MARIE STOPES

was $3.00 now only 98¢

FEDERAL JUDGE LIFTS BAN

on the famous book dealing with the intimate physical contacts of love in marriage

In lifting the ban on "Married Love" Federal Judge John M. Woolsey said this famous book "was neither immoral nor obscene, but highly informative.... It pleads, for a better understanding by husbands of the physical and emotional side of the sex life of their wives . . . I cannot imagine a normal mind to which this book would seem to be obscene or immoral."

American Biological Society, Dept. M169
319 East 34th St., New York, N. Y.

Enclosed is my remittance of 98c plus 15c for packing and delivery charges for which please send me in plain wrapper—all charges prepaid—one copy of the special American edition of Dr. Marie C. Stopes' famous book "Married Love" which originally sold for $3.00.

NOTE: Sold to Adults only—state age.

Name................................ Age........

Address................................

City................................ State................

Married Love, 1938

EARN MONEY Women DO FURCRAFT WORK AT HOME. Fine profits. No investment, no traveling. New, wonderful, money making craft for women at home. Need money? Then WRITE TODAY for particulars and FREE BOOK. No obligation. N. W. Fur Company, Dept. 3314 Omaha, Neb.

YARN WORLD'S FINEST LOWEST PRICES Satisfaction Guaranteed. FREE—Knitting Accessories with Order. FREE—16 Page Exclusive STYLE and Sample BOOK 1000 COLORS INSTRUCTIONS. WONOCO YARN CO., Dept. G, 371 Grand St., New York, N. Y.

SKIN RASH
RELIEVED....ITCHING STOPPED

For quick relief from itching of eczema, rashes, pimples, athlete's foot, and other externally caused skin eruptions, use cooling, antiseptic, liquid D.D.D. PRESCRIPTION. Greaseless, stainless, dries fast. Stops the most intense itching in a hurry. A 35c trial bottle, at drug stores, proves it—or money back.

D.D.D. *Prescription*

HAPPY RELIEF FROM PAINFUL BACKACHE

Caused by Tired Kidneys

Many of those gnawing, nagging, painful backaches people blame on colds or strains are often caused by tired kidneys—and may be relieved when treated in the right way.

The kidneys are Nature's chief way of taking excess acids and poisonous waste out of the blood. Most people pass about 3 pints a day or about 3 pounds of waste.

If the 15 miles of kidney tubes and filters don't work well, poisonous waste matter stays in the blood. These poisons may start nagging backaches, rheumatic pains, leg pains, loss of pep and energy, getting up nights, swelling, puffiness under the eyes, headaches and dizziness.

Don't wait! Ask your druggist for Doan's Pills, used successfully by millions for over 40 years. They give happy relief and will help the 15 miles of kidney tubes flush out poisonous waste from the blood. Get Doan's Pills.

▶ *Time-Fortune Magazines, 1933*

REPORTING
ON YOUR BUILDING AT
A CENTURY OF PROGRESS

NICOLAI & FARO
ARCHITECTS

ether or not you were among the many TIME
...ders to visit the TIME-FORTUNE Building at A
...tury of Progress in Chicago, you may be inter-
...d in its record.

...t offered visitors a place for rest and reading.
...world's largest magazine rack with over 1500
...iodicals from all over the world was in constant
... Here are outstanding facts about the building.

❧ ❧ ❧

...ISITORS TO BUILDING—91,000 a week. (A word to
...ertisers: thousands of these people were high grade
...ers in their respective towns, many of them learning
...ut the TIME idea for the first time. That's "dealer
...ience," the same strong kind that has been created,
... is being created by "The March of Time" on the
...o.)

...OOKLETS TO VISITORS—400,000. (Further acquaint-
...new friends with the TIME idea.)

...EW TIME SUBSCRIBERS—4,700 trial subscriptions.
...0 regular subscriptions.

- NEW FORTUNE SUBSCRIBERS—330.

- LETTERS WRITTEN AT BUILDING—246,000.

- POST CARDS—123,800.

- MAGAZINE MOST SUBSCRIBED TO (Visitors to the building could subscribe to any of the 1500 magazines dis-
played. No visitors were high-pressured, and TIME
charged no fee, received no pay for taking subscriptions.)
Not including TIME, FORTUNE and THE ARCHITEC-
TURAL FORUM the magazines most subscribed to were
Magazine Digest, Reader's Digest, Child Life.

- MOST FREQUENT BONER—middle aged ladies asking if
this was the place where fortunes were told.

- NUMBER OF PEOPLE WHO SAW THE BUILDING: Over
20 million eyes couldn't have missed the large reproductions of TIME and FORTUNE covers on the building.

- COPIES OF ARCHITECTURAL FORUM SOLD (July issue,
A Century of Progress Reference number, price $1.00):
3000.

- NET RESULT: Better than all expectations.

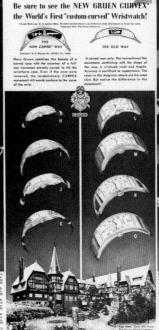

Bulova, 1935

Gruen, 1937

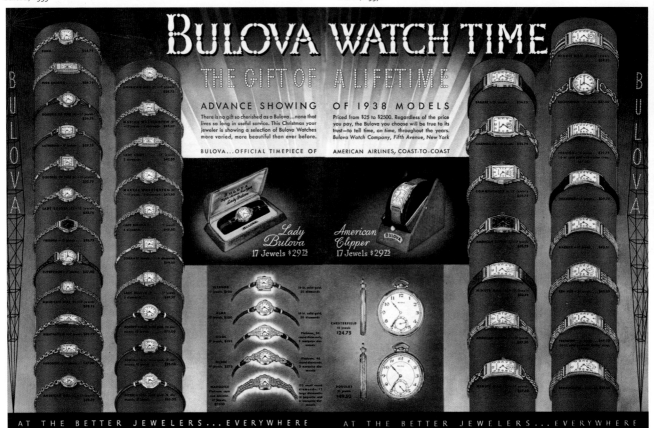

Bulova, 1937

Introducing to America

THE NEWLY IMPORTED BOXER

German Sieger and American Champion
Lustig vom Dom of Tulgey Wood

Shown for the First Time in America at the Mississippi Valley Kennel Club Show, St. Louis, Missouri, March 27th and 28th, Best of Breed, Winner of the Working Dog Group . . . Second Time Shown Tri-City Kennel Club Show, Moline, Illinois, March 30th and 31st, Best of Breed, Best of Working Dog Group, Best Dog in Show . . . Third Time shown, Chicago Kennel Club Show, Chicago, Illinois, April 3rd and 4th, Best of Breed, completing his American Championship in One Week—A Sensational Record.

TULGEY WOOD KENNELS

Mr. & Mrs. Erwin O. Freund, owners   •   Kennels at Hinsdale, Illinois

BUSINESS ADDRESS: 6733 West Sixty-Fifth Street • Chicago, Illinois • Phone Hemlock 8200

Tulgey Wood Kennels, 1937

They Just Can't Resist an
OUTDOOR COMPLEXION

BEAUTY may be only skin deep . . . but how are you going to enjoy life unless you stop 'em with an appearance of health and well-being? Take a tip from this lucky beach-comber, keep that *outdoor complexion*.

Bask in healthful, ultra-violet rays regularly every day right in your own home, snow or shine, beneath a G-E Sunlamp. Your favorite G-E dealer is ready with the latest G-E Sun-lamp models. Stop in and look them over. See how attractive they are. How little they cost to operate . . . actually only a few pennies a day.

Sunlamps by
GENERAL ⓖⓔ ELECTRIC

Ultra-violet rays, producers of Vitamin D, build up the calcium supply in the blood. They are essential in the cure and prevention of deficiency diseases. G-E Sunlamps are an efficient and reliable source of these rays. Prices start at $39.95. The model illustrated is the BM-8. Eastern list price, $44.95.

General Electric, 1939

Four-color process engraving, 133-line screen. Courtesy of The Dow Chemical Company. Prepared by MacManus, John & Adams, Inc.

INVESTMENT IN SHADE

Whether it's planted for shade or for beauty, a tree may very plausibly be acclaimed Public Benefactor, number one. And benefactors, too, are the advertisements that tell us how to protect our trees against the hazards of transplanting and save money while doing it. The handsome water color shown on this page not only speaks to the home owner in his own language, but also delights him by its unusual point of view.

Dow Chemical Company, 1938

ZANE GREY

Take Your Choice
of His Best Books

PROBABLY no living writer enjoys a wider popularity than Zane Grey. His books literally sell by the million. They are translated into nearly every foreign language. They've been filmed in color and made into feature talkies. Why? Because no one has caught the spirit of the Old West or written of it more glamorously than Zane Grey. And here are six of his best selling books which may be yours:

The Light of Western Stars
All the color of the Old Southwest, the perilous life of the Border, the lure of a woman's bright beauty, make this a fascinating tale.

The Mysterious Rider
Who was this strange solitary figure forever searching, searching—and what happened when "Hell-Bent" Wade rode into Bellounds Ranch?

The Heritage of the Desert
A young Easterner "goes Western," finds break-neck adventure, a lovely girl and a peace of mind that only the open places can give.

The Spirit of the Border
Here you will come close to the terror of Indian massacres, of conflict among Whites, of the strength and tenderness of pioneer love.

Wild Horse Mesa
Here is a rushing story of the wasteland, of love and cruelty and hate, all built around the greatest of wild stallions.

Forlorn River
A rousing tale of the days when cattle rustling was at its worst and of a young cowboy unjustly accused of being a thief.

And Still a Further Choice

Bambi
You'll believe animals are almost human when you read this exquisite story of a deer. By Felix Salten.

The Secret of Sea Dream House
Hair-raising happenings in a "deserted" pirate house in the Everglades. By Albert Payson Terhune.

The Indian Drum
An eerie mystery based on an Indian legend of the Great Lakes. By McHarg and Balmer.

Beau Ideal
The last of the foot-hearted Geste in the French Foreign Legion. By P. C. Wren.

The Virginian
Many critics say this is the greatest Western story of all time. By Owen Wister.

Touchstone
For twenty years their parents thought they were twins. And then—— By Ira Amos Williams.

Answers to Questions
Here's a splendid collection (5,000 in all) of the best questions and answers you've read in the newspapers.

The Royal Road to Romance
A daring young adventurer re-travels the trails of early explorers and conquering heroes. By Richard Halliburton.

How to Claim Your Copies

FOR any one of the books listed on this page, send us only two new or renewal subscriptions to *The Ladies' Home Journal* from people outside your family who do not live at your address. For any address in the United States send $1 for each 1-year subscription; $1.50 for 2 years; $2 for 3 years. Each subscription counts the same. For foreign and Canadian addresses, see title page. Mail the full amount you collect with your request for the books. Your own subscription may be included in your order, but it cannot count toward the books. We will forward the books at once, postage prepaid.

to any address* other than that of one of your subscribers. The request for the books must be accompanied by the full amount necessary; subscriptions sent previously do not count.

For three books, send three new subscriptions; or send five subscriptions for any six books. Only orders for two or more books will be accepted; do not send out subscriptions for one book.

*On account of imposts, no orders can be accepted for books to be shipped to foreign countries. And for each book ordered the Canadian or U.S. add 10c to cover duty.

Ladies' Home Journal

787 INDEPENDENCE SQUARE, PHILADELPHIA, PENNSYLVANIA

Upon request we'll be glad to send you an attractive booklet listing more than 100 delightful books.

Zane Grey, 1932

EDISON MAZDA LAMPS
GENERAL ⊕ ELECTRIC

For beauty and eye comfort
keep every lamp socket filled

There is an Edison MAZDA La
for every type of fixture

DON'T FORGET LAMPS
Take home a carton today for convenience and good lighting

WHEN you buy Edison MAZDA* Lamps, you get a General Electric product, improved by twenty-five years of research.

Edison MAZDA Lamps have the quality that assures full value of the current consumed. They are nationally advertised,

and there is a progressive Edison M Lamp dealer in your neighborhood

When buying lamps, always loo the name EDISON on the carton an marks MAZDA and ⊕ on the bulb.

*MAZDA—the mark of a research service

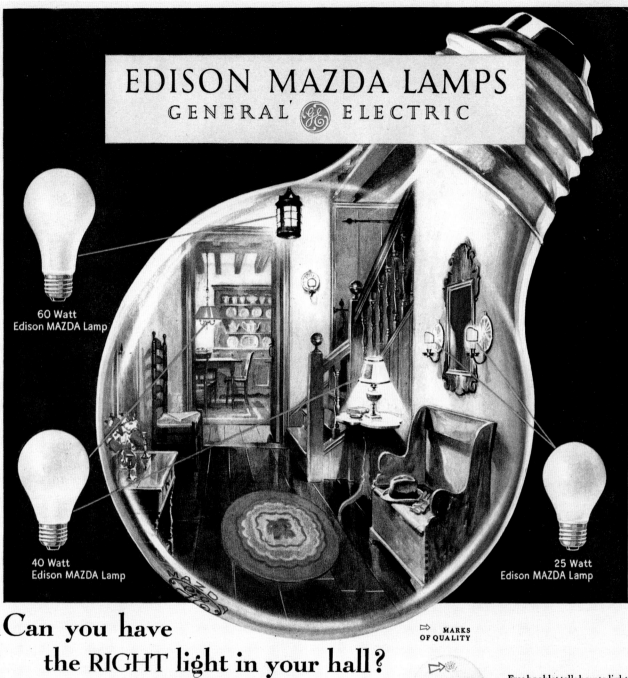

EDISON MAZDA LAMPS
GENERAL ⓖ ELECTRIC

60 Watt
Edison MAZDA Lamp

40 Watt
Edison MAZDA Lamp

25 Watt
Edison MAZDA Lamp

Can you have
the RIGHT light in your hall?

Is there a ceiling fixture for general illumination?
Is the stairway well lighted, to prevent missteps?
Is there good light at the mirror?
Does the light in your hall show it at its best?

THE FIRST IMPRESSION of your home will be formed as your guest enters the hall. A favorable first impression will be likely to influence later impressions.

Every hall should be equipped with a ceiling fixture to provide general illumination. The stairway should be well lighted. Dimness there may cause accidents. The importance of good light upon the stairs is emphasized if there are elderly people or small children in your home.

Callers will wish to make use of the hall mirror. A shaded lamp on each side of it will produce the most satisfactory light.

Use Edison MAZDA* Lamps for good lighting throughout your home. Their high quality assures *full value of the current consumed*.

When buying lamps, always look for the name EDISON on the carton and the marks MAZDA and ⓖ on the bulb.

*MAZDA—*the mark of a research service*

⇨ MARKS
OF QUALITY

Free booklet tells how to light
your home throughout

Few homes have enough light where it is needed. We have prepared a useful illustrated booklet which explains how best to light every room in your home. The coupon will bring you a free copy.

EDISON LAMP WORKS   S9
Nela Park, Cleveland, Ohio

Please send me the booklet entitled "How to Light Your Home."

Name...

Address..

A GENERAL ELECTRIC PRODUCT—

☞ THE MARK OF QUALITY

BE SURE to buy lamps that will give you all the light you pay for. Edison MAZDA Lamps, a product of General Electric, are tested under the requirements of MAZDA Service to give the *full value of the electric current you use for lighting.*

Good light is one of the most important among your daily necessities. It costs you less than any of the others, except air and water.

If there are children in your home, use plenty of good light from MAZDA Lamps to protect their eyes.

Edison MAZDA Lamps represent the latest achievements of MAZDA* Service, through which the benefits of world-wide research and experiment in the Laboratories of General Electric are given exclusively to lamp manufacturers entitled to use the name MAZDA.

MAZDA—the mark of a research service

EDISON MAZDA LAMPS
GENERAL Ⓖ ELECTRIC

General Electric, 1930

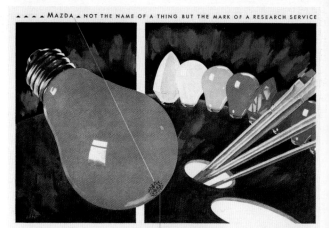

▲ ▲ ▲ MAZDA ▲ NOT THE NAME OF A THING BUT THE MARK OF A RESEARCH SERVICE

USE GENERAL ELECTRIC FLAMETINT AND INSIDE COLORED MAZDA LAMPS TO

Paint *with* Light

THE magic brush of the theatre is light. Use it freely in your own home to achieve the softness and beauty which make the Land of Make-Believe so attractive from "out in front." Ask your dealer in General Electric colored and decorative MAZDA lamps to show the following:

FLAMETINT lamps, whose mellow glow makes you think of candlelight and the ruddy warmth of an open fire. No living room really lives until its deep, easy chairs and cushion-piled couches are supplemented with the beckoning comfort of flametint. Paint with them for better living.

DECORATIVE LAMPS to give the final touch to modern decoration. Smart as Paris. New as tomorrow's sunshine. Unusual as an illustration by Erté. Every woman will think instantly of a dozen places to use them effectively because they are as beautiful unlighted as lighted.

COLORED LAMPS in a complete symphony of beauty—from the muted tone of pale ivory to the lusty notes of red and green suggestive of cheerfully painted breakfast rooms and gaily cretonned sun-rooms.

EXPENSIVE? Only a few cents more in most cases over the price you ordinarily pay for the famous standard line of inside-frosted MAZDA lamps which fill so many of your lighting needs. Inexpensive to burn as well. And remember, they come in the familiar blue carton. NATIONAL LAMP WORKS of General Electric Company, Nela Park, Cleveland, Ohio.

GENERAL Ⓖ ELECTRIC
MAZDA Ⓖ LAMPS

General Electric, 1930

SAVE THAT TWINKLE!

Eyestrain starts when children begin to use their eyes. That's the time you need to pay attention. Help their eyes develop normally: (1) by having their eyes examined regularly; (2) by providing lighting that helps them see safely.

The first step in securing good lighting is to use high quality lamp bulbs, the kind that don't waste electricity and that STAY BRIGHTER LONGER. Insist on MAZDA lamps made by General Electric.

Why take the chance of getting 30% less light for your money and of cheating your eyesight, by using inferior substitutes? The mark Ⓖ on the end of the bulb is sure protection against substitution. Look for it when you buy lamp bulbs.

15¢
60 WATTS AND SMALLER

G-E ALSO MAKES A LAMP FOR 10c. In 7½, 15, 25 and 60-watt sizes and marked Ⓖ

GENERAL Ⓖ ELECTRIC

General Electric, 1937

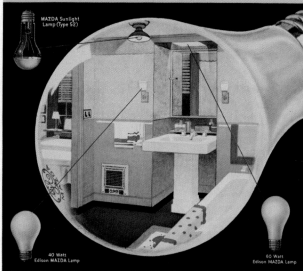

EDISON MAZDA LAMPS
GENERAL Ⓖ ELECTRIC

MAZDA Sunlight Lamp (Type S-2)

40 Watt Edison MAZDA Lamp

60 Watt Edison MAZDA Lamp

Is your bathroom Lighted the New Way?

Can you have the benefits of ultra-violet rays while bathing?

Is there good light at the mirror for shaving?

Can labels on bottles in the medicine cabinet be read easily?

THE new MAZDA* Sunlight Lamp (Type S-2), manufactured by General Electric, enables you to have ultra-violet-ray benefits comparable to those for which people travel to crowded beaches.

With a MAZDA Sunlight Lamp (Type S-2) in the bathroom ceiling fixture, the man of the house can enjoy the benefits of ultra-violet rays while shaving. Children and others can have these benefits while bathing.

This lamp will not operate in the ordinary socket. Special fixtures for the use of the MAZDA Sunlight Lamp (Type S-2) are now obtainable everywhere at small cost.

If you do not have a MAZDA Sunlight Lamp in your bathroom, use a 100 watt Edison MAZDA Lamp in the ordinary ceiling fixture and a 40 watt Edison MAZDA Lamp at each side of the mirror. A concealed luminous panel fixture with a 60 watt lamp will be a further aid for shaving and the use of the bowl. Good light in the bathroom is an inexpensive necessity.

When buying lamps, look for the name EDISON on the carton and the mark MAZDA and Ⓖ on the bulbs.

MAZDA—the mark of a research service.

MARKS OF QUALITY

Free booklet tells how to light your home throughout

Few homes have enough light when it is needed. We have prepared a useful illustrated booklet which explains how best to light every room in your home. The coupon will bring you a free copy.

Edison Lamp Works, Nela Park, Cleveland, Ohio

Please send me the booklet entitled "How to Light Your Home."

Name

Address

W-11

EDISON LAMP WORKS OF GENERAL ELECTRIC, NELA PARK, CLEVELAND, OHIO

General Electric, 1931

▶ *General Electric, 1937*

LIGHT UP WITH *Safety*

GENERAL 🅖🅔 ELECTRIC

MAZDA CHRISTMAS TREE LAMPS
STAY BRIGHTER LONGER

For a glowing Christmas tree, use General Electric MAZDA lamps . . . and watch young eyes sparkle as these famous lamps light up. G-E lamps do not burn out quickly . . . nor do they lose their brilliant color. (Standard colors are white, red, blue, green and orange.)

Not only will you light up for beauty, but the safeguards of General Electric manufacture and tests eliminate the hazards sometimes found in inferior bulbs. Why risk spoiling your Christmas when G-E Lamps stay brighter longer—and are safer?

General Electric makes only the bulbs. For best results you should insist that outfits and other lighted decorations be equipped with General Electric MAZDA Christmas Tree lamps. *And be sure, too, that spares and renewals bear the G-E trademark.*

"FAMOUS" CANDLES . . . le-shaped bulbs ow from tip to ith rich color. e in both series ltiple strings.

"ELECTRIC" CANDLES Small candles, with tiny electric lamps, that sparkle like the old-fashioned tallow candle. For series strings only.

"MULTIPLE" XMAS TREE LAMPS . . . In multiple strings all the lamps do not go out when one lamp goes dead, as they do in series strings.

"STANDARD" PINE CONE SHAPE . . . comes in white, red, blue, green and orange. For series strings only.

Your Keys to Chicago

Merry Christmas
Say it with flowers *By wire!*

Shop for the children and those close to your heart? Of course! But for out-of-town friends and acquaintance—those whose presents are always a difficult task—what could be more appropriate than to say "Merry Christmas" with flowers-by-wire! A grand idea! A marvelous gift—one that will never be forgotten. It's really fun to wire flowers. Easy, too—no wrapping, no mailing and sure, prompt delivery—if you select one of the 12,000 members of the Florists' Telegraph Delivery Association to wire your gift of happiness. Beautiful flowers, true artistry and service with a smile are to be found in every shop that displays the F.T.D. emblem. Look for it when you buy. And say "Merry Christmas" with flowers-by-wire this year.

FLORISTS' TELEGRAPH DELIVERY ASSOCIATION
AN INTERNATIONAL ORGANIZATION OF OVER 12,000 FLORISTS

Florists' Telegraph Delivery Association, 1937

The hazardous adventure of being a *baby*

"MAY my little one grow strong and sound" —it is the prayer of every mother. Cheerfully, throughout the crucial months of infancy, she dedicates each waking moment to make that wish come true.

And humane men, intent on easing her responsibilities, make certain she need never worry about the jars and jolts that distress so many babies. They design a "shock-proofed" carriage, scientifically constructed so as to safeguard sensitive little spines.

These Lloyd carriages have bodies of loom-woven fibre—reinforced with invisible steel wire in every upright strand.

They are upholstered with soft, luxurious fabrics. Their resilient springs are oil-tempered. They have gaily colored* balloon tires.

Particularly during National Lloyd Week, April 7 to 12, stores are making a special featuring of Lloyd carriages and strollers. There are many charming color finishes. Prices, due to the speed and manufacturing efficiency of the patented Lloyd looms, are easily within every family's means. And decidedly economical, too, is the colorful, smartly designed Lloyd loom-woven furniture now so much in evidence in so many nice homes.

*Smart and new are baby carriage tires in color, an exclusive Lloyd innovation

Lloyd LOOM Products
BABY CARRIAGES & FURNITURE
Menominee, Michigan
ORILLIA, ONTARIO, CANADA

NATIONAL **LLOYD** WEEK APRIL 7-12

For interesting information about Lloyd Baby Carriages or any of the other many Lloyd loom-woven products—Living Room and Porch Fibre Furniture, Steel Tubular Chairs and Stools, Juvenile Furniture, and Doll Carriages—simply address a request to Lloyd Loom Products, Dept. A., Menominee, Michigan.

Lloyd Loom Products, 1930

Improve your Bridge Game by tuning in with Bridge by Radio under personal direction of Milton C. Work. Covers both Auction and Contract. See newspapers for nearest station and time of broadcasting.

Easy Lessons in Auction Bridge—128 "winning" pages on bidding and play—10c.

Main Differences between Contract and Auction, by Milton C. Work—Free.

THE present revival of interest in the quaint old cross-stitch samplers and Godey fashion figures makes these four new Congress designs appeal to both the older and younger generation.

Used in complete ensembles of playing cards, score pads and tallies, they express the good taste of the hostess and make her parties a harmony of color and design.

The playing cards are produced by The U. S. Playing Card Company, Cincinnati, U. S. A., and Windsor, Canada, and that means they are of the finest quality. Sold in one, two, four, or six pack cases—ideal not only for parties but for gifts as well.

The score pads and tallies illustrated are made for The U. S. Playing Card Company by The P. F. Volland Company, Joliet, Illinois, whose Bridge party accessories and greeting cards are sold through twenty thousand leading merchants in the United States and Canada. Available in table units of one pad and four tallies, or in attractive boxes for two, three, or four table parties.

THE U. S. PLAYING CARD COMPANY
Cincinnati, U. S. A., and Windsor, Canada

Card players who prefer conventional back designs invariably use

BICYCLE PLAYING CARDS

They are the choice of clubs and tournaments everywhere because of their snap and finish.

Players who want cards of Bicycle quality with decorative color backs have made Bicycle Multicolor Cards an instantaneous success. Ask to see these new designs with tinted edges—another innovation.

THE U. S. PLAYING CARD COMPANY
Dept. 8-4, Cincinnati, U. S. A., or Windsor, Canada.
Please send items checked:
Easy Lessons in Auction Bridge—128 pages—10c
Main Differences between Contract and Auction—Free.
Name
Address

CONGRESS
PLAYING CARDS SCORE PADS *and* TALLIES...

Gateways, 1934 ◄ *Congress Playing Cards, 1930*

If typists were
ROBOTS

... then – any typist could be "set" to match the key tension of her typewriter. But typists are not robots. Each has developed her own individual touch. Therefore, to complement it, the typewriter must be readily adaptable to the exact finger pressure of the operator.

Royal alone makes this personalization possible. Touch Control, exclusive with the New Easy-Writing Royal, permits each typist to adapt the key tension to her exact finger pressure – to do this easily, instantly – by the simple turn of a dial!

Invite a demonstration of this sensational New Royal with its 17 major advances, including Improved Shift Freedom, Finger Comfort Keys, Automatic Paper Lock each designed to produce finer-appearing letters, increase efficiency, to decrease costs!

Royal Typewriter Company, Inc., 2 Park Ave., N. Y.
Branches and Agencies the World Over

THE NEW
EASY-WRITING
ROYAL
TYPEWRITER

Since 1848 every Kurtzmann has been built slowly, carefully — by master craftsmen ... Now, for the first time, this distinguished piano is priced throughout the United States at six hundred and forty-five dollars — the lowest price in Kurtzmann history ...You will find the Kurtzmann at leading piano stores from coast to coast. See it — play it — listen to its beautiful, resonant tone — a tone that will retain its beauty throughout the years

Six Hundred and Forty-five Dollars

CRAFTSMEN BUILD THE KURTZMANN

A DIVISION OF WURLITZER DEKALB, ILLINOIS

Kurtzmann Piano, 1935

No. 270/41/120 Hohner "L'Organola" Artists' Model. The latest development of Hohner perfection and workmanship. Casing, gallery and keys of mother of pearl. 41 treble keys, 120 bass keys. Four sets of hand made steel reeds. Three automatic octave coupler shifts on melody side and one on the bass side, provide a wide range of tonal effects. A truly magnificent instrument that will appeal to every lover of the Piano Accordion.

No. 200/25/12 Junior Model De Luxe. A favorite instrument for beginners. Choice of pearl white or pearl black finish.

No. 3053/34/80 Hohner "Imperial." An exquisite model, light and compact, finished throughout in white or black mother of pearl. An outstanding Hohner instrument.

Hohner "L'Organola" Console Model, a superb instrument featuring the curved keyboard, finished in white or black mother of pearl.

● Hohner Piano Accordions are offered in a wide range of sizes and prices, from the magnificent instrument pictured above to the simple eight and twelve bass models.

Regardless of size or price, all have the same uniform richness of tone, perfect construction and simplicity of playing that have won outstanding recognition for Hohner Piano Accordions as *"the world's best".*

The de luxe "Artists" Model shown above and the superb Hohner "Console" Model at the left are the latest achievements demonstrating Hohner leadership and supremacy in the field of Piano Accordions. Behind these marvelous instruments lies three quarters of a century of experience and development, as succeeding generations of craftsmen have steadily advanced the Hohner standard of quality and perfection.

As the Christmas Season approaches, the desirability of these popular and beautiful instruments for gift purposes is emphasized. For musical training—for the hours of joy and pleasure they bring—for pride of possession—few gifts equal a Hohner Piano Accordion.

Booklet describing complete line of Hohner Piano Accordions will be sent upon request.

HOHNER PIANO ACCORDIONS
M. HOHNER, INC., 351 FOURTH AVENUE, NEW YORK

Hohner Accordions, 1934

WHY NOT 40 HOURS FOR EXECUTIVES, TOO?

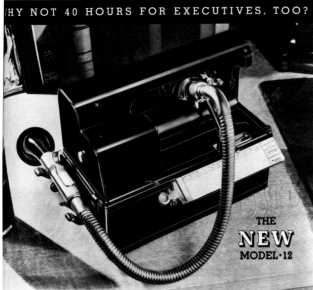

THE NEW MODEL·12

"The word DICTAPHONE is the registered Trade-Mark of Dictaphone Corporation, makers of Dictating Machines and Accessories to which said Trade-Mark is Applied.

DICTAPHONE

The shortening of the working week to forty hours need not hamper the executive whose creative type of work keeps him busy early and late. ● The new Model 12 will gladly work any number of hours a week if necessary. But the real purpose of this dictating machine is to enable you to do all your work in 40 hours—to double your ability to get things done. ● Find out how this new leisure for executives can be fitted into your life. Mail the coupon at the right for the new "Progress" portfolio.

DICTAPHONE SALES CORPORATION
420 Lexington Avenue, New York, N. Y.

Send me your "Progress" portfolio.

Name _____

Company _____

Street _____ City _____

Royal Typewriter, 1935 ◄   *Dictaphone, 1934*

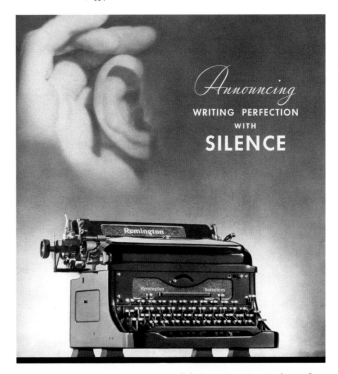

Announcing
WRITING PERFECTION WITH SILENCE

The NEW *Remington Noiseless—* is the climax of 60 years of typewriter experience. Its writing perfection is the result of dozens of Remington's pioneering developments. Its silence is the result of 24 years' refinement of the noiseless typewriter principle. Combining every known technical improvement into one superlative writing machine, this type-writer incorporates many new operator conveniences as well as new writing efficiency ...To head stenographers, to secretaries, to executives: We invite you to try this new machine at your leisure. May we also suggest the exchange of your present typewriter for *writing perfection with silence.* Look for Remington Rand in your telephone book. Or, write the Typewriter Division, Remington Rand Inc., Buffalo, New York.

Remington Typewriter, 1934

Only a movie camera gives you the complete record

Your visit to the New York World's Fair—

All your life you'll look back on it as a great experience. Packed with marvelous sights. Indescribable. Unique. Every day at the Fair you'll see more than you can absorb in a month of Sundays.

Think of being able to get the complete record with your movie camera. Think of taking it back home to show your friends—living it over again, time after time, with all its thrilling fun.

Thousands of people today are getting priceless records of life's great moments, with a movie camera. Be one of the lucky ones—take a movie camera with you wherever you go this summer. Let it double the fun of your vacation —give you a living souvenir you'll treasure always.

Only Eastman gives you Complete Equipment and Service . . . Ciné-Kodak—the home movie camera exactly suited to your needs . . . Ciné-Kodak Film . . . Processing Service that is world-wide and included in the price of the film . . . Kodascope—the projector that shows your movies clearly, brilliantly—Eastman all, and all designed to work together.

Be sure to stop at the Kodak Building—see the Greatest Photographic Show on Earth

There'll be Eastman experts there, who will advise you what to take with your Ciné-Kodak, and how to take it. And there you'll see the unique and gorgeous Cavalcade of Color—the "Greatest Photographic Show on Earth." Nothing like it has ever been seen before. Don't miss it . . . Eastman Kodak Company, Rochester, N. Y.

Life's great moments

To make 16 mm. Movies . . . Ciné-Kodak "E," the low-priced "sixteen" that has so many high-priced camera features, $39.50. Ciné-Kodak "K," most widely used 16 mm. home movie camera, $80—a new low price. Magazine Ciné-Kodak, 3-second magazine loading, $117.50.

To show 16 mm. Movies . . . Kodascope Model EE, Series II, capable, low priced, from $57.95. Kodascope Model G, Series II, Eastman's newest precision-built projector, from $112.95. Both complete with lens and lamp.

Ciné-Kodak
EASTMAN'S FINER HOME MOVIE CAMERAS

Ciné-Kodak, 1939

Movie "shots" for 10¢ apiece
with Eastman's new $29.50 Ciné-Kodak

Roll of film taking a couple of dozen scenes costs only $2.25—finished, ready to show

Your own adorable baby—in movies you make yourself. What will an occasional 10¢ buy that's half so precious?

An entirely new camera, an entirely new principle, makes one foot of film go as far as four. Each roll takes twenty to thirty news-reel shots.

And the roll costs only $2.25, finished, ready to run.

It's all so Simple

Make movies of the children, movies of your trips. Movies of interesting, exciting events. It's great sport. Vastly entertaining.

Ask to see Sample Movies

You show your movies with Kodascope Eight, the new all-electric projector, only $22.50.

Your Ciné-Kodak dealer has sample movies made with the Eight. Ask to see them projected. Or write for the booklet about this camera that gives you movie scenes at 10¢ apiece. Eastman Kodak Company, Rochester, N.Y.

Ciné-Kodak EIGHT *Eastman's New-Principle Movie Camera*

Ciné-Kodak, 1933

Now...you can make S-L-O-W motion COLOR movies with a *Filmo*
$55 8x film or 16 mm.

● Yes, you can now make s-l-o-w motion pictures of youth's lightning-swift movements and fleeting expressions—even in true-to-life *color*. Filmo captures movies of children, vacation days, travels, and sports for your repeated enjoyment—catches every fugitive detail faithfully, vividly. And all for only a few cents a scene.

With a Filmo, it is easy to make professional quality movies both indoors and outdoors. The film almost *drops* into place—takes but 20 seconds to load. Then look through Filmo's spyglass viewfinder, and *what you see, you get*.

The pocket-fitting, palm-size Filmo uses low-cost 8 millimeter film. Like all Filmos, it is made with the same precision construction that has made Bell & Howell equipment the choice of professionals. Has a fine lens, four speeds, and a single-frame exposure device that gives you the extra fun of making animated cartoons and titles.

See both 8 mm. and 16 mm. Filmo Cameras and Projectors—either silent or sound—at camera dealers' everywhere. Or write for informative booklets. Bell & Howell Company, Chicago, New York, Hollywood, London. Since 1907 the largest manufacturer of precision equipment for motion picture studios of Hollywood and the world.

GRADUATION OR WEDDING GIFT SUGGESTION

. . . Thousands appropriately give a Filmo to those who are *"starting out."*

MAIL COUPON FOR BOOKLET

BELL & HOWELL COMPANY
1841 Larchmont Avenue, Chicago, Illinois
Please send me the book, *How to Make Inexpensive Personal Movies.*

Name _____
Address _____
City _____ State _____

BELL & HOWELL

Bell & Howell, 1938

follow the STARS to WAAS & SON

For your recital needs

or school plays, you will require fancy fabrics and trimmings. We carry an extensive assortment in almost infinite variety and color, and will not only furnish samples, but will also submit valuable suggestions free. Write us regarding your problems.

Silk Hair (Silk-Mohair)
Wigs
Made especially for WAAS & SON.

All colors and styles. Brilliant colors—rose, blue, yellow, orange, pink, lavender and green. Also conservative black, white, blonde. $1.35.

Costume Materials

Spangled cloths . . Printed Vello . . (Large variety) . . Metaline fabrics . . Rayon Plush . . Armure cloth . . Silk nets . . Glazed tarlatane . . Plain tarlatane . . Crepe de chine . . Georgette crepe . . Metal cloths . . Dress silks (lustrous) . . Rosnina satins . . Ombre metallines . . Velveteens . . Taffeta Suisese . . Buckram . . Grisoline . . Algerine strips sport satin . . Costume lining . . Colored oil cloth . . Harlequin satins . . Costume satins.

For trimmings . . Peacock feathers . . Rhinestone trimming . . Voiles . . Organdies . . Two-tone Taffetas . . Ombre Georgette . . Sport Satins.

Accessories

Wigs . . Makeup . . Balloons . . Dancing Canes . . Buckram Hat Frames . . Feather fans . . Castinets . . Tambourines . . Costume jewelry and Costume accessories of every description.

Send for Samples

Waas & Son are prepared to send you complete sets of samples for same day your request is received! Natural original fabrics are featured only by us. There's no obligation whatever for this great help in planning your costume.

VELVETOE
(New Pad for Toe Slippers)

Combined pad for toe slippers made of soft velvet kid lined with Angora wool. Newest and most practical pad and only 50c pair.

Dancing Shoes and Supplies

Waas Grecco Sandals in seven charming colors—harmonize with any Grecian costume—blue, green, tan, natural, red, black kid, black suede and purple. Price $1.35.

The New "Bra-1-cee tap" Shoe, a splendid shoe embodying all the improved features in tap shoes. Black kid. Price includes aluminum heel and toe plates attached. $2.45. This shoe without toe plates only, attached, $1.95. Same without aluminum plates. Price, $1.75. Patent leather; as tap $4.95; tan; plates $2.45; toe and heel plates $2.50.

Aluminum Toe Plates protect a splendid slipper by enabling it to do sustained work without wear as in toe steps. Price 25c. For shoes. Price 25c.

Aluminum Toe Step-per for tap dancing on toe slippers, including cleats. Per pair, 35c.

Aluminum Heel Plate in 3 sizes. Send shoe size when ordering. Price 25c.

COSTUMES TO HIRE

The Waas organization is prepared to rent you well-made, authentic costumes for any plan, parade, minstrel, etc., in which the phrase are small sizes, that extensive importance in this work assures you of splendid garments, sanitarily selected and assembled. Estimates or information on request. Would you like costumes made to order? We will gladly send sketches and samples free on request.

Delen Toe Slipper. Last word in fit, comfort, neat support, neat appearance and wearing qualities. Black kid, $4.50. Pink, white or black satin, $4.65. Other colors dyed to order, $1.00 additional.

Famous Waas Ballet Slipper, finest black kid, new professional last. Sole oak leather with knife liner. Slips and left last, fully guaranteed. Finest ballet on the market at $2.25.

Bull and Toe Plate combination of aluminum. Per set, 50c.

The New "Hygeia" Supporter, in pink corset-rubber, eight inches wide. The important features are the kneaded silk front and the fact that the lower section is held up with Pac coups and can conveniently be down. The Hygeia supporter can be laundered easily. Price $2.00.

NOTE—Postage on all costumes and orders. I 8c for sets—30c for two—50c for three, etc. This amount should be included for postage. 27c flat fees!

New Big WAAS Catalogue No. 72—which illustrates everything needed in dancing school or on the stage. FREE copy will be sent on request.

TEACHERS, ATTENTION! Teachers, instructors and directors of dancing schools should ask for our special discount offer which permits a substantial saving on all our dancing school supplies.

WAAS & SON
123 South 11th St. PHILADELPHIA PA.
THEATRICAL DEPARTMENT STORE

Waas & Son, 1931

You're Making Movies with the "K" at Waikiki

● Bronze bodies soaring on a wave . . . this *is* the poetry of motion. Your Ciné-Kodak "K" will bring away the poetry, the motion, even the exotic color of strange places . . . for your movie screen at home. No disappointments with the "K"—it's simple, yet amazingly versatile. Loads with full 100 feet of 16 mm. film. Price, including case, from $112.50. Eastman Kodak Company, Rochester, New York. *If it isn't an Eastman, it isn't a Kodak.*

Ciné-Kodak "K"
EASTMAN'S FINEST HOME MOVIE CAMERA

Ciné-Kodak, 1934

FROM A KODACHROME ORIGIN

Life itself . . . Thousands are capturing its very essence with a movie camera

Don't fail to keep a movie record of that baby of yours.

Today all the world is discovering the pleasure of taking movies of children. Nothing is more fun at the time—and it gives you a record of absolutely priceless value, which you will treasure more and more as time goes on.

With Eastman's finer home movie cameras—Magazine Ciné-Kodak and Ciné-Kodak "K"—even the novice can get wonderful movies; clear, brilliant, pulsing with life and motion. These are the two most popular of all 16 mm. home movie cameras.

FULL-COLOR KODACHROME—And simply by changing your film—loading your Ciné-Kodak with Kodachrome instead of black-and-white—your movies will be flooded with gorgeous full color. Drop in at your dealer's—let him show you these 16 mm. Ciné-Kodaks. And some sample reels, both in black-and-white and full color . . . Eastman Kodak Company, Rochester, N. Y.

. . . AND FOR PROJECTION
For clearer, more brilliant projection, use Kodascope, the Eastman-made projector which teams so beautifully with Ciné-Kodak and shows your pictures at their best.

MAGAZINE CINÉ-KODAK loads in three seconds. You don't touch the film. It comes in a magazine. Just slip the camera into place, close the camera cover and shoot. Effortless loading is only one of six new features in this remarkable pocket-size movie camera. With fast *f*:1.9 lens, $125; including combination carrying case, $137.50.

CINÉ-KODAK "K" is the most widely used 16 mm. home movie camera—it's so simple, yet so fine. You get clear, brilliant movies at the touch of a lever. Loads with full 100 feet of 16 mm. film. With *f*:1.9 lens, $88.50; including carrying case, $100.

Ciné-Kodak
EASTMAN'S FINER HOME MOVIE CAMERAS

Ciné-Kodak, 1938

You're Making Movies with the "K" at Hialeah

● Bring away the life and action of interesting places, interesting people. Ciné-Kodak "K" keeps the perfect modern diary. It delights the beginner because it's so simple, the expert because it does so many things well. Your movies will be a success—from the first. You carry your whole "movie studio" in a 6 x 10 inch case. Ciné-Kodak "K" loads with full 100 feet of 16 mm. film. Price (case included) from $112.50. Eastman Kodak Company, Rochester, N. Y. *If it isn't an Eastman, it isn't a Kodak.*

Ciné-Kodak "K"
EASTMAN'S FINEST HOME MOVIE CAMERA

Ciné-Kodak, 1938

"HE ALWAYS SLEEPS WITH HIS LITTLE FIST THAT WAY"

The fleeting expression . . . the endearing gesture . . . snapshots catch these and hold them safe for you to treasure. Don't take chances with snapshots that will mean so much later—any camera is a better camera when you use Kodak Verichrome Film. Your pictures will be more truthful and expressive than ever. Always use Verichrome. . . . Eastman Kodak Company, Rochester, N. Y.

The snapshots you'll want Tomorrow—you must take Today

Kodak, 1933

THE READYSET TRAVELER

From the unbeaten track . . . from the originality of stylists and camera designers, comes the Readyset Traveler —unquestionably the most outstanding and practical innovation in camera creation of this beauty-conscious day.

In its distinctive specially-woven repp covering, colorful striping, platinum finish, and mechanical rightness there is a cosmopolitan air . . . an expression of the modern spirit that appeals to all who travel—at home or afar. For the Traveler looks like custom-made luggage . . . and *is* luggage—luggage to pack full of pictures.

The Traveler is a certified picture-taker. One you can count on for clear sharp pictures always.

You'll be proud to own, or give as a gift, the colorful, smart Traveler. For the thrill of its possession is surpassed only by the delight in its remarkable picture-taking ability. Ask to see it when you buy your next roll of film.

No. 1 Readyset Traveler—$13.00
(2¼ x 3¼ Pictures)

No. 1A Readyset Traveler—$16.00
(2½ x 4¼ Pictures)

Available
in four different color stripings

And the Traveler is one of the famous Agfa Ansco Readyset cameras . . . as nearly automatic as cameras can be and yet insure perfect pictures. No focusing, no shutter adjustments—just "Open, aim, shoot." As simple as that.

Agfa film—*the all- weather film*—takes good pictures anywhere . . . under the sun, or under a cloud. A size for every camera.

READYSET
TRAVELER
BY AGFA ANSCO

AGFA ANSCO OF BINGHAMTON, N
Agfa Ansco Ltd., 204 King Street East, Toronto, On

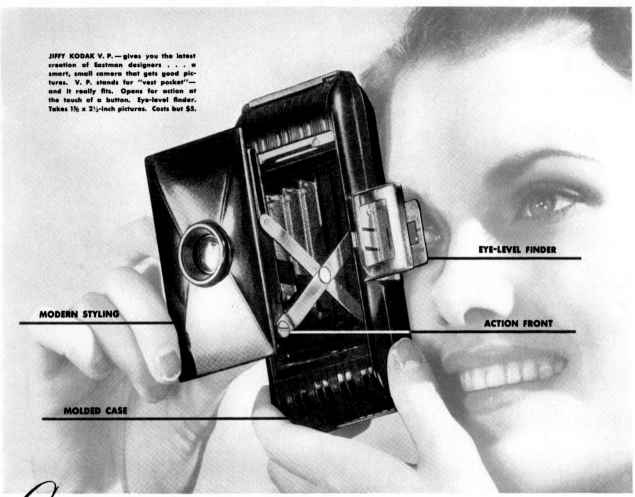

JIFFY KODAK V. P. — gives you the latest creation of Eastman designers . . . a smart, small camera that gets good pictures. V. P. stands for "vest pocket"— and it really fits. Opens for action at the touch of a button. Eye-level finder. Takes 1⅝ x 2½-inch pictures. Costs but $5.

EYE-LEVEL FINDER

ACTION FRONT

MODERN STYLING

MOLDED CASE

Check these new Kodaks against your old camera

KODAK SIX-20 (*below*)—America's most popular fine camera — rich in appointments, with etched side panels and enameled parts. Its keen *f*.6.3 lens makes snapshots at night with "SS" Film and Photoflood bulbs...its 1/100-second shutter gets children "on the go." Both eye-level and reflecting finders. For 2¼ x 3¼-inch pictures, $17.50. Other models from $14.

KODAK JUNIOR SIX-20, *f*.6.3 (*above*)—is offered at a remarkably low price for such fine lens and shutter equipment. The Kodak Anastigmat *f*.6.3 lets you make snapshots when you'd ordinarily put your camera away . . on dull days . . in the rain . . AT NIGHT with Kodak "SS" Film and Photoflood bulbs. Has both eye-level and reflecting finders. Three shutter speeds. Makes 2¼ x 3¼-inch pictures. Costs only $13.50. Other models, $10 up.

LIKE ANY OTHER SPORT, picture taking depends a lot on the equipment. Yet many people are still using cameras that were back numbers years ago.

Old models simply don't measure up to 1935 standards. Put yourself behind one of these new Kodaks and you boost your skill about 100%.

Lenses and shutters are better than you could ever before buy at the price. There's more convenience all around. Just look at the features.

Picture this modern world with a modern Kodak—this week-end. Your dealer has the camera you want. Kodaks from $5 up; Brownies as low as $1 . . . What else will bring so much lasting enjoyment?...Eastman Kodak Company, Rochester, N. Y.... *Only Eastman makes the Kodak.*

JIFFY KODAK—It works so fast it had to be called "Jiffy." Touch a button—"Pop"—it opens. Touch another—"Click"—it gets the picture. Focuses for near and distant subjects. There's extra smartness in its etched metal front and leather-like finish. Jiffy Six-20, for 2¼ x 3¼-inch pictures, $8. Jiffy Six-16, for 2½ x 4¼-inch pictures, $9.

Agfa Ansco, 1935 ◄ *Kodak, 1935*

Bug-A-Boo, 1938

Ozite Rug Cushion, 1930

Now! MOTH DAMAGE PROTECTION WITHIN EVERY BUDGET

At last, protection from moth worries is within *every* woman's means. *This* year a big roomy moth bag is given free with every pint can of Flit—two with every quart can.

This big, handsome, roomy moth bag holds three suits or as many as *five* dresses. All you do is spray the clothes carefully with Flit, pack them away, and forget them!

Flit gives you protection against moths, eggs and larvae. And Flit kills all forms of moth life DEAD—with the same promptness that it kills flies, mosquitoes and other flying insects.

No unpleasant odors...harmless to fabrics, humans or pets.

FLIT SPRAY DOES NOT STAIN

Flit Powder is a special, sure exterminator for crawling insects and fleas on dogs.

Copr. 1936, Stanco Inc.

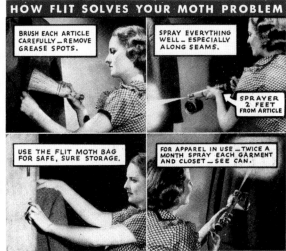

HOW FLIT SOLVES YOUR MOTH PROBLEM

BRUSH EACH ARTICLE CAREFULLY—REMOVE GREASE SPOTS.

SPRAY EVERYTHING WELL—ESPECIALLY ALONG SEAMS.

SPRAYER 2 FEET FROM ARTICLE

USE THE FLIT MOTH BAG FOR SAFE, SURE STORAGE.

FOR APPAREL IN USE—TWICE A MONTH SPRAY EACH GARMENT AND CLOSET—SEE CAN.

Flit, 1936

19,550,500 PERSONS ATTENDED SHOWINGS OF OUR HEALTH MOVIES FROM 1924 TO 1930

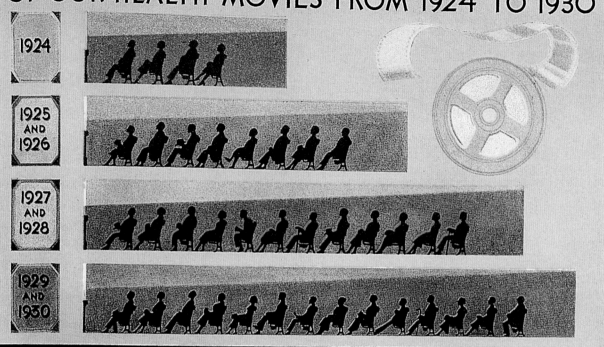

1924

1925 AND 1926

1927 AND 1928

1929 AND 1930

Each figure = 500,000 persons.

Courtesy of METROPOLITAN LIFE INSURANCE COMPANY—Four-color process, half-tone engraving, 133 screen

HOW THE METROPOLITAN NURSING SERVICE HAS GROWN

NUMBER OF VISITS TO INDUSTRIAL POLICYHOLDERS

MILLIONS
40
35
30
25
20
15
10
5

1909-1915 1909-1920 1909-1925 1909-1930

NUMBER OF CASES TREATED

1909 TO 1915

1909 TO 1920

1909 TO 1925

1909 TO 1930

Each bed = approximately 1,000,000 cases.

FOR PRINTERS — NUMBER 76 —

Motor Boats
Sea-Horses

Sea-Horse Prices

"Single," $125; "3," $150; "4," $160;
"10," $185; "12," $195; "16," $250;
"24," $285; "32," $325.

*All prices f. o. b. factory.
Partial payment terms.*

17½ ft. Service Runabout Boat, $485

*Sealite construction, V bottom, 5 ft. beam; 3
cross seats with lazybacks; weighs 395 lbs.;
true speed up to 26 m. p. h. with Sea-Horse
"32." Aquaflyer-type recess for motor.*

17½ ft. Aquaflyer, De Luxe Runabout

*Sealite construction, V bottom, 5 ft. beam; double
cockpit arrangement, with two upholstered
cross seats with lazybacks; weighs 450 lbs.; true
speed up to 19 m.p.h. with Sea-Horse "16,"
complete with motor, $925—up to 25 m.p.h. with
Sea-Horse 32, complete with motor, $995.*

15 ft. Knockabout Boat, $135

*Strong, lightweight; ½ in. cedar planking, hollow
and round construction; strong, bent white oak
ribs sheer to sheer, round bilge bottom, 4½ ft. beam.*

14 ft. Utility A Boat, $165

*Sealite construction, cedar deck, only 173 lbs.;
round bilge bottom, 52 in. beam, 3 cross seats,
ideal for yacht tender, camping, children.*

15 ft. Utility B Boat, $275

*Sealite construction, V bottom, 52 in. beam; 3
cross seats with lazybacks; weighs 227 lbs.; true
speed up to 22 m.p.h. with Sea-Horse "16."*

MATCHED UNITS MOTORS & BOATS

Matched Units Motors & Boats, 1930

Royal Blue, 1931

Evinrude, 1933

Eclipse Mower, 1939

SEE WHAT MIGHTY MECHANICAL MARVELS YOU CAN BUILD WITH
The Great New
ERECTOR

Hello Boys!

Look at that giant power plant! You build it yourself with the great new Erector. Piece by piece you erect its massive steel frame. Assemble its enormous fly wheel—pistons—governor. Mount its big, shining boilers. Then you hook up the powerful Erector electric engine and it throbs with action.

That's only one of the many exciting engineering models you can build with Erector. You can make that marvelous magnetic crane. Click the switch on the Erector Engine—pull the control levers and it raises or lowers—swings to the right or left, just as you command. Its magnet is so strong it grabs up steel girders before it touches them.

You can build *all* of the engineering models shown in the picture—and dozens more—with *one* Erector Set. Enormous drawbridges that actually open and close. Towering airplane beacon that revolves just like the real ones. All-metal airplane. Dump-trucks. And—with the new Erector Skyscraper Set —you can build skyscrapers as tall as you are.

You're a full-fledged engineer when you have an Erector—ready to build realistic, engine-driven models of the world's greatest mechanical marvels. There are more wonders—more exciting hours of fun—packed in an Erector Set than anything you can own.

A.C.Gilbert

Ferris Wheel
Built with the No. 7½ Set Operated with the new Erector Electric Engine.

NEW COLORS
MORE PARTS
Easier Model Building

The Great New Erectors are the finest ever made.

Look at this

SENSATIONAL
No. 7½ SET

Contains the powerful new Erector Electric Engine. Girders and structural plates finished in red, yellow and blue. Glistening boiler parts. The new snap rivets, gears and other engineering parts for building ferris wheel, magnetic crane, trucks, bridges and over 150 action models. With all these new features, only $10.95. Other sets from $1.00 to $25.00.

NEW
The Erector Electric Engine. Not just a motor—but a real engine complete with built-in gears.

NEW
Skyscraper parts. Builds realistic models of Radio City and other famous skyscrapers.

NEW
Big solid steel base plates and giant girders—make possible larger and stronger models.

NEW
Double feature. Snap rivets for speedy building —nuts and bolts for sturdy building.

See the Gilbert Hall of Science

The most stupendous boys' scientific exposition ever created. See the fascinating Gilbert Opto Kits—the mysterious Electric Eye—the Gilbert Chemistry Laboratory—Mysto Magic—the Gilbert Kaster Kit—and dozens of other thrilling sights. Look for these exhibits at your local toy store. Take your Dad along.

FREE! Gilbert Thrills Magazine

32 big pages packed full of exciting pictures and up-to-the-minute scientific information. True stories of how red-blooded boys have won fame and big awards in building Erector models—in making important chemical discoveries—and becoming masters of home craftsmanship. Regular price 25c. Free—combined with color catalog on the Great New Erector—to the first 50,000 boys who mail this coupon.

Mail this Coupon today

Mr. A. C. Gilbert, The A. C. Gilbert Co.
511 Erector Square, New Haven, Conn.
    Please send—free—Gilbert Thrills Magazine combined with big color catalog on the Great New Erector.

Name...

Street..

City.. State...................

Erector, 1935

Nationally Famous MUSICAL MASTERPIECES

by Celebrated Makers —

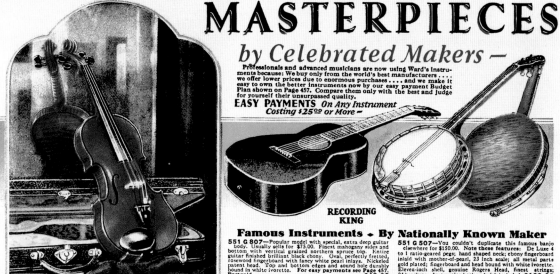

Professionals and advanced musicians are now using Ward's instruments because: We buy only from the world's best manufacturers . . . . we offer lower prices due to enormous purchases . . . . and we make it easy to own the better instruments now by our easy payment Budget Plan shown on Page 457. Compare them only with the best and judge for yourself their unsurpassed quality.

EASY PAYMENTS *On Any Instrument* Costing $25.00 *or More —*

RECORDING KING

Famous Instruments ◆ By Nationally Known Maker

551 G 807—Popular model with special, extra deep guitar body. Usually sells for $75.00. Finest mahogany sides and bottom with vertical grained northern spruce top. Entire guitar finished brilliant black ebony. Oval, perfectly fretted, rosewood fingerboard with fancy white pearl inlays. Nickeled patent head. Top and bottom edges and sound hole durably bound in white ivorette. For easy payments see Page 457. Postpaid.............................$48.00

551 G 507—You couldn't duplicate this famous banjo elsewhere for $150.00. Note these features: De Luxe 4 to 1 ratio-geared pegs; hand shaped neck; ebony fingerboard inlaid with mother-of-pearl, 23 inch scale; all metal parts gold plated; fingerboard and head bound with white ivorette. Eleven-inch shell, genuine Rogers Head, finest strings; 24 brackets. Instruction book and pick included. $100.00

MEINEL

Reproduction of Stradivarius 1725

So faithful is this re-creation of a genuine and highly treasured 1725 Stradivarius by Oscar Eugene Meinel himself, that it almost perfectly matches the tone qualities for which all Cremona Violins are famous.

The beautiful light amber color; the rare and wonderful graining of the two piece maple back; the moutan spruce top, and even to the marks of age, which are so much desired, are perfect. In years to come this master violin will be valued far beyond its purchase price. Carefully finished with 18 coats of special oil varnish. Bushed peg holes. Finest quality ebony pegs and tailpiece inlaid with solid gold. Imitation leather oblong case with silk plush lined. For easy payments see Budget Plan on Page 457. We Pay Postage.
551 G 675—Postpaid.............................$150.00
551 G 1088—Case Only. Postpaid.............25.00

Now! **Ward's Offers ROTH'S Three Finest Violins**

Finer reproductions of Stradivarius and Josef Guarnerius by one of the world's foremost violin makers—Ernst Heinrich Roth of Germany. Write us for the catalogue showing these old masters in actual colors.

G. PENZEL

Boehm System Metal Clarinet

551 G 559—One of America's best known metal Clarinets. Professional model—silver plated. Boehm system with 17 keys and 6 rings. Has the true clarinet tone found only in the higher grade wood instruments; intonation remarkably balanced; tuning barrel absolutely airtight. We believe this to be the finest single tube clarinet possible, at this price. Plush lined case included. For easy payments see Page 457. We Pay Postage.........$79.00

De Luxe "L'Orqanola" Accordion

HOHNER

120 Basses—41 Piano Keys

Superbly beautiful with marvelous tone. A magnificent Hohner accordion. **Range:** 41 Black and White piano keys; 3½ chromatic octaves, 120 basses. **Reeds:** Four sets of extra fine hand filed Treble reeds mounted on extra heavy aluminum blocks; individually tested to assure fullest tone and exact tune; 5 sets of Bass reeds. **Bellows:** 15-fold with special air-tight cloth. Gold or silver plated metal corner protectors. **Finish:** Frames and key board of special ivorette in either black or white finish. Leather clasps, bass and shoulder straps with felt backing. **Size:** 7½x18½ inches. Fine, plush lined carrying case. For easy payments see Budget Plan on Page 457. Not Mailable. Ship. wt. 55 lbs. Shipped Not Prepaid.
651 G 1112—White Finish Gold Plated Metal Trimmings.............................$350.00
651 G 1113—Black Finish Silver Plated Metal Trimmings.............................350.00

New Colorful Drum Outfit

DRUM MASTER

151 G 558—Popular professional drum outfit. Drum shells are laminated wood covered with the latest sparkling, sea green pearlette. Bass drum center support with tympani model rods. Outfit includes; Bass drum, 14 by 28 inches; Snare drum, 5 by 14 inches; Snare stand and Sticks; Beater with Spurs; 10 inch Tom-Tom and Holder; 13 inch Italian Cymbal and Holder; 13-inch Chinese Cymbal and Holder; 12 inch Pedal Cymbal, 10 inch Choke Cymbal, Traptable, Tambourine and Wood Block and Holder. For easy payments see Budget Plan on Page 457. Not Mailable. Ship wt. 60 lbs. Shipped Not Prepaid......$135.00

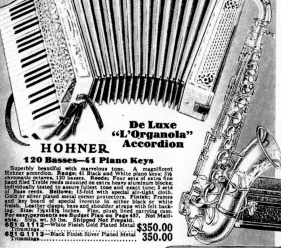

PREMIER AMERICAN

Eb Alto Saxophone

So positive are we that this E Flat Alto Premier-American (latest model of nationally known manufacturer) is the equal of any saxophone on the market that we want you to try it personally and compare it with the saxophone you have always considered the best. Then if for any reason it is not all you expected, return it and we will promptly send back the full amount you have paid. Here are a few of its many improvements—all suggested by professional players to make a better instrument. **1.** Special designed bowl for fullness of tone and ease of playing. **2.** Improved mouthpiece built to fit the mouth. **3.** New, scientific shaping of mouth pipe eliminates difficulty of playing high notes, gives full middle register, and extra volume on low. Strap, lyre, instruction book, and silk plush lined case included. For easy payments see Budget Plan on Page 457. We Pay Postage.
551 G 392—Silver plated, satin finish gold plated bell..............$95.00
551 G 391—Brass..................85.00

Regal

Made by One of the World's Largest Guitar Makers

Regal professional model. Genuine mahogany sides and back, and spruce top, especially reinforced with 14-spruce ribs for tone. Ebony fingerboard, nickel frets. Balanced, hand shaped neck. Postpaid.
551 G 753—Grand Concert Size Guitar.............$33.75
551 G 496—Tenor guitar same as 551 G 753, but tuned, fingered and played like a tenor banjo..........$33.75
551 G 579—Three-ply veneer cases, imitation leather, side opening. For above Guitars. State style wanted..............................$12.75

551 G 808—Genuine Regal Two-in-one Guitar (Hawaiian and Regular). Professional quality in tone and beauty at an unheard of low price.
Top of selected, clear grained eastern spruce reinforced with 14 spruce ribs for greater tone value; genuine mahogany back and sides. Fingerboard in silver color and black pearlette. Top beautifully decorated with scene of Diamond Head Honolulu. Outfit includes two books, one for Spanish playing and one for Hawaiian; set of picks and Hawaiian extension unit. Grand concert size. Postpaid.$22.75

Lionel Electric Trains, 1935

Mead Cycle Co., 1935

Hawthorne Bicycle, 1930

▶ *Daisy Air Rifles, 1939*

Buck Rogers
25th Century

HOW would YOU like to be Buck Rogers? ... How would YOU like to lead the earth's rocket ship fleet against the terrible Tiger Men of Mars ... the bird riders of Venus or the crafty Killer Kane and Ardala? Wouldn't that be SOMETHING? Boy!! Oh, Boy!!

Imagine yourself cruising through space thousands of miles per minute, wearing your interplanetary navigation helmet with its built-in radio antenna, and ear phones ... with your trusty rocket pistol in its holster, ready for instant action ... How'd you like THAT? Sure, it's 500 years in the future but right now you can own everything Buck uses—EVERYTHING—copied line for line from Buck's OWN equipment.

Look at that helmet, ... and that combat set, ... and that rocket pistol! Exact copies, every one of them, aren't they? ... Say, when you pull on that helmet, and strap on that combat set, you'll sure BE Buck Rogers himself.

Get yours NOW. Take Mother or Dad with you ... tell them how badly you need this equipment and that most Daisy dealers, leading department and chain stores have your complete outfit on hand. Of course if they're out of it, we'll send it to you, postpaid, for the prices shown.

Hurry ... be the FIRST one on your street to have all this 25th Century equipment. *Be Buck Rogers yourself.*

25th Century ROCKET PISTOL . . . .
It's an exact duplicate of Buck's and Wilma's *OWN* Rocket Pistols—the kind they use to fight the Tiger Men of Mars—and the scheming Killer Kane and Ardala. You can hear it "ZAP" for blocks but it's ABSOLUTELY HARMLESS 50¢*

(In some cities, on account of high freight charges, this price will be slightly higher.)

25th Century HOLSTER
It's different from ANY holster you ever saw ... Space Ships, Planets, Stars, in three colors, mounted on heavy, tough brown suede cloth. It's Buck Rogers' *OWN* holster—designed just for his famous Rocket Pistol . . . . 39¢*

(In some cities, on account of high freight charges, this price will be slightly higher.)

25th Century COMBAT SET . . . .
Absolutely the FIRST Interplanetary Combat Set. Buck Rogers' *OWN* Rocket Pistol, and his 25th Century Holster, together in a box showing scenes from Buck's thrilling adventures in space . . . . 89¢*

(In some cities, on account of high freight charges, this price will be slightly higher.)

25th Century Interplanetary Navigation HELMET . .
Buck always wears this. It has the full vision eye protector, ear phones and radio antenna found on Buck's *OWN* helmet. It's made of heavy brown suede cloth, with all metal parts highly nickel plated and polished. You CAN'T be Buck Rogers without this helmet . . $1.00*

(In some cities, on account of high freight charges, this price will be slightly higher.)

MADE BY THE MAKERS OF FAMOUS

DAISY AIR RIFLES

NRA WE DO OUR PART NRA

DAISY MANUFACTURING COMPANY · 240 UNION STREET · PLYMOUTH, MICHIGAN

Daisy Air Rifles, 1935

Daisy Air Rifles, 1935

Western Ammunition, 1935

Daisy Air Rifles, 1936

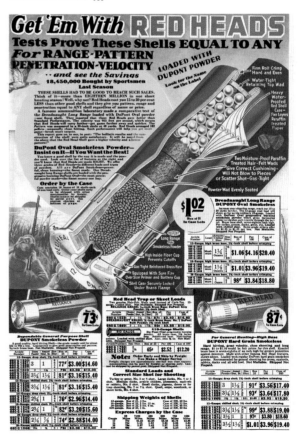

Red Heads Ammunition, 1931

FORMER RECORD UPPED 8 POINTS BY DETROIT POLICE IN INTERSTATE-INTERSERVICE MATCH

In addition to winning the Interstate-Interservice Match the Detroit Police placed second in the Colt Trophy Match, outranking New York City, both teams shooting 1156. Detroit teams also placed second and third in Sobol Trophy Match. Detroit Police Team, shown above, left to right: Reeves, Hemming, Team Capt. Marvin Driver, Sanderson, Lalonde.

FIVE NEW RECORDS HUNG UP IN .45 MATCHES

JONES, FLETCHER, HEMMING AND WARD BLAZE THROUGH WITH NEW RECORDS

In Medalists' Event Ten Shooters Tied or Bettered Previous Record

Gaining in both scores and number of entries heavy caliber shooting is fast coming into its own.

1939 Camp Perry won 5 records broken and one tied, Detroit boosting the Interstate-Interservice record up 8 points and Ward, the forty-fiver from California clipping six points from the old record in .45 Police competition.

Again the Colt National Match Model proved its amazing accuracy and downright dependability.

WARD
Noted .45 shooter that he is, Clarence Ward, Los Angeles, pushed the record on six points in the .45 Police match. Score 596. In this match all but three shots beat the former record. Ward also placed 2nd in the .45 Rapid-Fire.

SHAPIRO
Another Detroit Police officer who broke through to the two-A! Shapiro who tied the former record of 196 in the .45 Timed-Fire match. Like his brother officers, Shapiro shoots Colts in all matches.

HOLTZ
1st Sgt. E. W. Holtz, of the U.S. Cavalry, rode fast and lassoed a 269 to win the .45 Restricted Match.

VAN DOREN
C. L. Van Doren, civilian from California whose 270 led the field in the .45 Civilian Match.

COUSER
C. R. Couser, another of the U.S. Coast Guard fast steppers. He took the .45 Military Match with a 278.

FLETCHER
This is W. E. Fletcher, U.S. Marine ace who smashed the former record in the .45 Rapid-Fire event, scoring a 192.

CHAPMAN
Percy Chapman — U.S. Treasury Team — is the National Individual Champion. His was the team-A! Individual Champion. His was the team-A! champion shot a 293 possible, but like many of his class Chapman also placed second in the .45 Police Match and third in the American Legion Individual Aggregate.

U.S. Marines WIN NATIONAL PISTOL TEAM MATCH

The Marines loaded and how! They won the hard fought National Pistol Team Match with a score of 1315 shot in a driving rain. The U.S. Infantry Team came third, and the U.S. Infantry Team second. The match was shot too late to obtain a photograph of this team of crack shots.

WHALING
The Olsen Memorial is one of the most coveted Camp Perry trophies. This year it was won by Major W. J. Whaling of the U.S. Marines with a 579.

Shooters like the velvet smooth action found in the Colt National Match. They also like its target sights, particularly the rugged Stevens Double Adjustable rear sight that is so easily and accurately adjusted for windage and elevation. Combine these target refinements with the super-precisioned "match" barrel and you have a super-accurate heavy caliber arm.

Colt Automatic Pistol, 1939

Johnson Smith & Co., 1933

National Small-Bore Championship, 4 New Records with SUPER MATCH

FOR THE THIRD CONSECUTIVE YEAR, MORE SMALL-BORE MATCHES WERE WON WITH WESTERN SUPER-MATCH THAN WITH ANY OTHER BRAND OF AMMUNITION!

WESTERN SUPER-MATCH was again the outstanding small-bore ammunition at Camp Perry. For the THIRD CONSECUTIVE YEAR more small-bore matches were won with it than with any other brand of ammunition. It was used in setting 4 new World Records and in equalling another.

VERE F. HAMER, Woodstock, Minn., poured ten in with SUPER-MATCH for a World-Record 3192 in winning the National Small-Bore Championship the Critchfield Aggregate. He also won the Remington Trophy, 50 Meters Any Sights, tieing the record of 400 plus 200 plus 200.

WILLIAM B. WOODRING, Alton, Ill., hung up 3 new World Records with SUPER-MATCH: a sensational 400 — 37-x over the Dewar Course, Iron Sights, in the "400" Club Member's Trophy Match — a 400 — 39-x in the 50-Yard Any Sights All-Comers' — and a new record of 183 in the Pope Match. Woodring also won the 100-Yard Iron Sights All-Comers' score: 399 — 27-x — and was high Master

in 4 matches: the National Small-Bore Championship, score 3190 — the Preliminary Dewar, score: 399 — 35-x, the 100-Yard Any Sights, All-Comers': 400 — 26-x, and the 50-Yd. Iron Sights All-Comers', score: 400 — 34-x. *All SUPER-MATCH.*

KENNETH RECKER, Winter Haven, Fla., shot SUPER-MATCH and walked off with the U.S. Cartridge Trophy, score: 400 — 27-x. He was also high Master in the 100-Yard Iron Sights, All-Comers'. Score: 399 — 25-x.

GEORGE E. FROST and ARVEL FRANZ of Alton, Ill., topped the field with SUPER-MATCH in the Hercules Trophy Doubles, score: 393 — 14-x. Franz also won the Western Trophy, tieing the Camp Perry record of 400 — 32-x!

ROBERT R. LAUSTEN, Port Clinton, O., came through to win high Expert Class honors in the National Small-Bore Championship with SUPER-MATCH — and was also high Expert in the Austin Trophy, score 398.

J. T. GALLAHUE, Springfield, Ill., was high Master in the U.S. Cartridge Trophy Match, score: 400 — 22-x. He shot SUPER-MATCH.

WILLIAM PATRIQUIN, Ernest, Pa., was 2nd in the 50-Yard Any Sights Medalists', with SUPER-MATCH, score: 400 — 31-x.

L. A. POPE, Los Angeles, Cal., was high Expert in the Preliminary Dewar with SUPER-MATCH, score: 399 — 28-x.

Lt. M. E. KAISER, LaCarne, O., was high Expert in the 50-Yard Any Sights, All-Comers' with SUPER-MATCH: 400 — 36-x.

R. V. HIGH, Union, N.J., was high Expert in the 100-Yard Iron Sights All-Comers', with SUPER-MATCH, score: 399 — 21-x.

WORLD CHAMPION AMMUNITION

Western Ammunition, 1939

Detroit Police and U.S. Treasury Win With *Western*...8 Pistol Records!

EIGHT new Camp Perry pistol records were made with a red hot 1089 in winning the Interstate & Interservice .45 Automatic Pistol Team Match.

The DETROIT POLICE TEAM boosted the Camp Perry record 8 points with a red hot 1089 in winning the Interstate & Interservice .45 Automatic Pistol Team Match.

The U.S. TREASURY TEAM. No. 1 raised the Camp Perry record for the Colt Trophy 5 points to 1162. Three team members shot Western and the Detroit Police Pistol Team continued their record-shattering shooting with the World Champion Ammunition.

The U.S. TREASURY TEAM. No. 1 raised the Camp Perry record for the Colt Trophy 5 points to 1162. Three team members shot Western and the fourth, Winchester. The same team was 2nd in the N.R.A. Revolver Team Match with 1129 — 10 points higher than the previous Camp Perry record.

Ptl. ALF. W. HEMMING of the Detroit Police shot a remarkable 286 to win the .45 Pistol Medalists' Match — 7 points above the old record. Hemming also won the McGinley Trophy with Western, score: 288 — only 1 point under the Camp Perry record. He was 3rd in the Master Class of the N.R.A. Pistol Grand Aggregate, score: 1724, and placed 2nd in the .22 Rapid Fire with a 199 — 2 points above the old Camp Perry record.

Ptl. HARRY W. REEVES of the Detroit Police shot a perfect 300 in winning the Center-Fire Timed Fire Match — a new Camp Perry record! He placed 2nd in the Master Class of the N.R.A. Pistol Grand Aggregate, score: 1727. Reeves' 278 was high in the Police Class of the Olsen Memorial Trophy Match, emblematic of the national .45-caliber championship. He was also high in the Police Class of the .45 Timed Fire, with Western. He was 2nd in the N.R.A. .22 Pistol Championship, score: 293 — and placed 2nd in two other matches.

MELTON R. ROGERS of the U.S. Treasury Team is the new N.R.A. .22 Pistol Champion. His score of 296, made with Western SUPER-MATCH, is a new Camp Perry record! Rogers also placed 3rd in the McGinley Trophy Match, shooting Western, score 284. The two-man U.S. Treasury team of Melton R. Rogers and P. M. Chapman was 2nd in the Police Doubles, score 582. Both shot Western.

WALTER R. WALSH, U.S. Marine Corps Reserve, shot Western and placed 2nd in the .45 Timed Fire Match. His excellent score of 199 was high in the Military Service Class of the event.

Det. MAURICE W. LA LONDE of the Detroit Police set a new Camp Perry record of 75, with Western, in winning the Police Field Firing Match.

WORLD CHAMPION AMMUNITION

▶ *Remington Arms Co., 1932*

NITRO EXPRESS
HITS HARDER
REACHES FARTHER

KLEANBORE SHELLS:

GAME LOADS
NITRO EXPRESS
SHUR SHOT
TRAP LOADS
SKEET LOADS
ARROW EXPRESS
(Lacquered)

The Kleanbore Priming Mixture is patented—it cannot be duplicated by any other manufacturer.

OUTSTANDING FEATURES:

STABILITY
UNIFORMITY
SENSITIVENESS
PERFECT IGNITION
DEPENDABILITY
LONGER FLAME
NON-CORROSIVE

More Kleanbore .22's are sold than all other makes combined.

THE PROOF OF THE SHELL IS IN THE SHOOTING

There's a Kleanbore shell for every kind of shooting, and for every kind of shooting a Kleanbore shell will give the best results. For difficult long range shooting where you have to reach out and nail 'em at 50, 60, 70 yards and even at greater distances — it's Kleanbore Nitro Express that outshoots any shell on the market. At the traps — it's the Trap Load or Shur Shot Target Load. For all other upland or waterfowl shooting it's Game Loads or Shur Shot Shells.

They all come in distinctive green boxes. All the shells are green and on the side of each shell is "Kleanbore"—the name of America's Chosen Ammunition. Write for a descriptive folder. Address: Remington Ammunition Works, 812 Arctic St., Bridgeport, Conn.

REMINGTON ARMS COMPANY, Inc.
Originators of Kleanbore Ammunition

© 1932 R. A. Co.

4587

Go to your dealer and ask him to show you The Remington Standard American Dollar Pocket Knife

Make Your *❦*❦*❦*❦* **Christmas Gift a TOMAHAWK**
THE SPORTSMAN'S AXE

THOUSANDS of fellows will be made happy this Christmas with the best of all gifts—TOMAHAWK, the Sportsman's Axe! TOMAHAWK is as handy an article as a woodsman can carry . . . a keen axe, a fine hunting knife, an accurate compass and a book of matches—all the things you need most in the woods—compactly carried in a genuine leather pistol-type holster handy at your side. Every Pioneer will want one! Every Scout will want one! Every boy will want one! Already thousands of TOMAHAWKS are proudly carried by hunters and campers everywhere. Order your TOMA-HAWK early. As a Special Offer, we will engrave your name or nickname together with your Pioneer Chapter name or Scout Troop number on the handle of your TOMAHAWK free of charge. Act promptly, don't delay if you want your TOMAHAWK in time for Christmas. Send check or money order for $3.50 with the coupon properly filled in and we will send your TOMAHAWK, postpaid anywhere in the U.S.A. Your money back if not fully satisfied.

TOMAHAWK head forged from highest quality axe steel ground to keen edge, tubular steel handle, black knurled pistol-type grip, heavy chromium finish . . . Hunting knife, full size, 4½ in. razor sharp blade, pearl handle black and chromium trimmed, fits in axe handle . . . Compass guaranteed accurate, easy-to-read dial, metal case . . . Matches, compact book-type . . . Holster stoutly sewn of heavy russett leather, inner pockets for compass and matches, slotted to carry on belt. (Belt not included in TOMAHAWK outfit.) Hurry! Take advantage of the SPECIAL CHRISTMAS OFFER. Get your TOMA-HAWK handle engraved free of charge. Send check or money order for $3.50 today.

STANDARD PRODUCTS CO.
CLINTON,   MASS., U.S.A.

COMPLETE $3.50 POSTPAID

Special Christmas Offer

Tomahawk, 1935

Western Auto Supply Co.
Now in Our 21st Year of Service to Motorists

Offers Everything from a complete Camping Outfit

down to a Tent Peg . . . at Prices that SAVE You Money

Fishing Tackle, too

In the Outing Departments of most of our stores you will find proven tackle for every type of Western fishing . . . expertly selected for real service . . . and offered at typical "Western Auto" savings.

When each summer breeze stirs restless memories of winding road . . . of shaded dell . . . or rushing stream, there's no use fighting off that Gypsy urge much longer! It's time RIGHT NOW to overhaul the camping outfit—to bring it up to date, or plan a new one . . . and there's no better place to go for what you need than "Western Auto"! In the Outing Department of any Western Auto Supply Company store you'll find all that is new and practical . . . everything you need for greater comfort and convenience . . . and prices that enable you to own a better outfit for less.

Tents • Beds • Cots • Mattresses • Chairs • Tables • Cooking Utensils Stoves • Canteens • Vacuum Bottles • Outing Jugs • Lunch Kits • Outing Refrigerators • Luggage Carriers • Duffle Bags • Baby Seats • and many other outing needs—all priced to save you money

Western Auto Supply Co. More than 170 Stores in the West to Serve You
See Telephone Directory for the Address of Your Nearest Store

Western Giant Batteries	Penn Supreme Pennsylvania Oil	Auto Accessories of all kinds	Western Air Patrol Home Radios
Wizard and Wasco Batteries	West-well Pennsylvania Oil	Tools and Repair Parts	Motorola Auto Radios
Auto Electrical Needs	Long Run Western Oil	Cleaning and Polishing Needs	Garden Hose and Sprinklers
Long Run Auto Greases	Supreme Graphoid Lubricants	Paints for Home and Car	Bicycles and Accessories

Everything For Your Car at a Saving

National Carbon Co., 1932 ◄ *Western Auto Supply Co., 1936*

A HE-MAN'S KNIFE

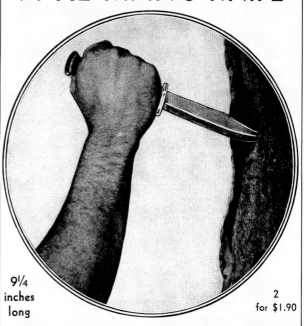

9¼ inches long

2 for $1.90

Complete with hard-wearing leather sheath

Only $1.00

YOU absolutely must have a good sheath knife when you go camping.

No experienced woodsman, camper, hunter or sportsman would think of setting out on the land and water trails without a thoroughly reliable sheath knife.

The new improved Pioneer Sheath Knife is the one for you. It is built to Deep-river Jim's specifications—and he had to have a knife that would stand the gaff. It's a he-man's knife, nine and a quarter inches long, with a tough, heavy blade of finely tempered Swedish steel, a guard for safety, and a husky, non-slip handle that fits your fist. The sheath is of high-grade leather, sewed and riveted—made to last, slotted for your belt and equipped with a snap-loop to hold it tight.

How do we sell this handsome, serviceable all-round sheath knife for only $1.00? The answer is that we make up thousands at a time and pass the large-production saving on to you.

You've simply got to have a Pioneer Sheath Knife. We sell this knife at a very low price and we do it on a money-back guarantee which makes certain that you'll be more than satisfied. Order it, look it over, and if you don't agree that it's a marvelous bargain, send it back to us in good condition and we will instantly refund your money. Obtainable nowhere except from The Pioneers' Dept. of *The Open Road*. Send for yours today!

- -

OPEN ROAD PIONEERS' CLUB   No orders sent outside   **3-37**
729 Boylston St., Boston, Mass.   U.S.A. and Possessions

I'm going to hit the trail, and when I do I want a Pioneer Sheath Knife in my belt. Enclosed

find . . . . (cash, check, money order). Please rush . . . . knife (knives) to me postpaid. (One knife $1.00; 2 for only $1.90).

Name . . . .

Address . . . .

City or Town . . . . .State . . . .

Pioneer Sheath Knife, 1937

How Scientific Skill brought a New Thrill to your Golf

DRY POLICE. Sturdy, weather-resisting "U.S." Raynster Rain Coats are worn by more policemen and firemen than any other water-proof coat made. They are absolutely weather-proof and water-proof, vulcanized to prevent leaks. Raynsters also come in stylish models for men, women and children.

"U.S." dared to turn the X-ray on your golf balls

Nearly every golfer in the country now knows the meaning of *true-center* in golf balls. The unique and revolutionary new true-center of "U.S." Golf Balls was brought to you through the unequaled experience of "U.S." scientists with almost every known type of rubber product.

Taking a further step, to make certain the *outside* of the ball stayed round and true, as well as the *center*, "U.S." engineers invented amazing new winding machines which wind the rubber thread far more accurately than was ever before possible.

Then "U.S." dared to turn the X-ray on golf balls—its own as well as others. In literally thousands of unbiased tests, the X-ray showed that only "U.S." Golf Balls had invariably perfect true-centers. They are round when you buy them and stay round when you play them. They spin long and true in flight. They do justice to your putting.

The knowledge and experience of the United States Rubber Company's 24 scientific laboratories stand back of each "U.S." product. The skill which gives you reliability and safety in "U.S." Royal Tires and "U.S." Industrial Belting—new beauty in "U.S." Royalite Flooring, new comfort in "U.S." Spring-Step Heels and "U.S." Keds—also puts a new thrill in the performance of "U.S." true-center Golf Balls. United States Rubber Company, General Offices: 1790 Broadway, New York, N. Y.

U.S. ROYAL

SALT LAKE CITY ELECTS KEDS. A few of the 1500 boys and girls who attended a Keds movie party at Salt Lake City, Utah. Every one of them wore "U.S." Keds. Boys and girls all over the country vote Keds their favorite sport and play shoe because Keds, with rugged canvas tops and anti-skid soles, are built for the hardest kind of wear. Keds are priced $1.00, $1.25, $1.50, $1.75 and up to $4.00. Look for the name "Keds" stamped on the shoe, just as you look for "U.S." on a golf ball or a tire.

FOR EVERYMAN'S RACING. Open-country driving speeds today approach racing speeds of a few years ago. Your tires must withstand new stresses and strains—around curves, over bumps, for hour after hour. Long, flat summer driving may heat tires up to 200° F. "U.S." Tires withstand every imaginable laboratory test. More—they stand up under the severest road tests made by our test cars under unfavorable driving conditions. And ask the "U.S." Tire dealer about the new "U.S." Heat Resisting Tube.

GERMANY'S LARGEST GAS PLANT selected this "U.S." Giant Conveyor Belt for carrying endless tons of coal. Over 800 feet long and nearly three feet wide, it has now given unusual service for nearly a year. The United States Rubber Company is the world's largest manufacturer of industrial rubber goods. Only "U.S." scientific skill with all kinds of rubber products could produce such outstanding yet radically different products as "U.S." Belting and "U.S." Golf Balls.

At the left is the story told by the X-ray—the perfect true-center of a "U.S." Ball and the distorted center of a similar-price ball of another make. In the new large-size ball, an *off-center* causes more wobble than ever.

At the right are the three popular "U.S." Balls. "U.S." *Royal*—long distance ball. "U.S." *444*—the "tough-cover" distance ball. "U.S." *Fairway*—the world's most popular 50¢ ball. See your pro today. He handles "U.S." Balls. In golfing, the big swing is to "U.S." *true-center* Golf Balls—just as in motoring the big swing is to "U.S." Tires.

© 1931, U. S. R. Co.

THE WORLD'S LARGEST PRODUCER OF RUBBER United States Rubber Company

U.S. Rubber Co., 1931

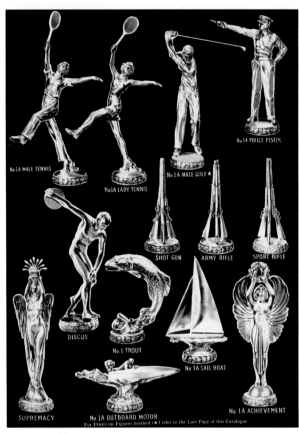

Statuette Trophies, 1933

Statuette Trophies, 1933

Macgregor, 1931

Macgregor, 1932

NEW KIND OF AUTO EYES

MAKES NIGHT DRIVING Safer than Day!

No more driving "blind" on a crowded highway at night! An astonishing new invention banishes night wrecks and smashups. Ends fear of running over children or animals. Mail coupon quick for the manufacturer's introductory Free Test Offer.

Fits Any Headlight---Ends Dangerous Dimming---Doubles Roadlight!

This new kind of Light even LOOKS entirely different. No wonder every installation brings a dozen more sales.

Lights up entire roadway, including ditches at side. Gives perfect illumination without shadows or flickering.

AT LAST! An amazingly queer yet simple invention lifts the curse of night driving from the motoring world. Actually like magic this altogether new discovery replaces the "bulb" in automobile headlights with truly amazing results. Road illumination is instantly doubled, yet glare is absolutely banished. Ordinary objects in the road, ruts, animals, obstructions, etc., are made clearly visible at least **three** times as far. Even cuts right through fog, mist, rain and snow. Instead of ordinary "direct" light, this beam is composed entirely of double-reflected or "infused" light. This new kind of beam pours down the highway ahead of you so far that you can actually see to go 70 miles an hour in safety.

Patent rights in this new lighting invention are fully protected. There is no wiring or installation. No extra upkeep. In the past, millions of motorists have paid from $10 to $25 for so-called spot-lights and driving-lights that at best are only make-shifts. This new method costs only a fraction as much and actually doubles road illumination with your present headlights! No wonder fleet owners, manufacturers, taxi and bus lines, etc., concerns like Wallace & Tiernan, N. J.; Blue & Grey Bus Line, W. Va.; Columbus, Fire Trucks, etc., are fast turning to this discovery as standard equipment.

Offered on Introductory Test

Every driver who ever rolled half blind down the highway at night knows exactly what such an invention means in added speed, nervous energy saved, perhaps fatal accidents banished. To prove as quickly as possible to motorists in every section what this invention will do, the manufacturer now makes a liberal FREE TEST OFFER. Simply mail the coupon for details.

HACHMEISTER-LIND CO.
Dept. R-1320   Pittsburgh, Pa.

Agent Makes $1,400 in One Week!

Full-time and spare-time workers. New FREE DEMONSTRATION Plan with SALES GUARANTEED. EXCLUSIVE TERRITORY. Sell in bunches to fleet owners. A real chance for $8 to $14 very first hour; $6,000 to $10,000 a year. Wehner, Pa., made $1,125 in 90 days' spare-time; Owens W. Va., made $500 a month; Davis, Pa., actually made $1,400 in one week! No limit for distributors. Use coupon for full details of money-making proposition. It's red-hot, ACT NOW!

HACHMEISTER-LIND CO.,
Dept. R-1320, Pittsburgh, Pa.

Rush details of your Free Test Offer; also facts about agent's money-making opportunities without obligation.

Name ....

Address ....

Town ....State.................

Hachmeister-Lind Co., 1931

SPORS PRESENTS A POPULAR
Tested Seller

NEWS!

There's big news in the making for selling! Spors Mystery box merchandise display! Designed by us for today's opportunities. These powerful, attention compelling displays should set a standard of high earnings and easy sales.

MYSTERY BOXES as illustrated are now being shown. Many orders for single deals are bringing repeat orders, one after another for five, ten, yes even fifty in some cases. Just six sales a day, grosses you nearly $77.00 in a week. Part time selling should pay you proportionally well.

And remember back of every "Mystery Box" is the Spors Guarantee of Satisfaction.

PROSPECTS EVERYWHERE

● ●

Operators Of:

Amusement	Taverns
Places	Barber
Drug	Shops
Stores	Clubs
Liquor	Fairs
Stores	Picnics
Pool	Church
Halls	Bazaars

BEAUTIFULLY DESIGNED

No. D1. Mystery Box Deal. It is made up of a beautiful, eye catching three color cabinet which contains 80 numbered surprises to be sold at 10c a sale. Brings in $8. Shipped express or freight. Weighs about 22 lbs.

Sells To Dealers $6.00 Cost You $3.95 -- Lots of 10 $38.50

MAKE QUICK SALES --- SURPRISES CHANGED FREQUENTLY

LOOK MEN BRAND NEW KNOCKOUT INVENTION

A·TOUCH·OF·A·BUTTON·HANDS·YOU·A·

LIGHTED CIGARETTE

*Just Touch
a Button . . .
Out Comes
a Cigarette
Automatically . . .
a Flame Appears
Automatically . . .
You Simply
Puff and Smoke!*

THERE ARE MILLIONS IN IT FOR SALESMEN

Imagine taking a shining, beautiful case from your vest pocket . . . you press a magic button . . . a miracle happens! AUTOMATICALLY your favorite brand of cigarette appears. AUTOMATICALLY at the same time there is a spark . . . a flame! A LIGHTED Cigarette is delivered right to your lips. You PUFF and SMOKE! Whoever imagined such a marvelous device? Yet it is HERE . . . PERFECTED . . . GUARANTEED! Ready for the waiting millions.

THE WHOLE COUNTRY IS WAITING FOR IT

This great invention is Brand New . . . Revolutionary . . . DYNAMIC! 30 million smokers—Men and Women . . . ready to BUY. Get your share of the millions of dollars to be made from this new smoke thrill. Show this magic device and smokers gasp in wonder. Everybody gets a "kick" from pressing the magic button and having a LIGHTED Cigarette delivered ready for smoking. Our first announcement of it brought back 60,000 reservations in only 10 days. N. O. Enwaver says, "Expect a thousand sales to movie people in California." Mark V. Hughes writes, "Believe I can sell 1500 in 60 days." N. P. Weaver advises, "Have orders for 250 . . . 10 salesmen ready to start."

SELF-SELLING, LOW PRICED FOR QUICK PROFITS

Think of *your* money-making opportunity. There are hundreds, thousands, tens of thousands of prospects in your territory. YOUR territory EXCLUSIVELY if you act quick! One demonstration may make a hundred buyers. Every buyer will talk, boost, advertise. Can't you see the wave of demand surging, overwhelming you with orders! Guess the price of the Magic Case—in rich, modernistic colors and designs! You'll probably guess several times what it sells for. And you'll be amazed when we tell you the profit you make on every sale. Think, man, THINK! Haven't you many a time hoped that LUCK would come to you in the form of a low-priced, self-selling, non-competitive article in demand by millions? At last . . . here's your opportunity for BIG MONEY.

15 DAY TRIAL OFFER

The facts we've given you fairly SCREAM "Big Profits." Just say the word and we'll wrap up a Magic Case and send it along for 15 days trial at our risk. If profits up to $95 a week are not too high for you mail the coupon today.

MAGIC CASE MFRS.
4234 Cozens Ave., Dept. G-4637, St. Louis, Mo.

G. F. Stayton, 1935

Lektrolite, 1933

Magic Case Mfrs., 1933   B. Max Mehl, 1935

Stark Bros. Nurseries, 1937

Jim Brown, 1931

Jim Brown, 1931

Jim Brown, 1931

Jim Brown, 1931

▶ *Jim Brown, 1931*

And the winner is...

Clean as a Whistle

If the sinister rubber glove was not enough, then surely the threatening surgical instruments would suffice in scaring consumers into thinking twice about using anything but the best to complete their personal regime. This aggressive marketing of a hygienic product played on the country's obsession with sanitation that had begun earlier in the century. While the nature of "toilet tissue illness" is never directly stated, the message is clear. Use Scott® Tissue, or face the surgeon's knife.

Nicht nur sauber, sondern rein

Sollte der scheußliche Gummihandschuh nicht reichen, dann würden die Furcht einflößenden Chirurgeninstrumente die Verbraucher bestimmt davon überzeugen, ihrem Allerwertesten nur mit einem Spitzenprodukt zu Leibe zu rücken. Diese aggressive Werbung für ein Hygieneprodukt konnte auf eine amerikanische Obsession hinsichtlich der Körperpflege bauen, die schon früher eingesetzt hatte. Der wahre Charakter der geheimnisvollen „Toilettenpapier-Krankheit" bleibt zwar im Dunkeln, doch die Botschaft ist eindeutig: Nimm Klopapier von Scott® oder sag dem OP-Tisch guten Tag.

Propre comme un sou neuf

Si les sinistres gants en caoutchouc ne suffisaient pas, la menace des instruments chirurgicaux devait achever de terrifier le consommateur qui aurait envisagé d'utiliser autre chose que le meilleur pour son hygiène intime. Cette campagne de choc pour du papier hygiénique exploitait l'obsession nationale pour la santé publique qui s'était développée plus tôt au début du siècle. Si la nature de « la maladie du papier toilette » n'est jamais explicite, le message est clair : utilisez Scott® Tissue, ou bien préparez-vous à passer sur le billard.

Limpio como una patena

Por si el siniestro guante de látex no infundiera ya bastante respeto, el instrumental quirúrgico adicional constituía sin duda un arma eficaz a la hora de incitar a los consumidores a adquirir los mejores productos para su higiene personal. Esta agresiva campaña de papel higiénico se hacía eco de la obsesión por la higiene que azotaba a los estadounidenses desde principios de siglo. Si bien en ningún momento llegaba a hablarse de una «enfermedad provocada por el papel higiénico», el mensaje era claro: «Utilice Scott® o tendrá que vérselas con el bisturí».

きわめて清潔に

この不気味なゴム手袋で効果がなくても、恐ろしい外科手術道具を見せれば十分だろう。最良の衛生用品以外は使わない方がいいということを認識させるには・・・。この強烈な衛生用品の販売広告は、20世紀前半に始まった国民の衛生強迫観念を利用している。「トイレットペーパー病」の本当のところはあからさまに書かれていないが、言いたいことは明らかである。スコット®ティッシュを使いましょう、そうしないと痛い目にあいますよ。

... often the only relief
from toilet tissue illness

THE annual reports issued by public hospitals show an astonishing percentage of rectal cases ... many of which require surgical treatment.

Physicians who specialize in ailments of this kind estimate that 65 per cent of all men and women over 40 suffer from some form of rectal illness.

Many of these cases are directly traceable to inferior toilet tissue. Harsh, chemically impure toilet tissue—made from reclaimed waste material.

As a safety precaution millions of women are equipping their bathrooms with the tissues that doctors and hospitals approve for safety—Scot-Tissue and Waldorf.

These two health tissues are made only from fresh new materials, specially processed to obtain an extremely soft, cloth-like texture. They are *twice as absorbent* as ordinary kinds.

Without this degree of absorbency, thorough hygiene is impossible.

You can rely on Scott Tissues to protect your family's health—just as doctors and hospitals rely on them to protect the health of their patients.

Eliminate a needless risk. Ask for ScotTissue or Waldorf when you order. They cost no more than inferior tissues. Scott Paper Company, Chester, Pa. In Canada, Scott Paper Co., Ltd., Toronto, Ont.

SCOTTISSUE, *an extremely soft, pure white, absorbent roll containing 1,000 sheets*
2 *for* 25¢
Price for U. S. only

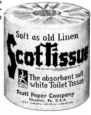

Soft as old Linen
ScotTissue
The absorbent soft white Toilet Tissue
Scott Paper Company
Chester, Pa. U.S.A.

The Waldorf
A Scott Tissue

WALDORF, *soft and absorbent, yet inexpensive. Any family can afford this fine tissue* 3 *for* 20¢
Price for U. S. only

Doctors, Hospitals, Health Authorities approve Scott Tissues for Safety

Scott Tissues, 1931

Their Romance Rocked the Foundations of an Empire!

Song Of The Flame, 1930

The Green Goddess, 1930

Parnell, 1937 ◄   Moby Dick, 1930

The Badman, 1930   ► Under A Texas Moon, 1930

Royal
of
merican
World!

Barrymore

John
Ethel
Lionel

TOGETHER
for the first
time on the
Screen!

The eyes of the motion picture world turned to Metro-Goldwyn-Mayer after the marvels of "Grand Hotel" were revealed to audiences. What next from this amazing producing company? Here is the answer! The most spectacular entertainment of our entire career! The last royal scandal of the present generation against a background of screen wonders never before attempted. And starring *for the first time together in films* the three Barrymores!

SAINT or DEVIL?

They came to worship, these gorgeous beauties of a debauched dynasty, and met a mad monk of hypnotic power.

in RASPUTIN

with
Ralph Morgan   Diana Wynward
Directed by Richard Boleslavsky

THE METRO-GOLDWYN MAYER LION
THE GREATEST STAR ON THE SCREEN

Rasputin, 1932

The Prince And The Pauper, 1937

Gunga Din, 1939

The Last Days Of Pompeii, 1935

The Sign Of The Cross, 1933

SAMUEL GOLDWYN
presents

THE
GOLDWYN
FOLLIES

IN TECHNICOLOR

with ADOLPHE MENJOU
THE RITZ BROTHERS
ZORINA · KENNY BAKER
Andrea LEEDS · Helen JEPSON
Phil BAKER · Ella LOGAN
Bobby CLARK · Jerome COWAN
THE AMERICAN BALLET

and introducing the comedy sensation of the world
EDGAR BERGEN & 'CHARLIE McCARTHY'
Story by BEN HECHT · Directed by GEORGE MARSHALL

Mr. Goldwyn has surpassed himself with his "Goldwyn Follies."
...JIMMY STARR
(L. A. Herald-Express)

Really great entertainment with highlights to please every taste.
...PAUL HARRISON
(N. E. A.)

Patrons of all types will receive "The Goldwyn Follies" with enthusiasm.
...FILM DAILY

Abounding in the lavishness and excellence which have become a tradition of Samuel Goldwyn.
IVAN SPEAR
(Box Office)

Excellent. Probably the best musical film I've ever seen.
...ALEX KAHN
(United Press)

RELEASED THRU UNITED ARTISTS

The
PINNACLE
of
SHOWMANSHIP
from the
MASTER
SHOWMAN . . .

"The Goldwyn Follies" sets a new standard for sheer screen beauty and sumptuous production, to cap its other merits as lush entertainment of exceptional box-office promise. Samuel Goldwyn gives it the works... talent from every popular field of entertainment... carrying out the best Goldwyn standard.

"The Goldwyn Follies" is an incredible blending of entertainment elements superbly effective and stunningly beautiful. Samuel Goldwyn has brought into being another hit attraction of the first rank, another proof of his showmanship. Its production elements set it apart from everything that has gone before and will set the world talking.

The GOLDWYN FOLLIES
in TECHNICOLOR

The Goldwyn Follies, 1938

THE GIFT THAT GIVES
YOU ALL OF MUSIC

...AN RCA VICTOR
PHONOGRAPH-RADIO

Richard Crooks famed concert and operatic tenor, is shown with his family listening to his newest Victor recording, from the Stephen Foster Album, on their new RCA Victor Phonograph-Radio Model U-109.

MAKE this the best of all Christmases with an RCA Victor Phonograph-Radio! Then the whole family can listen to the music of the world on Victor Records...then the heart songs that stir you most...the symphony you love...your favorite opera...the dance bands that please you...all are ready to be heard at an instant's notice. Then *your* children can grow up with the tens of thousands of others who are today learning to know and love fine music through Victor Records. Never before could you hear such a miracle of tone fidelity and beauty in recorded music as you can hear this year with the new RCA Victor Higher Fidelity Phonograph-Radio. Eight different models to choose from, and prices begin under $80!

RCA Victor Phonograph-Radio U-109—Shown above. Matches the perfection of Victor Higher Fidelity Records. Dynamic Volume Expander provides the same natural tone quality at any volume. Automatic record changer. Domestic and foreign reception. New RCA Victor Electric Tuning. Push a button — there's your station.

All prices f. o. b. Camden, New Jersey, subject to change without notice. RCA presents "The Magic Key" every Sunday, 2 to 3 p. m., E.S.T., on NBC Blue Network.

For Radio Tubes it pays to go "RCA All The Way"! First in metal — foremost in glass — finest in tone.

Above — This and your radio play Victor Records. RCA Victor Record Player R-91A, $19.95, transforms any modern AC radio into an electric phonograph-radio.

A SERVICE OF THE RADIO CORPORATION OF AMERICA

RCA Victor

RCA Victor, 1937

• To the left, a new design in the Heywood O.C. 920 series of Streamline Theatre Chairs. Note the protective Streamline edge around the back... the new turned front bottom board... and the swanky new aisle standard available in many modern color combinations.

THE *Tops* IN *Modern Style* !

HEYWOOD Streamline Seating gives you the absolute "tops" in style. These swanky, modern chairs will do wonders for houses that need reseating... will lend decorative flash and sparkle to any interior. Their well designed aisle standards... lustrous Streamline Edge around the back... trim tailoring... deck arm caps... and other distinctive features have made Heywood Streamline Chairs the favorite with prominent showmen... *and their patrons!* May we tell you more in detail about these stylish theatre chairs and why they will pay you dividends right at your box office?

• The Heywood Streamline Back has a protective, ribbed edge which prevents upholstery from soiling and wearing. Quickens house traffic, too, makes it easy for patrons to "spot" vacant seats.

HEYWOOD-WAKEFIELD
Established 1826
GARDNER, MASS.

Streamline Theatre Seating

Heywood-Wakefield, 1938

FROM THE SC... • FROM THE STAGE • FROM THE BALLET • FROM THE OPERA • FROM THE SCREEN • FROM THE RADIO • FROM THE STAGE • FROM THE BALLET • FROM THE OPERA

They all agree !

Hollywood is saying this is finest musical comedy ever made. I can honestly recommend it for your "must see" list.
... JIMMY FIDLER *(Radio)*

Samuel Goldwyn's "Goldwyn Follies" contains just about everything, expensive, lavish and crammed full of talent.
... LOUELLA O. PARSONS *(Universal Service)*

Is the finest musical in several seasons; every bit of entertainment value that could be gathered has been injected into it.
... DOUGLAS CHURCHILL *(Syndicate)*

One of finest color films yet made; is a work of art; rich in comedy and unusual entertainment; in a class by itself, maintaining the Goldwyn standard of quality.
... EDWIN SCHALLERT *(L. A. Times)*

A feast of beauty and comedy never before equalled... Goldwyn's supreme achievement.
. ELIZABETH WILSON *(Screenland)*

RELEASED THRU
UNITED ARTISTS

SAMUEL GOLDWYN presents *The* GOLDWYN FOLLIES IN TECHNICOLOR

The Goldwyn Follies, 1938

Greta GARBO
Robert MONTGOMERY
Joan CRAWFORD
Norma SHEARER
Wallace BEERY
John GILBERT
Marion DAVIES

IT'S WRITTEN in the STARS

Leo's crown fits him better than ever!

IF only you could take a peek through the telescope with Leo, what a thrill you would have watching M-G-M's brilliant stars, directors, writers and technical experts—all busy on the greatest production program in the history of this company. Week after week during the coming season new M-G-M hits will come out of that miracle city known as the M-G-M Studio. Mighty productions that are destined to take their place with such M-G-M triumphs of past seasons as "The Secret Six," "Reducing," "Our Dancing Daughters," "Anna Christie," "The Divorcee," "Min and Bill," "Paid," "Strangers May Kiss," "Trader Horn." *It's written in the stars* that Metro-Goldwyn-Mayer will again prove during 1931-1932 that it is the greatest producing organization in motion pictures.

"More Stars Than There are in Heaven" METRO-

Marie DRESSLER
Lawrence TIBBETT
William HAINES
Ramon NOVARRO
Buster KEATON
Alfred LUNT
The Theatre Guild Stars
Lynn FONTAINE

1931-1932 Will Be M-G-M's CROWNING GLORY

These famous stars and featured players will make the coming year the greatest in Metro-Goldwyn-Mayer history:

Marion DAVIES	Wallace BEERY	Joan CRAWFORD
Marie DRESSLER	Greta GARBO	John GILBERT
William HAINES	Buster KEATON	Robert MONTGOMERY
Ramon NOVARRO	Norma SHEARER	Lawrence TIBBETT
	Alfred LUNT	Lynn FONTAINE

Dorothy Appleby	Reginald Denny	Neil Hamilton	John Miljan	Irene Purcell
Lionel Barrymore	Kent Douglass	Helen Hayes	Ray Milland	Marjorie Rambeau
Edwin Bartlett	James Durante	Leila Hyams	C. Montenegro	C. Aubrey Smith
William Bakewell	Cliff Edwards	Jean Hersholt	Polly Moran	Ruth Selwyn
Charles Bickford	Phyllis Elgar	Hedda Hopper	Karen Morely	Gus Shy
Lilian Bond	Madge Evans	Leslie Howard	Conrad Nagel	Lewis Stone
Edwina Booth	Clark Gable	Dorothy Jordan	Ivor Novello	Ernest Torrence
John Mack Brown	Ralph Graves	Joan Marsh	Monroe Owsley	Lester Vail
Janet Currie	Charlotte Greenwood	Adolphe Menjou	Anita Page	Robert Young

In stories by the world's most brilliant writers. Directed by men who are making screen history.

You'll Soon APPLAUD

Marion DAVIES
in "Five and Ten"

Norma SHEARER
in "A Free Soul"

Marie DRESSLER
Polly MORAN
in "Politics"

Robert MONTGOMERY
in "The Man in Possession"

Greta GARBO
in "Susan Lenox, Her Fall and Rise"

and many others

GOLDWYN-MAYER

Metro-Goldwyn-Mayer, 1931

THEY'VE JUMPED FROM THE FUNNIES INTO THE MOVIES!

BLONDIE

and her folks... the BUMSTEADS!

WHAT A FAMILY!

America has fallen head over heels in love with them...

Here they are. (Top) PENNY SINGLETON as BLONDIE, and ARTHUR LAKE as DAGWOOD. (Center) Wee LARRY SIMMS as BABY DUMPLING. (Below, left) DAISY, the pup, as herself.

Perfect pictures, perfectly played, *perfectly hilarious!* Based on the famous comic strip by CHIC YOUNG. Screen play by RICHARD FLOURNOY. Directed by FRANK R. STRAYER.

They're Columbia Pictures!

ASK YOUR THEATRE when the next BLONDIE picture is showing... *and don't miss it!*

Blondie, 1939

You always see him on PARAMOUNT NIGHTS

Your Theatre Manager. He wouldn't be there if a poor picture had spoiled your afternoon or evening's entertainment. He's always there to greet you on Paramount nights because Paramount Pictures are consistently good entertainment. ❧ That does not mean the only good pictures are Paramount. It does mean that *all* Paramount Pictures are good, very often great, never anything but entertainment supreme. ❧ Just as with everything else, it pays to select your entertainment carefully and with pictures you need look no farther than the word *Paramount* to be sure of seeing the best show in town. ❧ Find out now when you can see those listed on this page and make it a point to see them all. ❧ *"If it's a Paramount Picture it's the best show in town!"*

PARAMOUNT FAMOUS LASKY CORP., ADOLPH ZUKOR, PRES. PARAMOUNT BLDG., N. Y.

Paramount Pictures

ON THE AIR! Paramount-Publix Radio Hour, each Saturday Evening, 10-11 P. M. Eastern Time over the Columbia Broadcasting System.

"PARAMOUNT ON PARADE"

Paramount's musical comedy supreme with a cast composed of the greatest stars of stage and screen. Like ten big Broadway shows in one—riotous comedy, song hits galore, dazzling Technicolor scenes—in this star-studded triumph of The New Show World!

GEORGE BANCROFT "LADIES LOVE BRUTES"

With Mary Astor and Fredric March. Directed by Rowland V. Lee from the play "Pardon My Glove" by Zoe Akins. Exciting, romantic melodrama with George Bancroft as the skyscraper king of New York wooing a beautiful society woman, played by Mary Astor.

"THE BENSON MURDER CASE"

William Powell, as "Philo Vance," is again called upon to solve the most baffling of all murder mysteries. How he does it is unfolded in this absorbing melodrama. With Jean Arthur, Paul Lukas, Eugene Pallette. Directed by Louis Gasnier from the novel by S. S. Van Dine.

Charles "Buddy" Rogers in "YOUNG EAGLES"

You've always wanted to see an aviation picture as great as "Wings." Here it is, starring Charles "Buddy" Rogers, hero of "Wings," directed by William Wellman, who produced "Wings." 100% dialogue throughout. Also in the great cast are Jean Arthur and Paul Lukas.

RICHARD ARLEN "THE LIGHT OF WESTERN STARS"

Thrilling, romantic all-talking, all-outdoors melodrama from the famous story by Zane Grey. Supporting Richard Arlen in the big cast are these great favorites—Mary Brian, Regis Toomey, Harry Green and Fred Kohler. Directed by Otto Brower and John Langan.

Paramount Pictures, 1930

ANOTHER GRAND PICTURE OPENS THE GATES OF MEMORY... rich with the emotion of years of beloved melody!

Darryl F. Zanuck and 20th Century-Fox bring you the newest and greatest in entertainment!

The stars of "Alexander's Ragtime Band"

TYRONE POWER ALICE FAYE

and the star who sings back the past you want to remember

AL JOLSON

Rose of Washington Square

with

WILLIAM JOYCE HOBART
FRAWLEY · COMPTON · CAVANAUGH

A 20th Century-Fox Picture

DARRYL F. ZANUCK In Charge of Production

Directed by Gregory Ratoff

Associate Producer and Screen Play by Nunnally Johnson

THE DRAMATIC STORY OF A GIRL ON THE LEVEL ABOUT LOVE... NO MATTER HOW IT TRICKED HER!

And in the swing of today... Gordon & Revel's latest hit, "I Never Knew Heaven Could Speak"!

Rose Of Washington Square, 1939

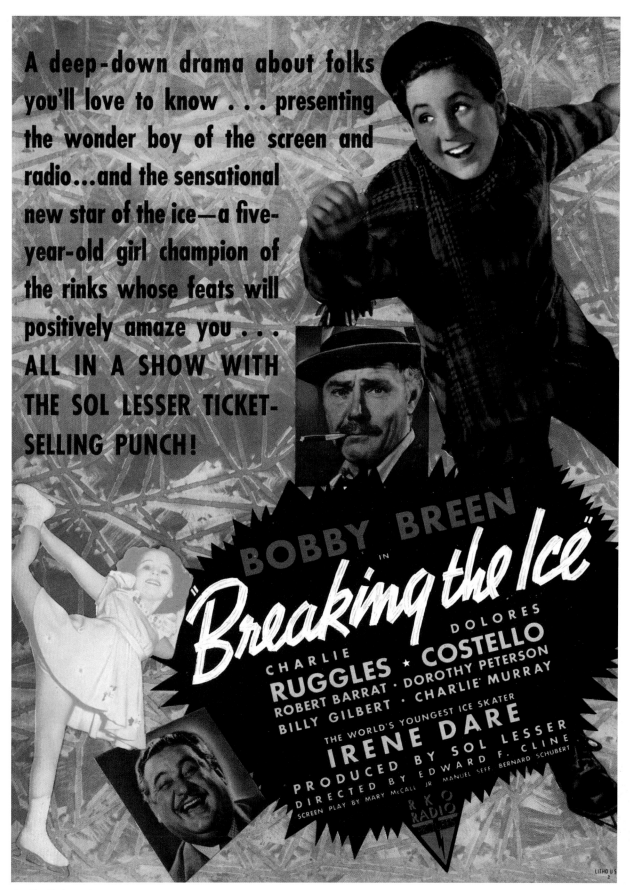

Breaking The Ice, 1938

FRED ASTAIRE
GINGER ROGERS

in

SHALL WE DANCE

with

EDWARD EVERETT HORTON ★ ERIC BLORE

JEROME COWAN ★ KETTI GALLIAN

WILLIAM BRISBANE and HARRIET HOCTOR

Music by GEORGE GERSHWIN ★ Lyrics by IRA GERSHWIN
Directed by Mark Sandrich ★ Pandro S. Berman Production

R K O
RADIO
PICTURES

SWEET SWING AND RED-HOT
BLUES! THEY'RE HEAD OVER
HEELS IN RHYTHM!

Refreshing as an April shower! . . . Exciting as a fire! . . . The world's gay dancing sweethearts, stepping to town higher, brighter than ever in their grandest
show of all! . . . Fred and Ginger surrounded by the screen's biggest comedy
cast . . . and three-score of Hollywood's hand-picked glamour girls! . . . **AND
THOSE GERSHWIN SONGS!** . . . "Let's Call The Whole Thing Off"—"Slap
That Bass"—"I've Got Beginner's Luck"—"They All Laughed"—"They Can't
Take That Away"—"Shall We Dance."

Carefree, 1938 ◄   *Shall We Dance, 1937*   ► *Marco Polo, 1938*

367

GARY COOPER

ROBERT LEE

in

The Adventures of

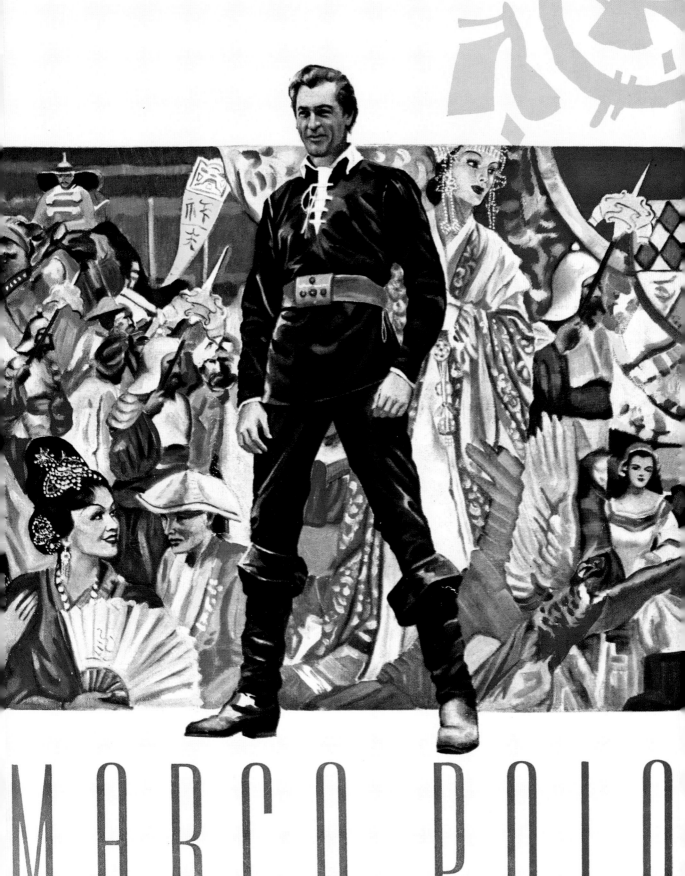

MARCO POLO

Hollywood Talent Parade, 1936

Top Of The Town, 1937

Warner Brothers, 1937

Time-Life, 1938

TAKE A LION WITH YOU
ON YOUR VACATION!

WANT to make sure of a roaring good time this summer? Looking for thrills, adventure, romance, fun? Remember Leo, the M·G·M lion! Look him up wherever you may be—at seashore or camp, at home or abroad—you're seldom more than a few miles away from a theatre where the world's greatest motion pictures are being shown! Drop in to see Leo. He'll be delighted to introduce you to the greatest stars on the screen today—acting for you in pictures that represent the world's best entertainment.

More stars than there are in heaven

METRO - GOLDWYN - MAYER

Metro-Goldwyn-Mayer, 1931

371

The Littlest Rebel, 1935

The Champ, 1932

The Little Princess, 1939

Huckleberry Finn, 1939

THE KENTUCKY OF GREAT
TRADITION HAS INSPIRED
A GREAT PICTURE...
IN ALL THE SPLENDOR OF
TECHNICOLOR!

Kentucky

with

LORETTA YOUNG · RICHARD GREENE
and **WALTER BRENNAN** · DOUGLAS DUMBRILLE
KAREN MORLEY · MORONI OLSEN
Photographed in TECHNICOLOR.

Directed by David Butler · Associate Producer Gene
Markey · Screen Play by Lamar Trotti and John Taintor Foote
From the story "The Look of Eagles" by John Taintor Foote
A 20th Century-Fox Picture
DARRYL F. ZANUCK in Charge of Production

*Proud romance ... beautiful
women ... chivalrous men ...
magnificent thoroughbreds! The
sport of kings climaxing when
the silks flash by at Churchill
Downs in the famed Kentucky
Derby! All against the warm
beauty of the Blue Grass country!*

Ask your theatre manager for KENTUCKY

Kentucky, 1939

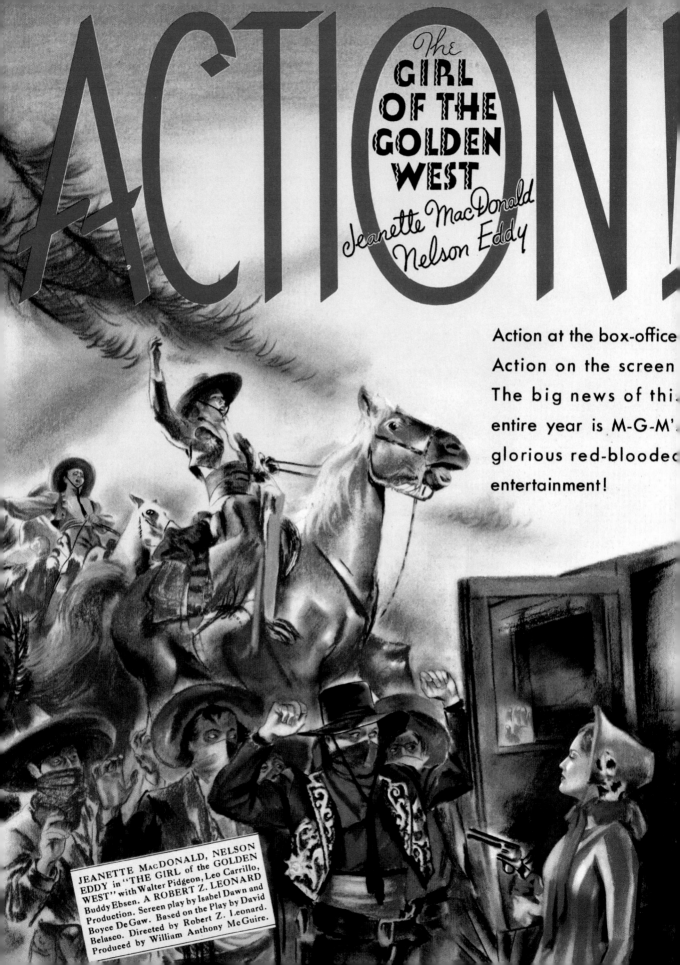

ACTION!

THE GIRL OF THE GOLDEN WEST

Jeanette MacDonald
Nelson Eddy

Action at the box-office

Action on the screen

The big news of thi...

entire year is M-G-M'...

glorious red-blooded

entertainment!

JEANETTE MacDONALD, NELSON
EDDY in "THE GIRL of the GOLDEN
WEST" with Walter Pidgeon, Leo Carrillo,
Buddy Ebsen. A ROBERT Z. LEONARD
Production. Screen play by Isabel Dawn and
Boyce DeGaw. Based on the Play by David
Belasco. Directed by Robert Z. Leonard.
Produced by William Anthony McGuire.

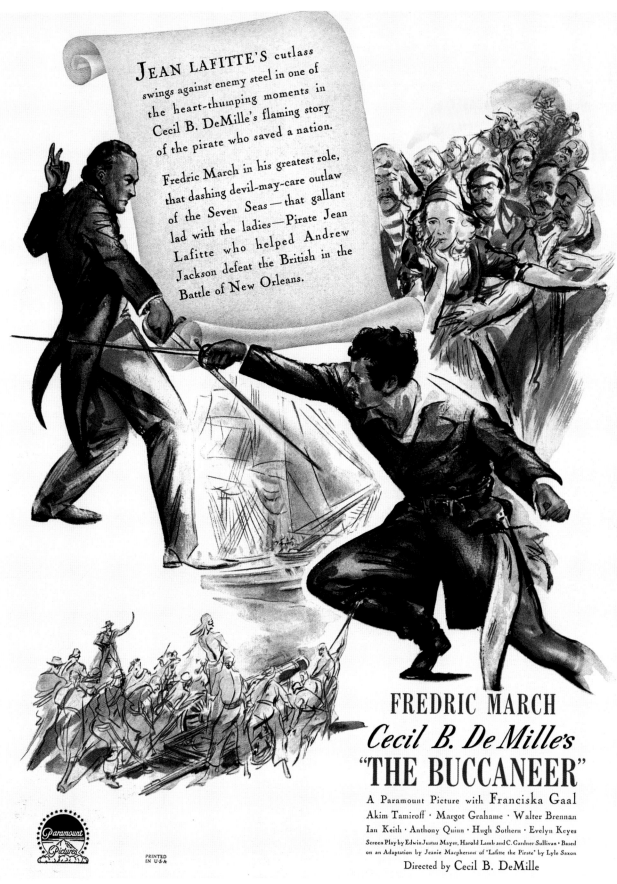

JEAN LAFITTE'S cutlass swings against enemy steel in one of the heart-thumping moments in Cecil B. DeMille's flaming story of the pirate who saved a nation.

Fredric March in his greatest role, that dashing devil-may-care outlaw of the Seven Seas—that gallant lad with the ladies—Pirate Jean Lafitte who helped Andrew Jackson defeat the British in the Battle of New Orleans.

FREDRIC MARCH
Cecil B. DeMille's
"THE BUCCANEER"

A *Paramount Picture* with Franciska Gaal

Akim Tamiroff · Margot Grahame · Walter Brennan
Ian Keith · Anthony Quinn · Hugh Sothern · Evelyn Keyes

Screen Play by Edwin Justus Mayer, Harold Lamb and C. Gardner Sullivan · Based
on an Adaptation by Jeanie Macpherson of "Lafitte the Pirate" by Lyle Saxon

Directed by Cecil B. DeMille

PRINTED
IN U·S·A

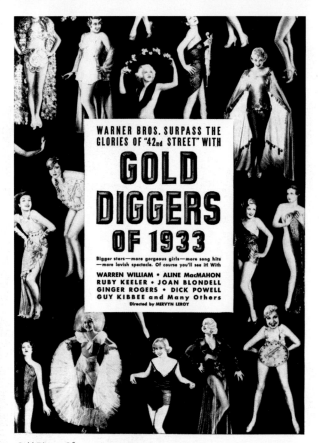

Gold Diggers Of 1933, 1933

Footlight Parade, 1933

Broadway Melody Of 1936, 1935

42nd Street, 1933

▶ *The Hurricane, 1937*

SAMUEL GOLDWYN
PRESENTS

THE HURRICANE

... the hunt for happiness ... relentless pursuit by an avenging law ... the merciless tropics—the glamour, the fragrant magic, the ecstatic beauty of star-strewn South Sea nights ... 'Midst this glorious setting, the exciting action of "THE HURRICANE" whirls to its tempestuous climax ... its vivid romance is lived by primitive children of nature unfettered by the chains of civilization ... a world of dreams is brought to life ...

C. Aubrey Smith, who portrays the role of Father Paul, the priest who aided the sweethearts to escape.

Mary Astor, at her brilliant dramatic best, as the compassionate wife of the Governor of Manukura Island.

Raymond Massey, as the relentless Governor, who pursued Terangi and Marama to their secret refuge.

Samuel Goldwyn has endowed "THE HURRICANE" with a magnificent cast including Dorothy Lamour, Jon Hall, Mary Astor, C. Aubrey Smith, Thomas Mitchell, Raymond Massey, John Carradine, Jerome Cowan and Mamo Clark, the Hawaiian beauty who played Clark Gable's sweetheart in "Mutiny on the Bounty", Movita Castaneda, the beautiful young Mexican, who played Franchot Tone's sweetheart in the same picture and Reri, the Tahitian who starred in "Tabu". Directed by John Ford, who won the Academy Award for "The Informer". Screenplay by Dudley Nichols. Released thru United Artists.

In "THE HURRICANE", Charles Nordhoff and James Hall, authors of "Mutiny on the Bounty", have created a vivid, stirring tale of love and adventure in the South Seas—and from it, Samuel Goldwyn—after expending an almost unbelievable fortune and two years of effort—has produced a motion picture that takes high rank with the screen's most brilliant offerings.

Dead End, 1937

Metro-Goldwyn-Mayer, 1937

The Charge Of The Light Brigade, 1936

Winterset, 1936

Dark Victory, 1939

MARLENE DIETRICH

"SHANGHAI EXPRESS"

All men desired her, this ravishing, mysterious creature whose scarlet life held many men—whose Love only one had ever known! Parted, they meet again, on the Shanghai Express—seething with intrigue, desire, hatred—hurtling through the night with a dead man at the throttle ... *Marlene Dietrich*, with an irresistible new warmth! The lover who comes back, *Clive Brook!* The year's greatest melodrama, *"Shanghai Express!"* See it—you'll live a thrilling new adventure in a night. And when the picture's over and you're home once more, you'll realize again how true it is when you say, *"If it's a Paramount Picture it's the best show in town!"*

WITH CLIVE BROOK

Anna May Wong, Warner Oland and Eugene Pallette. Directed by JOSEF VON STERNBERG

Paramount Pictures

PARAMOUNT PUBLIX CORP. ADOLPH ZUKOR. PRES. PARAMOUNT BLDG., N. Y.

MARLENE DIETRICH
as the "Blonde Venus"
Dietrich the glamorous — Exotic
beauty of "Morocco" — Tragic
heroine of "Dishonored" — Lovely
derelict of "Shanghai Express" —
Now more entrancing — more
gloriously luscious — as a girl who
played with love. Only Dietrich
can give such beauty, such dignity,
such allure to the scarlet letter!

MARLENE DIETRICH
in "BLONDE VENUS"
with HERBERT MARSHALL
CARY GRANT · DICKIE MOORE
Directed by JOSEPH VON STERNBERG

Shanghai Express, 1932 ◄ *Blonde Venus, 1932*

Metro-Goldwyn-Mayer, 1936

Only Angels Have Wings, 1939

Wuthering Heights, 1939

Captain Fury, 1939

The Charge Of The Light Brigade, 1936

Grimmer than that grim picture, "DRACULA," more gruesome and awe-inspiring than "FRANKENSTEIN," EDGAR ALLAN POE'S remarkable mystery story "MURDERS IN THE RUE MORGUE," laid in the dark caverns of Paris, will thrill you to your finger-tips. Beautifully enacted by

BELA LUGOSI and SIDNEY FOX
The Original "DRACULA"   Star of "STRICTLY DISHONORABLE"
Directed by ROBERT FLOREY

UNIVERSAL PICTURES

UNIVERSAL PICTURES CORPORATION   CARL LAEMMLE, President   730 FIFTH AVENUE, NEW YORK CITY

Murders In The Rue Morgue, 1932   ▶ *Love Affair, 1939*

you...
yourself...
...live their
LOVE AFFAIR"

RKO
RADIO
PICTURES

The Women, 1939

I Take This Woman, 1939

Roberta, 1935

Dinner At 8, 1933

▶ Mannequin, 1938

La 'Ardente Nuit

"Mannequin"
the drama of a shop girl's millions is the greatest Joan Crawford picture in five years!

JOAN
CRAWFORD
SPENCER
TRACY
in
MANNEQUIN
with
ALAN CURTIS
RALPH MORGAN
A Frank Borzage
Production
Screen Play by
Lawrence Hazard
A
Metro-Goldwyn-Mayer
Picture
Directed by
Frank Borzage
Produced by
Joseph L. Mankiewicz

"SURE, I LIKE A GOOD TIME!"

They called her a party wife. They said she "wasn't fit to be a mother." But *you'll* recognize Stella Dallas as one of the greatest, finest characters on the screen!

SAMUEL GOLDWYN

PRESENTS

STELLA DALLAS

WITH

BARBARA

STANWYCK

JOHN BOLES · ANNE SHIRLEY

From the novel by
OLIVE HIGGINS PROUTY
· *RELEASED THRU UNITED ARTISTS* ·

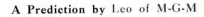

Flying Down To Rio, 1933

Goodbye Mr. Chips, 1939

Stella Dallas, 1937 ◄ *Personal Property, 1937*

Artists And Models, 1937

Just what the public ordered!

The sensational opening engagements of "A YANK AT OXFORD" confirm the astute choice of vehicle for a great popular idol. This two-fisted romance of a roving Yank is the stuff that makes even standing-room a pleasure!

(Note to the trade press from M-G-M and entire cast: "Thanks for those reviews!")

ROBERT TAYLOR in "A YANK AT OXFORD"
with Lionel Barrymore • Maureen O'Sullivan • Vivien Leigh
Edmund Gwenn • Griffith Jones • Directed by JACK CONWAY
Screen Play by Malcolm Stuart Boylan, Walter Ferris and George Oppenheimer • Original Story by Leon Gordon, Sidney Gilliatt and Michael Hogan • Based on an Idea by John Monk Saunders • Produced by Michael Balcon.
A Metro-Goldwyn-Mayer Picture

A Yank At Oxford, 1938

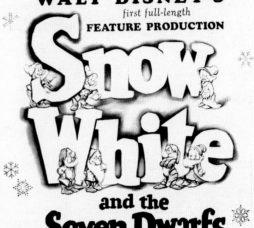

It took 1,000 ARTISTS THREE YEARS to make it!

The most anticipated picture in 20 years will be the show sensation of 1938—and for years to come!..The most amazing advance in screen entertainment since the advent of sound!..You'll gasp, marvel, cheer at its wonders as you thrill to an experience you've never lived through before!..Without a human actor, it's more human than all the dramas that ever came out of Hollywood!..Power to make you laugh, cry, throb with excitement!..Music to fill your soul—8 big songs, several as good as "The Big Bad Wolf"!..Romance, adventure, mystery, pathos, tragedy, laughter and beauty such as you must actually see and feel to believe!.. Truly the miracle in motion pictures — the new wonder of the world!

WALT DISNEY'S *first full-length* FEATURE PRODUCTION

Snow White

and the Seven Dwarfs

in the marvelous
MULTIPLANE TECHNICOLOR
Distributed by RKO RADIO PICTURES, Inc.

Snow White And The Seven Dwarfs, 1937

3 STAR HITS FOR YOUR HOLIDAY DISPLAYS

X1410
CHRISTMAS MURAL
40 IN. WIDE
20 FT. LONG

K 4
CHRISTMAS VILLAGE
REYKOTE
107 IN. WIDE
12 FT. LONG

D 35
DONALD DUCK
SANTA PANEL
40 IN. WIDE
72 IN. LONG

Reyburn's

DISPLAY MATERIALS *for* CHRISTMAS *1941*

SEE THESE THREE STAR HITS AND OUR OTHER HEADLINERS ON DISPLAY AT YOUR DISPLAY MATERIALS SUPPLY HOUSE.

FREE OUR 32 PAGE CATALOG SEND FOR YOUR COPY TODAY

THE REYBURN MANUFACTURING CO., Inc.
PHILADELPHIA, PA.
SHOWROOMS 1100 So. WABASH, CHICAGO   8 W. 36th ST., NEW YORK CITY

Reyburn Manufacturing Co., 1935

▶ *A Princess Marries, 1938*

A PRINCESS MARRIES

A NEW NOVEL ON A MODERN THEME
BY *Sylvia Thompson*

Author of "HOUNDS OF SPRING," "RECAPTURE THE MOON,"
"THE LILAC IS IN BLOOM," ETC.

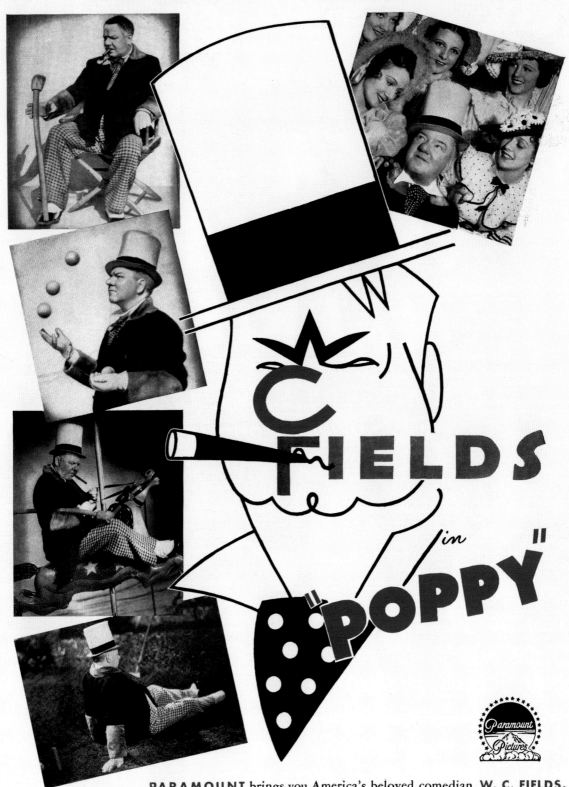

PARAMOUNT brings you America's beloved comedian, **W. C. FIELDS,**
as the one and only Professor Eustace McGargle in the musical comedy
"POPPY" with Rochelle Hudson . . . Directed by A. Edward Sutherland

11

Poppy, 1936

Boy Meets Girl, 1938

Strike Me Pink, 1936

Good News, 1930

Room Service, 1938

▶ Paramount, 1931

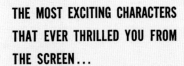

Algiers, 1938

Trader Horn, 1931

Theatre

▶ Stanley And Livingstone, 1939

"Dr. Livingstone, I presume?" Drama knows no moment more thrilling than when Stanley uttered those famous words in the heart of Africa!

nother master-performance by NCER TRACY twice Academy rd winner!

Twentieth Century-Fox presents
Darryl F. Zanuck's Production of

STANLEY *and* LIVINGSTONE

with the greatest acting cast ever assembled . . . starring

Spencer Tracy · Nancy Kelly · Richard Greene

with Walter Brennan · Charles Coburn · Sir Cedric Hardwicke
Henry Hull · Henry Travers · Directed by Henry King

Associate Producer Kenneth Macgowan · Screen Play by Philip Dunne and Julien Josephson · Historical Research and Story Outline by Hal Long and Sam Hellman

Magnificent Obsession, 1936

Anna Karenina, 1935

The Barretts Of Wimpole Street, 1934

Sylvia Scarlett, 1936

Jezebel, 1938

The Old Maid, 1939

Juarez, 1939

A Tale Of Two Cities, 1936

DRIVEN BY THE LOVE OF TWO WOMEN...
HE TORE CONTINENTS APART THAT SHIPS MIGHT SAIL THE DESERT!

Two women...one ever at his side, wanting anything he would give!...one haunting him with the image of eyes, lips, arms denied him! While lashed by his vision, men clawed the choking sand...crushed the wild Bedouin... to create the jugular vein of the world— the Suez Canal!

And when the savage black simoon roars in from the desert...twisting, torturing, destroying... you'll see spectacle and emotion the screen has never been able to capture before!

SUEZ

Production miracles performed in the desert for this great picture! Entire cities and palaces built! The Suez Canal reconstructed! Thousands of workmen and players! Carloads of motion picture equipment! Months of privation and danger!

A picture into which 20th Century-Fox poured all its vast resources... Darryl F. Zanuck all his production skill!

THIS IS ONE OF THE
MOVIE QUIZ
$250,000.00
CONTEST
PICTURES

A
**Twentieth Century-Fox
Picture**
with
TYRONE   LORETTA
**POWER · YOUNG
ANNABELLA**
J. Edward Bromberg · Joseph Schildkraut
Henry Stephenson · Sidney Blackmer
Sig Rumann · Maurice Moscovich
Nigel Bruce · Miles Mander · George Zucco
DARRYL F. ZANUCK
in Charge of Production

Directed by Allan Dwan
Associate Producer Gene Markey
Screen Play by Philip Dunne and
Julien Josephson based on a story
by Sam Duncan.

Suez, 1938

The Dawn Patrol, 1939

Stagecoach, 1939

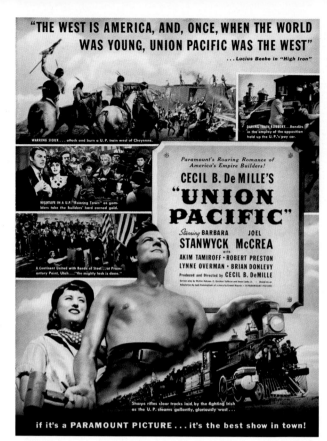

Union Pacific, 1939

Mutiny On the Bounty, 1935

Rulers Of The Sea, 1939

Dodge City, 1939

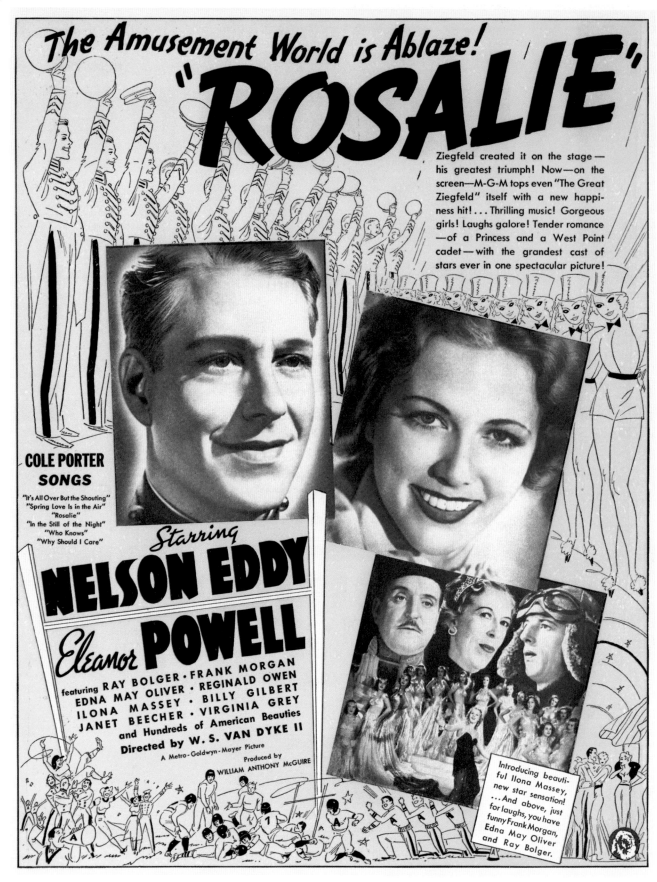

Rosalie, 1938

Manhattan Merry-Go-Round, 1938

Every Day's A Holiday, 1937

Hollywood Hotel, 1937

Top Of The Town, 1937

Charlie Chan's Chance

WARNER OLAND in another amazing adventure of Earl Derr Biggers' master sleuth! With eyes that see all, lips that tell nothing, Charlie Chan unmasks the most sinister crime of his career. Directed by John G. Blystone, with Alexander Kirkland, H. B. Warner, Marian Nixon, Linda Watkins . . . . A mighty murder mystery!

FOX

Charlie Chan, 1932

The Honorable Mr. Wong, 1932

HEADS UP, FILM FANS!

... for M-G-M's greatest film festival o'er land and sea!

Now all the heaven's a stage for Uncle Sam's fighting, flying men. You'll thrill as never before when you see the famed "Hi-Hats" wing into action! You'll grin as you watch the West Pointers getting a P G course in courage and daring! And you'll weep with the girls they leave behind as they soar into the skies to keep a date with the angels!

It took six months, thousands of men, $50,000,000 worth of equipment to make this exciting saga of the sky devils. You'll never forget it!

Wallace Beery
in
WEST POINT of the AIR

West Point Of The Air, 1935

The Dawn Patrol, 1930

Cock Of The Air, 1932

Sky Devils, 1932

Hell Below, 1933

TOGETHER AGAIN
in another **M-G-M** hit!

Ever since beautiful Joan Crawford and Bob Montgomery appeared together in "Our Blushing Brides" and "Untamed" we've been swamped with requests to co-star them again. You'll be delighted with the result.

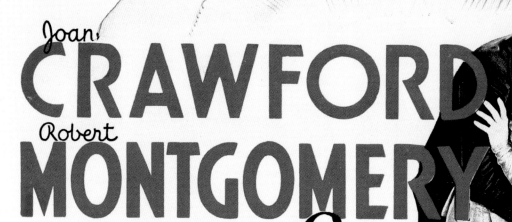

Joan
CRAWFORD
Robert
MONTGOMERY

in CLARENCE BROWN'S
production

Letty Lynton

Nils Asther's return to the screen is something to cheer. He's great in this romantic drama!

Beautiful Joan Crawford gives what many critics believe to be the most impressive performance of her career. Faced by her former lover and her husband-to-be she takes a course which leads to the very brink of tragedy. Once again Joan Crawford mingles tears and laughter, heart-throbs and thrills—again she captures the hearts of millions of her screen admirers! You'll compare it with the most thrilling picture you've ever seen!

with

NILS ASTHER
MAY ROBSON
LEWIS STONE

From the novel by Marie Belloc Lowndes

METRO-GOLDWYN-MAYER

King Of Burlesque, 1936

Anna Karenina, 1935

Letty Lynton, 1932 ◄   Waldorf Astoria, 1936

Nothing Sacred, 1937

And the winner is...

Some Liked It Sinful

Pre-Code Hollywood offered a variety of provocative films that provided more than just a titillating taste of the day's rapidly loosening sexual mores. By 1930, the Motion Picture Producers and Distributors of America (MPPDA) bowed to pressure from religious groups and the Federal government to clean up the nipples, the couples in bed together, the exposed navels. Under the direction of its president, Will Hays, the major studios agreed to a system of self-censorship. By 1934 the Hays Code was in effect, and films like *Illicit* were a thing of the past. It was not until 1968 that Americans were again treated to snippets of cinematic sin.

Manche mögen's heiß

Vor den Tagen der Selbstzensur ging es in vielen Hollywoodfilmen drauf, drunter und drüber – sie boten ein Spiegelbild der sich rapide lockernden Moralvorstellungen jener Jahre. Anfang der Dreißiger beugten sich schließlich die Motion Picture Producers and Distributors of America (MPPDA) der Forderung der Bundesregierung und verschiedener religiöser Organisationen, in Sachen Nippel, Pärchen im Lotterbett und blanke Bauchnabel aufzuräumen. Unter der Leitung des MPPDA-Präsidenten Will Hays stimmten die großen Studios einem System der Selbstzensur zu. 1934 trat der „Hays Code" in Kraft, und Filme wie *Illicit* gehörten der Vergangenheit an. Erst 1968 sollten die Amerikaner wieder Sündiges auf der Leinwand sehen dürfen.

Certains l'aimaient sulfureux

Dans les années 20, Hollywood produisit de nombreux films provocants. A partir de 1930, la MPPDA (Motion Pictures Producers and Distributors of America) finit par céder à la pression des groupes religieux et du gouvernement fédéral et consentit à faire le ménage. Adieu les seins nus, les couples montrés au lit, les nombrils à l'air ! Sous la direction de son président Will Hays, les principaux studios acceptèrent un système d'autocensure. Dès 1934, le « Hays Code » entra en vigueur et des films comme *Illicit* furent bannis. Il fallut attendre 1968 pour que les Américains aient à nouveau le droit d'entrevoir des fragments de péchés sur pellicule.

Los caballeros las prefieren pecaminosas

Antes de que se impusiera el «código ético», Hollywood producía toda suerte de películas provocativas. Todo acabó en 1930, cuando la Asociación de Productores y Distribuidores Cinematográficos de Estados Unidos, la MPPDA, acabó por sucumbir a la presión de grupos religiosos y del Gobierno federal para hacer desaparecer de las pantallas los pezones, las escenas de parejas en la cama y los ombligos al aire. Bajo la dirección del presidente Will Hays, los estudios más importantes se suscribieron a un sistema de autocensura. En 1934 entró en vigor el «Código Hays», y películas como la de este cartel pasaron a ser un vago recuerdo del pasado. Los estadounidenses tuvieron que aguardar hasta 1968 para volver a ver fragmentos eróticos en las películas.

罪深いのがお好き

映画制作倫理規定導入前のハリウッドは、過激な映画を次々と発表していた。性的モラルの束縛から急速に自由になっていった当時の嗜好をそそるにしても行き過ぎの感は否めなかった。1930年、宗教団体と連邦政府は当時ますます過激になっていく映画を容認しなくなった。アメリカ映画製作者配給者協会（MPPDA）は圧力に屈服して、映画産業界で道徳的にふしだらだと考えられるものを一掃した。なくなったのは、乳首、ベッドを共にするカップル、むき出しのへそ。MPPDA会長ウィル・ヘイズの指揮の下、主要な映画スタジオは自主規制制度に賛同してリージョン・オブ・ディーセンシー（良識連合）を組織した。1934年には、ヘイズ・コードとしても有名な映画制作倫理規定の適用が実施され、『イリシット』（禁断の愛）のような映画は過去の産物となった。1968年に、ようやくアメリカ国民は再び罪深いシーンをほんの少しだけ楽しめるようになった。

MARRIED LOVE

Or

ILLICIT

Which –
DOES THE MODERN GIRL PREFER?

SAFETY in marriage or daring adventures in stolen love? What is the real truth about this modern generation's attitude toward the once sacred convention of marriage? "ILLICIT" tells, frankly and fearlessly, the true-to-life story of one girl's amazing adventures in the dangerous business of *experimenting* with love.

featuring

BARBARA STANWYCK
CHARLES BUTTERWORTH · JAMES RENNIE · RICARDO CORTEZ · JOAN BLONDELL · NATALIE MOOREHEAD CLAUDE GILLINGWATER
Based on the play by
Edith Fitzgerald and Robert Riskin
DIRECTED BY ARCHIE MAYO

"Vitaphone" is the registered trademark of The Vitaphone Corporation

A WARNER BROS. AND VITAPHONE PRODUCTION

Illicit, 1931

Meet the girl men want to kiss

STYLE and BEAUTY

McCALL'S

The Weisbaum Bros., 1937 ◄ ◄ *Tangee, 1939* ◄ *McCall's, 1934*

Maybelline, 1937

Richard Hudnut Makeup, 1937

Irresistible Perfume, 1935

Seventeen, 1932

▶ *Maybelline, 1932*

RICHARD HUDNUT creates

MARVELOUS *The Matched* MAKEU

A harmonized makeu

What color are your eyes? Here's your key to correct makeup, your clue to new loveliness. For harmonizing, flattering shades of Marvelous Face Powder, Rouge, Lipstick, Eye Shadow and Mascara, find your makeup among these groups.

DRESDEN *type if your eyes are blue*

PARISIAN *type if your eyes are brown*

CONTINENTAL *type if your eyes are hazel*

PATRICIAN *type if your eyes are gray*

Harmonizing ROUGE · LIPSTICK · FACE POWDER · MASCARA · EYE SHADOW · 55¢ EACH

CHARM

THAT INDEFINABLE
SOMETHING ✦ ✦ ✦

IN COSMETICS EVEN
AS IN MOVIE STARS

JOAN BLONDELL
*Charming young star appearing
for Warner Bros. in "Illicit" and
"Other Men's Women."*

JUST as a new face brings added life and charm to a talking picture — so too, do these compacts bring an inestimable boon — a new charm — to the beauty problems of smart young women.

Delightful little factors in the fine art of makeup, they are at home in the smartest purses. Loose, cake, sifter and lipsalve compacts, plain or swivel lipsticks and even eyebrow pencils — each one cleverly cased in modern design and modish colors.

Away with the notion that beauty comes high! The fact is, most Deere beauty aids can be bought for as little as ten and twenty-five cents. Look for the name Ash's on the lipstick — the Deere guarantee of purity in every compact.

THE REICH-ASH CORP.
307 Fifth Avenue, New York

You may purchase these new Compacts at all Chain Stores

Reich-Ash Co., 1931

FOUNDATIONS OF BEAUTY

Beauty of face and beauty of hands achieved by care, Elizabeth Arden care . . . Cleanse, tone, soothe your skin at least twice daily with Miss Arden's matchless Ardena Cleansing Creams and Skin Tonic . . . Use her famous face powders . . . first, Illusion, soft and delicate, blended by Miss Arden herself for perfection of colour, sifted through fine silk to give it exquisite texture . . . then, sometimes, if you wish to acquire a particularly lovely, translucent look, over Illusion use Cameo Powder in another shade. Use her rich Hand Creams and Lotions to protect the delicacy and fineness of your hands.

New Hand Box $5	Ardena Skin Tonic . $1 to $15	Illusion Powder . $1.75 and $3
Cleansing Cream . . $1 to $6	Ardena Velva Cream . $1 to $6	Cameo Powder . . $2 and $3
Fluffy Cleansing Cream, $1 to $6	Orange Skin Cream . $1 to $8	Two-Powder Box $3

Elizabeth Arden

6 9 1   F I F T H   A V E N U E • N E W   Y O R K

Elizabeth Arden, 1939

GUERLAIN'S
GREAT NEW PERFUME

DARCY

« COQUE D'OR »

Richard Hudnut Makeup, 1936 ◄   Guerlain, 1939

VEGA

GUERLAIN

Guerlain, 1938

NEW— *actually good for your nails*

CUTEX CRÈME POLISH

CANNOT MAKE NAILS BRITTLE OR DRY

COVERS NAIL BLEMISHES

HAS GREATER BRILLIANCE

EASIER TO APPLY, WEARS LONGER

DOES NOT SETTLE IN BOTTLE . . .

- One great big advantage of Cutex Crème Polish is that it doesn't separate and settle in the bottle.
- The perfect companion to Cutex Crème Polish is the new Cutex Oily Polish Remover—contains a special oil to keep nails from becoming brittle.

Cutex was the first to give you Liquid Polish . . . then a complete range of Colored Polish . . . and now here's *Crème* Polish that is actually beneficial to your nails!

The new Cutex Crème Polish absolutely will not make your nails dry or brittle. So all of you can draw a deep breath again and stop worrying about broken or split finger nails.

And you won't believe it, but you'll find that the new Cutex Crème Polish goes on more divinely than ever, and that it wears even longer, without peeling or chipping. And has far more lustre than you've been accustomed to thinking was quite a bright lustre indeed!

Also you know how you hate those ugly ridges in your nails . . . and those annoying little white spots. Cutex Crème Polish covers them up completely . . . hides every blemish!

Now—you might expect Cutex Crème Polish to cost more. But it *doesn't!* You actually get it for exactly the same price—just 35¢ a bottle. Crème or Clear. And the convenient metal-handled brush never lets any bristles come out of the brush or the brush come off the handle.

7 lovely shades

Cutex Crème Polish comes in seven delightful, authentically styled shades . . . Natural, Rose, Mauve, Coral, Cardinal, Vermilion and Ruby. At your favorite store. Better stock up on the right shade for every frock and every open-toed sandal in your closet.

Northam Warren, New York, Montreal, London, Paris

Cutex, 1934

▶ *McCall's, 1933*

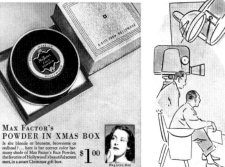

"Why wasn't I born a man?"

[The age-old cry of the sex destined to bear most of the world's troubles]

WHERE is the woman who has not, at some period in her life, used these very words? They sound like a complaint, but they are really a protest—a protest against those burdens of life which are wholly woman's.

Some of them still think—

Why do women use poisonous antiseptics in their desire for personal hygiene and surgical cleanliness? Of course they *do not need* to resort to poisons for this purpose, but many women still *think* they must!

If they would consult their own doctors they would find that cresol and carbolic acid have been displaced by a new, safe, non-poisonous antiseptic-germicide of great power, called *Zonite.*

Zonite is in a class by itself. No other non-poisonous antiseptic has one-quarter its germ-killing strength. Even when compared with the poisons, Zonite stands out supreme. It is far more powerful than any dilution of cresol or carbolic acid that can be safely allowed on the human body.

Women of the independent, enlightened type all over the world are today using Zonite for exclusively feminine purposes—undoubtedly more of them than are using any other germicide. They realize that Zonite is a genuine *personal antiseptic* for use on the body—not a disinfectant for tubs, buckets and staircases.

Zonite holds no poison-threat

Women all around you are using Zonite. Have *you* introduced it to your own special circle? Remember, Zonite is as safe as pure water. No injury to sensitive tissues with Zonite. No fear of accidental poisoning!

Zonite comes in two forms. The liquid is 30¢, 60¢ and $1.00. Zonite Suppositories are $1.00 a dozen. These dainty white cones provide a *continuing* antiseptic action. Many women use both.

"Facts for Women"—Sent by mail

This much-discussed booklet gives clear, concise information on the whole subject. Frank, authoritative, important. Send for it right away. Zonite Products Corporation, Chrysler Building, New York, N. Y.

ZONITE PRODUCTS CORPORATION   MC-35
Chrysler Building, New York, N. Y.
Please send me free copy of the booklet or booklets checked below.
☐ Facts for Women   ☐ Use of Antiseptics in the Home
NAME...
(Please print name)
ADDRESS..
CITY..STATE.........
(In Canada: Sainte Therese, P. Q.)

Zonite, 1933

▶ *Kotex, 1937*

Carefree Comfort FOR ANY WOMAN

Only Kotex has 3 types

for different women . . . different days

● **REGULAR KOTEX**—IN THE BLUE BOX. For the ordinary needs of most women—combines full protection with utmost comfort. Millions who are completely satisfied with Regular Kotex will have no reason to change.

● **JUNIOR KOTEX**—IN THE GREEN BOX. Somewhat narrower. Designed at the request of women of slight stature, and younger girls. Thousands will prefer Junior Kotex on days when less protection is needed.

● **SUPER KOTEX**—IN THE BROWN BOX. For those days when you desire a napkin with greater absorbency. Extra layers of Super Kotex give extra protection, yet it is no longer or wider than Regular.

QUEST. The *positive* deodorant powder, utterly effective, even on sanitary napkins. Use it with Kotex.

KURB TABLETS. To lessen the perception of pain and discomfort on certain days.

KOTEX BELTS. To make Kotex comfort complete. Patented clasps are safe, secure.

All 3 types at the same low price!

Guerlain, 1938

Guerlain, 1937

Guerlain, 1938

Guerlain, 1938

Guerlain, 1937

Gibbs French Wigs, 1935

Listerine, 1931

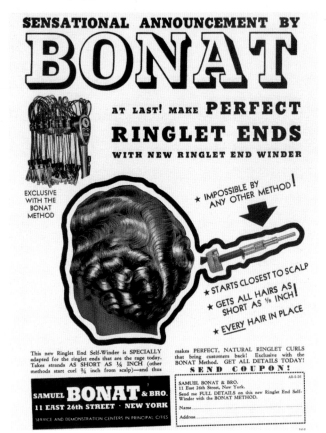

Bonat, 1936

Lucky Tiger, 1936   ▶ Gillette, 1939

You Get Shaves That Look And Feel Like A "Million" With This New *Gillette Blade* At ½ Price!

THIN Gillette BLADES
4 for 10
8 for 19c

Improved Kind Of Edges Protect Your Face From Smart And Irritation!

QUICK, easy, refreshing shaves that make your face *feel good* and look its very best! That's the kind of shaves you get with the Thin Gillette Blade every time! And what's more ... you save money, too! No wonder men everywhere are enthusiastic about the Thin Gillette. This top-quality blade is precision made to fit your Gillette Razor exactly ... and costs only 10c for 4. The steel is easy-flexing and hard enough to cut glass. Honed by an entirely new process, the edges are super-keen and absolutely uniform. Most men say this new blade out-performs and outlasts ordinary blades two to one. That's only the half of it. The Thin Gillette also protects your skin from the smart and burn caused by misfit blades. Remember—Gillette alone has the experience and facilities to make as fine a low-priced blade as this. Buy a package of Thin Gillettes from your dealer and get real shaving comfort for every penny.

You'll Enjoy Gillette's Exhibit In The Medicine Chest, Hall Of Pharmacy, World's Fair

Reputable Dealers Give You What You Ask For. Don't Gamble With Substitutes ... Insist On Gillette Blades!

aturally ... You Men Who Want Utmost Shaving uxury Demand The *Gillette Blue Blade*

Gillette BLUE BLADES King C. Gillette

OUTSELLS ANY OTHER RAZOR BLADE

5 for 25¢

TODAY'S Gillette Blue Blade is in every respect the finest razor blade ever produced. As such, it holds the world-wide preference of men who demand all that money can buy in shaving comfort. It is a luxury, to be sure, but one that every man can afford, for it actually *costs less than one cent a day!* With this in mind ... don't let anybody talk you out of utmost shaving satisfaction. Rely on your own judgment. Buy a package of Gillette Blue Blades from your dealer. They're guaranteed on a money-back basis.

Better Drying at less cost

Paidar Multiple Gas Dryer

Paidar Multiple unit gas dryer fits any room-capacity up to 12 hoods. Will dry 12 heads at the cost of one dried with ordinary dryers.

Paidar No. 2 Standard Gas Dryer

For those who wish the lowest cost of operation up to a capacity of 6 hoods. This Paidar gas dryer is very efficient, takes little space and is a small investment.

Paidar Improved Electric Dryer

is an outstanding example of low operating cost, and original investment. Every shop should have at least one for manicure table or waiting room.

Paidar Number Three

This is probably the most aristocratic of hair dryers. It has many features that make "has beens" of the general run of hair dryers yet the cost is comparatively low.

Full details on request

The Emil J. Paidar Company realizing that a dryer that is economical for one Beauty Shop can easily be extravagant in operation for another —has produced four models of dryers—two electric and two using gas.

If you will describe the anticipated drying requirements of your Beauty Shop giving gas and electric rates Paidar engineers will recommend the most economical method of serving your patrons.

Paidar Budget Plan Makes Payment Easy

EMIL J. *Paidar* COMPANY

Manufacturers of

1115 N. Wells St.   CHICAGO

Beauty Parlor Chairs	Barber Chairs	Lavatories, Etc.
Booths, Dressers	Mirror Cases	Barber Poles, Etc.
Hair Dryers	Display Cases	Manicure Tables, Etc.

32-34 West Twentieth St.
NEW YORK CITY

BETTER DRYERS AT NO ADDITIONAL COST

Emil J. Paidar Co., 1935

THEY CAN'T DUPLICATE IT!

Branded as impractical and impossible only four short years ago, CLAIROL today has revolutionized the entire hair dye industry and has definitely and positively created a new vogue —a new era—in hair beautification through color... cleansing, reconditioning and tinting in one quick treatment.

There is only one CLAIROL

CLAIROL

SHAMPOO OIL-TINT
Mury
BEAUTIFIES YOUR HAIR

LIGHT DRAB BROWN No 16 ★★★ TRIPLE STRENGTH
'INSTANT' CLAIROL

SHAMPOO OIL-TINT
Mury
BEAUTIFIES YOUR HAIR

FOLLOW THE LEAD OF THE COUNTRY'S LEADING BEAUTICIANS
See Page 81 This Issue

SHAMPOOS RECONDITIONS and TINTS

READ "EXPERT TEST-IMONY" OF LEADING HAIRDRESSERS ON PAGE 81 THIS ISSUE

Clairol, 1936

LOU GEHRIG says— *"Williams Softens My Tough Whiskers"*

LOU GEHRIG finds Williams *"Twin-Action"* Shaving Cream leaves his tough whiskers limp, wilted... easy to shave off

MEN like Gehrig, Bill Tilden, Barney Ross, Lawson Little—and thousands of ordinary mortals with tough, stubborn whiskers—are using Williams.

What's the reason? Because Williams Shaving Cream is "twin-action." It enables you to shave off the 40,000 hard, spiny hairs on your face without yanking or scraping your skin.

Here's how Williams quick-wetting cream attacks your beard:

FIRST, Williams rich, wet lather cuts through the oily film on each whisker—

drenches the "starchy" stiffness from the heart of each hair.

SECOND, it soaks and softens the tough outer skin on your face—allows your blade edge to reach down and clip off whiskers right at the base.

No longer will shaving menace your chin and your disposition. Gentle pressure of your razor, as it skims lightly over your face, takes off whiskers cleanly, smoothly—without scraping or irritation. Get a tube of Williams today.

FAMOUS ATHLETES WHO USE WILLIAMS SHAVING CREAM

LAWSON LITTLE · JOE MEDWICK · LOU MEYER · "BIG BILL" TILDEN · "PEPPER" MARTIN · GLENN HARDIN · BENNY FRIEDMAN · PAUL RUNYAN · NORMAN HILL · "STRANGLER" LEWIS · MURRAY MURDOCK · FRANK CROSETTI · JOHNNY FARRELL · "CHUCK" CONACHER · AB JENKINS · BILL SHAKESPEARE · FRED PERRY · LES PATRICK

Williams Luxury Shaving Cream
LARGE SIZE

After Shaving
This famous lotion closes skin pores... fights off acne spots ... leaves face smooth, refreshed.
Aqua Velva

Williams Shaving Cream, 1937

FOR THICK, HEALTHY HAIR

Gro-Flex Circulatory Massage

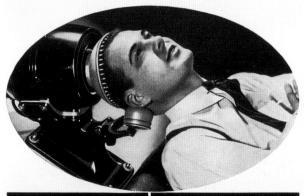

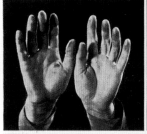 

NOT TEN FINGERS... BUT 400!

The 400 fingers of the Gro-Flex massage method for improving scalp conditions are equal to *forty pairs* of patient, willing hands.

Unlike human hands, however, Gro-Flex fingers do not slip... they do not get tired... they cover the entire head evenly, thoroughly.

Driven by an electric motor, the Gro-Flex fingers give a gentle, deep-down massage.

There are no oils, tonics or heat used. There's no harsh rubbing —just a soothing sensation. Scalp pores are cleansed, starved hair roots are nourished. Hair health comes from within the scalp.

Gro-Flex treatments are brief and relaxing. We invite you to visit one of our conveniently located shops for a demonstration.

Gro-Flex machines are available for home use. Ask about our attractive rental plan.

GRO-FLEX
HAIR CONDITIONING SHOPS

NEW YORK

1501 Broadway	*Paramount Bldg., Times Sq.*	**LAckawanna 4-3332**
17 East 42nd Street	*at Madison Avenue*	**MUrray Hill 2-2340**
30 Rockefeller Plaza	*No. 12, Concourse, R C A Bldg.*	**CIrcle 7-3996**
44 Wall Street	*10th Floor*	**BOwling Green 9-1272**

CHICAGO

118 West Randolph Street	*Hotel Sherman*	**Randolph 6426**

Gro-Flex, 1935

Lorraine, 1935 ◄ Lorraine, 1932

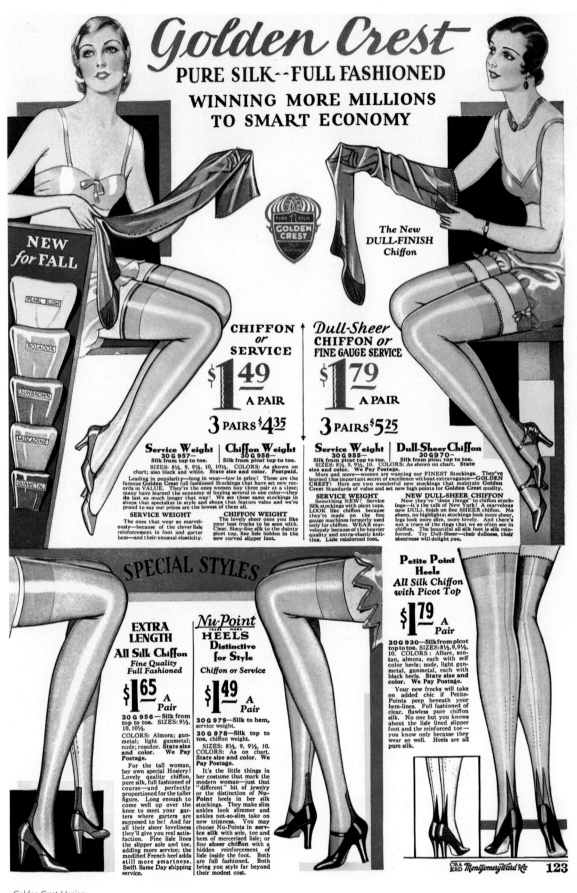

Golden Crest Hosiery

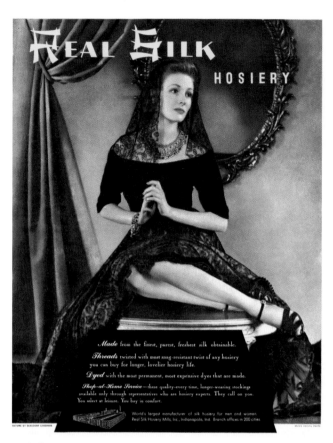

Real Silk Hosiery, 1939

Real Silk Hosiery, 1939

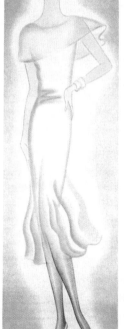

Exquisite colors . . wondrously lovely details of texture and finish . . Realsilk Hosiery pleases more women than any other hosiery sold! Perhaps because women have had a voice in its perfecting, during these ten years that Realsilk Hosiery has been sold to them by Realsilk Representatives in their own homes. Their comments . . suggestions . . have helped to make Realsilk the favorite

hosiery of chic women everywhere. Why not see these smart stockings, sponsored by a Fashion Committee of five famous women, in your own home, with your shoes and frocks? Realsilk Hosiery is sold only by Realsilk Representatives who call at your home. Branch offices in 250 cities in the United States and Canada. The Real Silk Hosiery Mills, Inc., Indianapolis, Indiana, U. S. A.

Lady Egerton
Neysa McMein
Lynn Fontanne
Elinor Patterson
Katherine Harford
the Realsilk Fashion Committee . .

Ask the Realsilk Representative to show you Realsilk's newest, sheerest stocking—style 100—invisibly reenforced for wear with low cut sandals. If he is not calling at your home regularly, 'phone your local Realsilk office.

the new **REALSILK** hosiery

Real Silk Hosiery, 1930

Our *Shop-at-Home Service* makes it easier for women to buy—Realsilk Representatives call on you—no shopping hurry —no parking worry . . . Our *Way* of manufacturing stockings makes them more economical for women to buy—pure, fresh silk — more snag-resistant twist—best and most permanent dyes . . . *These qualities* every time mean longer average wear.

World's largest manufacturer of silk hosiery for men and women.
Real Silk Hosiery Mills, Inc. Indianapolis, Ind. Branch Sales Offices in 200 Cities

Real Silk Hosiery, 1939

Corsets, 1930

Hats, 1930

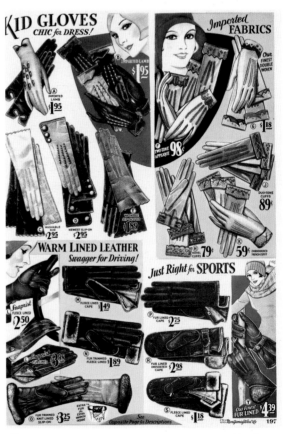

Gloves, 1930

▶ Lingerie, 1930

The PRINCESS INFLUENCE

B DANCE SET **$2.98**

C SILHOUETTE FITTED SLIP **$3.98**

E PURE DYE ALL SILK FLAT CREPE **$3.95**
HEAVY SILK CREPE DE CHINE REGULAR SIZES **$2.95** EXTRA SIZES **$3.98**

D COMBINATION **$1.98**

F DANCE SET **$1.98** STEP-IN **$1.69**

G LACE TRIM **$1.98** PLAIN TAILORE **$1.98**

ve Silk

Rayon Crepe Manj

Creations in All Silk Crepe de Chine

L GOWN **$2.98**

M GOWN REGULAR SIZES **$3.98** EXTRA SIZES **$4.98**

K CHEMISE **$2.98**

J SILK and RAYON TWILLED SATIN REGULAR SIZES **$1.98** EXTRA SIZES **$2.49** ALL RAYON TWILL REGULAR SIZES **$1.49**

N PANTIE **$1.00** VEST **89¢** BLOOMER **$1.00**

k and Rayon Satins

FINE QUALITY KNITTED RAYONS

U BRASSIERE TOP COMBINATION **$1.00**

P HAND MADE GOWN **$1.98**

CHARDONIZI

S VESTETTE **69¢** FANCY SHORTIE BLOOMER **$1.00** PLAIN SHORTIE BLOOMER **79¢**

T PAJAMA **$1.98**

O FAST COLOR PAJAMA **$2.98**

R 3 PIECE ENSEMBLE **$3.98** 2 PIECE PAJAMA **$1.98**

Z FAST COLOR 3-PIECE ENSEMBLE **$1.98**

W DANCE SET **$1.00** STEP IN

MUNSING *Wear* *presents* Foundettes

Munsingwear makes all styles of smart undergarments in all types of fabrics. For men, women and children.

UNDERWEAR · WATERWEAR · HOSIERY
SLEEPING AND LOUNGING GARMENTS · KNIT COATS
PULL-ONS · FOUNDATION GARMENTS

Brand New Foundation Garments of a Brand New Fabric, Invented by MUNSINGWEAR

You've never seen step-in girdles and foundation garments quite like these . . . for nothing like them has ever been created! Foundettes slim the hips, trim the waist, flatten the diaphragm and smooth the silhouette into smart and lovely lines. Yet, you've never worn anything quite so comfortable! Fashioned of specially processed two-way-stretch fabric . . . invented by Munsingwear . . . Foundettes will wash marvelously and wear wonderfully. They won't pull away from the seams or ravel back or curl. You'll like Munsingwear Foundettes for slimmer figures. And they're priced for slimmer purses. See these new Foundettes at a Munsingwear dealer near you. Munsingwear, Minneapolis.

LET MUNSINGWEAR COVER YOU WITH SATISFACTION

You *can* lose that bulge if *you send us the coupon below*

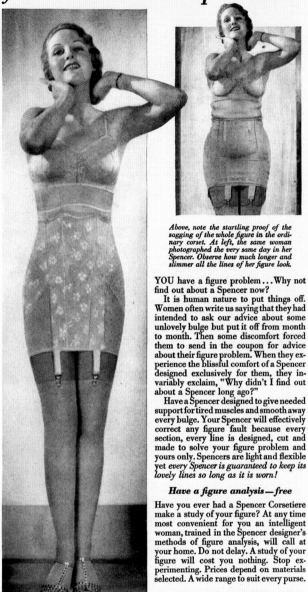

Above, note the startling proof of the sagging of the whole figure in the ordinary corset. At left, the same woman photographed the very same day in her Spencer. Observe how much longer and slimmer all the lines of her figure look.

YOU have a figure problem...Why not find out about a Spencer now?

It is human nature to put things off. Women often write us saying that they had intended to ask our advice about some unlovely bulge but put it off from month to month. Then some discomfort forced them to send in the coupon for advice about their figure problem. When they experience the blissful comfort of a Spencer designed exclusively for them, they invariably exclaim, "Why didn't I find out about a Spencer long ago?"

Have a Spencer designed to give needed support for tired muscles and smooth away every bulge. Your Spencer will effectively correct any figure fault because every section, every line is designed, cut and made to solve your figure problem and yours only. Spencers are light and flexible yet *every Spencer is guaranteed to keep its lovely lines so long as it is worn!*

Have a figure analysis—free

Have you ever had a Spencer Corsetiere make a study of your figure? At any time most convenient for you an intelligent woman, trained in the Spencer designer's methods of figure analysis, will call at your home. Do not delay. A study of your figure will cost you nothing. Stop experimenting. Prices depend on materials selected. A wide range to suit every purse.

Send for interesting free booklet "Your Figure Problem"

Look in your telephone book under "Spencer Corsetiere" and call your nearest corsetiere or send us the coupon below for booklet. This will not obligate you in any way.

••••••••••••••••••••••••••

Do You Want to Make Money?
Ambitious women may find business openings as corsetieres in every state. We train you. If interested, check here . . . . □

Also made in Canada and England at Rock Island, Quebec, and 4 & 5 Old Bond St., London, W. I.

••••••••••••••••••••••••••
Copyright, 1937, Spencer Corset Co., Inc.

Write Anne Spencer
for personal advice FREE on figure faults checked here.

November, 1937

Bulging hips
Bulging abdomen
Lordosis backline

Anne Spencer,
Spencer Corset Co., Inc.,
135 Derby Avenue,
New Haven, Connecticut.

Name_____
Address_____

SPENCER *INDIVIDUALLY DESIGNED* CORSETS

"I had a problem with ugly bulges
until I sent the Spencer coupon below"

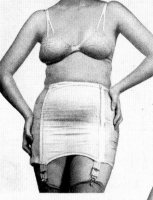

Above: Note the bulging of the hips and abdomen in the ordinary corset. At right the same woman in her Spencer. Hips are slenderized and the abdominal bulge is gone.

Are your hips a problem? Are you troubled with a bulging abdomen or a "spare-tire" of flesh around the waist line? Then follow the example of the young woman in the photograph and find out what a Spencer can do for you.

Your Spencer corset and brassiere will effectively correct any figure fault because every section, every line is designed, cut and made to solve your figure problem and yours only. Spencers are light and flexible yet *every Spencer is guaranteed to keep its lovely lines as long as it is worn!*

Have a figure analysis—free

At any convenient time, a Spencer Corsetiere, trained in the Spencer designer's methods of figure analysis, will call at your home. A study of your figure will cost you nothing. Stop experimenting. Prices depend on materials selected. A wide range to suit every purse.

Send for interesting free booklet "Your Figure Problem"

Look in your telephone book under "Spencer Corsetiere" and call your nearest corsetiere or send us the coupon below for booklet. This will not obligate you in any way.

"I've lost inches in my Spencer"

••••••••••••••••••••••••••
Copyright, 1939, Spencer Corset Co., Inc.

Write Anne Spencer
for personal advice FREE on figure faults checked here.

May 8, 1939

Bulging hips
Bulging abdomen
Lordosis backline

Anne Spencer,
Spencer Corset Co., Inc.,
133 Derby Avenue,
New Haven, Connecticut.

Name_____
Address_____

••••••••••••••••••••••••••

Do You Want to Make Money?
Ambitious women may find business openings as corsetieres in every state. We train you. If interested, check here . . . . □

Also made in Canada and England at Rock Island, Quebec, and 4 & 5 Old Bond St., London, W. I.

SPENCER *INDIVIDUALLY DESIGNED* CORSETS

Munsing Wear, 1933 ◄ *Spencer Corsets, 1937*

Spencer Corset, 1939

Trained Nurse Loses Fat
45 Pounds in 8 Weeks

Reduces Hips 10 Inches
With
New Battle Creek
Reducing Treatment

Miss Lola A. Sharp

Eat Big Meals. Fat Goes Quick—*Or No Cost*

"I had tried all kinds of reducing remedies without results. But I found BonKora different. It has taken off 45 pounds in 8 weeks. My hips reduced 10 inches. I wear dresses 4 sizes smaller. BonKora gave me new health, too. I am a trained nurse and I always recommend BonKora to my patients if they are stout."—Miss Lola A. Sharp, Trained Nurse, Bristol, Ind.

Trust a trained nurse to recognize the best way to lose her own fat. And thousands of men and women everywhere write that BonKora, the new Battle Creek Reducing Treatment, took off their fat even when other remedies had failed. It gave them new health and strength, too.

Loses 70 lbs in 14 Weeks

Mrs. F. W. Moran, 2349 Lake St., Kalamazoo, Mich., writes, "I lost 70 lbs. in 14 weeks taking BonKora. Reduced from 210 lbs to 140 lbs. It improved my health, too."

Mrs. Carrie Gray, 2954 Guilford Ave., Indianapolis, Ind., writes: "BonKora was recommended to me by a doctor as a safe remedy. I lost 27 lbs. in 7 weeks. Now weigh only 125."

How Many Pounds Would *You* Like to Lose?

15 pounds? 25 pounds? 70 pounds? More? Take BonKora, the new, safe Battle Creek Reducing Treatment.

BonKora takes off fat new "3-stage" way. Triple action; triple speed. Reduce fat all over if you wish. Or if you are just fat in certain parts—chin, shoulders, waist, hips or bust—this fat goes first. You can stop then, if you don't want to reduce elsewhere.

Don't starve. Take BonKora daily and you can EAT BIG MEALS of tasty foods you like as explained in BonKora package.

No dangerous drugs in BonKora. In fact this treatment *builds health* while reducing fat the *quickest way*. This new health, combined with new slender figures, makes users look YEARS YOUNGER, too.

Don't be fat any longer. Get BonKora, the new Battle Creek Reducing Treatment, from your druggist today. *Read special offer below.*

"YOU SURE ARE HEAVY MARY. WHY DON'T YOU TAKE BONKORA AND LOSE WEIGHT AS JANE DID"

TEST OFFER. Fat Goes Quick—*Or Pay Nothing*

No excuse for being fat any longer. Get slender; gain health; end tired feeling; look younger. The manufacturers of BonKora KNOW what it will do for you so they make this GUARANTEE: Get a bottle of BonKora from your druggist today. If not delighted with quick loss of fat, new health and younger looks, manufacturers refund money you paid for this bottle. *You don't risk a penny.* So start now to take BonKora, the new safe, pleasant Battle Creek Reducing Treatment.

BonKora—America's Biggest Selling Reducing Preparation

DISTRIBUTED BY BATTLE CREEK DRUGS, Inc. AT ALL DRUGGISTS
No Connection With Any Other BATTLE CREEK Organization

Your Druggist has BonKora or can get it quick from his wholesaler.' If not, write Battle Creek Drugs, Inc., Dept. 10, Battle Creek, Mich.

Battle Creek Drugs, 1933

Promise....

and fulfillment await the woman just discovering the telling power of figure beauty. For her, the modern way of youthful figure discipline...Foundettes.

Foundettes
BY MUNSINGWEAR

Minneapolis   New York   Chicago

Foundettes, 1939

Patterns

Preview these play-clothes, made up with Simplicity Patterns, in the better stores that sell the patterns . . . you'll find these stores clear across the country. And remember, in any event—"you're always in style when you dress with Simplicity."

Simplicity Patterns, 1935

DON'T BE A *Scarecrow* ON THE BEACH THIS SUMMER!

SKINNY!
CORRECT THIS SIMPLE MISTAKE AND PUT ON ALLURING CURVES!

Try This New Way of Correcting Iodine Starved Glands if You Want to Add

5 EXTRA LBS. THIS WEEK!

Skinny Men and Women Everywhere Amazed at Results

That's science's newest answer to skinny, rundown folks . . . scrawny men and women who can't seem to add an ounce no matter what they eat nor how good their appetite is. Already thousands of these so-called "naturally skinny" folks have been amazed and delighted with the ease with which they have added 3 to 8 lbs. in a single week. 15 to 20 lbs. of good solid flesh in 1 short month is not at all uncommon. And, best of all—more important than their new good looks and alluring curves—they feel like a million dollars! Here's the reason:

After years of scientific experimenting, experts have found that one of the greatest causes of skinniness is IODINE STARVED GLANDS. When these are corrected, weight seems to go on like magic. Kelpamalt, the new mineral-iodine concentrate from the sea—and perhaps the world's richest source of NATURAL PLANT IODINE, quickly gets right down to this common cause of skinniness and corrects it. It works "2 ways in 1."

First, its rich supply of easily assimilable minerals stimulates the digestive glands which produce the juices that alone enable you to digest fats and starches, the weight-making elements in your daily diet. And these minerals are needed by virtually every organ and for every function of the body. Second, Kelpamalt is rich in NATURAL IODINE—a mineral needed by the vital organ which regulates metabolism—the process through which the body is constantly building firm, solid flesh, new strength and energy. 6 Kelpamalt tablets contain more NATURAL IODINE than 486 lbs. of spinach or 1660 lbs. of beef. More iron and copper than 2 lbs. of spinach or 15 lbs. of fresh tomatoes. More calcium than 1 doz. eggs. More phosphorus than 3 lbs. of carrots.

Try Kelpamalt for a single week and notice the difference—how much better you feel. If you don't gain at least 5 lbs. of good, firm flesh in 1 week the trial is free. Kelpamalt costs but little at all good drug stores. If your dealer has not yet received his supply, send $1.00 for special introductory size bottle of 65 tablets to the address below.

Comparison of Minerals in KELPAMALT vs. VEGETABLES — 3 Kelpamalt tablets Contain:

1. More Iron and Copper than 1 lb. of spinach, 7½ lbs. fresh tomatoes, 3 lbs. of asparagus.
2. More Calcium than 1 lb. of cabbage.
3. More Phosphorus than 1½ lbs. of carrots.
4. More Sulphur than 2 lbs. of tomatoes.
5. More Sodium than 3 lbs. of turnips.
6. More Potassium than 6 lbs. of beans.
7. More Magnesium than 1 lb. of celery.

SEEDOL
Kelpamalt
Tablets

KNOWN IN ENGLAND AS VIKELP

Manufacturer's Note:—Inferior products—sold as kelp and malt preparations—in imitation of the genuine Kelpamalt are being offered as substitutes. Don't be fooled. Demand genuine Kelpamalt Tablets. They are easily assimilated, do not upset stomach nor injure teeth. Results guaranteed or money back.

SPECIAL FREE OFFER

Write today for fascinating instructive 50-page book on How to Add Weight Quickly. Mineral Contents of Food and their effects on the human body. New facts about NATURAL IODINE. Standard weight and measurement charts. Daily menus for weight building. Absolutely free. No obligation. Kelpamalt Co., Dept. 504, 27-33 West 20th St., New York City.

Naughty Nautical
JANE WITHERS
has a wardrobe of three
CATALINAS!
all made figure-flattering with
CONTROLASTIC*

LEAVE it to Jane to do things enthusiastically . . . whether it's playing a lively, lovable role in her new 20th Century Fox film, "Boy Friend" . . . or finding the slickest swim suits ashore or afloat.

Smart juniors . . . here's your cue . . . it's Catalina, made with Firestone CONTROLastic, the new elastic yarn that whittles the sprouting teen-age figure to bathing beauty proportions.

CONTROLastic's unique construction (3 to 5 wrapped layers of pure rubber in each tiny strand) makes it extra resistant to sun, air and water . . . keeps your Catalina lively and figure-flattering all season long.

Jane Withers wears, reading from top: Zephyr Wool and Celanese rayon with CONTROLastic. Puckerette of Celanese rayon with CONTROLastic. Hand-blocked Sunflower Print on rayon with CONTROLastic. All in misses' sizes in beautiful beach colors . . . . . Each $4

Write for free autographed picture of Jane Withers in full color, to Pacific Knitting Mills, Los Angeles. See Catalina Swim Suits at better stores.

*Reg. U. S. Pat. Off.

STYLED FOR THE STARS OF HOLLYWOOD AND YOU!

Catalina
SWIM SUITS
WITH *Controlastic*

This label pledges Multi-ply elasticity and figure control

PACIFIC KNITTING MILLS, LOS ANGELES, CAL.

Kelpamalt, 1935

Catalina Swim Suits, 1939

445

Playtime Toys with New Dash!

A "KAMPUS" KOAT $1.00

AA TANGO "SLAX" $1.00

B JACKET "SLAX," SCARF, All for $1.98

C FARMERETTE and HAT $1.00

D KNIT SHIRT 49c

DD GABARDINE "SLAX" 88c

E KNIT SHIRT 88c

F "SLAX" $1.29

G FARMERETTE and JACKET $1.98

H "ZIPPED" PLAY-SUIT WITH SKIRT $1.98 CHOICE — Plain or Print

J 3 PIECE $1.98

"House or Beach Coat, Play or Swim Suit, and Head 'Kerchief!'"

"Swishy" Rayon Taffeta

CONTRASTING PLEATS

B
NEW PLEATED BOTTOMS
99c

SELF COLOR PLEATS

EACH SLIP IN 2 LENGTHS

"Kno-back", Fitted, Brassiere-top Sl

C

RAYON TAFFETA	PURE-DYE PRE-SHRUNK RAYON CREPE
79c	**99c**

D

WEIGHTED SILK CREPE	PURE-DYE ALL SILK SATIN
$1 69	**$1 95**

E
RAYON TAFFETA!
IN 2 LENGTHS
NO PANEL
85c
WITH PANEL
95c

Set

F

G
WRAP-A-ROUND HOUSE COAT
99c
2-PIECE PAJAMAS
99c
HOUSE COAT AND PAJAMAS BOTH FOR
$1 89 SET

FAST COLOR

H
TOGS
with Dash and Zip
3-PIECE BOLERO PAJAMAS
$1 29
ZIPPER-FASTENED HOUSE COAT
$1 69
HOUSE COAT AND PAJAMAS BOTH FOR
$2 79

FAST COLOR

J
ZIPPER-FASTENED PANTIES

Style and Beauty

Fabrics

Metal Picture Buttons

McCall's, 1933 ◄ *Fabrics*

Fabrics

C.M.O. for Gay Variety in Smart New
TOPPERS

- SMART STYLES
- SMART LENGTHS
- SMART SHADES

C
ALL-WOOL
SMARTOWNE
SUEDE
$5.98

B
Voguish
SHAG-FLEECE
$4.98

A
Popular
CHARMOOR-
FLEECE
$3.98
RAY-BEST LINED

E
Fine, Soft
ALL-WOOL
SHAG-FLEECE
$7.98
RAY-BEST LINED

F
Popular
CHARMOOR-
FLEECE
$4.98
RAY-BEST LINED

FOR DESCRIPTIONS
PLEASE SEE
OPPOSITE PAGE

G
ALL-WOOL
SHAG-FLEECE
$5.98
RAY-BEST LINED

Toppers

▶ *Hockanum Woolens, 1938*

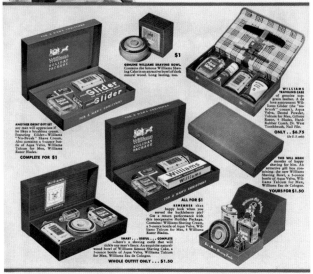

Williams, 1937

Montgomery Ward, 1937

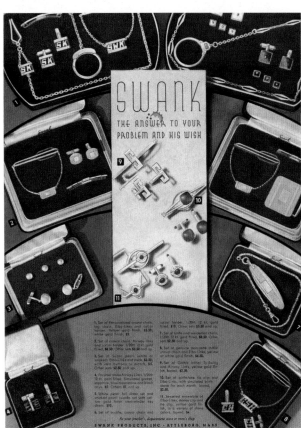

Swank, 1938

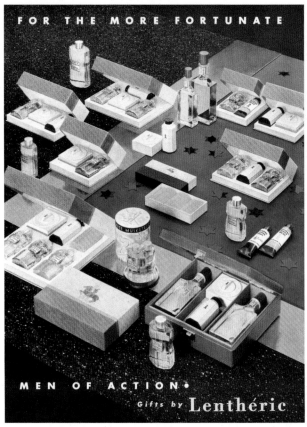

Lenthéric, 1938

▶ *Talon, 1931*

"Mist' Curley–yo' ain't got NUFF'N in dat bag!"

Well, I fooled George—for once. He told me he had been portering so long he could tell by hefting a bag just what was in it. Nor were his powers merely muscular. "Ex-ray eyes" he said he had.

So I asked him—"What's in my bag, George?" (It looked as husky as the steer it was made of, yet it was unbelievably light.)

And the old veteran hefted it, smiled—as though he thought I was trying to fool him. And finally—"Mist' Curley," he said, "Yo' ain't got *nuff'n* in dat bag!"

"Right, George," I said—I wouldn't spoil the old fellow's fun. But he was wrong. That bag contained plenty of a traveler's necessaries—yet with all its freight it was as light as the average bag is when stark empty! A Talon Slide Fastener accounted for that.

All other things equal, a Talon-fastened bag will be amazingly lighter than one that isn't. In other words, about *half* as heavy—and a dozen times more convenient! Bags equipped with Talons have neither clasps nor catches. They can be opened instantly—and as quickly closed. They're mighty smart-looking, too, if you're particular about that—and most of us are.

Whether for Summer vacation ventures or for a steady diet of travel, you'll want the advantages of Talons on the bag you buy. They'll stand all sorts of abuse—indefinitely. They won't stick, jam, or rust—if they're *genuine* Talons. And that's easy to tell. The genuine has TALON right on the pull-tab.

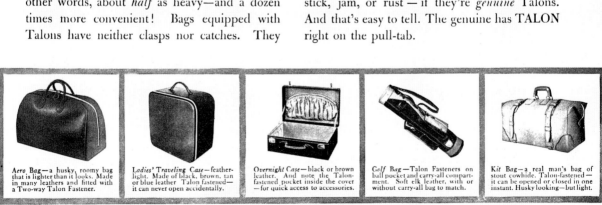

Aero Bag—a husky, roomy bag that is lighter than it looks. Made in many leathers and fitted with a Two-way Talon Fastener.

Ladies' Traveling Case—featherlight. Made of black, brown, tan or blue leather Talon fastened—it can never open accidentally.

Overnight Case—black or brown leather. And note the Talon-fastened pocket inside the cover—for quick access to accessories.

Golf Bag—Talon Fasteners on ball pocket and carry-all compartment. Soft elk leather, with or without carry-all bag to match.

Kit Bag—a real man's bag of stout cowhide. Talon-fastened—it can be opened or closed in one instant. Husky looking—but light.

TALON

Reg. U.S. Pat. Off.

THE SLIDE FASTENER
THAT ALWAYS WORKS

HOOKLESS FASTENER COMPANY, MEADVILLE, PENNSYLVANIA

NEW YORK · BOSTON · PHILADELPHIA · CHICAGO · LOS ANGELES · SAN FRANCISCO · SEATTLE

THEY FEEL RIGHT—A WELL-BALANCED RACQUET
AND THIS WELL-CUT *Skit-Suit*

HERE'S cool comfort and body ease you've never had before. SKIT-Suits by Munsingwear that look like shirts and shorts—so brief you don't know you're wearing them—so expertly cut and tailored they can't bag or bunch. And note the three special comfort features ... no-gap buttonless fly ... elastic leg-openings and waist band ... full seat coverage with elastic drop seat. Treat yourself to perfect comfort with SKIT-Suits. Also "by Munsingwear" is a complete line for men ... SKIT-Shorts, fancy shorts, knit underwear of every type as well as smart sox. Treat yourself to comfort and quality by asking for "Munsingwear." At quality stores. MUNSINGWEAR, Minneapolis.

Munsing Wear, 1937

B.V.D., 1937

Men's Underwear, 1931

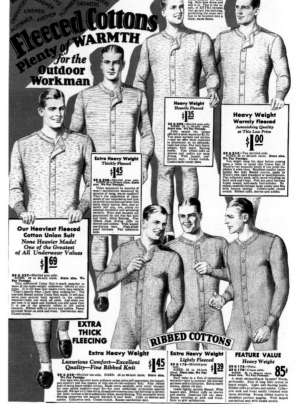

Men's Underwear, 1931

Allen-A Co., 1939

B.V.D., 1931

John David, 1937

Munsing Wear, 1933

▶ *Arrow Shirts, 1938*

Invitation to a Star Party

Dear Mr. Want-to-Shine:

This week every Arrow dealer in the whole land takes the wraps off the Shirt Stars for 1938 —and stages a big Style Party.

Besides a pre-view of the Shirts that will set the styles for the next six months, the show includes the season's blue-ribbon exhibit of Arrow Ties, Handkerchiefs, and Underwear.

We call this occasion *National Arrow Week*, and if you want to be first to wear what's new, it'll be worth your while to drop around.

Sincerely yours,

ARROW

NATIONAL ARROW WEEK • MAY 23 TO MAY 28

Let's make it an Easy Christmas

– with Realsilk's Shop-at-Home Service – *Gifts for Everyone*

Select at home

Phone local Realsilk office. Our representative comes to you. Serenely you sit and select.

Mailed for you

If you wish, we'll mail for you, direct to recipients.

In stunning packages

"MY DEAR—YOU CAN'T GO WRONG WITH ANYTHING HERE!"

choose your wrapping —Sparkling with cellophane, set off with ribbon, Christmas-y with stickers. Choice of wrappings for any size package.

"MY LOVE — JUST CHOOSE MY PRESENT FROM ABOVE"

☆ Why make Christmas *hard for yourself?* You have to give presents and you want to give right ones. Your question is, "How can I do my giving more appropriately—yet less nerve-wracklingly?" The answer is, "Ring up Realsilk! Have a Representative come right over with an entire Bag of Gifts." It's Christmas Shopping to the nth degree of ease. You sit, select, and order. At slight extra cost Realsilk handles all the other details—wrapping, enclosing cards, even mailing direct to receivers on any date you set. REAL SILK HOSIERY MILLS, Inc., Indianapolis, Indiana. Branches in 200 cities.

REAL SILK

Real Silk, 1938

The Newest Thing in Neckwear is a Famous Old Name!

It's in Zurich that Arrow, celebrated parent of billions of shirts and collars, gives its newest prodigy—the Arrow Tie—a glorious send-off.

Here, in this quaint Swiss town, live the world's slickest weavers. And here, in a fine old-world shop, these self-same weavers are working out special patterns and fabrics for Arrow ties.

They are really astonishing tie fabrics. Fabrics completely original in design. Fabrics which no other tie-maker can match at Arrow's price. Fabrics which make these new ties tops in value.

These sample fabrics created in Zurich are brought to America—duplicates woven on American looms. Then the ties are made up by Arrow's skilled workers, so that each tie will knot beautifully and resist wrinkling.

Result: Arrow ties are already becoming famous because Arrow is giving you exclusive, "expensive" ties for just $1 and $1.50.

ONE DOLLAR Above, you are some important new styles in summer ties. They are crêpes and foulards in original patterns developed by Arrow, brilliant values at one dollar. Your Arrow dealer will have these, or other equally engaging Arrow styles, on display, now. Cluett, Peabody & Co., Inc., Troy, New York.

If it hasn't an Arrow label it isn't an Arrow Tie

Arrow, 1937

WHAT COLOR SHOULD A TIE BE?

1 Any color. But Arrow—who makes the shirts and fine ties and has a paternal interest in both—implores you to bring them together harmoniously. For example, red or blue ties liven up well with blue shirts. Browns or greens ties with tan shirts. Burgundy or soft blue ties, with gray shirts.

2 You'll find plenty of color—correct, smart color—in Arrow patterned shirts and Arrow ties. But the idea is not to wear them all at once. Wear your boldest ties with your quietest shirts, more subdued ties with heavily patterned shirts.

3 Nearly any tie—plain, striped or patterned—can be worn with a white shirt. Solid colored ties, generally speaking, won't be happy with mild colored shirts. The plain tie should be worn only with patterned or white shirts.

4 The objective should be . . . contrast, done in good taste. Checked and figured ties with striped shirts, pin-stripes and solid colors with checked shirts, etc. This is particularly easy to achieve with Arrow Ties, because *Arrow Ties are designed to go with Arrow Shirts.*

No ordinary ties, these new Arrow ties.

They are ties whose patterns are selected from thousands of ideas gathered in France, England, Switzerland and America. Ties given the official blessings of the Arrow stylists, canniest of all style bigwigs. Ties with patented Arrow features. Ties featuring every worthwhile improvement known to neckwear men.

Ties whose rich fabrics, expert tailoring, patented features, all around *rightness* make them worth appreciably more than the $1 and $1.50 they cost. They're at your Arrow dealer's now.

$1.00 and **$1.50** Here are just a few of the new Arrow Ties. They cost only $1 and $1.50, and are worth more. See these and the many, many other handsome Arrow Ties at your own Arrow Dealer's. You'll be happily surprised with what Arrow has done for you. Cluett, Peabody & Co., Inc., Troy, New York.

ARROW CRAVATS

IF IT HASN'T AN ARROW LABEL IT ISN'T AN ARROW TIE

Arrow, 1937

HAND WOVEN
by the Spanish people
of New Mexico

New spring and summer patterns in these unique ties. Ideal birthday, anniversary, graduation gifts. Never sold in stores. Make selections here—order direct from weavers. Only $1 each—money back if not pleased.

Have you ever been in New Mexico? If so, you know that most of the people here are Spanish-speaking mountain folk whose ancestors settled this section in the 17th century.

Ever since, in their remote villages and placitas, many of these people have lived by raising sheep and weaving wool. It's a tradition with them. And this country, so colorful, seems to make these weavers natural artists.

Today I take the lovely fabrics produced by such Spanish weavers and have them made up into the beautiful neckties shown here.

Fascinating texture These fabrics are all wool—every thread of them—woven by hand on looms of a primitive type. That, and their soft native colors, is what gives these ties their unique character.

That is why a man who travels a lot, and who formerly bought most of his ties in London and Paris, recently said to me: "I can wear your ties with distinction anywhere. I never have one on that some well-dressed friend doesn't ask me where I got it."

And long life Then when men who have worn only silk ties learn by experience that my ties are cut and sewn so as always to tie right and "hang" right; when they find how wrinkles come right out of them after use; and that they can be cleaned again and again—then they say: "Why, you have the greatest tie value in the world!" Well, maybe I have. I do know that over a thousand *Sunset* readers have become enthusiastic customers.

Only $1 each — money back if not satisfied Yet I sell these fine tie for only $1 each, postpaid anywhere in U. S. Still better, if you order 5 or more ties now you may select one additional tie with my compliments—that is 6 for $5, or 7 for $6, and so on.

And you take no risk! The ties as shown here have been photographed directly by the modern color camera, and are as truly represented as it is humanly possible to show their colors. But if any tie I send you doesn't *fully* please you, or the person you give it to, send it back and exchange it—or *get your money back without quibble.* I must have satisfied customers.

How to order Order by the number opposite each tie. Please *print* your name and address. Enclose your check or money order (no stamps) for $1 for each tie—or $5 for 6. Money right back if you are not happy.

Note gift card at right Can you think of a nicer, more distinctive gift than some of these ties for a husband, son or friend—for a birthday, wedding anniversary or graduation? Tell me if you want them for this purpose and I will gladly enclose that attractive gift card.

WEBB YOUNG, *Trader*
116A Sena Plaza, Santa Fe, N. Mex.

Note the necklace at left It's made of corn kernels—corn that is grown naturally in blues, blacks, reds and yellows by the Pueblo Indians here. Best & Co., New York's leading fashion shop, has ordered hundreds of them for sale with sports wear. Why not be the first in your community to have this smart new piece of costume jewelry? Only $1, postpaid, boxed—and money back if you don't like it.

This tie has been hand-woven for you by the Spanish people of New Mexico at the request of

Webb Young, 1939

Arrow, 1932

Arrow, 1931

Arrow, 1931

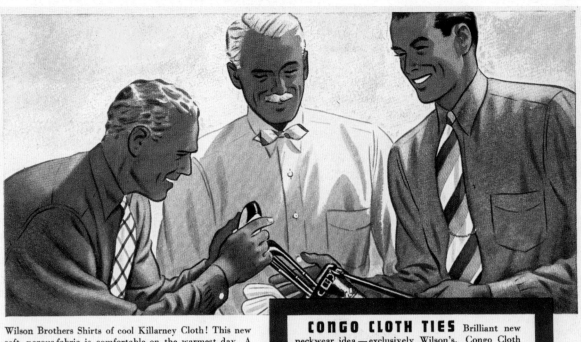

Wilson Brothers Shirts of cool Killarney Cloth! This new soft, porous fabric is comfortable on the warmest day. A novel random cord woven in gives it decidedly virile character. Two added aids to summer comfort are Wilson's new OBAN collar (light-weight, wiltproof) and V-shaped shirt body. In white, linen, dusty tones and pastel tints. $2.00.

CONGO CLOTH TIES Brilliant new neckwear idea — exclusively Wilson's. Congo Cloth Ties are tailored from the luxurious tropical suiting (DuPont spun rayon) specially adapted for neckwear. Drapes softly; resists wrinkling, spotting. Smart color combinations on light backgrounds. $1 (Bow ties, 75c).

STYLES THAT FLATTER YOUR
Summer Tan

SKIPPER SPORTWEAR

Left to right: Swim trunks with new built-in Support "U" (light inner lining of lastex that makes your waist trim as an athlete's) in pure wool, $3.95 . . . Jacket-style peasant-weave sport shirts with colorful overplaid and bright nubs of color, $3.95 to $5.00 . . . Skipper trunks in pure wool, $2.50 to $3.95 . . . Rayon polo shirts with jaunty Gaucho front, $1.00 to $3.50 . . . Polo shirts laced with knotted cord, $1.00 to $3.50. (*All in the season's smartest colors.*)

COPYRIGHT, 1937
WILSON BROTHERS

Now featured by leading men's stores and departments from coast to coast.

WILSON BROTHERS   CHICAGO NEW YORK SAN FRANCISCO

Also makers of Faultless Nobelt Pajamas, Faultless Nobelt Super Shorts, Buffer Hose

Wilson Brothers, 1937

▶ *Swank, 1936*

PERSONALIZED *Jewelry*

WITH A MAN'S OWN INITIALS.

Swank Jewelry accessories accent the correctness and individuality of a man's clothes—add zest to the fine art of dressing well.

Here is smart style . . . and quality, too! That's why Swank goes places with well-dressed men.

A wealth of new designs await you at jewelers, department stores, and men's shops.

● Set illustrated, Sterling Silver Buckle and
Tie Holder (either chain or bar type) $5
Other personalized jewelry $1 to $25

SWANK *JEWELRY ACCESSORIES FOR MEN*

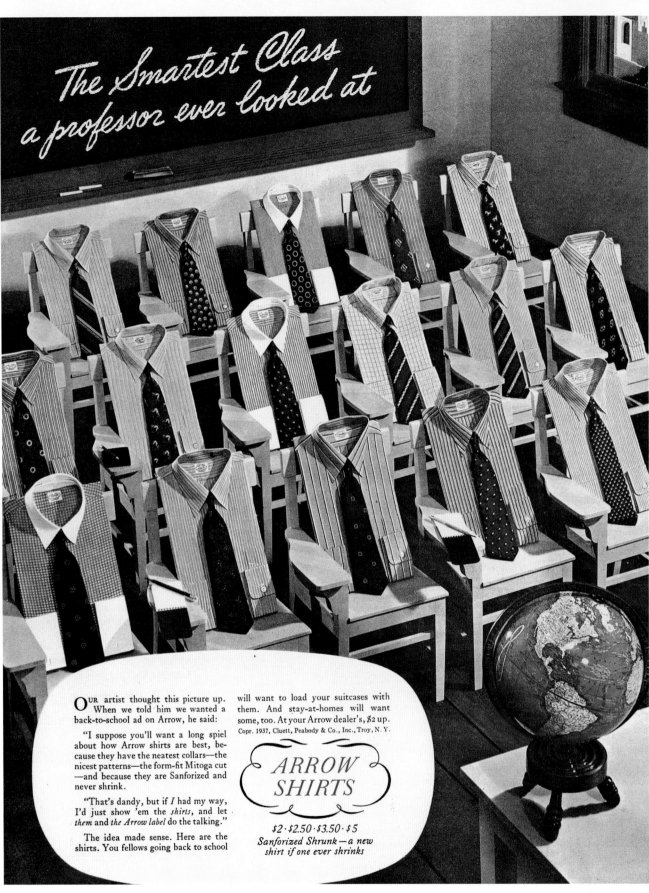

The Smartest Class
a professor ever looked at

OUR artist thought this picture up. When we told him we wanted a back-to-school ad on Arrow, he said:

"I suppose you'll want a long spiel about how Arrow shirts are best, because they have the neatest collars—the nicest patterns—the form-fit Mitoga cut—and because they are Sanforized and never shrink.

"That's dandy, but if *I* had my way, I'd just show 'em the *shirts*, and let *them* and *the Arrow label* do the talking."

The idea made sense. Here are the shirts. You fellows going back to school will want to load your suitcases with them. And stay-at-homes will want some, too. At your Arrow dealer's, $2 up.
Copr. 1937, Cluett, Peabody & Co., Inc., Troy, N.Y.

ARROW SHIRTS

$2 · $2.50 · $3.50 · $5
Sanforized Shrunk — a new shirt if one ever shrinks

Arrow, 1937

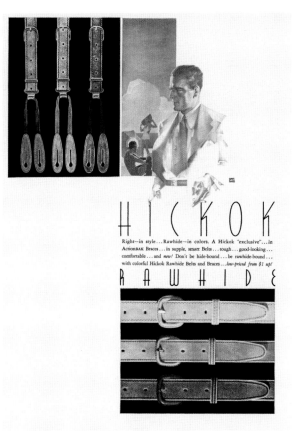

HICKOK

RAWHIDE

Right—in style...Rawhide—in colors. A Hickok "exclusive"...in ActionBAK Braces...in supple, smart Belts...tough...good-looking...comfortable...and *new!* Don't be hide-bound...be rawhide-bound...with colorful Hickok Rawhide Belts and Braces...*low-priced from $1 up!*

Hickok, 1939

CORONATION
ActionBAK Braces

LONDON STYLE...LUXURIOUS COMFORT

Sheer splendor...with deep regard for the proper thing!...that's the Coronation—the inspiration for the Hickok styles of the season. Correct color schemes of royal richness. Jewelry-like fittings...all incorporated with matchless ActionBAK comfort—exclusively Hickok.

Unhampered action—you move as you please and ActionBAK smoothly conforms. No nagging pull at hips or shoulders—no sagging trousers. This faultless service lasts, and ActionBAK style stays "like new"—because of Hickok long-life webbing, and extra-durable cable elastic cords. You will want more than just one pair of Hickok ActionBAK braces. HICKOK, Rochester, N. Y.

HICKOK
ActionBAK Braces

BELTS · BUCKLES · BRACES · GARTERS · JEWELRY

STYLE LEADERSHIP

Hickok, 1937

KNOX

Summer Fashion
CALLS FOR STRAWS

THESE THREE cool and casual gentlemen are men of taste, but each has chosen a different hat. We don't know which is the maiden's choice—she seems to be taking a strictly non-committal attitude.

It's even money which of these Knox Hats will register highest with you. There'll be occasions when each is correct.

The handsome lad at the right chooses for the moment a Knox "Comfit®" Straw

There's something spirited and youthful about the new Knox Straws!

which helps to set off his clean-cut features.

The serious chap in the center likes an easy hat and has it—a Knox "Nassau," an open-weave with a broad brim.

The good listener at the left goes in for a Knox Panama, with graceful, tapering crown and wide, snapped brim.

Summer's the season for smartness. With Knox Straws you'll be *properly* hatted for the summer season!

Wear a smart Knox Straw and celebrate the summer in style and cool comfort!

KNOX THE HATTER, FIFTH AVENUE AT 40th STREET, NEW YORK · · · AGENTS IN PRINCIPAL CITIES

Knox, 1937

Jayson

WHITEHALL by JAYSON

...ultimate in white shirts, heads a long list of the right Troy-tailored shirts for Spring better stores are featuring. To see them, ask for JAYSON by name...and enjoy the style and quality standards which have made millions prefer JAYSON shirts.

JAYSON shirts are guaranteed, without qualification, to give complete satisfaction. Will not shrink below marked size. F. JACOBSON & SONS, INC. 1115 BROADWAY, N.Y.

JAYSON SHIRTS PAJAMAS SPORTSWEAR

The JAYSON Whitehall shirt, illustrated, $2...Also available Jayson Whitehall pajamas $5.

Jayson, 1939

▶ *Hart Schaffner & Marx, 1936*

COLOR

PALM BEACH SUITS

It's very old fashioned to think that Palm Beach means a light color ● Palm Beach is the name of the most popular summer suit in the world: *The suit that lets your body breathe* ● You can have it in blue or brown or gray or white—in fact, a whole world of colors and patterns. ● The cloth is made by the famous GOODALL mills—by no one else—and is tailored by GOODALL experts into the smartest washable suits of the season ● You'll know you're getting the genuine when you see the trade marked label in the garment. Suits $17.75— Slacks $5.50—Dinner Formal $20.00. Goodall Company, Cincinnati, Ohio.

$17.75

TAILORED BY GOODA
Palm Beach
FROM THE GENUINE CL

This is a BOW TIE year!

IN HOLLYWOOD, Palm Beach and Broadway—the *bow* tie is unmistakably *the* tie style. And how fortunate for mankind that this week—and each succeeding week—you'll see a pronouncedly larger number of young men wearing smart bow ties.

In the first place, a bow tie is the most sensible tie any man can wear. It is truly correct. It is jaunty. A horizontal dash of tie-color is the dominant note of man's otherwise drab attire—and it relieves the monotony of vertical lines. It registers alertness. It breathes good grooming. It brings out the best in any man's face. It's on in a jiffy and amazingly comfortable with soft, semi-soft or starched collar.

The smartest bow ties are Spur Ties—the choice of millions. Tied by expert feminine fingers—they stay tied. And that secret of the phenomenal success of Spur Tie—the concealed, patented "Innerform" —permits you to adjust the wings to suit your *personal* fancy. You owe it to yourself to wear a Spur Tie—the smartest tie that ever set tie style. Step into a young men's store today and see those wonderful new spring Spur Tie colors and patterns —the smartest and most sensible ties that ever adorned masculine necks.

Insist that the Spur Tie red label shown above is on every tie and avoid inferior imitations. You can shape a Spur Tie in any way you like—fluffy or flat, severe or sportive—and the patented H-shaped Innerform holds it that way.

FREE

You'll enjoy this fascinating little book, "Off the Lot." Full of charming photographs. All about motion picture stars. For your copy write to Hewes & Potter, Inc., 65-SB Bedford Street, Boston, Massachusetts.

JOHN BOLES
Star in the Universal Picture Triumph "La Marseillaise"

John Boles, "The Golden Tenor of the talking screen," caps his great successes in "The Desert Song" and "Rio Rita" with "La Marseillaise"—the story of the song that inflamed a nation to red revolt and triumph. Laura LaPlante is the co-star in this burning love story.

Spur Tie

50¢ 75¢ $100

TIED BY HAND · · · IT STAYS TIED

HEWES & POTTER, Inc., 65-SB Bedford Street, Boston, Mass. 200 Fifth Avenue, New York. 120 Battery Street, San Francisco. 426 South Spring Street, Los Angeles. 412 S. Wells Street, Chicago. 1604 Arapahoe Street, Denver. Made in Canada by Tooke Bros., Ltd., Montreal. In Australia: Wallace, Buck & Goodes, Pty., Ltd., Sydney.

Palm Beach Suits, 1938 ◄ Spur Tie, 1930

THE ARISTOCRAT OF SUMMER FABRICS

PRIESTLEY'S NOR-EAST
They're Refrigerated by Nature SUITS

WRITE FOR A FREE STYLE
BOOKLET WITH A SAMPLE
OF NOR-EAST CLOTH

Priestley's
NOR-EAST
NON-CRUSH
REG. U.S. PAT. OFF.

At Better Men's
Stores Everywhere

$29.75

Here, at last, is the summer suit that makes LIFE worth living.

It's Priestley's Nor-East, the original worsted and mohair blend—the fabric that's refrigerated by Nature! It is actually *cool to the touch*, in addition to being feather-light and tissue-thin, yet holds its shape and style.

The cloth is imported—because only Priestley of England knows the secret of weaving this most luxurious of summer fabrics; the suits are styled and tailored by America's foremost maker of summer clothes. Your clothier can show you Nor-East in both light and dark colors, in plain shades and patterns. Ask for it!

★ TAILORED FOR READY-TO-WEAR EXCLUSIVELY BY L. GREIF & BRO., BALTIMORE ★

Priestley's Nor-East Suits, 1939

PRIESTLEY'S NOR-EAST--*it's refrigerated by Nature!*

THE ARISTOCRAT OF SUMMER FABRICS

Here is a summer suit different from any you have ever worn. For, in addition to being light and thin and porous, Priestley's NOR-EAST is *actually cool to the touch*—refrigerated by Nature! The cloth is imported—for only Priestley of England knows the secret of weaving this remarkable fabric.

It's non-crush, too! You can be sure it will hold its shape and style, despite heat and humidity!

Such a fabric deserves the very best of tailoring—and gets it! For NOR-EAST suits are handsomely tailored by America's foremost maker of summer clothes—styled in the soundest traditions of good taste.

This summer, you need not face a compromise between comfort and distinction—you can have *both!* Just ask your clothier for Priestley's NOR-EAST!

Priestley's
IMPORTED
NOR-EAST
NON-CRUSH
REG. U.S. PAT. OFF.

☆ At better men's
stores everywhere

$32.50

TAILORED EXCLUSIVELY BY
L. GREIF & BRO. ★ BALTIMORE

Priestley's Nor-East Suits, 1938

**THE UNIVERSITY
STYLE LEADERS SAY "IT'S DICKENS
BLUE FOR SPRING"**

Our style observers cover the leading universities throughout the United States for the latest style news. This spring it's Dickens Blue

You'll find it in tweeds stippled with colorful nubs. You'll find it in cheviots and unfinished worsteds—very little pattern

The 3-button coat is the favorite, 2 buttons to button; waist and hip lines are trim; the 2-button coat is next in order. Wherever our clothes are sold you'll find correct university style

HART SCHAFFNER & MARX

Hart Schaffner & Marx, 1930

The Standard Clothing House, Minneapolis

Minneapolis is famous for good flour; The Standard is famous for good clothes

We're going to change that childhood riddle, "Why does a miller wear a white hat?" to "Why do so many millers wear Hart Schaffner & Marx clothes?" The answer is because they not only like the clothes, but they like the store that sells them: The Standard

Clothing House of Minneapolis

Mr. Lynch and Mr. Nordstrom who are the owners of The Standard have been in the clothing business all their lives; they know how to give value and service, and how to build confidence

This store is typical of the many fine concerns throughout the United States who sell Hart Schaffner & Marx clothes. Find The Trumpeter in your community and you'll find clothes satisfaction

HART SCHAFFNER & MARX
New York   London   Chicago

Hart Schaffner & Marx, 1931

"And now, folks, Hart Schaffner & Marx present . . . THE THREE HILLBILLIES!"

TELEVISION'S going to be an awful shock in a case like this!

We won't take any responsibility, however, for what these Manhattan Hillbillies (who seem to be wintering in Florida) are about to broadcast. Chances are they never were west of the Hudson until they made a success at their mountaineer yodeling.

But we can commend them on the way they're turned out . . . regardless of their past history. They've evidently learned, like a lot of other men have today, that no matter whether you're behind a desk or a microphone it's important to be well-dressed!

Your local Hart Schaffner & Marx dealer can show you how easy it is to be well-dressed . . . and how inexpensively it can be done. See him tomorrow!

Robert Surrey

is Hart Schaffner & Marx top style reporter. And he is a very real person! Right now he is in Nassau. Next week he may be cruising on one of the sleek, smart Grace line ships. Or he may be in Bermuda! Or at Palm Beach! Or even at Sun Valley, the new winter sports paradise! For wherever well-dressed men congregate there you'll find Robert Surrey, sketch pad or camera in hand, accurately absorbing new style highlights. Highlights, which within a very short length of time, will appear in the smart, up-to-the-minute clothing tailored by Hart Schaffner & Marx. For instance, the gray and champagne shawl collar dinner jackets shown above give you just an idea of what the trend is in correct resort wear.

HART SCHAFFNER & MARX

THE TRUMPETER LABEL

A SMALL THING TO LOOK FOR . . . A BIG THING TO FIND

Hart Schaffner & Marx, 1937

THE
Lincoln
$10.00

KNAPP-FELT
THE NEW C&K HAT FOR THE MONTH
MADE BY THE CROFUT & KNAPP CO., FIFTH AVENUE NEW YORK

Knapp-Felt, 1930

Give him SCHICK'S APPEAL!

Free the face you love
from
"Razor-Blade-Skin"

GIVE the man of your heart a Schick Dry Shaver . . . be he father, husband, son or big brother. And the very first time he uses it . . . he'll bless you as the wisest of gift choosers.

"Shaving was never like this!" . . . he'll murmur tentatively, as he whisks off the whiskers, slick as you please . . . without lather or cream or any of the other messy accessories of old-style shaving.

But wait! Wait until his face has enjoyed a few weeks' vacation from cuts, nicks and abrasions. Then you'll see the EXTRA dividends of your gift . . . in his improved and refreshened complexion.

Then . . . in every way and every day . . . his Schick shaves will get better and better. He'll get "head barber" shaves invariably; swift, sleek, satin-smooth, and free from the slightest skin injury.

We won't bore you with the technical reasons why the Schick is imperatively the right dry shaver for you to choose. You see, Colonel Schick pioneered the whole dry shaver idea; spent 15 years to develop and perfect it. Many imitators have gone as far as they dared in infringing Schick patented principles. But it is the compromises they made to conceal infringement that keep their shavers so far behind the Schick in sweet, dependable and silken shaving performance.

If you'd like to enhance the "face value" of some man in your life . . . give him a Schick Dry Shaver.

Schick Dry Shavers come in 3 models—the new super-powered COLONEL SCHICK SHAVER, the new improved STANDARD SCHICK SHAVER and the SCHICK MAYETTE for women. All operate on AC or DC and men's models are equipped with either No. 7 shaving head for average beards or No. 10 for tough, coarse beards. Prices range from $12.50 for the Standard Schick Shaver to $23.00 for deluxe and gift sets.

SCHICK
DRY
SHAVER
THE CIVILIZED WAY OF SHAVING

SCHICK DRY SHAVER, INC., STAMFORD, CONN. Schick Dry Shaver, Inc., has no connection with the Magazine Repeating Razor Co., which manufactures and sells the Schick Injector Razor.

Schick, 1939

STETSON INTERNATIONAL COLORS

OVERHEARD AT THE GOLDEN GATE EXPOSITION

"Pretend you're not looking!"

JANET: Here come the cameramen! They must think you boys are distinguished international visitors.

PETE: Nice compliment, Janet. But I get it—it must be our new Stetsons.

JANET: Ah-hah! So that's how you suddenly got that continental air!

BILL: Sure! It's a trick Stetson does with their new International Colors!

PETE: *Didn't I tell you, Bill? Faint hat never won fair lady!*

STETSONS ARE PRICED $5 to $40

STETSONS MADE IN CANADA, FROM $3.50 • JOHN B. STETSON COMPANY, PHILADELPHIA, NEW YORK, LONDON, PARIS

Stetson, 1939

469

Blazers, 1931

Pioneers, 1930

Pacer, 1936 ◀ *Yukon Flannels, 1931*

Work Shirts, 1931

Overalls, 1930

TOUGHEST FABRIC of It's Kind for the Money!
HEAVY SUEDE Cloth
Shirts and Jackets!

Double Thickness ACROSS CHEST AND BACK

Warm, Soft-Like Suede Leather!
Wind-Proof, Storm-Proof
A Super-Service Jacket for All Weather Wear

$3.98

35 G 800—Tan suede only.
HALF SIZES: 14 to 17-inch neck. Order same size as size of shirt you wear. We Pay Postage.

You'll say it's one of the finest you ever bought. A Super-Jacket that looks like suede leather—a double thickness cotton Suede Cloth windbreaker that is built to withstand the severest weather—that laughs at wind and storm—offered to you at the lowest imaginable price for a garment of this character. We added reinforcements across the chest and back—giving you more strength, and at the same time more warmth. It is styled with two big, button-down pockets—just the kind an active man needs. The genuine Jack-O-Lastic Web bottom keeps it around your body snugly—warmly. You'll say it's the most comfortable jacket you ever wore. Regardless of where you buy it, you couldn't find a garment that would give you more enjoyable wear for so little money.

TALON HOOKLESS FASTENER *Down Front*
Something New for the Great Outdoors

$4.95

35 G 735—Red. **35 G 736**—Green.
35 G 737—Brown.
HALF SIZES: 14 to 17-inch neck. Order same size as size shirt you wear. We Pay Postage.

Send your old jackets to their "Happy Hunting Grounds." Here is something new, something different, something better. It's on or off in a jiffy because it has a Talon Hookless Fastener with new pull, that locks. Can be closed at any point from top to bottom and stays there. No buttons to fumble and fuss with. One pull and the jacket is open or closed. It keeps out every breath of wind, and gives you such a snug fit around the neck. Constructed of the finest double cotton Suede Cloth we could find. The flat collar can be turned up around the neck. It also features our new 2-in-1 pocket—a smaller pocket on a larger one.

Men! How's This for a Shirt Bargain!
Looks Like Leather

$1.35

35 G 727—Tan.
35 G 728—Gray.
HALF SIZES: 14 to 17-inch neck. State size. We Pay Postage.

Men! Here is shirt value. Fine cotton Suede Cloth Shirt in coat style with two big button-through pockets. Generously proportioned, giving ease and freedom of action. The smart suede finish closely resembles leather. Suitable for most any kind of weather and our price is exceptionally low for this quality. Every man should have one for general utility wear—and at our low price every man can afford one.

DOUBLE WEIGHT for Rough Wear

We Pay Postage

To Please the Boys

Double Weight
Cotton Suede Cloth Shirt
Looks and Feels Like Leather

$2.79

35 G 753—Dark Brown. **35 G 754**—Gray.
35 G 755—Tan.
HALF SIZES: 14 to 17-inch neck. State size. We Pay Postage.

Our most popular Suede Shirt. Warm Suede Cloth of soft, double weight cotton yarns closely woven to resemble suede leather. A great shirt for severe weather protection. Practically wind-proof. Coat style. Two large button-down flap pockets. Flat collar. Faced sleeves. Washable. Warm—comfortable—economical.

Extra Heavy
Cotton Suede Cloth

$2.79

35 G 730—Tan only.
HALF SIZES: 14 to 17-inch neck. State size. We Pay Postage.

It stops the wind and in addition it **wears**! The fabric is a sturdy, **double weight** Cotton Suede Cloth with a soft, smooth finish resembling leather. Jack-O-Lastic web bottom retains its elasticity and fits the hips snugly and warmly. Convertible collar. Two flap pockets; and at a price that means real savings!

Double Weight
Suede Cloth Jacket

$1.98

35 G 880—Tan only.
SIZES: 6 to 16 years.
State age-size. We Pay Postage.

As sturdily constructed as our men's Jackets, it answers the needs of the liveliest boy. This Jacket is of double Suede Cloth—a heavy, cotton fabric with a soft nap characteristic of suede leather. Practically wind-proof. Coat style. Adjustable cuff. Button-through slash pockets. Jack-O-Lastic Web bottom. Every detail of construction is just as you want it.

Sturdy Shirt
Cotton Suede Cloth

$1.29

35 G 907—Tan.
35 G 908—Gray.
HALF SIZES: 12 to 14-inch neck. State size. We Pay Postage.

Very low price. Any boy would like to own this Cotton Suede Cloth Shirt. Has the feel and appearance of soft leather. Ruggedly constructed for husky boys. Closed front style. Two big, button-through pockets. The collar and cuffs are interlined for extra wear and warmth. Will stand the strain of hard play.

Men's Wear, 1931

473

Men's Shirts, 1931

Men's Wear, 1931

Boy's Coats, 1931

Knickers, 1931

▶ *Men's Hats, 1930*

C.M.O. STYLE-LEADERS FOR 1938!

SEE PAGES 274 TO 318 FOR OTHER BARGAINS IN MEN AND BOYS' WEA

Popular Wide Waistbands
METAL-INITIALED

$1⁹⁹   **$2⁹⁸**

WIDE 24-INCH BOTTOMS

Natty Glen-plaid slacks in popular Hollywood style with extra-wide 4-inch waistband and 5-button closing, enriched with initials in metal. Of fine-spun, hard-finished Cotton Worsted with woven plaid pattern, in your choice of five popular colors. Extra wide 24-inch cuffed bottoms. So low priced! COLORS—At left. SIZES—Waist 28 to 36 inches; inseam 28 to 34 inches. State waist, inseam, color, and PRINT initials desired.
3 K N65—Price $1.99 Shpg. wt. 1 lb. 12 ozs.

The STYLE'S as hot as red pepper - - - see the wide, 4-inch "two-fingered" extension waistband with metal initials - - - the pleats, the buckled straps, and wide 22-inch bottoms. And the FABRIC'S smart and exceptionally Good - - - Cassimere, about 2/3 Wool, balance Cotton and Rayon in herringbone weave. A "stand-out" buy. COLORS—At right. SIZES—Waist 28 to 36 ins.; inseam 28 to 34. State waist, inseam, color, and PRINT initials.
3 K N28—Price $2.98 Shpg. wt. 2 lbs.

COLORS: LIGHT GRAY, LIGHT TAN, DARK GRAY, DARK BROWN, DARK BLUE

COLORS: MEDIUM BLUE, MEDIUM BROWN, MEDIUM GRAY

THE LATEST SPORT SHIRT **79c** CHOICE OF 2 CLASSY COLOR-COMBINATIONS

COLLEGIATE SLACKS **$2⁹⁵** EACH CHOICE OF 2 POPULAR COLORS

"Swellegant" newest collegiate-style slacks with pleats, and wide inch waistband with ring-decorated straps fastening with buttons. Fine Flannel, about 1/3 Wool, balance Cotton and Rayon, with smart tone windowpane pattern. 22-inch bottoms. Excellent value! COLORS—Light-gray, or Light-tan. State waist, inseam, and color.
3 KN30—SIZES—Waist 28 to 36 ins.; inseam 29 to 34. Price $2. Shpg. wt. 1 lb. 12 ozs.

A "rah-rah" shirt - - - the most dapper you'll see on the camp. Back, sleeves, and collar in one shade; front contrasting-colored. Fine Quality Knitted Combed Cotton Jersey. A "beaut!" COLORS—Navy-with-gray, or Gray-with-maroon. State color and s
3 KV15—SMALL fits chest 34-36 ins.; MEDIUM 37-40; LARGE 41-44 . . . 7 Shpg. wt. 8 ozs.

INITIALS MONOGRAMMED
WITHOUT EXTRA CHARGE

WE WILL EMBROIDER ANY 2 OR 3 LETTERS ON SHIRTS SHOWN BELOW

WHITE BLUE

SHIRT WITH TIE AND TIE-CLASP **89c** EACH SET

DEEP BLUE / WHITE / TAN / LIGHT BLUE / GRAY

79c 3 FOR $2²⁵

BLUE WHITE RED

NEW RODEO SHIRT **$1²⁹**

CHOICE EITHER IN EITHER COMBINA 49

SPECIAL VALUE!
An outstanding bargain in a set consisting of one monogrammed Good Quality, fast-color Cotton Broadcloth shirt, a neat-looking tie, and a tie-clasp with

SANFORIZED-SHRUNK
It sets the pace in outstanding value. "Quality" features you'd never expect in a shirt priced so low - - - "Sanforizing" and embroidered initials. Of Fast-color Good Quality Cotton Broadcloth. Very

Embroidered horseshoes on the collar, and cord lacings through the 12 eyelets, make this slipover shirt

Cool, easily-laundered shirts in snappy styles. Of Cotton, mesh. COLORS—White-with-navy, or

Puritan Sportswear, 1939

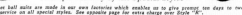

Basket Ball Shirts

Men's Wear, 1938 ◄ *McGregor Sportswear, 1936*

Pep Squad Outfits

477

THREE GREAT **AIR-LIGHT** *STETSONS*

From Old Westbury to Santa Barbara, these new Air-Light hats are seen at the fastest games. Left: a low-creased crown and full brim distinguish Stetson's "Open Road" -- $6. Right: "Casino," in pewter gray, is a Superior Air-Light, finished with the exclusive Selv-Edge -- $10.

Drop in at your dealer for a look at these new Air-Lights. Feel their softness and wisp-like weight . . . see how they will take any shape you wish and take it smartly. For all their lightness, these hats are full-blooded Stetsons . . . able to keep their smart style-lines as long as you wear them. John B. Stetson Company, Philadelphia, New York, London, Paris. Stetsons are also made in Canada.

Only two ounces of felt in these versatile Air-Light styles. Stetson's "Whippet," shown with the "Tailored Edge," is an advanced style -- at a new price -- $7.50.

STETSON HATS

Air-Light Stetsons, from $5. Other Stetsons, from $7.50 (unlined from $7) to $40

Stetson Hats, 1937

FOLLOW THE "METAL" *URGE TO SMARTNESS*

Winning colors at any big game this Fall are these new metal-shade felts. Left: Stetson's "Chatwood" in antique bronze...a softly furred "metal blend" felt that touches new heights of color smartness. Right: "Ballinger" in Anaconda ...with its wider brim blocked in a rolling curl. Ask to see it, too, in smart gun-metal gray.

Hard to choose between these new Stetsons isn't it? Each one is tops for its type . . . and tops for quality, too. That's why Stetsons are world famous. Men know that smart Stetson style will endure to the last day of wear. John B. Stetson Company, Philadelphia, New York, London, Paris. Stetsons are also made in Canada.

STETSON HATS

Stetsons, from $7.50 (unlined, from $7) to $40. Air-Light Stetsons, from $5.

Stetson Hats, 1937

Stetson Presents

PADDOCK GREEN AND SORREL TAN

America's race-meets, hunt-meets, horse-shows...colorful, thrilling ...drawing the smart world as never before. This inspired Stetson to set a new style-pace for Spring 1938 with a series of colors derived from the world of thoroughbreds. Right: A "Sorrel Tan" snap brim, welt edged, worn with center crease spread out at back. Left: Stetson's new "Paddock Green" in a distinguished pork-pie shape with saddle-stitched brim.

The smart shapes and "Thoroughbred Colors" of these Stetsons are new as tomorrow. But Stetson felt, unchanged with the years, has the same rugged quality that has made the name Stetson famous the world over. John B. Stetson Company, Philadelphia, New York, London, Paris. Stetsons are also made in Canada.

Stetson Hats

STETSON HATS ARE PRICED FROM $7.50 (UNLINED, $7) TO $40. AIR-LIGHT STETSONS, FROM $5

Stetson Hats, 1938

DOBBS
IN RAINBOW MIXTURES *Field + Stream*
...A HAT FOR TRUE SPORTSMEN

Hours upon hours of patient handwork are devoted to producing a smart felt hat with the soft velvety texture of Dobbs Field & Stream! No machine method could ever duplicate the feeling of richness you experience as you circle your hand over this superb hat. And nothing but skillful fur-blending by experts could produce the radiant Rainbow Mixtures—exclusive with Dobbs Field & Streams hats...Again Dobbs sets the style!

Dobbs
Representatives in Fine Stores Everywhere

$7.50
Other Dobbs Hats $5 to $20

NEW YORK'S LEADING HATTERS • 711 FIFTH AVENUE AT 55TH STREET • 380 PARK AVENUE AT 53RD STREET • NEW YORK

Dobbs Hats, 1939 ▶ *Knox Hats, 1939* ▶▶ *French Line, 1932*

Perfectly suited

BY JANTZEN

The Swing

The "Swing" (illustrated) in tune with the rhythm of Youth! Gay three-color contrast—or in solid colors—created of whipcord Kava Knit fabric. *Tailored-in elastic Brä-Lift for youthful uplift* $6.95

Other Jantzen Creations $4.50 to $10.95

De Luxe Half-Hitch

De Luxe Half-Hitch (illustrated) The Trunks of the Year! Superbly tailored from a rope-stitch Kava Knit. Hawaiian beach-patrol side stripes. $3.95

Other Jantzen Trunks $2.95 to $4.95

•

A reproduction of this Petty painting without descriptive copy will be sent on receipt of 10c in stamps or coins.

Suited for stunning appearance, for perfect fit, for glorious comf
Briefly, skillfully cut, the new Jantzens give you a world of sun expos
and free-as-a-breeze action for swimming, diving and beach fun. K
Knit fabrics of luxurious quick-to-dry wool in fresh new versions h
magical knitted-in qualities through the magic of Jantzen-Stitch
mean *figure-control for women* and trim athletic smartness for men.
the water and out, you are assured a perfect, *permanent* fit. See the
Jantzens at your favorite store or shop. Jantzen Knitting Mills, Portla
Oregon; Vancouver, Canada; London, England; Sydney, Australia.

Jantzen

JANTZEN KNITTING MILLS,
Dept. 301, Portland, Oregon

Send me style folder in color
featuring new 1937 models.

WOMEN'S ☐   MEN'S ☐

Name

Street

City

A Jantzen always attracts attention! Because it's America's finest fitting swimming suit! It's the best precaution against a distressing appearance—in the sea or on the sands. Cruise into any good shop and see the new models in the fashionable Kava-Knit fabrics. Upon receipt of 10c in coin or stamps we'll gladly send you a reproduction of this Petty painting without advertising. Address Dept. 241, Jantzen Knitting Mills, Portland, Oregon.

"One of us must flag that ship with our Jantzen"

Jantzen, 1936

"RUNNING IMPROVES MY FIGURE?— SILLY, IT'S JUST MY JANTZEN!"

● Presenting the new Jantzen Glamour Fabrics

VELVA-LURE ☆ SUEDE-SHEEN SATIN-KNITS ☆ KNIT-IN PRINTS

the most radiant stars of summer's bright stage. Their creation is unquestionably the outstanding swim suit news of the year. They are new, amazingly new. They were developed by Jantzen exclusively and are made only *by Jantzen*. Gorgeous textures have been developed in these luxurious Glamour Fabrics. Velva-Lure and Suede-Sheen are soft, gleaming, velvety; Satin-Knits are rich, radiant, lustrous; Knit-in-Prints, of vibrant color and gaiety. *The miracle of Lastex yarn* has been added for just the right amount of two-way stretch that holds the body in youthful sculptured lines. These astonishing tailored Jantzens with Positive Uplift give a new meaning to figure-control in a swim suit for women and set a new standard of trim athletic appearance for men. In the water and out they fit with wrinkle-defying perfection. See these new Jantzen Glamour Swim Suits at your favorite shop or store. Note their rich sheen and beauty of texture. *Feel* their appealing softness. Test their amazing elasticity. Jantzen Knitting Mills, Portland, Oregon; Vancouver, Canada; Sydney, Australia; London, England.

Left: The **ZIP-IN,** a sparkling new Jantzen half-skirt model tailored in gorgeous "Velva-Lure", $7.95. Skirtless model in "Satin-Knit", $5.95. Other Jantzen models, $4.95 to $7.95.

Right: Tops in design, tailoring, fit and fabric is the new **STREAMLINER** in Suede-Sheen, luxuriously soft and rich, $4.95. Other Jantzen trunks $2.95 to $4.95.

Jantzen
MOLDED-FIT SWIM SUITS

JANTZEN KNITTING MILLS, Dept. 241, Portland, Oregon.
Send me style folder in colors, featuring new 1939 models.

Women's ☐ Men's ☐

Name
Street
City

Jantzen, 1939

You, Too, May Get a Heavenly Tan Like This

WITHOUT PAINFUL BURNING

HERE'S a marvelous scientific product, SKOL, that actually filters out those rays of the sun that cause blisters and ugly, painful redness.

● Skol lets you bask in the sun for hours. Lets you tan comfortably, beautifully, even if you are blond. Made after a formula originally developed in Sweden for snowburn, Skol is now used on beaches in 25 countries.

Be sure to apply Skol before you go out in the sun and again after each swim! It's not greasy, doesn't show, won't pick up sand. Skol Company, Inc., New York.

SKOL
BLOCKS OUT HARMFUL SUN-RAYS
ADMITS BENEFICIAL SUN-RAYS
RELIEVES SUNBURN—NON-OILY

SKOL COMPANY, INC., NEW YORK

NOT OILY—NOT GREASY

This is the WRONG way to try to get your tan. You burn painfully first —look lobster-red and unattractive...*suffer*

This is the RIGHT way to encourage a lovely tan. Use Skol and tan gloriously without redness or painful burning

Jantzen, 1937 ◄ *Skol, 1939*

SETTING THE STAGE FOR A SUCCESSFUL SUMMER SWIM

"Acele," the acetate yarn de luxe, takes to the sea

"ACELE" DEPARTMENT, DU PONT RAYON COMPANY, INC., EMPIRE STATE BUILDING, NEW YORK CITY

Acele, 1936

▶ *Burdine's, 1934*

Interwoven, 1934

Interwoven, 1934

Interwoven, 1935

Interwoven, 1936 ▶ Interwoven, 1934

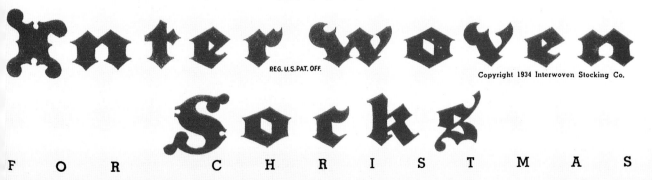

MAKE NO MISTAKE

CHOOSE

Interwoven

REG. U.S. PAT. OFF.

Copyright 1934 Interwoven Stocking Co.

Socks

FOR CHRISTMAS

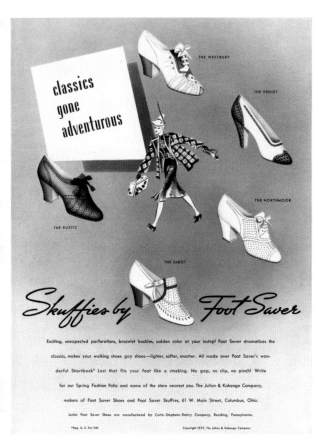

classics
gone
adventurous

THE WESTBURY

THE HENLEY

THE NORTHMOOR

THE RUSTIC

THE SABOT

Skuffies by Foot Saver

Exciting, unexpected perforations, bracelet buckles, sudden color at your instep! Foot Saver dramatizes the

classics, makes your walking shoes gay shoes—lighter, softer, smarter. All made over Foot Saver's won-

derful Shortback® Last that fits your foot like a stocking. No gap, no slip, no pinch! Write

for our Spring Fashion Folio and name of the store nearest you. The Julian & Kokenge Company,

makers of Foot Saver Shoes and Foot Saver Skuffies, 61 W. Main Street, Columbus, Ohio.

Junior Foot Saver Shoes are manufactured by Curtis-Stephens-Embry Company, Reading, Pennsylvania.

®Reg. U. S. Pat. Off.   Copyright 1939, The Julian & Kokenge Company

Foot Saver, 1939

They never tread the beaten path

As mass manufacture reduces more and more things to a dead level of
similarity, the product of individual craftsmanship stands out in sharp relief.
Fine leather working is not a lost art in the making of Nettleton Shoes.
They, like the men who wear them, reflect character which does not tread
the beaten path. A. E. Nettleton Co. H. W. Cook, Pres., Syracuse, N.Y.

Nettleton

GENTLEMEN'S FINE SHOES

PRICED TEN TO TWENTY DOLLARS

The ALGONQUIN
Hand-sewed vamp. Remark-
ably comfortable. An exclusive Nettleton Pattern.
Ten Dollars

TRY THE
PENCIL TEST

Nettleton, 1936

Roblee, 1939 ◄ *Children's Clothes, 1930*

Sweaters, 1930

Everests Feature NEW Boudoir Fashions

Smart Kid Trim Felt 79¢
Daintiest, staunchest, most cheerful Felt House Slipper you perhaps have ever seen for the money. The color effects are charming; mottled Felt body; chic wing tip and covered spring heel; spicy rayon ribbon and rosette trim. A treat for the eye, and a joy to the foot—for the sole and heel are of padded chrome leather.
SIZES: 3 to 8. No half sizes. State size. Postpaid.
24 G 3504—Royal purple.
24 G 3505—Rose and gold.
24 G 3506—Frost blue. 79¢

Warm Felt Leather Sole $1.15
Very low price for so much genuine comfort, and the adequate support most feet need, even in the restful House Slipper. Thick, warm Felt—in lovely shades—to especially remember at gift time. Another of our most popular Everests, with dainty ribbon cutout-trim and gay little pompon. Flexible leather sole and low heel, with easy rubber lift.
"I've never found a nicer house slipper for the money"—"exactly what I wanted, so low priced, too!"—so write our customers. Postpaid.
SIZES: 2½ to 8. State size.
24 G 3955—American Beauty.
24 G 3954—Alice Blue.
24 G 3953—Taupe. $1.15

Crepe Silk D'Orsay $1.49
The foot that slips into this lovely D'Orsay—will find new feminine flattery, along with ideally restful support. Fashioned to a queen's taste—from rich Crepe Silk, with dainty rayon braid binding, and a rare boudoir touch in the feathery ostrich fancy, which Paris sets to the outer side. Within—a delectable lining of contrasting rayon brocade. Soft padded chrome leather sole to match shoe; dressy 1¾-inch covered heel with leather top.
HALF SIZES: 3 to 8. State size. Postpaid.
24 G 3501—All red.
24 G 3502—Black with peach ostrich trim.
24 G 3503—All blue. $1.49

$1.25 Plush Collar Covered Heels
← This lovely Slipper will head your gift list, we know. So new—so richly tailored. Fine smooth Felt, with soft padded chrome leather sole, shapely arch supporting shank, and 1½-inch felt covered Cuban heel with leather lift. Figured plush in a softly harmonizing tone, makes a very rich collar. Dainty braid; Frenchy pompon.
SIZES: 3 to 8. No half sizes. State size. We Pay Postage.
24 G 3507—Plum.
24 G 3508— Alice blue. $1.25

Leather Lift on Heels

98¢ Shank Support
Comfortable Felt Slipper. Mild fawn color trim on deep vivid sapphire blue; an eye-feasting combination. Silk Pompons. Padded chrome leather sole, light firm shank support, and easy low rubber heel.
SIZES: 3 to 8. No half sizes. State size. Postpaid.
24 G 3929. 98¢

$1.49 Pajama Slipper
Soft quilted Satin; rayon braid trim; feathery maribou halo. All blue, or black with peach maribou, matches shoe. Trim shank and counter support; 1½-inch heel; leather top. Very feminine and very comfortable.
SIZES: 2½ to 8. State size. Postpaid.
24 G 3514—Alice blue.
24 G 3515—Black. $1.49

95¢ Dressy! Inexpensive
Dainty, fashionable D'Orsay, for lounging or restful house wear. This splendid imitation kid-leather effect looks almost like the real kid, and the lines are just as you would find in the higher priced slippers. Dainty contrasting rayon lining. Dressy medium toe; easy padded chrome leather sole; restful supporting shank, 1½-inch Cuban heel with leather top.
SIZES: 3 to 8. No half sizes. State size. Postpaid.
24 G 3404—Red.
24 G 3405—Black. 95¢

$1.39 Fine Kid D'Orsays
A rare thing—to find such Slipper beauty with assured economy. For this is a genuine $2 value. Fine, soft genuine Kid leather, which molds so perfectly on foot-flattering lines. Blue, red or jet black; all have daintily contrasting rayon lining. Soft padded chrome leather sole to match; light supporting shank, trim medium toe last; very smart 1½-inch covered heel with leather top.
HALF SIZES: 3 to 8. State size. Postpaid.
24 G 3401—Black.
24 G 3402—Red.
24 G 3403—Blue. $1.39

59¢ A Great Bargain
The tremendous volume of business we do on this low-priced Boudoir Slipper is highest proof of its nation-wide popularity. Those who have tried it, know it to be the equal of similar slippers selling everywhere from 79¢ to 89¢. Durable Felt which stands for warmth and plenty of service. Dainty pompon and rayon ribbon trim to match. Luxurious ease—in the soft padded chrome leather soles and spring heels.
SIZES: 3 to 8. No half sizes. State size. Postpaid.
24 G 3916—Brown.
24 G 3919—Sapphire.
24 G 3917—Old rose. 59¢

$1.29 Juliettes Leather Soles
For those who enjoy the higher more cozy-warm back, and a fine supporting sole—for all comfort wear about the house, or perhaps hours in the sick room—here is the ideal Everest Slipper. Well-chosen trim gives it the smart two-tone effect. A fluffy plush border edges the high back; the cutout front-applied border is laced with lustrous fancy ribbon, and the prim little two-tone tab is a real boudoir touch. Good quality Felt; restfully flexible oak leather soles; rubber heels. Many stores sell this up to $2.00. Postpaid.
SIZES: 2½ to 9. State size.
24 G 3942—Brown.
24 G 3943—Claret red.
24 G 3944—Alice blue. $1.29

Felt Hi-Lo → 98¢
Just unbutton the trim collar and turn it snugly up around the ankle. This particular Hi-Lo is a bit smarter than the ordinary, because of its new floral-pattern collar, introducing a pleasing ground tone that harmonizes so nicely. Thick, warm, soft Felt, with padded chrome leather sole and heel.
SIZES: 3 to 8. No half sizes. State size. We Pay Postage.
24 G 3509—Brown.
24 G 3510—Blue. 98¢

For Real Comfort

Soft Wool Lining

Genuine Sheepskin $1.49
For that extra-fluffy warmth—this Genuine Sheepskin Slipper; a cozy treat for the foot unusually sensitive to the cold. Even the soft roll collar will turn up snugly about the ankle. Full fluffy sheep wool lining. Gay red pompon. More cheer for the cold days.
SIZES: 3 to 8. No half sizes. State size. We Pay Postage.
24 G 3400—Natural tan.

$1.69 Paris "Vani-Tea"
Rich Crepe Silk; dainty braid trim and foxy satin ribbon bow. Quilted Silk sock lining to match. Soft padded chrome leather sole; supporting shank; 1½-inch heel; leather top. We Pay Postage.
SIZES: 2½ to 8. State size.
24 G 3516—All Nile green.
24 G 3517—Black with peach bow. $1.69

$2.49 Back-Strap "Mule"
Height of all boudoir chic—the new back-strap Mule in rich black Satin with gorgeous pink satin lining. Silvered strap tab. Flexible oak leather turn sole; 1½-inch covered heel. Hard to beat this value!
SIZES: 2½ to 8. State size. We Pay Postage.
24 G 3511—Black. $2.49

$1.00 Choice of Kid or Patent Leather
Wish her a happy Birthday or a Merry Christmas with a pair of these inexpensive, feminine little Everest favorites—the dainty silk pompon style. Soft as a glove; so easy to slip into the overnight bag. Lovely choice of blue, black or gay red Kid, or glowing black Patent Leather. Padded chrome leather soles and heels, and a snug felt lining—for complete foot joy. Young moderns—collegiates—youthful matrons—call this their favorite.
SIZES: 3 to 8. No half sizes. State size. Postpaid.
24 G 3903—Black patent.   24 G 3901—Black kid.
24 G 3902—Red kid.   24 G 3904—Blue kid.
Per pair. $1.00

Trim and Neat 89¢
Smarter, more restful lounging or bedtime hours—sure to be spent in these inexpensive, feminine little Felt Everest Slipper. Its soft, restfully padded sole and heel insure easy, noiseless tread. The trim collar carries a harmonizing floral design; dainty rayon braid edges the high front, and the chic little pompon rests on a cutout felt medallion. You save money at this price.
SIZES: 3 to 8. No half sizes. State size.
24 G 3512—Alice blue.
24 G 3513—Flame red. 89¢

Shoes, 1930

GUARANTEED SIX MONTHS
Over 1,250,000 Pairs Sold SINCE FIRST INTRODUCED

$3.85

Ward's Six Months' Guaranteed Work Shoes are of the very best quality leather, and will give you at least six months of service. Should they fail to wear six months, we will replace them with a new pair of shoes charging you only for the number of days you had the old pair, and crediting you with the number of days they failed to wear. This Guarantee applies to 24 G 1820 and 24 G 1825 only.

WARD'S GREATEST WORK SHOE VALUE

During the past twenty years over 1,250,000 pairs of this famous ALL SOLID LEATHER Work Shoe have faithfully fulfilled the Six Months' Guarantee. Year by year the sales pile up. This is positive proof of the brute strength and wearing qualities which men everywhere have found by actual experience are contained in this ACE of Work Shoes. Read about the famous construction points shown below.

The secret of their amazing durability lies in the careful selection of materials and superior construction. Uppers are tanned by a special process to render them "barnyard proof." The heavy oak tanned soles are selected by experts to insure the long wear required of them. All solid leather, every inch of them. State size. Postpaid.

24 G 1820—Brown. 24 G 1825—Black.   24 G 1820—Brown. 24 G 1825—Black.
SIZES: 5 to 12. Wide   SIZES: 13 and 14. Wide
width.....................$3.85   width.....................$4.85

ALL SOLID LEATHER

1. Soft, heavy barnyard-proof uppers.
2. Solid leather counters.
3. Solid leather heels.
4. Triple stitched and reinforced with rivets.
5. Strong full grain leather insoles.
6. Double soles, oak leather outsoles and oak leather middle soles; double nailed and sewed construction.
7. Full vamp, not cut off under the tip; and hard box toe.

Skowhegan Shoe Grease
Increases the wear and helps to make them waterproof. Contents 5 ounces. We Pay Postage.
24 G 5740........17¢

Steel Shank—Riveted Arch   High Grade

High grade Corrective Style Work Shoes that assure working comfort the moment you put them on. You don't need to "break them in." Uppers and high-grade leather soles are specially treated to give them barnyard resistance—soft black or brown chrome leather (known as elkskin). A steel shank and riveted arch eliminate foot fatigue. Leather heels. Genuine Goodyear welt construction. It pays to buy quality!
SIZES: 6 to 12. Wide width. State size. We Pay Postage.
24 G 1890—Brown tip toe.
24 G 1891—Black moccasin toe. Per pair.............$3.98

$3.98

SOLID LEATHER
Two Full Soles
Outside Counter
Goodyear Welt Construction

$7.59

16-In. "Oil King" Hi-cuts
Others Ask Up To $12.00
Oil Tanned Leather Uppers

"Don't see how you can sell such fine shoes for so low a price." . . . "Never have found anything to beat them." That's the way men talk about these famous quality "Oil Kings"—our best 16-inch Hi-cuts. Specially built with all-leather construction. The most practical for hunting, hiking, mountain climbing—also for hard work in oil fields, lumber camps and other places where your boots MUST stand the gaff.

Heavy oil tanned brown chrome leather uppers. Outside leather counter. Special heavy oak leather outsoles and oak tanned middle sole. Genuine Goodyear welt construction. Oil tanned chrome leather tongue and vamp lining. Leather heels. Plain toe, army officers' style. Full bellows tongue. A super-built Hi-cut you'll be glad to own. Men, you'll find no other to compare with it unless you pay several dollars more.
SIZES: 6 to 12. Wide width. State size. We Pay Postage.
24 G 2036......................$7.59

Tip Toe
Leather Heels

Plain Toe
Rubber Heels

$2.49

Two Roomy, Durable Work Shoes

Built of sturdy leathers throughout. Smooth brown leather uppers—comfortable all the day through. Oak tanned leather soles. Nailed and sewed. Hard box toe; leather heels.
SIZES: 6 to 12. Wide width. State size. We Pay Postage.
24 G 1801—Tip toe......$2.49

Wide plain soft toe is very comfortable. Strong smooth brown leather uppers—soft, pliable and extra tough. Durable oak tanned leather soles, nailed and sewed. Solid, live rubber heels.
SIZES: 6 to 12. Wide width. State size. We Pay Postage.
24 G 1863—Plain toe.....$2.49

$6.98 $6.59

Composition Soles

Chocolate color chrome leather oil tanned uppers. Comfortable moccasin toe. Genuine Goodyear welt construction; sewed all around heel. Wonder-Wear composition rubber outsole, heavy oak tanned middle sole. Height 16 inches. Rubber heels. Weather-proof welt. Leather counters. Leather lined vamp.
SIZES: 6 to 12. Wide width. State size. We Pay Postage.
24 G 2031..................$6.98

Double Soles

Quality second only to our famous "Oil King." Strongly made of solid leather. Soles are double oak leather. Genuine Goodyear welt construction. Uppers are heavy brown leather (known as elkskin). Moccasin toe; cloth lined vamp; leather heels. Leather counter, full bellows tongue. Straps and buckles. Height 16 inches.
SIZES: 6 to 11. Wide width. State size. We Pay Postage.
24 G 2048..................$6.59

$6.98

Goodyear Welt 18-Inch Hi-cuts

Uppers are heavy, pliable, chrome tanned leather (known as elkskin), reinforced with strong stitching. Highest quality oak bend leather double soles. Goodyear welt construction. Sewed all around the heel. Solid leather heel and counter. Weather-proof welt excludes dampness. Bellows tongue. State size. We Pay Postage.
24 G 2042—Brown with tip toe. SIZES: 6 to 11, width C; also sizes 5 to 12, width D, E, EE.
24 G 2038—Black with tip toe. SIZES: 5 to 12, Width EE.
24 G 2041—Pearl color with moccasin toe.
SIZES: 6 to 12. Width EE. Per pair........................$6.98

Boots, 1930

491

There's STYLE in Friendly Leathers

just as in Friendly lasts and patterns

LOOK at the leathers shown on this page and you will see what is smart for men's shoes this fall and winter. From the fashionable Scottie Buck, on through the special St. Andrews Grain, Surrey Calf, Iceland Seal, and others; all are aristocrats of leathers—fine leathers from which fine Friendly Shoes are made.

Every leather has been selected for a special reason and purpose. Some are heavy, some are light, some are smooth grain, others have a patterned grain that brings out the character of the leather. And each is fashioned over correct, specially measured lasts, with smart pattern designs that match the fall and winter fabrics and colors in men's apparel.

See these shoes at your Friendly dealer's in all the new lasts and patterns for fall and winter. Or, if you prefer, there is the Frank Jarman Custom Shoe at $6.50.

NEW FRIENDLY STYLES

NEW FRIENDLY LEATHERS (Left to Right)

$5 THE JARMAN "FRIENDLY" SHOE Friendly to the Feet

JARMAN SHOE COMPANY · A Division of General Shoe Corporation · NASHVILLE, TENNESSEE

Jarman Shoes, 1935

Jarman Shoes, 1939

Keds

make news

Keds Yeoman oxfords are made of tire duck in six bright colors. Crepe soles have layers of ground cork. Shock-proof insoles.

For dignified interludes, Keds Veranda oxfords (above) with molded heels. Shock-proof insoles. White and navy blue.

Keds Bike oxfords (below). Natural tire duck with brown leather-finish saddle. Flexible arch cushions, extension type soles.

Excel on the courts with Keds Majestic oxfords. Flexible arch cushions for comfort. Blue striped bumpers and red suede-finish soles for color.

Flexible arch cushions make for extra comfort in Keds Hyannis oxfords. Vulcanized crepe soles. White and navy blue.

Tire duck makes soft moccasin vamps in Keds Dartmoor oxfords. Extension welt-type foxing. Creped soles. Shock-proof insoles. Brown, navy and natural.

They are not KEDS unless the name KEDS appears on the shoes.

United States Rubber Company

Keds, 1939

Nunn·Bush

Ankle fashioned Oxfords

Nunn-Bush Genuine White Buck Styles $8.50 to $10.50

Your PERSONAL APPEARANCE Deserves the Difference Ankle-Fashioning Makes

If every man knew what every Nunn-Bush salaried craftsman knows — every man would be wearing Nunn-Bush shoes.

You wear sports oxfords for better appearance. Treat yourself to the finest money can buy! Learn why Ankle-Fashioning is winning the Lifetime loyalty of innumerable men.

$7.85 to $12.50

NUNN-BUSH SHOE COMPANY
MILWAUKEE   NEW YORK   SAN FRANCISCO

Ask your local Nunn-Bush merchant about the built-in Nunn-Bush Weight Distributor Arch.

Nunn-Busch, 1937   ▶ *Real Silk, 1932*

The *Psychology of* Psocks

by GROUCHO MARX

ADVERTISER'S NOTE—We engaged Groucho Marx to write this advertisement, reimbursing him at his regular rate. The result is a hilarious burlesque of the Realsilk Representative calling on Mr. Marx on his Hollywood set and making the sale.

is a true *p*story, which I have trans- from the Russian, first, however, g on a neat Russian blouse to get the " of that difficult language. It con- the sox-life of the former Grand Duke chidor ("Tiger Rose") Marxisoxsky.

E DAY a commoner came to my castle llywoodograd. He caught the Grand e with a hole in his sock. Imagine ng the Grand Duke with a hole in his Imagine catching anyone with a hole sock. I felt chagrin creeping all over blushed through my tunic.

e commoner took one look at the rosy toes and playfully said, "This little ent to market; this little pig stayed ."

nough," I cried, "quit profaning the d Duke's toes and come to the point." ly I threw my *mantilla* over the of- ng members.

Don't let the hole in the sock get your ky," he said. "You'd be surprised how holes in socks, or stockings for that er, go on under cover. In fact, I just from the exclusive Malibu Beachsky on, where I found three leading men an ingenue with holes in their hosiery. ped them, and I can help you, too."

You have moved me strangely," said the d Duke. "Who are you?"

he Realsilk Man—come to bring you lad tidings of wonderful socks—wholly ut holes—and of such quality that Grand

Dukes, and even people with regular jobs, are proud to sheathe their feet within them."

He started firing questions at me rapid-fire.

"Is your sox-life a happy one?

"Can a Grand Duke do first-class duking in socks like those you now wear?

"Do you feel at ease when you take off your shoes in company?"

By this time we were both in tears. I dried his and vice versa.

"Shako," I said at last, doffing my own with a bow, "but why are you taking so much trouble just for a poor old broken-down Grand Dukeovitch?"

"You look good for at least a dozen pairs of these non-rippable, extra quality, super-guarded toed, double-decked soled, hand-somely patterned, longer-wearing famous Realsilk socks. I feel sure that I have shown you the error of your previous sox-life. Shall I put you down for two or four dozen pairs?"

Of course, a Marxisoxsky never takes the first figure offered, so I got him down to one dozen pairs before I bought. And I can truth-fully say, it was the turning point in the Grand Duke's life.

Now, on the set, when the boys and girls have recess from the hurly-burly of lights, cameras, sound mixers, directors and gag-men, and have gathered together for a moment's relaxation, instead of importuning me to do my card tricks, bird calls, or ocarina solos, they say:

"Grouchidor, show us your socks," —and I'm proud to say that I do!

To *Women*: If you have read this sock ad please know that the Realsilk Representative who calls at the home also brings a complete line of women's fine hosiery and lingerie, as well as wearables for all members of the family.

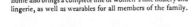

THE SOCKS WITH SEVEN EXCLUSIVE FEATURES

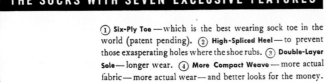

① **Six-Ply Toe**—which is the best wearing sock toe in the world (patent pending). ② **High-Spliced Heel**—to prevent those exasperating holes where the shoe rubs. ③ **Double-Layer Sole**—longer wear. ④ **More Compact Weave**—more actual fabric—more actual wear—and better looks for the money. ⑤ **Longest Silk Leg Found in Any Socks**—the bigger the foot size, the longer the leg. ⑥ **Double-Thick Garter Bands**—non-rippable —comfortable. ⑦ **Triple-Fast Hygienic Dyes**—fast to light, washing and perspiration. Color cannot harm the feet. Real-silk Hosiery Mills, Inc., Indianapolis, U. S. A. World's largest manufacturers of silk hosiery. Branches in 250 cities.

Keds, 1937

Jarman Shoes, 1937

How 24 "U.S." Laboratories helped bring Glory to Heroes of Air and Land

The Zeppelin's Crew, the Davis Cup Team, put their faith in Keds!

A dangerous lurch of the Zeppelin's cat walk—a lightning drive at the critical moment of a championship tennis match—footwork must not fail! That is why the United States Rubber Company, makers of Keds, concentrate all their vast store of knowledge about rubber and fabric to make Keds the most reliable shoe of its kind in the world.

For eight years, practically every member of the American Davis Cup Team has worn Keds. "The Shoe of Champions" has helped win victories on every championship tennis court in America and Europe.

On the Graf Zeppelin's epoch-making flight around the world, Keds assured safe footwork through gale and calm. There are 24 scientific laboratories

in the United States Rubber Company. Each contributes to Keds' high quality. The same knowledge and skill which produce "U. S." Royal Tires, "U. S." Royal Golf Balls, "U. S." Royalite Flooring that outwears marble, produce in "U. S." Keds a shoe of rugged stamina.

There's nothing exclusive about Keds except their high quality. You can buy them—for your tennis matches, for your adventurous voyages, for your camping—at most good shoe stores for as little as $1.00 and as much as $4.00, depending upon the model you choose. They are not Keds unless the name "Keds" is on the shoe.

United States Rubber Company

General Offices, 1790 Broadway, N. Y.

Keds now come in many colors. Here at the left is Keds "Gladiator"—which has red and black soles, and trimmings and uppers of white or suntan.

There are more than 31 different Keds—star models for basketball and tennis, play shoes, camp shoes, beach clogs, pumps and oxfords.

Keds sell for $1.00, $1.25, $1.50, $1.75, and up to $4.00. The more you pay the more you get—but full value whatever you spend.

Ask for Keds by name and be sure of this—that the name "KEDS" is plainly stamped on every shoe you buy.

Keds
REG. U. S. PAT. OFF.
THE SHOE OF CHAMPIONS

THE WORLD'S LARGEST PRODUCER OF RUBBER

United States Rubber Company

Klassy Kicks, 1933 ◄ *U.S. Rubber Co., 1931*

They're on..

..they're off
as quick as a wink!

trim as a glove
light as a slipper

NO SNAPS • NO BUCKLES • NO FASTENER

Paris says

tres chic!

YOU'LL be delighted with Gaytees, particularly if you'd rather not bother with fasteners and such. Gaytees are the new silhouette outershoes that *slip* on—and off—with one quick pull. They gently *give* as they go over your toe, and then settle neatly around your ankle into snug, tailored lines that achieve the smartest kind of effect!

The Parisian fashion world is tremendously enthusiastic about these new Gaytees. That famous designer of women's shoes, Ducerf-Scavini, says, "The *shape* of this outershoe which moulds

itself to the foot, gives a slenderizing effect the ankle which has never been seen befor And Jenny, distinguished style authority, ad "Gaytees achieve that supremely difficult ta for an overshoe—of keeping the foot in un trusive relationship to the ensemble as a whol

But to appreciate the distinctly differe character of Gaytees, you should try them o your own shoes. There's no time like the pres —drop into any of the better shops today a ask for *slip-on* Gaytees—made only by United States Rubber Company.

slip on
Gaytees
REG. U. S. PAT. OFF.

ALSO IN SNAP AND KWIK SLIDE FASTENER STYLES

Enna Jetticks, 1938

Daniel Greens Shoes, 1935

Gaytees, 1932 ◄ *Shuglov, 1932*

Odette Shoes, 1939

KIDDIES PLAY SUITS
REG. U.S. PAT. OFFICE

This Label Means Wear

Our BIG Special — Three Sturdy FABRICS

An Outstanding Value 69¢

Mothers — here's a world of protection and wear for very little money. A complete garment. Material is medium weight cotton fabric in stripes or checks. Full sized. Firmly stitched seams button front, drop seat.
SIZES: 2 to 8 years. State age-size.
42 G 5986 — Blue and white hickory stripe............69¢
42 G 5984 — Blue and white pin checks............69¢
42 G 5925 — Blue and white stripe Victory Cloth......69¢
SIZES: 9 to 12 years.
42 G 5927 — Blue and white stripe Victory Cloth...........79¢

Our Best! 5 Long Wearing Washable Fabrics
CHOICE 88¢ Each

Double Knees Double Seat

A real bargain this sturdy Kiddies' Play Suit. Soft finish Silver Cloud suiting or Pin Stripe Cloth with dark blue trim. Rust-proof nickel buttons, triple stitched seams. Drop seat.
SIZES: 2 to 8 yrs. State age-size. Postpaid.
42 G 5921 — Blue and white pin stripes...88¢
42 G 5924 — Silver Cloud blue and gray stripes..88¢

Pioneer Jrs. Two Denims

Tough, closely woven materials go into Pioneer Jr. Play Suits. All seams triple stitched. Closed top. Bright nickel rust-proof buttons.
SIZES: 2 to 8 years. State age-size. Postpaid.
42 G 5991 — 2-45 heavy blue denim...88¢
42 G 5992 — Blue and black genuine Morocco striped denim.......88¢

Strongly Sewed Double Knees

Full sized Kiddies' Play Suits with rip-proof seams. All points reinforced. Rust-proof nickel buttons. Drop seat. Very low cost.
SIZES: 2 to 8 years. State age-size. Postpaid.
42 G 5972 — Blue and white hickory............88¢
SIZES: 9 to 12 years.
42 G 5973 — Blue and white striped hickory............98¢

79¢ Hickory Stripe, Blue Denim or Two-Oxen Chambray

A PLAY Suit that is a whole garment in itself. Let your youngster wear this sturdy suit for knockabout play, and save his other clothes for dress wear. Every seam is triple-stitched to withstand the strain of small-boy play. Pockets provide space for usual collection of nails and marbles. Drop seat. Button front.
SIZES: 2 to 8 years. State age-size. We Pay Postage.
42 G 5922 — Blue denim.............79¢
42 G 5947 — Genuine 2-oxen blue chambray...............79¢
42 G 5971 — Blue and white hickory stripe..................79¢

Low Priced Economy Overall 49¢

Full cut, sturdily stitched genuine Stifel stripes or blue double and twist denim.
SIZES: 2 to 8 yrs. State age-size. Postpaid.
42 G 5968 — Genuine stifel blue and white stripe...........49¢
42 G 5969 — Plain blue denim......49¢

Double Seat and Knees 85¢

Plenty of wear for active boys. Sturdy quality blue denim or fine weave tan khaki jean. A genuine Kiddies' Play Suit. Rip-proof drop seat feature. Seams triple stitched. Full cut. Double thickness of material at seat and knees.
SIZES: 2 to 8 years. State age-size. We Pay Postage.
42 G 5918 — Blue denim............85¢
42 G 5919 — Tan khaki jean.......85¢

Give Him A Young America Play Suit

FRUIT-OF-THE-LOOM Wash Suits

Sold by Mail Only by Ward's, With Label in Suits
$1.00 Each
State Second and Third Choice
SIZES: 2 to 8 years. State age-size. We Pay Postage.
40 G 3704 — Blues, tans and greens, combination trim. All same or similar to styles shown. Each...$1.00

Stop! I Am the Law! $2.39

What little boy doesn't like to play policeman? Get your boy this strongly made outfit consisting of jacket, long pants...

Be a Real Aviator $3.69

A smart, strongly made Aviator Play Suit that will delight any boy and make him feel "just like a real aviator." Fine quality durable khaki twill. Smartly tailored coat, trim breeches, over-... hat, imitation...

Let's Play Wild West $2.39

Your boy will get loads of fun from this Wild West Suit. The fancy trim is strong khaki pants, sturdy plaid flannelette shirt will stand rough wear. Included in this outfit...

The Big Chief $1.65

Bright trimmings feature this good weight tan khaki Indian Outfit. Headdress has twelve highly colored feathers. The 95c suit is of lighter weight khaki. Postpaid.
EVEN SIZES: 4 to 14 years. Tan only.

Ride 'Em Cowboy — Just Off the Ranch $3.25

A new Cowboy Outfit sold by mail only by Ward's. Sure to please every real boy. Pants made of extra heavy khaki, with bright pointed trimmings. Heavy flannelette assorted plaid shirts...

7-Piece Cowboy Suit $1.39

For only $1.39 you get a Cowboy Suit that will please your boy and help keep his better clothes for dress wear. Long pants of durable khaki have imitation leather fringing. Waist is strong cotton...

Whoopee! Every Boy Wants This Tom Mix Suit $3.75

Genuine Tom Mix Cowboy Outfit. Just what every boy wants when he plays wild west or rodeo. Outfit is strong khaki twill, with chaps of cotton flannel. Fast-color painted decorations on the imitation leather chest plates and chap trimmings. Wool felt Carlsbad Junior hat; lariat; toy pistol and holster...

Tom Mix Cowboy Suit

Kiddies Play Suits, 1930

► *Shoes, 1931*

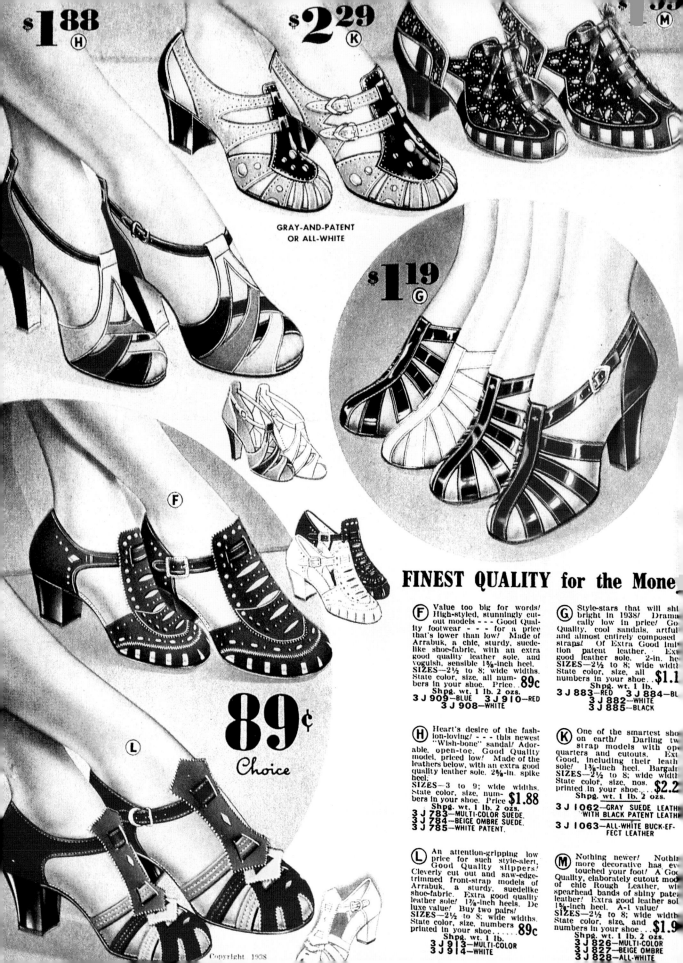

1^{88} (H)

2^{29} (K)

$^{$}$ (M)

GRAY-AND-PATENT
OR ALL-WHITE

1^{19} (G)

(F)

(L)

89¢
Choice

FINEST QUALITY for the Mone

(F) Value too big for words! High-styled, stunningly cut-out models - - - Good Quality footwear - - - for a price that's lower than low! Made of Arrabuk, a chic, sturdy, suede-like shoe-fabric, with an extra good quality leather sole, and voguish, sensible 1⅝-inch heel. SIZES—2½ to 8; wide widths. State color, size, all numbers in your shoe. Price..89c
Shpg. wt. 1 lb. 2 ozs.
3 J 909—BLUE   3 J 910—RED
3 J 908—WHITE

(G) Style-stars that will shi bright in 1938! Drama cally low in price! Go Quality, cool sandals, artful and almost entirely composed straps! Of Extra Good imi tion patent leather. Ext good leather sole. 2-in. he SIZES—2½ to 8; wide width State color, size, all numbers in your shoe...$1.1
Shpg. wt. 1 lb.
3 J 883—RED   3 J 884—BL
3 J 882—WHITE
3 J 885—BLACK

(H) Heart's desire of the fashion-loving! - - - this newest "Wish-bone" sandal! Adorable, open-toe. Good Quality model, priced low! Made of the leathers below, with an extra good quality leather sole. 2⅝-in. spike heel.
SIZES—3 to 9; wide widths. State color, size, numbers in your shoe. Price $1.88
Shpg. wt. 1 lb. 2 ozs.
3 J 783—MULTI-COLOR SUEDE.
3 J 784—BEIGE OMBRE SUEDE.
3 J 785—WHITE PATENT.

(K) One of the smartest sho on earth! Darling tw strap models with op quarters and cutouts. Ext Good, including their leath sole! 1¾-inch heel. Bargai SIZES—2½ to 8; wide width State color, size, nos. $2.2 printed in your shoe.
Shpg. wt. 1 lb. 2 ozs.
3 J 1062—GRAY SUEDE LEATH WITH BLACK PATENT LEATH
3 J 1063—ALL-WHITE BUCK-EF-FECT LEATHER

(L) An attention-gripping low price for such style-alert, Good Quality slippers! Cleverly cut out and saw-edge-trimmed front-strap models of Arrabuk, a sturdy, suedelike shoe-fabric. Extra good quality leather sole! 1⅞-inch heels. De luxe value! Buy two pairs! SIZES—2½ to 8; wide widths. State color, size, numbers printed in your shoe.....89c
Shpg. wt. 1 lb.
3 J 913—MULTI-COLOR
3 J 914—WHITE

(M) Nothing newer! Nothin more decorative has eve touched your foot! A Goo Quality, elaborately cutout mod of chic Rough Leather, wi spearhead bands of shiny pate leather! Extra good leather sol 1¾-inch heel. A-1 value! SIZES—2½ to 8; wide width State color, size, and numbers in your shoe...$1.9
Shpg. wt. 1 lb. 2 ozs.
3 J 826—MULTI-COLOR
3 J 827—BEIGE OMBRE
3 J 828—ALL-WHITE

Copyright 1938

And the winner is...

Americans Wanted More

In the midst of the Depression, when depleted wallets were the norm, people were looking for more of everything—more money, more food, more woman. Gone was the flat-chested flapper of the previous decade. Many American women subscribed to a new standard of beauty, perhaps inspired by full-figured movie icons like Mae West. The mere sentiment of selling extra pounds to women was unique to the time. By decade's end standards of beauty took another turn, and the lean, mean look became the ideal for the remainder of the century.

Darf's auch etwas mehr sein?

Während der Depression, als Schmalhans Küchenmeister war, hätte es für die Amerikaner von allem etwas mehr sein dürfen – mehr Geld, reichhaltigeres Essen, üppigere Frauen. Der flachbrüstige Flapper-Look war passé. Viele amerikanische Frauen folgten dem neuen Schönheitsideal, das durch kurvenreiche Filmstars wie Mae West verkörpert wurde. Schon die bloße Idee, Frauen mit zusätzlichen Pfunde zu beglücken, dürfte einmalig sein. Als der Krieg und die damit verbundene Rationierung drohten, änderte sich das Schönheitsideal erneut, und für den Rest des Jahrhunderts war der ranke und schlanke Look angesagt.

Toujours plus !

En pleine Dépression, alors que la plupart des bourses étaient vides, les Américains en voulaient toujours plus : plus d'argent, plus de nourriture, plus de féminité. Adieu les garçonnes à la poitrine plate des années folles ! De nombreuses Américaines adoptèrent les nouveaux canons de la beauté, sans doute inspirés par de plantureuses idoles de cinéma comme Mae West. Vendre des kilos supplémentaires aux femmes était propre à cette époque. A la fin de la décennie, marquée par la menace de la guerre et le rationnement, les critères de beauté changèrent à nouveau et la silhouette svelte redevint l'idéal féminin jusqu'à la fin du siècle.

Más y más

En plena Depresión, y con los bolsillos vacíos, la población estadounidense pedía más de todo: más dinero, más alimentos y mujeres más femeninas. De ahí que se evaporara el gusto por las mujeres sin pecho, tan en boga en la década precedente. Muchas estadounidenses se sumaron al nuevo patrón de belleza, inspirado en estrellas cinematográficas de curvas sugerentes, como Mae West. En aquellos tiempos, vender a las mujeres la ilusión de engordar unos quilos era una baza segura. Hacia finales de la década, el patrón de belleza dio un nuevo giro y las mujeres esbeltas devinieron el ideal que se impondría durante el resto del siglo.

アメリカ国民は豊かさをお望み

大恐慌のまっただ中で、財布が空っぽなのが一般的な時代、人々はすべてにおいて豊かさを探し求めていた――有り余るお金を、豊富な食品を、豊満な女性を。1920年代の、小さな胸をした当時の現代娘はいなくなった。おそらくメイ・ウェストのようにグラマーな映画界のセックス・シンボルに刺激されてのことだろう、アメリカ女性の多くは新たな美しさの基準を歓迎した。このミラクル体重増加フォーミュラの広告女性はルーベンスが描く女性像ほど豊満ではないし、女性に余分な体重を売るという考えもこの時代だけに特有のものに過ぎない。1930年代の終わりには、戦争の脅威とそれに続く物資供給制限にともなって美しさの基準は別の転機を迎えた。痩せて、貧相な外見がその後の理想となった。

I HAVE PLENTY OF DATES SINCE I'VE PUT ON 10 POUNDS

Skinny? New easy way adds 5 to 15 lbs. *quick*

DOCTORS for years have prescribed yeast to build up health. But now with this new yeast discovery in little tablets you get far greater results — health, and also solid, attractive flesh—*and in a far shorter time!*

Not only are thousands quickly gaining beauty-bringing pounds, but also clear, radiant skin, freedom from indigestion, constipation and nervousness, glorious new pep.

This amazing new product, Ironized Yeast, is made from special *brewers' ale yeast* imported from Europe—the richest yeast known —which by a new process is concentrated 7 times—*made 7 times more powerful.*

But that is not all! This rich yeast is then ironized with 3 special kinds of iron.

Day after day, as you take Ironized Yeast tablets, watch flat chest develop, skinny limbs round out attractively, skin clear to beauty—you're an entirely new person.

Results guaranteed

No matter how skinny and weak you may be, this marvelous new Ironized Yeast should build you up in a few short weeks as it has thousands. If you are not delighted with the results of the very first package, your money instantly refunded.

Special FREE offer!

To start you building up your health right away, we make this absolutely FREE offer. Purchase a package of Ironized Yeast tablets at once, cut out the seal on the box and mail it to us with a clipping of this paragraph. We will send you a fascinating new book on health, "New Facts About Your Body," by a well-known authority. Remember, results are guaranteed with the very first package — *or your money refunded.* At all druggists. Ironized Yeast Company, Inc., Dept. 128, Atlanta, Ga.

Posed by professional models

Ironized Yeast Co., 1935

Every woman a
meal-time magician..

Thanks to this Quality tuna.

White Star Tuna, 1939 ◄◄ *Sperry Flour, 1939* ◄ *Baker's Chocolate, 1933*

"We're glad we live here"

Now, more than ever, children adore the good things made with Crisco, the <u>miracle</u> shortening

Look! The new super-creamed Crisco offers you
5 new cooking miracles!

1. *A miracle of creaminess for you!* This new Crisco was creamed and creamed, over and over. What a help in making cakes! No more beat—beat—beat till your arms "drop off." You'll find it easy to mix this new fluffy Crisco with sugar and eggs—*in only 30 seconds!*

2. *And your cakes will be miracles!* . . . so much fluffier you'll be delighted! This wonderfully fluffy Crisco is the creamiest shortening of all—it gives cakes an airy-light texture. And the creamy flavor of Crisco is the secret of more delicate-tasting cakes.

3. *Now for you—miraculously tender pastry.* And here's how! Use the new super-creamed Crisco—it blends much finer, giving you a pastry mix that needs very little water. Your dough will be much easier to handle. And—"Oh!—what tender pies you

make!" your husband and children will tell you.

4. *Miraculous fried foods for all the family!* Fry the pleasant way with Crisco—with no smoke or smells. Get fried foods that make you hungry at first sight!—as crisp and brown outside as if broiled—as wholesome and tender inside as if baked! The kind children can eat safely.

5. *Best miracle of all—miraculous digestibility!* Now children *can* take their choice of "grown-up" foods like pies and fried foods—if you use Crisco, the lightest vegetable shortening. As doctors know, with Crisco it's easier to cook light, digestible foods. Yet Crisco foods give extra-energy—just what fast growing youngsters need most!

Try Crisco today! Your cooking will be easier—your dinners will be grand surprises—and your family's digestions will be happier!

SAVE MONEY! Get a saving on the price per pound of Crisco—buy the thrifty 3-lb. size! This is the handy size to use when you make cakes, pies and fried foods! Don't crowd this 3-lb. Crisco in your refrigerator. Crisco is different! It keeps fresh and creamy on a handy kitchen shelf.

TRADEMARK REG. U. S. PAT. OFF.

Crisco, 1937

▶ *Twins, 1937*

TWINS

THE DONUT TOWER looms high above the beautiful San Francisco World's Fair... and attracts thousands of hungry Fair-goers who are discovering that Tested Quality Donuts are the tastiest treasure on Treasure Island!

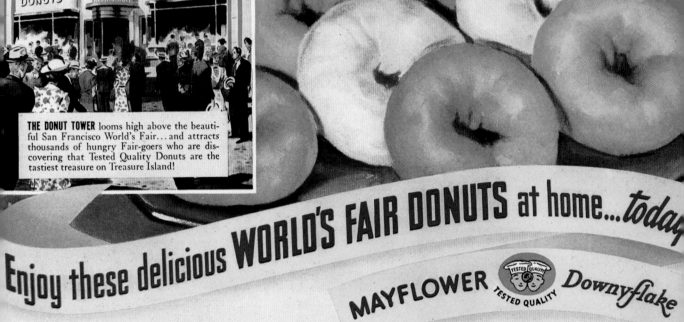

Enjoy these delicious WORLD'S FAIR DONUTS at home... today

MAYFLOWER · TESTED QUALITY · Downyflake

HOORAY! Now *you* can enjoy these melt-in-your-mouth donuts that millions of people at both World's Fairs are raving about! Your own baker, donut shop, or food store has these *extra-special* donuts that bear the famous Seal of Tested Quality.

LOOK! Is it any wonder they're America's *prize* donuts? For Tested Quality Donuts are made from certified milk... selected quality eggs... sun-ripened wheat... and pure vegetable shortening! Give the children all they want with their milk or cocoa... Tested Quality Donuts are wholesome, pure, and digestible.

SURPRISE your family with this grand taste-treat *today*. You will find these special donuts under various brand names, including Mayflower and Downyflake. Just be sure the Tested Quality Seal is on the package and you can be sure you're getting the best donuts in town!

THE DONUT CASINO, at the New York World's F is a striking monument to the glorious good of Mayflower Tested Quality Donuts. Cro are flocking here—and to the Donut Palac the Amusement Area—for these delicious don

DOUGHNUT CORPORATION OF AMERICA

LOOK FOR THIS SEAL ➤

★ *Different* ★ *Delicious* ★ *Digestible* ★ *Doughnuts*

TESTED QUALITY

Doughnut Corporation of America, New York City · Canadian Doughnut Corporation, Ltd., Toronto, Canada
British Doughnut Co., Ltd., London

FREE TRIPS TO EITHER FAIR! — **88 CASH PRIZES** — Here chance of a lifetime... to spend your vacation at the San Fran or New York World's Fair (whichever you prefer) with all eling expenses paid! Or you may win one of 88 cash prizes! enter the World's Fair Donut Recipe Contest. It's easy—it's Ask your local dealer for *free* entry blank containing full de

Swans Down Cake Flour, 1935

Baker's Chocolate, 1938

Donuts, 1939 ◄ Pillsbury Cake Flour, 1931

Mazola Salad Oil, 1936

PROTECT YOUR BABY

with Foods 57 you know are SAFE!

GIVE baby the food values your doctor wants him to have! Give him Heinz Strained Foods—and play safe. For Heinz Baby Foods bear the Seal of Acceptance of the American Medical Association's Committee on Foods—and that's important. Ask your doctor. He knows the importance of this Seal. He knows that prepared foods which have been accepted by the Committee can be relied on for desired nutritional values.

If you could only watch Heinz Strained Foods being prepared, you would never again spend long hours in your kitchen, cooking and straining baby's food! Luscious, garden-fresh vegetables—sun ripened beauties from model farms ... immaculate Heinz kitchens with modern, scientific equipment glistening in cleanliness ... and Heinz' famous cooks! What a combination! No wonder Heinz Strained Foods are so laden with flavor, so wholesome in nourishment, so rich and ripe in color!

You'll notice, too, that Heinz Strained Food tins are enamel-lined. That's for added protection of flavor. Even in cooking, Heinz excludes flavor-robbing air. When you open a tin of Heinz Strained Foods, you'll know that these luscious puréed vegetables are just as fresh from the garden—possibly even fresher—than the foods you yourself prepare. And babies seem actually to prefer the Heinz taste!

Try Heinz Strained Foods today. Protect your baby's diet—and give yourself a much-needed rest from daily hours of kitchen toil. Your doctor will approve. Then, call your grocer and tell him to send you all nine kinds. They're surprisingly economical!

9 KINDS—1. Strained Vegetable Soup. 2. Peas. 3. Green Beans. 4. Spinach. 5. Carrots. 6. Tomatoes. 7. Beets. 8. Prunes. 9. Cereal.

HEINZ *Accepted* STRAINED FOODS

© 1935 H. J. Heinz Co.

Schoolboys! Schoolgirls! Mothers!

$12,000

Free!

Bread ENERGY FOR Vitality!

Bread, 1934

Diamond Crystal Salt, 1937

Morton's Salt, 1930

Land O' Lakes, 1935

Morton's Salt, 1938

Swift's Brookfield Butter, 1934

Swift's Brookfield Butter, 1934

Swift's Brookfield Butter, 1935

Swift's Brookfield Butter, 1935

▶ *Bordon's, 1939*

Always FRESH!

MAZOLA is always of the same high quality, packed under the most modern, sanitary conditions and comes to you in bright, clean, sealed-tight tins —ALWAYS FRESH!...This delicately flavored, pure vegetable oil is *itself* as good and wholesome to eat as the corn from which it comes...Once you try Mazola, you will always prefer it for your Salad Dressings.

Comes to you all ready to press out and set up. No cutting or pasting. Complete instructions with each Bakery. 56 different pieces. Everything you need to play Wholesale Baker—Retail Baker—and House-to-House Baker. A thrilling and realistic trip through Bakeryland. You can actually turn the dough mixer, put loaves of bread in the oven, haul baked goods in the truck, put cakes, doughnuts, bread and pies in the display cases and take them out again just as real bakers do. You have never seen anything like it. Be the first in your neighborhood to have this fascinating Play Bakery. *Send for yours TODAY!*

To parents This unusual offer is made for two reasons:

First, to induce you to buy and serve the delicious bread made for you by the modern baker—to induce you to find out how the baker saves you time and money, how he gives you and your children the vigor that comes from the rich, quick nourishment of baked foods.

Second, to bring to your children a new and exciting form of amusement that will keep them happy and occupied for hours at a time. Besides being real fun for children of all ages, this Play Bakery will help them to learn many interesting facts about modern commercial baking—one of our oldest and most essential industries.

To teachers Teachers who are interested in the project method of education are invited to avail themselves of this opportunity to procure, for their classroom use, an authentic presentation of the equipment and methods used in the production and sale of commercially baked foods.

USE THIS HANDY COUPON

Pillsbury Flour Mills Company, P. O. Box 511
Minneapolis, Minnesota

Please send me a PLAY BAKERY. I enclose a wrapper (label, or sales slip) taken from a loaf of baker's bread, and 10c in coin.

NAME ....

ADDRESS ....

CITY ....

HERE'S HOW YOU GET IT!

Buy a loaf of any baker's bread (any kind). Send the label, or brand name cut from wrapper, or the sales slip, with 10c (in coin, not stamps) and your name and address to Pillsbury Flour Mills Company, Box 511, Minneapolis, Minnesota. Your Play Bakery will be mailed promptly, and postpaid. This offer is good in the U. S. A. only, and expires October 15, 1936.

IT PAYS TO PATRONIZE YOUR BAKER

Mazola Salad Oil, 1935 ◄ *Pillsbury, 1936*

Aunt Jemima, 1939

Vermont Maid Syrup, 1931

Aunt Jemima, 1935

▶ *Shredded Wheat, 1939*

WHILE THEY LAST
FREE!
WITH 2 PACKAGES OF WHEATIES

NEW "SHIRLEY TEMPLE" OCCASION DISH

Hello Everybody Shirley Temple

Shirley Temple, Fox Films' "Little Bunch of Personality and Charm," whose latest picture, "Heaven's Gate" will soon appear throughout the United States. The very first time Shirley tasted Wheaties, she said: "Um-m-m, these are good!"

This Fascinating Dish Is Worthy in Every Detail to Carry the Name and Picture of Its Famous Child-Actress Sponsor, Shirley Temple. Fashioned of Exquisite Sapphire Blue "Scalloped" Glass, It Will Not Only Be a Delight to Your Child, But at the Same Time a Gay and Valuable Addition to Your Table. It May Be Used for Relishes, Bonbons, Jams, Nuts, Fruits, Etc.

GIVEN FREE AT YOUR GROCER'S
When You Buy 2 Packages of
WHEATIES
The Sensational New Whole Wheat Flake Cereal for Children

Offer Made Solely to Induce You to Prove *in Your Own Home* that Here, at Last, Is One Cereal Your Child Will Eat Without Coaxing or Arguing

OH! WHERE DID YOU GET THIS LOVELY SHIRLEY TEMPLE DISH? ISN'T IT ADORABLE?

IMAGINE....THEY GIVE IT FREE AT THE GROCERS WHEN YOU BUY 2 PACKAGES OF WHEATIES! THE CHILDREN LOVE IT — AND IT'S SO HANDY FOR RELISHES, NUTS, CANDIES AND ALL SORTS OF THINGS

ACCEPT FREE
FROM YOUR GROCER TODAY!
Hurry and Get Your Dish . . . Before Too Late!

And Start Your Child Eating a Great Big Breakfast of Whole Wheat Mornings

ALL you do is go to your grocer—buy two packages of Wheaties—and he will give you this lovely "Shirley Temple" Occasion Dish, fashioned of exquisite sapphire blue "Scalloped" glass. But act at once! Don't disappoint your child by waiting till these bowls are all gone.

By accepting this gift, you introduce to your home this newest, most remarkable cereal for children . . . Wheaties!

Wheaties are real whole wheat . . . magically transformed! Whole wheat in a form so delicious, so utterly tempting that children "go for" it like a party dish. Crispy, crunchy, golden brown flakes . . . as gay and alluring to a child as a French confection. Yet—whole wheat that, with abundant milk or cream, sugar, and some kind of fruit, comprises a breakfast that helps to provide essential food-energy and also to build strong bones and solid flesh. So much so, that it is known today among stars of sport everywhere as a "Breakfast of Champions!"

Get Wheaties from your grocer today, and accept this beautiful "Shirley Temple" Dish. You'll be glad you did.

GOLD MEDAL FOODS, INCORPORATED
of Copr. 1935, by General Mills, Inc.
GENERAL MILLS, INC., MINNEAPOLIS, MINN.

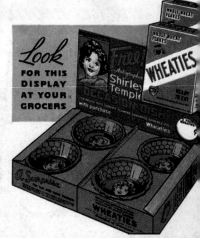

Look FOR THIS DISPLAY AT YOUR GROCERS

3-Minute Oat Flakes, 1931

Bisquick, 1935

Wheaties, 1935 ◄ Post Toasties, 1934

Quaker Puffed Wheat, 1935

I'm *Strong* for it !

My mother got me started eating Shredded Wheat because, believe it or not, I wasn't always such a husky kid. It made me feel pretty good and the coach at school said it was okay. Us fellows can't be bothered fussing about food. We got to have something that sticks to our ribs and doesn't give us stomach ache. Pop eats Shredded Wheat, too, every single morning. Mother knows her stuff, all right!

NATIONAL BISCUIT COMPANY

"Uneeda Bakers"

Be sure to get the package with the picture of Niagara Falls and the N. B. C. Uneeda Seal.

SHREDDED WHEAT

Shredded Wheat, 1934

▶ *Cream Of Wheat, 1937*

The "Champp"

-he needs your help, mother!

GIVE HIM PLENTY OF THIS VITAL FOOD ENERGY EVERY DAY

The "champ" to his playmates... but you know, mother, he is still a very little chap who burns up each day more bodily energy in proportion to his size than a grown-up.

Breakfasts are supremely vital now. For he gets up in the morning with his energy supply at a low point. His system calls for, craves, demands food energy to help him face the tremendously active hours just ahead.

Delicious Cream of Wheat will help supply abundantly that daily food energy . . . and will release it for use speedily, without burdening even delicate digestions.

Join the millions whose children have thrived on Cream of Wheat during the past 42 years!

Sticks to the ribs! Young systems crave nourishment like this. Cream of Wheat offers carbohydrate for quick food energy, protein for muscle building. Yet it is digested with ease. Digestion begins right in the mouth!

Quick food energy of the sort your own doctor will tell you your child needs for activity and growth. This famous hot cereal provides it abundantly. As part of an adequate diet, it also helps stimulate steady, natural weight gains.

CREAM OF WHEAT

Less than ½ cent a serving is the low cost of Cream of Wheat. This cereal cooks up to 6 times its original volume, so that each package yields over 50 generous helpings. It pays to make Cream of Wheat your family breakfast cereal!

3½ million bowls served daily! That's how youngsters love delicious, steaming hot Cream of Wheat. Only the best hard wheat from leading growing areas —heat-treated, purified and blended—can yield such matchless flavor. Order Cream of Wheat today. It's quick and simple to prepare.

IMPORTANT: The Council on Foods of the American Medical Association has awarded to Cream of Wheat the "Seal of Acceptance". This officially indicates that this famous hot cereal and the advertising for it are acceptable to the Council.

ACCEPTED AMERICAN MEDICAL ASS'N.

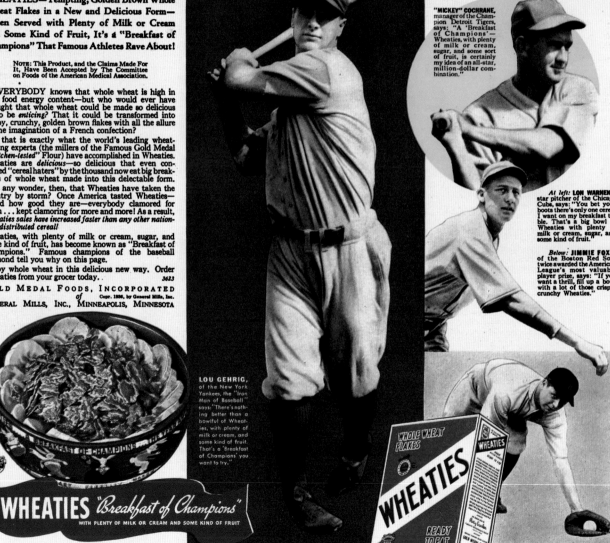

CHAMPIONS OF BASEBALL

INVITE YOU TO TRY A

"Breakfast of Champions"

WHEATIES—Tempting, Golden Brown Whole Wheat Flakes in a New and Delicious Form— When Served with Plenty of Milk or Cream and Some Kind of Fruit, It's a "Breakfast of Champions" That Famous Athletes Rave About!

NOTE: This Product, and the Claims Made For It, Have Been Accepted by The Committee on Foods of the American Medical Association.

EVERYBODY knows that whole wheat is high in food energy content—but who would ever have thought that whole wheat could be made so delicious as to be *enticing?* That it could be transformed into crispy, crunchy, golden brown flakes with all the allure to the imagination of a French confection?

Yet that is exactly what the world's leading wheat-milling experts (the millers of the Famous Gold Medal "*Kitchen-tested*" Flour) have accomplished in Wheaties. Wheaties are *delicious*—so delicious that even confirmed "cereal haters" by the thousand now eat big breakfasts of whole wheat made into this delectable form.

Is it any wonder, then, that Wheaties have taken the country by storm? Once America tasted Wheaties— found how good they are—everybody clamored for them . . . kept clamoring for more and more! As a result, *Wheaties sales have increased faster than any other nationally distributed cereal!*

Wheaties, with plenty of milk or cream, sugar, and some kind of fruit, has become known as "Breakfast of Champions." Famous champions of the baseball diamond tell you why on this page.

Enjoy whole wheat in this delicious new way. Order Wheaties from your grocer today. . *3623*

GOLD MEDAL FOODS, INCORPORATED
of Copr. 1936, by General Mills, Inc.
GENERAL MILLS, INC., MINNEAPOLIS, MINNESOTA

"MICKEY" COCHRANE, manager of the Champion Detroit Tigers, says: "A 'Breakfast of Champions'— Wheaties, with plenty of milk or cream, sugar, and some sort of fruit, is certainly my idea of an all-star, million-dollar combination."

At left: LON WARNEKE, star pitcher of the Chicago Cubs, says: "You bet your boots there's only one cereal I want on my breakfast table. That's a big bowl of Wheaties with plenty of milk or cream, sugar, and some kind of fruit."

Below: JIMMIE FOXX, of the Boston Red Sox, twice awarded the American League's most valuable player prize, says: "If you want a thrill, fill up a bowl with a lot of those crispy, crunchy Wheaties."

LOU GEHRIG, of the New York Yankees, the "Iron Man of Baseball" says: "There's nothing better than a bowlful of Wheaties, with plenty of milk or cream, and some kind of fruit. That's a 'Breakfast of Champions' you want to try."

WHEATIES *"Breakfast of Champions"*
WITH PLENTY OF MILK OR CREAM AND SOME KIND OF FRUIT

WHOLE WHEAT FLAKES

WHEATIES

READY TO EAT

Wheaties, 1936

"IF YOU WANT THE TOPS... *TRY* A *Breakfast of Champions*"

JOE MEDWICK

Baseball's Leading Batter in 1937

Tomorrow Morning Try Wheaties

Yes—they're wheat. *Whole wheat*—in gold-brown toasted flakes! But they taste like whole wheat never tasted before. A new taste. A taste so supremely delicious it has made Wheaties America's fastest growing cereal over the past four years.

But that's not all—Wheaties are crisp. Roasted and toasted to a turn. So crisp they crackle and crunch. Remember—Wheaties are whole wheat with all of its famous food-energy properties retained.

Wheat has always been the basic cereal food of most Americans. It is a source of good body-building protein and supplies a greater percentage of minerals than such grains as corn and rice.

Thus, in Wheaties you get these two things which you want in the ideal breakfast food: The substantial "rib-sticking" food values of whole wheat. PLUS a taste that makes every dish an invitation for another.

Wheaties and the advertising claims made for them are accepted by the Council on Foods of the American Medical Association. Try Wheaties. Order from your grocer today by name W-H-E-A-T-I-E-S. Tomorrow morning join Joe Medwick and other famous champions, in a "Breakfast of Champions"—Wheaties with milk or cream, sugar and some kind of fruit. Copr. 1938, General Mills, Inc.

"Breakfast of Champions" is a reg. trade mark of General Mills

GENERAL MILLS, INC., MINNEAPOLIS, MINN.

IF IT'S A *"Breakfast of Champions"* You Want, This is the Dish—
WHEATIES With Milk or Cream, Sugar and Some Kind of Fruit

FIRST TIME JOE MEDWICK FACED A PROFESSIONAL PITCHER, *HE LINED THE BALL* OVER THE RIGHT FIELD WALL; *THE SECOND TIME, OVER* THE LEFT; *THE THIRD TIME*, OVER THE *RIGHT*; and *THE FOURTH* time, OVER THE *LEFT*. Then He Was Told He Was *TOO YOUNG* to Play!

JOE MEDWICK GOT 26 HITS IN 51 TIMES AT BAT *With His Famous* 'BIG BETSY'—A 47-ounce BAT—SIX OUNCES *HEAVIER than THAT USED by his* TEAM-MATES

And It's Tops With These Stars, Too...

Mel Ott   Joe Di Maggio   Lefty Grove   Carl Hubbell   Bob Feller   Hank Greenberg

Wheaties, 1938

Snap! Crackle! Pop!

SURPRISED? Yes indeed, everybody is surprised when they first hear Kellogg's Rice Krispies crackling out loud in milk or cream. A crisp, cheery call that seems to say—"Listen . . . . get hungry!"

Serve Rice Krispies any time and you'll enjoy them. And when children eat Rice Krispies at supper, or you have a bowlful for a bedtime snack, they promote sound sleep.

Rice Krispies are nourishing and easy to digest. Extra delicious with fruits or honey added. Sold by grocers everywhere. The WAXTITE bag inside the package keeps them oven-fresh. Made by Kellogg in Battle Creek. Quality guaranteed.

SOMETHING EXTRA! On the back of every package of Kellogg's Rice Krispies is a Mother Goose story as told by Kellogg's Singing Lady. Children love these stories, and since new ones are constantly appearing, the more Rice Krispies you buy, the more stories you get.

Kellogg's RICE KRISPIES

Listen...hear!

MEOW GOES THE CAT

BOW-WOW GOES THE DOG

OINK-OINK GOES THE PIG

and *Kellogg's* RICE KRISPIES go

snap! crackle! pop!

You may wonder why Kellogg's Rice Krispies crackle in milk or cream. That is a secret that Kellogg will always keep, but the crunchy crispness and delicious flavor of Rice Krispies is always yours to enjoy.

Adults as well as children welcome the sound of Kellogg's Rice Krispies and their unusual goodness. Nourishing and easy to digest. Extra delicious with fruits or honey added. When Rice Krispies are eaten at the nursery supper or for a bedtime snack, they promote restful sleep.

Grocers everywhere sell Rice Krispies. The WAXTITE bag inside the red-and-green package keeps them oven-fresh. Easy to prepare. Economical too. Many generous servings for a few cents. Made by Kellogg in Battle Creek.

LOOK! On the back of every package of Kellogg's Rice Krispies is a delightful Mother Goose story as told by Kellogg's Singing Lady. New stories appear constantly, and children all over the country eagerly look for them. The more Rice Krispies you buy the more stories you get.

Kellogg's RICE KRISPIES

Kellogg's RICE KRISPIES
crackles IN CREAM

Rice Krispies, 1935

"SHALL I PUT THIS IN THE PACK FOR YOU?"

12" x 15½" Full-Color Copy of this Vernon Grant painting. Free of Advertising Matter. With frame and glass. For only four Kellogg's Rice Krispies package-tops and 25c.

● How would you like to pull *this* plum out of your pile of Christmas gifts? In its *full size*, it is even more beautiful and amusing than it appears here! Christmas Day—and every day—will be brighter, cheerier, merrier with this gay little fellow grinning from the wall! Send for him, or any of the six pictures, now.

Package-tops from Kellogg's Rice Krispies are easy and pleasant to get! For this is one of the most *enjoyable* cereals you ever tasted. It's grains of *real* rice . . . flavored to their very cores by a secret Kellogg method . . . toasted till they turn so fluffy, golden, and crunchy that they *crackle* in milk or cream! Your grocer sells Kellogg's Rice Krispies. Order your packages from him *today!*

SO CRISP they crackle in milk or cream!

snap! crackle! pop!

Kellogg's RICE KRISPIES

Kellogg's RICE KRISPIES

Rice Krispies, 1938

Rice Krispies *Speaking*

crackle! pop! snap!

from the cereal bowl

BROADCASTING the biggest treat of flavor and crispness you ever tasted! Toasted rice bubbles so crisp they snap, crackle and pop in milk or cream!

Kellogg's Rice Krispies are extra delicious with fresh fruits or berries. Sweeten with honey for variety. Delightful for any meal.

One of the best cereals for children ever made. Wholesome rice . . . easy to digest . . . in a tempting form that youngsters can't resist. Splendid for the evening meal.

Convenient. Economical. Always oven-fresh in the sealed WAXTITE bag. No wonder Rice Krispies are the most popular rice cereal in the world. Sold by all grocers. Made by Kellogg in Battle Creek.

Listen!- *get hungry*

Kellogg's RICE KRISPIES
crackles IN CREAM

snap! crackle! pop!

Rice Krispies, 1935 ◀ *Rice Krispies, 1933*

Now...Corn in Tempting "Bubbles"...

SOMETHING ENTIRELY NEW FOR BREAKFAST!

Looks Different...Tastes Different ...Has 4 added Food-Elements not combined in any other well-known Corn Cereal ! [AND THERE'S A REASON IT STAYS CRISP IN MILK OR CREAM!]

HOW WOULD YOU like to have something new, and different, and thrilling, for breakfast—something totally different from anything you ever ate before?

If you would, here's something that will surely appeal to you.

It is a new cereal . . . a corn cereal . . . but it doesn't taste like any corn cereal you've ever known. It's wholly new in form. Entirely new in taste.

We set out deliberately to make a cereal that would be different. We made it in bubbles, as you can see at the left. Airy, dainty bubbles that melt in your mouth . . . Bubbles so crisp and tempting they'll delight you!

And they stay crisp, too . . . do not get all soaked in milk or cream as flat flakes cereals do. Scientific tests *show* they stay crisp longer. The way they're made is the reason!

We Consulted Nutrition Experts

Before making KIX we consulted leading experts in nutrition. Then we "tailor-made" this cereal. During the process of manufacture we added four

food-elements not combined in any other well-known corn cereal!

We added Vitamin B to it. That's the vitamin needed to help promote good appetite and healthy nerves.

We added Vitamin D—"sprayed" to it. That's the vitamin needed for bones and teeth.

Then we added concentrates of Calcium and Phosphorus—minerals required for bodily development.

In short, we added four vital foodfactors not combined in any other ready-to-eat corn cereal!

Corn KIX helps balance the diet. Combats certain common dietary deficiencies.

Thus you'll want to serve it for breakfast every morning. Why not get two packages at your grocer's and start tomorrow?

"Mm-m! They're Grand!"

"Talk about good things to eat — I'm just crazy about KIX, and so are all the other kids in the neighborhood. We eat big bowlfuls for breakfast every morning and ask for more!"
Comments like that are typical of children all over the country.

Corn KIX is made by General Mills, Inc., Minneapolis, Minn.

It's Taking America by Storm!

WHY NOT GET A PACKAGE TODAY?

corn **KIX**

Kix, 1939

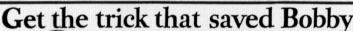

Beech-Nut Gum, 1932

▶ *Nabisco, 1938*

sert a problem?
ing a tea?
ldren's party?
e to nibble?

"Have a Cookie!"

HERE are America's favorite cookies —and some good suggestions for serving them.

See how they can simplify your many daily menu problems...help out in entertaining...make home a more delightful place to be.

N. B. C. cookies are made from the finest ingredients. They're delivered to your food store "home-made" fresh!

See Your Food Dealer for a wide variety of National Biscuit Company crackers and cookies for every occasion.

ERT IN A MINUTE. There are no wrinkles on the brow of the provident housewife who delicious OREO SANDWICH on hand. This combination of two luscious chocolate cookies creamy fondant filling is a scrumptious dainty to top off a meal—and how folks go for it!

AFTERNOON TEA
Serve these VANILLA WAFERS with pride—they're the finest made. Rich in creamy butter, eggs and milk. Special mixing makes them feather light.

ANILLA WAFERS

ARROWROOT BISCUIT

CHILDREN'S PARTY
No upset stomachs from wholesome ARROWROOT BISCUIT—made with easily digestible arrowroot flour. Nourishing milk, eggs and butter in them, too.

FIG NEWTONS

NICE FOR NIBBLING
When your family gets a yen for something sweet—FIG NEWTONS are the perfect answer. Rich cake filled with real honest to goodness fig jam, made from *selected* figs.

LOF
CT
G

PRODUCTS OF NATIONAL BISCUIT COMPANY

Refuse substitutes; buy the advertised brand every time!

for Easter

As correct as a gardenia in your button hole for the Easter parade, is a timely gift to make someone happy on this glad spring holiday! And what, may we ask discreetly, is more fitting than . . . this piquant Chocolate Bazar by Johnston . . . 100 luscious pieces to the pound . . . Smartly boxed in metal, at two and four dollars . . . There are Johnston agencies in all good neighbourhoods.

Johnston's
CHOCOLATES

Johnston's Chocolates, 1930

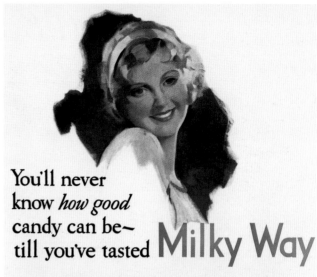

You'll never know *how good* candy can be— till you've tasted Milky Way

UNTIL you actually experience the thrill for your- self, you can't imagine what it's like. No one can tell you that it tastes like this or like that, because it doesn't taste like *anything else in the world.*

The only way to find out what you've been missing is to eat a Milky Way. Take a good, hearty bite through that rich, thick, milk chocolate coating, through that golden layer of creamy caramel and through that flavory center. When you taste the blending of those three flavors, then you'll be able to talk with authority about candy.

It tastes good because it really *is* good, in every sense of the word. It is a milk confection, rich in whole milk, malted

milk, finest milk chocolate and fresh eggs. Every single ingredient is the very best that money can buy.

Each shipment of ingredients is carefully tested for quality, and then used *the same day it arrives.* That's one reason for the wonderful freshness of Milky Way . . . plus the fact that it sells so fast that dealers must keep fresh supplies on the way constantly.

Milky Way is so pure, so full of quality, so skillfully and carefully made, that it has created completely new standards of candy excellence. It is so easily digested that it is the ideal sweet for children as well as adults.

Eat one today . . . now . . . and know how good candy really *can* be.

MARS, INCORPORATED   CHICAGO, ILLINOIS

Milky Way, 1931

Shirley Temple's

SIX FAVORITE DESSERTS

FREE AT YOUR GROCER'S!

Grown-ups as well as little Shirley, love these original, tempting dishes! Ask your grocer for this clever set of six different recipes and let your family enjoy the same desserts often served in Shirley's home.

Top Row:
"CURLY TOP'S" FAVORITE: Apple sauce custard with peanut-butter crumbs and puffs of meringue. SHIRLEY'S 7th BIRTHDAY CAKE: Orange juice flavoring, orange-custard filling, and cocoanut frosting. HOLLYWOOD SHORTCAKE: Fluffy-light gingerbread, fresh strawberries and whipped cream.

Bottom Row:
CHOCOLATE "PUDDING-TART": Real Rocky Road pudding served in a flaky pastry shell. "POOR LITTLE RICH GIRL" CAKE: An ice cream "sandwich", made with cake and chocolate sauce. STUDIO-LUNCH COOKIES: Inexpensive, crisp cakes made of "sugar and spice and everything nice."

TO MAKE THESE DESSERTS EXACTLY AS SHIRLEY TEMPLE PREFERS THEM, BE SURE YOU USE DRIFTED SNOW, THE "HOME-PERFECTED" FLOUR

Get your copy of Shirley Temple's favor- ite desserts from your grocer before they're all gone!

Because they're the choice of a world famous star, don't think these desserts are difficult or costly. You'll make them per- fectly by using Drifted Snow "Home- Perfected" Flour. Variation in flour quality causes one-half of all baking failures. To save you from this, Drifted Snow Flour is tested by Sperry's staff of 117 Western homemakers, living in many states. Only

flour which they find gives uniform results under all conditions is sold as Drifted Snow "Home-Perfected" Flour. That's why it will give you better baking, save you from failures and waste.

Remember, everybody will want Shirley Temple's desserts. Get your copy free at your grocer's and order a sack of Drifted Snow "Home-Perfected" Flour. Then you can make these dishes just the way the little star loves them.   © 1936, Sperry Flour Co., S. F.

36 more recipes!
In addition to the Shirley Temple's des- serts, Sperry offers underall conditions as sold as Drifted Snow "Home-Perfected" Flour.

LOOK FOR THIS DISPLAY AT YOUR GROCER'S

FREE RECIPES

36 RECIPES

DRIFTED SNOW *Home Perfected* **FLOUR**

Sperry Flour, 1936

The thing to do . . .
Give

Whitman's
CHOCOLATES

"What a charming box."
"What a delightful variety of chocolates."
"Such freshness . . . and delicious flavors."

IT's easy to imagine the exclamations of delight that will greet your Valentine gift of Whitman's Chocolates. For Whitman's is a double messenger of good taste—it says "I know *quality*"—and it says "Only the finest for *you.*" See these packages direct from Whitman's, at your dealer's *now.*

VALENTINE'S DAY
FEBRUARY 14th

The SAMPLER

The FAIRHILL

Only hearts marked Whitman's contain Whitman's Candies   Copyright, 1937, Stephen F. Whitman & Son, Inc.

Whitman's Chocolates, 1937

The Happy Moment
— when the show is over

BEECH-NUT GUM

Most popular gum in America is Beech-Nut Peppermint. Try our Spearmint, too, if you enjoy a distinctive flavor!

PEPPERMINT FLAVORED
ALWAYS REFRESHING
BEECH-NUT GUM
PEPPERMINT

BEECH-NUT SPEARMINT Gum

BEECHIES
Gum in a crisp candy coating ... doubly delightful that way! Peppermint, Spearmint, Pepsin.

Beech-Nut SPEARMINT
5¢
BEECHIES

Beech-Nut PEPPERMINT
5¢
BEECHIES
CANDY COATED GUM

Beech-Nut PEPSIN
5¢
BEECHIES
AID DIGESTION

Beech-Nut ORALGENE Chewing Gum
WITH DEHYDRATED MILK OF MAGNESIA
FOR THE TEETH

ORALGENE
The new firmer texture gum that aids mouth health and helps fight mouth acidity. "Chew with a purpose."

SEE THE BEECH-NUT CIRCUS
Biggest Little Show on Earth!
A mechanical marvel, 3 rings of performers, clowns, animals, music 'n' everything! Now touring the country. Be sure to see it when it visits your city.

The Beech-Nut Circus

Beech-Nut Gum, 1937

Everybody knows Charms. Everybody likes them. Charms are absolutely pure candies made from the finest ingredients. Every flavor is superbly delicious. Serve Charms at parties... keep several packages always on hand.

CHARMS COMPANY   NEWARK, N. J.
Walter M. Lowney Co., Ltd.   Montreal, Canada

The purity and goodness of Charms are now further protected by this *improved*, convenient package. They remain always clean and fresh. A trial package will convince you.

Charms, 1937

Wrigley's Gum, 1935

For beauty of lips and neck-line enjoy Double-Mint Gum. Every day! Wherever and whenever convenient. It's a natural beauty exercise.

WRIGLEY'S DOUBLE MINT CHEWING GUM

PEPPERMINT FLAVOR

DOUBLE DISTILLED PEPPERMINT

Baby Ruth, 1939

Baby Ruth, 1937

Wrigley's Gum, 1935 ◀ *Curtiss Candy Co., 1933*

Beech-Nut Gum, 1938

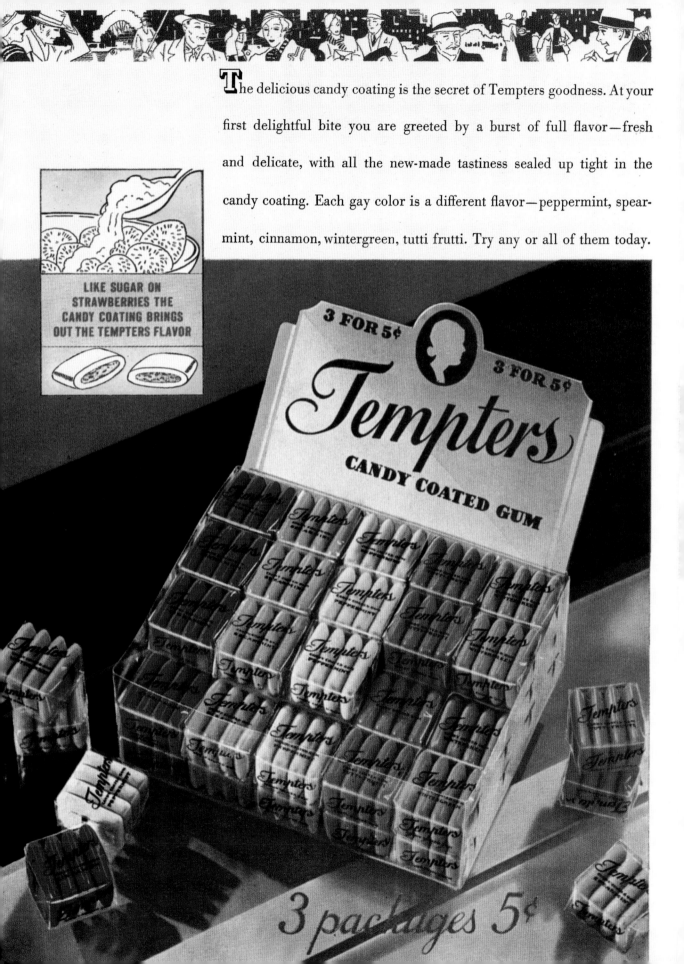

The delicious candy coating is the secret of Tempters goodness. At your first delightful bite you are greeted by a burst of full flavor—fresh and delicate, with all the new-made tastiness sealed up tight in the candy coating. Each gay color is a different flavor—peppermint, spearmint, cinnamon, wintergreen, tutti frutti. Try any or all of them today.

LIKE SUGAR ON STRAWBERRIES THE CANDY COATING BRINGS OUT THE TEMPTERS FLAVOR

3 FOR 5¢
3 FOR 5¢

Tempters
CANDY COATED GUM

3 packages 5¢

The Flavor of 35 *Real Cherries*

is actually used by Royal for a single package of Cherry Gelatin

Only the finest, juiciest cherries...the pick of the crop...are selected for Royal. Blemished or under-ripe cherries are culled out—discarded.

ROYAL CHERRY FLAVOR
ROYAL *Quick Setting* GELATIN DESSERT
CHERRY FLAVOR

For a colorful dessert, serve Royal Cherry Gelatin with pear halves, maraschino cherries and fresh mint

You can tell the difference instantly between ROYAL and flat-tasting, artificially flavored gelatins

PLUMP red cherries...hand-picked and bursting with juice—that's what you taste in Royal Cherry Gelatin.

Not artificial "chemical flavors" made in a test tube! *Real* cherries are used to get that rich, natural taste...the flavor of 35 to 50 cherries for every single package.

You can *smell* the difference the instant you pour on the hot water. With Royal you get just the delicious fragrance of the fruit itself. Never a trace of the unpleasant odor so often noticed in ordinary gelatin desserts.

All 7 Royal flavors are made from pure, wholesome fruit. That's important, Mother, in a dessert so necessary for your children.

Let your whole family enjoy Royal Gelatin today. But be sure to ask for "R-O-Y-A-L"

Seven pure fruit flavors: Cherry, Raspberry, Strawberry, Pineapple, Lemon, Lime or Orange. Also the new Royal Gelatin Aspic, unsweetened, for making jellied meats and salads.

FREE— *Beautiful New Recipe Book:* Over 100 recipes. Natural color photographs. "Movie" directions for moulding and unmoulding. Send front of Royal Gelatin or Royal Pudding package (any flavor).

Royal Gelatin, Product of Standard Brands Incorporated
691 Washington Street, New York City, Dept. G-34
I enclose package front. Please send "Royal Desserts and Salads."

Name
Address
City   State
Copyright, 1936, by Standard Brands Incorporated

Royal Gelatin, 1936

Beech-Nut Gum & Candy, 1937

Jell-O, 1935

Beech-Nut Gum & Candy, 1936

Royal Gelatin, 1937　　　　　▶ *Best Foods, 1936*

Kraft, 1936

Best Foods & Hellmann's, 1939

Best Foods & Hellmann's, 1937

Miracle Whip, 1939

▶ Coca-Cola, 1931

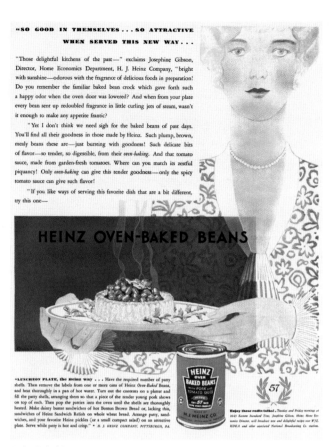

"SO GOOD IN THEMSELVES ... SO ATTRACTIVE WHEN SERVED THIS NEW WAY ...

"Those delightful kitchens of the past—" exclaims Josephine Gibson, Director, Home Economics Department, H. J. Heinz Company, "bright with sunshine—odorous with the fragrance of delicious foods in preparation! Do you remember the familiar baked bean crock which gave forth such a happy odor when the oven door was lowered? And when from your plate every bean sent up redoubled fragrance in little curling jets of steam, wasn't it enough to make any appetite frantic?

"Yet I don't think we need sigh for the baked beans of past days. You'll find all their goodness in those made by Heinz. Such plump, brown, mealy beans these are—just bursting with goodness! Such delicate bits of flavor—so tender, so digestible, from their oven-baking. And that tomato sauce, made from garden-fresh tomatoes. Where can you match its zestful piquancy! Only oven-baking can give this tender goodness—only the spicy tomato sauce can give such flavor!

"If you like ways of serving this favorite dish that are a bit different, try this one—

HEINZ OVEN-BAKED BEANS

"LUNCHEON PLATE, the Heinz way . . . Have the required number of patty shells. Then remove the labels from one or more cans of Heinz Oven-Baked Beans, and heat thoroughly in a pan of hot water. Turn out the contents on a platter and fill the patty shells, arranging them so that a piece of the tender young pork shows on top of each. Then pop the patties into the oven until the shells are thoroughly heated. Make dainty butter sandwiches of hot Boston Brown Bread or, lacking this, sandwiches of Heinz Sandwich Relish on whole wheat bread. Arrange patty, sandwiches, and your favorite Heinz pickles (or a small compact salad) on an attractive plate. Serve while patty is hot and crisp." • H. J. HEINZ COMPANY, PITTSBURGH, PA.

Enjoy these radio talks! Tuesday and Friday mornings at 10:45 Eastern Standard Time, Josephine Gibson, Heinz Home Economic Director, will broadcast new and delightful recipes over WJZ, KDKA and other associated National Broadcasting Co. stations.

H. J. HEINZ CO.

Heinz Baked Beans, 1930

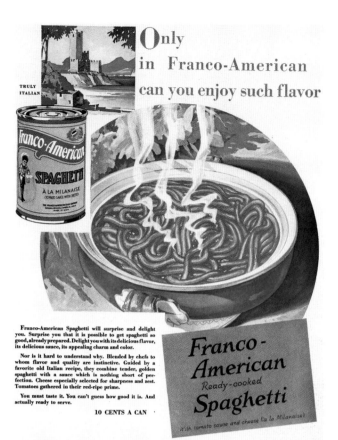

Only in Franco-American can you enjoy such flavor

TRULY ITALIAN

Franco-American SPAGHETTI À LA MILANAISE (TOMATO SAUCE WITH CHEESE) THE FRANCO-AMERICAN FOOD COMPANY

Franco-American Spaghetti will surprise and delight you. Surprise you that it is possible to get spaghetti so good, already prepared. Delight you with its delicious flavor, its delicious sauce, its appealing charm and color.

Nor is it hard to understand why. Blended by chefs to whom flavor and quality are instinctive. Guided by a favorite old Italian recipe, they combine tender, golden spaghetti with a sauce which is nothing short of perfection. Cheese especially selected for sharpness and zest. Tomatoes gathered in their red-ripe prime.

You must taste it. You can't guess how good it is. And actually ready to serve.

10 CENTS A CAN

Franco-American Ready-cooked Spaghetti

With tomato sauce and cheese (à la Milanaise)

Franco-American Spaghetti, 1932

a Symphony of spice and prize Heinz tomatoes !

The wholesome goodness of prize, Heinz-bred tomatoes and rare spices transforms humdrum dishes into savory masterpieces

MEN the world over—from famous chefs to hungry husbands—call Heinz Tomato Ketchup a triumph in the art of spicery! Small wonder too—for this lively, wholesome sauce lends irresistible lure to scores of masculine dishes.

The ancient rule for good spicing is "nothing too much—all things in right proportion". That's the secret of Heinz Tomato Ketchup. No single spice predominates but many flavors are skilfully blended.

A dash of Heinz Ketchup is sheer inspiration for casserole dishes, omelets, gravies, salad dressings and sauces of many kinds! Literally, it brings to your table a world of flavor—for Heinz experts travel around the earth to find the rare spices that give it zest. Through the

Straits of Banda to Amboyna, to Ceylon and Zanzibar where forest trees blossom like pinks in an old-fashioned garden—they search for the choicest of seasonings!

Ketchup making takes time. Big, glistening tomatoes—almost bursting with juice—come straight from the fields to our near-by kitchens. They are sorted, washed, sieved and cooked with pure granulated sugar, Heinz own spices and mellowed vintage vinegar. When the ketchup is boiled down, thick and heavy, it is quickly poured steaming hot into sparkling bottles. Can you smell the aroma? Does it make you hungry? Of course! So, head your grocery list with Heinz Tomato Ketchup. Order "doubles" —one bottle for the table and another for the shelf beside the stove.

Heinz
TOMATO KETCHUP

Tune in Heinz Magazine of the Air. Full half hours—Monday, Wednesday and Friday mornings, 11 E.S.T., 10 C.T., 9 M.T., 8 P.T., 11 noon Pacific time—Columbia Network.

Heinz Spaghetti, 1930 ◄ *Heinz Ketchup, 1936*

SHE USED TO BE A DOUBTER !

... BUT HER DOUBTS TURNED TO AMAZEMENT WHEN HER SISTER PERSUADED HER TO TRY THIS QUICK, EASY WAY TO MAKE BETTER JELLIES AND JAMS.

HERE'S HOW SHE WAS CONVINCED!

MY! THIS IS EASY!

Mrs. Baker had always used the old, "long-boil" method. Consequently she didn't believe jelly-making could be easy. But finally she tried the "short-boil" way, with Certo. (Notice easy way of squeezing juice from the jelly bag with a potato masher!)

NOW I ADD CERTO !

I NEVER SAW ANYTHING SO SPEEDY !

LOOK AT ALL THE EXTRA GLASSES, TOO !

When it came to boiling her jelly . . . what a difference with Certo! Following the easy Certo recipe, she just brought her fruit juice and sugar to a boil . . . added Certo . . . brought to a boil again . . . and boiled hard exactly ½ minute. Presto! The jelly was done!

And now came the biggest surprise of all! The Certo recipe called for only 2 cups of juice . . . Yet when her jelly was skimmed and poured, Mrs. Baker had 11 glasses . . . about four more than she would have had if she'd used the old, long-boil way. (Because of the short boil,

no juice boiled away . . . That's why she got those extra glasses.) Furthermore, the whole job took her less than 15 minutes, after she had her juice ready. Her sister explained that jams were just as easy to make, and more economical also, with Certo!

HOW CLEAR AND SPARKLING !

AND ISN'T IT DELICIOUS ?

And what a relief to have no worry about failures! With Certo, any fruit makes perfect jelly . . . firm, yet tender; clear and sparkling. The flavor is much finer, too (no "boiled-down" taste). Short boiling retains all the natural flavor of the fresh, ripe fruit itself.

NO MYSTERY ABOUT CERTO!
... What it is ... how it acts

CERTO is just natural fruit pectin . . . the substance in fruit that makes jellies jell. Fruits vary in the amount of pectin they contain. Many don't contain enough to make them jell. When you use Certo, with the special Certo recipe for each fruit,

you are getting just the balance of pectin, sugar and fruit juice needed for perfect jam or jelly. Certo eliminates worry about failures . . . saves time, money, work . . . gives much better flavor! You can buy Certo at any grocer's. A product of General Foods.

89 TESTED RECIPES UNDER LABEL

Underneath the label on every Certo bottle is a book of easy, accurate jam and jelly recipes. Different fruits require different handling. That's why Certo gives you separate recipes for each fruit . . . 89 in all! Follow each recipe exactly. © 1935, G. F. Corp.

CERTO

Certo, 1935

547

Royal Baking Powder, 1936

Libby's Corned Beef, 1930

Stahl-Meyer, 1937

Swift's Premium Meats, 1938   ▶ Parade of Progress, 1939

ARADE OF PROGRESS

Stokely's Foods, 1937

Swift's Premium Meats, 1934

Heinz Baked Beans, 1934

Spam, 1938

Libby's Meats, 1935

MILD SAVOR... UNMISTAKABLY PREMIUM

ROUNDS of English muffin—white and gold of poached Brookfield Eggs — Hollandaise — and, crowning touch, criss-cross slices of Premium Bacon. Not just ordinary bacon, but Swift's Premium—mild, savory, tantalizing, with that inimitable Premium taste.

Swift & Company

BE SURE IT IS SWIFT'S PREMIU
*The new Premium "Savor-tite" Ha
ready cooked in the sealed contain
bears the familiar blue Premium lab
The uncooked hams and bacon ca
other identifying marks as well—
word Swift in brown dots down the
length of the side—the markings on
rind and parchment wrappers.*

Swift's Premium
Hams and Bacon

National Biscuit Co., 1934

Certo, 1937

Swift's Premium Meats, 1930 ◄ Sunshine Crackers, 1935

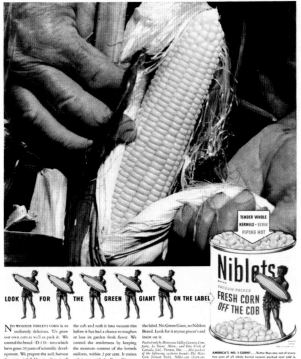

Niblets, 1939

Planter's Peanuts, 1930

Velveeta, 1939

Planter's Peanuts, 1930

▶ Ritz Cracker, 1937

There's RITZ... one friend I always recognize!

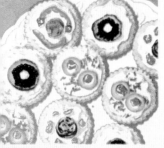

Campbell's Soup, 1933

Campbell's Soup, 1939

Campbell's Soup, 1934

Campbell's Soup, 1931

▶ *Asparagus, 1931*

If home menus were **PRINTED** *these dishes would have French names*

ERVE this enticing hot dish at home—and it is called "asparagus." But downtown—on the ɔd menu of the *maître d'hôtel*, it sparagus *Polonaise*."

, it's the same simple dish you may at home, but—the *maître d'hôtel* ciates *the better-touch* that asparaves the menu, and he names his ng asparagus dishes accordingly.

ll, why not use the same method me—except the printed menu? his: serve Asparagus *Polonaise* tow for dinner. And *c-a-l-l* it Aspar*Polonaise;* get the family to call it agus *Polonaise*. And note the effect ır good salesmanship on the appef everybody at the table.

Asparagus Polonaise

e's the recipe: Turn California Canned agus into a saucepan and heat, using the in the can. Allow 6 to 8 spears for each :. While this is heating, melt 2 table of butter in a frying pan, and add ½ soft bread crumbs. Fry until a golden, ing brown, then add ¼ teaspoon of emove from the fire, add a chopped, ooked egg, and pour over the asparagus, he tips. This recipe will make a real gus treat for four persons.

How very easy it is! Really, it's remarkable how many *better-touch* dishes you can make with asparagus. And it's surely a delight to see how enthusiastically the family will welcome them.

Nor need you ever hesitate to serve asparagus—in breakfast omelets, in luncheon salads, or as hot dinner dishes—for asparagus is a non-fattening delicacy. It fits any diet. It fits every appetite. And that's all the more reason why you should have a supply always on your pantry shelf—both tips and long spears.

California Canned Asparagus is not only a wonderful day-round delicacy, but it is a most convenient food to use.

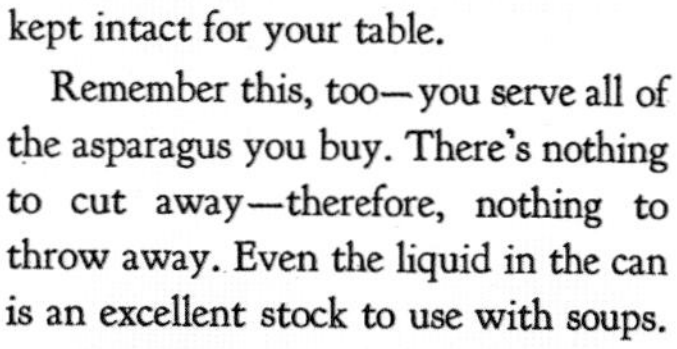

Tips with Chicken à la King

It is ready to serve just as it comes from the can—with all its tender freshness kept intact for your table.

Remember this, too—you serve all of the asparagus you buy. There's nothing to cut away—therefore, nothing to throw away. Even the liquid in the can is an excellent stock to use with soups.

And now there's a new asparagus recipe book—"This Business of Tempting Appetites"—containing dozens of different asparagus dishes to help you keep your menus worthy of your cooking skill. Write for your copy tonight. It's free, of course!

Canners League, Asparagus Section, Dept. 482
800 Adam Grant Bldg., San Francisco, Calif.

Please send me free of charge, the new recipe book, "This Business of Tempting Appetites."

Name ____________________

Address ____________________

City ____________ State ____________

CALIFORNIA CANNED

Asparagus

The World's Most Popular Salad and Vegetable Delicacy

EVERYWHERE...

....the sunny, sparkling favorite!

(*N*ote: When a soup is so good that it goes round the world—that's news for your appetite.)

Many a traveler to foreign shores has come back with a twinkling eye and a merry story about discovering Campbell's Tomato Soup in some far off corner of the earth. And no wonder, for its deliciousness, its tang and zest have made friends for it everywhere. It is far and away *the world's most popular soup.*

And this is why: For over a quarter of a century, choice tomatoes have been specially bred for it in Campbell's hothouses and gardens. Fine, sweet table butter is used to make it still smoother and even more nourishing. The most skillful seasoning adds the final exquisite touch. And, following Campbell's special recipe, internationally known chefs bring this greatest of soups to such perfection that every time you eat it you will say there is not another tomato soup like it.

News is news. But tasting says it all so much better. Why not serve Campbell's Tomato Soup tomorrow?

The wish I wish
This very minute
Is for a plate
With Campbell's ir

Campbell's Soup, 1936

Campbell's Soup, 1935 ◄ Campbell's Soup, 1931

Campbell's Soup, 1934

ALL PURE and WHOLESOME

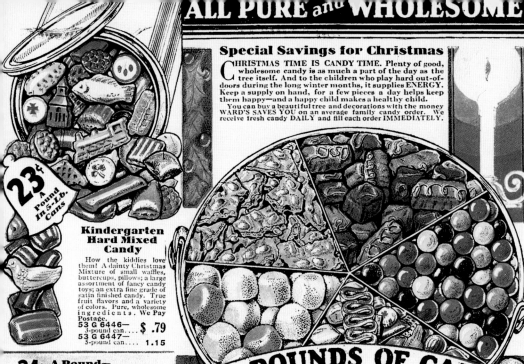

Special Savings for Christmas

CHRISTMAS TIME IS CANDY TIME. Plenty of good, wholesome candy is as much a part of the day as the tree itself. And to the children who play hard out-of-doors during the long winter months, it supplies ENERGY. Keep a supply on hand, for a few pieces a day helps keep them happy—and a happy child makes a healthy child.

You can buy a beautiful tree and decorations with the money WARD'S SAVES YOU on an averaged family candy order. We receive fresh candy DAILY and fill each order IMMEDIATELY.

23¢ A Pound. In 5-Lb. Cans.

Kindergarten Hard Mixed Candy

How the kiddies love them! A dainty Christmas Mixture of small waffles, buttercups, pillows; a large assortment of fancy candy toys; an extra fine grade of satin finished candy. True fruit flavors and a variety of colors. Pure, wholesome ingredients. We Pay Postage.
53 G 6446—
3-pound can.... $ .79
53 G 6447—
5-pound can.... 1.15

4-Quart Size Aluminum Kettle and 5 Lbs. Candy

A wonderful double value! Candy for the children and a useful 4-quart aluminum kettle for mother. Delicious assortment of brilliant satin finished hard candies in a large assortment of shapes. A marvelous variety of fruit flavors and bright colors that always delight the children. Made of pure, wholesome ingredients. We Pay Postage.
553 G 6496—
5 pounds candy in 4-quart kettle for $1.86

Cans and Kettle

TEN POUNDS OF CANDY IN USEFUL PAIL

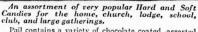

24¢ A Pound— In 5-Pound Boxes

An assortment of very popular Hard and Soft Candies for the home, church, lodge, school, club, and large gatherings.

Pail contains a variety of chocolate coated, assorted flavored creams; assorted, rich fruit-flavored gumdrops; golden brown, fresh crispy peanut brittle; assorted flavored round candy fruit balls; and a popular hard satin finished Christmas mixed candy, freshly made and brightly colored. Each kind of candy is in separate compartment. You will find the galvanized pail very useful.

Fill the empty ornamental holiday boxes, pictured below, with this tempting assortment. Also fine for Santa's use in filling Christmas stockings. We Pay Postage.
553 G 6475—10 pounds candy in galvanized pail. $2.69

Bargain Price Both for $2.69

Crimp Ribbon Mixture

Extra Quality! A fine Old-Time Mixture. Satin finished hard candy, an assortment of pillows, waffles, crimp ribbon, cut rock, broken taffy and many other designs. Various flavors and brilliant colors. An assortment which has proved a big favorite with many of our customers. Like all Ward's candies the ingredients are pure and wholesome. You can depend on quick, accurate service. Postpaid. $ .76
53 G 6471—3-pound box............
53 G 6472—5-pound box............ 1.20

Empty Holiday CANDY BOXES

Folding Boxes with tape handles. Fine for filling with candy to hang on Christmas trees, for Sunday schools, clubs, lodges, etc. We Pay Postage. 53¢
53 G 6699— 30 one-pound boxes............53¢
53 G 6698— 30 half-pound boxes.........33¢
53 G 6697—100 half-pound boxes.........94¢

Fancy Butter Cream

25¢ A Pound— In 5-Pound Box

The eating qualities and purity of this Assortment for the little ones cannot be beat. Soft, tender butter creams made of extra fine, pure, wholesome ingredients. A large assortment of elephants, horses, cows, turkeys, dolls, corn, Santa Claus and many vegetable signs, distinctively colored and appetizingly. We Pay Postage.
53 G 6784—1-pound box............
53 G 6785—2-pound box............
53 G 6786—5-pound box............

French Cream Bonbons

One of the most popular and best known assortments of Christmas Candies. An assortment of deliciously flavored and brightly colored soft crystallized creamy bonbons, jellies and creams with jelly tops in many different shapes and designs. We Pay Postage.
53 G 6598—2-pound box............ $ .59
53 G 6599—5-pound box............ 1.34

Church and School Assortment

30 Pounds Candy With 60 Boxes **$6.39**

53 G 6450—Just the thing for very large groups of children. Enough candy to gladden 60 little hearts! You get 5 pounds each of Chocolate Drops; Gum Drops; French Cream Bonbons; Orange Slices; Ribbon Mixed Candy; and Cut Rock—six kinds of candy. And we include 60 gay, colorful empty boxes to fill with the candy—half a pound in each box. We Pay Postage.

60 Empty Boxes, Half-Pound Size, Included With 30-Lb. Box of Candy

Assorted Fruit Balls

One of the most popular Hard Candies among the children. Assorted flavors and colors. We Pay Postage.
53 G 6738—1-pound can.............32¢
53 G 6739—2-pound can............61¢

Cocoanut Buttercup

Crispy, lustrous, satin finished jacket; assorted colors and flavors filled with creamy macaroon cocoanut. A delightful wholesome tidbit, enjoyed by everyone. A superior grade as only pure and wholesome ingredients are used. We Pay Postage.
53 G 6463—1-pound can............
53 G 6464—3-pound can............

Tropical Fruit Jellies

Extra tender and luscious Jelly Drops. A fine, tempting true fruit flavors and colors. A member of the family will enjoy these quality jellies. We Pay Postage.
53 G 6481—2-pound box............
53 G 6482—5-pound box............

MISS JUNE CLYDE
POPULAR HOLLYWOOD STAR

Candy, 1930 ◄ *Diamond Walnuts, 1934*

561

Libby's, 1938

Lynden Chicken Fricassee, 1938

Libby's Vegetables, 1934

Wessen Oil, 1934 ▶ Dole Pineapple, 1939

WE WANT
DOLE
PINEAPPLE
GEMS

DOLE
PINEAPPLE GEMS
FROM HAWAII
CONTENTS 14-OZ. SHOW

WANTED

omething *different* in fruit. Some-
ng that is appetizing and easy to
gest. It must be convenient and
omical to serve . . . and, above all, a
e and a size that small children can
eat without help.

FOUND

In Hawaii and at grocers everywhere, just what was "wanted"—Dole
Pineapple "Gems"! New and most inviting.
Golden spoon-sized cuts of luscious
pineapple from the juiciest and tenderest part of the fruit.

REWARD

Reward comes to those who serve
"Gems" and to those who eat them—
new color, new luscious flavor, new ideas
for breakfast, and for luncheon
and dinner, appetizers, salads and
desserts. And children love "Gems"!

Sunsweet Prunes, 1938

Sunsweet Prunes, 1934

Dole Pineapple, 1931 ◀ Libby's, 1934

Libby's, 1934

· NEW TREAT FROM HAWAII · · ·
SPOON-SIZE CUTS FROM THE TENDEREST,
JUICIEST PART OF THE PINEAPPLE

DOLE PINEAPPLE GEMS

TRULY HAWAIIAN

Dole Pineapple, 1939

Dole Pineapple, 1935

DOLE PINEAPPLE JUICE

Dole Pineapple, 1938 ◄ *Dole Pineapple, 1935*

Dole Pineapple, 1937

He: *Where, except in Hawaii, can you find such delicious pineapple juice?*

She: *Right over on the mainland by asking your grocer for unsweetened DOLE Hawaiian Pineapple Juice.*

Hawaiian Pineapple Co., Ltd., also packers of Dole Sliced Pineapple, Crushed, Tidbits, and the new Royal Hawaiian Spears, all in the vacuum-sealed cans. Honolulu, Hawaii, U. S. A.— Sales Offices: San Francisco, Calif.

Dole Pineapple, 1937

▶ *Dole Pineapple, 1934*

om these happy islands . . . a pure, golden juice to delight your taste

ese incredibly beautiful islands of Hawaii
with the romance and joy of distant ages
I find that pure, unsweetened Hawaiian
apple Juice has long increased the delight
ving. The finest Hawaiian pineapples are
E-grown. In a modern plant, with every
in the juicing process rigidly controlled,
ure, unsweetened juice is extracted from

these luscious pineapples and swiftly vacuum-
packed in sanitary cans for your protection. Lift
your own glass of cool golden DOLE Pineapple
Juice and say, as they do in the Islands, "Aloha
Nui!"..."A Toast of Friendship and Delight"...
A Toast of good cheer and refreshing goodness!
Hawaiian Pineapple Co., Ltd., Honolulu, Hawaii.
Sales Offices: 215 Market Street, San Francisco.

OLE PINEAPPLE JUICE

The Greatest Gift of all is *Health!*

This Christmas, Give a Box of Rich-Juiced
Sunkist Seedless Navel Oranges
(Now Specially Featured by Your Dealer)

WHAT could better express the warmth of holiday greetings than a box of Sunkist California Oranges —time-honored Christmas fruit!

Golden-skinned—rich with the extra wealth of flavor bestowed by all-year sunshine—they carry in appearance, in taste, in thought, the wish for a happy, healthy year to come.

The Cost Is Reasonable

Sunkist Oranges are plentiful now. Dealers' prices suggest the answer to *several* gift list problems.

Just be sure you order the Sunkist kind. The California Navel Oranges now in season have no seeds — are easier to peel, slice and segment—have *more* of the soluble solids for healthfulness and flavor.

Sunkist
Seedless Navel
Oranges
FROM CALIFORNIA
RICHER JUICE . . . FINER FLAVOR
EASIER TO PEEL, SLICE AND SEGMENT

Two Ideal Christmas Gifts

Give a Sunkist Electric Fruit Juice Extractor, the quick way to whiz out juice—and get more of it! Two models—at your dealer's or sent direct. *(Left)* Sunkist Junior: ivory glass bowl, chromium finish body, black base. Only $12.95, delivered, U.S. *(Right)* Sunkist Juniorette: small but sturdy. Complete with strainer and glass, $6.95, delivered, U. S.

All Four Protective Food Essentials

They give you all four of the now-known prot food essentials—vitamins A, B and C, and cal Guard teeth and gums. Aid digestion. Build u alkaline reserve in a natural way.

So buy a box also for yourself. Start drinkin glasses of fresh Sunkist Orange juice every day *vigorous health.*

FREE—Recipe and Health Booklets

Many delightful fresh fruit drinks are inc among 200 ways to serve oranges and lemons booklet, "Sunkist Recipes for Every Day." of citrus fruits in the healthful diet is fully discus "Fruits That Help Keep the Body Vigorous." Both Write address below. Copr., 1935, California Fruit Growers

ADDRESS—CALIFORNIA FRUIT GROWERS EXC
DEPT. 112, BOX 5030, METRO. STATION, LOS ANGELES,

3 to 12 years — Watch these years when your children's sturdy bodies are at stake

It's the "three to twelve" years that doctors agree are so critical in building the strong, sturdy bodies—the ruddy health—that is every child's birthright. And it's these years, most of all, when they need an abundance of the *sunshine vitamin* that plays so important a part in building strong bones and sound, well-developed teeth.

Most foods, you know, are lacking entirely in this precious vitamin. And especially now, during the winter months when the sun's rays themselves are least effective, you'll find doctors urging Cocomalt as part of every child's regular diet to supply this vital need.

But Cocomalt is much more than a delightful "something-to-drink" that contains Vitamin D. It is really a completely balanced *natural* food drink that combines in scientific proportion the nourishing elements ideally suited to growing children. And it's so delicious, with a flavor so definitely its own, that youngsters take to it as eagerly as they take to playtime.

Not too rich or heavy. Not too sweet. Wholesome. Easy to digest—it helps digest other foods. A wonderfully inviting hot drink for breakfast, a "Mother-may-I-mix-it-myself?" treat—hot or cold after school . . . Why not start now to make it a part of your children's daily diet—and your own as well? You may get Cocomalt at your grocer's in half pound, one pound, and the economical five pound family size.

MORE PRECIOUS THAN DIAMONDS

Few natural foods contain this precious rare vitamin. Yet doctors say Vitamin D—the Sunshine Vitamin—is one of the most important elements for building strength and vitality. That's why Cocomalt should be a part of every child's (and grown-up's) regular diet. It aids in the prevention of rickets (soft bones, bowel legs) and helps build strong bones, sound teeth and sturdy bodies.

Have data Vitamin D make boses strong and healthy? — Read the fascinating story of the Sunshine Vitamin and how it works in the body, as told in the booklet "Children of the Sun." It's FREE—Send the Coupon.

R. B. Davis Company, Hoboken, New Jersey
Please send me free booklet "Children of the Sun."

Name
Street
City
State

HOT OR COLD

Cocomalt
A Delicious Food Drink
Chocolate Flavor
DELICIOUS · NUTRITIOUS

ADDS 70% MORE NOURISHMENT TO MILK

Cocomalt, 1930

REFRESHING!

Straight from Hawaii, the land of tropical fruits and flowers, comes this new, *refreshing* beverage—DOLE pure, unsweetened Hawaiian Pineapple Juice. Drink a cool glassful of this golden fruit juice in the morning before you start the serious business of living. It picks you up and starts you on your way refreshed. Here is pineapple juice which, in flavor and aroma, measures up to your most exacting ideas of how freshly-squeezed pineapple juice should taste.

DOLE Hawaiian Pineapple Juice actually provides quickly available energy because the juice is extracted from field-fresh, *fully-ripened* pineapples in which the easily assimilated fruit sugars (source of energy) have been fully developed. A good source of vitamins A, B and C. It carries the Seal of Acceptance of the American Medical Association's Committee on Foods.

DOLE Pineapples, grown on our plantations, are carefully picked at the exact time when sunshine, rain and soil have ripened them to perfection. DOLE vacuum-packing seals the important nutritive elements and the field-fresh flavor within the can. Available at grocers everywhere. Look for the name "DOLE" stamped on top of the can.

In the morning or mid-afternoon a glass of DOLE Hawaiian Pineapple Juice provides you with quickly available energy . . . And late in the evening a long, cool glass is refreshing and satisfying.

DOLE PINEAPPLE JUICE

Dole Pineapple, 1934

"Father's fussy, too — he insists on Del Monte"

Pure Natural Unsweetened

Wise father—wise little girls! But really, *anybody*, fussy or not, would want more of a juice like this—after a single, delicious, golden glassful!

What a flavor. . . . *What flavor!* It's *sun* created! Mellow and ripe-tasting. Every little juice-drop simply fragrant with tropic richness.

Really *natural* tasting juice. From the finest pineapple! You just know that it is! And packed *fresh*. The way you'd expect DEL MONTE to pack it!

Yes, even a child can notice its special goodness. So think what a thrill *you'll* get—knowing what pineapple juice *should* taste like! Just try it.

Del Monte QUALITY
UNSWEETENED PINEAPPLE JUICE

IT'S DEL MONTE PINEAPPLE JUICE

Sunkist Oranges, 1935 ◄ *Del Monte, 1937*

THE Del Monte VARIETY SHOW

IT'S IN TOWN

A GALAXY OF OLD FAVORITES ★ NEW STARS
★ HEADLINERS FOR EVERY MEAL ★

★ STARRING ★
THE WORLD-RENOWNED
DEL MONTE FRUITS
PEACHES
PINEAPPLE · PEARS
and a distinguished cast

THE CELEBRATED
DEL MONTE VEGETABLE FAMILY

THE 2 SPARKLING
DEL MONTE JUICES

DEL MONTE THE GREAT COFFEE

Del Monte BRAND QUALITY CANNED FOODS

The Del Monte VARIETY SHOW "FIND-OUT" EVENT
MAR 15 APR 18

WATCH YOUR GROCER'S WINDOWS this month

It's a real variety show. And some great star, sure to win applause, DEL MONTE Pears, near you is "stage manager!"

On his shelves and in his windows this month, you'll find an all-star cast of DEL MONTE Foods—specially featured in one gorgeous ensemble.

And what headliners! DEL MONTE Peaches —good for an encore, any time! DEL MONTE Pineapple—big, thick slices from the No. 2½ out all the DEL MONTE Foods your grocer is offering this month. Give the whole DEL MONTE troupe of "variety acts" on your table, and do its great "variety act" on your table. And raise the curtain on better meals!

Del Monte, 1936

From luscious sun-ripened fruit, grown to perfection in Hawaii, comes DOLE Pineapple Juice . . . . Pure, natural, unsweetened . . . . Truly Hawaiian

Dole Pineapple, 1938

▶ *Dole Pineapple, 1938*

PURE, NATURAL UNSWEETENED JUICE FROM SUN-RIPENED PINEAPPLES. FLAVOR AND ZEST THAT ARE TRULY HAWAIIAN

DOLE
PINEAPPLE JUICE

Sunkist Orange Juice, 1931

Welch's Grape Juice, 1932

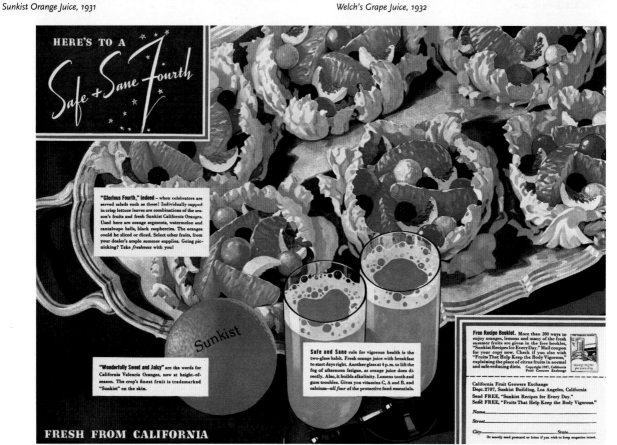

Sunkist Oranges, 1937

Sunkist Oranges, 1935

Sunkist Oranges, 1938

Golly, Mis' Maria

FOLKS JUS' CAN'T HELP HAVIN' A FRIENDLY FEELIN' FOR DIS HEAH COFFEE!

Molasses and January—the boys who "tote aroun'" the coffee to all the Show Boat guests—know what people think of Maxwell House Coffee!

Smiles of satisfaction always greet the mellow, rich, full-bodied goodness that's in every cup of this fine coffee.

For Maxwell House has *everything* that goes to make a coffee delicious...

It is the same matchless blend of choice coffees that the aristocrats of the Old South knew and loved many years ago. No other blend has ever quite compared for rich, satisfying flavor.

ROASTER-FRESH ALWAYS

It brings you, too, the fragrant freshness of the roasting ovens. Packed by the exclusive Vita-Fresh process, Maxwell House always comes to you as fresh and full-flavored as the very hour it was scooped warm from the roaster. And no coffee can be fresher than that!

And it is ground by a newly developed process that assures you perfect uniformity and delicious flavor in every cup

of coffee... whether you make it by the drip, percolator or any other method.

Why don't you try Maxwell House Coffee today? We think you too will be delighted with the smooth, delicious flavor of this famous blend.

And you'll find the price surprisingly low. Millions have learned that it costs no more, in fact, than many coffees of lower quality standards. Maxwell House Coffee is a product of General Foods. It is always Good to the Last Drop.

FRESH AS THE HOUR IT LEFT THE ROASTER — A BLEND THE YEARS HAVE NEVER MATCHED

VITA-FRESH MAXWELL HOUSE Coffee HIGH GRADE

MOLASSES AND JANUARY stop their fun-making long enough to "another cup of coffee" for Maria, Captain Henry's sister. Hear stars of the Maxwell House Show Boat—one of radio's greatest sh every Thursday night. Hear, also, the lovely voices of Lanny Ross, A Hanshaw, Conrad Thibault and Mary Lou, and the glorious music Voorhees and his Show Boat Band. A full hour of gorgeous entertai —every Thursday night! N.B.C. Coast-to-Coast hook-up. ⊙ G. F. Co

MAXWELL HOUSE... GOOD TO THE LAST DROP

The ALL·PURPOSE *Beverage*

SAY GEAR-AR-DELLY

and the ALL·PURPOSE TIN

A *cup* of Ghirardelli's serves every beverage purpose, just as a *tin* of Ghirardelli's serves every *chocolate* purpose. Serve delicious, hot Ghirardelli's wherever an appetizing invigorating beverage is called for ... whether at bedtime for restful, natural sleep ... or for children after school ... for bridge luncheons ... parties ... breakfast ... or for picnics (take it in your Thermos).

Use Ghirardelli's Ground Chocolate for every recipe calling for chocolate ... whether for beverage (see simple directions below) ... or for cakes ... or puddings ... or cookies ... or parfaits ... sundaes ... sauces ... yes, even for chocolate pie-crust! *Full* chocolate flavor, and the convenience of powdered form.

Say "Gear-ar-delly" to your grocer

★ This Recipe Packet is *free* send the coupon below

Listen to the informative, entertaining Ghirardelli radio programs ... NBC: Tuesdays at 10:50 A.M.; Columbia-Don Lee System: Thursdays at 3 P.M. (4 P.M. in Mountain Time zone)

RECIPES

Ghirardelli's Ground Chocolate is equally useful in cooking and baking, or for making delicious hot chocolate beverage . . . When you have a treasured recipe which calls for old-style cake or solid chocolate, use Ghirardelli's instead for more delicate flavor, simpler method, and for economy . . . Use this formula: If your recipe calls for solid chocolate, use ¼ cup of Ghirardelli's Ground Chocolate for each "square" or "ounce" of solid chocolate called for. If it calls for *unsweetened* chocolate, decrease the sugar in your recipe by one tablespoon for each ¼ cupful of Ghirardelli's you use. Four tablespoons make a quarter-cupful. Many useful and delicious chocolate recipes in the Sweet Sixteen Recipe Packet . . Send the coupon for one — *sent free*.

GHIRARDELLI'S *Ground* CHOCOLATE

Maxwell House Coffee, 1934 ◄ *Ghirardelli's Chocolate, 1932*

Tea, 1938

Tea, 1938

Lipton's Tea, 1939

Lipton's Tea, 1938   ▶ *Lipton's Tea, 1938*

NATURE'S FULL FLAVOR
Captive!
...TILL YOU SAY THE WORD

ANOTHER REASON WHY EVERY 7ᵀᴴ FAMILY IN AMERICA BUYS A&P COFFEE

Nature seals the full flavor of coffee in the coffee bean. That's why A&P's famous coffee is delivered to our stores still in the bean. Not until the very instant you buy it, is Nature's flavor seal broken. In this way, and only in this way, do you get the full, fine, fresh flavor of coffee at its best. And you get precisely the correct grind for *your* coffee pot.

Down in South America, A&P maintains its own staff of 60 coffee experts, who buy only the *pick of the plantations.* And from then on through testing, shipping, blending, roasting, and grinding at our own stores, every detail is under A&P's control . . . that's why A&P Coffee is coffee at its best!

Ordinarily such superb quality coffee would be expensive — but because we eliminate many in-between profits and extra handling charges you save worthwhile money on every pound of A&P Coffee you buy. Thousands save up to 10¢ a pound.

So whether you buy A&P Coffee for its glorious flavor or its amazingly low price, you are the winner! Convince yourself next time you buy coffee.

THIS DIAL, WITH SEVEN DIFFERENT GRINDS, WILL BE SET AT THE PRECISELY CORRECT GRIND FOR YOUR TYPE OF COFFEE POT. CORRECT GRINDING IS EXTREMELY IMPORTANT.

See this coffee ground before your eyes at your A&P Store. Laboratory tests prove that A&P Coffee sold in the bean and ground at the moment of purchase, has more flavor, finer flavor, fresher flavor. You will appreciate this superb flavor in every cup of A&P Coffee.

Ground exactly right. Order for Regular Pot (coarse), Percolator (medium), Drip (fine), Vacuum Pot (extra fine).

JOIN THE SMART THOUSANDS WHO SAVE UP TO 10¢ A POUND ON THESE FINE, FRESH COFFEES

EIGHT O'CLOCK COFFEE — RED CIRCLE COFFEE — BOKAR COFFEE

No costly containers are needed to preserve the freshness of A&P whole bean coffee. A&P makes its own inexpensive bags.

You always get the pick of the plantations and yet you pay amazingly low prices for fine, fresh A&P Coffee.

A&P offers you three superb blends of coffee — Eight O'Clock, mild and mellow — Red Circle, rich and full bodied — Bokar, vigorous and winey. Buy one of these fine, fresh coffees at your A&P Store.

AT ALL A&P FOOD STORES

A&P Coffee, 1939

Richer in theol...it
Awakens the Senses

WITHOUT any undesirable after-effect, tea quickens the tempo of life. It pleasantly stimulates the flow of thought, and sharpens the perceptions. Gently but surely it brings to both body and mind an increased sense of well-being and enjoyment.

These facts about tea have long been known and appreciated by the most cultivated peoples in all parts of the world.

What you like in tea is *theol.* This fragrant, flavor-bearing oil is present in all tea, but in varying amounts. Some teas are rich in it — some poor.

More theol is found in *Tender Leaf* Tea than in any but the most costly blends, not ordinarily found in grocery stores. It is made up of the tender leaves alone. They are picked at the height of flavor — during the favorable dry season.

Your grocer carries *Tender Leaf* Tea in two convenient sizes, conveniently priced. Try *this* tea, richer in theol. It lifts you up — and doesn't let you down.

TENDER LEAF TEA — Orange Pekoe and Pekoe — 7-OZ. NET WT.

Tender Leaf Tea, 1934

"Here's MY SECRET *in buying tea!"*

ADDED VALUE IN FLAVOR PROTECTION

TAKE this tip from tea: It is especially delicate and sensitive. Not only does its exquisite flavor escape easily, but it also needs protection from strong odors of surrounding products. That is why so many wise and careful tea-packers safeguard tea with Cellophane transparent wrapping.

You'll get the same enjoyable result when you buy coffee, or dainty, crispy wafers, or any other taste-tempter — if you choose the kind that comes in Cellophane.

SEND FOR THIS NEW BOOK! How to make all sorts of useful, colorful things: Flowers, lampshades, belts, book jackets, gift wraps, party favors, table decorations, etc. Also weaving and crocheting with Cellophane. 32 pages, over a hundred illustrations. Easy to do — and lots of fun! Send 10c. coin or stamps: Dept. T, Du Pont Cellophane Company, Inc., 350 Fifth Avenue, New York City.

Cellophane DU PONT
"Cellophane" is the registered trade-mark of the Du Pont Cellophane Co., Inc.

Canada Dry Ginger Ale, 1938 ◄ Cellophane, 1935

GINGER SNAP!

Got lots of ginger? You need it in this fast world. So try re-fueling occasionally — with Canada Dry! Picks you up...braces, refreshes you! Canada Dry's famous secret process-brings out the full, rich flavor of the world's finest ginger root. With your next meal or whenever you feel the need of a lift...call for Canada Dry. It's gingervating!

Drink Canada Dry Ginger Ale

IT'S GINGERVATING!

Picks you up . . . aids digestion

Copyright 1939, Canada Dry Ginger Ale, Inc. "The Champagne of Ginger Ales"

Canada Dry Ginger Ale, 1939

Perrier, 1934

PERRIER — OF COURSE

*Every Bottle of Perrier Water is
the Perrier Spring in Miniature.*

Perrier Water improves the flavor
of the best whiskey and brandy. It
makes a fine, smooth highball. Imparts to still wines its delightful effervescence. In fact, Perrier glorifies
everything with which it is mixed.
Small wonder that it is the first
choice in table waters wherever fastidious people gather.

Perrier

The Champagne of Table Waters.

Sole Agents for the United States **E. & J. BURKE, LTD,** Long Island City, N. Y.

Perrier, 1934

The Clicquot Club's
CHAMPION THREESOME !

THEY'VE never won a cup in their lives.* . . . But
you should see the goblets and glasses they've filled!
Here is Clicquot Club Pale Dry . . . a really dry
ginger ale. There's wonderful water in Clicquot. It's
pure—not purified. Drawn from deep rock sources,
it comes so cold and clean from the earth that even
distillation is unnecessary! Jamaica's choicest ginger is
carefully blended with certain taste-heighteners that
must be aged to attain their full, delightful zest.
   CLICQUOT CLUB Golden is a more mellow "gingery"

drink—penetrating to the very roots of thirst! Pour it
into a glass and watch the sparkling bubbles start a
gay dance that doesn't end till you drain the last drop!
You can be sure CLICQUOT CLUB Golden is pure and
safe—a wholesome, delightful drink for the children!
   CLICQUOT CLUB Sparkling Water "Soda" is that same
pure water from the earth's depths. Carbonated to an
indescribably fine point, under refrigerated pressure,
its liveliness lasts—long after the cap has been lifted!
   A dealer close by you has these delicious CLICQUOT
beverages . . . in all their various sizes. Look him up
today. . . . Clicquot Club Company, Millis, Mass.

*However, Clicquot points with pride to Gold Medals won at
the San Francisco Exposition in 1915, and at Paris in 1928.*

Clicquot Club PALE DRY
A really dry ginger ale, tangy
and zestful . . . with an aroma
all its own. In full-quart and pint
sizes, and in 12-ounce and split
sizes for hotel and club service.

Clicquot Club GOLDEN
A rich, mellow ginger drink, with
the old Jamaica flavor . . . Aged ingredients blended with crystal-
pure water from deep rock sources.
In full-quart and full-pint sizes.
   Clicquot Club SARSAPARILLA. The
standard for 36 years. In split sizes.

Clicquot Club "SODA"
A pure sparkling water from deep
rock sources, not purified with
chemicals. Highly carbonated. In
full-quart and 12-ounce bottles;
also split sizes for hotels and clubs.

**A FULL QUART
IS 32 OUNCES**
And a full pint is 16
ounces. CLICQUOT CLUB
comes in *full pints* and
full quarts. Also in special hotel and club sizes.
Net bottle contents are
required by law on all
labels. So look before
you buy, for full value!

AN EXTRA DRINK! In every two of Clicquot Club's full-quart or full-pint, honest-
measure bottles, you will find 8 *extra* ounces . . . enough *extra* ginger ale to make an added drink!

Clicquot Club, 1935

"SAY! IF WE COULD ONLY MAKE BUBBLES LIKE THAT !"

There's a long, active life in store for highballs
mixed with White Rock. Prove it yourself.
Pour out a glass of straight White Rock. Even
after thirty minutes, if you listen carefully, you
can still hear its bubbling activity. It's a *mineral*
water, too. ON THE ALKALINE SIDE . . . BETTER FOR YOU

White Rock Water, 1938   ▶ *Mission Dry, 1930*

a Trees and Desert Buttes, California

Your Morning Nip
...Transformed

GOOD News for devotees of the breakfast glass of nge or grapefruit juice! re is pure California t juice in bottles ith the stimulating rkle of sweetened on juice and car- ated water added whet morning appe- s...Now, children will take to r daily health drink with a :...eager for the bubbly glass a its tempting new taste ... erica's modern table bever- is none other than your old y favorite, MISSION DRY, *beverage of the century*. This cious flavor which captured

the country overnight is as wel- come in the morning as at mid- night... and the sparkling purity of MISSION DRY permits gener- ous serving to children as well as grownups... Insist on MISSION DRY, the original or- ange dry... look for the distinctive black bottle.

In two juices ... orange or grapefruit ...wherever the choicest bottled bev- erages are dispensed or sold.

MISSION DRY *Sparkling*

The original orange dry ...the original beverage in black bottles

ORANGE LEMON or GRAPEFRUIT

MISSION DRY *Sparkling*

SERVE ICE COLD

Between scenes of Paramount's super picture of Rome, THE SIGN OF THE CROSS — Fredric March as Marcus Superbus, Claudette Colbert as Empress Poppaea and Director Cecil B. DeMille.

PHOTOGRAPHED IN NATURAL COLORS BY NICKOLAS MURAY

The pause that refreshes "stops the show"

Director DeMille plays host to Marcus Superbus (Fredric March) and Empress Poppaea (Claudette Colbert) with a pause for ice-cold Coca-Cola. Underneath the grandeur that was Rome, they're hard-working actors. Getting hot, tired and thirsty — just as you and I . . . *The pause that refreshes* means to bounce back to normal. Paramount's Hollywood studio provides for it with a fountain in the restaurant and bottled Coca-Cola on the sets. In the part you play in this workaday world, it's ready around the corner from anywhere — and so easy to keep a few bottles in your refrigerator at home.

The pause that refreshes
...directed by Lubitsch

Drink

Coca-Cola

Delicious and Refreshing

COCA-COLA CO., ATLANTA, GA.

as Chevalier *and* MacDonald

finish the famous waltz in Metro-Goldwyn-Mayer's

super picture **"The Merry Widow"**

A photograph of "The Merry Widow" in production. Director Lubitsch invites Prince Danilo (Maurice Chevalier) and The Merry Widow (Jeanette MacDonald) to pause for an ice-cold Coca-Cola, served from M-G-M's famous studio soda fountain.

You have to be on the set to see one scene that's a part of every picture in Hollywood. It's *the pause that refreshes* with ice-cold Coca-Cola. When there's more work ahead and need of good cheer and awakened energy, the director himself often commands this pause. And everybody takes part,—to be refreshed and feel fit, ready for the next scene.

Coca-Cola, 1933 ◄   *Coca-Cola, 1934*

Coca-Cola, 1937

Coca-Cola, 1934

Coca-Cola, 1935

Coca-Cola, 1938

"Take off . . . refreshed"

You're off to a flying start when you start refreshed. So no wonder you find people enjoying *the pause that refreshes* with ice-cold Coca-Cola at airport soda fountains. Thirst asks nothing more.

THE *FEEL* OF REFRESHMENT
MAKES TRAVEL MORE PLEASANT

Coca-Cola, 1938

Pure refreshment

Everybody welcomes *the pause that refreshes* with ice-cold Coca-Cola . . . at bright and cheerful soda fountains. It's a moment that brings friends together . . . to enjoy the pure refreshment of this sociable drink.

"THIRST ASKS NOTHING MORE"

Coca-Cola, 1938

Its taste holds the answer

"Delicious and refreshing." That's ice-cold Coca-Cola . . . the drink everybody knows. Good things from nine sunny climes poured into a single glass. Your thirst asks nothing more.

THIRST STOPS HERE . . .
FOR ICE-COLD COCA-COLA

Coca-Cola, 1939

And the winner is...

Coffee, Tea, or Mam-my
Long before decaf coffee became an American staple, Sanka®was offering "the mister" a 97 % caffeine-free beverage. In marketing this product as a luxury item—a popular advertising strategy—black stereotypes were exploited to appeal to a more elitist consumer. Discomforting as this ad may be, little has changed in today's mainstream advertising mix.

Kaffee, Tee und Kulleraugen
Lange bevor die Amerikaner entkoffeinierten Kaffee zu einem ihrer Grundnahrungsmittel machten, bot die Firma Sanka®dem weißen Herrn und Meister einen zu 97 % koffeinfreien Kaffee an. Um einer elitären Klientel dieses Produkt als Luxusgut anzudienen – eine populäre Werbestrategie –, bediente man sich rassistischer Stereotypen. So unangenehm einem diese Anzeige nun erscheinen mag, viel hat sich bis heute nicht geändert.

Café, thé ou nounou ?
Bien avant que le café décaféiné ne devienne un produit de base pour les Américains, Sanka® proposait déjà une boisson à 97 % sans caféine. Pour commercialiser ce produit comme article de luxe (une stratégie publicitaire fréquemment utilisée), les Noirs étaient exploités comme stéréotypes pour cibler un consommateur plus élitiste. Aussi dérangeante que soit cette affiche aujourd'hui, les recettes des publicités grand public n'ont guère changé depuis.

Café, té... o la bebida especial de la casa
Mucho tiempo antes de que el café descafeinado se convirtiera en un alimento básico en Estados Unidos, Sanka®ofrecía «al señor» una bebida con tan sólo un 3 % de cafeína. En aquella época, una de las estrategias publicitarias populares para comercializar un producto como bien de lujo consistía en utilizar estereotipos de sirvientes negros para atraer a los consumidores más elitistas. Y por muy incómodo que resulte este anuncio, las cosas no han cambiado tanto en la publicidad actual.

コーヒー、紅茶、それとも黒人のばあやが入れたものにする？
カフェイン抜きのコーヒーが人気商品となる以前に、サンカ®は、97％カフェインレスのコーヒー飲料「ミスター」を発売していた。広告を出すにあたり、この商品をぜいたく品として上流階級にアピールするために、黒人に対する固定観念が利用された。この広告を見るときまり悪いような気分になるのは、おそらく今日の大半を占める広告構成とまったく変わりないからだろう。

"You ain't goin' to let the Mister drink coffee <u>at night</u>, is you?"

PERHAPS you're in the same boat as "the Mister." Perhaps the caffein in coffee keeps *you* awake, too.

If so, you can now enjoy coffee at any hour—and sleep the sleep of the just! . . . How? By drinking Sanka Coffee.

Real coffee—and real *sleep!*

Sanka Coffee is real coffee—with 97% of the caffein removed. No fear of sleeplessness, indigestion, jumpy nerves. But, you may ask, does decaffeinated coffee taste as good as other coffees? Every bit! The only thing caffein ever added to coffee was regrets. It isn't even responsible

for that cheery glow. That comes from coffee's own steaming warmth and bracing flavor.

Sanka Coffee is a blend of the choicest Central and South American coffees—roasted to the peak of brown perfection. You prepare it as you've always prepared coffee—boil, percolate or drip. You delight in the same appetizing aroma—the same rich, satisfying flavor.

For proof—make the night-test!

To prove it, drink your first cup of Sanka Coffee at night. Next morning you'll know, from actual experience, that you've discovered a delicious

coffee you can enjoy morning, noon *and* night—without regret!

Packed in vacuum-sealed cans, Sanka Coffee comes to you as fresh and fragrant as the day it was roasted. Your grocer sells it—ground or in the bean—with the guarantee of absolute satisfaction or your money back. Or send in the coupon and 10¢ for a sample can. Sanka Coffee is a product of General Foods. Get a pound to-day.

 Sanka Coffee has been accepted by the Committee on Foods of the American Medical Association with the statement: "Sanka Coffee . . . is free from caffein effect and can be used when other coffee has been forbidden."

Sanka Coffee

REAL COFFEE · 97% CAFFEIN-FREE · *DRINK IT · AND SLEEP!*

General Foods, Battle Creek, Mich. L.H.J.—4-33

Enclosed find 10¢ in stamps to cover the cost of mailing and packing, for which please send me a ¼-lb. sample can of Sanka Coffee.

Name_____

Street _____

City_____ State_____
This offer not good in Canada

Sanka Coffee, 1933

589

On the ground he'll want this new gasoline

IN the air his hand commands smooth-flowing power never marred by troublesome knock or ping.

Of course he wants the same kind of smooth responsive power in his car . . . as do you, and every other motorist who seeks the best.

Now comes SKY CHIEF . . . the answer to this wish. You, yourself, will say there has never been a gasoline like it . . . so brilliantly eager . . . so effortless in its acceleration and pull.

This gasoline is a triumph of high anti-knock quality, instant volatility and surging power adroitly merged to give you a maximum of road enjoyment.

SKY CHIEF is waiting for you now. It costs no more than other premium gasolines. Look for it now beside the famous Fire-Chief pump . . . at Texaco Dealers all over America.

TEXACO Sky Chief

. . . for those who want the best

SKY CHIEF sells for about half the price you paid in 1920 for the then regular gasoline, illustrating the continued success of the petroleum industry in providing the public with better products at lower prices.

FACTS (for the technically minded) VOLATILITY: Sky Chief combines an instant and sustained volatility which gives record quick-starting and acceleration . . . without tendency to vapor lock. ANTI-KNOCK: Its extremely high anti-knock quality permits a higher peak of efficiency and power without knock or ping. ECONOMY: Because you get more work from a given amount of gasoline, there's a distinct saving. Sky Chief shortens miles, stretches gallons, flattens hills.

Texaco Dealers invite you to tune in The Texaco Star Theatre — full hour of all-star entertainment — Every Wednesday Night — Columbia Network — 9:00 E.D.T., 8:00 E.S.T., 8:00 C.D.T., 7:00 C.S.T., 6:00 M.S.T., 5:00 P.S.T.

Texaco, 1939

THIS is the Guarantee behind every FIREBALL Reflector Button

BACK of every Fireball Reflector Button is the responsibility of an organization financially strong and technically exacting. From the molding and annealing of Fireball lenses of optical glass to the relentless final testing, every Fireball button is engineered and manufactured with scientific precision.

Each aspheric Fireball lens is individually inspected by means of an optical projector that magnifies its image. If this image shows the slightest imperfection the lens is rejected. Focal variation as little as 1/1000 of an inch is detected and corresponding adjustment is made in the position of the reflector. This is an important feature of Fireball construction, made possible by the use of a separate reflecting unit of highly polished chromium. The lenses are hermetically sealed into the rustless shells after all moisture has been extracted from the air inside these shells. The buttons are then subjected to the "driving test," projecting their reflection against a mirror at the distance and angles of exposure to approaching headlights. Twice every day samples are taken from the production line for laboratory check. These are first frozen at 7 degrees below zero; then placed immediately on an electric stove and heated to 180 degrees. This is both a shock test and a test to prove that no moisture remains in the air inside the shells. From the stove these buttons are plunged into cold water, repeating the shock test and proving that the buttons are watertight.

In normal service no reflector buttons will ever receive such cruel treatment as that to which every Fireball is subjected before it leaves our hands.

Write For Catalog

THE NATIONAL COLORTYPE CO., INC.
BELLEVUE, KENTUCKY (Opp. Cincinnati, Ohio)

National Colortype Co., 1938

INDIGO

Old AS THE PYRAMIDS . . .
New AS THE 20TH CENTURY

While the pyramids of Cheops were yet young, dyers of Thebes were using indigo. For more than five thousand years, the rich blues of natural indigo were prized for their beauty and fastness.

Then, in 1866, Adolph von Baeyer, a famous German professor, became curious about this age-old dyestuff. He determined to penetrate the secret of its atomic structure.

To his amazement he found that indigo was composed of hydrogen, oxygen, carbon and nitrogen atoms surrounding two benzene residues — the identical substances present in coal-tar products!

It remained only for chemical science to achieve complete synthesis of these elements and a manufactured indigo would result.

Thus, out of this venturesome professor's research grew a new and better way to produce indigo.

Moreover, chemists later discovered that by substituting bromine atoms for hydrogen, various shades of blue were secured. Other variations brought forth yellows, oranges, reds and violets.

The World War dramatically shut off our accustomed European source of these dyestuffs. But, promptly, on behalf of American fabric producers, The Dow Chemical Company undertook to perfect its own process for producing indigo and its derivatives.

These manufacturers well know how speedily and successfully Dow mastered the problem. Incidentally, to Dow also went the distinction of being the first producer of synthetic indigo in this country.

Dow has maintained a distinct leadership in this field. Currently it produces twenty-six different indigoid products. Each is notable for its purity, fastness and uniformity of color. Each is a tangible tribute to Dow research, resourcefulness and ability to produce well.

THE DOW CHEMICAL COMPANY, MIDLAND, MICH.
Branch Sales Offices: 30 Rockefeller Plaza, New York City · Second and Madison Streets, St. Louis · 135 S. La Salle St., Chicago

Dow
CHEMICALS INDISPENSABLE TO INDUSTRY

RCA Victor, 1933 ◄ *Dow Chemicals, 1937*

Transparent Woman

A new substance you can see through made it possible to construct the Transparent Woman. At various exhibits you will be able to view this unique Oil-Plating in your engine it would remarkable model of the complete human body, made visible, clear through. Now if there could just be a similar fine way of showing you the insides of your automobile engine being Oil-Plated by Conoco Germ Processed Oil—patented. No other oil forms Oil-Plating. If you could just see seem like the first really permanent lubrication to you. Can't drain away because it plates to every part . . . can't burn right up . . . can't leave any un-oiled bare spots. Whether you're hustling through a 5000-mile trip, or starting and stopping on a hundred daily errands, your engine stays 100% Oil-Plated. Even without seeing it, you know how Oil-Plating helps. Because when the Conoco Mileage Merchant checks your radiator—and your Germ Processed oil—you "don't need anything." Continental Oil Co.

CONOCO GERM PROCESSED MOTOR OIL

Conoco, 1937 ► *Mc Call Co., 1931*

TENITE *AN EASTMAN PLASTIC*

A PROBLEM OLD AS GLASS

··· AS SOLVED FOR RCA VICTOR

Since glass was first made, craftsmen have sought simple ways of framing it or attaching it to other materials securely, without strain.

A method newly found by plastic molders is to cast directly around glass a frame of Tenite. Tenite-framed glass is in effect one piece—an air-tight, dust-tight, vibration-proof unit which can readily be fastened to wood or metal.

Outstanding examples of this new plastic art, here illustrated, are the Tenite frames molded around the dial glasses of 1938 RCA Victor radios.

Sound manufacturing economies and added sales appeal mark the success of this application. Neither wood nor metal could have duplicated Tenite's perfect union with glass, its lustrous beauty, its flexibility of design or its low assembly cost.

Tenite offers industry more than a new grip on glass. Many manufacturers are finding that their products can be molded of Tenite more economically than they can be cast or machined from any other material. For reasons of beauty, serviceability and cost, Tenite is displacing wood, metal and rubber in a wide variety of everyday uses—steering wheels, door knobs, combs, pencils, buttons, toys, typewriter keys, fish baits, goggles.

TENITE BOOK ON REQUEST

Tenite is a tough, practically unbreakable plastic made of Eastman cellulose acetate, in all colors—plain, variegated, transparent, opaque. Custom molders will gladly tell you about its suitability for your product. Or write us direct for a 52-page book on Tenite and its uses.

TENNESSEE EASTMAN CORPORATION
KINGSPORT, TENN.
(SUBSIDIARY OF EASTMAN KODAK COMPANY)

Tenite Plastic, 1937

▶ *Tenite Plastic, 1939*

Millions steer with TENITE

TENITE STEERING WHEELS are now in the hands of millions of automobile drivers. These plastic wheels—molded over a metal core—have the horn-like toughness and beauty of Tenite combined with the rigidity of metal.

Lustrous color—warmth to the touch—a smooth dirt-resistant surface—and a total absence of exudation that soils hands or gloves—these are the qualities of Tenite which have made it the most widely used plastic for car interior appointments.

In scores of industries, large and small, products are now being molded of Tenite more economically than they could be cast or machined of any other comparable material. High-speed production, reduced finishing operations, added beauty and serviceability are advantages of Tenite which contribute to profitable sales.

Tenite Book on Request

Tenite is a tough, practically unbreakable plastic made of Eastman cellulose esters in an unlimited range of transparent and opaque colors. Leading custom molders will tell you more about its advantages—or write us direct for a 52-page book on Tenite and its uses. Tennessee Eastman Corporation (Subsidiary of the Eastman Kodak Company), Kingsport, Tennessee.

TENITE AN EASTMAN PLASTIC

Myers Water Systems, 1932

THE NATIONAL CASH REGISTER COMPANY ANTICIPATED THE NEW NEEDS OF THESE CHANGING TIMES. ● NOT BY ANY MAGIC OF MIND OR PATTERN OF PALMISTRY. BUT BY VIRTUE OF 50 YEARS' EXPERIENCE FEELING THE PULSE BEATS OF A THOUSAND DIFFERENT TYPES OF BUSINESS. ● NATIONAL ENGINEERS HAVE DEVELOPED NEW CASH REGISTERS, ACCOUNTING MACHINES AND SYSTEMS THAT WILL RECORD AMERICA'S RETURN TO DOING-BUSINESS-AT-A-PROFIT. ● THESE NEW PRODUCTS ARE THE RESULT OF A MAJOR INVESTMENT IN RESEARCH, NEW TOOLS, NEW DIES, NEW SALES IDEAS, NEW SERVICE PLANS. ● FOR MONTHS, OUR PLANTS HAVE BEEN WORKING FULL BLAST, BUILDING THESE MACHINES WHOSE "BRAINS" PROVIDE THE ADDED INFORMATION TODAY'S BUSINESS MAN MUST HAVE. BE HE A MANUFACTURER, A BARBER, A RETAILER, OR A BOOT-BLACK. ● THE NATIONAL CASH REGISTER COMPANY IS PROUD OF THE CONTRIBUTION IT IS AGAIN ABLE TO OFFER AMERICAN BUSINESS.

National Cash Register, 1933

Burroughs Adding Machine Co., 1930

Plaskon Co.,

▶ *NCR Co., 1930*

It's Plastics Picking Time down South

How Chemistry Helps Create New Materials From Nature's Crops

Below Mason and Dixon's line, there's a drift of white across the map. Snowy cotton dapples fields that yesterday were waving green Tomorrow, you will wear it as cloth, write on it as paper, put it to a thousand uses as plastics.

Plastics from *cotton?* Yes—from cotton, from wood pulp and from chemicals that have their genesis deep in the earth as coal and limestone, on the earth as corn, above the earth as elements of the very air itself. To these basic elements, Chemistry adds its acids, plasticizers and solvents, while industry provides its scientific processes and its craftsmanship.

The result? A flood of man-made plastics materials undreamed of a generation ago, bringing new articles of universal usefulness. From steering wheels to hair ornaments, from transparent flower boxes to colorful radio cabinets, the list of products made from plastics is well-nigh endless.

Such is another service of Chemistry to Industry...helping produce new materials for a new age to better serve the needs of all mankind MONSANTO CHEMICAL COMPANY, St. Louis.

HOW MONSANTO SERVES
Monsanto Chemical Company produces 31 chemical products used in the manufacture of plastics. In addition, its Plastics Division at Springfield, Massachusetts, produces these plastics:

Cellulose Acetate • Cellulose Nitrate
Cast Phenolic Resin • Vinyl Acetals
Polystyrene • Resinox Phenolic Compounds
Sheets • Rods • Tubes
Molding Compounds • Castings
Vue-Pak Transparent Packaging Materials

MONSANTO CHEMICAL
SERVING INDUSTRY...WHICH SERVES MANKIN

STOPPING THE SOIL THIEF...
THE TERRACING SHOW-DOWN

Bigger than the job of digging the Panama Canal or building the Mississippi Levee—the biggest of all earth-moving projects is that of constructing terraces to check the erosion that robs United States farms of 3,000,000,000 tons of soil each year.

Pioneer in building track-type tractors, "Caterpillar" has pioneered, too, in developing machines and methods to build better terraces at less cost. With terracing machines, and with "Caterpillar" Diesel Tractors to supply low-cost power to pull those machines, costs have reached new lows. Leading the field, "Caterpillar" provides over 70% of the power terracing equipment used today.

Get the SHOW-DOWN on "Caterpillar" performance on modern terracing operations, and on countless other power tasks. Caterpillar Tractor Co., Peoria, Illinois, U.S.A.

CATERPILLAR
DIESEL

Caterpillar, 1935

Westinghouse, 1939

Color Photography *Takes Wing!*...

A new technique in advertising art is here—the COLAIRPHOTO!

Now the same marvelous natural color effects that have recently been achieved in photographic close-ups of flowers and portraits are possible from the air—as illustrated above.

The Finlay Color Process... developed and perfected for aerial photography by Captain Ashley C. McKinley, offers advertising agencies a new and startling method of achieving *realism*.

For instance, what a grand opportunity for illustrating a steamship account? Or a roofing product? Or a picturesque hotel?

Who could resist the lure of Pinehurst... Bermuda... Hawaii... or Southern California—in natural color?

Perhaps the editor of a college year book, glancing at this page, will find inspiration for a novel series of campus views, photographed from the air in full color.

The possibilities are endless and the prices are only slightly higher than the conventional black and white aerial photograph.

Look into this new medium. Let us show you some sample COLAIRPHOTOS and talk with you about its possibilities.

ASHLEY C. McKINLEY, Inc., Two West Forty-fifth Street, New York City

COL**AIR**PHOTO ... *Aerial Photography In Natural Color*

Monsanto Chemicals, 1939 ◄ *Ashley C. McKinley, Inc., 1933*

Timken—The Dominant Bearing In Heavy Duty Oil Field Equipment

You'll find Timken Tapered Roller Bearings on the really tough jobs everywhere because they ENDURE. In the oil fields, for example, where machinery takes a terrific beating, more Timken Bearings are used in heavy duty equipment than any other make of anti-friction bearing. In fact, in ALL industry—wherever wheels and shafts turn—you will find Timken Bearings. Timken Bearings stand supreme because of Timken's correct design and Timken's 38 years of engineering development and experience. Such sweeping recognition must make you see the advisability of insisting on Timken Bearings when buying automotive vehicles—oil field equipment—construction machinery—railroad cars and locomotives—metal rolling mills or any kind of modern industrial machinery. The Timken Roller Bearing Company, Canton, Ohio.

TIMKEN BEARING EQUIPPED

Timken, 1934

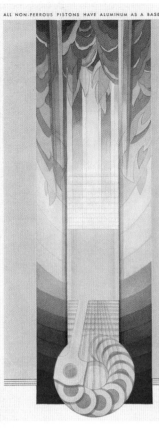

Alcoa Aluminum, 1931

Republic Steel Co., 1933

Technicolor, 1930

Kewanee Boiler, 1936 ▶ *Buick, Oldsmobile, Pontiac Sales Co., 1932*

TURN TO THE "MAN WHO CAN TAKE THE PLACE OF THE SUN"

WHEN your children's last "Good-bye, Mother", is said and they're off to school for another year, turn to your telephone and make certain of your winter's heat . . . so essential to a family's health.

Call your coal merchant; he can replace the sun's summer warmth with clean heat in your home all winter from Famous Reading Anthracite . . . that sootless, smokeless, longer burning, absolutely safe, economical hard coal.

Make your coal merchant your heating adviser. He can tell you how to get safe, automatic heat with hard coal . . . or how to make your present furnace deliver more heat at lower cost.

He has, or can get for you, Famous Reading Anthracite . . . Nature never made nor has man discovered a finer fuel.

Use Reading Anthracite this winter and enjoy plenty of steady heat at low cost.

Send for a free copy of "The Book of Better Heating", an easy-to-read handbook about taking care of any kind of heater using solid fuel. It will aid you to have better heat at lower cost. Write the P and R*, Room 725-S, Reading Terminal, Philadelphia, Penna.

*The Philadelphia and Reading Coal and Iron Company

FAMOUS READING ANTHRACITE

THAT BETTER PENNSYLVANIA HARD COAL

Reading Anthracite, 1931

▶ *Republic Steel Co., 1934*

The entire Republic organization is young, aggressive, alert to the changed production and merchandising conditions of today—and ready to help industry to meet them

KEEPING A STRIDE AHEAD

● Republic's service to industry goes far beyond the meeting of mere tonnage requirements. ● It lies in the constant development of new steels for new uses—in constructive, technical help to fabricators, manufacturers, architects and engineers—in new ideas, new products, new ways of doing things. ● Republic has always had the courage to pioneer—the ability to keep a full stride ahead. That spirit carried along by a young, aggressive organization has made Republic the world's largest producer of alloy steels. ● It is responsible for Enduro, the perfected stainless steel, for Toncan, the rust-resisting iron—for "electric weld" pipe, the Agathon alloys and Republic's other modern metals. ● Republic representatives are easy to reach. You will find them alert, progressive—ready to be of service.

REPUBLIC STEEL CORPORATION

GENERAL OFFICES ✈ R ✈ YOUNGSTOWN, OHIO

AND CARBON STEELS • TONCAN IRON • STAINLESS STEEL • PIPE AND TUBULAR PRODUCTS • BARS AND SHAPES • HOT AND COLD ROLLED STR
• BLACK, BLUE ANNEALED AND GALVANIZED SHEETS • SPECIAL FINISH SHEETS • TIN PLATE • NUTS, BOLTS, RIVETS, ETC. • WIRE PRODUCTS • DIE ROLLED PRODUC

The mystery that took 15 years to solve

A GULF scientist and his associates watched exultantly as the first few drops of golden liquid fell into a test tube.

They were, they believed, on the trail of a completely new refining process—*a process that would produce the finest motor oil the world had ever known.* Yet, unless some one could unravel a scientific mystery, that oil would remain forever a mere laboratory curiosity!

For the new process called for a rare chemical—aluminum chloride—which was prohibitive in cost. No one in the history of chemistry had been able to solve the mystery of how to produce it at a reasonable price.

Yet solved it was—*after 15 solid years of relentless research!* In the end, Gulf scientists had brought the cost of aluminum chloride down to earth. They had made commercially practicable the "Alchlor process" for refining motor oil

(so called from aluminum chloride). They had produced a motor oil that literally deserved the title "world's finest."

That phenomenal motor oil is Gulfpride.

How does the Alchlor process make Gulfpride the world's finest motor oil? Like this. Gulf first makes a fine Pennsylvania motor oil, an oil you would be glad to pay a premium price for . . . and gets out of it 20% residue—containing carbon, gum, and sludge-formers! This Gulf-owned process actually starts where others stop.

That is why Gulfpride gives you the greatest insurance against motor wear that money can buy. It practically eliminates the formation of carbon. It takes you miles farther before you need to add a quart!

Use Gulfpride once, and you will understand why it exceeds every set of quality standards ever written for motor oil, including those of the U. S. Government . . . why leading air lines have chosen it to lubricate all their planes.

At 35¢ a quart (includes Federal tax only) Gulfpride, we believe, will cost you less per mile. Moral: When you change your oil for summer, change to Gulfpride. At the Orange Disc.

Gulf Oil Corporation . . . Gulf Refining Company

THE WORLD'S FINEST MOTOR OIL

100% Pure Pennsylvania · In sealed Cans only

Gulf Refining Co., 1937

This man spends his life keeping you out of second gear

THIS man is engaged in a curious occupation. He is working to make sure that 2,000,000 motorists will be able to drive their cars up hills in high gear.

For this man is one of the control chemists of the Gulf Refining Company. And the machine he operates is an uncanny device which ferrets out and records the "hill power" of gasoline.

Every day, samples of Gulf gasoline are placed in this machine for testing. The engine

is started—and the detonation of the gasoline, or "engine knock," is translated into electrical energy and recorded on a dial. If the electric finger of the gauge falls below the standard that Gulf has set for it by so much as a hair's breadth, the entire lot of gasoline is re-processed.

With the aid of machines such as this, the Gulf Quality Control Laboratory can check Gulf gasoline against competing motor fuels. Without stirring from the laboratory, Gulf chemists can predict which of a dozen motor fuels will best thrust

a car up Pike's Peak or Lookout Mountain.

Thus, Gulf chemists can, and do, make sure that the gasoline you buy under the Gulf disc is unsurpassed by any other fuel of its price.

This, and other Gulf Laboratory tests, have a deep significance for you, the motorist. For they are unceasing assurance that, whether you buy a tankful of Gulf Gasoline, a filling of Gulf motor oil, or any other product wearing the Gulf name, you get the best that engineering science and manufacturing vigilance can produce.

© 1934, GULF REFINING CO., PITTSBURGH, PA.

GULF REFINING COMPANY

Gulf Refining Co., 1934

The Indispensable Partner of Industry

FROM the cereal you eat at breakfast to the bed in which you sleep at night, virtually everything that touches your daily life has been shaped or made possible by machinery.

Were the machines of America to cease turning, civilization as we know it would fall. Overnight, the clock would be turned back three hundred years.

And this Machine Age of ours would not be possible without the helping hand of lubrication. For without its proper lubricant,

every machine in America would soon grind itself into uselessness.

Gulf is proud of the part Gulf Industrial lubricants have played in the progress of American Industry. From its Research Laboratories have come scores of new lubricants which have made possible fresh magic of the machine. And through the services of its lubrication engineers, Industry has been able to solve many a puzzling manufacturing problem.

A special Gulf oil ministers to the machinery that makes the shoes you wear. Another helps

clothe you by keeping the busy spindles of great textile mills whirring smoothly. Still others of Gulf's 400 Industrial lubricants are indispensable partners of the machines that produce America's steel and lumber—the building materials of the nation.

Yes, Gulf is proud of its part in pioneering new aids to Industry.

And Gulf looks forward to playing an even greater part in producing things that make industry more productive and life more livable. © 1934, GULF REFINING CO., PITTSBURGH, PA.

GULF REFINING COMPANY

Gulf Refining Co., 1934

A Place in the Sky

UP from this airport roars a great air-liner, bound for its conquest of time and space.

It is a passenger plane of Eastern Airways, whose fleet of ships is powered and lubricated by Gulf. Its flight is another tribute to Gulf's place in the sky.

Today, from Maine to Mexico, Gulf supplies fuels and lubricants to the winged ships that ply the airways. Many leading air-lines use Gulf products only. Travelers fly millions of miles a year in planes served by Gulf.

Certainly no company is better fitted by experience to hold a leading place in com-

mercial aviation. For since 1916 Gulf has worked to develop special petroleum products for aviation use. Gulf has kept a step ahead in producing better gasolines, better oils, to meet the extraordinary demands of air travel.

This organization also blazed new trails by testing its aviation products in actual service before placing them on the market. Gulf's own ships—a "laboratory of the air" —have been a familiar sight at airports for many years.

But perhaps the most conclusive proof of

the quality of Gulf aviation fuels and lubricants is that they have helped establish no less than six world's records, including those set by the famous St. Louis Robin.

Gulf's record of pioneering and achievement in aviation is not only significant to those who fly, but to all who use petroleum products of any kind.

For the same vision, the same courage, the same drive which carried this company to success in the air, is reflected today in the quality of the 654 products which bear the Gulf name. © 1934, GULF REFINING CO., PITTSBURGH, PA.

GULF REFINING COMPANY

Gulf Refining Co., 1935

▶ *Gulf Refining Co., 1935*

Mile-stone on a road that has no end

ON a downtown corner in a well-known Eastern city is a new and significant building.

It is a service station—one of the most complete and luxurious that may be found anywhere in America. Its beauty is unusual. Yet its significance lies in the fact that here, in stone and steel, is a prediction.

For this service station is an indication of what tomorrow may bring to the highways of America. It offers new and thoughtful conveniences to the travelling public. It is a milestone on the road toward the day when major service stations may be, in effect, depots of travel rather than ports of call.

Gulf believes that motoring is still in a stage of comparative infancy. It believes in its increasing importance in the American scene. And as this form of transportation grows in magnitude, the scope, comforts and facilities of service stations must broaden with it.

With this in mind, Gulf is constantly studying traffic flow and traffic trends, to the end of offering still other small but important comforts to road-weary motorists.

For Gulf believes that good service is only the beginning of better service. It is an evolutionary process which, because of the very nature of the industry we serve, can have no end. © 1935. GULF REFINING CO., PITTSBURGH, PA.

GULF REFINING COMPANY

Republic Steel Co., 1934

Jones & Laughlin, 1934

Kinner, 1930

Dow Chemicals, 1939   ▸ Alcoa Aluminum, 1931   ▸▸ Oldsmobile, 1930

TOUGH—Aluminum Alloy Pistons face a firing squad hundreds of times a minute and *Live*

"Load"—"Ready"—"Aim"—"Fire" —Like a command to a firing squad, your foot on the throttle gives the signal. A wall of exploding flame hits the pistons—but Lynite Pistons are not made to be "killed in action." They are just naturally *tough*.

But mere toughness is not enough. Lynite Pistons are made of light, strong alloys of Alcoa Aluminum, which weigh only ⅓ as much as old-fashioned piston material, and conduct heat many times faster. There lies the difference—*such a difference* that manufacturers, placing perform-ance and your operating economy ahead of price, deliberately pay more for aluminum alloy pistons to give you advantages like these: longer piston life; cooler engines; less carbon; reduced vibration; less wear on bearings and cylinders.

Buy cars equipped with aluminum alloy pistons and you get more performance for your automobile dollar. When replacing pistons in your present car be sure to specify Lynite Pistons made of the light, strong alloys of Alcoa Aluminum. ALUMINUM COMPANY of AMERICA; 2497 Oliver Building, PITTSBURGH, PENNA.

REG. U. S. PAT. OFF.

What a proving ground! Nearly 2 Billion miles of driving each year by owners of these cars* equipped with aluminum alloy pistons.

AUBURN	ESSEX	NASH
AUSTIN	FORD	PACKARD
CHRYSLER	FRANKLIN	PEERLESS
CORD	GRAHAM	PIERCE-ARROW
DE SOTO	HUDSON	PLYMOUTH
DE VAUX	HUPMOBILE	REO
DODGE BROS.	JORDAN	RQLLS-ROYCE
DUESENBERG	LINCOLN	STUDEBAKER
DU PONT	MARMON	STUTZ
DURANT		WILLYS-KNIGHT

*From Automotive Industries

LYNITE PISTONS
AND CONNECTING RODS
MADE OF ALCOA ALUMINUM

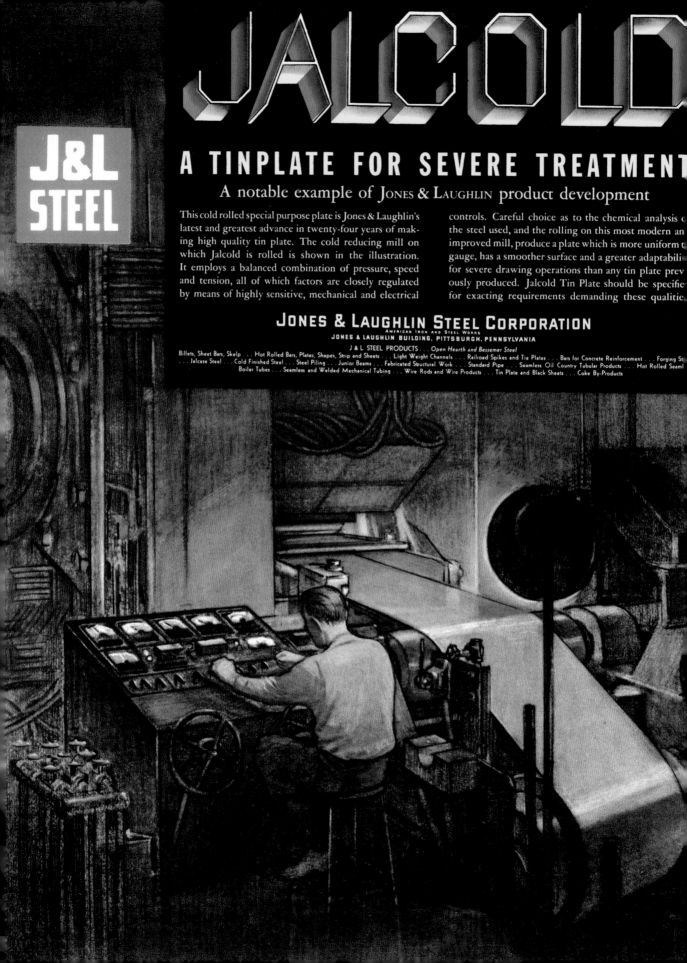

"To save time is to lengthen life—"

"ACCELERATION, rather than structural change, is the key to an understanding of our recent economic developments."

—FROM THE REPORT OF PRESIDENT HOOVER'S COMMITTEE ON RECENT ECONOMIC CHANGES

THE PLOD of the ox-cart. The jog trot of the horse and buggy. The rush of the high-powered motor car. The zoom of the airplane. Acceleration. *Faster* speed all the time. ⌇ Speed and more speed in production, transportation, communication, and as a result, more wealth, more happiness, and yes, more leisure for us all. ⌇ Scientific research has been the pacemaker of this faster, yet more leisurely, existence. At a steadily increasing rate it is giving us hundreds of inventions and improvements which speed up work, save time and money, revolutionize life and labor in the modern age. ⌇ Conceive

how much time modern electric lighting has saved the American people—not to mention the billion dollars a year in lighting bills saved by the repeatedly improved efficiency of the MAZDA lamp. Think of the extraordinary democratization of entertainment and education made possible by the radio tube! ⌇ Both these benefits to the public owe much to the steady flow of discovery and invention from General Electric laboratories. So do the X-ray and cathode-ray tubes, the calorizing of steel, atomic-hydrogen welding, the generation of power for home and industry at steadily lower costs. ⌇ The G-E monogram is a symbol of research. Every product bearing this monogram represents to-day and will represent to-morrow the highest standard of electrical correctness and dependability.

FOR THE HOME—General Electric and its associated companies manufacture a complete line of electric products including G-E MAZDA and G-E Edison MAZDA lamps, G-E refrigerators, G-E fans, G-E vacuum cleaners, G-E wiring systems, Edison Hotpoint heating appliances, and G-E motors for other household electric products. ⌇ ⌇ ⌇

FOR INDUSTRY—Several thousand electric products and appliances, including generating and distributing apparatus, motors, electric heating apparatus, street lights, floodlights, traffic lights, airport lights, Cooper Hewitt lights, Victor X-ray apparatus, motion-picture apparatus, electric locomotives and equipment, and street-car equipment.

GENERAL ELECTRIC

General Electric, 1930

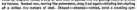

Lifted by magnetic hands, a strip of cold steel is pushed into the glaring mouth of a white hot furnace. Masked men, moving like automatons, drag it out again—blinding hot—hurling off a million tiny meteors of steel. Shaped—reheated—welded, amid a crackling symphony of noises, it rolls down the skids for finishing, cutting, threading, testing, shipping.

.. A MIGHTY SPECTACLE OF STEEL

Picturesque and awe inspiring is this mighty spectacle of steel—the making of pipe by the "lap-weld" process, which, with the "butt-weld" process, holds an important place in the manufacture of pipe. But Republic, alert to changing trends in industry and never content to let well enough alone, has expended $10,000,000 in acquiring and developing a newer method—faster, more economical and far better in results—the instantaneous Electric Weld. Originally used for welding small tubing and conduit, this process now handles sizes up to

sixteen inches. Large users, insisting upon the most rigid standards of quality, have already purchased over four thousand miles of Republic Electric Weld Pipe. Repeat orders, constantly coming in from these original buyers, give tangible evidence of satisfactory service. The pipe of the future will be Electric Weld—and Republic, by its large investment in this revolutionary process, has merely given further evidence of its adoption of a program of continuous improvement and constructive contribution to better products of steel.

REPUBLIC STEEL CORPORATION

HEADQUARTERS: YOUNGSTOWN, OHIO

ALLOY AND CARBON STEELS . TONCAN IRON . STAINLESS STEEL . PIPE AND TUBULAR PRODUCTS . BARS AND SHAPES . HOT AND COLD ROLLED STRIP . COKE . PIG IRON

PLATES . BLACK, BLUE ANNEALED AND GALVANIZED SHEETS . SPECIAL FINISH SHEETS . TIN PLATE . NUTS, BOLTS, RIVETS, ETC. . WIRE PRODUCTS . DIE ROLLED PRODUCTS

Jones & Laughlin, 1934 ◄ *Republic Steel Co., 1931*

THIS YEAR—OWN AND ENJOY A PITCAIRN AUTOGIRO

A scene—not of "some day" but today. This paved courtyard may permit the Pitcairn Autogiro to taxi closer to the door than on some estates, but even the country place of moderate size may have a lawn entirely adequate for the practical use of the Pitcairn Autogiro. If yours is such an estate or if you will select a neighboring field, a Pitcairn representative will gladly demonstrate the complete practicability of this modern American scene. The 1932 Pitcairn Tandem affords greater speed and comfort than before. Full visibility for both pilot and passenger, and dual controls, permit sharing the full enjoyment of flying. With its security now an accepted fact, owning a Pitcairn Tandem is something just as practical to think of for 1932 as a fine motor car. Write for Pitcairn descriptive literature.
PITCAIRN AIRCRAFT, INC., PITCAIRN FIELD, WILLOW GROVE, PA.

Pitcairn Autogiro, 1932

▶ Sterling Engine Co., 1930

The Thrill of Winged Flight

whether in aeroplane or modern runabout, which is virtually a water plane, is similar in both.

A 200 horsepower Sterling Petrel engine drives this Sea-Lyon runabout at over 40 miles per hour. That the thrill may be prolonged, continued on indefinitely, as you will, this Petrel is built 16% larger (779 cubic inches) and with greater power at useable revolutions — 2000 R.P.M.

(Any comparable engine, of 678 cubic inch piston displacement, must turn 300 to 500 revolutions faster, with tremendously increased effort, to equal the Petrel.)

The Sterling Petrel's fuel consumption is satisfactorily less per mile. . . . . . It is safely carbureted.

STERLING ENGINE COMPANY

1270 Niagara Street   Buffalo, N.Y., U.S.A.

12 to 565 H.P.

STERLING

invites you to visit their
Thirtieth Annual Exhibit at the

NATIONAL MOTOR BOAT SHOW

GRAND CENTRAL PALACE, NEW YORK CITY

January 18 to January 26, 1935

Advance models in both gasoline and oil engines, ranging
from 12 to 1000 horsepower.

STERLING   ENGINE CO.
1270 NIAGARA ST.   BUFFALO, N. Y.

Sterling Engine Co., 1935

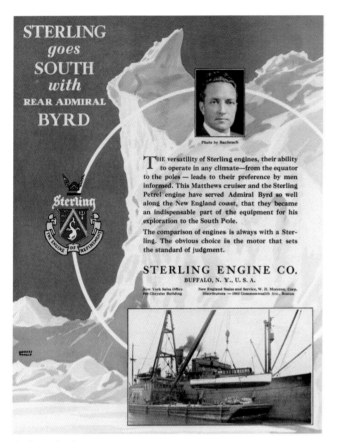

Sterling Engine Co., 1934

Sterling Engine Co., 1934

Sterling Engine Co., 1932

Sterling Engine Co., 1931

FROM moonlight on Rio's Botafogo Crescent to California's golden sunshine · · · · from Palm Beach to the Riviera · · · · wherever sport and romance ride the waters, there you find Dodge Boats · · · · Flashing beauty to give the eye a new delight · · · · fleeting speed to bring new thrills to sportsmen · · · · amazingly low prices well within the reach of thousands who never before could satisfy their wish to own a fine boat · · · · From the 16-foot runabout at $945 to the 45-mile speedster at $4500, Dodge Boats present the utmost in value at the world's lowest prices · · · · Planked with genuine mahogany, the bottoms double planked, with ribs and frames of stout white oak, today's Dodge Fleet excels even the previous craftsmanship of Dodge · · · · The smallest of the fleet makes 30 miles an hour and the largest rides with ease at the racing speed of 45 miles · · · · The Dodge catalog shows and describes all Dodge Boats in 16, 21, 25 and 28 foot lengths, open and closed models · · · · A copy will be sent free on request.

DODGE BOATS

Dodge Boats, 1930

NOW DODGE BOATS join with tarpon, sailfish and sunshine to lure the northern sportsmen · · · · A constant stream of boats flows out from Newport News for southern waters to meet the imperative demand for fine boats at low prices · · · · More Dodge Boats are on their way to South America and Europe's winter playgrounds on the sunny Riviera · · · · Still more hundreds now speeding through the great Dodge plant will accumulate there in anticipation of the Spring demand for these fleet, sleek boats · · · · a demand that will surely outstrip the unprecedented acceptance of last year · · · · With the new year now begun Spring is truly just around the corner · · · · For those whose eagerness is keen, Dodge suggests an order for a Dodge Boat to be delivered when and where you will · · · · months of anticipation added to still more months of joyous realization · · · · Dodge Boats in 16, 21, 25 and 28-foot lengths, with speeds of 30, 35, 38 and 45 miles an hour, suit every boating purpose · · · · Prices of $945, $2100, $2500 and up to $4500, F. O. B. Works, meet every requirement of every purse · · · · Complete catalog on request.

DODGE BOATS

Dodge Boats, 1931

STERLING ENGINES

Matthews 46 foot enclosed bridge deck cruiser. Speed with single Sterling Petrel .20 miles plus, with twin Sterling Petrels, 26 miles.

JUDGE VALUE BY COMPARISON

The Sterling Petrel 180-225 H.P. engine is the better buy for Matthews cruisers. The staunchly built heavily timbered hulls, intended for years of seaworthiness, beautifully refined, require power. Petrel engines contribute years of smooth service with ordinary attention, are more carefully built and longer tested, so that the hazard of "running in" the engine is eliminated. The patented Sterling piston is successful. The engine is lower in height, reducing the center of gravity, but has a long connecting rod, reducing piston side thrust and cylinder wear.

Sterling builds all high powered engines with a counter weighted dynamically balanced crankshaft, accepting a handicap of its added cost, to reduce the forces which otherwise deteriorate an engine. And the Petrel is almost 15% larger than engines of comparative price! Quieter running at less effort, eliminates the need of ever removing the engine from the boat for bearing attention. The additional cost of the Petrel is slight—but more than compensated in desirable attributes, which you are invited to consider. Investigate before you buy.

MODELS FROM 18 TO 565 H.P.

STERLING ENGINE COMPANY • BUFFALO, N.Y., U.S.A.

Sterling Engine Co., 1932

The Record Breaking
FAIRFORM FLYER

36' Fairform Flyer, built by Huckins Yacht Corp., Jacksonville, Fla. Equipped with twin Dolphin Special 6 cylinder Sterling engines 290 H. P. each, 1930 R.P.M.

Modern in design and speed, equipped with established seasoned engines, the new Fairform Flyer suggests a late afternoon cruise—the antithesis of the lawn party of the 'eighties. Or, perhaps a week end journey of exploration—new scenery, open space, relaxation, and kindred terms, that prepare you for Monday with a feeling of having rediscovered America. · · · · ·

STERLING ENGINE COMPANY
BUFFALO, NEW YORK, U.S.A.

W. H. Marston Corp., Distributors, Boston   Bruns, Kimball & Co., Distributors, New York

Sterling Engine Co., 1930   ▶ *Dodge Boat & Plane Co., 1931*

An entirely new deal from the wheels up

. . . that's what Alcoa Aluminum makes possible

LYNITE PISTONS
AND CONNECTING RODS
take punishment and like it

Made from the strong alloys of Alcoa Aluminum which weigh only ⅓ as much as other piston metals, Lynite Pistons and Connecting Rods are naturally light in weight. They are tough —and more than that—they carry off the inferno of heat that surrounds your high compression engine many times faster than metals formerly used.

Keep full strength! Slash weight in half! Such are the revolutionary advantages offered to the automotive field—to all transportation—by Alcoa Aluminum and its light strong alloys.

And with these possibilities at their command, engineers inevitably think of an *entirely different* car, truck, bus, railroad coach, street or subway car, airship and airplane. At once, they plan *completely different* units that will go faster, ride more comfortably and reduce operating costs to far lower levels.

Already the new movement has begun. Take these examples. In the truck field there is the chassis shown above. The frame itself, the differential and rear axle housings—in fact almost everything from trunions to top is made of Alcoa Aluminum. Result, the completed chassis weighs 1½ tons *less* than

a similar one made of steel. In the bus field a new "aluminized" coach has been built that is 4000 lbs lighter. One of the highest powered stock passenger cars has many of its engine, chassis and body part made of aluminum alloys—to be exact, a total of 135 different aluminum parts.

Alcoa Aluminum can be cast, stamped, pressed o forged. It is readily plated with chromium or nickel It is rolled into structural shapes and sheets from which passenger cars, truck and bus bodies, rail road coaches, and street cars are made. Shapes and sheets are carried in stock. There are also available strong aluminum alloy plate in sizes up to 35 ft long, 120 inches wide and ¾ inch thick; rivets bolts and screws. Write for the handbook "Alcoa Aluminum and Its Alloys." Address ALUMINUM COMPANY *of* AMERICA 2497 Oliver Building, PITTSBURGH, PENNSYLVANIA

ALCOA ALUMINUM

Salute to the pioneers of swift travel
...the "aluminized" trains of today

LYNITE PISTONS
AND CONNECTING RODS

for speed boats
or giant planes

"Miss America," racing through a cloud of spray—the giant DO-X steadily soaring through the skies from continent to continent —both were aided by pistons made of the light strong alloys of Alcoa Aluminum. Weighing only ⅓ as much as old-fashioned piston metals, these alloys lift thousands of tons, every running minute, from all types of motors. They are tough. They carry off heat *many* times faster.

As much as 70,000 pounds of dead-weight stripped from a single de-luxe passenger car! 9,000 pounds saved on a single tank car! No wonder that "aluminized" trains are speeding into favor with railroad after railroad.

Equal in strength to structural steel, the light, strong alloys of Alcoa Aluminum are only ⅓ as heavy. That's why the president of a world-famous railroad—itself a large user of aluminized cars, has said: "This lighter metal . . . will add a third to the carrying capacity of trains."

All forms of transportation are sisters under the skin. With aluminized equipment, all can save vast quantities of power, make starting and stopping smoother and easier, can provide greater riding comfort and safety. Street cars can be as much as 12,000 pounds lighter. Buses with "aluminized" bodies can relieve gas, oil and tires of the burden of a ton or more of excess dead-weight. From ½ ton to more than 3 tons can be lifted from standard truck bodies and chassis.

Standard structural shapes of the strong alloys of Alcoa Aluminum, in sizes up to 10 inches in depth and 90 feet in length, are carried in stock.

Available also are strong Alcoa Aluminum alloy plate in sizes up to 35 feet long, 120 inches wide and ¾ inch thick; sheet, rivets, bolts, nuts, screws, etc. Send $1.00 for the handbook, "Structural Aluminum." Address ALUMINUM COMPANY *of* AMERICA; 2497 Oliver Building, PITTSBURGH, PENNA.

ALCOA ALUMINUM

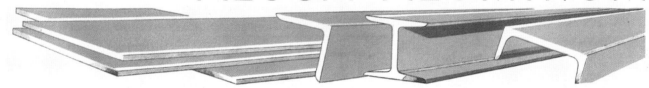

Alcoa Aluminum, 1932 ◄ *Alcoa Aluminum, 1932*

Peer into the Future
Alcoa Aluminum is revealed
a shining symbol of strength...light weight...enduring beauty

Even as we look, the present passes. A decade slips by and the desire for the stimulating contacts of city life has increased our urban population twice as fast as the country at large.

Crowded metropolitan space demands expansion—but how? Probably through buildings rising tier upon tier; overhead traffic lanes; roof space for aeroplane landings; aerial sidewalks; terraced parks—buildings mounting ever upward.

Peer into the future and Alcoa Aluminum is revealed. Weighing only one-third as much as metals now commonly used, Alcoa Aluminum is destined to play a prominent part in future building development.

Alcoa Aluminum resists corrosion. It need not be painted. It will not streak adjoining surfaces. It can be cast, forged,

drawn, extruded, welded and riveted. On the exterior of buildings its beauty is already seen—its light weight and strength utilized. For the interior trim and furnishings of office buildings, stores, and residences its decorative charm is employed. Providing the architect with a metal that lends itself readily to design and fine detail; that insures permanence; that saves handling of unnecessary dead-weight; that cuts cost of erection, Alcoa Aluminum will find ever-increasing use.

In each of our offices we have competent representatives, who are familiar with the decorative and structural uses of each of the special Alcoa Aluminum alloys. The services of these representatives are available to architects. ALUMINUM COMPANY of AMERICA; 2497 Oliver Building, PITTSBURGH, PA.

ALCOA ALUMINUM

Alcoa Aluminum, 1931

MODERNIZED WITH ALCOA ALUMINUM

Just a few of the many products that have been improved by using ALCOA Aluminum. Our development engineers have information on what these light, strong alloys can do and how done for products in your industry. Please write us!

Overhead Cranes 1, 3, 5	Radio Parts 1, 3, 5
Wheelbarrow 1, 2, 3, 5	Dashboard Motors 1, 2, 3, 4
Lifting Jacks 1, 2, 3	Window Sash 1, 2, 3
Bayonet Equipment 1, 3, 5	Spray Guns 1, 2, 3, 4
Meter Boxes 1, 3, 5	Collapsible Tubes 2, 5
Scaffolds 1, 3, 5	Roller Skates 2, 4
Sewage Disposal Equipment 3, 5	Refrigeration Insulation 1, 3
Railway Section Cars 1, 3, 5	Store Fronts 2, 3
Office Equipment 1, 3	Traffic Markers 3, 4, 5
Coin Changers 1, 3	Bolts 1, 3, 4
Diesel Engines 1, 4, 5	Connecting Rods 1, 4
Fire Extinguishers 2, 3	Golf Clubs 2, 5
Lighting Fixtures 2, 3, 5	Milk Coolers 3, 5
Surveying Equipment 1, 3	Pneumatic Tools 1, 3, 5
	Roofing 1, 3, 5

1 For Lighter Weight	2 For Sales-Appeal
3 For Corrosion Resistance	
4 For Greater Strength	5 For Economy

MOVING MOUNTAINS *at* BOULDER DAM
25 *tons at a time*

Catching 10-ton jagged rocks from a power-shovel dipper, hauling 25-ton loads up 21% grades—a dump truck with an ALCOA Aluminum body that dwarfs all others, is literally moving mountains at Boulder Dam.

The world's biggest dump body, carrying tons more load, yet weighing tons less than similar steel bodies...on the world's toughest job...of *course* it's *made of the light, strong alloys* of ALCOA Aluminum! Wherever modern progress makes new and greater demands on metals, men are turning to ALCOA Aluminum.

Somewhere there's new power, new efficiency, new sales appeal waiting for your company. ALCOA Aluminum is ready to help you find it. And that holds whether it's a new tube for tooth paste or a modern train for swifter transportation.

Here are alloys with the strength of structural steel, yet only 1/3 the weight. Alloys that resist corrosion; that are non-contaminating, non-magnetic, high in heat and electrical conductivity. Alloys, available for every purpose, in every form and size, from structural shapes to die, sand and permanent mold castings. From extruded shapes, forgings and plate to sheet, foil, tubing, etc., etc. Available even in the form of paint pigment (ALCOA Albron Powder) that brightens plants, guards against rust, weathering, smoke, acid fumes.

The light strong alloys of ALCOA Aluminum are looking for new and harder jobs—big and small. If your company has one, address ALUMINUM COMPANY of AMERICA; 1802 Gulf Building, PITTSBURGH, PENNSYLVANIA.

ALCOA ALUMINUM

Alcoa Aluminum, 1934

200,000 H.P.
UNDER HER HOOD_

AND SHE RELIES ON THE MAKERS OF MOBILOIL FOR VITAL ENGINE PROTECTION

A Short Story about the Newest Atlantic Record Holder.. the World's Finest Oil.. AND YOUR CAR!

LAUNCHED SEPT. 26, 1934...christened "Queen Mary"...she put to sea on her maiden voyage, May 27, last year. The British said she was not out for the record. But four trips later she won the right to the coveted Blue Ribbon for speed supremacy!...joined the Normandie, the Bremen, Europa, Rex and others that have held it.

What has this to do with your car? Just this: every North Atlantic record-breaker has been lubricated by the makers of Mobiloil. Which just about makes Mobiloil the world's Blue Ribbon motor oil, doesn't it? It does. Mobiloil is the world's largest-selling motor oil today. Use it in your car...and you have the best!

MOBILOIL AND MOBILGAS SOCONY-VACUUM OIL COMPANY, INC.

Pullmann Co., 1937 ◄ *Socony-Vacuum Oil Co., 1937*

Gulf Refining Co., 1935

John Morrell & Co., 1935

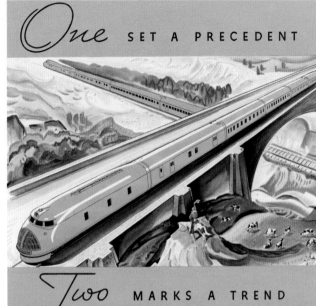

Alcoa Aluminum, 1935

Alcoa Aluminum, 1935

With TIMKEN At The New York World's Fair

The exhibit of TIMKEN Products at the New York World's Fair has been acclaimed one of the outstanding features of this, the greatest show of all time.

Strikingly original in conception, wonderfully beautiful in its gorgeous color scheme and brilliant lighting effects, the Timken Exhibit emphasizes the keynote of the Fair "The World of Tomorrow" in a manner that captivates every visitor. But the Timken Exhibit has other claims to pre-eminence apart from its originality and beauty. Never before for example, has such a comprehensive display of bearings been seen in one place. Here are shown TIMKEN Bearings ranging from a few ounces in weight to one weighing more than *three tons*; bearings for every possible application in industry and transportation—from automobiles to railroad trains and from precision machine tools to huge steel rolling mills. Equally impressive are the displays of other TIMKEN Products; including TIMKEN Alloy Steels, TIMKEN Alloy and Carbon Steel Seamless Tubing, TIMKEN Rock Bits, and TIMKEN Fuel Injection Equipment for fuel oil burning engines.

Nor is novelty lacking, for as a demonstration of the precision with which TIMKEN Bearings are made there is a machine capable of measuring the thickness of a human hair in hundred-thousandths of an inch! Visitors can measure their own hair on this machine and keep the measurement records for souvenirs. Naturally this is one of the most popular spots in the entire Fair.

All in all the Timken Exhibit is a truly remarkable achievement—an attraction no visitor can afford to miss. You will find it in the Metals Building adjacent to the Trylon and Perisphere.

THE TIMKEN ROLLER BEARING COMPANY, CANTON, OHIO

TIMKEN

TRADE-MARK REG. U. S. PAT. OFF.

COPYRIGHT 1939, BY THE TIMKEN ROLLER BEARING COMPANY

Timken, 1939

EMPIRE STATE—world's largest office building—between Grand Central and Pennsylvania Terminals—an internationally famous site—the logical address for New York City offices

▼

EMPIRE STATE

FIFTH AVENUE AT 34th STREET, NEW YORK

OFFICERS

ROBERT C. BROWN
Vice President & Treasurer

ALFRED E. SMITH
President

J. HOLLOWAY TARRY
Secretary

DIRECTORS

PIERRE S. DUPONT   MICHAEL FRIEDSAM   ALFRED E. SMITH   JOHN J. RASKOB   ELLIS P. EARLE
AUGUST HECKSCHER   LOUIS G. KAUFMAN

READY FOR MAY 1931 OCCUPANCY

For Rental Information Inquire
H. Hamilton Weber, rental manager, or your own broker

Empire State Building, 1930

EMPIRE STATE BUILDING
NEW YORK

THE WORLD'S LARGEST AND TALLEST OFFICE BUILDING

The Empire State Building: designed by Shreve, Lamb & Harmon; under construction at 5th Avenue, 33rd and 34th Streets, New York City by Starrett Bros. and Eken, Inc... to be 85 stories high, the largest and tallest office building in the world, with twelve hundred and thirty-two elevator entrances by Dahlstrom.

DAHLSTROM METALLIC DOOR COMPANY
JAMESTOWN, N.Y.
With offices in all principal cities

ARCHITECTS: SHREVE, LAMB & HARMON
CONTRACTORS: STARRETT BROS. AND EKEN, INC.

Elevator Entrances by
DAHLSTROM

· 113 ·

Empire State Building, 1930

COPPER for vertical surfaces
THE TREND OF TOMORROW

THE Bullock's-Wilshire Building, Los Angeles, is an interesting example of the modern trend in building design and construction. Copper used on vertical surfaces makes for unusual effects at lower construction costs.

John Parkinson and Donald B. Parkinson, Architects, comment as follows: "In designing Bullock's-Wilshire Building it was our desire to use metal in plastic form for the ornamental portions, and for the tower, in combination with masonry, in order to accent the vertical lines

of the building, and to add interest to the facade, which might otherwise become quite monotonous on account of its extent.

"On account of the beautiful color, the natural variation in tone, together with its permanence and workability, we adopted copper without hesitation.

"The verde antique finish was developed by the use of acids, so that when the building was finished the final color effect was established. The color tones, we believe, will improve with natural weathering."

The Bullock's-Wilshire Building, Los Angeles, is the work of John and Donald B. Parkinson, architects. Sheet metal installed by the Forderer Cornice Works, San Francisco. Builders—P.J.Walker Company.

COPPER & BRASS
RESEARCH ASSOCIATION
25 Broadway, New York

CENTURIES OF SERVICE PROVE THE DURABILITY OF COPPER AND ITS ALLOYS

Copper & Brass, 1931

STARTED!

BOULDER CANYON PROJECT
and a New Era in
LOS ANGELES'
INDUSTRIAL GROWTH!

WITH THE DRIVING of a silver spike into a railroad tie on September 17, 1930... the continued development of the Los Angeles industrial area is guaranteed for generations to come.

Between the massive shoulders of Boulder Canyon, billions of added wealth will pour into the Southwest... millions of new population... unlimited low cost water and power. This new source of water and power will create tremendously rich new markets, besides stabilizing the phenomenal population growth disclosed by the 1930 census. And Los Angeles is assured its posi-

tion as a world leader in profitable and low cost industrial production.

Planning your Pacific Coast plant requires consideration of the Boulder Canyon project... the two are inseparably welded. Foresight today promises rich rewards when this gigantic development is completed, the manufacturing importance of today's Los Angeles will be trebled in the immediate future.

Bureau of Power and Light engineers are organized to render exceptional consultation service. Upon request, a very complete survey of your water and power requirements will be made in a comprehensive, confidential report.

Secretary of the Interior, RAY LYMAN WILBUR, said regarding the future benefits of the Boulder Canyon project:

"It is as if our country had suddenly had a new state added to it, for the new and wider use of this controlled water will care for millions of people and create thousands of millions of wealth."

BUREAU OF POWER AND LIGHT
City of Los Angeles

Boulder Canyon Project, 1930   ▶ *Empire State Building, 1931*

CRES OF SUNLIT OFFICE SPACE

EMPIRE STATE
AN INTERNATIONALLY KNOWN ADDRESS
FIFTH AVENUE AND 34TH STREET NEW YORK
H. HAMILTON WEBER, Rental Manager, EMPIRE STATE BUILDING, CAledonia 5-8347 or Your Own Broker

OFFICERS
Alfred E. Smith, President
Robert C. Brown   J. Holloway Tarry
Vice-President, Treasurer   Secretary
                   DIRECTORS
Alfred E. Smith   August Heckscher   Ellis P. Earle
    Pierre S. Du Pont   John J. Raskob
        Louis G. Kaufman

© Hiram Myers Photo

- ABOVE: Animated spectacular 60 x 35 ft. in dimensions, incorporating 1200 ft. of tubing and 4500 bulbs, built in Montreal by Claude Neon General Advertising, Ltd., using 25 Jefferson Transformers.
- LEFT: Novel theatre front in Minneapolis by Vent and Canopy Company, incorporating 10 Jefferson Transformers.

On Unique Spectaculars -- Small Shop Signs -- Anywhere -- Dependability Comes First

The smallest sign is just as important to its owners as the largest. . . . And trouble with any sign takes a slice of your profits to make it right.

That is why so many leading contractors standardize on Jefferson Transformers—use them on every installation of every size. These contractors know that Midpoint Grounded, Balanced Design, pioneered by Jefferson, is unequaled for dependable, efficient and economical operation — that improvement has followed improvement on Jefferson Transformers, each development adding to sturdiness, length of life, economy, or convenience of installation.

Get complete information on the Jefferson Line for all requirements by writing for Bulletin No. 352-LT. JEFFERSON ELECTRIC COMPANY, Bellwood (Suburb of Chicago), Illinois. Canadian Factory: 535 College Street, Toronto.

- The Midwest Neon Company, Sioux City, Iowa, built and installed this theatre front at Pipestone, Minn., using 27 Jefferson Transformers.

JEFFERSON *Luminous Tube* Transformers

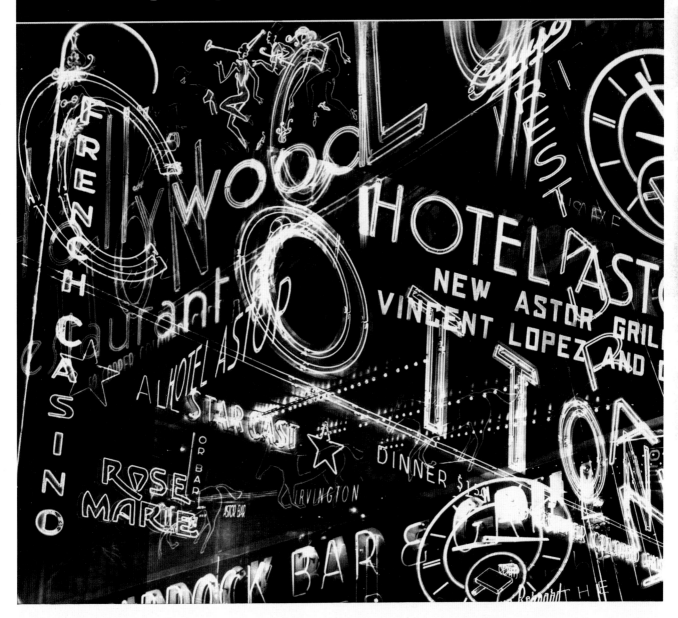

A new sign language...written in Glass!

IN New York and London, in Denver and Shanghai, along the Main Streets of the world, dusk brings forth a million vivid electric signs that make the night alive. There is a new sign language... written in glass!

Neon has been called the light that changed the night-time face of the world. But before neon could attain widespread use, it fell to Corning research to develop special colors and special glass that would work easily into all the shapes required.

All the tubing for neon signs is made at Corning on machines which can make many miles of it a day. Other machines developed by Corning, make most of the lamp bulbs for the entire nation.

Corning research has found many new uses for glass in the home, in science and industry. Consider for example, the new "Pyrex" brand top-of-stove ware that can be used over an open flame. The new fibre glass, as soft as eiderdown, for house and industrial insulation. And research is

only beginning to explore its other uses. Consider also the power lines and radio stations insulated with glass. The hundreds of places in industry where inventive minds have used glass to replace other materials less proof against exposure, acid and wear! For more of the story of glass research in America, write today for your free copy of a new illustrated book, "Corning Glass Works presents..." Corning Glass Works, Corning, New York.

CORNING
means
Research in Glass

Jefferson Transformers, 1935 ◄ *Corning Glass, 1935*

Outdoor Advertising reaches the public when it is on the move...convenient to the point of sale

IN 1908 the California Fruit Growers' Exchange appropriated $7,000 and began to advertise its Sunkist Oranges. In 1934 this advertiser has *this* to say (in January 15 issue of Sales Management), about Outdoor Advertising:

"We believe that in our poster advertising we link five strong factors in the accomplishment of our marketing program. We use pictures, little text. We reach every Sunkist prospect, since even those who know little English understand pictures and learn to know the trademark. Color, the basic appeal in Sunkist display, tempts the appetite and adds force through the dramatic size of posters."

Outdoor Advertising delivers circulation, according to actual traffic count, to guarantee thorough coverage of any market entered.

It impresses that circulation by dramatic simplicity, dominating size, full color—and with a reiterative persistence that is inescapable.

By exerting this irresistible influence upon prospective buyers when they are out of doors, ready to buy, Outdoor Advertising bridges the gap between advertising read or heard indoors and the point of actual purchase.

As a part of many a sound merchandising plan, Outdoor Advertising has proved its economy, demonstrated its power, built profitable sales. Actual examples of what Outdoor Advertising can do to promote the sale of your product at low cost will be supplied upon request. Investigate now while space is still available.

OUTDOOR ADVERTISING INDUSTRY

OUTDOOR ADVERTISING INCORPORATED

1 PARK AVENUE, NEW YORK • 165 WEST WACKER DRIVE, CHICAGO

ATLANTA • BOSTON • CLEVELAND • HOUSTON • LOS ANGELES • ST. LOUIS • BALTIMORE • CINCINNATI • DETROIT • KANSAS CITY • PHILADELPHIA • SAN FRANCISCO

Outdoor Advertising Industry, 1934

America is outdoor-minded! The motor car made it so. I am materially aided in reaching and selling my market thru Outdoor Advertising. And it pays!

A.H. Reeke

PRESIDENT
REEKE-NASH MOTOR CO.
CLEVELAND, OHIO

This is the story of successful selling. It is the experience of one of America's foremost distributors. He has proven the effectiveness of the Outdoor message. An outstanding sales record confirms his contentions.

¶ Today—the purchasing power of the nation is on the highways. We are a nation of Outdoor enthusiasts. Ever on the go . . Doing things . . Going places.

Mental reactions are fast. We are headline readers. Selling must be geared to the market.

¶ Outdoor Advertising dominates the motoring millions . . Color commands the eye. The message flashes. A mental impression is registered. Constant repetition builds the buying impulse. Desire is created. A decision is made. Business results.

THE CENTRAL OUTDOOR ADVERTISING COMPANY

1028 CARNEGIE AVENUE
CLEVELAND

320 VANCE STREET
TOLEDO

Central Outdoor Advertising Co., 1930

"We tickle the palate *through the eye*"

SWIFT knows that the eye-line is the direct line to the appetite. Swift stays where all eye-lines must meet—on the big, dominating, outdoor displays.

▶ With everyone always going somewhere, the national mood is outdoor minded. We make our decisions on the run. We buy what our eyes tell us to buy. We act—when the urge to action is ever before us. No wonder

outdoor advertising is the prime motivating force in most of the buy-words we use . . . *the force that makes a trade-mark a real mark of trade.*

▶ Positive are the results that come with outdoor advertising. For it is the one advertising medium that knows no waste basket. It stays where it is put. And it is put where every man and his family must see it and do see it every day of their lives.

▶ If twice told tales are better, the multi-told message of outdoor displays becomes the one inescapable factor in our lives. It makes us see. It makes us think. It makes us decide. It makes us act. It works with no "time off." Its hours are all hours. It makes the first sale and the repeat sale. It doesn't merely prompt —it pushes. It is the one sure force that will help your business today.

THE CENTRAL OUTDOOR ADVERTISING COMPANY, Inc.
1028 Carnegie Avenue, CLEVELAND, OHIO · · 320 Vance Street, TOLEDO, OHIO

Central Outdoor Advertising Co., 1930

"We are believers IN THIS KIND OF *Advertising*"

TO "COVER THE EARTH" with S-W Paints and Varnishes, the Sherwin-Williams Company have long known that the earth must first be covered by S-W advertising. They know, too, that the people who live on this earth live outdoors, think outdoors, buy outdoors. They "cover them" by strategic Outdoor Display, not only in their home city but from coast to coast. ¶ Outdoor displays of this spectacular nature tell a story through the eye, day and night, and Sherwin-Williams are strong believers in this kind of advertising. ¶ Since these displays were built Sherwin-Williams have had any number of fine comments about them. They have put still further

interest and snap into their important Cleveland activities, tying up splendidly with their national advertising campaign. ¶ That important part of the earth known as the North Ohio Market, with its three million purchasing-minded and prosperous populace, is covered with S-W thoroughness by the coordinated Central Outdoor facilities. You can win and hold that market both quickly and economically if you use the Central plan for your business. ¶ Now that sales costs must stand up under constant scrutiny, you should have that plan before you. Next year's program must make sales *with* profits. Be sure you know why Central can do just that for you.

THE CENTRAL OUTDOOR ADVERTISING COMPANY, Inc.
1028 Carnegie Avenue, CLEVELAND, OHIO · · 320 Vance Street, TOLEDO, OHIO

Central Outdoor Advertising Co., 1930

"Covering the Earth" from Cleveland

PAINT represents itself universally—even at night—in large areas of color.

So, likewise, does OUTDOOR ADVERTISING. The two are closely related in basic characteristics. And in function, each is an indispensable tool of the other. Much of our outdoor display *is* paint . . . and is, at the same time, the means of advertising and selling paint.

For nearly seventy years— since the time of its establishment as a small shop in Cleveland—the Sherwin-Williams

Company, world's largest makers of paints and varnishes, has been a consistent user of Outdoor Advertising, a potent implement of business.

As a result—in large part—of which, the trademark of the familiar paint can pouring over the globe is known to millions. And the Sherwin-Williams Company attributes much of the S-W brand preference, trademark recognition and dealer identification to its use of the outdoor medium.

Quoting Mr. G. A. Martin, president of Sherwin-Williams: *The people*

retain impressions made by color on the eye as they travel the highways. We are great believers in this method of keeping our name and trade-mark constantly before the public. No advertising program of ours would be complete without a substantial allotment for outdoor painted display.

The power of Outdoor Advertising, in giving impetus and momentum to sales, has been proved many times, and for many different kinds of merchandise. Complete facts, suggesting its possibilities for application to your product and your selling plans, will be supplied on request.

THE OUTDOOR
ADVERTISING
INDUSTRY

SERVICE THROUGHOUT THE UNITED STATES

OUTDOOR ADVERTISING INCORPORATED
National Sales Representatives for the Majority of the Industry

One Park Avenue, New York
165 West Wacker Drive, Chicago

ATLANTA · BOSTON · CLEVELAND · HOUSTON · LOS ANGELES
ST. LOUIS · BALTIMORE · CINCINNATI · DETROIT · KANSAS CITY
PHILADELPHIA · SAN FRANCISCO

Central Outdoor Advertising Co., 1934

MAÑANA ... Alert management knows well enough where economies can be effected, profits increased . . . through changes in policies and methods. • Reforms are planned in principle . . . but their execution must await the assembling and organizing of detailed information. • And under the day-to-day pressure of routine business, action is postponed until a tomorrow that never comes. • Our service ends costly procrastination . . . accelerates action . . . converts indefinite plans into a specific program of improvement. • Our business is one of fact finding for management.

R. A. LASLEY INC. • ENGINEERS • Chrysler Building, New York

DISTRIBUTION · PRODUCTION · RESEARCH

OBJECTION SUSTAINED . . . Objection or no objection, lawyers will continue to ask leading questions • So will business. Business still asks leading questions . . . finds out what it wants to find out . . . proves the point it wishes to prove with market research. Without benefit of independent counsel this evidence forms the record . . . guides production . . . dictates the policy of promotion . . . maps the sales strategy. And oftener than not, misses the mark! • If you want to know what your customers think of you and your product, individually and collectively, and how they came to have these opinions, we can help you. Our business is one of fact finding for management, of asking direct, *not* leading, questions.

R. A. LASLEY INC. • ENGINEERS • Chrysler Building, New York
DISTRIBUTION—PRODUCTION—RESEARCH

R. A. Lasley Inc., 1934 ◄ *R. A. Lasley Inc., 1934*

IMPACT

ACCORDING TO WEBSTER: The single instantaneous striking of a body in motion against another body.

ACCORDING TO YOUNG & RUBICAM: That quality in an advertisement which strikes suddenly against the reader's indifference and enlivens his mind to receive a sales message.

YOUNG & RUBICAM, INCORPORATED · ADVERTISING
NEW YORK · PHILADELPHIA

Young & Rubicam, 1930

★ TUG O' WAR ★

Modern advertising is a tug o' war. One advertiser trying to pull the consumer in one direction, his competitor pulling in another.

★

Victory goes with strength. But do not confuse strength with bulk. More powerful than "dominating space" is the skill that sways feelings, convinces minds, commands action.

★

YOUNG AND RUBICAM·INC ADVERTISING NEW YORK PHILADELPHIA

· 95 ·

Young & Rubicam, 1930

we are running the wooden Indians out of advertising

The Cigar Store Indian was carted off to the Curio Shop because he couldn't sell

* Into his job stepped a lot of attractive youngsters. They changed the smoking and tobacco-buying habits of the nation, wrote new industrial history.
* Yet until just recently even they had something of the Wooden Indian about them. For the mechanical limitations of the color cameras made them fix their expressions and freeze their gestures while the pictures were being taken.
* But today the last Wooden Indian is banished from advertising illustration by a new color camera so fast that the living models need never "pose" a gesture or expression. Now we can photograph them in *full action, as well as full color*—moving, breathing, living people.
* That's how the picture on the facing page was made. The match spurts . . . the first fragrant puff curls up . . . the camera clicks! Natural, unposed . . . convincing because it's REAL!
* The same sort of Sales-Making illustration is good advertising for almost any product. And we can make it for you here in our studio. From it our engravers know how to make plates that will reproduce faithfully on the printed page the sharp brilliance of the originals. These plates may be either printed right here at our press or sent out to magazines or other printers.
* We offer you every facility of a large and completely equipped printing establishment. Printing by almost every process, engraving, binding, mailing, etc., etc. We can handle any part of any printing job, no matter how large or how small, or take undivided responsibility for turning it out complete, on time and to your entire satisfaction.

R. R. DONNELLEY & SONS COMPANY
THE LAKESIDE PRESS

350 E. 22nd St., Chicago ·Telephone Calumet 2121 ★ Eastern Sales Office: 305 E. 45th St., New York · Telephone Murray Hill 4-7000

R.R. Donnelley & Sons, 1934

▶ *Frigidaire, 1935*

FOURTH MILLION

ODAY three million genuine Frigidaires have been built and the manufacture of the 4th million has begun. Throughout the world Frigidaire has set the standard for efficient automatic refrigeration. Into millions of homes it has brought a higher plane of living—a better standard of health. And constantly, through the years, Frigidaire has been improved. Benefiting from the suggestions of users, and the engineering facilities of General Motors, it has offered better arrangement of food space—

snow-white porcelain on steel inside and out, the Cold Control, the Hydrator, light that flashes on at the opening of the door—more ice, automatic ice tray release, automatic reset defrosting, and remarkably low operating cost. In an endless flow, General Motors has added to Frigidaire improvements and conveniences that have set this one make apart from all other refrigerators.

Three million Frigidaires have been built—and the greatest single influence in the choice of Frigidaire by new buyers is the

enthusiastic recommendation of its users.

The manufacture of the 4th million has begun. There are sixteen beautiful models that represent further new standards of value—every one equipped with Frigidaire's newest contribution to its future users, the Super Freezer—which provides a *complete refrigeration service* in every model.

The Frigidaire '35's are here. And we are proud of the fact that we can offer them at prices that will make them available to new millions of homes.

12,000 MILES
from repair parts

IF MACHINERY SHOULD BREAK DOWN AT THIS MINE, IT WOULD TAKE SIX MONTHS TO GET SPARE PARTS

NEW CALEDONIA ← → FIJI ISLANDS ← → HONOLULU ← → SAN FRANCISCO ← → NEW YORK

World's most isolated power plant
uses Gargoyle Lubricants to safeguard equipment

There are no power consultants on the South Sea island of New Caledonia—no spare parts within 12,000 miles. Should machinery break down in Mutual Chemical Company's chrome mines, operations would come to a halt for at least six months. Lubrication *must be* correct.

So these mines guard against machinery breakdowns by the use of Gargoyle Lubricants.

Gargoyle D. T. E. Oil Extra Heavy used in these Diesel engines and Gargoyle D. T. E. Oil Heavy Medium used in the air compressors, are the grades recommended and used by the engine builders. These are the identical oils that are available for use in your plant—in New York or New Caledonia.

You'll find Gargoyle Lubricants used in industrial plants in every corner of the globe and in most leading plants in world industrial centers. Plants in Manchester, England, and Pittsburgh, Pa., for instance, can obtain spare parts quickly, but even a few hours' interruption might disrupt production schedules. So the same Gargoyle Lubricants keep machinery running smoothly.

Plant operating records, written in every language, prove that the use of Gargoyle Lubricants and Socony-Vacuum engineering service reduces power consumption from 3% to 10%, lowers maintenance and repair expense, speeds up production, insures against breakdowns.

Any Socony-Vacuum representative will be glad to show you how correct lubrication has helped lower unit production costs in leading plants in your own industry.

Socony-Vacuum Corporation, 26 Broadway, New York City. Branches and distributors throughout the world.

SOCONY-VACUUM
CORPORATION

GARGOYLE
Lubricating Oils

Socony-Vacuum Co., 1934

▶ Monsanto Chemicals, 1939

MONDAY MIRACLE

Chemistry's newest contribution to soap works a washday transformation

STAPLE of the grocer's shelves, busy servant of the laundry and home, soap has been taken for granted by those it serves...until today. Fashion has brought innumerable changes in the clothes that soap must wash ...now the soap industry brings a fundamental new advancement to soap itself.

Chemistry developed it, the progressive American soap industry has applied it to the working of a million "Monday Miracles" in homes and laundries. Your own family's garments are benefiting today from this improvement in many of the best known brands of soap.

From elemental phosphorus, chemistry created a new soap ingredient, tetrasodium pyrophosphate. As a result, industry is producing soaps that clean clothes shades whiter, keep colors fresh and bright, free garments from graying scum, leave tubs clean and ringless. These new soaps are kinder to the hands, gentler on fabrics, create an uprush of cleansing, sudsy bubbles even in hard water.

Such is another step in the ever-quickening progress of Industry ... translating the work of Chemistry into terms of widespread usefulness to all mankind. MONSANTO CHEMICAL COMPANY, St. Louis.

HOW MONSANTO SERVES

Industry applies products of Monsanto Chemical Company to thousands of uses in the service of all mankind. A few of these are:

PHOSPHOTEX (Tetrasodium Pyrophosphate) — a detergent aid for soaps.

VINYL ACETAL — new plastic for automobile safety glass, amazingly tough and elastic, permanently transparent.

PENTACHLOROPHENOL — to eliminate wood degrading organisms and termites.

ACCELERATORS, ANTIOXIDANTS—for production of longer-wearing automobile tires and other rubber products.

FERRISUL (Ferric Sulfate) — for treatment of water, sewage and industrial wastes.

MONSANTO CHEMICALS
SERVING INDUSTRY...WHICH SERVES MANKIND

FOUR WORLDS
beneath one roof...Four
groups of human beings,
bounded on four sides by
economic pressure; living,
loving, hoping—a symbol
of America today...To
share their fortunes is
not to exploit them
but to understand them.

E·R·SQUIBB & SONS
MANUFACTURING CHEMISTS SINCE 1858

E.R. Squibb & Sons, 1934

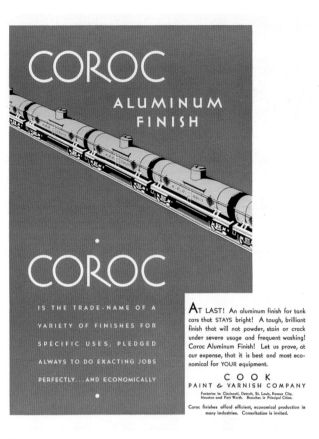

Coroc, 1931

SERENELY BEAUTIFUL – FOR ALL TIME

THE MATCHLESS BEAUTY of Rock of Ages granite is as imperishable as the faith and ideals which a memorial should proclaim.

In but a single quarry, cutting deep into a wooded Vermont hillside, is found granite of the fine, hard texture and uniform blue-gray color which distinguish Rock of Ages. Throughout the centuries it will stand un-marred—defiant of heat, of cold, of storm, of time itself.

By selecting Rock of Ages granite, you eliminate all speculation as to the beauty and character of the finished memorial. The Rock of Ages certificate of perfection, which your memorial craftsman will unhesitatingly give you, is an uncompromising guarantee, not only of the material, but of Rock of Ages craftsmanship as well.

Write for our helpful booklet "HOW TO CHOOSE A MEMORIAL"

ROCK of AGES
THE *DISTINCTIVE* BARRE GRANITE

ROCK OF AGES CORPORATION...BARRE, VERMONT

Edison, 1931 ◄ *Rock Of Ages Co., 1930*

PRECISION

Precision in Sterling engines is attained, not by the speediest production methods, which this company has always maintained cannot produce full load engines of reliability, but by machining to closest tolerances, and then accurately fitting by hand. Main bearings, for instance, are line reamed by machine; then "blued" in by the original hand process. Pistons are slowly machined that the ring grooves shall be concentric and devoid of any inaccuracies. Cylinders are honed, one at a time, to micrometer exactness.

Building Sterling Petrel engines to their present leading status has required 4 years. They graduate into 1931 without a single mechanical change; unmatchable
in developing 200 H. P. at 2000 R.P.M.,
in power at a safe engine speed,
in turning the larger propeller,
in possessing the only 7 bearing crankshaft that is fully counter-weighted and in true dynamic balance
and in being
safely and economically carbureted.

STERLING ENGINE COMPANY
1270 Niagara Street
Buffalo, New York, U.S.A.

W. H. Marston Corp., 1043 Commonwealth Ave., distributors, Boston

Reuss, Kimball & Co., 5th Ave. at 12th St., distributors, New York

Sterling Engine Co., 1930

4-POINT CHAIN SUSPENSION

VIBRATION
POSITIVELY PRODUCED
EFFECTIVELY ENDURED

The suspension of the Vibrator Screen by four forged link chains eliminates the possibility of transmitting any lateral vibrations to the supporting structure or building. The chains act effectively as dampeners of any resultant vibration tendency in the sub-frame. For installation where long suspension chains are required special chain weights are attached midway from screen to support. This standard feature with S-A Vibrator Screens is only one of the important design phases of which you will wish to know. The catalog is ready that describes and illustrates the general design of all the six different sizes. Each size is available in single, double and triple deck assemblies.

S-A VIBRATOR SCREEN
STEPHENS-ADAMSON MFG. CO.
AURORA, ILLINOIS ∴ LOS ANGELES, CALIFORNIA ∴ BELLEVILLE, ONT., CANADA
When writing advertisers, please mention ROCK PRODUCTS

S-A Vibrator Screen, 1930

WHITE PORTLAND CEMENT
IS INDISPENSABLE TO THE CONSTRUCTION INDUSTRY

STUCCO
TERRAZZO
CAST STONE
MORTAR
SWIMMING POOLS

● The architectural preference for concrete does not rest solely upon its manifest stability and workability. It is also founded on artistic considerations. White or colored concrete, in many forms, is now being used in almost every type of building because it produces results that are as attractive as they are permanent. ● Medusa White Portland Cement, plain and waterproofed, produces concrete of the same great strength and durability as regular Gray Portland Cement. It can be tinted as desired, for clear, uniform, permanent color effects. ● Medusa White is the *original* White Portland Cement. For 25 years it has been the outstanding White Cement, used all over the world for better results and better appearance. A few of the hundreds of uses for this White Portland Cement are shown at the left.
MEDUSA PORTLAND CEMENT COMPANY, 1002 Engineers Bldg., Cleveland, Ohio

MEDUSA
WHITE PORTLAND CEMENT
PLAIN AND WATERPROOFED

Medusa, 1931

3 DAY
FREIGHT AREA
63,500,000 population
Fifty-four Billion
Spendable Income

2 DAY
FREIGHT AREA
43,000,000 population
Thirty-nine Billion
Spendable Income

OVERNIGHT
TRUCKING
AREA
16,000,000 population
Seventeen Billion
Spendable Income

FROM
Philadelphia
The Work Shop of the World

▸ ▸ ▸ ▸ you can reach more people with less effort than from any other center in the United States. To speed up distribution, locate your plant in Philadelphia. Send for information. Philadelphia Business Progress Association, 1442 Widener Building.

Address Department P for booklet, "Production and Distribution in the Philadelphia Area."

DIRECT SAILINGS (WITHOUT LIGHTERAGE) FROM THE PORT OF
PHILADELPHIA TO PRINCIPAL SEA PORT COUNTRIES OF THE WORLD

PHILADELPHIA
BUSINESS PROGRESS ASSOCIATION

Philadelphia, 1930

▶ Popular Mechanics, 1932

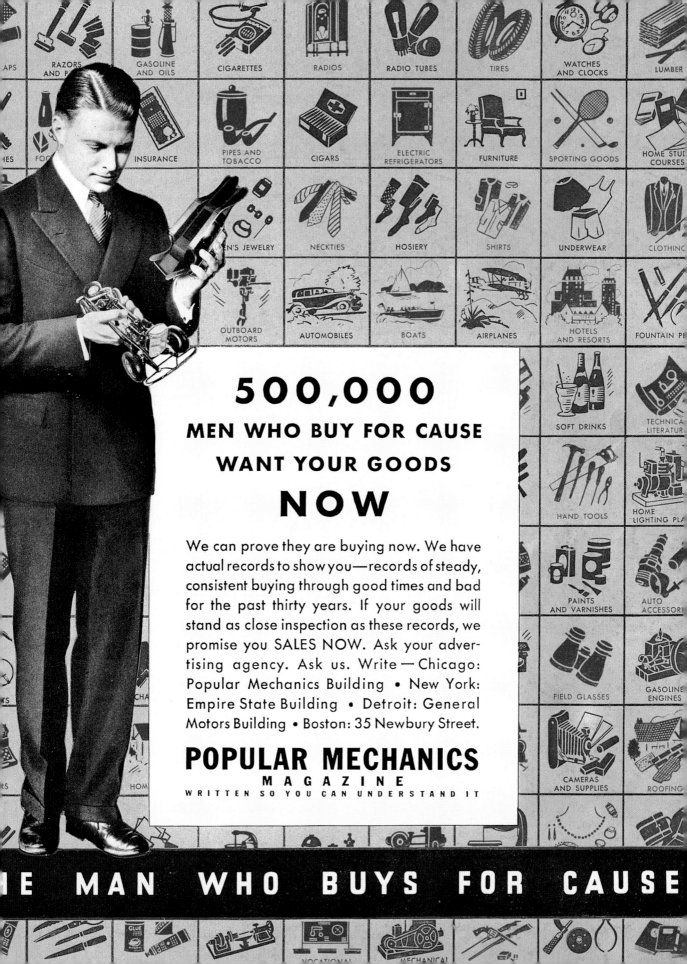

Bendix Products, 1934

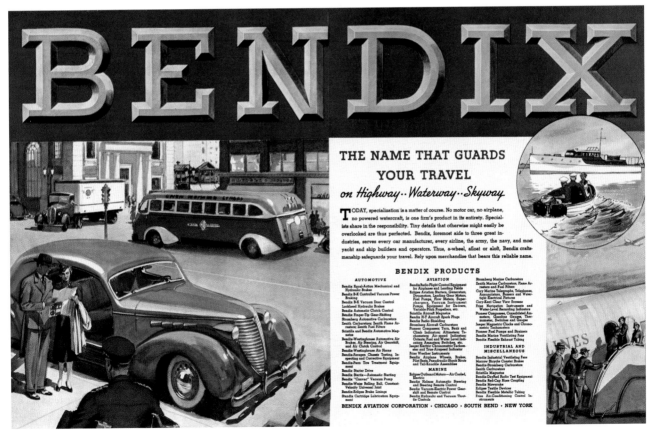

Country Gentleman, 1936 ◀ Bendix Products, 1937

HIGHLAND WROUGHT IRON
brings to modern industry a metal that endures, and has endured, for ages

In the Marne Valley, France, the Gauls buried a chief sitting in his chariot, 400 years B. C. The skeleton is found lying in its cave between the wrought iron tires of the chariot wheels. All else is crumbled, dust to dust. Only the bones remain of the man, only the wrought iron remains of that chariot of 2300 years ago.

Today wrought iron is made by the Highland Iron and Steel Company of a quality to endure for untold years.

Highland Wrought Iron is being adapted constantly to new uses by architects, railroads, oil fields and refineries, public utilities, ship builders and other industries. They choose Highland Wrought Iron because it resists rust, corrosion, fatigue and progressive fracture.

This tough metal is puddled and rolled until it acquires super-endurance. Its two principal characteristics are—first, stratified internal structure which prevents progressive fracture, and—second, myriad layers of Iron Silicate which stop rust at the surface.

We deliver Highland Wrought Iron in bars, billets and rods, from which it is forged into an ever-growing diversity of finished products, a few of which follow: For architects—gates, grilles,

gratings, railings, fences, hinges, knockers, lighting fixtures, window sash, cornice supports, stone anchors, spikes, nails, etc. For railroads—locomotive draw bars, engine and tender truck equalizers, valve yokes, spring hangers, engine bolts, stay bolts, etc. For oil fields and refineries—tank plates, roofing, sucker rods, nuts and bolts.

The public utilities are interested in it for high tension transmission towers, transformer stations, and "pole hardware." Ship builders favor it because it resists rust in salt air and salt water.

No man can foresee the full extent to which Highland Wrought Iron will come into service. Hundreds of unexpected economical uses have already been found by the engineering and metallurgical staff of the Highland Iron and Steel Company. Inquiries are invited from all who could profit by a metal of superior endurance, ductility and resistance to rust.

The integrity of Highland Wrought Iron, and the service rendered users by the Highland Iron and Steel Company, accord with the Acco Giant symbol of Quality which represents the American Chain Company, Inc., and Associate Companies.

ACCO
A group of Basic Industries under the management of American Chain Company, Inc.

These are the Acco Industries:
AMERICAN CHAIN COMPANY, Inc., and ASSOCIATE COMPANIES

American Chain Company, Inc.	Highland Iron and Steel Company	Wright Manufacturing Company
American Cable Company, Inc.	The Hensley Manufacturing Company	Dominion Chain Company, Ltd.
Andrew C. Campbell, Inc.	Page Steel and Wire Company	(Niagara Falls, Ontario, Canada)
Ford Chain Block Company	Pratt & Cady Company	British Wire Products, Ltd.*
Hazard Wire Rope Company	Reading Steel Casting Company, Inc.	Parsons Non-Skid Company, Ltd.*
	The Rubber Shock Insulator Corp.	(*Both of London, England)

Ask for further information. The uses of Highland Wrought Iron are so numerous and often so unusual that The Highland Iron and Steel Company would be glad to discuss the subject with anyone who will write, addressing the inquiry to 400 West Madison Street, Chicago.

This is one of a series of Acco institutional advertisements.

ACCO, 1931

In the *Kalevala*, the Finnish epic, the divine smith—Ilmarinen—forged a bride of gold and silver for Wainamoinen, who was pleased at first to have so rich a wife, but soon found her intolerably cold—his house comfortless...

of warmth – and comfort – and cheer . . .

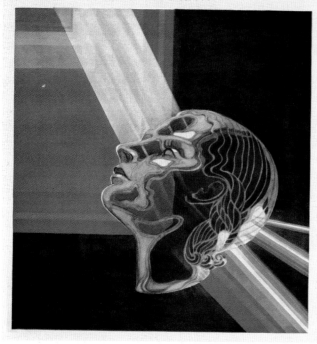

for in spite of furs and fires she froze everything that touched her, chilled everything surrounding her. : : : The old saga thus points, of course, in its forceful—if indirect—way, to the *flesh-and-blood* woman as the bestower of warmth, of comfort, in the household. And indeed, of the many-sided nature of woman, this ability to create from any background an atmosphere of warmth and comfort and cheer and peace, is the most remarkable. : : : To work with such materials as fall to her hands—in such an abode as falls to her lot—to pass on to other women those particular little ideas of her own that she has found best—to accept from them ideas she may like . . . to *blend* all these and other things into that saving atmosphere we call Home, is the prerogative solely of woman. And it is as near to a divine achievement as can be attained on this earth.

Perhaps one good reason why McCall's is now read in 2,450,000 homes

is because it is edited to pass on to women those ideas of others that

help to make for warmth, and comfort, and cheer in the home

McCALL'S
A MAGAZINE FOR WOMEN

McCall's, 1930

▶ *Cudahy Packing Co., 1932*

Into the amphibion class with its inherent advantages for transport service, Douglas has introduced a plane of startling performance . . . and typical Douglas dependability. It has the ability to alight on water or land closest to the heart of cities, and to fly straight to its destination, irrespective of terrain. It has a speed of 150 m.p.h., maneuvers on one motor. It is comfortable . . . quiet, and is custom=finished to accommodate eight or ten. May we send detailed information? Douglas Aircraft Company, Inc., Santa Monica, California.

A Douglas Amphibion of the Wilmington-Catalina Airline fleet. The line maintains a 10-trip schedule daily between the Southern California mainland and the island.

Amphibion
CUSTOM BUILT BY
DOUGLAS

FIRST AROUND THE WORLD

"NEXT STOP.. CHINA!"

Hᴵɢʜ ᴏᴠᴇʀ ᴍᴀɴɪʟᴀ's ᴛʀᴏᴘɪᴄ ꜱʜᴏʀᴇꜱ, a modern clipper 3 days out of the Golden Gate clears the mists . . . circles to westward . . . disappears over the horizon, China-bound! No mere flight of fancy, this . . . no imaginative dream of the far distant future!

When this giant 25-ton air-liner roars away on the last leg of the California to the Orient run . . . it will mark the completion of plans and routes studied and charted for years. *It will inaugurate the first scheduled trans-oceanic air service in the world . . . linking the new world with the old!*

To the men of Pan American Airways goes the honor for this thrilling achievement . . . to the vision and resourcefulness of its engineers and the efficiency of its pilots and navigators.

Already, initial test flights have thrilled the world with the amazing smoothness and the mathematical precision with which they have been accomplished. Already, a chain of bases has been laid across the Pacific at Midway Island, Wake Island and Guam to Manila.

Of fundamental importance, at these bases of supply, are Socony-Vacuum lubricants. Hundreds of barrels of Aero Mobiloil have been transported to the islands, ready to play their part in the reg-ular operation of Pan American's mighty motors!

Thus again, as in the epoch-making flights of the past . . . the Wright brothers' pioneering flights . . . Lindbergh's dash to Paris . . . the U. S. Army 'round-the-world flight . . . and as in the present vast operation of the Deutsche Luft Hansa throughout Europe and South America . . . Socony-Vacuum lubricants have been chosen to perform . . . where *unfailing* performance is vital!

Today, in 63 countries of the world . . . flyers, as well as motorists, mariners and manufacturers, look to Socony-Vacuum for the finest petroleum products that modern methods can produce.

Douglas Aircraft Co., 1931 ◄ *Socony-Vacuum Oil Co., 1935*

All
STERLING
POWERED

Colossal projects, driven by Sterling engines, completed visions of master engineers, are active testimony to the character of Sterlings. What other marine engine has so qualified industrially, in such an array of imposing and successful applications?

Lakehurst, telescoping mooring mast, Sterling Viking 8 cylinder engine, 565 H.P., 1200 R.P.M.

New York City, fireboat, 5 Sterling Viking 8 cylinder engines, total 3000 H.P., 1200 R.P.M.

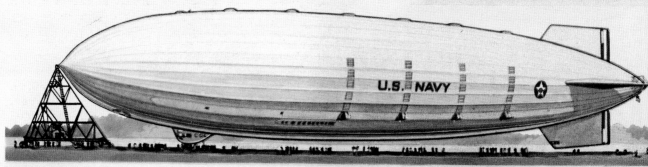

Akron, Ohio, mooring mast, Sterling Dolphin 8 cylinder engine, 240 H.P., 1200 R.P.M.

St. Paul, cruising house-boat, 125′ long, 25′ beam, 2 Sterling Petrel reduction gear engines, 180 H.P. each, 600 R.P.M., built by Joseph Dingle Boat Works.

Chicago, WASP, 88′ fast cruiser, designed by Grebe, built by Great Lakes, driven by 2 Sterling Viking 8 cylinder engines, total 1130 H.P.

The Navy mooring masts at Lakehurst Akron and Sunnyvale; the giant New York City fireboat, only gasoline-electric boat most powerful fireboat in the world; th great Portland and Tacoma fireboats, and many others; bridges, pumps, generators locomotives, rail motor cars, all equippe with Sterling engines, all requiring specifi technical knowledge, are evidence tha Sterling maintains a progressive organiza tion.

Every Sterling model is scientifically engi neered and most carefully built. Ever model, compared in terms of power and mechanical attributes, typifies 25% greate value. Prices are interestingly low.

STERLING
ENGINE COMPANY
BUFFALO, NEW YORK, U.S.A

Wings for a Comet

CUTTING the pylons at 300 miles an hour, airplanes in the annual Thompson Trophy Race on Labor Day flashed into the straight-away with incredible speed —speed unthought of even five short years ago.

Faster, ever faster, go these winged comets.

Two Thompson Trophy Race winners have set official world land plane speed records, and two others have set unofficial records. Thus the leading American air classic with its impressive awards encourages—and assures—constant improvement in the speed and safety of our country's aircraft.

That airplane safety may become as axiomatic as automobile safety, Thompson continues the annual Trophy Race as a challenge to aeronautical engineers—as a proving ground for planes.

THOMPSON PRODUCTS, INC.
Cleveland · Detroit · St. Catharines, Canada
Manufacturers of Motor and Chassis Parts Made to Car Builders' Specifications

MFRS. OF THE THOMPSON SILCROME VALVE
PIONEERS OF THE NEW SILCROME-X VALVE

Thompson Products

The Thompson Trophy, Premier Speed Award at the NATIONAL AIR RACES, Cleveland

Sterling Engine Co., 1933 ◄ *Thompson Products, 1935*

You will never really go hunting until you go in a *Douglas Amphibion*
...where you revel in inaccessibility, miles away from any blind that can be reached by other means
of travel...where you pick your own horizon and settle down any place on water or a likely
place on land. You'll be there hours...days sooner, winging along at 125 m.p.h.
in a comfortable cabin, custom-finish for eight. There is ample reserve for a speed of 150
m.p.h. if you want it, and assurance that either motor will carry the load. May we forward literature? *Douglas Aircraft Company, Inc., Santa Monica, California, U.S.A.*

Amphibion
CUSTOM-BUILT BY
DOUGLAS

FIRST AROUND THE WORLD

Douglas Aircraft Co., 1931

SECURE AND PRACTICAL FOR RECREATION AND UTILITY

Open areas surrounding almost any country club offer room for the owner of a Pitcairn Autogiro to fly directly to his golf game. Requiring little room to take off and even less to land, the pilot owner can fly directly to the scene of almost any sporting event. The practicality of such use has long ago been demonstrated by those owners of the Pitcairn Autogiro who have flown to football games, race tracks, hunt meets and other social gatherings in many locations. The ability to land on and take off from any reasonably sized open ground with security frees the pilot from the necessity of seeking a safe landing only at the large airport. The 1932 Pitcairn Tandem has been refined in design for greater speed and pleasure. Improved streamlining and more engine power add to speed. Tandem cockpits that afford the full visibility so desirable to the amateur flyer, have dual controls to permit sharing the sport of flying. A demonstration can be arranged at the point where you would use your own Autogiro. Write for descriptive literature.
PITCAIRN AIRCRAFT, INC., PITCAIRN FIELD, WILLOW GROVE, PA.

PITCAIRN
autogiro

Pitcairn Autogiro, 1931

D O U G L A S
Amphibion

Fostered by the United States Army and Navy through rigid requirements, American aviation today is recognized for its dependability and safety. ɔ ɔ The years that Douglas has been associated in building to these inflexible standards for the service of the Government now finds reflection in its new Amphibion...a craft that carries on the name which has been gained by Douglas... that dependability must be paramount. ɔ The Amphibion, custom-built by Douglas, is now available. Speed 150 M.P.H. 600-800 H.P. Twin motors, each capable of carrying the entire load. Passengers and crew 8. ɔ ɔ You are invited to write for specifications.

DOUGLAS AIRCRAFT COMPANY INC. SANTA MONICA, CALIFORNIA

DOUGLAS FIRST AROUND THE WORLD

Douglas Aircraft Co., 1931

D O U G L A S
Amphibion

Years hence, the same lad who sits beside his father now in the Amphibion cabin will himself be at the controls...of this same ship. ɔ ɔ The life span of a Douglas plane is yet to be determined. The first Douglas mail planes, built in 1926, still fly...daily. ɔ ɔ And the Douglas of today, unwilling to accept past standards, must be an even better craft. ɔ ɔ You are invited to write for complete specifications of the Custom-built Amphibion. ɔ ɔ 600-800 H.P. 60-150 M.P.H. Twin engines, each capable of carrying the entire load. Passengers and Crew 8.

DOUGLAS AIRCRAFT COMPANY, INC. SANTA MONICA, CALIFORNIA

Douglas Aircraft Co., 1931 ▸ Douglas Aircraft Co., 1931

D O U G L A S
Amphibion

The performance of the Douglas amphibion is startling...yet Douglas engineers have not sacrificed seaworthiness for performance · The Douglas amphibion is twin-engined...either motor will carry the full load...safely! · The Douglas amphibion is custom-built. We invite you to study its specifications and performance...write for particulars · Speed range 60—150 m.p.h. Horsepower 600—800. Passengers and crew 8

DOUGLAS AIRCRAFT COMPANY INC. SANTA MONICA ·CALIFORNIA

DOUGLAS FIRST AROUND THE WORLD

Half Way Across the Pacific

Of course, the Motor Control is Cutler-Hammer

In this electrical age, Motor Control is ever in the vanguard of civilization's onward march, for electric motors now do the back-breaking work wherever men go. Water must be pumped. Air must be moved. Tools must be turned. The needs of the machine shop, homes or hotel on tiny Wake Island, Mid-Pacific station of the Pan-American Airways, are the same as those in your own home town. . . . Being isolated several *thousand* miles from any help, however, makes people very serious about the choice of Motor

Control. No one likes the inconvenience, the waste of time, or the repair costs of mechanical troubles, but on Wake Island such troubles could become a near-calamity. So the Motor Control for Wake Island, delivered there on one of the earliest trips of the famous China Clipper, is all *genuine* Cutler-Hammer Motor Control.

Cutler-Hammer Motor Control is an outstanding choice wherever the importance of reliable, trouble-free electric motor performance is recognized. Many factories use Cutler-Hammer Motor Control exclusively . . . specify it by name for every motor or motorized machine purchased and refuse to accept any substitute. A majority of all electric motor builders recommend Cutler-Hammer Motor Control. Leading machinery builders feature it as standard equipment. A host of independent electrical wholesalers carry adequate stocks for your convenience. CUTLER-HAMMER, Inc., *Pioneer Manufacturers of Electric Control Apparatus*, 1259 St. Paul Avenue, Milwaukee, Wisconsin.

Cutler-Hammer, 1938

▶ *Westinghouse, 1936*

...INGS FOR THE IRON HORSE

...ennsylvania Railroad's new
...c highway from New York
...shington opens another stir-
...apter in the annals of trans-
...tion. Heretofore railroad
...fication was primarily de-
...to the improvement of termi-
...d main line suburban service,
...nel operations, and the haul-
...f heavy freight over steep
...tain grades. Today it becomes
...ew order of railroad modern-
...n on major trunk lines...
...ents a definite advance in the
...mical readjustment of rail-
...facilities to the demands of
...rn travel.

...his advance, Westinghouse has
...d a major role, consistent with
...ong tradition of co-operation
...the Transportation Industry.
...e Westinghouse Electric and
...ufacturing Company was
...d on that tradition. Its foun-
...nvented and brought to bril-
...fruition the Westinghouse
...Brake. Its first great achieve-
...was the successful promulga-
...of the alternating current
...m... upon which is based the
...sylvania's system for main
...electrification.

...this great project, Westing-
...e brought the wealth of a half-
...ury of experience and engi-
...ng progress. A conspicuous
...ple of Westinghouse enter-
...on every front where elec-
...y is helping to build a new and
...er economic civilization.
...tinghouse Electric & Manufac-
...g Co., East Pittsburgh, Pa.

NATURE'S AIR IS BEST

WHEN a new June sun coaxes blossoms from plant and tree . . . when the morning grass glistens with warm dew and puffy snow-white clouds float over a sapphire sky . . . then instinct tells us Nature's air is at its best and all mankind yearns to answer the call of the great outdoors.

Healthful warmth like that of a fine June day—made so by Nature's own formula—is brought to your home through all the winter months by the Holland Vaporaire Heating System.

No longer need any one pay the penalty of obsolete heating methods. No longer need any one live in stifling, stagnant, baked-dry air . . . Holland's simple, compact, electrically-controlled home heating and air-conditioning system warms, humidifies and circulates the air you breathe. You enjoy a refreshing, exhilarating indoor atmosphere.

In winter, a moist balmy current of warmth circulates through every room and keeps the proper temperature constant. The air changes completely every few minutes.

In summer, a power-driven, airplane-type propeller sends zestful, cooling breezes through the whole house—making hot, sultry days and nights comfortable.

Every Holland Vaporaire Heating System is accurately engineered and custom built to fit the exact requirements of the home it serves. One company plans, builds, sells, installs and finances. Responsibility is undivided. Comfort and satisfaction are guaranteed by Holland's written bond.

Get the facts. There's a direct factory branch in your community. Simply telephone. Have a Holland heating engineer call. No obligation . . . Vaporaire Division, HOLLAND FURNACE COMPANY, Holland, Michigan.

FREE HEATING ENGINEERING SERVICE

Holland's Complete Heating Survey is the modern way to heating comfort. Holland Surveys include humidity reading, chimney draft tests, show you how to save fuel and money through proper heat distribution, disclose fire risks, and reveal the reasons some rooms are hard to heat. Have a Complete Heating Survey made by Holland heating engineers without delay. No cost—no obligation.

World's largest installers of home heating systems, operating three large factories and 554 factory branches from coast to coast

HOLLAND VAPORAIRE HEATING

THE ELECTRICALLY CONTROLLED AIR-CONDITIONING SYSTEM FOR WINTER HEATING AND SUMMER COOLING

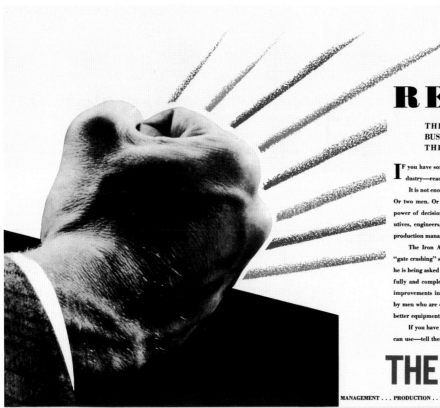

The Iron Age, 1931

Holland Vaporaire Heating, 1931 ◄ American Radiator, 1936

Kelvinator, 1936

And the winner is...

Between World Wars

Long before the shadow of war was cast on the United States, one of the country's first modern peace organizations was lobbying Americans to consider an alternative. Founded in 1936, World Peaceways was instrumental in convincing Franklin D. Roosevelt to stave off involvement in World War II during the 1930s. Their aggressive series of magazine ads, billboards, and radio programs— some featuring babies on butcher blocks or disabled WW-I vets who had been all but forgotten—also reminded the country that, in contemporary warfare, there could be no such thing as a noncombatant US citizen.

Zwischen den Kriegen

Lange bevor düstere Kriegswolken am Horizont aufzogen, versuchte eine der ersten modernen Friedensgruppen des Landes, den Amerikanern Alternativen aufzuzeigen. 1936 gegründet, war World Peaceways maßgeblich daran beteiligt, Franklin D. Roosevelt davon zu überzeugen, das Land aus dem Zweiten Weltkrieg herauszuhalten. Mit aggressiven Reklametafeln, Radiospots und Anzeigen – einige zeigten Babys auf Schlachterblöcken und die schon fast in Vergessenheit geratenen Kriegskrüppel des Ersten Weltkriegs – erinnerten sie die Nation daran, dass es in einem modernen Krieg keine unbeteiligten Zivilisten mehr gibt.

Entre deux guerres mondiales

Bien avant que l'ombre de la guerre ne s'abatte sur les Etats-Unis, l'une des premières organisations pacifistes américaines faisait campagne contre l'éventualité d'un conflit armé. Fondée en 1936, World Peaceways contribua à convaincre Franklin D. Roosevelt de retarder l'intervention de son pays dans la Seconde Guerre mondiale. Ses campagnes de choc dans les magazines, à la radio ou sur les panneaux d'affichage (certaines montrant des bébés sur des tables de boucher ou des soldats de la Grande Guerre revenus infirmes, puis oubliés) rappelèrent également aux citoyens américains que, dans la guerre moderne, il n'y avait pas de non-combattants.

El período de entreguerras

Tiempo antes de que la sombra de la guerra se cerniera sobre Estados Unidos, una de las primeras organizaciones por la paz nacidas en el país actuaba como grupo de presión conminando a los norteamericanos a que contemplaran alternativas al enfrentamiento bélico. Fundada en 1936, la World Peaceways desempeñó un papel esencial durante los años treinta, al convencer a Franklin D. Roosevelt de no involucrar al país en la Segunda Guerra Mundial. Sus descarnadas campañas en la prensa escrita, en vallas publicitarias y en programas radiofónicos mostraban a bebés sobre tablas de carnicero y a veteranos de la Primera Guerra Mundial lisiados y desatendidos. Con ello, se recordaba a la población que, en época de guerra, no tendría cabida el ciudadano estadounidense no combatiente.

大戦のはざまで

戦争の黒い影が合衆国に忍び寄る前、最初の近代的平和組織が、参戦か不戦かよく考えるようにとアメリカ国民に働きかけた。1936年設立のワールド・ピースウェイズには抑止力があり、フランクリン・D・ルーズヴェルトを説得して、かろうじて1930年代の第2次世界大戦参戦を食い止めさせた。彼らの積極的な一連の雑誌広告、屋外看板、ラジオ番組——肉屋のまな板の上の赤ちゃんや、すでに忘れ去られたも同然の不具の第2次世界大戦の退役軍人を主役にしたものもあった——は、この国には戦争にかかわらない合衆国市民は存在し得なかったということも再認識させた。

To be killed in action

He's going to grow up to go to war?

No—he's never going to grow up at all. If another war comes, he and his mother and thousands upon thousands like them are going to "die in action."

"Impossible!" you say. "They're non-combatants." Don't be silly—there'll be no such thing as non-combatants in the next war.

Wide-cruising submarines, and bombing planes will laugh at front lines. Gas—gas so powerful that one drop on your skin will kill you—will not be particular whose skin it touches. There will be no haven, no sanctuary, no safety. *Everyone* will suffer.

And for what? *Glory*—where was it in the last war?

Victory—where was it in the last peace?

With that cruel lesson still fresh in mind, is another war to be forced upon us—a war infinitely more horrible, more futile, and more lasting in its harm than the last?

That is for you to decide!

What to do about it

Hysterical protests won't avert another war, any more than will "preparedness."

Civilization must build its own defense out of human reason and intelligence, properly organized and applied.

To every reasonable and intelligent man and woman in America goes the responsibility of doing his or her share to avert the coming war.

World Peaceways offers a practical plan of how you *can* help. Write for it. There is no obligation involved in your inquiry, except the obligation to your conscience and to your conviction that *there must be no more wars.* World Peaceways, Inc., 103 Park Avenue, New York City.

World Peaceways, 1935

"... and here's our new bathroom"

IT'S REALLY THE OLD ONE MADE OVER

TWO SIMPLE CHANGES, and almost any bathroom becomes up-to-date and attractive. Let's look at your own. Is it about average size, 6 x 9 feet? Then for less than $20 you can work wonders with a floor of Armstrong's Inlaid Linoleum, a trimly tailored floor, securely cemented in place.

Change number two provides the smart, modern walls every careful housekeeper wants. And all with very little bother or outlay of money, thanks to Armstrong's

Linowall. This new material is quickly installed right over old walls. Then *no more refinishing!* For Linowall is permanently beautiful and, like Armstrong's Linoleum, doesn't mind a splashing or even a spilled medicine bottle.

Our new book, "Floor Beauty for New Homes and Old," tells charmingly how to brighten up bathrooms, kitchens, and other

rooms of your home. Full color illustrations show convincingly what a big difference modern Armstrong Floors and Walls can make.

Your copy will be sent for 10¢ to cover mailing costs (20¢ in Canada.) Address Armstrong Cork Company, Floor Division, 974 Mary Street, Lancaster, Pa. (Makers of cork products since 1860.)

Armstrong's Linoleum Floors

FOR EVERY ROOM Ⓐ **IN THE HOUSE**

PLAIN • INLAID • EMBOSSED • JASPÉ • PRINTED • ARMSTRONG'S QUAKER RUGS and ARMSTRONG'S LINOWALL

Armstrong's Linoleum Floors, 1934

"Their guest room made me feel at home the moment I stepped into it ... so comfortingly cozy ... so alive with loveliness." Thus another guest expresses the welcome so carefully built into this room by a smart hostess. She began, as many decorators do today, with the floor ... a spread of modestly colorful plaid (Armstrong's Embossed Inlaid No. 5470). It's restful and quiet underfoot—and just as kind to the hostess as to the guest. A quick dusting cleans it. Occasional touching up with Armstrong's Linogloss Wax (self-polishing) keeps its colors glowing. What is true of this guest room can be true of any room in your home—an Armstrong Floor will help you double its beauty. Your merchant has scores of designs to choose from—and he'll be glad to give you exact prices if you tell him your room measurements.

Decorating Ideas by the Bookful

We have prepared a 36-page book for you, full of ideas that will help you brighten your home. Ask for "Floors That Keep Homes in Fashion," illustrated with room photographs in full natural color. Just send 10¢ (40¢ outside U.S.A.) to Armstrong Cork Products Company, Floor Division, 3606 Mary Street, Lancaster, Pennsylvania. (Makers of cork products since 1860.)

The most satisfactory way to install linoleum on wood floors is to insist on a permanent job cemented over felt.

ARMSTRONG'S LINOLEUM FLOORS
for every room Ⓐ *in the house*

PLAIN • INLAID • EMBOSSED • JASPÉ • PRINTED • ARMSTRONG'S QUAKER RUGS and ARMSTRONG'S LINOWALL

Armstrong's Linoleum Floors, 1936

FAMOUS FOR FINE FOOD, Grauel's Market, Baltimore, is also becoming famous for its fine, trade-attracting floor—a special design in Armstrong's Linoleum installed by John R. Livezey, designed by J. P. Pfeiffer & Son, Baltimore (Marbelle No. 03 with strips of jade green). Table and counter tops are also Armstrong's Linoleum.

BUY-APPEAL FROM THE FLOOR UP is the plan of this modern market. "Despite keen competition, this plan is paying attractive trade dividends," enthusiastically reports Mr. Harry Grauel, the proprietor. "Folks like the fine, spick-and-span appearance of my Armstrong Floor. It has eye-appeal and *buy*-appeal. It's my best silent salesman!" Mr. Grauel will also tell you that Armstrong's Linoleum Floors, when trimly and properly cemented in place over felt, can take street-floor traffic, that such floors cut cleaning to a minimum, and do away with expensive floor refinishing. When the photograph above was taken, this floor hadn't been washed, waxed, or polished in a month, although it had received a daily sweeping. You see it reproduced just as the camera caught it—no tracks, traffic lanes, or scuff marks. Your local linoleum merchant can demonstrate two other big virtues of modern Armstrong Floors ... cushioning comfort underfoot, and a price that should appeal to any careful business executive. Let him tell you the whole story of floors that put showmanship in selling.

WE'LL SEND YOU a most helpful portfolio of different business interiors if you write for "Better Floors for Better Business." It also brings you the wear, care, and cost story in concise, quick-reference form. No charge (4¢ outside U.S.A.). Armstrong Cork Products Company, Floor Division, 3711 City Street, Lancaster, Pennsylvania. (Makers of cork products since 1860)

ARMSTRONG'S LINOLEUM FLOORS
Custom-Laid or Ⓐ *Standard Designs*

PLAIN • INLAID • EMBOSSED • JASPÉ • LINOTILE • CORK TILE • ACCOTILE • RUBBER TILE • ARMSTRONG'S LINOWALL and ARMSTRONG'S QUAKER RUGS

Armstrong's Linoleum Floors, 1934 ◄ *Armstrong's Linoleum Floors, 1937*

I like that store .. they never try to sell you substitutes

WHEN you want a long-wearing, labor-saving, dollar-saving rug, do as this housewife did. Go to a store that sells genuine Congoleum with the Gold Seal pasted on the face of every pattern. Genuine Congoleum has a waterproof, sanitary surface that is the easiest thing in the world to clean. These rugs lie flat without fastening. And they outwear cheaply made substitutes by a wide margin. Look for the Gold Seal when you buy.

CONGOLEUM-NAIRN INC. . . . KEARNY, N. J.

In Canada: Congoleum Canada, Ltd., Montreal

"Grace, you really ought to go and see the new Congoleum patterns. You can see them all at the place where I bought this ... I like that store—they don't try to sell you substitutes." *The pattern Helen chose is "Norfolk," Congoleum Gold Seal Rug No. 670. Room decorated by Gimbel Bros., N. Y.*

CONGOLEUM
REG. U.S. PAT. OFF.

Gold Seal Rugs

AND BY-THE-YARD

Congoleum, 1934 ▶ *Armstrong's Linoleum Floors, 1931*

APPY LANDINGS

for young airmen who haven't won their wings

THESE are adventurous days for air-minded young America. Models to be built. Test flights to be made. Maps to be studied. And that Saturday afternoon air meet and circus!

But even intrepid aviators must have an airport. So Flight Commander (that's mother, of course) does some very special planning.

The closet becomes a chart room. The bed a handy storehouse. A little more magic—and the floor is just the happiest landing field a busy boy could wish for.

It won't tell tales on him for one thing—the Accolac-Processed surface is spot-proof, stain-proof. It's built for hard service—every color inlaid. It helps quiet noise, soften footsteps. And it's springy and warm, too—cemented firmly in place over linoleum lining felt.

The happiest part of this Armstrong floor is its pleasing design. This is just one of innumerable motifs you can plan with Armstrong's Linoleum. Some, called Linosets, come all ready for quick installation. Others can be worked out in plain, or marble, or Jaspé linoleum to suit your fancy. Your local linoleum, furniture, or department store merchant will tell you the whole story of these Armstrong Floors of individual design.

Plans for this room free

In the meantime, our Bureau of Interior Decoration would like to send you complete working plans for this young airman's room—color scheme, furniture details, floor plan. Plus a bookful of other equally unusual interiors called "New Ideas in Home Decoration." Just send 10¢ to cover mailing. Address Armstrong Cork Company, Floor Division, 339 Lincoln Ave., Lancaster, Pennsylvania. (Makers of cork products since 1860.)

Some day a very lucky son of a very famous flyer may have a room like this. At least we hope he'll have as happy a landing place for his imaginary flights as the Armstrong's Linoleum Floor shown. Embossed Inlaid No. 3221 forms the field, while plain blue, tan, and yellow linoleum are used for the center inset design. Two designs below are: left, Linoset No. 2; right, Jaspé No. 010.

Armstrong's *Linoleum Floors*
for every room in the house

IN · · · INLAID · · · EMBOSSED · · · JASPÉ · · · PRINTED · · · *and* ARMSTRONG'S QUAKER RUGS

A little money buys a lot of leisure . . .

YOU know how hard it is to keep old-fashioned rugs clean—how easy it is for back-breaking cleaning-drudgery to steal away a big share of your summer hours of leisure.

But this drudgery and a Congoleum Rug simply can't exist in the same room. So, wherever you plan to spend your summer—see to it that drudgery spends it somewhere else.

That's easy to arrange. Lovely Congoleum Gold Seal Rugs—for porch, dining room, kitchen, living room—all for surprisingly little money. That's the answer.

Flat-lying, sanitary, rain-proof—these rugs can be cleaned with a whisk of a damp mop—as free of germs, dirt and grime as you will be free of drudgery, when Congoleum Rugs come into your home.

Go to your dealer now. Ask for Congoleum Gold Seal Rugs, and (for your own protection) see that the Gold Seal is pasted on the face of the pattern.

CONGOLEUM-NAIRN INC., KEARNY, N. J.
In Canada—Congoleum Canada Ltd., Montreal

CONGOLEUM
GOLD SEAL RUGS

ONLY genuine Congoleum Rugs have that in-built durability imparted by the exclusive Multicote Process. So to safeguard you against inferior rugs that will not last like real Congoleum, we paste a big Gold Seal right on the pattern-side of every genuine Congoleum Gold Seal Rug.

If the material offered you does not bear this Gold Seal, it is not Congoleum. Ask for Congoleum Gold Seal Rugs by name. And make sure you get them.

Congoleum, 1931

donald deskey

noted designer of furniture and fabrics, and member of the American Union of Decorative Artists and Craftsmen, tells decorators of American homes

what he thinks of
EMBOSSED LINOLEUM

As a fitting background for his newest designs in furniture and fabrics, Mr. Deskey selects this new Embossed effect in Armstrong's Linoleum (No. 5226). "This floor," says Mr. Deskey, "captures the play of lamplight particularly because of its textured surface."

IN homes of today good taste calls for some new habits in floors," declares Donald Deskey. "One reason for this happy change is the group of new Embossed Inlaid Linoleum effects introduced by Armstrong.

"In my opinion, Embossed Linoleum is an exceptionally fine floor for many types of rooms. It possesses all the practical virtues that have always characterized linoleum, plus this one very decided advantage—a textured surface you can see and feel. I've watched this textured surface under the play of lamplight, of sunlight. It gives a decorative and still a structural feeling to the floor. Colors are softened, enriched by it. Never can an Embossed Floor be accused of a drab appearance.

"To those who wish to keep their homes in tune with the better things that are being done in home furnishings, my advice is to see these latest contributions for floors—Embossed Inlaid Linoleum."

That's easy advice to follow. Next time you are shopping, stop in at a good linoleum, furniture, or department store. There you can get complete information about the reasonable cost of an Armstrong Floor, the new spot-proof, easily cleaned Accolac-Processed surface, the trim, custom-like way any floor you select will be installed.

For suggestions on just what floor designs will look best in your home, write to our Bureau of Interior Decoration. "New Ideas in Home Decoration," a color-illustrated book by Hazel Dell Brown, will be sent you promptly. Expert help in planning every part of room decoration will be given free. With your request enclose 10¢ to cover postage (Canada, 20¢).

Address Armstrong Cork Company, Floor Division, 941 Mary St., Lancaster, Pennsylvania. (Makers of cork products since 1860.)

Armstrong's Linoleum Floors
for every room in the house

PLAIN   •   INLAID   •   EMBOSSED   •   JASPÉ   •   PRINTED   •   and ARMSTRONG'S QUAKER RUGS

Armstrong's Linoleum Floors, 1931

The old floor was a problem
— but Muriel solved it

Here's Muriel and her friends having "kitchen party" after the movies. "Don't bother about crumbs," says Muriel, "this new rug is a perfect cinch to clean." *The pattern shown is "Isabelle," Congoleum Gold Seal Rug No. 674. Kitchen installed by Abraham & Straus, Brooklyn, N. Y.*

WHEN Muriel and her mother went shopping, they followed the golden rule of rug buying—Look for the Gold Seal. This Gold Seal identifies the one and only genuine Congoleum—both rugs and "by-the-yard." The one way to be sure of complete satisfaction is to buy only rugs that have the Gold Seal pasted on their patterns. Fascinating new Congoleum designs for every room in the house are now on display. You'll enjoy seeing them.

CONGOLEUM-NAIRN INC., KEARNY, N. J.
Makers of the famous easy-to-clean Sealex Linoleum and Sealex Wall-Covering
In Canada: Congoleum Canada, Ltd., Montreal

CONGOLEUM
Gold Seal Rugs
AND CONGOLEUM BY-THE-YARD

Armstrong, 1936 ◄   *Congoleum, 1934*

The real color and graining of
KNOTTY PINE
in "STAINLESS SHEEN" floor covering

There's a gracious charm . . . an inviting warmth . . . a cheery, homespun flavor to Pabco Knotty Pine . . . bringing a new note of hospitality and friendliness into a home!

And, it's a floor covering that you can use in a wide variety of rooms . . . living rooms, dining rooms, breakfast rooms, bedrooms, dens and rumpus rooms . . . either in town or country.

Like all Pabco rugs and yard goods, its non-porous Stainless Sheen surface is surprisingly easy to keep spotlessly clean . . . with no other aid than a damp mop! No moisture nor grease can penetrate the extra-thick enamel; no dirt nor germs can find a hiding place!

Also, this Stainless Sheen surface is sturdier . . . far more durable.

See Pabco Knotty Pine . . . and other new Pabco patterns in rugs and yard goods . . . at your local floor covering store . . . today! You'll be thrilled at how much floor beauty you can buy for just a few dollars!

The Paraffine Companies, Inc.
New York   San Francisco   Chicago

PABCO
FLOOR COVERINGS

PABCO *Guaranty* RUGS and PABCO *Warranty* YARD GOODS

Pabco Floor Coverings, 1938

CLOSE HARMONY between floor and walls

. . . . a new way to remodel old kitchens

Walls—"Green Beryl" design in Sealex Wall-Covering No. 7961. Floor—the "Andalusia" pattern, Sealex Linoleum No. 7327.

Be ready for your husband the next time he compliments your cooking— the next time he says, "This pie is better than the ones mother used to make." Remind him, ever so sweetly, that you could do still better— if only your kitchen were more gay and cheerful. And then—

Show him this picture. Explain that this is a brand new idea in kitchens . . . floor and walls built of two intimately related materials — Sealex Linoleum and the new Sealex Wall-Covering. This gives the room a "unity" of color and texture that greatly increases its charm.

Tell him that Sealex remodeling produces expensive-looking results at a cost that really won't ruin him financially. These materials are perfectly suited for remodeling. No costly preparatory work is necessary. The materials are applied right over the old floor or walls.

Point out that Sealex will make you a much more agreeable wife, for this flooring is resilient—makes every step you take seem lighter—keeps you from getting tired and cross. Furthermore, both these Sealex materials are stain-proof and easy-to-clean. You're through with temper-trying scrubbing.

Your final argument is to take him by the arm and lead him to a store that sells Sealex. No one can possibly resist the fascinating new Sealex patterns now on display in the stores.

CONGOLEUM-NAIRN INC., KEARNY, N. J.
Also manufacturers of the famous Congoleum Gold Seal Rugs.

"Court" Pattern,
Sealex Linoleum No. 7340

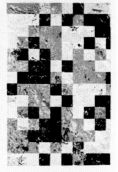

"Mosaic" Pattern,
Sealex Linoleum No. 3240

SEALEX
REG. U. S. PAT. OFF.

FLOORS AND WALLS

These floors do their part for Better Business

THERE'S a brighter spirit—a quicker pulse—in today's business world. And a floor that reflects this spirit serves as a pleasant pick-me-up for customers and employees alike.

No matter what your business may be, a sunny new floor of Armstrong's Linoleum will help it gain a firmer footing in today's march towards recovery.

In great banks and modest shops—in magnificent hotels and corner lunch counters—you'll find Armstrong's Floors doing their part—faithfully, cheerfully.

Armstrong Floors keep their life and color with a minimum of care.

They stay the way you like to see them for years.

There are scores of Armstrong Floor designs to choose from, suited to different tastes, different uses, different budgets. And the cost? It will not be much. There is a merchant in your neighborhood able and willing to give you an accurate estimate. He will install your new floor permanently over linoleum lining felt, with only the slightest interruption of business.

BETTER BUSINESS BOOK FREE
"Public Floors of Enduring Beauty" shows many Armstrong's Linoleum Floors that are building business for merchants the country over. Your copy is free (Canada, 25¢). Or, if you're interested in residence floors, enclose 10¢ (Canada, 20¢) for a beautiful book on practical decoration. Ask for "Floor Beauty for New Homes and Old." Armstrong Cork Company, Floor Division, 979 Race Ave., Lancaster, Pa. (Makers of Cork Products since 1860)

Armstrong's Linoleum Floors
CUSTOM-LAID OR (A) STANDARD DESIGNS

PLAIN • INLAID • EMBOSSED • JASPÉ • LINOTILE • CORK TILE • ACCOTILE • RUBBER TILE and ARMSTRONG'S LINOWALL

Armstrong's Linoleum Floors, 1934

FLOOR SHOWMANSHIP has made the Ambassador Hotel a famous rendezvous at the Nation's Capital. For the gay Armstrong's Linoleum Floor has been an irresistible invitation to the smart set who dine here nightly. It's been two years now since this Armstrong Floor started welcoming guests to the Ambassador. Yet, despite the unusually severe wear, this floor looks as fresh as the day it was installed. This is just another practical example of the service you can expect from Armstrong's Linoleum in your own place of business. An example, too, of how you can now have floors specially designed to match any decorative motif. Such floors put showmanship into a business interior. And put a real saving into your pocket, for they cut maintenance costs to a minimum. Ask your local merchant to give you all the facts and figures of these better floors for better business.

THE AMBASSADOR HOTEL, Washington, D. C., has spread color and comfort underfoot with this specially designed Armstrong's Linoleum Floor in cadet blue, ruby, and white. Trimly tailored and cemented in place over cushioning felt, such a floor also offers the advantage of lowered maintenance costs, and satisfactory service over many years.

Write for Free Book, "Better Floors for Better Business." Illustrates all types of business interiors that have put floors on the sales force. Armstrong Cork Products Company, Floor Division, 3709 Liberty St., Lancaster, Pa. (Makers of cork products since 1860)

ARMSTRONG'S LINOLEUM FLOORS
Custom-Laid or (A) Standard Designs

PLAIN • INLAID • EMBOSSED • JASPÉ • LINOTILE • CORK TILE • ACCOTILE • RUBBER TILE • ARMSTRONG'S LINOWALL and ARMSTRONG'S QUAKER RUGS

Armstrong's Linoleum Floors, 1937

GAY AS A JUNE DAY is every day in this roomful of summer sunshine.

And gay indeed is the woman who has discovered how easy it is to capture such lasting good cheer for her home. You'll make that discovery the moment you visit your favorite merchant and see the lovely new fashions in Armstrong's Linoleum Floors. They'll let you be a bit daring with color. They'll help you plan rooms that are different, rooms that will turn out just as you hoped. The room above is but one example. Here's something quite new in linoleum—a plaid design in six-inch marble blocks, No. 640—that invites the generous sprinkling of color in walls, furniture, and drapes. The result is a refreshing harmony, a cheering, summery atmosphere. So cheering, too, when cleaning time comes! This floor is brushed clean in a jiffy. And it's kept new and bright with occasional applications of Armstrong's Linogloss Wax. Is it any wonder that so many, many women are modernizing their homes with Armstrong's Linoleum Floors?

Year-Round Comfort is a welcome feature of this most refreshing room. For every step on the Armstrong Floor is cushioned, quieted. Linoleum itself is springy, and the most comfortable of floors when firmly cemented over felt . . . A good reason, too, why this floor will last for years of service. Note the unusual color scheme of chartreuse, lemon-yellow, and salmon, the silver ceiling and the rainbow rug. (Complete specifications of this room will be sent on request.)

"Floors That Keep Homes in Fashion" is a new 36-page book you should have before you spend a penny in fixing up your home. Natural color photographs of all types of interiors will help you see just how your own rooms will look. Write, enclosing 10¢, and we'll send you a copy (in Canada, 40¢). Address Armstrong Cork Products Company, Floor Division (Dept. J-12), Lancaster, Pa.

ARMSTRONG'S LINOLEUM FLOORS
for every room (A) in the house

PLAIN • INLAID • EMBOSSED • JASPÉ • PRINTED • ARMSTRONG'S QUAKER RUGS and ARMSTRONG'S LINOWALL

Armstrong's Linoleum Floors, 1935

Mom says stay out of her kitchen. She just scrubbed the kitchen floor and doesn't want us tramping over it. I-w- ... Gee ... just when we wanted to make some m'lasses taffy, too ...

Say, Billy—if we had a Congoleum Rug Mom wouldn't always run us out of the kitchen. Mrs. Fisher has one, and she never fusses about her kitchen floor . . . let's ask Mom to get one!

And, Madam, this Gold Seal is your guarantee that it's genuine Congoleum! Imagine the children giving me this idea! I never dreamed real Congoleum Rugs cost so little.

This cheerful kitchen says ... "Youngsters welcome!"

With an easy-to-clean Congoleum Rug on the floor, even Mother enjoys the children's kitchen parties! And her purchase gives her every penny's worth of value . . . for she made sure there was a Gold Seal pasted on the face of the pattern. Only genuine Congoleum . . . Rugs and By-the-Yard . . . can carry this Gold Seal. The pattern shown in the kitchen is "Medbury"—Congoleum Gold Seal Rug No. 409. Room size rugs, up to 9 feet by 12 feet, $4.50 to $9.95. Larger sizes equally low priced.

CONGOLEUM
Gold Seal Rugs
and Congoleum by-the-yard
NONE GENUINE WITHOUT THIS GOLD SEAL ➡

CONGOLEUM-NAIRN INC., KEARNY, N. J.; IN CANADA: CONGOLEUM CANADA, LTD., MONTREAL
Also sole manufacturers of the famous easy-to-clean Sealex Linoleum and Sealex Wall-Covering

A charming pattern for perpendicular convenience—"Gretchen," Congoleum Gold Seal Rug No. 402.

"Bucca[?]"—Congoleum Gold Seal Rug No. 607, recalls the Candlewick motif of Colonial days.

Congoleum, 1935

Armstrong's Linoleum Floors, 1938

Congoleum, 1936

Pabco, 1936

Cambridge Tile Co., 1937

▶ Armstrong's Linoleum Floors, 1932

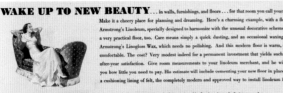

WAKE UP TO NEW BEAUTY ... in walls, furnishings, and floors ... for that room you call your own.

Make it a cheery place for planning and dreaming. Here's a charming example, with a floor of Armstrong's Linoleum, specially designed to harmonize with the unusual decorative scheme. It's a very practical floor, too. Care means simply a quick dusting, and an occasional waxing with Armstrong's Linogloss Wax, which needs no polishing. And this modern floor is warm, quiet, comfortable. The cost? Very modest indeed for a permanent investment that yields such year-after-year satisfaction. Give room measurements to your linoleum merchant, and he will tell you how little you need to pay. His estimate will include cementing your new floor in place over a cushioning lining of felt, the completely modern and approved way to install linoleum floors.

This room is filled with new beauty ideas—twin beds made up as one, built-in vanity table, figurines instead of pictures, and a specially designed floor of Armstrong's Rust Jaspé Linoleum with Plain Black interliners. Complete specifications sent on request.

YOUR COPY IS READY! Send 10¢ (U.S. and Canada only) for our new 36-page book, "Floors That Keep Homes in Fashion," showing all types of rooms in full color. It explains free decorating service, Armstrong Cork Products Company, Floor Division, 3704 Mulberry Street, Lancaster, Pa. (Makers of cork products since 1860)

ARMSTRONG'S LINOLEUM FLOORS

for every room Ⓐ in the house

PLAIN · INLAID · EMBOSSED · MARBELLE · JASPÉ · RAYBELLE · PRINTED · QUAKER RUGS and LINOWALL

Armstrong's Linoleum Floors, 1937

THE
Mayfair
Chair
BY
KARPEN
A STUDY IN ELEGANCE
Genuine (Honduras) Mahogany
SPECIALLY PRICED
AT YOUR DEALERS $49.50 PLUS FREIGHT
★
Write for Booklet
"Charm that Endures"

KARPEN
Guaranteed
FURNITURE

COVERED IN GENUINE CHASE *Velmo* CHOICE OF COLORS
GUARANTEED MOTH PROOFED

S. KARPEN & BROS.

CHICAGO   NEW YORK   LOS ANGELES   SAN FRANCISCO

Karpen Furniture, 1937

A CHARMING
LIVING ROOM
All Day—

A BEDROOM
THAT *Night*

How you can add
Another Bedroom
FOR AS LITTLE AS $34.75

HOW many times have you wished for an *extra bedroom*... a truly comfortable place where you'd feel free to invite guests to spend the night ... a room that would come in handy when the children are home from school or when relatives arrive unexpectedly?

Well, you *can* have that room, and it won't cost a dollar for remodeling, or increase your rent a cent! For, when you bring one of these new Simmons Studio Couches into your home, you automatically add another bedroom!

Go Beautifully In So Many Rooms

There's hardly a room in your home where one of these attractive new couches would

not prove a handsome addition. Delightfully modern, in a wide range of authentic styles and charming fabrics, they meet the most discerning decorative requirements.

During the day, your living room, den, library, spare room or one-room apartment reflects a new note of smartness and hospitality. At night, you can always solve your extra-bedroom problem in a jiffy.

Easily Converted into Double or Twin Beds

Each of the many attractive Simmons Studio Couches can be *quickly* converted

into a marvelously comfortable double bed or twin beds. No fuss or bother, for they make up just as easily as an ordinary bed.

The Countess Studio Couch, illustrated above, is available in a choice of many beautiful fabrics, cord trims. Complete with Simmons inner-spring mattress. $34.75.

See New Sofa-Bed Creations by Simmons

Your dealer has other Simmons couches and a beautiful new group of Simmons Sofa-Beds—smart sofas concealing two Simmons beds. Simmons Company, Merchandise Mart, Chicago, Illinois.

SEPTEMBER 7TH FIRST SHOWING BY LEADING STORES

SIMMONS
Studio Couches

BY THE WORLD'S LARGEST MAKERS OF BEDS · SPRINGS
MATTRESSES · STUDIO COUCHES · METAL FURNITURE

Simmons Studio Couches, 1937

HERE'S A FLOOR THAT SAYS,

"Let's dance" AND MEANS IT!

Can Armstrong Floors take the traffic? Our best answer is to point out their popularity for restaurant and dance room floors. Above, you see one of the latest proofs—the famous Arcadia, The International Restaurant, in Philadelphia. Here the Armstrong Floor does the same double duty it will be asked to do in your own business home: first, to attract trade by its fresh, smart beauty; and second, to keep all its snap, dash, and eye-appeal regardless of a most severe day-and-night drubbing.

Your local linoleum merchant can tell you of other sales-attracting Armstrong installations, can show you other Armstrong Floors that give no hint of their years and years of active service. See him. Get the money-saving facts.

Dancing feet can't mar the beauty of this custom-built Armstrong Floor in the Arcadia, The International Restaurant, Philadelphia, Pa. The special design (orange with insets of black, white, and silver gray) indicates the unlimited effects possible with modern Armstrong's Linoleum. *Floor installed by Livezey Linoleum Floors, Inc. Armand D. Carroll, architect.*

Ask for This Decorating Service

Our Bureau of Interior Decoration will gladly work with you or your architect in creating floor effects that best suit your place of business. This free service is explained in our new book, "Public Floors of Enduring Beauty." All types of business interiors are illustrated. Send for this free helpful book. (In Canada, 40¢.) Armstrong Cork Products Company, Desk D3, Floor Division, Lancaster, Pennsylvania.

ARMSTRONG'S LINOLEUM FLOORS

Custom-Laid or *Standard Designs*

PLAIN · INLAID · EMBOSSED · JASPÉ · LINOTILE · CORK TILE · ACCOTILE · RUBBER TILE and ARMSTRONG'S QUAKER RUGS

Armstrong's Linoleum Floors, 1935

▶ *Sherwin-Williams Paints, 1936*

Painting by Rockwell Kent

BEAUTY AND

(Copyright 1936), Sherwin-Williams Co., Cleveland, O.

PROTECTION

No one knows paint like a painter

PAINTERS know paint. Know it from every angle. Know it from the standpoint of beauty, of service, of protection. No one knows paint like a painter!

And 8 painters in every 10 use Dutch Boy White Lead—use it because it retains its beauty longer—because it gives a protective coating that doesn't crack or scale and therefore saves the expense of burning and scraping when repaint time rolls 'round—because with Dutch Boy they obtain the exact tints and shades your individual taste demands.

Remember, when your painter writes "Dutch Boy White Lead" into his estimates he is assuring you of a custom-made paint, a paint mixed to order for your particular job. Depend upon him. No one knows paint like a painter!

Write for "The House We Live In", a free booklet giving many helpful suggestions on the decoration and protection of the home. Address the branch nearest you.

NATIONAL LEAD COMPANY

New York, 111 Broadway—Buffalo, 116 Oak Street—Chicago, 900 West 18th Street—Cincinnati, 659 Freeman Avenue—Cleveland, 820 West Superior Avenue—St. Louis, 722 Chestnut Street—San Francisco, 235 Montgomery Street—Boston, National-Boston Lead Co., 800 Albany Street—Pittsburgh, National Lead & Oil Co. of Pa., 316 Fourth Avenue—Philadelphia, John T. Lewis & Bros. Co., Widener Building.

8 PAINTERS IN EVERY 10 USE DUTCH BOY
(According to an impartial, country-wide survey)

DUTCH BOY
WHITE LEAD

100 LBS. NET
DUTCH BOY
WHITE LEAD

Save the surface and you save all—dog's head

Dutch Boy Paint, 1930

Mr. *and* Mrs. Valspar

"Aren't these colors lovely, Val?"

"Whenever I start painting with these colors, Val, I just can't leave them alone," continues Mrs. Valspar.

"Yeah," agrees Val, "just like eating peanuts."

The famous Valspar Boiling Water Test

Transform *"The Den"*

THE SAME ROOM, THE SAME FURNITURE—PLUS VALSPAR AND NEW DRAPES.

"GOSH! . . . It's hard to imagine it's the same room," says Mr. Valspar, their color-spree in 'The Den' having ended in mutual admiration of their accomplishment.

"I think we worked out a pretty attractive color scheme, Val, don't you?" returns Mrs. Val, recalling the night she had curled up in the old wing chair when they planned the "transformation."

"But, it's even better than we anticipated," concludes Val, "and if credit goes where it belongs 'The Valspars' should be saluted."

Thousands of other families have been equally gratified with Valspar. Whenever there is any "finishing" to be done to beautify the home . . . . Valspar is invariably the finish used! A welcome companion on every journey into Colorland!

For Valspar, experienced and reliable old guide, blazes the trail for many delightful color pilgrimages . . . indoors . . . outdoors. Wherever the chosen surface calls for painting, varnishing, enameling or lacquering, there is always the right Valspar for the need . . . always the right color or combination of colors.

There is the certainty of Valspar Quality to add to the success of your color efforts. Quality in the sense that Valspar can "rough it" in any weather or climate and still retain its beauty . . . a waterproof, wearproof, weatherproof finish proved in service.

Always remember! The name Valspar includes Clear Varnish, 4 Hour Enamel and Lacquer in most popular colors, a complete range of House Paints, Flat Wall Paints, Porch and Floor Paints. Every penny invested in Valspar pays out satisfaction . . . with interest.

HEADQUARTERS
VALSPAR FINISHES
The store that displays this headquarters sign is the place to obtain your Valspar in just the "finish" and color you desire.

VALSPAR FINISHES
· VARNISHES · · PAINTS · · LACQUERS · · ENAMELS ·

Valspar Finishes, 1930

▶ *Ward-O-Leum, 1931*

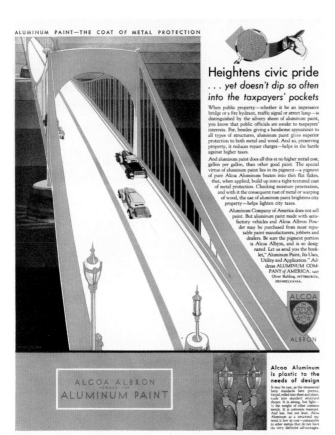

Alcoa Aluminum Paint, 1932

Sherwin-Williams Paints, 1931

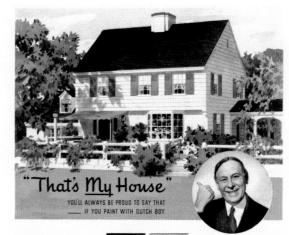

Pittsburgh Plate Glass Co., 1937 ◄ *Sherwin-Williams Paints, 1937*

Dutch Boy Paint, 1936   ► *Armstrong, 1932*

THE "CENTURY"

Characteristic of Hettrick quality is this new modern styled glider. Tubular chrome front rail and white enameled back rail; torpedo type arms with chrome trim and fitted with ash receiver in each arm; sturdy embossed end panel; fluted metal front panel. Three individual sections of spring with nine coils in each. Ball bearing suspension; anti-sway lock; opens up to form a bed as shown on page 45. Six individual cushions covered with waterproofed Textileather, filled with cotton linters and double rope piped with stayform binding.

Spring Steel Chair—Constructed of heavy spring steel. Cushions are covered with waterproofed Textileather, filled with cotton linters and double rope piped; metal arm rests.

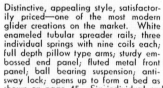

No. K-1577

No. K-1376	Sh. Wt. 150 lbs.	$42.10
No. K-1371	Sh. Wt. 150 lbs.	42.10
No. K-1374	Sh. Wt. 150 lbs.	42.10
No. K-1577 Spring Steel Chair	Sh. Wt. 55 lbs.	14.88

No. K-1376

No. K-1371

No. K-1374

THE "CORANADO"

Distinctive, appealing style, satisfactorily priced—one of the most modern glider creations on the market. White enameled tubular spreader rails; three individual springs with nine coils each; full depth pillow type arms; sturdy embossed end panel; fluted metal front panel; ball bearing suspension; anti-sway lock; opens up to form a bed as shown on page 45. Six individual cushions covered with waterproofed Textileather, filled with cotton linters and double rope piped with stayform binding; painted with the finest enamel pigments obtainable and baked in a modern infrared ray oven.

Spring Steel Chair—Constructed of heavy spring steel. Cushions are covered with waterproofed Textileather, filled with cotton linters and double rope piped; metal arm rests.

No. K-1586

No. K-1368	Sh. Wt. 150 lbs.	$36.66
No. K-1360	Sh. Wt. 150 lbs.	36.66
No. K-1366	Sh. Wt. 150 lbs.	36.66
No. K-1586 Spring Steel Chair	Sh. Wt. 55 lbs.	14.88

No. K-1368

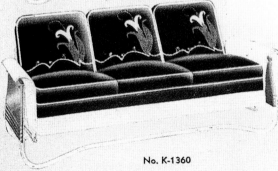

No. K-1360

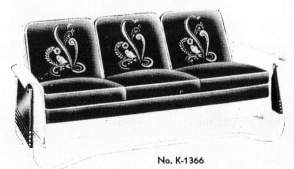

No. K-1366

There's a Hettrick Glider for Every Purpose and Every Purse

Emil J. Paidar Co., 1936 ◄ *Hettrick Gliders, 1935*

FLOOR PLAN AND DECORATIVE SCHEME AS DESIGNED FOR A CLIENT

An office such as this is not the result of chance. It is the product of experienced planning, talented designing and skillful execution. It should also reflect the personality of its occupant and harmonize with the nature of his business or profession.

The William F. Wholey Company, Inc. offers a specialized planning and decorative service to assist executives in creating offices of distinction.

Studies of individual requirements and sketches will be made for prospective clients, without obligation.

The WILLIAM F. WHOLEY CO. Inc.
Equipment Specialists
11 East 36th Street, New York

Decoration ~ *Furniture* ~ *Office Planning*

William F. Wholey Co., 1930

CHAIRS OF 'GLASS'

for Contemporary Cinderellas

Jewel setting for your lady. So magically inspired, it's like foretelling the future by gazing into a crystal. Knockout for a Manhattan terrace . . . for a country garden. Brilliance for an interior. Cora Scovil thought it up. Here is an original working model. Dupont's Plastex is the 'glass.' Chair to order, $175.

HIDE-OUT FOR A MAN

Leather on the walls in cheerful tangerine. Leather on deep twin barrel chairs in tobacco brown. A place for his books and drinks. A chance to try his hand at Rachmaninoff or Cole Porter on his own Minipiano. True Bachelor's quarters . . . even if you do have a daughter at Vassar. P. S. You can duplicate the works right to the wallpapers for $742.62.

HOW TO LIVE FOR TODAY AND TOMORROW AS SEEN IN A&S HOUSE OF PLANES FOR 1957 . . . INTERIOR DESIGNS BY ELEANOR LE MAIRE

Abraham & Straus, 1937

Office of Gerald M. Lauck, Vice-President, N. W. AYER & SON, INC., New York

THIS MAN TOLD US HIS TASTES—

He has his coffee, his neckties, his home as he likes them, so can you think of any good reason why his office should not reflect his tastes, as well?

Our illustration shows the kind of room Mr. Lauck likes to live in. As a good part of our living is done in our offices, such congenial surroundings are bound to make our work more pleasurable; more constructive.

In offices created by the Wholey organization, you will always notice a fine blending of authentic decorative treatment, masculine comfort and practical conveniences for the busy executive.

OFFICE PLANNING **WHOLEY** INTERIOR ARCHITECTURE · DECORATION · FURNITURE
THE WILLIAM F. COMPANY INC. 11 EAST 36. NEW YORK

William F. Wholey Co., 1931

SEE THIS AND MANY OTHER

Stunning New Designs

NOW ON DISPLAY AT YOUR KROEHLER DEALER'S

A very moderate investment will add this beauty and comfort to your home. Kroehler's enduring 5-Star Construction at a surprisingly low price is possible only because of Kroehler's large manufacturing facilities. Unvarying hidden quality in furniture has built Kroehler from a small beginning in 1893 to the world's largest furniture manufacturer operating ten great factories. Watch newspapers for your Kroehler dealer's announcements on these striking new designs. Kroehler Mfg. Co., 666 Lake Shore Drive, Chicago, Ill., or Stratford, Ont., Canada.

Kroehler Swedish Modern Suite No. 2000 in turquoise. Background suggests a contrasting wall color. Drapes could be a berry wine and rug a tobacco brown.

KROEHLER
WORLD'S LARGEST FURNITURE MANUFACTURER

Kroehler, 1939 ▶ William F. Wholey Co., 1932

The W. F. W. Co. Inc. 1931

It Didn't Just Happen!

Being counsellors to many of the country's largest advertisers, The J. Walter Thompson Advertising Corporation recognizes the value of competent counsel in their own problems.

Months before their new Wall Street offices were to be occupied, the needs and inter-relations of their departments were being charted on the drawing boards of the Wholey designing staff.

Under the Wholey plan, no detail of office design is left to chance, nor need furnishings be selected from sketches alone. At the Wholey Showrooms, three floors are devoted to complete offices, reception rooms, board rooms . . . where decorative treatments and furnishings to suit all purposes and budgets may be compared, and preferences definitely established.

Valspar Enamels, 1937

Imperial Wallpapers, 1935

Lullabye Furniture Co., 1935

Hettrick Play Equipment, 1935   ▶ ▶ W & J Sloane, 1933

Standard Plumbling Fixtures, 1931

Plumbing Fixtures, 1931

Libbey-Owens-Ford Glass Co., 1937 ◄

Pittsburgh Plate Glass Co., 1937　　　► *Crane Co., 1930*

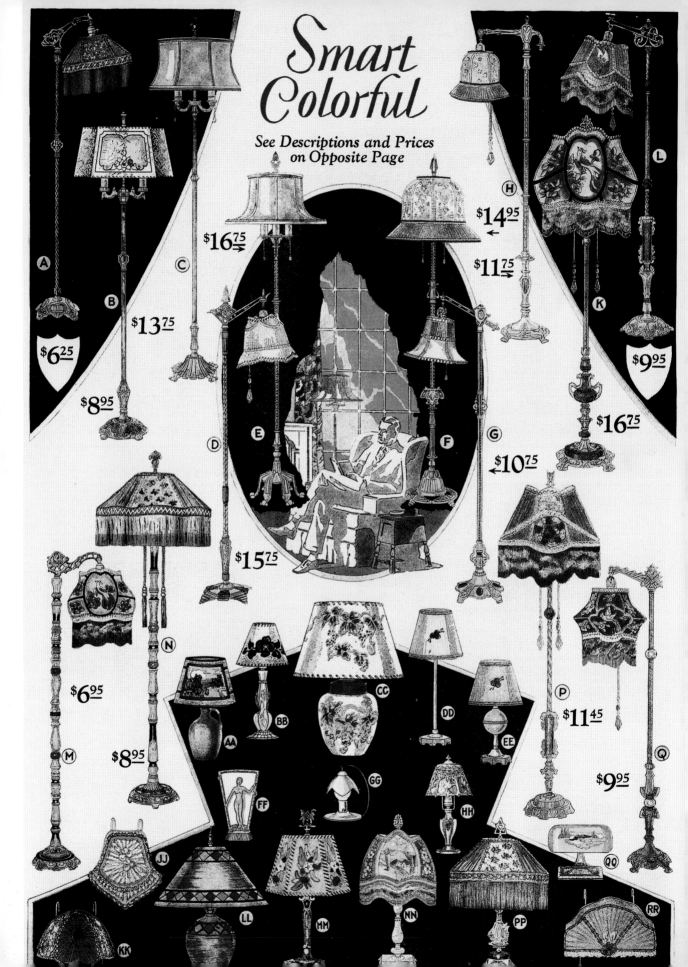

Smart
Colorful

See Descriptions and Prices
on Opposite Page

A

$6.25

B

$8.95

C

$13.75

$16.75

D

E

$15.75

F

G

$10.75

H

$14.95

$11.75

K

L

$9.95

$16.75

M

$6.95

N

$8.95

P

$11.45

Q

$9.95

AA

BB

CC

DD

EE

FF

GG

HH

JJ

KK

LL

MM

NN

PP

QQ

RR

A Quilted Mattress

Palmer Quilted Mattress, 1936

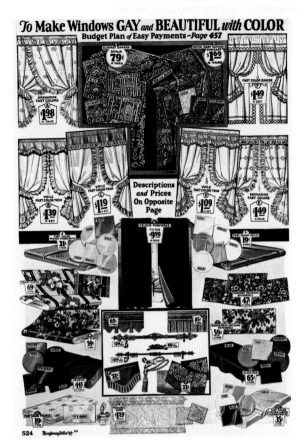

Curtains, 1931

Lamps, 1931 ◄ Rembrandt Lamps, 1935

Westinghouse Lamps, 1936

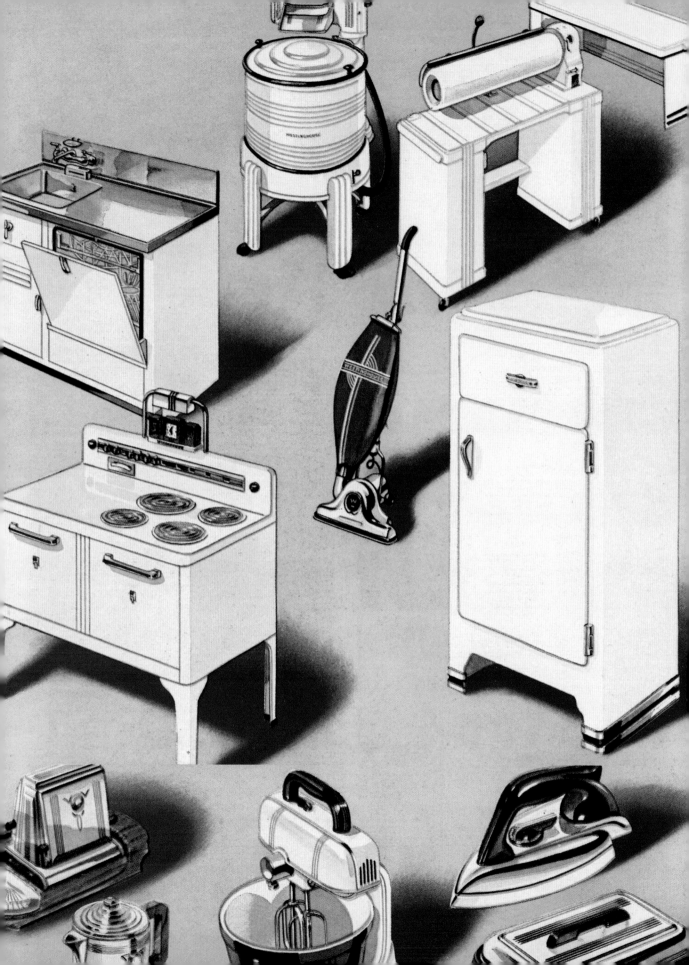

Kalamazoo, 1937

Westinghouse, 1936 ◀ General Electric, 1931

Kalamazoo, 1937

Magic Chef, 1931

General Electric, 1930

General Electric, 1931

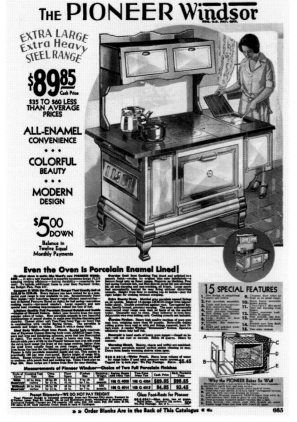

Pioneer Windsor Range, 1930

General Electric, 1935

▶ *Westinghouse, 1936*

"It's a joy to work in a Kitchen like this"

NOW YOU CAN HAVE ONE...__EASILY__

● Imagine the thrill of having a beautiful, modern kitchen where everything is convenient . . . where electricity cooks meals automatically . . . even prepares frozen salads and desserts . . . then does the dishes!

The Westinghouse Kitchen Planning Department will design such a kitchen for your home, arranging it scientifically to save all extra steps and motions. The layout will include the modern appliances you now have, plus the equipment you will want for a *completely* modernized kitchen. A friendly budgeting plan makes it surprisingly easy to obtain all this beauty and convenience on a simple step-by-step plan.

In celebration of its Golden Jubilee year, Westinghouse brings to America's kitchens the most modern, beautifully styled electric appliances you have ever seen. The line is headed by the Westinghouse Golden Jubilee Refrigerator that sets a new standard of refrigerator value . . . the sensational Golden Jubilee Ranges with their new "Economizer" speed units that cut electric cooking costs 18% . . . and a complete line of great Golden Jubilee appliances for every home need.

On the next page is shown a beautiful 7-color portfolio that tells the whole entrancing story. On its 24 big pages are "before" and "after" pictures of kitchens, showing what *you* can accomplish, economically. Mail coupon with 10c to cover partial cost. Portfolio will be sent you at once.

WESTINGHOUSE GOLDEN JUBILEE
1886 1936

Every house needs

Westinghouse

Yea Man
THEY SHOLY DO COME CLEAN SINCE
MONEL
CAME TO OUR HOUSE

The Monel tank in this
RUUD GAS WATER HEATER
is guaranteed against rust and corrosion for 20 years!

YEA MAN! Hot water that is hot! That's the kind this heater delivers for 24 hours in the day. And every drop is clean, clean, CLEAN! No rust-discoloration to stain your fine linens. No yellowish tint to make your bath as uninviting as a mud puddle. Because the tank inside that Ruud Gas Water Heater is made of solid, rust proof Monel.

Draw a big, black line under that word *solid*. It's important. It means a tank that is rust proof inside, outside and all the way through — not plated, coated or clad. It means a long-lasting, money-saving tank that is guaranteed against failure or leaks due to rust or corrosion for 20 years.

Today — take the first step towards trouble-free, economical hot water service. Investigate the Ruud Gas Water Heater with Monel tank guaranteed for 20 years. Your gas company, plumber or dealer in bottled or tank gas will be glad to tell you all about it. Write today for an interesting booklet "Go Gas for Hot Water". Remember, these heaters burn gas — the modern economical fuel. The International Nickel Company, Inc., 73 Wall Street, New York, N.Y.

See the Ruud and Monel Exhibits at the San Francisco Exposition and at the New York World's Fair.

MONEL

Monel, 1939

Gas Heaters, 1931

Wardway Gyrator Washer, 1931

Easy Washer, 1931

Beautiful new washer

that saves hours of drudgery

A NEW 2-TUB EASY DAMP-DRYER WASHER WITH STARTLING IMPROVEMENTS

To the youthful modern woman of America, EASY presents this glorious new and improved washer. Superb in beauty! Vibrant in color! Spectacular in performance! Never before have you seen a washer like it. Note its streamline gracefulness. Its two smart beige porcelain enameled tubs. Its glistening harmonizing top. It is beautiful when you buy it — and it will stay that way.

Only EASY Offers
All These Extra Advantages

Replacing the old-fashioned wringer is the new and improved EASY Damp-Dryer in a separate tub with these decided advantages over wringing: • It has no wringer — no exposed revolving wringer rolls. All moving parts are enclosed. It is ABSOLUTELY SAFE. • It ends slow piece-by-piece hand-feeding into a wringer by automatically whirling the water out of a tubful of clothes in less than two minutes. The clothes rest easily in the Damp-Dryer and do not move as the water is extracted.

There is no squeezing, twisting or friction. No deep, hard creases in clothes. • This improved EASY takes out more water than wringing does . . . Leaves clothes evenly damp-dry. You hang your clothes on the line in the sun and air just as you always have but they dry faster. In bad weather clothes can be line-dried quickly indoors. • It puts no strain on fabrics. No broken buttons. No torn clothes. No cracked silks. No stretched woolens. • It washes and damp-dries bulky things like blankets and feather pillows which will not go through a wringer.

Washes and Damp-Dries
at Same Time

This new EASY washes and damp-dries at the same time. Eight pounds of clothes can be washing while eight more pounds are being damp-dried. • If you prefer, it washes, rinses and then damp-dries with but one handling of the

clothes until ready for the line. • It empties itself without your lifting heavy pails of water. An efficient automobile-type pump does this burdensome task for you.

Choose Your Favorite Type of Washer

The new EASY with its wonderful extra features can be had in either the famous EASY Vacuum Cup type or agitator type washer. Both models are remarkably efficient. Both sell at the same low price—on most convenient terms. • See this latest and most advanced of modern washers today. See how it saves washing time . . . Saves rinsing time . . . Reduces line-drying time . . . Saves ironing time . . . Saves mending time. Compare its extra time and labor-saving features with those of any other washer. • Thousands of EASY dealers are listed in the phone books of America. If no dealer is listed under "EASY Washer" in your phone book, write us for his name.

Syracuse Washing Machine Corporation
Salar and Spencer Sts., Syracuse, N.Y.

697

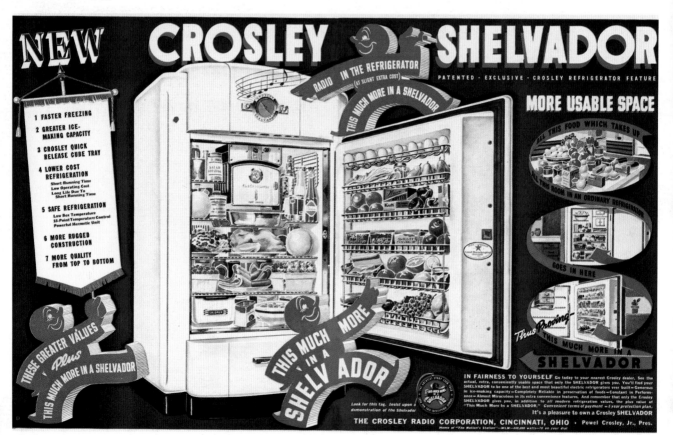

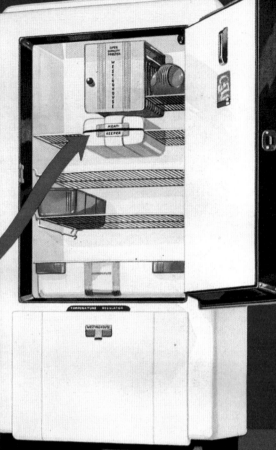

For the first time a place to keep MEAT properly!

ONLY WESTINGHOUSE OFFERS THIS

Kitchen-proved
MEAT-KEEPER

Greatest improvement in years! A big, covered, ventilated, all-porcelain meat compartment that keeps your steaks, chops, and roasts *fresher* for days *longer*. It conserves needed moisture at Safety Zone temperature. Gives the new 1938 Westinghouse Kitchen-proved Refrigerator the *most complete* food storage facilities ever developed. Together with the new glass-top Humidrawer for vegetables, the new Super-capacity Froster, Zoned Temperature Regulator, and improved Economizer Mechanism it makes possible Kitchen-proved Savings in *food*, *time*, and *money* like these:

1 Saves FOOD

Big food savings plus the low prices of the 1938 Westinghouse make it your budget's best friend. $1.07 on leftovers, $1.03 on quantity buying ... these weekly average savings in 102 Proving Kitchens amount to

$9.10 a month
Kitchen-proved

2 Saves TIME

Ice cubes frozen in 56 minutes! That's average fastest time in 102 Westinghouse Proving Kitchens! Frozen desserts in 65 minutes! And a whole week's food shopping in one or two trips to the store.

SHOPPING TRIPS CUT IN HALF

Kitchen-proved

3 Saves MONEY

Operating cost amazingly low! Average, 62 cents a week less than previous methods of refrigeration in 102 Proving Kitchens! Only 4/5 of a kilowatt-hour daily average current consumption.

10 HOURS OUT OF 12 IT USES NO CURRENT AT ALL

Kitchen-proved

Get Personal Proof: Your nearest Westinghouse dealer can give you facts and figures on Kitchen-proved Savings in homes like yours. Find his name in your classified telephone directory under "Refrigerators, Electric." Westinghouse Electric & Manufacturing Co., Mansfield, Ohio

Westinghouse *Kitchen-proved* Refrigerator
EVERY HOUSE NEEDS WESTINGHOUSE

A WORD FROM THE WIVES

"WE WANT A REFRIGERATOR!"

THE BEAUTIFUL NEW
GE Triple-Thrift
REFRIGERATOR

1. SAVES ON PRICE!
2. SAVES ON CURRENT!
3. SAVES ON UPKEEP!

"SAY IT with posies and sweets on birthdays and anniversaries, but at an important giving-time like Christmas, *we want a big, new General Electric Refrigerator!*" That's the word from the wives this year, so the Santa Claus in your home needn't hint for gift suggestions!

Thank your lucky stars that it's a G-E she wants! For now you can buy a bigger, roomier model—the world's finest refrigerator—and *save three ways!* You *save on price*. You *save on current*. You *save on upkeep*.

MATCHLESS ECONOMY

The new G-E Triple-Thrift Refrigerator is priced within easy reach of your budget. It uses far less current—probably only a fraction of what your old-fashioned refrigerator now consumes. Backed by five years' performance protection and an unparalleled record for operating economy, this new G-E with

its automatic Thrift Unit, will save you money year after year.

There are 12 models of the G-E Triple-Thrift Refrigerator from which to choose. Two strikingly distinctive styles, Monitor Top and Flatop. All have the famous sealed-in-steel mechanism that G-E pioneered over ten years ago. And now, *oil cooling*, another proved advancement assures even quieter operation, less current consumption and more *enduring* economy.

SHE WANTS A G-E

Make this a G-E Refrigerator Christmas! Give *her* the gift she wants most—the gift that she'll be proud to own for years to come! General Electric Company, Appliance Division, Nela Park, Cleveland, Ohio.

● The new General Electric brings you all the advanced features for greater convenience and economy. Faster freezing speed. Easy-out ice cube trays. Wide-range temperature control and defroster. Full-width sliding shelves (even the top shelf slides). Stainless steel super freezer. Interior lighting. Thermometer. And ample cold producing capacity for the most torrid of heat waves.

GENERAL GE ELECTRIC
TRIPLE-THRIFT REFRIGERATORS

General Electric, 1937

▶ *Certified ICE Member, 1936*

Cold ALONE *is not enough!*

INSIST ON MODERN *Air Conditioned* REFRIGERATION

...is something entirely new in refrigerators for the home—
...nditioned refrigeration. Because the modern *ice* refrigerator
...conditioned, it gives you *three-way* protection: Constant
...proper moisture and clean-washed air. So the modern *ice*
refrigerator does more than simply keep foods
cold. It protects them against rapid drying
out—keeps them fresh and flavorsome.

A modern *ice* refrigerator keeps food flavors
from mingling. It constantly collects all food odors
and disposes of them through the outlet. These new
refrigerators cost so much less than other types

that you can almost refit your entire kitchen with the saving. They neve
get out of order. They are so handsome that you will be proud
own one...so efficient that you need ice only once in several day
See them before you buy. Consult your local ice dealer.

BE MARY PICKFORD'S GUEST... Join the jolly "Parties at
Pickfair", her Hollywood home...one of the most famous in
the world. Al Lyons and his noted
Cocoanut Grove Orchestra. Your
favorite motion picture stars as
guests. Every Tuesday evening at
10 P. M., E. S. T., Columbia Broadcasting System.

...mblem is a mark
...iency and quality
...gn of purity and
service.

THE NEW STANDARD OF REFRIGERATOR VALUE

Westinghouse
Golden Jubilee **REFRIGERATORS**

WESTINGHOUSE
1886 W 19
GOLDEN JUBILEE

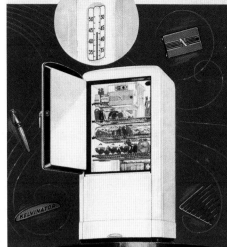

Westinghouse, 1939

Kelvinator, 1936

Westinghouse, 1936 ◄ Frigidaire, 1935

um·m·m!

um·m·m!

m·m·m!

Yo' next range should be a
GENERAL ELECTRIC!

A GENERAL ELECTRIC RANGE simplifies the art of good cooking. Without specialized cooking skill you can serve delicious meals that will turn delicate appetites into roaring, robust hunger, that will tempt the most finicky taste.

The automatically controlled, precision temperatures of a G-E Range eliminate failures. Health giving vitamins and all the delicious natural flavors of foods are served at the table —not cooked away in the kitchen.

General Electric, the world's largest manufacturer of electrical products—the leader in electrical research and development for more than half a century, has *modernized electric cookery.* The famous G-E Hi-Speed Calrod heating unit gives swifter and far more economical cooking heat— is more durable and lasts longer.

In easy utility, in matchless performance, in outstanding beauty, General Electric Automatic Electric Ranges are years ahead—yet you pay no premium. G-E prices are low—no more than you might pay for an ordinary electric range.

General Electric Ranges are beautifully styled in the modern mode of kitchen design. They can be placed flush against the walls and adjoining cabinets. General Electric Company, Specialty Appliance Dept., Sec. M7 Nela Park, Cleveland, Ohio.

GENERAL ⊕ ELECTRIC
AUTOMATIC RANGES

Automatic precision temperature control.

Centralized panel control. All switches grouped at point of greatest utility.

Stain resisting porcelain enamel cooking surface.

3 Hi-Speed Calrod surface units.

Thrift Cooker with pudding pan.

Oven (16″ x 14″ x 18″) with two fast heating Calrod units.

New sliding oven shelves.

Aluminum smokeless broiler pan.

Large warming oven equipped with Calrod heating unit.

Two large storage drawers on self-aligning roller bearings.

10 Distinctive G-E Range Models. Prices start as low as **$69**⁵⁰ F.O.B.

General Electric, 1935

▶ *Westinghouse, 1931*

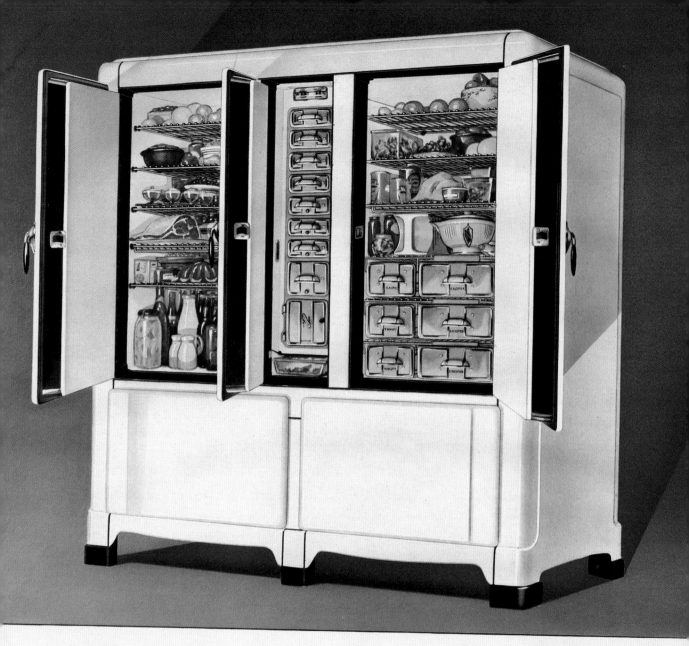

KELVINATOR

the Finest in Electric Refrigeration

IF you knew as much as we do about the 20th Anniversary Kelvinator, we are sure you would agree with us, heartily. Without boasting—and with no intention of disparaging the other fine electric refrigerators being built to-day, we do believe the new 1934 De Luxe Kelvinator *is* the finest in electric refrigeration.

Of course, we are proud of it! Why shouldn't we be? We know how it is engineered—how it is built—of what fine materials it is made—and how it will perform. We know the tradition behind it. We know the brilliant record our engineers and designers have made as *pioneers* in the industry during the past

twenty years—the longest experience in the industry. And finally, we know this is their greatest achievement.

The Kelvinator management extends a cordial invitation to the readers of Fortune in all the corners of the globe—an invitation to visit the nearest dealer and inspect the 20th Anniversary Kelvinators. Wherever Fortune goes, a Kelvinator dealer is very likely to be found. . . . KELVINATOR CORPORATION, *14287 Plymouth Road, Detroit, Michigan. Factories also in London, Ontario, and London, England.* 1914

General Electric, 1939

Kelvinator, 1937

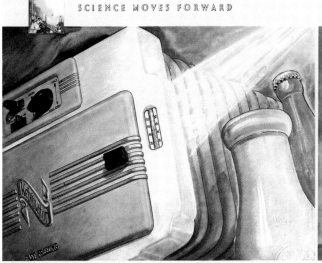

Kelvinator, 1934 ◄ Kelvinator, 1936

NOW

HERMAN NELSON Invisible RADIATOR

BEHIND THAT
GRILLE IN THE
WALL...THERE'S
A RADIATOR THAT
SAYS, "THIS BUILD-
ING IS MODERN"

THE HERMAN NELSON

Makers of the *Herman Nelson Invisible Radiator*, for residences, apartments, hotels, offices and monumental structures—the *Univent*, for the ventilation of schools, offices, churches and all buildings having an acute ventilating problem—the *Herman Nelson hiJet Heater*, for economical distribution of heat in factories, mills, garages, warehouses, and smaller buildings.

Herman Nelson, 1930

▶ *Lane Cedar Hope Chests, 1939*

Western Air Patrol Radios, 1938

Toastmaster, 1937

Bullocks, 1933 ◄ *Toastmaster, 1938*

Toastmaster, 1931

Graybar ad

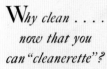

GraybaR

EVERYTHING ELECTRICAL

Why clean . . . .
now that you
can "cleanerette"?

"What! Eight o'clock already! And a million things to clean!"

"Well, I'm certainly off to a good start!"

"Imagine! I used to dread cleaning mattresses!"

"My! Even the curtains are easy this way!"

"And now this old coat looks like new!"

"Presto! Now it's a handy little plant sprayer!"

"Now, I know why Jim swiped my Cleanerette!"

. . . . . . the Handy Cleanerette

$13.50

The Graybar Cleanerette, at only $13.50, is the quickest, easiest way yet discovered to clean stair carpets, mattresses, car interiors, clothes . . . and what difficult spots *have* you! . . . But its usefulness doesn't stop there. With the clever Vaporette attachments (also moderately priced) it sprays insecticides and deodorants . . . protects clothing . . . deodorizes kitchens . . . etc., etc.! . . . Actually, this "handful of vacuum cleaner" is a *whole cleaning outfit in itself!* Convince yourself! Glance at the pictures at left. Then mail the coupon!

GRAYBAR ELECTRIC CO.
Gentlemen: Please tell me all about the Cleanerette and the Vaporette attachments.

Name ....
Address ....

Tune in on the Graybar Hour every Tuesday—10 to 10:30 P. M., E. S. T.—Columbia Network.

Graybar, 1930

Hoover ad

Years ahead! **HOOVER**
CLEANING ENSEMBLE
keeps colors fresh

Dirt and color can't exist in the same room. When dirt burrows in, color goes down with it. The crispest color scheme you can contrive is defeated—by a dirt-mask!

Take the dirt mask off your rugs and room fabrics with the new beauty treatment for homes—Hoover Color-Cleaning. It keeps colors fresh! The method is exclusive—like that of no other cleaner. A Color-Restorer (patented Agitator) flutters hidden dirt from carpets, brings out hidden color. Light, deep-working Cleaning Tools take the dirt mask from other furnishings. As unseen dirt comes out, colors come back. You can show your room with pride—it's color-clean again.

Free Color-Cleaning of one rug and one piece of furniture. Phone your local Hoover dealer for this rest, by his neighborhood representative. See how Hoover Cleaners handle dog hair and moth nuisances. Try any of the three Hoovers—One Fifty Cleaning Ensemble, Ensemble in Brown, new Hoover "305". Five million people have owned Hoovers—you can, too, for as low as $1.00 a week, payable monthly. THE HOOVER COMPANY, Factories: North Canton, Ohio; Hamilton, Ontario.

Hoover, 1939

General Electric ad

From June Bride to July Homemaker

. . . IN SIX EASY STEPS!

WHY not play fairy godmother when you select a present for a bride? Why not give her the prolonged youth, the smooth, unruffled brow, the success in cooking that comes with handsome easy-to-use General Electric Hotpoint home appliances?

Here are six gifts every bride really wants. Choose one, choose all. There's magic in their performance and beauty in their being. And the whole world knows that when a gift bears the General Electric Hotpoint trademark, it has to be good. Your nearest General Electric Hotpoint dealer has these appliances on display. See them. They settle the question of what to give your favorite bride, or mother—or yourself.

AUTOMATIC TOASTER—

PORTABLE MIXER—

COFFEE MAKER—

A LA CARTE COOKER—

PHANTOM IRON—

WAFFLE IRON—

You'll always be glad you bought a G-E

GENERAL ELECTRIC
Hotpoint

General Electric, 1937

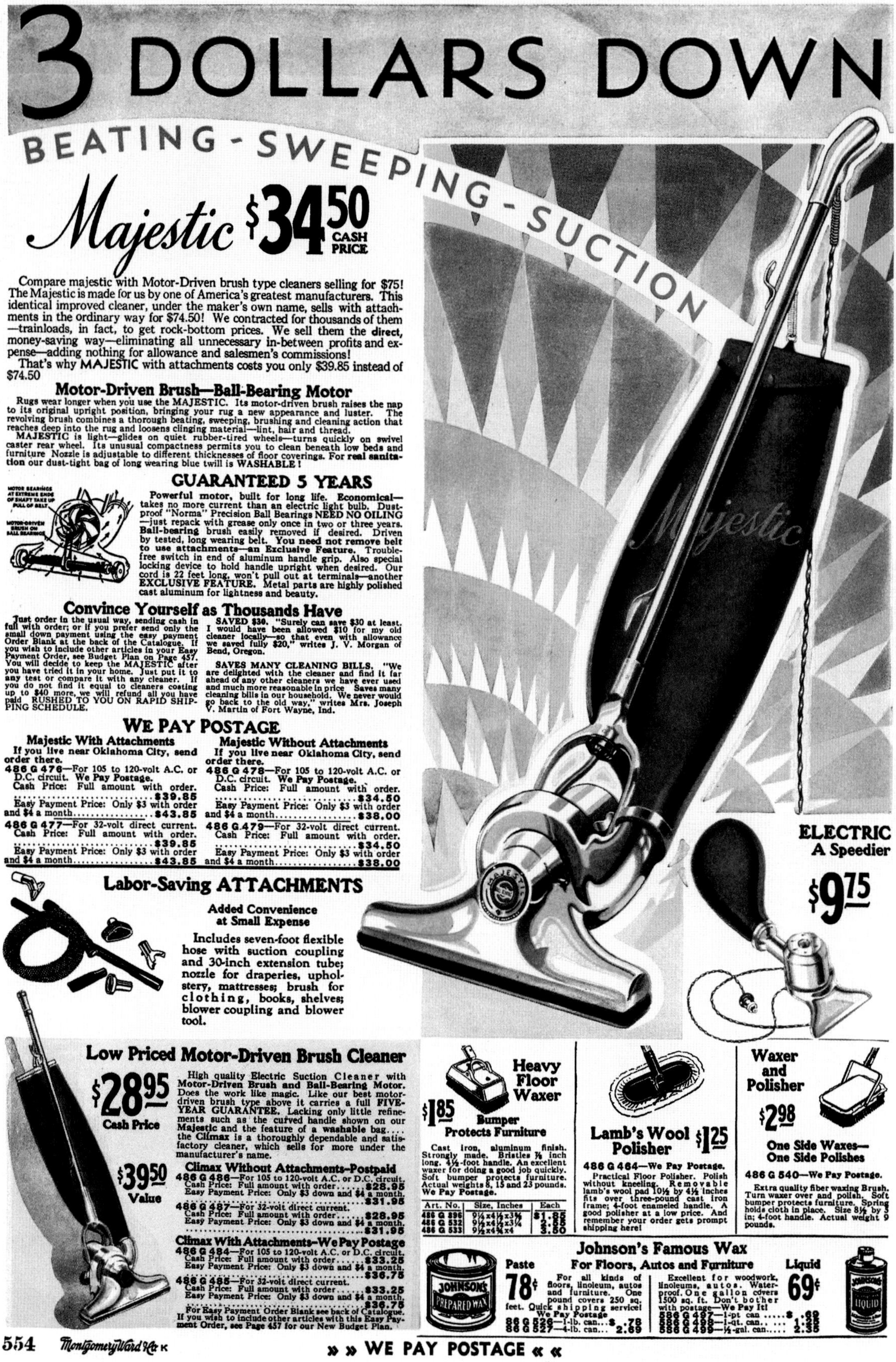
3 DOLLARS DOWN
BEATING - SWEEPING - SUCTION
Majestic $34.50 CASH PRICE
Compare majestic with Motor-Driven brush type cleaners selling for $75! The Majestic is made for us by one of America's greatest manufacturers. This identical improved cleaner, under the maker's own name, sells with attachments in the ordinary way for $74.50! We contracted for thousands of them —trainloads, in fact, to get rock-bottom prices. We sell them the direct, money-saving way—eliminating all unnecessary in-between profits and expense—adding nothing for allowance and salesmen's commissions!
That's why MAJESTIC with attachments costs you only $39.85 instead of $74.50
Motor-Driven Brush—Ball-Bearing Motor
Rugs wear longer when you use the MAJESTIC. Its motor-driven brush raises the nap to its original upright position, bringing your rug a new appearance and luster. The revolving brush combines a thorough beating, sweeping, brushing and cleaning action that reaches deep into the rug and loosens clinging material—lint, hair and thread.
MAJESTIC is light—glides on quiet rubber-tired wheels—turns quickly on swivel caster rear wheel. Its unusual compactness permits you to clean beneath low beds and furniture Nozzle is adjustable to different thicknesses of floor coverings. For real sanitation our dust-tight bag of long wearing blue twill is WASHABLE!
GUARANTEED 5 YEARS
Powerful motor, built for long life. Economical—takes no more current than an electric light bulb. Dust-proof "Norma" Precision Ball Bearings NEED NO OILING —just repack with grease only once in two or three years. Ball-bearing brush easily removed if desired. Driven by tested, long wearing belt. You need not remove belt to use attachments—an Exclusive Feature. Trouble-free switch in end of aluminum handle grip. Also special locking device to hold handle upright when desired. Our cord is 22 feet long, won't pull out at terminals—another EXCLUSIVE FEATURE. Metal parts are highly polished cast aluminum for lightness and beauty.
Convince Yourself as Thousands Have
Just order in the usual way, sending cash in full with order; or if you prefer send only the small down payment using the easy payment Order Blank at the back of the Catalogue. If you wish to include other articles in your Easy Payment Order, see Budget Plan on Page 457. You will decide to keep the MAJESTIC after you have tried it in your home. Just put it to any test or compare it with any cleaner. If you do not find it equal to cleaners costing up to $40 more, we will refund all you have paid RUSHED TO YOU ON RAPID SHIPPING SCHEDULE.
SAVED $30. "Surely can save $30 at least. I would have been allowed $10 for my old cleaner locally—so that even with allowance we saved fully $20," writes J. V. Morgan of Bend, Oregon.
SAVES MANY CLEANING BILLS. "We are delighted with the cleaner and find it far ahead of any other cleaners we have ever used and much more reasonable in price Saves many cleaning bills in our household. We never would go back to the old way," writes Mrs. Joseph V. Martin of Fort Wayne, Ind.
WE PAY POSTAGE
Majestic With Attachments
If you live near Oklahoma City, send order there.
486 G 476—For 105 to 120-volt A.C. or D.C. circuit. We Pay Postage.
Cash Price: Full amount with order. $39.85
Easy Payment Price: Only $3 with order and $4 a month $43.85
486 G 477—For 32-volt direct current.
Cash Price: Full amount with order. $39.85
Easy Payment Price: Only $3 with order and $4 a month $43.85
Majestic Without Attachments
If you live near Oklahoma City, send order there.
486 G 478—For 105 to 120-volt A.C. or D.C. circuit. We Pay Postage.
Cash Price: Full amount with order. $34.50
Easy Payment Price: Only $3 with order and $4 a month $38.00
486 G 479—For 32-volt direct current.
Cash Price: Full amount with order. $34.50
Easy Payment Price: Only $3 with order and $4 a month $38.00
Labor-Saving ATTACHMENTS
Added Convenience at Small Expense
Includes seven-foot flexible hose with suction coupling and 30-inch extension tube; nozzle for draperies, upholstery, mattresses; brush for clothing, books, shelves; blower coupling and blower tool.
ELECTRIC A Speedier $9.75
Low Priced Motor-Driven Brush Cleaner
$28.95 Cash Price
$39.50 Value
High quality Electric Suction Cleaner with Motor-Driven Brush and Ball-Bearing Motor. Does the work like magic. Like our best motor-driven brush type above it carries a full FIVE-YEAR GUARANTEE. Lacking only little refinements such as the curved handle shown on our Majestic and the feature of a washable bag.... the Climax is a thoroughly dependable and satisfactory cleaner, which sells for more under the manufacturer's name.
Climax Without Attachments–Postpaid
486 G 486—For 105 to 120-volt A.C. or D.C. circuit.
Cash Price: Full amount with order $28.95
Easy Payment Price: Only $3 down and $4 a month. $31.95
486 G 487—For 32-volt direct current.
Cash Price: Full amount with order $28.95
Easy Payment Price: Only $3 down and $4 a month. $31.95
Climax With Attachments–We Pay Postage
486 G 484—For 105 to 120-volt A.C. or D.C. circuit.
Cash Price: Full amount with order $33.25
Easy Payment Price: Only $3 down and $4 a month. $36.75
486 G 485—For 32-volt direct current.
Cash Price: Full amount with order $33.25
Easy Payment Price: Only $3 down and $4 a month. $36.75
For Easy Payment Order Blank see back of Catalogue. If you wish to include other articles with this Easy Payment Order, see Page 457 for our New Budget Plan.
Heavy Floor Waxer
$1.85
Bumper Protects Furniture
Cast iron, aluminum finish. Strongly made. Bristles ⅞ inch long. 4½-foot handle. An excellent waxer for doing a good job quickly. Soft bumper protects furniture. Actual weights 8, 15 and 23 pounds. We Pay Postage.
Art. No. | Size, Inches | Each
486 G 896 | 9¼x4½x3¾ | $1.85
486 G 532 | 9½x4½x3¼ | 2.55
486 G 533 | 9½x4¾x4 | 3.50
Lamb's Wool Polisher $1.25
486 G 464—We Pay Postage.
Practical Floor Polisher. Polish without kneeling. Removable lamb's wool pad 10½ by 4½ inches fits over three-pound cast iron frame; 4-foot enameled handle. A good polisher at a low price. And remember your order gets prompt shipping here!
Waxer and Polisher
$2.98
One Side Waxes—One Side Polishes
486 G 540—We Pay Postage.
Extra quality fiber waxing Brush. Turn waxer over and polish. Soft bumper protects furniture. Spring holds cloth in place. Size 8½ by 5 in; 4-foot handle. Actual weight 9 pounds.
Johnson's Famous Wax
For Floors, Autos and Furniture
Paste 78¢
For all kinds of floors, linoleum, autos and furniture. One pound covers 250 sq. feet. Quick shipping service!
We Pay Postage
86 G 526—1-lb. can... $ .78
86 G 527—4-lb. can... 2.69
JOHNSON'S PREPARED WAX
Liquid 69¢
Excellent for woodwork, linoleums, autos. Waterproof. One gallon covers 1500 sq. ft. Don't bother with postage—We Pay It!
586 G 497—1-pt can ..... $ .69
586 G 498—1-qt. can..... 1.25
586 G 499—½-gal. can..... 2.35
JOHNSON'S LIQUID
554 Montgomery Ward & Co K
»» WE PAY POSTAGE ««
Majestic Sweeper, 1931

Chosen for another FAMOUS LINER *becaus*
of its glorious COLORFUL TONE

THE palatial Franconia, famous Cunard liner—most luxurious of World Cruise Steamships—chooses Majestic
Radio for the 1930 cruise.

Again honored as the radio unaffected by changing
latitude and various conditions—again recognized as the
master of distance—the new Majestic is selected to entertain the Franconia's passengers on their six-months
cruise round the world.

Picking up foreign stations from Algiers to Stamboul,
from Bombay to Shanghai—reaching across dark jungles
and tropic seas—Majestic brings in program after
gram in that unrivaled COLORFUL TONE that is ex
sively Majestic's.

Chosen for the world flight of the Graf Zeppeli
chosen for the world cruise of the Franconia—chosen fo
of America's finest trains—chosen by over two mil
owners—Majestic must unquestionably be your cho

A trial in your home will convince you. No cost,
obligation. Call your dealer—and ask about Majest
convenient payment plan.

GRIGSBY-GRUNOW COMPANY, CHICAGO, U. S. A. • WORLD'S LARGEST MANUFACTURERS OF COMPLETE RADIO RECEIV

*Licensed under
patents and ap-
plications of R.
C. A. and R. F.
L. also by Lekti-
phone, Lowell &
Dunmore and
Hogan License
Associates.*

*TUNE IN Majestic
Theatre of the Air over the
Columbia Broadcasting
System every Sunday eve-
ning from 9 to 10, Eastern
Standard Time. Famous
headliners of the stage and
screen.*

Majestic Radio

MIGHTY MONARCH OF THE AIR

RCA Victor, 1938

RCA Victor, 1936

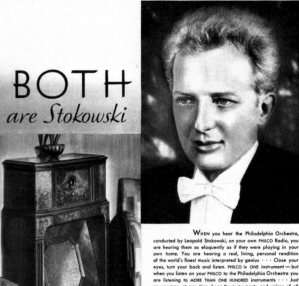

Majestic Radio, 1930 ◄ *General Electric, 1936*

Philco, 1932

Build your Summer Cabin with Shevlin Log Siding

WHEN you are considering the material for your outdoor cabin you may remember having admired certain snug, woodsy cabins of peeled pine logs. In all probability many of these cabins were actually built of Shevlin Log Siding, since this new building material looks like log construction and is being widely used for mountain, beach and lake retreats.

Shevlin Log Siding makes weather-proof cabins with none of the costly, uncomfortable disadvantages of real log structure. It saves the labor and expense of felling, stripping, and hauling. Made of pine with a rounded log surface, it blends fittingly with its surroundings and can be finished in charming weather-beaten effects.

Finished with ship-lap edge, one "log" fits the next to make a tight structure with minimum labor. And it is reasonable in first cost, can be easily obtained from the nearest lumber dealer and can be put up by any carpenter—or by yourself.

Shevlin Log Siding is made from native timber—California White Pine (Pinus Ponderosa), Pondosa Pine and also Norway Pine. On the Pacific Coast it is made by The McCloud River Lumber Company, McCloud, California, and the Shevlin-Hixon Company, Bend, Oregon.

Cabin of Shevlin Log Siding owned by Dr. Kenneth Bulkley. Architect, Wilbur Tusler.

SHEVLIN PINE

SEND FOR FREE BOOKLET—"Log Cabins Up To Date." Write to:

Shevlin, Carpenter & Clarke Company
Dept. 517, 900 First National-Soo Line Building, Minneapolis, Minnesota
Or Nearest Sales Office:

SAN FRANCISCO: . The McCloud River Lumber Company, Dept. 517, 1030 Monadnock Building.
LOS ANGELES: . The McCloud River Lumber Company, Dept. 517, Petroleum Securities Building.
BEND: . . . . . . The Shevlin-Hixon Company Dept. 517, Bend, Oregon.
NEW YORK: . . . N. H. Morgan, Sales Agent Dept 517 1205 Graybar Building.
CHICAGO: . . . . Shevlin, Carpenter & Clarke Company, Dept 517, 1866—208 South LaSalle Street Building.
TORONTO: . . . Shevlin, Clarke Company, Ltd., Dept. 517, 1806 Royal Bank Building.

Shevlin Log Siding, 1931

THE ARCHITECTURAL FORUM has the honor to announce the publication of an entire issue written and designed by and devoted to the new and unpublished work of

FRANK LLOYD WRIGHT

Edgar Kaufmann House, Bear Run, Penna.   Hedrich-Blessing

The Editors believe that this issue is the most important architectural document ever published in America. Here is the first and only record in print of what we have come to call the Modern Movement, from its inception to its present-day interpretation. In more than 100 pages of photographs, plans and drawings you will see architecture as thoroughly indigenous to America as the earth and rocks from which it springs.

SAYS WRIGHT OF ORGANIC ARCHITECTURE:
"This type of Architecture, suited to the modeling of the surrounding hills, bespeaks the materials and methods under which and by way of which the buildings themselves were born."

OF AMERICA'S YOUNGER ARCHITECTS:
"We have technology and technologies to throw away, technicians to burn, but still we have no architecture. We need an architecture so rich in this life of today that just because of it life will be better worthwhile."

OF THE SMALL HOUSE:
"To give the little American family the benefit of industrial advantages of the era in which they live, something else must be done for them than to plant another little imitation of a mansion. The house of moderate cost is not only America's major architectural problem, but the problem most difficult to her major architects. I would rather solve it with satisfaction to myself than anything I can think of."

—FRANK LLOYD WRIGHT

THE ARCHITECTURAL FORUM is published by the Publishers of LIFE, TIME, and FORTUNE at 330 East Cermak Road, Chicago, Illinois. Single copies of the Frank Lloyd Wright issue are available there upon remittance of $2 per copy.

Frank Lloyd Wright, 1937

And the winner is...

Placating the Patron

"The customer is always right," coined by American department-store owner H. Gordon Selfridge for his new London store in the early 1900s, had been adopted as a hallmark of American business by the 1930s. Like much advertising, the claims of GF Allsteel® were well founded, but went to extremes by suggesting that an office would gain "greater character and dignity" through the use of its furniture. Nonetheless, the overriding idea that the customer is always right endures as a principle of business today.

Alles für König Kunde

Der von dem amerikanischen Warenhausbesitzer H. Gordon Selfridge Anfang des 20. Jahrhunderts für seine neue Londoner Filiale geprägte Slogan „Der Kunde hat immer Recht" war in den Dreißigern zum Leitspruch in der amerikanischen Geschäftswelt geworden. An der Werbebotschaft von GF Allsteel® war sicherlich etwas Wahres dran, doch mit der Behauptung, man verleihe seinen Büroräumen mit ihrem Mobiliar „mehr Charakter und Würde", schoss man vielleicht etwas über das Ziel hinaus. Aber die Auffassung, der Kunde habe immer Recht, hat zumindest in der amerikanischen Wirtschaft bis heute überlebt.

Comment caresser le consommateur dans le sens du poil

Dans les années 30, le monde des affaires américain avait fait sienne la devise « Le client a toujours raison », inventée au début du siècle par H. Gordon Selfridge pour son grand magasin londonien. Comme dans la plupart des publicités, les affirmations de GF Allsteel® étaient fondées, mais elles ne craignaient pas d'en rajouter en suggérant qu'avec ses meubles, un bureau « gagnerait en personnalité et en dignité ». Il n'en reste pas moins que l'idée selon laquelle le client est roi prévaut encore aujourd'hui.

El cliente siempre tiene razón

En los años treinta, la industria y el comercio norteamericano habían hecho suyo el lema «El cliente siempre tiene razón», acuñado por H. Gordon Selfridge al inaugurar sus grandes almacenes Seldfrige's en Londres a principios del siglo xx. En este caso, como en casi toda la publicidad, y pese a su indudable calidad, GF Allsteel® exageraba un tanto al afirmar que su mobiliario confería a cualquier oficina «más carácter y dignidad». No obstante, no hay que olvidar que la idea de que el cliente siempre tiene razón sigue siendo uno de los principios comerciales en la actualidad.

顧客のご機嫌取り

「お客様は常に正しい」。アメリカ人の百貨店創業者 H・ゴードン・セルフリッジが1900年代初めにロンドン店をオープンしたときにつくりだした格言である。1930年代、アメリカ企業は優良企業の証としてこの考えを取り入れていた。他の広告のようにGFオールスチール®の主張は確固たるもので、同社の家具を使えばオフィスに「もっと個性と気品」が生まれるでしょう、とはまた極端である。そうはいっても、お客様は常に正しい、ということを他のすべてに優先させる考えは、今日のビジネスの基本原則として存続している。

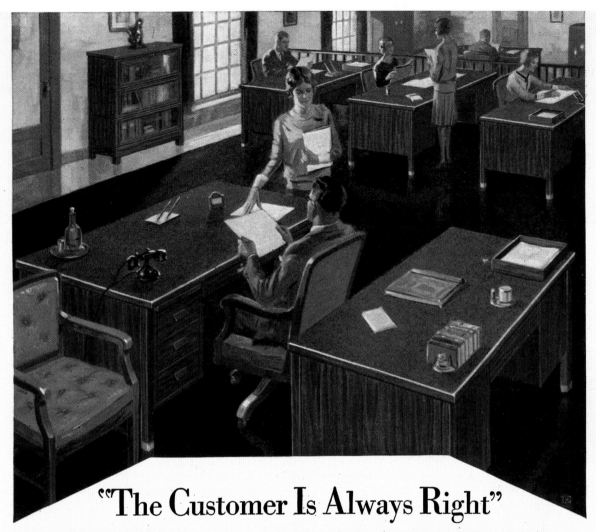

"The Customer Is Always Right"

AND his opinion of you and your business is just what you make it.

Let him find you and your co-workers in modern surroundings, equipped with the tools of modern business.

GF Allsteel Equipment supplies that up-to-the-minute touch in appearance. And because its utility is known and recognized, it never fails to create an impression of character and progress.

It brings you the strength and stamina of steel, for permanence; the resistance of steel to wear, to fire, to dampness, to every hazard of hard use; and the baked-on enamel finishes, possible only with steel, for enduring beauty.

With GF Allsteel Equipment, work is done with less effort and more speed.

Business leaders everywhere have proved that. And they have also found inspiration for workers in these finer offices, and a greater character and dignity that impresses every visitor.

THE GENERAL FIREPROOFING COMPANY

Youngstown, Ohio · Canadian Plant, Toronto
BRANCHES AND DEALERS IN ALL PRINCIPAL CITIES

"Serves and Survives"

COMPLETE OFFICE EQUIPMENT

[Commercial Desks · from $45 to $80
Executive Desks · from $175 to $500
Slightly higher in the West and South]

THE GENERAL FIREPROOFING CO. L.D. 868
Youngstown, Ohio
Please send me a copy of the GF Allsteel Office Equipment Catalog.

Name_____
Firm_____
Address_____
City_____ State_____
1-95-30

DESKS ·· FILES ·· SAFES ·· SHELVING   FILING SUPPLIES

GF Allsteel, 1930

Different - but Symbols of the Same Idea

There is scarcely a section of this nation that is not witnessing today dramatic evidence of the progressiveness of the American railroads.

This evidence may take the form of faster freight and passenger schedules, wider use of air-conditioned cars, door-to-door handling of freight, lower rates, or constant improvements in the all-important roadway.

Or it may find more spectacular expression in new streamlined trains—marvels of colorful utility linking fresh beauty to new standards of comfort and service for the traveler.

In whatever form you see these examples of enterprise—whether in the workaday running of the railroads or spotlighted in dramatic steam engines, impressive electrics or sleek new Diesels—you see different symbols of the same idea.

That idea is to provide the American people with *the safest, most serviceable and progressive transportation system in the world.*

We believe if you'll look about you with an understanding eye, you'll see surprising proof of how superbly that idea is being served.

Association of AMERICAN RAILROADS

SAFETY FIRST— friendliness too!

American Railroads, 1936

When THOROUGHBREDS
speed down the track . . .

Great names in racing...War Admiral ...Gallant Fox...Cavalcade...are linked with the Kentucky Derby. Great names in railroad transportation...THE GEORGE WASHINGTON ...THE SPORTSMAN...THE F.F.V....are traditionally associated with the turf classic. For Louisville is one of the many travel-Meccas in *The Chessie Corridor*, the picturesque east-west travel way served by this distinguished fleet of smooth-riding, air-conditioned trains.

Mile after mile, from the windows of these trains the view is constantly changing, continually fascinating. Pages of American history turn back as you cross storied Virginia, the glorious Blue Ridge and Alleghany heights, or follow the shining beauty of the Ohio River...And sweet repose crowns your day in a quiet sleeping car where a comfortable berth invites you to *Sleep Like a Kitten.*

GO THE MOST INTERESTING WAY...

THROUGH THE CHESSIE CORRIDOR

CHESAPEAKE AND OHIO LINES

"A-L-L A-B-O-A-R-D The George Washington!" ST. LOUIS, Union Station; CHICAGO, 12th Street Central Station; INDIANAPOLIS, Union Station; LOUISVILLE, Central Station; CINCINNATI, Union Terminal; WASHINGTON, Union Station; PHILADELPHIA, Pennsylvania R.R. Station; NEW YORK, Pennsylvania Station.

SWITZERLAND
LAND OF Variety

1939 Gala Event
SWISS NATIONAL EXPOSITION
ZURICH
May to October

You have a date at DEL MONTE

Del Monte is America's greatest resort—three hours south from San Francisco's Treasure Island!

Here are four championship golf courses, miles of forest bridle paths, sunny pools, ocean beaches.

And in the center of these 20,000 acres—where Spring is all year 'round—the world's gayest hotel!

For new, free book and colored picture map of Del Monte's Monterey Peninsula, write Carl S. Stanley, Manager, Del Monte, California

HOTEL DEL MONTE
and Del Monte Lodge at Pebble Beach

You can change your surroundings as quickly as your mood. The majestic grandeur of towering crags is but a few hours delightful ride from the calm and intimate beauty of the lake country. Whatever your vacation desire, you will find it in Switzerland!

NO VISAS— NO MONEY FORMALITIES
Ask your travel agent or write for booklet V-1

Swiss FEDERAL RAILROADS
475 Fifth Avenue, New York

PEACEFUL Sweden
LAND OF SUNLIT NIGHTS

Visit Sweden's romantic medieval castles and lovely Chateau country...colorful Dalecarlia where quaint traditions and bright national costumes bring bygone centuries to life...age-old Visby, city of ruins and roses...gay and modern Stockholm, most beautiful of Europe's capitals. These and other sights await you in peaceful Sweden...a land of tranquil beauty, enhanced by the mystic twilight of the midnight sun. ★ Sweden is the gateway to the Scandinavian wonderlands and the Baltic region. Convenient connections from England and the Continent. Eight days direct from New York in modern luxury liners ★ This will be a Scandinavian Travel Year, so book early.

Ask your travel agent or us for "LANDS OF SUNLIT NIGHTS" free booklet suggesting delightful Scandinavian tours. Swedish Travel Information Dept. V.

SWEDISH TRAVEL INFORMATION BUREAU
630 FIFTH AVENUE NEW YORK

Combining convenience with charm and dignity—The Westbury attracts distinguished guests from everywhere.

Ideally located in the quiet East side residential section—adjacent to Central Park...shopping and theatrical centers.

Single, Double Rooms and Suites
Furnished or Unfurnished
Serving Pantries
Monthly and Yearly leases
TWO RESTAURANTS • POLO BAR

THE Westbury
MADISON AVE. at 69th ST., NEW YORK
Direction KARL P. ABBOTT
Ross W. Thompson, Mgr.

American Airlines, 1939 ◄ Chesapeake & Ohio Lines, 1938   Travel, 1939   ► Southern Pacific, 1937 ►► Pennsylvania Railroad, 1938

Here comes the *Daylight!*

Southern Pacific's new streamlined train
between Los Angeles and San Francisco

Let us stand by the tracks of Southern Pacific's Coast Line, as thousands now do every day, and listen . . .

North and South the shining steel stretches along the shore. There is no sound but the soft murmur of the surf.

Suddenly from far off comes a musical note, rising. Round a curve flashes a streak of color. Here comes the Daylight, *the most beautiful train in the West!*

Southern Pacific's streamlined *Daylight* is the West's newest and finest train, linking Los Angeles and San Francisco in a glorious daylight trip, streaking along the edge of the Pacific Ocean for more than a hundred breathless miles. Two identical trains give daily service in each direction. Costing $1,000,000 each, custombuilt from stem to stern, they are pulled by the largest, most powerful streamlined locomotives in the world.

Step inside the *Daylight* and see the beauty and luxury that have already won the West. Notice the wide, soft seats in the coaches. They are cushioned with sponge rubber and turn to face the extraordinarily large windows. Each seat has an individual light and recessed ash tray. Note how the color scheme changes in every car, and how harmonious and restful the colors are — smoke gray, Nantes blue, French green, apricot, tan.

Here is the tavern with its big, deep semi-circular leather lounges — and the coffee shop, with a horseshoe-shaped counter where light meals are served.

Now, the diner. Observe the cheerful colors and the bright flowers on the tables. Notice that tableware and linen bear the winged *Daylight* emblem. All of it was especially designed for this train.

Finally, the parlor car, with its supremely comfortable chairs, and the parlor observation car that ends the train in a smooth, windowed curve.

The *Daylight* is, of course, completely air-conditioned. There is radio reception in every car except the diner. First class, tourist and coach tickets are all honored on the train. (Parlor cars are restricted to first class tickets, plus a nominal seat charge.)

No extra fare

You can travel between Los Angeles and San Francisco in the *Daylight's* luxurious coaches for our lowest fares:

$9⁴⁷   **$14**

ONE WAY   ROUNDTRIP

Coach passengers enjoy full use of the *Daylight's* diner, tavern and coffee shop.

The *Daylight* operates on the fastest regular schedule in history between San Francisco and Los Angeles, leaving each city daily at 8:15 a.m. and arriving at 6 p.m.

For a booklet in full color describing the *Daylight*, write F. S. McGinnis, Dept. SU-6, 65 Market St., San Francisco, California.

THE TAVERN is a delightful place to gather with your friends. Service on the *Daylight* is characterized by real western hospitality.

Southern Pacific

PENNSYLVANIA RAILROAD PRESENTS

A FLEET OF MODE

Bar Lounge: Designed in collaboration with the Pullman Company by Raymond Loewy, creator of smart modern interiors. Interestingly placed divans .. conversation corners in richly cushioned fabrics .. low broad upholstered settees .. venetian blinds .. a magnificent mural, facing long triple-panelled mirrors .. a fan-wise bar within easy hail. Soft shades predominate in the color scheme and lighting which are soothing, not flamboyant.

Master Suites (on Broadway and Liberty Limiteds) Something entirely new in private accommodations. Two rooms, not one. The first, a handsome lounge in soft colors, with radio and other modern furnishings (at night, twin beds); the second, a private bathroom with shower.

NISM

Observation Cars: Here the designer's art is conspicuously evident. Cresc shaped divans . . low tabourets . . deep carpeting . . lounge chairs inform arranged, the lighting soft but radiant. The whole effect distinctively casual in a smart club. A richly appointed buffet adjoins the main lounge. Anyt missing ? Yes, the open observation platform. Now it is glass-enclosed lux

ES INTO SERVICE WEDNESDAY, JUNE 15, 1938, LED BY A NEW AND FINER

BROADWAY LIMITED

First All-Room Train in History.. Daily Between New York and Chicago.. 16 Hours!

RACK TRAINS are reborn—a whole fleet of them. liant innovations in comfort and style. Even car ghts and dimensions change. All this, achieved by aboration of Pennsylvania Railroad and Pullman npany engineers and Raymond Loewy, noted designer.

l it's all yours to enjoy in air-conditioned travel on nsylvania Railroad routes uniting New York, Phila- hia, Baltimore, Washington and other leading cities h Chicago and St. Louis.

new types of private accommodations, a wider ge than ever before available on any train. In ad- on to new versions of drawing rooms, compart- ts, double bedrooms, you now have . . the Master

Suite, the Roomette, the Duplex. Each has a definite individuality, and all have nice soft beds — 6 feet, 5 inches long — and private toilet facilities.

Nor is that all. New personality is given the fleet leader . . *Broadway Limited*. Staffed with valet, barber, mani- curist, maid and train secretary, this leader becomes an all-room Pullman train. Privacy for every passen- ger. New-style diners, too—excitingly different. Faster schedule also — New York to Chicago in 16 hours !

Coupled with the new electrified mileage east of Harrisburg, this *Fleet of Modernism* now makes travel on the Pennsylvania Railroad even more attractive than ever before. Enjoy it !

Roomettes give you private little world of you own. Comfortably compac this accommodation pro vides . . personal toilet an washing facilities, illum nated mirror, enclosed ward robe and, at night, a ful length bed which dips dow at your finger's touch

BY DAY *a cheery sitting roo* **BY NIGHT** *a cozy bedroo*

Pennsylvania Railroa

RIDE THE MOST BEAUTIFUL TRAIN IN AMERICA

See a hundred miles of Pacific Ocean on your Southern Pacific California trip!

THE TAVERN on the *Daylight* is lined with cozy leat[her] booths and illuminated with soft, colored lights. In [this] congenial atmosphere, you'll spend happy hours w[hile] California's beautiful coastal scenery glides by.

63,060 passengers in three months, 143,851 in six months, 198,540 in nine months! That's the impressive record of Southern Pacific's new *Daylight*, the most beautiful train in America. Every day this brilliant streamlined train speeds between Los Angeles and San Francisco over the route of the California Missions, through rolling mountains and rich valleys, following the very edge of the Pacific Ocean for more than a hundred miles.

Whether your Pacific Coast destination is Los Angeles, San Francisco, Portland or Seattle, you can include this *Daylight* trip in your ticket by going west on *one* of Southern Pacific's Four Scenic Routes and returning on *another* SP route (see explanation at right).

Costing more than $2,000,000, custom-built from stem to stern, the twin *Daylights* are the "flagships" of an impressive fleet of brand new trains recently placed in service by Southern Pacific. In the year just past, the thrifty *Californian* and *San Francisco Challenger*, the royal *Forty-Niner*, the new *Cascade*, the *Sunbeam* in Texas and the giant new streamliner *City of San Francisco* joined the *Golden State Limited*, the *Overland Limited*, the *Sunset Limited* and the other famous trains that serve the Southern Pacific West.

HOW TO SEE TWICE AS MUCH ON YOUR TRIP WEST

The *Daylight* is just one bonus you enjoy on a Southern Pacific ticket to the Coast. We have Four Scenic Routes to California (see map). By going on one of these routes and returning on another one, you see a different part of the United States each way. You see *twice as much* of California and the West as you would by going and returning on the same route. You enjoy the *Daylight* ride between Los Angeles and San Francisco. And from most eastern and midwestern places, such a "go one way, return another" SP ticket costs you not one cent more rail fare than the usual back-and-forth round trip.

FOUR SCENIC ROUTES TO CALIFORNIA

1 SHASTA ROUTE
2 OVERLAND ROUTE
3 GOLDEN STATE ROUTE
4 SUNSET ROUTE

FREE TRAVEL SERVICE! For Southern Pacific's libe[ral] illustrated travel guide, *How to See the Whole Pacific C[oast]* write O. P. Bartlett, Dept. SE-3, 310 So. Michigan Av[e,] Chicago. He will also send you a post card for you to m[ail if] you wish a detailed routing, with costs. No charge fo[r this] service. No obligation.

Southern Pacific's representatives in principal eastern [cities] are authorities on the West. They will be glad to perso[nally] assist you plan your trip. See your telephone director[y.]

SOUTHERN PACIFIC

THE WEST'S GREATE[ST]
TRANSPORTATION SYST[EM]

Companion of Mountains

For more than a thousand miles, the majestic grandeur of Rockies and Cascades accompanies the North Coast Limited, newest of transcontinental trains, between Chicago, Twin Cities and Spokane, Portland, Tacoma, Seattle.

NORTHERN PACIFIC
YELLOWSTONE PARK LINE

Travelers to and from the Northern Pacific Coast and California enthusiastically commend the "New North Coast Limited Way." For Western travel information, address E. E. Nelson, 304 Northern Pacific Ry., St. Paul, Minn.

New North Coast Limited

Northern Pacific, 1930

New North Coast Limiteds

CORNER OF CARD ROOM IN THE OBSERVATION-CLUB CAR

Seasoned travelers are experiencing keener enjoyment from their trips to California by going the **New North Coast Limited** way between Chicago, the Twin Cities and the Northern Pacific Coast.

NORTHERN PACIFIC
YELLOWSTONE PARK LINE

These luxurious new trains with their improved roller-bearing smoothness have set a new standard of transportation service, along a scenic route, the beauty of which changes, but does not wane, with the seasons.

For Western travel information or posters of the American Rockies, address E. E. Nelson, 302 Northern Pacific Railway, St. Paul, Minn.

Northern Pacific, 1930

NEW 20ᵀᴴ CENTURY LIMITED

Sensational new air-conditioned streamlined train brings hitherto unknown comforts for New York-Chicago travelers, starting June 15th!

CLEAR THE TRACKS for a stirring new chapter in American travel! On June 15th comes the new, streamlined 20th Century Limited—thrillingly new, from headlight to observation lounge.

On its 36th anniversary America's most distinguished train, in its new, sleek, streamlined beauty, presents many features heretofore unknown in travel of any kind.

Every accommodation in this epoch making train, built by the Pullman-Standard Car Manufacturing Company, will be an individually air-conditioned private room, with complete toilet facilities and clothes locker, air-conditioned with individual temperature and ventilation control, and a really home-like bed. There are new-style compartments, bedrooms, drawing rooms and roomettes—America's first all-room train!

The roomy, air-conditioned dining, bar lounge and observation cars, exterior of locomotive and many new features of the train are designed by Henry Dreyfuss, one of America's foremost industrial designers.

As the new "Century" speeds its way between New York and Chicago—faster than ever before—you are undisturbed by motion or noise of travel, so carefully has this great super-streamlined train been designed and engineered. The new 20th Century Limited, over the famous Water Level Route is built to give you the smoothest, safest ride in America!

NEW YORK—CHICAGO 16 HOURS
Beginning June 15th
Lv. New York 6:00 P.M. Ar. Chicago 9:00 A.M.
Lv. Chicago 4:00 P.M. Ar. New York 9:00 A.M.
Daylight Saving Time

Never before a dining car like this! A never-to-be-forgotten restaurant — a colorful combination of gayety and dignity — where passengers will enjoy the art of famous Century chefs.

The new "Century's" Bar-Lounge is spacious...restful...hotel-like and air-conditioned. Its large windows provide daylight cheerfulness, while at night its unique lens lighting system gives the illusion of daylight.

The new "Century" Roomette affords privacy and room to move around before retiring. It costs no more than a section!

When you are ready to retire you merely lower the bed from the wall. Adjust temperature and ventilation as you desire.

The new "20th Century" private drawing room is a spacious living room by day, with full private toilet facilities.

THE WATER LEVEL ROUTE
YOU CAN SLEEP!

NEW YORK CENTRAL SYSTEM MORE THAN EVER—
IT PAYS TO RIDE THE CENTURY

Southern Pacific, 1938 ◄ 20th Century Limited, 1938

Chesapeake & Ohio, 1937

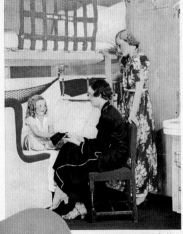

Pullman, 1937

Western Trains, 1935

▶ *Italien Line, 1932*

Christmas Present

A happy, carefree cruise Round the World . . . designed to your order . . . starting whenever you choose . . . taking 85 days to two years.

Luxurious Living
ALONG THE SUNSHINE ROUTE

World-famed President Liners have broad play-decks and an outdoor swimming pool . . . every stateroom outside (with real twin beds) . . . menus made up from the best the whole wide world affords.

Visits to 21 Fascinating Ports
PHILIPPINE DUGOUT AND VINTAS

Exciting days and nights in the great cosmopolitan ports of Cuba and Panama, California, Hawaii, Japan, China, the Philippines, Malaya, India, Egypt, Italy, and France . . . 14 fascinating far-flung countries.

Stopovers and Sidetrips Anywhere
PEKING SIDETRIP

Weekly sailings from New York, Los Angeles and San Francisco allow stopovers and sidetrips anywhere en route . . . continuation on the next or another of these world's only regular-world-cruising ships.

Low Shore Costs
INDIA HAS BRAND NEW THRILLS

Ask your own Travel Agent for all details. Or write Dollar Steamship Lines, 604 Fifth Avenue, New York; 110 South Dearborn Street, Chicago; 311 California Street, San Francisco. Offices in other principal cities.

Round the World
CRUISES TO ORDER
COST JUST $854 FIRST CLASS

•

DOLLAR
Steamship Lines

COMING IN JUNE!

THE "NORMANDIE"

Largest...most luxurious and beautiful of modern ships ...the "Normandie" will set new standards of comfort and safety in ocean travel for many years to come.

On June 3 there will arrive in New York not merely another big liner, but a *different kind of liner . . . a super-liner.*

Neither size nor speed was the first consideration of the engineers who plotted her dynamic lines. Those qualities came later, as the result of a fresh approach to the basic problem of assuring our passengers maximum safety and convenience.

For the decoration of this super-liner ...fifty years ahead of her time ...the foremost artists of France were called into consultation. The *Normandie* decor ... executed with the inimitable finish of French craftsmanship . . . is beyond anything you have ever seen in brilliance.

Imagine a ship 1029 feet long ... 79,800 tons ... a dining-salon 400 feet in length, walled with molded glass, and entirely air-conditioned . . . a sun deck, clear of all obstructions, as long as two city blocks ... an eighty-foot swimming pool ... virtually every cabin in First Class with bath or shower, many with private decks . . . a completely equipped theater . . . radio-telephones constantly in touch with both shores ... a staff of 1200 to assure your comfort.

Need we say that the chef and his corps of assistants are even now engaged in an amiable conspiracy to raise your appreciation of French Line food to new and quite entrancing heights?

You must see this ship! ... The arrival of the *Normandie* in New York harbor with a distinguished passenger list will be an event in maritime history. Your Travel Agent can tell you more about her . . . and (if you are quick) arrange for early reservations. . . . French Line, 610 Fifth Avenue (Rockefeller Center), New York City.

French Line

Other Sailings to England and France: ILE DE FRANCE, April 13, May 18, June 29 • PARIS, April 20, May 11 • LAFAYETTE, April 27, June 1 and 29 • CHAMPLAIN, April 6, May 4

S. S. "NORMANDIE" FIRST ARRIVAL IN NEW YORK, JUNE 3. FIRST SAILING FROM NEW YORK, JUNE 7. ADDITIONAL SAILINGS: JUNE 22, JULY 10 AND 31, AUGUST 21, SEPTEMBER 4

French Line, 1935

THE SOUTHERN ROUTE IS THE

LIDO DECK ROUTE TO EUROPE

Look at their gleaming decks—Lido Decks! At a glance you discover the secret of one of the greatest travel pleasures of today. To cross on the sparkling Southern Route ... and to travel on ships built for sunshine, for blue-dark waters, for Riviera life at sea!

Once across the Gulf Stream you discard your top coat ... the sun is shining! Everybody is on deck in sport clothes— playing or promenading.

It makes little difference which vessel. The Rex ... holder of the prize Blue Ribbon of the Atlantic. The Conte di Savoia

... world's only gyro-stabilized liner. The Roma, original Lido vessel. The Conulich liners Saturnia or Vulcania ... each with a whole deck of private verandah-suites. Or the de luxe Conte Grande. Each is a true "sun-ship" ... offering an added thousand miles of cruising east of Gibraltar at no added cost!

ITALIAN LINE

Write for literature to LOCAL TOURIST AGENT or our nearest office—New York 1 State Street; Philadelphia 1601 Walnut Street; Boston 40 Arlington Street; Cleveland 644 Arcade; Union Trust Building; Chicago 333 North Michigan Ave.; San Francisco 580 Post Street; New Orleans 1906 American Bank Building; Montreal Architect Building, 1155 Beaver Hall Hill; Toronto 159 Bay Street.

Italian Line, 1935

Lido Entertains at Sea

Engaging little groups . . . on open air verandahs . . . or around a sunny, outdoor pool. Wherever they gather, Lido's distinguished guests are entertained with deft and gracious skill.

For superb luxury . . . for the matchless freedom of the Southern Route's world famous "outdoor life at sea" . . . and for congenial fellow-travelers—on your trip to Europe—go Lido!

Choose the Rex or gyro-stabilized Conte di Savoia for speed . . . or, for a more leisurely crossing, select the Roma, Saturnia or Vulcania. Consult your TRAVEL AGENT or Italian Line, 624 Fifth Ave., New York. Offices in Philadelphia, Boston, Cleveland, Chicago, Los Angeles, San Francisco, New Orleans, Montreal, Toronto.

Italian Line

Dollar Steamship Lines, 1935 ◀ Italian Line, 1939

". . . . AND SUPERB SERVICE IS ONE REASON I ALWAYS GO HAPAG-LLOYD!"

Ask the Hapag-Lloyd trans-Atlantic Commuters

FROM Hapag-Lloyd Commuters you will learn about the deep and satisfying enjoyment of an Atlantic crossing to Europe. They form a majority of Hapag-Lloyd passengers and they will tell you that these lines have thoroughly mastered the art of pleasing. This year, go Hapag-Lloyd—then you, too, will want to repeat your trip many, many times.

These nine great ships provide Luxury, Speed, Comfort, in frequent sailings with arrivals of clocklike precision in England, Ireland, France, Germany. BREMEN • EUROPA • Giant Lloyd Expresses to Cherbourg, Southampton and Bremen, with the swift COLUMBUS adding calls at Ireland. NEW YORK • HAMBURG • DEUTSCHLAND • HANSA • Popular Hapag "famous Four" to Cherbourg, Southampton and Hamburg, frequently adding Ireland. ST. LOUIS • BERLIN • Our lowest rate liners. Germany via Galway-Southampton.

The 1939 edition of "Your Trip To Europe" is now available. Send coupon for this 250-page book of helpful information about European and trans-Atlantic travel.

Hamburg-American Line
North German Lloyd
57 Broadway, New York, N. Y.
I enclose 25 cents (stamps accepted) for the revised 1939 edition of the 250-page travel book, "Your Trip To Europe".

Name
Address
City_____ State_____

YOUR TRAVEL AGENT, or

HAMBURG-AMERICAN LINE • NORTH GERMAN LLOYD

57 Broadway 669 Fifth Avenue
New York, N. Y.

Offices and Agencies in Principal Cities of United States and Canada

Hamburg-American Line, 1939

THE *Lido Life* *synonymous with the* SOUTHERN ROUTE

"Lido" is an Italian word . . the Lido Deck an Italian Line creation! In daytime, with the sun streaming down, here is the Lido of gay cabanas and beach costume. In the ghostly evening, stars and shaded lamps utterly transform the setting! Now you are formal—festive—as on the terrace of a Riviera casino, with the moon and the Mediterranean everywhere.

Only on the Southern Route can the "Lido life" be properly enjoyed. For a speedy crossing, choose the Rex, fastest liner afloat, or the Conte di Savoia, only gyro-stabilized liner. The Roma and Augustus offer the same Lido delights on a more leisurely itinerary—likewise the Cosulich liners Saturnia and Vulcania, which include as many as nine and ten ports en route. And remember that all six vessels offer 1000 miles or more of cruising "east of Gibraltar" at no extra cost!

Write for illustrated literature to local agent or our nearest office. — New York: 1 State Street; Philadelphia: 1601 Walnut Street; Boston: 86 Arlington Street; Cleveland: 944 Arcade, Union Trust Building; Chicago: 333 North Michigan Avenue; San Francisco: 386 Post Street; New Orleans: 1806 American Bank Building; Montreal: Architect Building, 1133 Beaver Hall Hill; Toronto: 159 Bay Street.

ITALIAN LINE

Italian Line, 1934 ◄ *Grace Cruises, 1935*

Hawaii via Matson Line

☆ Whether your whim is solitude or congeniality, the choice is *your own* in this lanai, or veranda suite, aboard the S. S. Lurline...a luxurious apartment,

opening onto your strictly "private deck"...a universe glass enclosed or open at your will...Your own private horizon! ☆ See your travel agent

or Matson Line, New York, 535 Fifth Ave.; Chicago, 230 North Michigan Ave.; San Francisco, 215 Market St.; Los Angeles, 730 South Broadway;

Seattle, 814 Second Ave.; Portland, 327 Southwest Pine St.   S. S. LURLINE · S. S. MONTEREY · S. S. MARIPOSA · S. S. MALOLO

Matson Line, 1934

Lady in Waiting

She might have served at the court of Versailles, this femme de chambre from Brittany. Pleasant and deft and courteous, she invents a hundred little unobtrusive attentions to make life a luxurious affair. For she is bred, through long apprenticeship, in the French Line tradition of service. ● Every voyager on France-Afloat is accorded such devotion as Royalty itself enjoys. Merely to wish is to be obeyed. There is a whole regiment of attentive stewards and stewardesses ...who not only speak English, but seem actually to interpret one's unspoken whims. And every attendant, from the four-foot page-boys to the maître d'hôtel, is concerned, personally and intimately, with life's amenities. ● How could a French Line crossing be anything but Sybaritic! The food, for example, is considered by connoisseurs to be the flower of French cuisine ... and it is served with an engaging and appropriate grandeur. (Enter caviar ... capped by the claws of a life-size eagle sculptured in gleaming ice!) Everything about France-Afloat ...the atmosphere, the appointments, the company ... contributes to a thoroughly successful crossing. ● May we point out that in spite of its many luxuries, a French Line passage costs no more! Any travel agent will be glad to arrange your booking ... and there is no charge to you for his services.... French Line, 19 State Street, New York City.

French Line

MONTAGE CREATED FOR THE "FRENCH LINE" BY HALICKA, PARIS

PARIS. June 9 and 30, July 21, August 11 and 30, September 19, October 6 ● ILE DE FRANCE. June 16, July 7 and 28, August 18, September 8 and 29, October 20 ● LAFAYETTE. June 13, July 3, August 25, September 15 ● CHAMPLAIN. June 2 and 23, July 15, August 4, September 22

French Line, 1934

SPECIAL REDUCED FARES
Low Summer Rates

● Never before have such attractive rates to the Orient been offered to the American public. Round trip summer rates to Yokohama are now equivalent to approximately one-and-one-half minimum rates first, cabin, second, and tourist classes. ● Deluxe first, second, and cabin classes from San Francisco and Los Angeles via Honolulu. Every comfort of the twentieth century on great new express motor liners. Magnificent dancing salons ...tiled swimming pools...gymnasiums...public rooms, the work of European stylists...and menus that would make any languid appetite laugh in eager anticipation. ● Also

N·Y·K·LINE
(Japan Mail)

New York, 25 Broadway, 545 Fifth Avenue · San Francisco, 551 Market Street · Seattle, 1904 Fourth Avenue · Chicago, 40 North Dearborn Street · Los Angeles, 605 South Grand Avenue · or any Cunard Line office. Consult your local tourist agent. He knows.

....TO THE ORIENT

splendid new cabin and tourist cabin motor liners almost as luxurious ... from Seattle and Vancouver direct to Japan.

JAPAN, CHINA and the PHILIPPINES
From Pacific Coast to Japan and Return

FIRST CLASS	CABIN CLASS	TOURIST CABIN
$465	$375	$195 UP

Now is the time to see the wonderful lands of the East. Full details as to rates and the exceptional service given on N.Y.K. ships are described in beautifully illustrated literature. Call or write to Department 19.

N.Y.K. Line, 1932

to Europe— *with the Greatest of Pleasure!*
(and also the utmost in VALUE)

The "Club Manhattan" and "Club Washington" are gay and smart—feature all-American orchestras.

FOR many a veteran traveler, a single feature of the *Manhattan* and *Washington* can be well worth the trip. Often it's the genuine shipboard hospitality...a cuisine long world-famous...perhaps a detail of service or entertainment which reveals a management well schooled in the "fine art of knowing how." Combine *all* the features of these luxurious ships, and you have a crossing which gives new meaning to pleasure at sea ... and unsurpassed travel *value*. Cabin Class from $186; Tourist from $127. Weekly sailings with the *Pres. Harding* and *Pres. Roosevelt*, Cabin from $141.

U.S. Lines

U.S. Lines, 1939

THE TEA CEREMONY—INTRODUCED BY THE SHOGUN ASHIKAGA YOSHIMASA

THE visitor to Old Japan is always delighted with the gracious ceremonies to which even the simplest acts are elevated. How perfectly this artistic reverence prepares one for the wonders of the Blossom Empire—its mirror lakes and painted valleys, the centuries-old craftsmanship, all the ancient loveliness of shrines and temples.

Most pleasantly surprising is the existence side by side with these ancient beauties of the modern miracles of traveling comfort and convenience. Swift, super-luxury express trains whisk the traveler from city to city. Large, modern hotels await him everywhere with all the familiar facilities and services. Automobiles spin into the remotest sections. Even the favorite sports are amply provided for—golf, tennis, baseball, riding or flying.

The Japan Tourist Bureau (a non-commercial organization) maintains an office in New York in addition to widespread facilities in Japan for the special service of visitors. It will be honored to help plan your itinerary, arrange all the details of accommodations, and serve you while in Japan, without additional cost. It will make your visit to "The All Year Paradise" an unforgettable experience.

The wonderlands of Japan, Korea, Manchuria and China are reached from the United States and Canada by frequent steamships sailing from San Francisco, Seattle and Vancouver. Full information will be furnished by any tourist agency or by the Japan Tourist Bureau. Write for Booklet.

JAPAN
TOURIST BUREAU
c/o Japanese Gov't Railways, One Madison Ave., N. Y. City
c/o Nippon Yusen Kaisha, 545 Fifth Ave., N. Y. City

Japan Tourist Bureau, 1930

Lido after dark

THE CONTE DI SAVOIA . . . MIDNIGHT!

THE miraculous Southern Route sun has gone down . . . and the scene changes utterly. Instead of beach slacks . . . it's "white tie and tails". Instead of deck tennis, fencing, traps . . . it's music and champagne . . . or Asti Spumante, if you prefer to "do as the Romans do", as you probably will. For of course this is an Italian ship, offering all the warmth and subtlety of Italy's wines and table delicacies as well as those of other countries. Daytime Lido brought first fame to the Italian Line, with its sweeping play-decks and pools. Lido after dark brings the crowning mark of elegance to your Wintertime outdoor crossing.

Choose the great Rex, the gyro-stabilized Conte di Savoia, or the charming Roma, for an express voyage. Or enjoy the more leisurely route of the Vulcania or Saturnia, with their eight or nine extra ports to entertain you on the way. All are true Lido leaders . . . by day or night!

The leading **TRAVEL AGENTS** *in your city are our representatives. Consult them freely—their services are gratis. Or apply to our nearest office: New York, Philadelphia, Boston, Cleveland, Chicago, Los Angeles, San Francisco, New Orleans, Montreal, Toronto.*

ITALIAN LINE

Winter takes a Lido holiday

LIDO DECK—Conte di SAVOIA

WINTER goes a-summering on the Southern Route! Though the calendar wears a frosty look, it knows no power to change the bright skies, the blue waters, the friendly temperatures . . . as your Italian liner approaches mid-ocean, skirts the Azores, pauses at Gibraltar and moves serenely on into the placid Mediterranean.

"Lido" takes command! Thanks to the beneficent weather . . . and thanks many times over to the design and construction of Lido ships . . . your Winter crossing is transformed into a beach-revel of warmth and

The Thermometer Tells the Story! . . . 69° is a fairly normal noon temperature on a typical Southern Route crossing . . . though it may be freezing at home. Ask your Travel Agent for our illustrated weather-map booklet giving comparative statistics: "Why It's Called the Mild Southern Route".

sunshine. For this is the *open-air* way to all Europe, especially in the cold months. Board the great Rex, the gyro-stabilized Conte di Savoia or the charming Roma, for an express voyage. Or treat yourself to the leisurely nine or ten port itinerary of the popular Vulcania or Saturnia . . . if you can afford the time to *see more* on your way to Europe.

In either case, be sure to pack your favorite beach-robe and sandals!

The leading **TRAVEL AGENTS** *in your city are our representatives. Consult them freely — their services are gratis. Or apply to our nearest office: New York, Philadelphia, Boston, Cleveland, Chicago, Los Angeles, San Francisco, New Orleans, Montreal, Toronto.*

ITALIAN LINE

Main Lounge S.S. Lurline—Photograph taken enroute to Hawaii.

Hawaii

S. S. LURLINE • S. S. MARIPOSA
S. S. MONTEREY • S. S. MALOLO

★ Hawaii has some neat solutions to happiness and peace of mind. The countless pleasure devices of your Matson-Oceanic liner give you the first delightful sense of them. More diversions daily than you ever thought a day could offer, as you sail through balmy weather touched with a magic found only in the South Seas. *So easy to go.* Only 5 days over to the Islands from California. Any time that suits you is the right time to sail, for you can always count on meeting summer in Hawaii. Low fares make the voyage a real investment.

So easy to continue . . . down through the South Seas. It is only 15 days to New Zealand from California . . . but 3 days more to Australia. Via Hawaii, Samoa, and Fiji. *Modest fares* your key to these charmed regions.

Fascinating booklets and interesting details at your travel agency, or

Matson Line • Oceanic Line

New York, 535 Fifth Avenue—Chicago, 230 North Michigan Avenue
San Francisco, 215 Market Street—Los Angeles, 730 South Broadway
Seattle, 614 Second Avenue—Portland, 327 Southwest Pine Street

Matson Line, 1934

Dining Saloon S.S. Lurline—Photograph taken enroute to Hawaii.

Hawaii

S. S. LURLINE • S. S. MARIPOSA
S. S. MONTEREY • S. S. MALOLO

Booklets full of ideas free at your travel agency, or

Matson Line • Oceanic Line

New York, 535 Fifth Avenue—Chicago, 230 North Michigan Avenue—San Francisco, 215 Market Street—Los Angeles, 730 South Broadway—Seattle, 614 Second Avenue—Portland, 327 Southwest Pine Street

All the good things of life are on their native soil in Hawaii. You sample them in generous measure on Matson-Oceanic liners—palatial new ships inspired by the Islands they serve. At your command a whole cargo of clever devices for your entertainment and comfort.

Your only duty . . . go anywhere and do anything . . . whenever you wish. Sounds like a millionaire's idea of a vacation . . .

and *is*. But all the happy people sailing to Hawaii are not millionaires. Just people who know where to get the most for their time and money. It's only a 5-day sail to the Islands from California.

The inspiration of these magic regions invite you to continue through the South Seas. Only 15 days to New Zealand from California. To Australia . . . only 18! Via Hawaii, Samoa, Fiji. At modest fares.

Matson Line, 1934

JAPAN

THE AOI FESTIVAL HONORING THE KAMIGAMO JINSHA AND SHIMOGAMO JINSHA SHRINES.

Ceremonials out of the 6th Century offer one key to the real life of Japan today — fast limited trains and the great hotels offer another! 1932 visitors may enjoy it all — the ancient and the modern — at unexpected low cost on a series of scientifically planned inclusive tours prepared by the Japan Tourist Bureau, a non-commercial organization.

On a 14 day trip, for a small average expenditure per day, you may enjoy Yokohama, Tokyo, Kyoto, Kobe, see Miyanoshita, the shrines of Nikko and the Kamakura Buddha, motor to Fujiyama, feed the sacred deer at Nara, glimpse the choicest regions of the Empire. In 21, 28, 35 or more days an even wider territory may be covered at correspondingly low cost. All tours may be made independently or with a talented courier.

1932 is the year for your Japan visit . . . Steamship fares are the lowest in the world, considering service and the distance traveled. Hotels and living expenses are most reasonable. Start your plans by sending for illustrated literature describing the above tours.

Japan, Korea, Manchuria and China are reached from the United States and Canada by the Nippon Yusen Kaisha, Osaka Shosen Kaisha, Canadian Pacific, the American Mail Line and the Dollar Steamship Line. Full information will be furnished by any of their Lines, any tourist agency, or by the Japan Tourist Bureau % Japanese Gov't Railways, One Madison Ave. N.Y.C. or % Nippon Yusen Kaisha, 551 Fifth Ave., N.Y.C.

An Economical
Travel Opportunity
for 1932 . . .

JAPAN
TOURIST BUREAU

Japan Tourist Bureau, 1932

Good-Bye
to all that!

RACKETS and riveters . . . cross-town traffic and subways . . . brownstone fronts with basement entrances . . . conferences and conventions and sales charts . . . six o'clock friends and parlor games . . . aren't you in your soul of souls fed up with them?

The sulphur and molasses season is at hand. Now is the time when executives come back from lunch wondering why nothing tastes good any more. Now is the time, also, when smart people give themselves a taste of good salt air and a few weeks abroad.

"Seymour," they say (if their budget includes a Seymour), "get out the trunks. We're off on the Vasty Deep." Or if, like most of us, they have no Seymour, they just pack a few bags, hail a taxi, and say: "Pier 57, North River."

And presto! the moment they set foot on deck, they're in France! . . . Bronzed and mustachioed tars, whose Breton forefathers saw America before Columbus . . . well-trained English-speaking servants within call . . . all is well-ordered for these fortunate travelers. They speed eastward . . . eating marvelous food . . . basking . . . walking

. . . dancing . . . and in general doing whatever they darn well please. And they step ashore feeling already a different person altogether!

Ask your travel agent about voyaging on France Afloat . . . and as the skyline vanishes from view, wave your hand, sniff the salt breeze, and say: "Good-bye to all that!" The French Line offices in the larger cities of the United States and Canada, or at 19 State Street, New York City.

French Line

ILE DE FRANCE, April 8, April 30 •• LAFAYETTE, April 16, May 21 •• DE GRASSE, April 5, May 10
ROCHAMBEAU, April 30 •• PARIS, May 14 •• FRANCE (West Indies Cruise, April 8), April 22, May 27

French Line, 1931

SO THE LUSITANIA WENT DOWN

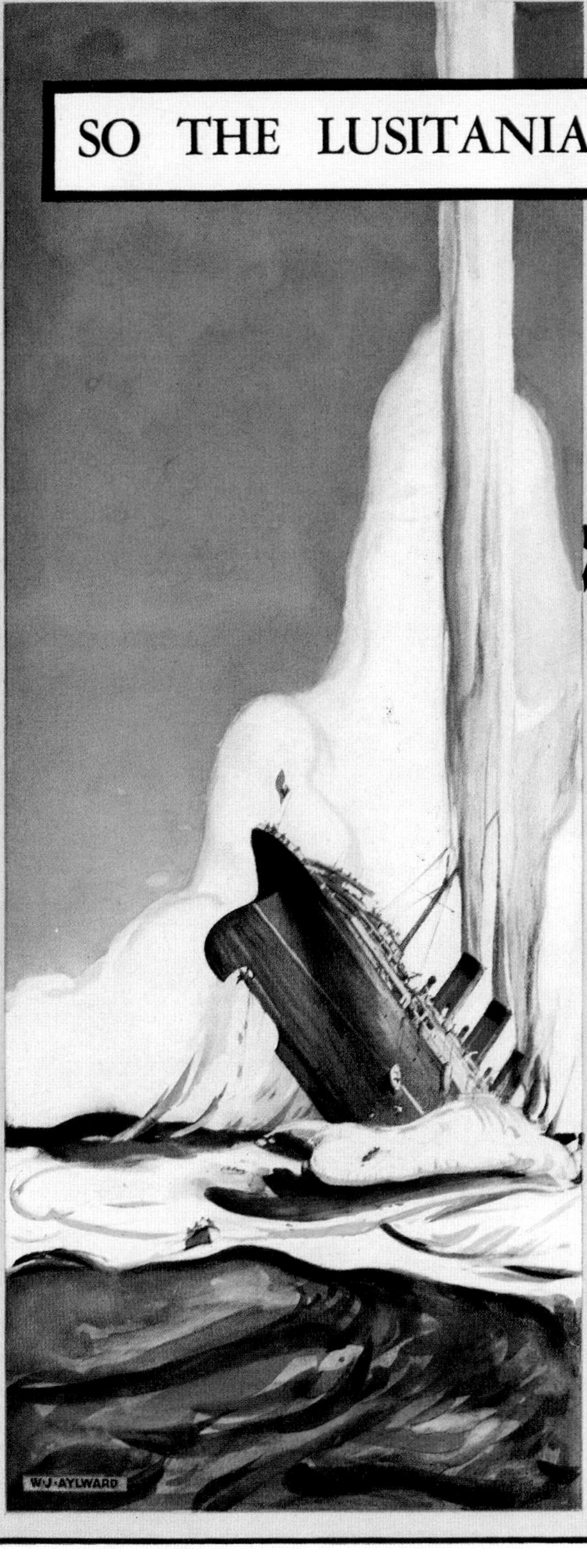

Well, what of it?

★

"What of it?" you cry. "The whole world was shocked. For days the newspapers talked of nothing else."

Well, but what of it? After all, it was a little thing.

How many Lusitanias would have to go down to carry all the dead and missing soldiers and the dead civilians of the great World War?

One Lusitania a day.
For a year.
For 10 years.
For 25 years.
For 50 years.

One Lusitania a day for 70 years, or one a week, beginning nearly a century before the discovery of America by Columbus and continuing to the present hour.

That is the number of Lusitanias that would be required to carry the dead. The dead of all nations who died in the war.

This advertisement, written by Bruce Barton, painted by W. J. Aylward and presented here through the co-operation of FORTUNE and the courtesy of the AMERICAN MAGAZINE, is the first exhibit of an educational campaign dramatizing the horrors of war; a campaign which Henry Ewald has called "a bold, practical plan which dwarfs all former use of advertising." Co-operation to develop this campaign into a persistent, extensive, efficient drive for Peace is invited by World Peaceways, Hotel Roosevelt, Madison Avenue at Forty-fifth Street, New York City.

World Peaceways, 1934

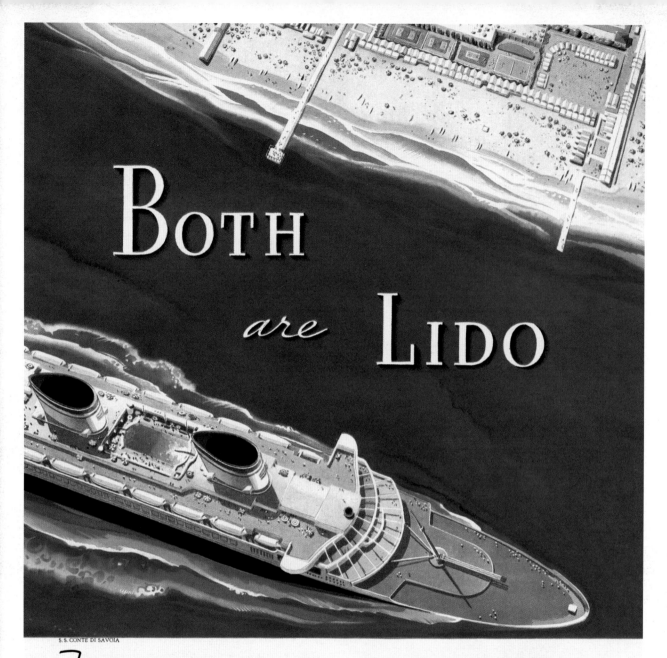

S.S. CONTE DI SAVOIA

*T*he Lido of Venice . . . and the Lido of Italian liners . . . are sisters under the sun! The famed strip of golden, warm sands, splashed by the turquoise of the Adriatic and set off by the glories of Venice across the Lagoon . . . sees its splendor, its color, its charm, its *Lido life* mirrored on the sweeping decks of the super-liners Rex and Conte di Savoia . . . leaders of the equally famed Italian Line fleet!

Smart Europe flocks to Venice's Lido "in season". Smart America more and more is flocking to the Italian Line's Lido in *all* seasons— because of the outdoor delights, the mildness, the serene comforts of the Southern Route crossing, at any time of the year.

Soon you will be going abroad again. This time, give your trip the added glamour of a Lido crossing . . . and the added 1000 miles or more of Mediterranean cruising at no added cost. There are two ways to go—a direct, express crossing to Naples, Genoa or Nice on the Rex or Conte di Savoia . . . or a leisurely itinerary embracing as many as ten fascinating ports on the popular Roma, Saturnia or Vulcania. And at the end of your Lido voyage, fast trains will speed you to European capitals!

The leading TRAVEL AGENTS *in your city are our representatives. Consult them freely—their services are gratis. Or apply to our nearest office: New York, Philadelphia, Boston, Cleveland, Chicago, San Francisco, New Orleans, Montreal, Toronto.*

ITALIAN LINE

Italian Line, 1937

► *Oceanic Steamship Co., 1934*

NEW ADVENTURE

A view of Sydney harbor . . . evoking admiration for Australia and the youthful vitality of its young civilization . . . playing . . . building . . . achieving a new order on the world's oldest continent. Strange contrasts—almost within sound of today's busy traffic—unique survivals of human and animal life found in no other part of the world. A voyage to this South Seas continent offers a *new adventure*.

Join a Matson *"South Pacific Cruise" personally escorted all-inclusive-cost—to Australia! via Hawaii! Samoa! Fiji! New Zealand!* Never before in travel! A 46-day cruise from California, *every month of the year*. No more than 5 days between ports. Smart elegance of magnificent liners . . . *"Mariposa"* or *"Monterey"* . . . emphasizing your enjoyment of the voyage. Similar attractive fares if you travel independently. ☆ *Your travel agent is an authority, see him for information, or any of our offices.*

The OCEANIC STEAMSHIP COMPANY
MATSON LINE

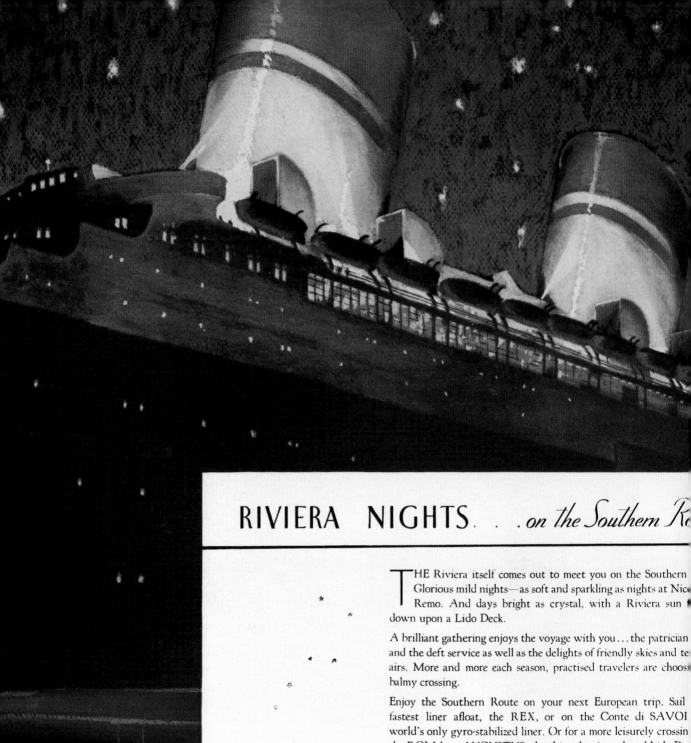

RIVIERA NIGHTS... *on the Southern R*

THE Riviera itself comes out to meet you on the Southern
Glorious mild nights—as soft and sparkling as nights at Nic
Remo. And days bright as crystal, with a Riviera sun
down upon a Lido Deck.

A brilliant gathering enjoys the voyage with you...the patrician
and the deft service as well as the delights of friendly skies and te
airs. More and more each season, practised travelers are choos
balmy crossing.

Enjoy the Southern Route on your next European trip. Sail
fastest liner afloat, the REX, or on the Conte di SAVOI
world's only gyro-stabilized liner. Or for a more leisurely crossin
the ROMA or AUGUSTUS, the ships that introduced Lido Dec
the Cosulich liners SATURNIA or VULCANIA, each offe
entire deck of verandah-suites! On any ship you enjoy an extra th
miles or more of cruising east of Gibraltar at no extra cost. For i
tion and rates, take advantage of the expert service given by yo
travel agent, or apply to our nearest office.

ITALIAN LIN

Children of the Sea ___

The eyes of young Raleigh, in Millais' famous painting, hold dreams as vast as the ocean. He, like all his race, was a child of the sea. And Quartermaster Suter, at the helm of the Aquitania, shares the same high heritage — fortified and defined by years of Cunard White Star training.

You will sense, aboard Cunard White Star liners, something stronger than routine or a master's orders. These officers and seamen feel a responsibility greater than any that could be written in a book of rules . . . a code of honor that has come down to them from fathers and grandfathers before. Racially and by training, they are Children of the Sea. Even in the lowliest of those who serve you, this heritage inspires an ancient and compelling pride in their calling . . . a feeling that cannot be taught, that can only be explained as part of the British tradition. From your host at the Captain's Table down to "Boots" who does your shoes, each delights in making you feel that tranquil hospitality which is Britain's own. The new "Queen Mary" . . . sailing from England May 27, from New York June 5 . . . will be distinguished not only by her size and power and luxury, but by the men and women who serve aboard her — true Children of the Sea.

TO FRANCE AND ENGLAND

Express Service: Next Sailings . . . Berengaria April 3 and 22 . . . *Aquitania* April 15 . . . Cabin Class $208 up. *Liverpool and Channel Services:* Next Sailings . . . *Corinthia* April 4, *Britannic* April 6, *Alaunia* April 9, *Andania* April 11, *Samaria* April 17 . . . Cabin Class $129 pp. *Tourist Class* in all ships, from $107, *Third Class* from $82. Cunard White Star Deferred Payment Plan available if desired, an exclusive feature.

*FROM BRIDGE TO ENGINE ROOM . . . CHILDREN OF THE SEA
Left to right: Commodore Sir Edgar T. Britten, R.D., R.N.R. appointed to command the "Queen Mary" . . . and in Atlanta, Baltimore, Boston, Chicago, Cleveland, Detroit, Los Angeles, Minneapolis, New Orleans, Philadelphia, Pittsburgh, Portland (Me.), Portland (Ore.), San Francisco, Seattle, St. Louis, Washington, Halifax, Montreal, Quebec, Saint John, Toronto, Vancouver, Winnipeg.*

The British Tradition distinguishes Cunard White Star

Book through your local agent or Cunard White Star Line, Offices at 25 Broadway and 638 Fifth Avenue in New York . . . and in Atlanta, Baltimore, Boston, Chicago, Cleveland, Detroit, Los Angeles, Minneapolis, New Orleans, Philadelphia, Pittsburgh, Portland (Me.), Portland (Ore.), San Francisco, Seattle, St. Louis, Washington, Halifax, Montreal, Quebec, Saint John, Toronto, Vancouver, Winnipeg.

Cunard White Star, 1936

Now see America by Grace Line

TO South America

Modern Grace Line "Santa" ships sail to South America from New York every week—from California every other week. Cruises outside 32-day trips to Lima, Peru; 39-day tours far into the Andes to Cuzco and the interior of Peru; and 39-day cruises to Valparaiso and Santiago, Chile. Stop-over privileges permit visits to the lovely Chilean Lake Region and Buenos Aires. En route Panama Canal, Havana and 12 to 17 other Caribbean and South American cities, depending on route selected. Connections at all ports with Pan American-Grace Airways (flying time Santiago to New York, four days, from other points proportionately less).

BETWEEN NEW YORK AND California OR MEXICO CITY

Grace Line presents fortnightly cruises and rail-water trips between New York and California or Mexico City—the only cruises visiting en route Colombia, Panama, El Salvador, Guatemala and Mexico, with an additional stop at Havana eastbound. These splendid Grace "Santa" ships offer all outside rooms with private, fresh water baths; outdoor, tiled swimming pools; light, airy dining rooms high up on promenade decks; gymnasiums; Dorothy Gray Beauty Salons and pre-release talking motion pictures. One of these luxurious Grace "Santas" sails every two weeks from New York and from San Francisco and Los Angeles.

For illustrated literature, itineraries, fares and all-expense cruises, consult your travel agent or Grace Line, New York, Boston, Pittsburgh, Washington, D.C., Chicago, San Francisco, Los Angeles, Seattle.

The beach deck and tiled swimming pool on the "Santa Lucia", sistership of the "Santa Rosa", "Santa Paula" and "Santa Elena".

July in the Lake Region of Chile, where our seasons are reversed—A natural color photograph by Ivan Dmitri.

Italian Line, 1934 ◄ *Grace Line, 1937*

Workers' Club, Moscow

16 Days in 4 Great Cities
of the SOVIET UNION $192*

Visit the new and the old in highly individual cities of Soviet Russia where gigantic new planning is altering social forms and yet preserving the notable art treasures of olden times. *Leningrad* with its palaces and "Hermitage" art gallery . . . *Moscow* with its famous Kremlin and intense activity . . . *Rostov* with its enormous collective farming and communal life with theatres, clubs, and sport fields . . . *Kiev* with its Byzantine art and Ukrainian music and theatre.

INTOURIST provides everything — hotels, meals, all transportation, sightseeing, theatre tickets, Soviet visa, and the services of English-speaking guides.

*Second Class, two together; $240 for one alone.
Greatly reduced rates for three or four together.

Other unusual tours: *Moscow and Leningrad,* 7 days, $85; *Moscow, Kharkov, and Kiev,* 10 days, $110 up; *Volga Tour,* 16 days, $160 up; three tours to *Turkestan;* Industrial Tours. Write for General Booklet L 4.

INTOURIST, INC.

261 Fifth Ave., New York; 304 N. Michigan Blvd., Chicago; 756 S. Broadway, Los Angeles. Or see your own travel agent.

TRAVEL IN THE
SOVIET UNION

Intourist, Inc.,1931

German Railroads Information Office, 1936

Hamburg-American Line, 1935   ▶ *Hamburg-American Line, 1934*

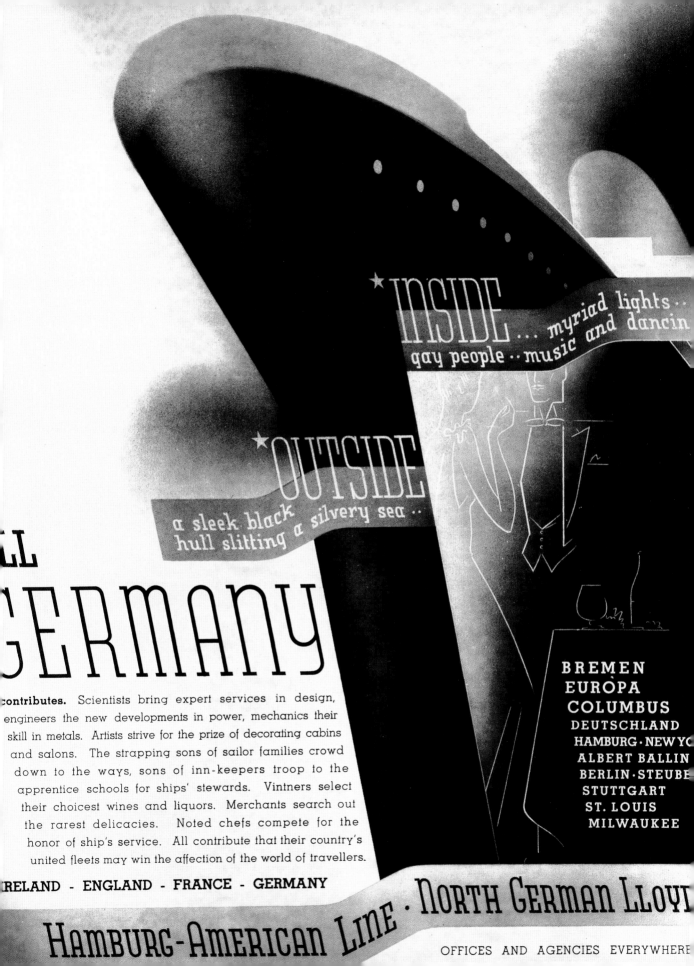

★ INSIDE ... myriad lights.. gay people ·· music and dancin

★ OUTSIDE a sleek black hull slitting a silvery sea ..

LL GERMANY

contributes. Scientists bring expert services in design, engineers the new developments in power, mechanics their skill in metals. Artists strive for the prize of decorating cabins and salons. The strapping sons of sailor families crowd down to the ways, sons of inn-keepers troop to the apprentice schools for ships' stewards. Vintners select their choicest wines and liquors. Merchants search out the rarest delicacies. Noted chefs compete for the honor of ship's service. All contribute that their country's united fleets may win the affection of the world of travellers.

BREMEN
EUROPA
COLUMBUS
DEUTSCHLAND
HAMBURG · NEW YO
ALBERT BALLIN
BERLIN · STEUBE
STUTTGART
ST. LOUIS
MILWAUKEE

RELAND - ENGLAND - FRANCE - GERMANY

HAMBURG-AMERICAN LINE · NORTH GERMAN LLOYI

OFFICES AND AGENCIES EVERYWHERE

TRAVEL AT REDUCED RATES TO YOUR FAVORITE
SUMMER RESORT
IN *Pullman* SAFETY & COMFORT

DARK TANS
for Fair People

Now that you're here for the New York World's Fair, it would be a shame to miss seeing Bermuda. This coral isle is within 40 hours of New York by sea . . . and only 5 by air.

Here, to Bermuda, come sun-worshippers from all the world, to pilgrimage on beaches of pinkish coral sand. They are gathered there this very morning.

Observe their pleasant ritual: Lying relaxed, they face the sun (you can see the effect of these devotions in the golden bronze of their skins). They sip long, cold drinks. They discourse lightly on the excellence of Bermuda golf . . . the low price of English and continental goods . . . the fun of bicycling to formal dances . . . the magnificence of the view from St. David's and Gibb's Hill Lighthouses.

Surely, you owe it to yourself to see this enchanting and colourful spot before you return from the Fair.

BERMUDA IS WITHIN EASY REACH OF THE NEW YORK WORLD'S FAIR

YOU CAN GO BY SEA OR BY AIR— Luxury liners travel from New York to Bermuda in 40 hours . . . a round-trip total of nearly 4 days of shipboard life. Sailings from Boston, too. ● Splendid new transatlantic planes now take off from New York and Baltimore, Maryland, and descend at Bermuda 5 hours later . . . an enchanting experience in the sky. ● A wide choice of accommodations is provided by Bermuda's many hotels and charming cottages. ● No passport or visa is required for Bermuda.

Bermuda

PLEASURE ISLAND

Bermuda, 1939

Hawaii, 1932

Hawaii, 1931

Bermuda, 1934

Bermuda, 1939

THE ISLANDS OF
Hawaii

★ Oahu, Honolulu's island, is one of the four main counties of the Hawaiian group. The others—Kauai, Maui and Hawaii—share Oahu's advantages, but offer their own individual beauty and diversion,

Outrigger Canoe Club
WAIKIKI

ROBERT MACK   COPYRIGHT HAWAII TOURIST BUREAU 1936

★ *At play in Honolulu. Natural color photograph taken in Hawaii*

Waikiki—*the world's most famous beach is only part of Hawaii's great diversity!* All of her islands are rimmed by superb beaches . . . white sands, black sands, "barking" sands . . . shaded by slanting coco-palms, washed by lazy surf. You may swim in perfect comfort at any time by clock or calendar . . . midnight or noon . . . January or June!

Behind her shorelines, high-speed motor-roads wind through verdured canyons . . . past plantation-lands . . . and climb to the inspiring summits of great volcanoes.

Behind her gaiety and varied pleasures is *Hawaii, the community,* modern and Ameri-can. A community of fine schools . . . lovely homes . . . shops that are fashion centers. A land of boundless energy . . . imparting to all an unique joy of living.

When you turn westward to these isles like no other place in the world . . . let us know your sailing-date, that we may welcome you . . . with scented necklaces fresh woven from our native flowers . . . the Aloha *lei* greeting, proud tradition of Hawaii! Nowhere else does a community say "how-do-you-do" with such sincerity and grace. *Write us by all means.*

From routine to rapture is an instant change! Swift, luxurious steamships sailing from Los Angeles, San Francisco or Vancouver, B. C. speed over this glorious sea-way in less than five days. Our booklet, "Nearby Hawaii" and "Tourfax" bulletin contain complete information, invaluable in planning your visit. Free, from your railway, steamship, or travel agent, or Hawaii Tourist Bureau, 40 Main Street, San Francisco, Calif.; 722 West Olympic Boulevard, Los Angeles, Calif.

This Bureau, with headquarters at 765 Bishop Street, in Honolulu, is a non-profit organization, maintained by

THE PEOPLE OF HAWAII

to enable you to obtain accurate information on any subject concerning the entire Territory of Hawaii, U.S.A.

Hawaii WILL LIVE IN YOUR HEART *forever*

Matson Line to *Hawaii*

NEW ZEALAND · AUSTRALIA · *via* SAMOA **· FIJI**

Complete details of exhilarating Matson South Pacific voyages may be secured from all Travel Agents or Matson Line— Oceanic Line, New York, Chicago, San Francisco, Los Angeles, San Diego, Seattle, Portland.

Hawaiian hotel reservations at the beautiful Royal Hawaiian and Moana at Waikiki may now be made when you book steamer passage. An added convenience for Matson travelers.

S.S. LURLINE · S.S. MARIPOSA · S.S. MONTEREY · S.S. MALOLO

Hawaii's floral beauty photographed in natural color.

Southern Pacific, 1939

Californians, Inc., 1937

Southern California, 1935 ◄ *Southern California, 1937*

Southern California, 1934

Follow the Vogue of Royalty

SEE THE HAUNTING BEAUTY OF CANADA ..LOVELIEST OF ALL AT *Banff* AND *Lake Louise*

IN THE CANADIAN ROCKIES

Warm Sulphur Swimming Pool at Banff Springs Hotel—Amid Majestic Peaks

★ A true Alpine kingdom—this realm of grandeur. Mile-high snow peaks. Hotels with the spacious air of castles. Swim pools of warm sulphur and fresh water. Trail rides and hikes on top of the world with cowboys and Swiss guides. And by night fun reigns in brilliant ballrooms. Come up this summer—see Canada's crowning glory. Travel the Columbia Icefield Highway ...America's newest, most spectacular drive...from Lake Louise.

Special rates for guests staying at Banff Springs Hotel or Chateau Lake Louise a week or longer.

Air-conditioned transcontinental trains. Low round-trip fares to Banff, North Pacific Coast, California, Alaska.

Ask Your Travel Agent or Nearest Canadian Pacific Office
NEW YORK · BOSTON · PHILADELPHIA · CHICAGO · SAN FRANCISCO · MONTREAL
and other large cities in U. S. and Canada

Lovely LAKE LOUISE *Columbia* ICEFIELD HIGHWAY

BRING YOUR CAMERA
$1,000 IN CASH PRIZES
Capture this brilliant paradise in color photos. Gleaming glaciers, purple peaks, mountain flowers, Alpine sunlight. Ask for contest details. 47 Cash Prizes.

Canadian Pacific
WORLD'S GREATEST TRAVEL SYSTEM

Banff Springs . . .  Cosmopolis
of the   Canadian Rockies

LIKE a continuous smart English houseparty . . . nonchalant, brilliant, informal. So go the stimulating days under the hospitable roof of Banff Springs Hotel, in the heart of the Canadian Rockies. Mornings . . . every one to his tastes . . . along with interesting companions. Pony rides up trails over 8,000 feet high. A climb up Sulphur Mountain. Golf on a $350,000 course with glacial river hazards. Luncheon, prepared by famous chefs. Archery with Indian bows . . . speedy tennis on red clay courts . . . canters on well-groomed saddle horses . . . motor trips to lovely Lake Louise, dips into a warm sulphur pool topped off with icy cold plunges. And then tea time in the lounge.

Now the scene takes on a more formal tone, tweeds and sports dresses give place to the graceful evening mode. And after a perfect dinner with exquisite music . . . and a light opera by the gay *Cruisaders*, a tete-a-tete under a silvery moon, with the stars looking down on Bow Valley's exquisite panorama.

Come up this summer and stay! . . .

Special monthly rates, European Plan for typical room with bath, *single* — $8.00 up per day, *double* — $12.00 up. Period suites for two, $28.00 up. Special servants' quarters. Room rates about 20% lower during May, June, Sept. But arrange for all summer long. American Plan also, May 15th — June 15th and Sept. 7th to 30th, for stay one week or longer, room with bath and meals, *single* — $10.00 per person per day, *double* — $18.00 per day. **Hotel opens May 15th.** Reservations, rates, information, from any Canadian Pacific Office: New York, Boston, Philadelphia, Buffalo, Washington, D. C., Detroit, Chicago, San Francisco, and all important cities in the United States. *Canada:* Montreal, Winnipeg, Vancouver.

Banff
SPRINGS HOTEL

Canadian Pacific

Low fares—Pacific Coast Excursions—May 15—Sept. 30.
Ask for Pacific Coast Tours, Alaska, Conducted Tours Folders.

Canadian Pacific, 1939 ◂ Canadian Pacific, 1939

THE GLACIERS ARE BIGGER

The largest glaciers in the world are along the coast of Alaska. You can snowball upon them in summer—yet in June and July, wild flowers in profusion fringe their edges!

A most unusual country is Alaska. Imagine, if you will, a land where a baseball game can be played at midnight without artificial light! Where totem poles stand next to telephone poles in modern towns. Where vines grow three inches over night, in gardens near glacial fields of ice.

Travel by train across America. We have *air-conditioned* trains which are cool, clean, quiet and safe. Relax as you ride. Arrive at Seattle, refreshed and ready to sail. How much vacation time have you? Two weeks, three, or four? We can give you an Alaskan trip to exactly fit your time and pocketbook. And nowhere in the world can you find a vacation paradise to equal this enchanted land. May we figure costs from your home town?

in ALASKA

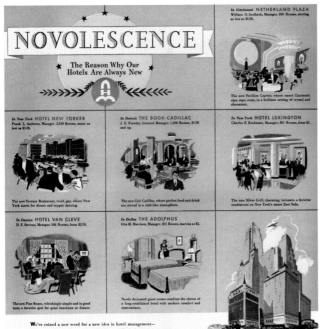

National Hotel Management Inc., 1935

Greyhound, 1932

Alaska, 1935 ◀   The Waldorf Astoria, 1931

Greyhound, 1935

YOU CAN SEE ALL THE WORLD
Right here in America!
GREYHOUND MAKES IT POSSIBLE

1. Black Forest, Germany . Washington Forests
2. Rhine Valley . . . . Columbia River
3. Mt. Fujiyama, Japan . Mt. Hood, Oregon
4. Normandie, France . . . Oregon Apples
5. Mt. Vesuvius . . . . . . Mt. Lassen, Cal.
6. Lake Bracciano, Italy . Crater Lake, Ore.
7. Arabian Deserts . . . . Nevada
8. Australian Trees . . Cal. Giant Redwoods
9. China . . . . . . San Francisco Chinatown
10. Sutherland Falls, N. Z. . Yosemite Falls
11. Transvaal, S. Africa . Nevada Gold Mines
12. Vineyards of Italy . . . . . Fresno, Cal.
13. Himalaya Mts. . . . . Sierra Nevada Mts.
14. Old Spain . . . . . . California Missions
15. Petra, Arabia . . . . . Grand Canyon, Ariz.

16. Dead Sea, Palestine . . . Salton Sea, Cal.
17. New South Wales . Arizona Silver Mines
18. Isle of Capri . . . . . Catalina Island
19. Sahara Desert . . . . Yuma Sand Dunes
20. Monte Carlo . . . . Agua Caliente
21. Egypt (near Cairo) . . Ariz. Petrified Trees
22. Inca Temples, Peru . . Casa Grande, Ariz.
23. Arlsburg Grotto, Austria . Carlsbad Caverns
24. Spanish Bull Fights . . . . Juarez, Mexico
25. Alaska . . . . . . Glacier National Park
26. New Zealand Geysers . . . . Yellowstone
27. Issyk Kul, Russia . . . . Great Salt Lake
28. Australia . . . . . Dakota Wheat Fields
29. Swiss Alps . . . . . Rocky Mt. Nat. Park
30. Odessa, Russia . . . Kansas Wheat Fields

31. Liberian Villages . . . Taos Indian Pueblos
32. Austrian Salt Mines . Hutchinson, Kansas
33. Bolivia, Lead & Zinc Mines . Joplin, Mo.
34. South Africa . . . . . . Kansas Kafir Corn
35. Cheviot Hills, England . . Missouri Ozarks
36. Baku, Russia . . . . . . Amarillo Oil Fields
37. Kimberley, Africa . Arkansas Diamond Mines
38. Baden-Baden, Germany . Hot Springs, Ark.
39. Monterrey, Mex. . . . . San Antonio, Texas
40. Argentine Pampas . . . . Texas Ranges
41. Sicily, Orange Groves . Rio Grande Valley
42. Nile Valley, Egypt . . . . . Texas Cotton
43. Russian Steppes . . . . Montana Plains
44. Gelsivore, Sweden . Hibbing Iron Mines

45. Killarney Lakes . . . . Minnesota Lakes
46. Yangtze River, "Big Muddy" Missouri R.
47. Holland Dairies . . . Wisconsin Dairies
48. Dellie des Edroith, France . Wisconsin Dells
49. Brussels, Belgium . Kansas City (horse show)
50. Buenos Aires, Argentina, Chicago Stock Yards
51. Munich, Germany . . . St. Louis Breweries
52. Brooklands, England. Indianapolis Speedway
53. Cairo, Egypt . . . . Memphis (cotton port)
54. Epsom Downs, England. Churchill Downs, Ky.
55. Dnieper Project, Russia . . Muscle Shoals
56. Birmingham, England . Birmingham, Ala.
57. Cuban Sugar Cane . . . . . . Louisiana
58. Kiel Canal, Germany . Houston Ship Canal
59. Marseilles, France . . . . . New Orleans

61. Nova Scotia . . . Evangeline Land, La.
62. Italian Riviera . . . . Gulf Coast
63. Yokohama, Japan . Belding Silk Mills, Mich.
64. Holland . . . . . Holland, Mich. (tulips)
65. Citroen Auto Plant, Paris . . Detroit, Mich.
66. Fingal's Cave, Scotland. Mammoth Cave, Ky.
67. Scotch Highlands . . . Great Smoky Mts.
68. Parthenon, Greece . . Parthenon, Nashville
69. India (Jain Colossus), Atlanta, Ga. (Stone Mt.)
70. Tuileries Gardens, Paris. Magnolia Gardens,
Charleston, S. C.
71. Bruges, Belgium . Bok Carillon Tower, Fla.
72. Waikiki, Hawaii . . . . . Florida Beaches
73. Malay Tropics . . . Florida Everglades
74. Victoria Falls, S. Africa . . . Niagara Falls

75. London, England . . . . Ottawa, Ontario
76. Paris, France . . . . . Montreal, Canada
77. Brighton Beach, Eng. . Bar Harbor, Maine
78. St. Moritz, Switzerland . Lake Placid, N.Y.
79. Jena, Germany . Rochester, N.Y. (cameras)
80. Hull, England . . Gloucester, Mass. (fishing)
81. All Nations . . . . New York City
82. The Ruhr, Germany . . . . Cleveland, O.
83. The Saar, Germany . . . . Pittsburgh, Pa.
84. Belleau Wood, France. Gettysburg, Nat. Park
85. Jap. Cherry Blossoms . . Washington, D. C.
86. Pont d'Arc, France . . Natural Bridge, Va.
87. Lancashire, Eng. . . Piedmont Textile Mills
88. Turkey . . . . . . Carolinas (tobacco)
89. English Fox Hunting . . Virginia Hunt Clubs

The whole world is at your finger-tips! Strange and thrilling scenes from every foreign land—interesting people, customs, and industries of every nation—all are found right here within the borders of America—and all can be reached in short, pleasant trips by Greyhound bus.

This unusual map cannot begin to tell the story. You will at once think of other places right in your home state, which can as easily be compared with foreign scenes, natural and man-made wonders, mountains, lakes, rivers ... they count up into thousands! The cost of reaching them by Greyhound is exceedingly low—far less than operating even a small private automobile, yet comfort, safety and convenience of schedules are exceptional. Why not plan your *round-the-world-cruise-at-home* for this very summer?

PRINCIPAL GREYHOUND INFORMATION OFFICES

CLEVELAND, OHIO . . . . . . E. 9th & Superior
PHILADELPHIA, PA. . . . . . . Broad St. Station
CHICAGO, ILL. . . . . 12th & Wabash
NEW YORK CITY . . . . Nelson Tower
BOSTON, MASS. . . . . . . 230 Boylston St.
WASHINGTON, D. C. . 1403 New York Ave., N.W.
DETROIT, MICH. . . . . Tuller Hotel
CINCINNATI, OHIO . . . . . 109 East 7th St.
CHARLESTON, W. VA., 1101 Kanawha Valley Bldg.

SAN FRANCISCO, CALIF. . . Pine & Battery Sts.
FORT WORTH, TEX. . . . . 8th & Commerce Sts.
MINNEAPOLIS, MINN. . . . 509 6th Ave., N.
LEXINGTON, KY. . . . . . . 801 N. Limestone
NEW ORLEANS, LA. . . . . 400 N. Rampart St.
MEMPHIS, TENN. . . . . . 146 Union Ave.
RICHMOND, VA. . . . . . . 412 East Broad St.
WINDSOR, ONT. . . . . . 1004 Security Bldg.
LONDON, ENG., A.B. Reynoldson, 49 Leadenhall St.

The GREYHOUND LINES

MAIL THIS FOR INFORMATION, PICTORIAL FOLDERS

Send this coupon to Greyhound information office nearest your home (listed at left), for complete information on any trip you may plan. We will give rates, suggest routes, enclose informational folder. Jot down the city or place you wish to visit, on margin below. No obligation. Paste the coupon on a penny post card if you wish.

Name _____

Address _____

City _____ — SP6

"RIDE WITH US
in this $20,000 AUTOMOBILE!"

NEW YORK

at far less cost than driving a small private car

NOT EVEN THE SWANKIEST FOREIGN-BUILT LIMOUSINE CAN MATCH THESE FEATURES!

4-POSITION RECLINING SEATS   DIFFUSED TUBULAR LIGHTING

HEALTHFUL HEATING, VENTILATION   LONGEST WHEELBASE FOR EASIEST RIDE

Hear this cordial invitation! It comes from the army of friendly and cosmopolitan people who have made more than *forty million* trips by Greyhound in the past year. "A $20,000 automobile!" you say—"Why, even the snootiest foreign-built limousine doesn't cost that much money. How can *I* afford to travel in such a car?"

As a matter of fact, we doubt if you could purchase the new Greyhound Super-Coach for even that sum—as private automobiles are sold. It is actually worth a lot more, with its brilliantly designed aluminum alloy construction, deep-cushioned chairs adjustable to four positions, diffused tubular lighting, healthful heating and ventilation, advanced safety features found in no ordinary automobile. And remember, the service of America's most skilful drivers comes with the coach.

Would you believe that one can ride to nearly any part of America or Canada in this luxurious cruiser, at a third the cost of driving a small private car? More amazing, Greyhound fares have come steadily *down*, through the years, as comfort and convenience have gone *up*—despite the advance of nearly all living costs. In this new year, Greyhound offers America's biggest dollar's worth of travel— and that goes for trips to the next city or across the continent. *See for yourself.*

The **GREYHOUND** LINES

PRINCIPAL GREYHOUND INFORMATION OFFICES

Cleveland, O. . . . . . . E. 9th & Superior	San Francisco, Cal. . Pine & Battery Streets
Philadelphia, Pa. . . . . Broad Street Station	Ft. Worth, Tex. . . . 905 Commerce Street
New York City . . . . . 245 W. 50th Street	Lexington, Ky. . . . . 801 N. Limestone
Chicago, Ill. . . . . . . 12th & Wabash	Memphis, Tenn. . . . . 527 N. Main Street
Charleston, W. Va. . . 155 Summers Street	New Orleans, La. . 400 N. Rampart Street
Minneapolis, Minn. . 509 Sixth Avenue, N.	Cincinnati, Ohio . . . . 630 Walnut Street
Boston, Mass. . . . . . . 60 Park Square	Richmond, Va. . . . 412 E. Broad Street
Washington, D.C.,1403 New York Ave., N.W.	Toronto, Ont. . . 1501 Royal Bank Bldg.
Detroit, Mich.,Washington Blvd. at Grand Riv.	London, England . . . .
St. Louis, Mo. . . Broadway & Delmar Blvd.	. . A. B. Reynoldson, 49 Leadenhall Street

For You—Bright Pictorial Booklets All About Winter Playgrounds

Break the spell of Winter with a trip to sunshine cities of the South or West! Mail this coupon to nearest information office, listed at left, for thrilling rotogravure section "FLORIDA AND GULF COAST" ☐, or colorful folders "CALIFORNIA, ALL THE WEST" ☐, "ACROSS AMERICA THROUGH SOUTHWEST" ☐. (Please check which one.) If fares and information on any special trip are desired, jot down place you wish to visit, on line below.

Name

Address

SP-1

The American Way..*of getting places!*

☆ The amazing speed and superb comfort of Flagship travel and the dependability of American's nation-wide day-and-night service provide a striking example of the American public *getting what it wants.* There are many who are not yet aware of the extent, the economy or the convenience of air travel. To these people, regular Flagship patrons say: "Fly once, and you'll fly always!" Call your Travel Agent today for Flagship schedules and fares. Or phone the nearest office of American Airlines, Inc.

AMERICAN AIRLINES *Inc.*
ROUTE OF THE FLAGSHIPS

American Airlines, 1939

T. RIEBER, CHAIRMAN OF THE BOARD OF THE TEXAS COMPANY, *says:*

"When I fly coast to coast, I prefer the TWA Way."

Above: Mr. Rieber and action-scenes along the far-flung Texaco front.

"WHEN I fly coast to coast, I prefer the TWA Way. For it has been my experience that the smooth-flying ships of the Lindbergh Line, with their excellent sleeper berths, make an overnight trip a real pleasure and land me at my destination rested and refreshed.

"Further, I would like to congratulate TWA on the excellent service rendered, both by the alert officers who command and run these great new super-liners and by TWA's charming and intelligent group of air-hostesses."

PEOPLE WHO KNOW FLY TWA
THE LINDBERGH LINE

TWA now offers you insurance at the same low rates which apply to rail or steamship service.

FASTEST SLEEPER SERVICE COAST-TO-COAST

THE ROUTE THAT LINDBERGH CHOSE

TWA, 1938

NEW WORLD'S RECORDS BY UNITED AIR LINES

☆ With a new fleet of 3-mile-a-minute, Wasp-powered Boeings, United Air Lines is giving the fastest service ever maintained with multi-motored planes. New York-Chicago is a morning, afternoon or evening flight. Chicago-Pacific Coast an overnight journey. And New York-California a trip of less than one day. These are world's records.
☆ The public's response to this service is to use it. During 1933 United Air Lines carried approximately 125,000 passengers. Another world's record.
☆ United's new Boeing planes make every provision for the passengers' comfort. Heated spacious cabins.

☆ Adjustable reclining chairs for relaxation or for sleeping during night flights.
☆ United Air Lines' year-round service utilizes every known aid to aviation. Multi-motored planes manned by two transport pilots. Two-way radio. Directive radio beam. Lighted airways. Frequent weather reports.
☆ Fly with United Air Lines — the fastest and most interesting way to travel. ☆ For schedules, tickets or reservations to 137 cities . . . call United Air Lines' ticket offices, Hotel Porters, Travel Bureaus, Postal or Western Union. ☆ Air Express — Phone Air Express Division, Railway Express Agency. Use Air Mail — it speeds business.

UNITED AIR LINES
Subsidiary of United Aircraft & Transport Corporation

United Air Lines, 1934

Off the CATAPULT

Poised on the catapults of the U. S. Navy's battleships and cruisers are swift observation scout airplanes — ready to flash into the air on scouting missions far in advance of the fleet.

The latest addition to this important class of airplane is the new Vought-Sikorsky observation scout — a sleek trim monoplane of superior performance. Descended from the famous Vought "Corsair," first service type ever to operate from the catapults, the new Vought-Sikorsky airplane reflects more than twenty years of experience in the production of airplanes for the United States Navy.

UNITED AIRCRAFT
CORPORATION
East Hartford, Connecticut

★ PRATT & WHITNEY ENGINES ★ VOUGHT-SIKORSKY AIRPLANES ★ HAMILTON STANDARD PROPELLERS

United Aircraft, 1939

▶ *Hockanum Woolens, 1938*

Healthful tropic sunshine — Hawaiian cane sugar

A real world traveler — Hawaii's golden Pineapple

Coast down the white crest of Waikiki's surf-*this winter!*

Waikiki! A soft breeze sways the coco palms above you, and shakes a crimson carpet from the royal flame tree. Idly you watch a slim outrigger speed in on a foaming roller. The native beach boys clowning in the water. Those nice looking girls that were on the boat coming over. They're five shades darker now. A great ship noses out to sea . . . to the South Seas? What does it matter? A *don't care* laziness steals over you.

Hawaii's lure. It haunts you. First on board ship, as you neared the magic isles . . . then, when you lived its beauty and its song. Too soon it must go home with you. But that's the finest thing of all— it will go with you . . . yours to live with and smile with, always. Of Hawaii, Mark Twain said, "Other things leave me, but it abides: other things change but it remains the same. For me its balmy airs are always blowing . . . in my nostrils still lives the breath of flowers that perished twenty years ago."

Come this winter! There are no seasons in Hawaii. Winter rages . . . somewhere else. There's so little variation throughout the year that the native language has never found need for a word similar to "weather." Come and enjoy the sports you like best,

in strange settings. You'll find a new relaxation and you'll find a *new self*.

Luxurious hotels edge coral sand. Modest cottages and inns hide beneath shady palms.

An Inexpensive Trip

A trip to Hawaii need not be expensive. A roundtrip from the Pacific Coast, including all expense afloat and ashore can be made for less than $350. some lower than $300.

The *Hawaii Tourist Bureau* will, upon request, mail you FREE, authoritative information about the islands—costs, what to see and do, etc.

For a special book on Hawaii, profusely illustrated in full color, with picture maps, enclose ten in coin or stamps to defray handling charges.

HAWAII

HAWAII TOURIST BUREAU
(OF HONOLULU, HAWAII, U. S. A.)
225-B BUSH STREET, SAN FRANCISCO or 1151-B SO. BROADWAY, LOS ANGELES

MATSON Line from SAN FRANCISCO
215 Market Street, San Francisco
730 So. Broadway, Los Angeles
535 Fifth Avenue, New York

814 Second Avenue, Seattle
140 So. Dearborn Street, Chicago
271 Pine Street, Portland, Ore.

LASSCO Line from LOS ANGELES
730 So. Broadway, Los Angeles
685 Market Street, San Francisco
215 East Broadway, San Diego

140 So. Dearborn Street, Chicago
535 Fifth Avenue, New York
412 Thomas Building, Dallas

ANY TRAVEL AGENT WILL GIVE YOU FULL PARTICULARS

Hawaii Tourist Bureau, 1931

AMERICA ON PARADE

SKY CHIEF   SKY QUEEN   SKY MASTER   SUN RACER

SKY KING   SKY EMPRESS

Every day and every night scores of passengers on TWA are gaining new appreciation of America's beauty. They thrill to the spectacle of California—are speechless
at the splendor of Grand Canyon from the sky. The whole colorful West—Sky City
of Acoma, Inscription Rock, Boulder Dam, Enchanted Mesa, Painted Desert—delight
beyond all expectation. Even the fertile farmlands of the Mississippi Basin are surprisingly interesting. And the approach to New York, the world's greatest city, presents a view that cannot be surpassed.

On business or pleasure, by day or by night, your flight across America via TWA
will seem all too short. Douglas Skyliners on all schedules, each equipped with Gyro-
Pilots and Automatic Stabilizers, assure smooth, steady, comfortable flight. Call any
TWA office, Pennsylvania R.R., or leading hotels and travel bureaus.

fly TWA

THE *Lindbergh* LINE

TRANSCONTINENTAL & WESTERN AIR, INC.

FASTEST SHORTEST ...COAST TO COAST

TWA, 1935

And the winner is...

Basking in Post-Olympic Glory

Published in 1938, this ad from the German Tourist Board invites unsuspecting tourists to visit the land where "the world marches on". The copy offers the traveler the opportunity to experience Deutschland's glorious past, Berlin's gay nightlife, and romantic operas and festivals. Coyly bypassing any references to a Nazi presence—save for the party flag flying on the beach—and the firmly entrenched dictatorship of Adolf Hitler, invitations such as this would quickly evaporate as the country's aggressive pogrom began to breach German borders.

Deutschland sonnt sich im Glanze Olympias

1938 lud das deutsche Fremdenverkehrsamt ahnungslose Touristen ein, das Land zu besuchen, in dem die Zeit (im Stechschritt) „voranmarschierte". Der Text verhieß dem Reisenden eine Begegnung mit Deutschlands ruhmreicher Vergangenheit und dem schillernden Nachtleben Berlins, romantische Opern und Festspiele. Sieht man von der Hakenkreuzfahne am Strand ab, vermied man tunlichst jeden Hinweis auf das Nazi-Regime und Adolf Hitlers Terrorherrschaft. Als Deutschland jedoch begann, seine Grenzen neu zu ziehen, verschwanden diese Anzeigen rasch.

Les lauriers post-olympiques

Publiée en 1938, cette publicité de l'office du tourisme allemand invite les touristes à visiter le pays « qui va de l'avant ». Le texte propose au voyageur de découvrir le glorieux passé de l'Allemagne, la joyeuse vie nocturne de Berlin, avec ses opéras romantiques et ses festivals, mais reste très évasif quant à la présence nazie (exception faite du drapeau du parti flottant sur la plage) et à la dictature fermement établie d'Adolf Hitler. Ce genre d'invitation disparut rapidement à mesure que les rumeurs de pogroms se répandirent hors des frontières.

Gloria postolímpica

Este anuncio del Ministerio de Turismo alemán, aparecido en 1938, invitaba a los turistas más despistados a visitar la tierra «donde el mundo se ponía en marcha». En el texto se ofrecía al viajero la oportunidad de conocer de propia mano el pasado glorioso de Deutschland, de disfrutar de la animada vida nocturna de Berlín y de acudir a óperas y festivales románticos. Esquivando con cierta timidez las referencias a la presencia nazi (salvo por la bandera del partido que ondea en la playa), así como la dictadura firmemente consolidada de Adolf Hitler, las invitaciones de este tipo se desvanecieron en el aire tan pronto como los escarnios del país empezaron a traspasar las fronteras de Alemania.

オリンピック後の栄華に浸って

1938年に発行されたドイツ観光局のこの広告は、無邪気な旅行者を「世界が進撃する」地へ招いている。宣伝文は、ドイツ帝国の輝かしい過去、ベルリンのきらびやかなナイトライフ、夢のようなオペラや催し物を体験するチャンスだと誘いかけている。浜辺にたなびく党旗以外、ナチの存在とアドルフ・ヒトラーの独裁権を確実に保守していることにはうまく触れないようにしているものの、この国の猛然たるユダヤ人虐殺がドイツの国外へ及ぶにつれて、このような案内はあっという間に消えてなくなることだろう。

Plan Now

FOR A GLORIOUS TRIP
TO
GERMANY

• Turn romantic pages of history in Germany. The time-mellowed ruins of ancient castles, the tomb of Charlemagne, the elaborate Guild Halls of medieval cities, the Romanesque and Gothic cathedrals of Cologne, Freiburg, Worms and Speyer, and Frederick the Great's palace of Sanssouci . . . these and many others . . . What glories of the past they echo! . . . What message of romance they bring you—as you tour through Germany . . . while operas and festivals, stage-craft and symphonies evidence in word and music the undying genius of Goethe, Wagner, Beethoven and Bach.

But the world marches on in Germany, also . . . Here you will find 20th Century progress. Or all modern sports and many that are uniquely German — piloting gliders on the Wasserkuppe or breasting the Rhine in a Faltboot. Then, too, there are great cities like Berlin, with their gay night life, splendid theatres, hotels and restaurants . . . And centers of culture, art and merrymaking like Munich, as famed for its museums as for its brew . . . Dresden, Nürnberg, Frankfurt, Stuttgart, Bayreuth, Weimar — all with a connotation of their own.

As for scenery: the Bavarian Alps, the Black Forest, Harz and Thuringia . . . the castles and vineyards of the Rhine and its gentle-flowing tributaries, the fruit trees and gardens of the Bergstrasse, the lovely sweep of sea and sky along the Baltic and North Sea. And the charm of Germany's famous health resorts.

Travel on swift streamliners of the German Railroads. The famous "Flying Hamburger" covers 186 miles in 137 minutes. All rail fares reduced 60%.

All this you can enjoy, and more . . . in perfect comfort whether in hotel, train or steamer . . . good living at moderate prices, *still further reduced by the use of registered Travel Marks.* And the German Railroads grant you *60% reduction of rail fares.* Now is the time to see Germany. Begin planning your trip today.

CONSULT YOUR TRAVEL AGENT AND WRITE FOR BOOKLET 48

GERMAN RAILROADS INFORMATION OFFICE

665 Fifth Avenue at 53rd Street, New York, N. Y.

65

German Railroads Information Office, 1938

Index